Divine Sensibility

"With this volume, *Divine Sensibility*, Edmond Zi-Kang Chua concludes his trilogy on Asian systematic theology that saw the light of day in less than three years, giving a new meaning to 'prolificity.' Building on his second volume, *Experience, Culture and Religion in Systematic Theology*, Chua attempts a reinterpretation of evangelical systematic theology that remains faithful to its creedal affirmations on divine revelation, divine transcendence, divine identity, divine immanence, divine creation, and on humanity as the image of God and at the same time is open to contemporary insights on psychological wellbeing, cultural diversity, and religious plurality. Such a theological reconciliation of apparently opposite viewpoints is a herculean task that Chua discharges with scholarly depth and pastoral sensitivity. Evangelical conservatives and liberal theologians will have to judge whether Chua's efforts are successful, but there is no doubt that his reinterpretations of Christian *loci theologici* respond to an urgent need in the academy and the church. I strongly encourage a careful reading of Chua's trilogy."

—**Peter C. Phan**, The Ignacio Ellacuría Chair of Catholic Social Thought, Georgetown University

"Dr. Chua is a rising scholarly star within the broad evangelical tradition of Christianity. While remaining true to core evangelical values, Chua probes beyond any narrow perspective to explore the interface of theology with diverse disciplines and contexts. His approach to a fresh discussion of key Christian doctrines is both academically thorough and delightfully innovative. *Divine Sensibility*, the third volume in his systematic theology, is an ambitious work that is both challenging and rewarding. For anyone with an interest in contemporary evangelical theology, and especially hermeneutics, this work is a must-read."

—**Douglas Pratt**, Honorary Professor in Theological and Religious Studies, University of Auckland

"Once again, Chua has delivered a very distinctive conservative Evangelical theological enquiry that is not hostile to religious diversity. Based within conservative worldviews that some may find uncomfortable, Chua nevertheless seeks for openness to others and uses psychology, religious studies, and deep textual reading of the biblical text and Christian thinkers to offer theological readings that are both traditional and original. Whether one agrees with his arguments, Chua's voice stands apart and deserves attention."

—**Paul Hedges**, Professor of Interreligious Studies, Nanyang Technological University

Divine Sensibility

A Biblical and Contemporary Systematic Theology

Edmond Zi-Kang Chua

WIPF & STOCK · Eugene, Oregon

DIVINE SENSIBILITY
A Biblical and Contemporary Systematic Theology

Copyright © 2025 Edmond Zi-Kang Chua. All rights reserved. Except for brief quotations in critical publications or reviews, no part of this book may be reproduced in any manner without prior written permission from the publisher. Write: Permissions, Wipf and Stock Publishers, 199 W. 8th Ave., Suite 3, Eugene, OR 97401.

Wipf & Stock
An Imprint of Wipf and Stock Publishers
199 W. 8th Ave., Suite 3
Eugene, OR 97401

www.wipfandstock.com

PAPERBACK ISBN: 979-8-3852-4983-1
HARDCOVER ISBN: 979-8-3852-4984-8
EBOOK ISBN: 979-8-3852-4985-5

VERSION NUMBER 11/13/25

Scripture quotations marked (ESV) are from The ESV® Bible (The Holy Bible, English Standard Version®), © 2001 by Crossway, a publishing ministry of Good News Publishers. Used by permission. All rights reserved.

To a new generation of evangelicals

"What is seen was not made out of things that are visible."
—Heb 11:3 ESV

Contents

Abbreviations | ix

Part 1: Creation's Imaging of the Divine

Introduction | 3

Chapter 1: The Christian Doctrine of Divine Revelation: The Experience of God in the Succession of Time | 14

Chapter 2: The Christian Doctrine of Divine Transcendence: The Experience of God in the Freedom of Space and Trust | 50

Chapter 3: The Christian Doctrine of Divine Identity: The Experience of God in the Plurality of Encounter | 94

Chapter 4: The Christian Doctrine of Divine Immanence: The Experience of God in World Religions | 155

Chapter 5: The Christian Doctrine of Divine Creation: The Experience of God in Self-Acceptance | 196

Part 2: Humanity's Imaging of the Divine

Introduction | 259

Chapter 6: The Christian Doctrine of Humanity: Sociality as Essential to Divine and Human Personhood | 271

Chapter 7: The Christian Doctrine of Adoption: Divine-Human Communion as Imperative for Full Personhood | 311

Chapter 8: The Christian Doctrine of Faith: Divine-Human Communion as Critical for Clear Knowledge of God | 344

CONTENTS

Chapter 9: The Christian Doctrine of Incarnation: Jesus as Revelation of God's Eternal Humanity | 377

Chapter 10: The Christian Doctrine of Perfection: Divine Work as Human Capacitation | 407

Works Cited | 443

Subject Index | 463

Scripture Index | 471

Abbreviations

BDB	*A Hebrew and English Lexicon of the Old Testament. With an Appendix Containing the Biblical Aramaic*, edited by Francis Brown, S. R. Driver, and Charles A. Briggs
CF	*The Christian Faith: An Introduction to Christian Doctrine*, Colin E. Gunton (1941–2003)
CG	*Der christliche Glaube nach den Grundsätzen der evangelischen Kirche im Zusammenhange dargestellt*, Friedrich Daniel Ernst Schleiermacher (1768–1834)
Civ.	*De civitate Dei* (*The City of God*), St. Augustine of Hippo (354–430)
Conf.	*Confessiones* (*Confessions*), St. Augustine of Hippo
Contr. Ar.	*Orationes contra Arianos* (*Against the Arians*), St. Athanasius of Alexandria (293–373)
De Cher.	*De Cherubim*, Philo Judaeus (15–10 BC to AD 45–50)
DG	"Der dreifaltige Gott als transzendeter Urgrund der Heilsgeschichte," Karl Rahner (1904–84)
DHT	*The Dictionary of Historical Theology*, Trevor A. Hart (ed.)
Dsa	*De servo arbitrio*, Martin Luther (1483–1546)
ECRST	*Experience, Culture and Religion in Systematic Theology: An Integrative and Pluriform Methodology*, Edmond Zi-Kang Chua (b. 1982)
Ep.	*Epistola*
ET	English translation

ABBREVIATIONS

Fid. orth.	*Expositio accurata fidei orthodoxae* (English translation, *An Exact Exposition of the Orthodox Faith*), John of Damascus (675–749)
Gal.	*Galatervorlesung*, Martin Luther
GD	*Gereformeerde Dogmatiek*, Herman Bavinck (1854–1921)
GGG	*'God-ness', 'God-ity', and God: A Historical Study and Synthesis of the Christian Doctrine of the Divine Being*, Edmond Zi-Kang Chua
Gingrich	*Shorter Lexicon of the Greek New Testament*, edited by F. Wilbur Gingrich and revised by Frederick W. Danker
Gla	"De gratia et libero arbitrio," St. Augustine of Hippo
Heid. Disp.	*Die Heidelberger Disputatio* (*Heidelberg Disputation*), Martin Luther
Inst.	*Institutio Christianae religionis* (*Institutes of the Christian Religion*), John Calvin (1509–1564)
KD	*Die Kirchliche Dogmatik* (*Church Dogmatics*), Karl Barth (1886–1968)
LSJ	*A Greek-English Lexicon* (Henry George Liddell, Robert Scott, and Henry Stuart Jones)
LT	Latin translation
LXX	Septuagint
MG	*Die Menschlichkeit Gottes*, Karl Barth
MHT	*The Moody Handbook of Theology*, Paul Enns (b. 1937)
NBD	*New Bible Dictionary*
NDT	*New Dictionary of Theology*, Sinclair B. Ferguson, David F. Wright, and J. I. Packer (eds.)
NICNT	*The New International Commentary on the New Testament*
NIDNTT	*The New International Dictionary of New Testament Theology*
NIGTC	*The New International Greek Testament Commentary*, I. Howard Marshall and Donald A. Hagner (eds.)
NTDNTW	*The NIV Theological Dictionary of New Testament Words*
Or.	*Oratio*

ABBREVIATIONS

Orthodox Faith	*An Exact Exposition of the Orthodox Faith* (English translation of John of Damascus' *Expositio accurata fidei orthodoxae*)
RD	*Reformed Dogmatics* (English translation of Herman Bavinck's *Gereformeerde Dogmatiek*)
Röm.	*Römervorlesung*
STEA	*A Systematic Theology from East Asia: Jung Young Lee's Biblical-Cultural Trinity*, Edmond Zi-Kang Chua
Summa	*Summa Theologiae* (*Summary of Theology*), St. Thomas Aquinas (1224/5–74)
Syst. Theol.	*Systematische Theologie* (*Systematic Theology*), Wolfhart Pannenberg (1928–2014)
TAP	*The Trinity in Asian Perspective*, Jung Young Lee (1935–96)
TCG	*Theology for the Community of God*, Stanley J. Grenz (1950–2005)
Trin.	*De Trinitate* (*The Trinity*), St. Augustine of Hippo/*De Trinitate* (*On the Trinity*), Richard of Saint Victor (d. 1173)
WA	Weimarer Ausgabe (Weimar edition of Luther's works)

Part 1: Creation's Imaging of the Divine

Introduction

A CONSERVATIVE EVANGELICAL INTERPRETATION of the Bible is often associated with ideas of a divine predetermination of human action calling into question the place of human freedom and ethical responsibility, a lack of affinity with insights of modern psychology,[1] an inveterate uneasiness, if not subtle intolerance, toward other religious traditions[2] as well as natural science. Notwithstanding this state of affairs, it is in fact possible to read and engage the Bible from a conservative evangelical standpoint, assuming all the theological categories of the Christian tradition, without marginalizing key scriptural emphases on human ethics and decision-making, psychological wellbeing and axiology, the value of natural science, and the idea of goodness in other religious traditions.[3]

---

1. A recent study revealed that conservative evangelical views are correlated with "more negative attitudes towards mental health help-seeking." Lloyd, et al., "Psychological Distress." In this study, conservative or fundamentalist evangelicalism is defined in terms of several theological tenets: biblical inerrancy, a literal scriptural hermeneutic, an exclusive understanding of salvation as received only through Christ, and an imperative to evangelize and help non-Christians receive a spiritual regeneration. On the use of "non-Christian" in reference to other religious traditions as well as their adherents, we acknowledge Peter Phan's concern regarding its potentially offensive, pejorative, and condescending implications and use the term only in a sociological sense for convenient discourse. Phan, *Joy of Religious Pluralism*, 99, 110n9.

2. Speaking of the evangelical church today, Douglas Pratt observes, "Often we assume that in order to be true to our Christian identity, we need to resist the encroachment of another religion: we think we need to exclude, rather than be open to, the religious other. Many Christians around the world take this position in one form or another." Pratt, *Being Open, Being Faithful*, 148.

3. Cf. the "respectful" yet "innovative" approach taken by Barth, *KD* IV.2, §64.2 (ET, Bromiley, p. 108).

PART 1: CREATION'S IMAGING OF THE DIVINE

Purpose

In a world fractured by religious tensions that arise partly from different groups' non-negotiable need to adhere to particular creeds and confessions, it is more critical than ever to begin and continue a work in academia (from where tenable ideas and theories percolate into the province of practitioners) that articulates and promotes a method that eschews a relativization of confessional distinctives but rather reconciles deeply-cherished confessionalisms with an undiluted respect and appreciation for beliefs in other religious and non-religious traditions. I propose to do this from within the Christian evangelical tradition, formulating a system of Christian doctrine centered around the paradigm of God as a sensible divine being whose image is reflected in creation and humanity whilst applying a historical-grammatical hermeneutic.

Angle

Divine Sensibility will formulate a Christian systematic theology from an evangelical perspective, discussing doctrines related to the conception of God as one whose ontological and moral primacy and character are reflected in created and human realities. The teaching of Scripture will be primary and foundational for the articulation of theological doctrine, and the hermeneutical approach that will be adopted is the historical-grammatical method.

Objective

The major object of *Divine Sensibility* is to bring evangelical Christian systematic theology into deep and constructive doctrinal conversation with some oft-neglected yet essential methodological domains; namely, psychology and cultural and religious studies. A reasoned and informed conviction that guides the work is that many aporia or at least internal tensions in Christian dogmatics, ranging from the problem of exclusivism vis-à-vis truth and value in other religious and non-religious traditions to the question of divine sovereignty vis-à-vis the reality of evil, human injustice, and suffering, exist chiefly to the extent that theology ignores or fails to grapple sufficiently with the fact that key doctrinal systems emerged during periods of vastly different sociopolitical complexion when access to information in various domains of knowledge requisite for the proper and accurate interpretation of Scripture was lacking.[4] Among other things, the book endeavors to forge and model a biblical and evangelical path between a fundamentalist evangelical and liberal theological approach.

Coverage

This book will discuss ten Christian doctrines; namely, the doctrines of divine revelation, divine transcendence, divine identity, divine immanence, divine creation, humanity, adoption, faith, incarnation, and perfection.

Main Arguments

A key premise of this work is that religious or non-religious confessionalism does not necessarily entail interreligious tension or conflict but, given a sufficiently contextualized approach, is able to promote profound respect and appreciation for other religious and non-religious traditions; the work's main contribution is to demonstrate that it is possible to formulate a Christian evangelical systematic theology that does just that without having recourse to a relativization of confessional distinctives.

The book draws attention to the shared human experience of knowing ourselves as other than the source of our being and moral orientation and therefore as dependent on the actual source of our being and moral orientation, God comprising a Divine Nature, a substrate on which all existence depends for its being and capacities, as well as an entitative Trinity.

On this premise, interreligious diversity of beliefs may be apprehended in a manner where religious and non-religious differences are

---

4. Hermeneutics is determined by the content of Scripture (e.g., God is love and saves sinful humanity through faith in the self-sacrificial atonement effectuated by the Lord Jesus) read with an appreciation of insights from other fields of inquiry including psychology, culture, and other religious traditions (salvation and Christian living do not negate the role of emotionality, cultural insight and presupposition, and the equal validity and legitimacy of other religious traditions). On the basis of a preliminary and provisional outline of biblical teaching provided by such a hermeneutic, a full-fledged doctrinal system can be developed. Cf. Barth, *KD* 4.3.1, §69.1 (ET, Bromiley, p. 32) and Joseph O'Leary's argument for an "interreligious control of trinitarian discourse" in O'Leary, "Demystifying the Trinity," 241–42.

not seen as mutually antithetical but rather complementary through a threefold classification of religious and non-religious differences of belief: differences that are non-opposed and accessible to introduction; differences that are focused and accessible to extension; and differences that are polemical and accessible to functional equivalence.

Ultimately, what matters from a newly-interpreted biblical-theological perspective, contextualized to modern domains of psychology and cultural and religious studies, is that adherents of every religious and non-religious tradition maintain their different convictions without compelling others to adopt their beliefs while recognizing that moral attitude and behavior alone are of real and binding importance.

Religious exclusivism is considered from the standpoint of a personalist slant in the development of evangelical theology in which the decisive influence of figures such as Augustine of Hippo and Martin Luther is situated in the context of a deeper discussion regarding their own personal experiences of conversion. Divine sovereignty as raising a problem for the ubiquitous experience of evil, injustice, and suffering is interpreted in terms of God's legal claim over all creation's obedience, the freedom of created moral agents to obey or do otherwise, and God's sovereignty as deterrent, delegative, withheld forbearingly, and as general. Furthermore, the divine-human relationship as conceived in feudal-monarchical terms since Anselm of Canterbury will be critiqued from the standpoint of biblical teaching in the context of an analysis of differences between individual-individual and state-citizen (or state-subject) relations.

Ultimately, God's very being, nature, and character is disclosed by the very humanity of the incarnation of Christ, not as a transformation—incidental to God's essence—underwent in order to fulfill purely instrumental ends that could not be fulfilled by earlier prophets or an utterly transcendent God including exemplifying to human beings how they ought to live (on the assumption that people would not understand God in God's infinitude) and dying in atonement of human sin (on the Platonic assumption that God being immortal is not capable of undergoing death). Contrary to being simple, immutable, impassible, and infallible, as well as seemingly unheeding toward numerous desperate human cries for succor, God's essence undergoes a complete transformation, relative to preexisting and older theologies, in the direction of humanity; God's moral sense is situated on the same plane as that of humankind, the only difference being that God's morality is unparalleled in degree.

INTRODUCTION

The timeline of creation in Genesis 1 is given a new interpretation as a spiritual and devotional resource affording a regular weekly pattern for the practice of meditation and piety in ancient Israelite society.

Procedure

The theological foundations that will undergird *Divine Sensibility* are faith, Scripture, tradition, reason, experience or psychological wellbeing, cultural diversity, and religious plurality, taking account of the role of each of these domains in theological construction, as well as the potential influence of these fields on the Christian understanding of God.

Potential Impact on the Field

Given its purpose, approach, and aims, *Divine Sensibility* is geared toward pioneering and suggesting, in an informed and evidential manner, a way of being deeply creedal and confessional as an adherent of any religious or non-religious tradition, without taking a historical-critical approach to the Bible or a progressive theological perspective, while treating other religious and non-religious traditions with full seriousness, respect, and appreciation. *Divine Sensibility*'s potential impact will mainly be in the academic field and subfield of evangelical theology and evangelical hermeneutics respectively.

Relation to Works in the Subject Area

In exemplifying a new approach to evangelical Christian systematic theology proposed and outlined in an earlier work; namely, my book, *Experience, Culture and Religion in Systematic Theology*, a work discussed in my article, "Pope Francis on the Religions as a Path to God," *Divine Sensibility* is closest in theme and perspective to those works while developing new doctrinal motifs. As a matter of fact, *Divine Sensibility* forms the final installment in a three-volume systematic theology comprising *A Systematic Theology from East Asia: Jung Young Lee's Biblical-Cultural Trinity*, a critical, comparative, and constructive formulation of the theological system of a twentieth-century Korean-American United Methodist theologian as a general approach for a comprehensive systematic theology; *Experience, Culture and Religion in Systematic Theology: An Integrative and*

PART 1: CREATION'S IMAGING OF THE DIVINE

Pluriform Methodology, articulating a method and specific approach for, as well as reassessing and reinterpreting four core doctrines in, a biblical and contemporary systematic theology which is more fully elaborated, with a reassessment and reinterpretation of ten key doctrines, in the present work, *Divine Sensibility: A Biblical and Contemporary Systematic Theology*. As a systematic theological treatise, *Divine Sensibility* seeks to enounce Christian doctrine in a viable yet also coherent and comprehensive way. In this regard, *Divine Sensibility* occupies a similar intellectual space to any historical or contemporary systematic theological work including, but not limited to, Millard Erickson's *Christian Theology*, Wayne Grudem's *Systematic Theology*, Robert Jenson's *Systematic Theology*, and Stanley Grenz's *Theology for the Community of God*, the key distinction being that *Divine Sensibility* engages in theological formulation from the standpoint of a methodology that gives close attention to the role and influence on theological construction of psychological wellbeing, cultural diversity, and religious plurality.

In Karl Barth, the "humanity of God" (in his lecture, "Die Menschlichkeit Gottes") refers to the uncoerced and voluntary eternal decision of the sovereign and immutable God, who is Lord, Creator, Preserver, Savior, and Redeemer, to create and be with and for humankind, as a "man-encountering God" as much as "God-encountering man" as opposed to being an abstract God in Godself (and leaving humankind to be abstract people in themselves for whom God is nothing more than a "pious notion", a symbol of human religiosity, religious morality, religious potentiality, and religious self-consciousness, therefore in a monologue as opposed to a dialogue with God). Such a conception of God affirms and is concerned for humankind, substituting Godself for humankind so as to deliver them from their perversity, helplessness, and misery through a history and dialogue of God's speech and acts directed to humankind, into an authentic and loving communion and covenant-partnership with humankind, a communion grounded, fixed, circumscribed, and ordered (with humankind as God's inferior) by God alone.

The visible product of this divine disposition, movement, and action in favor of humankind, comprising as it does a human community of faith walking in the example of Christ himself and characterized by the all-important quality and practice of "fellow-humanity" in a "Christocratic brotherhood", an expression of the divine relational character in human persons, as paradigmatically and archetypally has first happened with Christ, the incarnate Word of God, justifies the term, the humanity of God. Indeed Barth believes the object of theology to be the intercourse and commerce between God and humankind.[5]

Where Barth seeks to advance a theological tradition in which humankind is placed in an analogical relationship with God, in which humankind is exhorted to be like God in morality in ways fitting to humankind without proposing that the human moral nature of Jesus corresponds to the eternal morality of God in the divine essence, a move regarded in the Christian tradition as an encroachment on the mystery and prerogatives of the divine infinitude, an opinion with which we disagree, *Divine Sensibility* is distinct from Barth's work in that it does take that further step.

Intended Audience

Divine Sensibility is written mainly for evangelical Christian scholars and academically-inclined pastors dissatisfied with a status quo in which evangelical theology seems to lack the intellectual power, imagination, and will to engage more fully with diversity that is so much a part of living in the modern world. The academic research monograph will provide these potential readers with an all-embracing, internally coherent, and cogent theological framework, rooted in an evangelical-scriptural hermeneutic and employing traditional theological categories, accompanied by careful exposition of problematic passages in Scripture often adduced in support of religious exclusivism.

Outline

Each main chapter will proceed in the following manner: provide an outline of various major conceptions of the doctrine or doctrinal dimension in question while introducing an innovative interpretive option which seeks to express a more holistic balance of the seven sources of Christian theology; namely, faith, Scripture, tradition, reason, experience (psychological wellbeing), cultural diversity, and religious plurality; consider relevant theological, philosophical, historical, sociopolitical, cultural, and psychological background in a way that discloses the new interpretive possibility as a logical, sensible, and cogent choice, in an epistemological

---

5. Barth, *MG*.

section; and formally articulate and explicate the new doctrinal option, in a doctrinal formulation section.

What follows is a brief description of each chapter of the first part of the book.

Chapter 1: The Christian Doctrine of Divine Revelation: The Experience of God in the Succession of Time

In contradistinction to a traditional theological scheme which enunciates and justifies the role of Christian Scripture as a divinely inspired and authoritative work in relation to other types of religious text, this chapter articulates a theory of universal revelation based on principles of human morality with the following content: God is the divine being who offers sincere and unconditional love through God's reality and existence as the basis of all that exists, without whom nothing which is and lives can be or live, and as the giver of all good things, including a moral-centered identity in which an individual can draw endless fulfillment from God, terminating the need for pathological desires of a religious nature. The modes by which people can know God as revealed in the succession of time, constituting a precondition for the reception of any sacred text or religious tradition, are humility, gratitude, and hope.

Chapter 2: The Christian Doctrine of Divine Transcendence: The Experience of God in the Freedom of Space and Trust

Whereas a traditional theological conception frames God's ontological difference or transcendence in terms of dimensionality, this chapter formulates a doctrine of a formal and qualitative divine transcendence with the following content: God's transcendence is to be understood, formally, through the freedom of space, in terms of how the Divine Nature grounds and makes possible all of existence and, qualitatively, through the mode of trust, in terms of how the trinitarian entitative God exists in a loving relationship and serves as a moral guide to humankind individually and collectively.

INTRODUCTION

Chapter 3: The Christian Doctrine of Divine Identity: The Experience of God in the Plurality of Encounter

In a classical theological conception, God's identity is typically confined to specific religious or social experiences. In contradistinction to that, this chapter enounces a doctrine of divine identity as established in a plurality of encounter with the following content: God establishes God's identity through plural forms of encounter by human beings with God, whether this be the Divine Nature or the Trinity. As Divine Nature, God is fundamentally posited in a certain manner of reality, as a specific non-conscious and non-personal structure of ontology and morality to which no change or alteration can be made, not even by God, yet such change or alteration is essentially unnecessary, given that the structure that constitutes the Divine Nature is already perfect as a supreme ontological and moral framework, there being no possibility of adding to its glory. As Divine Nature, God is encountered through higher-level reflection on the possibility of existence, activity, and fulfillment, and a discernment of what is true, good, and beautiful in things which exist, in a broad-ranging sense on the basis of a long-term observation of reality in its concreteness, as well as the moral guidance such a Nature affords a person as a moral agent. In this way, people encounter God as Divine Nature through the structure of reality, including their own existence, as well as the inner voice of morality or conscience. As Trinity, God is encountered through God's self-distinguishing religion-specific manifestations as figures of biblical history encountered and as attested in Scripture for the benefit of posterity, as well as inner moral guidance, particularly that which alludes directly to the message of Christianity.

Chapter 4: The Christian Doctrine of Divine Immanence: The Experience of God in World Religions

A theology of world religions typically struggles to reconcile religious difference with divine truth, in some cases upholding divine truth in a specific religious group and in others sacrificing objective divine truth to safeguard the equality of religious difference. This chapter, however, adopts an integrative and pluriform approach to religious difference which upholds both objective divine truth and the equality of religious difference. Such a doctrine has the following content: God is immanent in all world religions, a truth borne out in human religious experience.

PART 1: CREATION'S IMAGING OF THE DIVINE

There is no contradiction between major religious and philosophical traditions in terms of their moral vision for humanity as responsible, caring, and compassionate toward God (or gods, the divine, or ultimately significant), self, and other, traits often mirrored in divine or human religious figures in many of these traditions. The very fact that a system of beliefs and practices exists as a religion or metaphysical philosophy suggests that some foundational claims are made about how a person should lead their lives in a way that will be most meaningful and beneficial to themselves and others. This implies that morality is at the heart of every religious or metaphysical philosophical tradition. A prescription for the way in which people ought to conduct themselves such that they do not cause harm to self, others, and the world around them but contribute towards the flourishing of each person lies at the center of every tradition. Some degree of harmony can be striven for between religious and philosophical traditions through discussing differences which are non-opposed and accessible to introduction, focused and accessible to extension, and polemical and accessible to functional equivalence, yet what ultimately matters is that all religious and philosophical traditions already promote and advance moral inspiration and support in the context of a human community. That they do this constitutes the quintessence of religion and metaphysical philosophy.

Chapter 5: The Christian Doctrine of Divine Creation: The Experience of God in Self-Acceptance

In contradistinction to a traditional Christian apprehension of God's creation in terms of processes by which God accounts for the reality of all existence, this chapter proposes a doctrine of a two-stage creation of spiritual beings and material bodies which successfully overcomes theodictic and logical quandaries associated with a conception of God as an omnipotent personal being. Our doctrine has the following content: God is revealed as a divine community of love through the sober acceptance that all entities and things are of equal value and worth, both within a species and across species, and the survival instinct and structure of living beings and plant life. The destructive capacities of those who envision human and material reality in a fissiparous way make evident that all of existence, regardless of social messaging, personal opinion, and against the strongest convictions to the contrary, is indebted to and obligated under the truth that all things are of equal worth. This state of affairs, along with a human need for respect, discloses the universal value God places on each entity and object, in which each entity or object is designed to have and display its intended creational value through its individual function, and intimates an ultimate desire, through an ultimate valorization, attesting to the existence, personhood, and agency of a Creator. The human capacity for compassion discloses the reality of an atoning higher power. Similarly, the survival instinct and structure of living beings and plant life point to a principle of vitality, the possibility of each entity and object's being, nature, existence, activity, and flourishing indicate an ontological principle, and the moral consciousness, inclination, and agency of entities so endued suggest a moral principle, making for a common witness of moral agents, living beings, and plant life to an ontological and moral principle which gives vitality. A biblical doctrine of creation is capable of harmonization with biological evolutionary theory. Direct creation and a unity of ontological principle and entitative divinity cannot be admitted on account of logical and theodictic considerations.

1

The Christian Doctrine of Divine Revelation

The Experience of God in the Succession of Time

CHRISTIANITY IS A REVELATORY religion; the ultimate authority behind its sacred texts is God alone, who has transmitted a message of salvation through prophets, apostles, and God's own Son, the Lord Jesus Christ, the divine-human Son of God and second person of the triune godhead. The doctrine of revelation sits at the epistemological head of Christian theology, defining the sacred incontestability or lack thereof of the value to be placed by Christians upon the teachings of the Christian Scriptures in relation to other forms of knowledge.

There is a diversity of views regarding the revelatory nature of the Christian Scriptures. Some are of the opinion that the Bible is not to be classified as divine revelation in any way (non-revelation). Those of such a persuasion may be inclined to the viewpoint that the Bible, while of high literary value, is nevertheless a human work of spiritual and theological inspiration (non-revelation: comprehensive).[1] Others are minded to conceive of Scripture as a mode of truth originating in

---

1. Cf. Erickson, *Christian Theology*, 174–75. Such a view is found in progressive Christianity and considers the Bible to be a collection of documents by various authors, edited and compiled into a single whole, presenting in different genres the spiritual and religious insight of its authors and of persons written about by these authors. See Chia, "Progressive Christianity."

God, but subsequently corrupted through the intervention of religious figures (non-revelation: corruptive).[2]

The Bible has also been regarded as a cognitive or theological-specific type of divine revelation. In the first case, God is thought to have revealed Godself as a majestic Creator and moral lawgiver through the

---

2. This view is found in Islamic tradition. See Reynolds, "Scriptural Falsification," 189. Be that as it may, there is strong and copious internal evidence that both the Old and New Testament portions of the Christian Scripture were faithfully transmitted from the time of divine dictation or inspiration. The Old Testament was unimpeachably transmitted under the custodianship first of the priests, Levites, and elders (from 1450 BC to 400 BC), who kept the complete book of the law (the Torah, comprising the five books of Moses; namely, Genesis, Exodus, Leviticus, Numbers, and Deuteronomy)—which God dictated to Moses on Mount Sinai and the latter wrote on papyrus scrolls, used in ancient Egypt, from which Moses came, as early as 2900 BC (Exod 24:4)—beside the ark of the covenant (Deut 31:24–26), read the whole law of God to all the Israelites in seven-year cycles (Deut 31:9–13), and preserved the book for the king to make a copy so that he will be able to read it throughout his life, keep its statutes as an expression of the fear of God and thereby avoid treating his fellow Israelites with contempt or deviating from the law of God, that his dynasty might be assured (Deut 17:18–20), Joshua, Samuel, and Jeremiah adding to this book in their time (Josh 24:26; 1 Sam 10:25; Jer 36:27–28), this book of the law being faithfully transmitted, such that a reference to it was made during the reign of King Jehoshaphat of Judah during the early ninth century BC (2 Chr 17:9); during the reign of King Josiah of Judah in the late seventh century BC (2 Kgs 22:8); during the time of Daniel, who was exiled to Babylon around the beginning of the seventh century BC and was able to read Jeremiah (specifically the part in 25:11–12), which had already become part of the Scripture (Dan 9:2), when God promised to preserve Scripture (Dan 12:4, 9); during the time of Zechariah, who ministered during the sixth century BC (Zech 7:12); and during the time of Ezra the scribe and founder of a guild of scribes, that is, between the fifth and fourth centuries BC (Ezra 7:6, 10; Neh 8:1–2); second, through the scribes themselves who made copies of the autographs (400 BC to AD 200); and finally the Masoretes, Jewish scholars who devoted their lives to the transmission of the Scriptures (AD 500 to 1000). The accuracy of the scribal transmission of the Old Testament has been demonstrated by a comparison of manuscript portions (dating to between the third century BC and the first century AD), recovered along with the rest of the Dead Sea Scrolls and representing every Old Testament book except Nehemiah and Esther, with the Leningrad Codex, the earliest complete Old Testament manuscript (AD 1008), yielding few variations. As for the New Testament, these writings of the apostles and their associates were transmitted through scribes who made copies of the originals, of which we continue to have an abundant number, 5,300, with the earliest complete manuscript being the Codex Sinaiticus (fourth century AD), which is consistent in terms of the Alexandrian text type and features with papyrus fragments dated to as early as the second and third centuries AD, such as the Papyrus 75 (P75)—dated to AD 175 to 225, which contains parts of Luke and John—whose text is a close match to that in the Codex Sinaiticus. See Skariah, "Perfection Preservation," 286–99, 310–13; Capua, "Papyrus-Making"; Editors of Encyclopaedia Britannica, "Jehoshaphat"; Editors of Encyclopaedia Britannica, "Josiah"; Gigot, "Daniel"; Bright, "Ezra"; Editors of Encyclopaedia Britannica, "Zechariah"; Windle, "Three Oldest Biblical Texts"; Andrews, "Unveiling the Truth."

natural order, encompassing the natural world as well as the human conscience and sense of morality, and allied philosophical reasoning, while the Scripture supplies a new knowledge of God above and beyond that which a human mind is able to secure through logical processes grounded in observation of the external and internal world of humankind (cognitive revelation).[3] In the other case, though the Bible is to be treated as divine revelation, it is infallible only in regard to its theological and spiritual message, and not also in terms of the historical and scientific facts it reports (theological-specific revelation).[4]

Some theologians believe the Bible to provide specific revelation in two forms. First of all, the Bible transmits divine revelation in a propositional sense, through verbal affirmations, negations, descriptions both literal and metaphorical, and other statements, all thought to have originated from God through the superintendence of the Holy Spirit inspiring specific authors from different stations of life and historical-cultural circumstances to put to writing ideas and sometimes words or always exact words from God, which may include attestations to direct divine speech, human prophetic speech, human speech, divine and human actions, and references to preexisting material (specific revelation: conceptual/textual).[5]

Second, the Bible may be seen to convey divine revelation by means of a direct personal experience of God in which God takes from the text of the Bible, which in itself constitutes only a record of past revelation, since revelation can only be conceived as direct and personal, or from the message of a preacher, in addition to direct divine speech and action, and brings these records, references, and applications of past revelation to life as the direct, personal revelation of God, spoken by Jesus the Word of God, with the Father and the Holy Spirit (specific revelation: existential).[6]

We reject the conception of the Bible as non-revelation. To the extent that the Bible attests to the actual lives, theologically significant deeds, and claims of prophets, apostles, and Christ himself, as well as the

---

3. This view is otherwise known as natural theology. Cf. Erickson, *Christian Theology*, 129–32. Friedrich Daniel Ernst Schleiermacher developed the conception of a natural theology in the direction of a universal human experience of utter dependence on God: *CG* §4.1–4 (ET, Tice, Kelsey, and Lawler, pp. 18–27).

4. The view of Augustus Hopkins Strong. See a summary of this view in Enns, *MHT*, 164–65.

5. Cf. Erickson, *Christian Theology*, 175.

6. Barth, *KD* 4.1, §60.1 (ET, Bromiley, p. 368); Barth, *KD* 4.3.1, §69.2 (ET, Bromiley, pp. 96–101).

Trinity in action in the world, these are already affirmations of divine revelation. If so, God has a means of keeping the content of revelation unsullied by religious and political maneuvering.

The conception of the Bible as cognitive revelation is also to be rejected in view that, in the case of the claim of natural revelation, it is assumed that nature itself has the power to commend itself to the human mind and spirit as a revelation of the divine being, power, and glory. It is impossible, however, in the absence of any preexisting religious or philosophical tradition developed on the basis of divine revelation, with any degree of certainty or confidence to construct from hints in nature alone a picture of God and God's ways in the world. Instead, the Scripture serves as a revelatory tool of hermeneutics through which elements and attributes in the world and humanity may be properly assessed, interpreted, expounded, and applied.

Moreover, the Bible's revelatory function is not to be circumscribed and limited to a religious or theological sphere, rendering Scripture an inadequate witness to historical record and scientific observation. If the Bible could not be trusted in regard to matters of history and phenomenal observation, fields in which facts pertaining to actual events and processes are committed to record with historical writings treated as factual attestations (as far as their historicity may be directly or indirectly established), then the ability of the Bible to establish credibility in the events it records as actual is severely compromised. The specific genre of a biblical passage is to be identified so as to allow for a proper interpretation of the text.

We concur with the propositional and existential conception of divine revelation in and through the Bible, proposing to combine these constructions by recourse to the distinct but related ideas of divine revelation coming in the forms of the Bible *inspired* (in the written, canonical text) and the Bible *inspirited* (in the Holy Spirit's directing of the reader's or hearer's attention to a particular text or idea in the Scripture, concomitant with the Spirit's exposition and application of the same).

Concurrently, we have no desire to limit the scope of divine revelation to the Christian Scriptures. Instead, we suggest that the scriptures of all mainstream religious traditions around the world are products of divine revelation, in different ways, according to the classical interpretation of each religious tradition.[7] All that these scriptures assert is to be taken

---

7. How differences and even ostensible contradictions between religious and nonreligious traditions may be reconciled will be seen in the fourth chapter.

with utmost seriousness, in culturally adapted ways, taking special care to interpret each passage according to its genre and literary placement. Furthermore, the interpretation of each Scripture may be conditioned by definable central themes arising from an introspective experience of God in the succession of time, space, and the rest of the created order.

In what follows, I seek to lay the epistemological foundations and formulate the doctrinal character of a view of the Bible as providing reliable revelation from God, concurring with God's revelation in other religious and non-religious traditions through a moral matrix (universal revelation: morality-centered), and articulate a doctrine of divine revelation which is grounded in the experience of God in the succession of time.

Epistemology

What if existence were not a sequence of events, one coming after another? What if human beings were nothing more than statues of marble, having already in their physical forms a complete fulfillment of function with respect to themselves, simply for the fact that there is no self-consciousness in a statue and therefore no self?

If there were no conscious self, there would be no need to seek fulfillment for such a self; the existence of a self-consciousness appears to presuppose some need for self-completion. A perfect and complete self is capable of existing, yet such an entity would have no reason to undergo a passage of time, or at least no self-directed impetus for participating in a flow of events. In positing human beings as incomplete selves in time, God affords them immense motivation for being part of the flow of time in the midst of history.

In our many interactions with our personal environments, we look for the completion of ourselves. We imagine we can find our fulfillment in material gains. We are disappointed. Recalibrating our approach to life, we turn to relationships and all too often our inner evils spill out and plunge our lives into ultimate chaos. We seek a sense of groundedness in our status, titles, and power, never predicting that fatigue would ensue from having to expend far more effort in maintaining a grip on authority and control than joy may be secured therefrom, and hollowness from the ultimate realization arising from the limits of mortality imposed upon human persons.

We fail to grasp that without an acceptance of incompleteness, there can be no true completion. Fulfillment consists neither in material possessions, nor pleasurable relationships, nor intoxicating power and admiration. Temporal beings must content themselves with the fact that happiness can only arrive in a gamut of concrete and momentary forms, disappearing almost as soon as they are perceived.[8]

If the sources of happiness can hardly be manipulated, one should not be so presumptuous as to fancy that happiness itself may be controlled. There is wisdom in living in the moment, provided it does not insulate us from living in other, almost immediately succeeding moments. Whether time is an enemy or friend depends to a significant extent on our ability to embrace it as a moment in our individual existence, an event before which we stand as autonomous beings, capable of absorbing its life-force and vitality and spitting out the bones of evil and malice.

It is needful to learn ways to distill from the vessel of each incident the inherent value of happiness through returning to a profound appreciation of the non-givenness of human existence and the presumption of the mountain of expectations and hopes built upon it.

To what end does a person who has lately overcome a life-and-death experience hold no further wishes as to how their lives should go and relinquish their ability to be disappointed by setbacks and failures in the course of their human existence?

One may contend that being delivered from almost-certain annihilation might be deemed a great gain in itself, and this cannot be disputed. And yet, there seems to be something exceptional about the alteration in the attitude of a person who has been saved from falling over the cliff of existence, which we do not really find in those who experience success upon success.[9] The one who has been salvaged from destruction,

---

8. A leitmotif of Ecclesiastes is the idea that the human pursuit of a sense of achievement through assiduous and dogged effort, a sense of satisfaction through pleasure-seeking, and a sense of control through pursuing wisdom and piety are wrongheaded in light that any advantage that might accrue will prove to be transient or only temporary (consider the frequent use in Ecclesiastes of the term, *hebel*, signifying "vapor" or "breath" to indicate caducity, insubstantiality, worthlessness, or futility [BDB], beginning with the second verse).

9. Can a person pride themselves on having attained success apart from God? To the extent that they achieved a certain level of accomplishment in their lives through sheer determination, due to a strong desire for some good that arrives as a result of that success, what is that good except something which God created, and what is the quality in the human being that enables them to discern and pursue that good but what God conferred upon the human individual? It is left to them only to approve of what God

as opposed to the one for whom life has been a sheer fount of blessing and favor, by virtue of remembering their state of continual precariousness through being so very nearly brought to the point of annihilation, is divested, at least momentarily, of any presumption or pretension; they are relieved of burdens they never had to bear, stumbling blocks which occlude the right perception of the blessedness of each passing moment, succeeding incident, and ensuing event.[10]

---

does through them, as a form of enjoyment God confers on them.

10. We ought to take quiet joy whenever we experience setbacks or losses, since our mortal life ends someday, and it is our failures and losses, not our successes and gains, which prepare us emotionally for the day we lose our earthly existence, when all that we once had is no more. As a matter of fact, life is an exercise in learning to decrease and disappear, at least until the mortal end of human existence which precedes an ultimate resurrection. Concerning the reason suffering is seen as beneficial for Christian growth, this is on account that a major hindrance to spiritual maturity is a certain largeness of our ego, a sense of entitlement and even arrogance, whereby we visualize the things we possess and even those we envy others the possession of as things we own or think we should own rather than as gifts from God. Losing gratitude for our blessings and constantly hankering after more in grievous dissatisfaction, we allow these visible or socially advantageous objects to dictate how much we are worth; we lose sight of our own inherent value as those posited with the capacity and privilege to be moral agents, unaware that our proclivity to locate our self-worth in the things we have or we wish to possess is due to how early on in life when we needed to be affirmed and protected those who ought to have done us that service turned the affirmation we needed into a transaction where we receive affection contingent on fulfilling specific conditions for social approval. We grew to become people who, in order to feel secure and accepted, endlessly require and strive for social affirmation which is granted mainly on the ground of satisfying conditions such as having wealth, professional or familial success, status, or power. All this is invariably regarded as a possession rather than a gift in view of its perceived importance in securing our self-worth, a perspective that can only engender unceasing tension, rivalry, and outright conflict. In this context, suffering helps a person come to their senses regarding how all that they have is a gift from God instead of their own permanent possession and they are more easily able to embrace gratitude toward God and both gratitude and grace toward others. The way toward joyful contentment is through empathy; to the extent that one is able to translate oneself imaginatively into the actual or potential dire and bleak circumstances of those who are presently suffering or might come to suffer physical, psychological, or spiritual oppression to a considerable degree and perhaps on a large scale, they would be able to experience a sense of being astonishingly fortunate and therefore blissful, though not in such a way as to be indifferent towards the needs of sufferers. Empathy is the mainspring of the most deeply sacrificial altruism in which a person so values the wellbeing of another that they would go to the extent of acting affirmatively to engender or preserve a state of wellbeing for that person even if it means suffering great material deprivation, physical suffering, or even the loss of one's own life. For a definition of empathy as a feeling of oneself into the plight of another along with the application of the concept to God and an etymological observation, see Lee, *God Suffers for Us*, 12.

For this reason, God approves not just of being in time but also the ever-present and almost always undesirable possibility of non-being in time. Those who are not prepared for death are not prepared for life either. It is as we emotionally compass the imminence of non-being, whether it be in time or on account of our ontological emptiness, that the key is conferred on us to unlock the mysteries of life in a world of glittering attractions and seductive false promises.

As such, the Lord Jesus decries those who pursue security in their lives as those who have indeed forfeited it, whereas he commends those who spurn the stability of their being in favor of his teachings which incline toward a contemplation of human mortality such as he himself and his disciples will undergo by reason of persecution (Matt 10:38–39). God is desirous of our personal happiness, our beatitude even, and yet such happiness can only come about through our living in time with great and incisive clarity concerning our state of being and existence.

Time itself supplies the driving force for seizing a sense not just of any purpose whatsoever, but only of a divinely ordained purpose. In the absence of any purpose, or of, just as bad, an erroneous purpose, time constitutes a terror of conflict or rivalry on some scale, at least a great, energy-sapping, moping boredom, no less than a horrible curse, for oneself, if not for others as well. Without spiritual illumination and philosophical enlightenment, the unending cycle of day and night means very little.

To this end, the transition from rest to work and back to rest again is vividly marked by the presence and withdrawal of the light of God, who commands that eternal radiance to shine into human activity and orientate all that we do, with a view to nothingness being given its proper place instead of a chaotic and formless blackness returning to overwhelm our existence through our self-destructive spiral into domination and meaninglessness.

God's wisdom for attaining to human happiness and self-fulfillment infuses our lives with newfound indestructible and inalienable meaningfulness, inspiriting the psychologically bone-dry with a fiery and undying motivation to hold fast to that wisdom from above so as to distill happiness from the vessel of event. In that the doctrine of the supreme being and God as Creator underlies this philosophical approach, it constitutes God's gift of purpose bestowed upon human beings who have been posited and, in that manner, caused to dwell in the intersection between events in time. To affirm a non-givenness of being, existence, and life is implicitly to affirm a divine source and origin of all existence excepting its own.

On a naturalistic view, in which all things just are, without rhyme or reason, without origin or purpose, no higher or more transcendent form of existence or reality may be owed one's being, and whatever exists may just be a fact of life, not due or connected to any further rational cause. Even in this case, however, it must needs be quested what the principle is that results in things being the way they are, though there may ultimately be no underlying essence beneath that principle, which may very well be uncaused.

Is any gratitude owed to an impersonal essence of existence? One may not be grateful to such an essence and root, but surely one can be thankful for it. If I am fatigued after a long day of sales work, and I fall into a comfortable couch, while I may not verbally express my thanks to the chair, is it not possible at all that I experience at least a tinge of happiness directed toward that felicitous piece of furniture?

Non-givenness is, I contend, possible even without the assumption that a personal God exists and originates all that is. An atheist who lacks such a basic attitude of thankfulness is sorely lacking in a crucial personal attribute, one which will see them through the mists and blazes of enervating boredom and tumultuous competition.

Taking the issues in their turn, why is an individual ever short on interest, on enthusiasm? A mental illness most frequently associated with such a symptom is clinical depression or major depressive disorder, a persistent and disruptive form of depression in which a person loses a verve for life, experiences a sense of personal unworthiness and suicidality, among other symptoms.[11] In a meta-analysis of 184 studies, individuals who were subjected as children to maltreatment, whether it be sexual, physical, emotional abuse, or emotional, physical neglect, were more than twice as likely as those without these experiences to suffer from clinical depression; furthermore, almost half of all the patients who experience depression attested that they were ill-treated in these ways as children.[12]

With the benefit of an anecdotal example, it is possible to reconstruct the psychological etiology of one type of an individual in the grip of the silent ravages of ennui. It might be that such a person has been

---

11. American Psychiatric Association, "What Is Depression?"
12. Nelson et al., "Childhood Maltreatment."

rejected by a parent or caregiver and left feeling nothing but personal isolation, loneliness. We have been constituted interpersonal beings with social needs, and try as we might, we can never function as healthy individuals without the meaning, purpose, responsibility, and determination with which love infuses a person.

To what end is a life of affluence, entertainment, or popularity if a person is unable to consolidate their personal identity around a network of other persons who sincerely care for them? Such a person cannot experience a sense of security, confidence, strength, and safety given that trust has had no opportunity to develop in the context of a healthy, interpersonal relationship. The friendship and affection of a caregiver assures a child that they are well taken care of, that they have nothing to worry or be anxious about, that whatever the harms that may subsequently await them at some corner, they have already built up the resilience to confront those fears and engage in self-rescue.

In this way, the individual becomes more than a single, isolated entity compelled to face a brutal and cold world on their own—this would be impossible. Yet, were there to be even just one person who faithfully discharges their God-given obligation to care for a child in their moment of need, especially during the first year of life, this would be sufficient to transform the equation, simply because herein a model is afforded, a representation of a single, caring individual which is capable of being projected onto the rest of the world of many other individuals. Ah! the soul thinks, perhaps that other person is just like the one who cared for and loved me. There develops a natural penchant for pro-social attitudes, behaviors, actions inclined toward the formation of many other and healthy relationships.

Now consider an opposite example, where a person has never had a chance to develop a healthy representation of the other person, for the reason that they have never experienced love and affection as a child, only neglect, abuse, or even violence at the hands of those who ought to have cared for them. It is very easy for such a child, now an adult, who experiences the world as unsafe, to lose their way in life, to know not what they ought to pursue, to feel no care or drive to succeed in life in the ways their peers do, to fail to fathom the meaningfulness of their very existence.[13] Some may develop atypical coping mechanisms including constructed identities.

---

13. Cherry, "Erikson's Stages of Development."

There are male persons known to me who have experienced gender dysphoria and come from a context in which the parent of the opposite sex was domineering and even abusive towards them as children while the parent of the same sex proved to be meek and subdued amid conflict. These gravitated towards the opposite gender in terms of identity and role whilst developing an intense aversion against their biological-based gender identity, role, appearance, and genitals. They experienced pronounced fear, in response to which they assumed the gender identity of the opposite-sex parent in view of the strength they modeled in contrast to their same-sex parent, in a subconscious desire to strengthen themselves against future episodes of abuse. Other individuals may assume the identity of what is typically perceived to be the physically stronger sex.[14]

None of these hapless individuals are to blame for their predicament, though personal misery should never serve as a pretext for sin, such as any engagement in self-harm. They have merely suffered as victims, forced to bear the frustrating and tormenting consequences of the actions of those who have neglected or abused them. The latter sometimes derive a perverse pleasure from seeing their victims afflicted, while those who suffer as a result of their unwarranted, unjust, and irresponsible behavior are consigned to undergo pain for many years, sometimes lasting for a lifetime. These victims have to undergo far more struggle as adults than many others, put in a position of having to overcome psychological tendencies and temptations to replicate the evil to which they were subjected.[15]

---

14. Such correlations between abuse and gender identification in anecdotal examples should not be used to pressure or compel transgender persons to seek trauma-related therapy or identify back with their biological sex; it is the prerogative of the adult individual alone which gender identity they choose to assume. There is typically a recognition among transgender persons that biological sex is a physical quantity that may be defined and determined in some way for the majority of individuals, whereas gender identity relates to the whole different dimension of a desire or decision to see oneself as a member of a particular gender group, in itself an important attribute of members of the gender in question, and quite possibly also to adopt the demeanor, dress code, and physical attributes (through surgical intervention) of the gender identified with. Consequently, transgender persons belong in a protected class of their own and should not be compared with any other gender class, much less discriminated against, mocked, or physically harassed.

15. It may not be possible to change a person and stop them from mistreating oneself, but it is imperative to recognize that the brunt of the emotional injury reposes in an inner ambiguity created within the soul of the mistreated person. A child or a person affected by childhood trauma, being incapable at the stage of childhood of

It is not that perpetrators of abuse contrive these propensities, or possess them on account of being especially wicked or depraved. Rather, in all probability they acquiesced as children in the commission of acts of neglect and abuse against them, accepting these as patterns of thinking, feeling, and acting that are right and proper. And who is to blame for doing that? They were only children. They are not to be faulted for what was done to them, only what they choose to do with the fact of what was done to them. There is much for these persons to work on in the way of growing into maturity and finally becoming adults, yet not many are cognizant of their own unhealthy ways of functioning as human persons, simply repeating history, and the processes of abuse are perpetuated through them, even as they continually grapple with the pain of living. A disengagement of life is bequeathed for victims of neglect and abuse by a failure to attain at a young age the sense that the world can perhaps be unsafe, but can also be quite safe, and on account of the latter, livable.

Research shows a significant link between child sexual abuse and revictimization during adolescence and adulthood and a significant risk of maltreatment for children whose mothers experienced child maltreatment themselves. This leads to the assessment that abuse is capable of being perpetuated from parent to child, in which abused children become involved in abusive relationships characterized by being abused or committing abuse, including abuse against their own children, in a manner similar to the way in which they themselves were abused. Why this happens may be due to, among other reasons and possibilities, emotional responses to childhood abuse of resentment, insecurity, escapist idealization, an inability to empathize, or a need to feel more powerful by committing abuse against another person.[16] Some psychologists are of the

---

differentiating between their own actions and the way their caregivers treat them, will wonder whether they have done anything at all to deserve that mistreatment and they will also feel aggrieved at the injustice they have endured. Yet because they are unsure concerning whether they had a role to play in bringing about the incident of mistreatment, they condemn and devalue themselves whilst feeling distressed over the behavior of the other person, but they may remain unwilling to confront the issue because of a fear of abandonment or rejection. This two-pronged psychological assault can be managed and reduced to a unidirectional phenomenon comprising only a sense of injustice by one's grasping of the fact that the unjust treatment one has received imputes nothing about the value of the person who has been hurt, that they have not deserved their mistreatment on account of being wicked or irresponsible in some way and that they retain the fullness of their worth and have a right to maintain full confidence in it. See Gillis, "Child Trauma Survivors."

16. Hébert et al., "Child Sexual Abuse and Revictimization"; Armfield et al., "Intergenerational Transmission of Child Maltreatment"; Hartney, "Cycle of Abuse."

PART 1: CREATION'S IMAGING OF THE DIVINE

view that empathy is innate to human beings, and yet maternal neglect and familial conflict may lead to this being squelched, with the result that formerly empathetic children grow up to reflect the non-empathy shown toward them, perhaps even in horrifying ways like a fatal shooting by a six-year-old boy of a female classmate of the same age.[17]

And what of competition? Why do people covet what others possess, whether it be wealth, status, power, or pleasure? Why has the world and human existence become for these individuals a locus of rivalry, a site for one-upping the other person, for proving oneself to be worthy or even the best of the best? Some level of competitiveness is required to fend for oneself in a world of limited resources characterized by an exclusion of those who do not meet certain standards such as, in a modern society especially, academic achievement.[18]

One suspects, however, that human beings do not function ideally when they so fundamentally attach their sense of self-worth to their accomplishments. The very fact that people in the present time spend extortionate durations following or discussing the public lives of celebrities, decking out their own social media accounts with frequently embellished posts publicizing the wonderful week they spent overseas with family members, giving their hours of leisure to their work (though in some cases, this seems to be a necessity), going out of the way to converse about past achievements, speaking in hushed tones of those they know who have come to attain certain admired occupations, and being unwilling to gracefully retire and walk into their senior years, suggest a crisis of sorts of personal identity.

For some, human existence is characterized by restiveness and gaping dissatisfaction. One is aware only of the extent to which they do not measure up to some other person in terms of their lifestyle or professional success. Given that identity is formed during adolescence in Erikson's schema, in which a teenager develops the set of beliefs, values, and ideals with which they will face the opportunities and challenges of life in constant interaction and negotiation with their parents and caregivers, it is highly possible that the essential foundations of an adult worldview, for all its benefits and defects, are laid during this period.[19] There already appears to be some anecdotal correlation between the occupations ideally

17. See Kalb, "Learning Right from Wrong"; Maxouris, "6-Year-Old Boy Fired a Gun."
18. Cf. Markovits, "Meritocracy Debate."
19. Cherry, "Erikson's Stages of Development."

preferred in Singapore as a case in point, at least on the part of the older generation; namely, those of a doctor or lawyer, and the messaging conveyed to children by their parents which the former will carry with them into their adulthood.

Quite possibly, and in this regard I draw from the personal experience of an individual with whom I am closely acquainted, many individuals of this bent were not treated unconditionally with dignity during their formative years; they may have been repeatedly told by those whose opinion matters most to them that apart from their achievements in school they could not be anything worth. They swallowed the lie hook, line, and sinker, and developed into physically mature persons whose emotional immaturity inexorably shows up in their incapacity for a peaceful coexistence with other persons, their incapability to lose or to fail, for their personal identity and worth are wrapped up in the extent to which they succeed in the fields in which they work or operate, or come to possess desirable external assets.[20]

Such individuals tend to clutch tightly onto what little success they have already attained, even if only external, and are also drawn to exclusivist systems, these averring the specialness of their adherents on the grounds that solely their specific belief systems are true and only those who have been personally chosen, endorsed, and aided by a divine being can accept these beliefs, so that the very acceptance of some creed implies approval by God and the chosen status if not wisdom of the human person in the fact of their agreement with God in what they ought to believe and practice as well as their commitment to those beliefs and practices.[21] Due to the fact that a sense of security in accomplishment is directly tied to the wellbeing of the individual self, such persons, by their own willful and wrongful choice, tend to make a show of strength, including trampling on those regarded as weaker, though they themselves are weak internally. Empathy and reciprocity are thrown out the window.

In the two categories of disengagement and competitiveness, the self is not accorded sufficient space to develop and become strong. With the person who is anxious and terrified that they will not be able to

---

20. Gillis, "Conditional Parental Love."

21. These may believe that God continues to be pleased with a believer who turns to Christ whenever they experience sinful thoughts, feelings, desires, and commit sinful actions, given that faith is accounted of such supreme value that any participation in sin cannot possibly overshadow its contribution to personal salvation or cast any aspersions on that salvation.

contend successfully with perceived and actual threats in the external environment, the conscious self does not even have a place in which it can be rooted, but fears to be itself, with all the obligations and responsibilities that this brings. The game of being and existence in the world, as it were, has not even begun.

With the individual whose self-worth is wrapped up in its success in attaining certain goods or levels of achievement, the self feels safe enough to continue in its existence, yet it deeply feels that its validity is constantly open to challenge and threat. Such a self does not feel confident enough that it can hold its head up high in the world among other selves; it thinks and feels that it requires a crutch of some sort, an aegis and panoply, a shield of protection and sword with which it can fend off any potential attack on its worthiness. This it finds in the various measures of personal success so popular in many societies, whether it be social approval, status and power, wealth, or some other thing. In both cases, the self is under threat. It is either not validated in its very existence, or it is constantly harried by criticisms from every direction that it is less than others, inferior and deserving of shame.[22]

Both groups are to be pitied and proffered any necessary assistance that might be appreciated. Each will surely benefit from drawing happiness and inner delight out of any event they might encounter, using the sieve that is death to a complacency pertaining to their being and existence, and presumption that they deserve some level of a quality of life.

To be sure, each group will need to work differentially upon rebuilding and restoring their damaged and compromised identities by renouncing deceptive and wrongful ways of thinking, feeling, desiring, and acting, and finding a partner who is able to offer a love unconditional, one which sincerely cares for the person afflicted with disengagement as a result of neglect or abuse during childhood, and one which valorizes the person afflicted with competition as a result of being told that they mattered not apart from their accomplishments.

Who is God, save such a one? God is one who offers sincere and unconditional love through God's reality and existence as the basis of all that exists, without whom nothing which is and lives can be or live, and as the giver of all good things, including an identity in which an individual can draw endless fulfillment from God, terminating the need for pathological desires of a religious nature.

22. According to marriage and family therapist John Amodeo, shame is a universal feeling. Amodeo, "Sneaky Obstacle."

Doctrinal Formulation: Morality-Centered Universal Divine Revelation

God is the divine being who offers sincere and unconditional love through God's reality and existence as the basis of all that exists, without whom nothing which is and lives can be or live, and as the giver of all good things, including a moral-centered identity in which an individual can draw endless fulfillment from God, terminating the need for pathological desires of a religious nature. The modes by which people can know God as revealed in the succession of time, constituting a precondition for the reception of any sacred text or religious tradition, are humility, gratitude, and hope.

Discussion

God is the divine being who offers sincere and unconditional love through God's reality and existence as the basis of all that exists, without whom nothing which is and lives can be or live, and as the giver of all good things, including a moral-centered identity in which an individual can draw endless fulfillment from God, terminating the need for pathological desires of a religious nature.

Sincerity is too often in short supply. Aside from the numerous occurrences of crimes of confidence game, marital infidelity is rife in an intimate relational context where trust is most to be expected—but all too frequently betrayed. How, then, do we define the attribute of sincerity? Sincerity is closely tied to integrity and a sense of personal commitment and responsibility: the desire and willingness for a person to express just what they actually know or feel about a person or situation, and to do just what they have promised.

Being heavily dependent on the relational setting, sincerity differs between relationships of varying intimacy. The expression of sincerity on the part of a sales representative will differ from that in parenting, marriage, or faith. In the case of the salesperson, sincerity entails only being truthful about the product they are attempting to sell and persuading potential customers to purchase rather than fudging the limitations or irrelevance of the product for a particular potential client just to close a deal and fulfill a sales quota so they may be confirmed or advance in their profession, even if only for reasons of financial survival.

PART 1: CREATION'S IMAGING OF THE DIVINE

With a parent, sincerity looks like a commitment not just to attend to a child's immediate physical needs and enforce familial obligations but also to be emotionally connected with them, recognizing their independent personhood, growing need to exercise autonomy and, more important than any other factor, the fact that they have feelings as well. To a sincere parent, a child is not merely a physical, mental, or emotional burden, an accidental product of an episode of uncontrolled romance carried too far, a tool to bring delight to a parent or accomplish ends they were never personally able to achieve. Children do not exist for the glory of their parents, to make for pleasurable lunch or dinner conversations among friends or relatives as to how much they may have achieved at school, work, or even in their personal or public life, according to rubrics of success customary in any community or society. They exist as persons in their own right. In a marriage marked by integrity, spouses realize that they have come together in order to give to one another, physically obviously but also relationally and emotionally; they do not regard each other as objects of romantic or sexual pleasure or an instrument to live the high life (1 Cor 7:3–5).

Lamentably, many have imported false and deleterious notions of the ways in which people should treat one another in various contexts, some of which we have already discussed, into a relationship of faith with God. At times, people imagine God to be like an unethical salesperson, peddling a product that is the message of the church in order just to gain converts and increase tithes, obfuscating certain putative "uncomfortable truths" about the Bible which, if known more widely, would supposedly turn a great many from a religion that is regrettably thought (by overly many individuals) to be all about hypocrisy, judgmentalism, monetary gain, personal fame and power of pastors, evangelists, and apologists, willful distortion of historical facts, cultic obsession with unusual beliefs and practices, and more. Alternatively, God is wrongfully conceived much like an emotionally neglectful parent who does only what is necessary to keep God's children alive but is in every other way derelict or a loveless spouse, using people only for the pleasure or glory they can bring.[23]

In infinite stark contrast to these false notions, God is a divine being who offers a love characterized by the deepest sincerity, integrity,

---

23. While God wills that people should praise and glorify God, this is not the sole purpose of human existence, which is primarily oriented toward seeking a deep conviction of God's love.

and responsibility. In a classical theological discussion of the divine will, God is believed to be taught by the Bible to possess a will that is both natural and necessary.

Voluntas naturalis is a nod in the direction of the acknowledgment that God's will is utterly unbounded by any personal or moral obligation to anyone or anything, including Godself; God's will belongs to God's own nature, and is always exercised freely, as an expression of God's moral and personal essence.

Voluntas necessaria, on the other hand, describes the state of affairs into which God brought Godself by engendering the whole of creation, by which, also, God's personal and moral obligations toward the created order are brought into being. It is to be noted that God's natural will most properly and most fully expresses the state of obligation or lack thereof in which God stands in relation to God's creatures. Whilst existent and thereby having already been generated, these creatures continue to possess no claim to God's providential care to promote their wellbeing.[24] Were God to be so minded, God could very well, without the slightest stain on God's conscience, choose to do away with all that God originated, as very nearly happened in the time of Noah.

God's will is said to be "necessary" only, simply, and purely in the sense that going by God's unchanging moral nature as God has revealed this to be most clearly through the person of the Lord Jesus Christ, God is not perceived, foreseen, or expected to bend what is almost a rule or necessity of God's moral existence, without the implication that God is driven by an internal necessity.[25] Therefore, God's will is necessary only because it expresses God's unchanging and good moral nature, and not because creatures, having been made, came to possess some hold over God to obligate God only to treat them well, all the time.

The Divine Nature having brought all things and people into existence, God does not take the easy way out when God's relationship with human beings becomes difficult, but bears with the human creation (understood as posited) through thick and thin, evil and righteousness, anguish and joy, constantly guiding them through many sorrowful betrayals, hoping interminably for the better and ideal world God lovingly

---

24. For an exposition of the different aspects of God's will, see Barth, *KD* 2.1, §31.2 (ET, Haire, pp. 590-97).

25. Cf. Barth, *KD* 4.2, §64.2 (ET, Bromiley, p. 41), in relation to God's willing of the incarnation of Christ.

anticipates. God chooses the human person, every individual, as an eternal choice, an eternal elect.

That God is without beginning is deeply entrenched and very well preserved in the Christian tradition. To aver God as being originless is highly problematic for propositions from a Christian faith tradition that assert that God's existence is indisputable from a logical-experiential standpoint. For if it is thought that an uncreated first cause of libertarian freedom must exist in order to account for the reality of the universe we are familiar with, there is patently nothing to account for the existence of that first cause itself.[26]

To the extent that the existence of the first cause is rootless in an ontological sense, its determination is also without necessity. Unlike creatures whose nature is dictated by the character of its process of origination, such as a human fetus which takes on all the general and many specific biological characteristics of its parents, God is without cause or origin, lacking in connection to a forebear, predecessor, or causal principle, and therefore without any imperative basis for the specific and particular determination of all God's moral and instrumental attributes. Whereas a human fetus has to possess the biological attributes of its parents, God or the first cause is without any such need.

As a matter of fact, as opposed to being conceived as infinite, the first cause may just as reasonably be speculated to be some finite source of all living and non-living entities after itself. The material tenor of the universe may be proposed to have developed from built-in mechanisms within this finite origin, while the moral nature of rational entities can be said to arise with the conferring of such moral attributes by the finite source. In this case, the entire universe is conceived to have been present in this finite origin in seed form in the beginning, only to grow and evolve out of this initial state. With such a theory of ultimate origins, it will not be necessary to include the participation and activity of spiritual personal and moral agents.[27]

It is just as conceivable and logical as a traditional Christian conception of God as the Creator of all things, that the universe started off

---

26. Cf. Loke, *Cosmological Arguments Revisited*, 29–30.

27. It is no more challenging to apprehend the process by which a non-personal source produces all ontological and moral reality than understand why a supreme personal being exists in its determination and how such a being could generate anything at all—that is to say, there is no necessary relationship between a Creator (personal or not) and its power to create.

at a primitive stage of a big bang, or began from an intermediate stage in which many of the living and non-living elements already existed by being posited without cause. The door to the most fanciful speculation and conjecture is opened very wide through a doctrine of an uncaused first cause; hence, no metaphysics has any claim to rational superiority over another, though one which promotes morality is better (because of the ability to promote human and ecological flourishing) than one that neglects or opposes it. It has to be acknowledged that the most majestic account of a divine origin or causation of the cosmos is ultimately an arbitrary belief, for the very fact that God's existence under this view is without reason, without explanation. Indeed, God is not responsible for God's existence. God cannot be said to have willed Godself into existence without falling into the logical contradiction of affirming the existence of a thing prior to its existence as a cause of its own existence.[28]

Furthermore, an infinitely eternal Creator and first cause is without even logical clarity and coherence. Infinity as a concept is without basis in reality. At best, infinity functions as a purely conceptual tool which takes its point of departure from what is observable, measurable, and finite. The concept does this without actually being rooted in any way in reality on account of the fact that it negates and eludes all human experience, description, consideration, and analysis. Infinity consists in that which is beyond the finite boundaries of human experience. However, the moment these boundaries are conceived and specified, the mind is stimulated to imagine what might lie beyond them, and thus the boundaries of the conceivable begin to expand without limit, rendering it an impossible task to ever touch the infinite. A simple way to put a finger on the impossibility of such a task is to speak of a biggest number, of which there can be none, for the moment a person declares that a particular figure is sufficiently large, one may add just one unit to that number and it instantly becomes larger than the previous number. The process can be repeated endlessly.

To the extent that God is a concrete reality rather than a mathematical abstraction, God cannot be said to exist as infinity. To speak of God as existent infinitely in eternity is effectively to declare time or at least experience (in this case, that of eternal communion within the godhead) to be infinite. Yet time or experience as a concrete aspect of reality cannot be infinite, because it is concrete rather than an abstraction. It is possible,

---

28. Cf. Van Til, *Introduction to Systematic Theology*, 327–28.

PART 1: CREATION'S IMAGING OF THE DIVINE

however, to imagine the Divine Nature as an instrumental framework, arising spontaneously at a point before which there is no possibility of any existence, that accounts for the existence, growth, maturity, fulfillment, and wellbeing of all living and non-living entities in the universe without a conceivable limit to the development of the universe.[29]

Although this is not the sole logical possibility for the origin of the universe, it is felt to be sufficiently aligned to the account of cosmological origins afforded in the biblical witness, which there is sufficient reason to believe gives reliable testimony to the events it depicts and confidence to believe that its origin is itself reliable in its self-testimony. The relational dimension of the godhead as attested in Scripture is accounted for by a doctrine of God in entitative form, in which God as Trinity exists as a finite agent of ultimate authority, working hand in glove with its spiritual moral agents, the angelic host, as well as its human agents, to steward all of the cosmological order.

There is therefore no revelation in nature of a personal God, whether glorious or humble according to the preoccupations of theologians, apart from the guidance of a Christian or other monotheistic tradition or of a supreme spiritual ontological principle in the absence of guidance from a Hindu or other impersonal theistic tradition.[30] Consequently, Scripture

---

29. There is a physical explanation for every physical phenomenon yet not for why there is a physical explanation for every physical phenomenon, for why things are shaped the way they are, partake of the qualities in which they partake, and why they even are or exist in the first place. As the ontological and moral source of all that is, God, in any name given to God by the various religious and non-religious traditions, as the Divine Nature (as opposed to the entitative Trinity) is the fundamentum, substratum, and ultimate source of all the defining principles of both the physical and human universe; namely, the four fundamental forces of nature (gravity, electromagnetism, the weak force, and the strong force), the fact that the human mind structures all reality and objects of perception in accordance with a spatiotemporal framework (as per Kant's two forms of intuition) and categories of human understanding such as quantity (unity, plurality, totality), quality (reality, negation, limitation), relation (inherence and subsistence or substance and accident, causality and dependence or cause and effect, community or reciprocity), and modality (possibility, existence, necessity), as per Kant's twelve categories of understanding, but in a transcendental realist compatibilist understanding, in which space-time and the dimensions indicated by the twelve categories of understanding do actually exist in an objective and cognitively accessible universe concomitant with a human mind that is able and given to perceive these realities. Rehm and Biggs, "Four Fundamental Forces of Nature"; Janiak, "Kant's Views on Space and Time"; Thomasson, "Categories." The multiverse proposal brings us no closer to a complete and definitive resolution of the issue insofar as it falters on the question of what makes it necessary for a number of universes to exist according to and representing the mathematical laws of probability.

30. Cf. Barth, *KD* 3.1, §40 (ET, Edwards, pp. 11, 25); González, *Reformation to*

itself declares how it is by faith that the creative origin of the universe in the invisible Word of God may be grasped (Heb 11:3).

The conception of a metaphysical and moral principle remains, however, as an intrinsic concomitant of human nature and existence, given the ongoing relative stability of essences and entities in the universe and the presence and operation of a conscience, a moral compass which channels human thinking, feeling, desiring, willing, and acting in the direction of that which is agreeable to behaving in a manner in which one wishes others to behave towards themselves, and congruent with the pursuit of psychological and physical safety, with love, and with respect for self and the other. This baseline conviction as to the metaphysical constitutes all that is necessary, intellectually, for the adequate and abundant flourishing of human existence and community.

As to the indictment in Rom 1:18–23 against those who fail to recognize God's character as bearer of an "eternal power" and "divine nature" (Rom 1:20 ESV) instead of existing in the form of physical idols of animals and anthropomorphic figures, we observe that there is no particular or explicit reference to a personality of a single divine being such as we find in Christian Scripture and theological tradition. In point of fact, this passage can be harmonized with the ultimate ontological and moral principle that atheists are able to accept.[31] They will patently not designate such a principle a god of any shape or sort, yet they will be able to acknowledge that a higher principle exists above their own

---

Present, 50. Hence, too, the New Testament discourses in a number of places concerning the fact that those have been guided by the Spirit of God who are able to profess faith in the Lord Jesus Christ as divine Son of God incarnate, come to die in atonement of our sins. See Jonathan Edwards, commenting on 1 Cor 12:3 and 1 John 4:2–3, inter alia, in "Marks of Work of True Spirit," 2.1, p. 266. In addition, the use of the concept of monotheism in this volume is not calculated to imply an interreligious hierarchy as part of a secular evolutionary framework in which monotheism is seen as a development from polytheism and the monotheism/polytheism dichotomy has been deployed politically and rhetorically since its seventeenth-century invention, with monotheism supposedly being associated with a higher level of civilization and polytheism a more backward mode of knowledge and experience. Rather, the reference to Christianity and Islam as monotheisms in this work is merely intended at registering the conception of God at the heart of each of the two religious traditions as a single being rather than a group of separate and independent beings. For a critical discussion of the way the monotheism/polytheism and religion/non-religion antitheses have been tied historically, in view of their emergence from within a European colonial matrix, to contextual interpretations of religion (!) by those from North America or Western Europe who are white Protestant middle- or upper-class males, see Hedges, *Christian Polytheism?*, 4–6.

31. Chua, "Religions as Path to God," 263.

existence, originating and sustaining all that is, all even that they are in their moral nature. This principle of being and morality can very well be recognized as eternal in its power or effect, reach, or scope, in that it has always existed. In addition, it possesses a very transcendent dimension of being and reality, a nature that exists above all existence and provides a foundation for their being and persistence. Such a nature alone and in itself is recognizably divine and sacred in a Hindu tradition of belief in an impersonal supreme ultimate.

The personal conviction that the existence of a personal Creator is based on faith is contrary to the theological philosophy of Thomas Aquinas, who imagined the origination of all things in a personal first cause to be the conclusion of a logical analysis of the existence of the universe. In the second of Aquinas' five ways, the way of causation, he posits that causes in the world are themselves accounted for by other causes. And yet, it is not observed nor is it conceivable that the existence and reality of a cause could be explained by recourse to a process of self-causation, for this would be to presuppose that a thing preexists itself, a contradiction in terms. As such, all causes in the world are ultimately effects of their own respective causes, and to preclude an infinite regress, it is necessary to posit the existence of a first cause which ends the sequence of origination of all things at the beginning.[32] Such a view is subject to my earlier critique regarding the arbitrariness of any assertion concerning the nature of a putative uncaused first cause. If so, the Christian conception of God as the Divine Nature stands as a most cogent explanation because such a structural framework for ontology and morality, rather than some random physical process, is able to account not just for material-biological but also spiritual datum such as the human soul and the spiritual-paranormal domain.[33]

It has to be said that any radical materialist attempt to deny the existence of the soul and attribute spiritual occurrences to mental activity is by its very nature self-defeating and deleterious because it undermines the entire concept of human rights which is based on the notion of the infinite worth of a human individual as something far more than an aggregation of atoms and molecules. On a radical materialist view, the rights of an individual are subjugated to any prevailing societal

---

32. Aquinas, *Summa* 1a, Q. 2, Art. 3, co.

33. The reference to the paranormal as added support for the Christian claim of divine reality comes from Samuel Wen-Sheng Chua; for a theory of the origination of the universe via random processes, see Holden, "God Did Not Create the Universe."

priorities and people can be "justifiably" harmed or murdered without compunction, compunction itself being possible only on accepting the human being as a moral subject.

God offers unconditional love.

Most parents do not desire that harm befall their children. Most do not love their children only for what they can give to them; they may only believe that if their children are unable to attain certain levels of achievement, they will more likely than not have to face increased hardship in finding their place in the world. Hence, these parents compel their children to do whatever is necessary to achieve certain goals or markers of success. They do not realize how they are effectively contributing toward the creation of a personal identity in their child in which success and accomplishment take centerstage and crowd out the more essential qualities of gratitude, goodwill, and compassion which should characterize every human person.

There are indications in research that the formation of an identity based on achievements on the part of teenagers is correlative with mental health issues such as anxiety and depression, whereas those raised in such a way that they feel truly valued by their parents tend to also demonstrate a healthy degree of self-esteem.[34] An obsessive desire of any sort is unnatural, because it reveals a fundamental sense of personal inadequacy, a dependence on external goods to prop up one's selfhood in the absence of self-value.

God bestows upon each human person an unconditional gift of God's love, not at all subject to the vagaries and vicissitudes of human behavior. There is nothing that a human creature can bring to the table in such a way as to enrich the life of God, and God does not require anything from the hand of the human creature in order to add to God's plenitude, for it is already perfect and complete.[35]

As the giver of all good things, God endues every person with a moral-centered identity from which they can draw endless fulfillment from God, repudiating the need for pathological desires of a religious nature.

---

34. Huddleston, "The Most Successful Kids."
35. Cf. Barth, *KD* 4.2, §68.2 (ET, Bromiley, p. 777).

PART 1: CREATION'S IMAGING OF THE DIVINE

Any religion is constituted by a vision of human fulfillment embedded in a human heart. More than an organizational motto or societal ethos, it is a deeply held personal conviction regarding the thing or set of things, as well as how these things may be secured, that is believed to generate not just profound gratification but bring about a total or ultimate self-actualization.

Every major world religion promotes moral good and ethical ways of achieving this. For this reason, a pathological religious desire refers not to the beliefs of any religious group or faith tradition, but rather the tissue of personal aspirations by which an individual is occupied, distracted, and hampered from making advances along the quintessential human quest for moral improvement and repentance.

A persistent personal vision comprehensively, systematically, and almost exclusively oriented towards winning the competition to decide the fittest in some sector of human life, whether it be social approval, status or power, wealth or affluence, may be considered an idolatrous personal religion.[36] Such idolatry is a tireless and frenetic cycle of human endeavor originated from a dysfunction of psychological processes of relation. The need to service an impossible and insatiable demand arises from a failure of psychodynamic development in which normal, healthy patterns of relation are marred by a violation of the fundamental code of empathy that governs all human behavior.

This is how a pathological mode of relation may be unwittingly nurtured in a person. The essential desire of a child is to find itself in a place or world in which it can know that it is safe, loved, and respected. Should the environment in which it grows up be riddled with indications of threat to its personal safety, physical or emotional, demonstrations that it is treated as a mere instrument or transactional element, or manifestations of being deprived of autonomy through mollycoddling, the child will variously develop into a person who accepts aggression or violence or the use of such on others, being treated as an instrument or treating others as instruments to get what they want in life, or embraces being deprived of their autonomy through overprotection or doing the same to others.[37] The mind of a child is very pliable and capable of being molded through interactions with early life caregivers

---

36. Barth, *KD* 4.1, §60.2 (ET, Bromiley, p. 421): "A man's god is that which is supreme for him."

37. Cf. Bernstein, "Kids' Self-Esteem."

such as their own parents or adults who have impacted their lives in some significant, positive or negative, way.

This is why it is necessary to steadfastly renounce association with aggression or violence, transactionalism, and mollycoddling, in order to cut the flow of life to internal and external activities that bring harm to oneself or others. Such a confession and approach cannot possibly have any moral force without the understanding that our very being and ethics are undergirded by an ultimate and divine source not just of our existence but also our moral nature. Without such a being or essence taking the side of good morality, the question of right or wrong would at best be eternally undecided amid a dualism of options, both equally right and good.[38]

Yet we know from the Bible that God is on the side of those who oppose aggression and violence of any sort, who repudiate a transactional mentality in interpersonal relationships, and who are against a culture of overprotection which serves to stifle the autonomy, independence, and growth of an individual.

In relation to aggression and violence, God is attested in the Scriptures as a being of peace.[39] Christ is one whose character is gentle rather than quarrelsome or disputatious, merciful, compassionate, empathetic, and kind rather than riding roughshod over the weak, vulnerable, and sensitive (Matt 12:15–21). He is one whose apostle he commanded to instruct the church at Rome that they should do everything within their power to live in peace with all people (Rom 12:18).

Far from a transactor who treats other people as instruments or tools to fulfill his agenda, the Lord Christ loves with sincerity purely for the good of the other person. He died as a ransom in service of the other (Mark 10:45). The fact that he gave up his own life without actually standing to gain anything beyond what he already had originally, that is, his divine status in the presence of worshipping angels which he temporarily relinquished so as to enter the world as a servant of servants, suggests that whatever he did in the way of becoming incarnate and executing the salvation of humanity through dying on the cross

---

38. This is more than a question of regulating behavior to safeguard social order. Having a stronger moral compass as opposed to focusing on their academic performance as a source of self-esteem is connected with better mental health outcomes in college students. Dittmann, "Self-Esteem."

39. 1 Cor 14:33, Rom 14:17; Gal 5:22. In this case, God is the giver of a fruit of the Holy Spirit characterized by peace, among other facets, in which the gift of such a fruit corresponds to the moral character and essence of the giver.

as an atoning sacrifice, even if it led to the resurrection, declaration of himself as the Son of God, ascension, and future effective kingship, he did out of an untainted desire for the eternal wellbeing of the objects of his salvific and redemptive activity.[40]

What of being an overprotector? Can the Lord Jesus be said to be someone like that? Jesus is not one who stifles our sense of personal autonomy and responsibility by usurping our role as individual persons (Matt 12:15–21). Even as God constitutes the undergirding source of all that exists, their maturity, fulfillment, and wellbeing, that Divine Nature does not divest any human person of their freedom to make their personal choices, especially in relation to their moral decisions.[41]

The very possibility of a moral malformation should alert us to the fact that we may not always rightly understand ourselves, others, or the situations in which we are caught in any interpersonal relationship, especially those marked by conflict. Even if we perceive that an injustice has been done to us, we may perhaps be wrong about this and functioning merely as a self-justifying bully.[42] The scriptures and the Lord in the

---

40. Those who hold on to status do not grasp that titles and authority are at best provisional realities in the proper functioning of human society according to its intended purpose.

41. It is fair to ask regarding the place of the doctrine of an immanent-economic Trinity characterized by simplicity in this theological formulation. After all, classical theologians such as Augustine of Hippo have interpreted God's actions in the scriptural witness in terms of God's operations upon creation and human persons rather than a direct intervention on the part of the immutable and impassible godhead. Patristic and later theologians who espoused the doctrine of divine impassibility strike a further distinction between Christ's divine and human natures and have argued that Christ's attitudes and actions were only analogically representative of the character of the absolute God which is forever inscrutable and inaccessible to human knowledge and perception. As such, affirmations regarding God's character cannot simply be made on the basis of what Scripture represents God as discovering, feeling, saying, or doing. This rubric, while well-attested in classical theology, is very much a function of classical Greek philosophy rather than a necessary implication of the scriptural testimony, and it is not adopted in the formulation of our theological system, which draws a straight line between what Scripture attests about what God discovers, feels, says, and does, and what God actually discovers, feels, says, and does, thereby affirming the immanence of God while reconceptualizing divine transcendence not as literal absence and spiritual presence but literal presence, the triune God actually indwelling the hearts of believers and directly operating in many parts of the world in the Holy Spirit and, just as importantly, the Divine Nature ontologically undergirding all reality and making its existence, character, and activity possible. Therefore, God cannot be said to be in a cup, though God as Divine Nature ontologically undergirds the reality and function of the cup. See Chua, *ECRST*, 77–107.

42. Cf. Barth, *KD* 4.1, §60.2 (ET, Bromiley, pp. 420–21).

scriptures both speak of a chronic and nettlesome form of blindness (John 9:39–41).[43]

This involves failing to perceive the truth of oneself, others, and a situation of interpersonal relationship and conflict due to stark differences in one's convictions regarding interpersonal ethics. The commonality among the aggressor, transactor, and overprotector is that they constantly put themselves in the right whenever the question arises as to whether they may perhaps be mistreating in some way another person. They do this not very consciously in fact, but only because the presuppositions underlying their primary mode of relating with another person are questionable, yet unquestioned, ones.

An aggressor, for instance, firmly believes, and this is backed by all the power of emotionality shaped by abusive experiences of their formative years, that it is right and par for the course that they are treated, and that they ought to treat others, with aggression and violence. A similar state of affairs obtains with the transactor and overprotector. Having no objective and fair plumbline by which to measure the way they relate with others, they fight tooth and nail to maintain and defend their position vis-à-vis the other person, the actually aggrieved party.

In this respect, the aggressor, transactor, and overprotector are oblivious to the reality of their maltreatment of the other person; as a matter of fact, they endlessly attempt to vindicate their treatment of the other as right, all because they have effectively been overcome by a defective worldview, a twisted and dysfunctional personal ideology and principle, system, and framework of personal relation, because this was the way they were formed psychologically, socially, and relationally, and they know of no other way; this was the system to which they were introduced and into which they were inducted when it was time to look for clues and answers as to how they should think, feel, and behave.

The Lord Jesus remarks of the personal ideology of the Pharisees that it is symptomatic of a certain inability to see, and this only in the context of the former's appearing to them, with his authoritative teaching and example, to which their system of personal ideology proved to be strongly antithetical on account of the fact that the systems of identity and relation are completely different, even mutually exclusive. They were raised, formed, nurtured, and shaped as aggressors, as those who do not

---

43. Cf. Barth, *KD* 4.3.1, §69.2 (ET, Bromiley, p. 84).

recognize the spiritual and psychological suffering they inflict on those they were meant to properly guide and serve (Matt 23:4).

Jesus, in contrast, specialized in lifting heavy burdens from the shoulders of the weak, vulnerable, and misguided flock (Matt 11:28–30), not that he had no responsibilities whatsoever to impart, but that with him the burden of false guilt and faux remorse was forever banished, and those who walked with him, though they made great personal sacrifices, yet did so with a cheerful heart, having the right understanding of who they were, who the other was, and the reality of the situation of an interpersonal relationship and situation of conflict.

As such, it was as though a great light had shone on the spiritually blind, and they loved the darkness rather than the light, doubling down on their past ways of thinking, feeling, and acting rather than abjuring them in favor of the ways of the Lord (John 3:16–21). These are rightly judged by the Lord.

The modes by which people can know God as revealed in the succession of time, constituting a precondition for the reception of any sacred text or religious tradition, are humility, gratitude, and hope.

Memory is a necessary condition for the perception of time. Without recollection of the past, if all we knew were the present instant, which we forgot as soon as it passed, there would be no experience of succession and therefore time. Another necessary condition is a spiraling movement of the present, the death of each moment and the coming to be of a subsequent next moment.

If all that there was is memory, there would be no experience of succession, only a replay in any order, not necessarily chronological, of past events. But if what just occurred a moment ago is remembered, and if what is currently happening slipping into the past to make way for a new moment from the future in the present, then the perception of succession and time becomes possible.

Therefore memory, the brain's retention of what it processed to have happened in the recent or still-accessible past, as well as sensation and experience, the brain's processing of what is currently happening but in fact has already become a very recent past by the time it is processed, are both necessary for a sense of the passage of time.[44]

---

44. Augustine defines memory in terms of both the mind's presence to itself and things recollected. Augustine, *Trin.*, 14.3.11.14 (ET, Hill, pp. 383–84).

The flow of time seems to hasten with occupation with some activity and to slow when the passage of time itself is a personal focus. We surmise that this is because the mind measures time according to change. With a busy schedule, the mind organizes its experience of succession according to distinct transitional phases between events of a day, and has no or very little awareness of the movement of time outside these transitional points.

Those who set themselves to a major task which requires protracted periods of sustained activity such as writing a doctoral dissertation or conducting some other form of research or investigation tend to find that time flies; in this context, the mind is preoccupied with completing the task, measuring change according to significant milestones and being less aware of the transition points introduced by other activities, such as a break from research, or a personal errand. Without the consciousness of the movement of time from hour to hour, the mind is not subject to impatience over the slowness of the passage of time, which it does not even notice in the first place.

When however the mind is able and minded to concentrate on the passage and flow of time, there are many more transitional points, between each minute and each hour, and hence the mind is more rigorously aware of the movement of time. The mind measures the slowness or speed with which time moves by the frequency with which it is aware of time within a specified period. If this frequency is low and there are fewer transitional points, such as in the case of a person with a busy schedule, time seems to make haste, and if it is high and there are more transitional points, as with a person who keeps looking at the clock or their watch out of excitement for what is to come, boredom, or because they are in the midst of doing something they have been compelled to do, time becomes sluggish. When the remaining time becomes saliently limited, such as to a person with a terminal illness and only five months left to live, time speeds up as a function of the many things a person feels they need to do before they finally depart, and appears to be insufficient. Time also hastens when a person dreads an approaching future event.

It is precisely because the number of transition points in a sequence of events is an index of the subjective perception of the speed at which time passes that those who remember very little of their whole past tend to feel that their lives have elapsed quickly. Hence, the subjective perception of the passage of time is linked with memory.

PART 1: CREATION'S IMAGING OF THE DIVINE

There is very little substantive difference between time itself and a sense of purpose, calling, or mission. Time in reality is given by God in succession that in the fact that all things are always drawn into the past, we may know *humility* in grasping how we also will be drawn into emptiness apart from the sustaining powers of God, that in the fact that we live in the present or the very recent past we may know *gratitude* for the fact that we remain in vitality by the provision of God alone, and that in the fact that the present is always being replaced by an oncoming future we may embrace *creativity* and *hope* for a better future for ourselves, others, and the world, a truly moral and humane future.

Humility, gratitude, and creative hope. These are qualities which are found in all world religions which endorse and support a human existence that is rooted in spirituality and yet functional and productive in the world.[45] They can even be found, with certain adjustments, in atheistic systems, where they can be recast as humility, thankfulness, and creative hope on the basis of an ultimate moral principle and ontological process.

To this end, it is a general statement and affirmation about God that is inclusive of other religious and philosophical traditions. In any theological proposition or system of such propositions, it is always critical to begin from, think alongside, and end with reflections having an eye to the beliefs and practices of other religious and philosophical traditions. The reason this is important is because each theological or philosophical system of thought has an equal claim to divine revelation.

---

45. For all their supposedly irreconcilable differences, religious traditions have much in common with one another. For all its emphasis on the importance of believers knowing and incarnating the holy character of the God they worship and adore, Christians are exhorted not to "separate" or "detach" themselves from the affairs and concerns of the world but rather to "prepare" themselves to participate and be "involved" in as complete a manner as possible, yet only to bear the fruit of God's love rather than lay hold of worldly pleasures or be entangled in carnal enmities. This is not very different, is it, from a Hindu ethical ideal of "detached activism" (*karma-yoga*) which avoids the Scylla of fully embracing the carnality of the world (*dharma* or "world-affirmation") and the Charybdis of shunning society completely (*mokṣa* or "world-negation"), in which an ethical act is performed not in order to attain some benefit but purely for its own sake. The Buddhist tradition urges adherents to observe the discipline of equanimity, in which a disciple learns to relinquish a posture of desire or aversion with regard to people or things desired or disliked respectively through bringing these thoughts and feelings to an end by determined effort, whilst encouraging ethical action in what is a *via media* between self-indulgence and self-denial. See Chung, "Jesus, Glory of God"; Crawford, *Hindu Bioethics*, 22–23; Olendzki, "Devadaha Sutta," 36–37.

This is not to say that a specifically Christian construal of theology does not make any particular claims not discoverable in other religious traditions or that Christian theology, to the extent that it still does so, should desist. To be sure, Christian theology, like any other religious theology, is based on specific sacred texts or scriptures. These didactic documents lay claim to deeper, even divine, truth, and originate in specific historical periods and in particular places and cultures.

They do, of course, make statements and affirmations which are not directly or explicitly found in any other religious or philosophical tradition. Even then, these differences and distinctions *are not* ultimately significant for the moral timbre of all relationships in the world, between God, the divine, or the ultimate (including the relationships between the divine persons in a triune godhead); humanity (including the relationships among human persons); and the animate and inanimate fellow residents and parts of the natural world.

Chiefly, from a Christian point of view, we are interested in the question of whether our specific conception of salvation impinges in any way on the validity of other religious or philosophical traditions. In particular, we are keen to know if members of other religious or philosophical traditions are at all "saved", if the relationship between God and them is made good in some way, whether self-identical or other.

Prescinding from the subject of what non-Christian religious and philosophical traditions hold dear as a central object of their respective systems, the Christian conception of salvation deals with, if the testimonies of the Epistles to the Romans and Hebrews, as well as other New Testament documents, hold any weight, the so-called problem of human sinfulness and its implications on the relationships between and among God, humanity, and the rest of the created order. Most importantly, at least in Christian tradition, the relationship between God and human beings both as a whole and individually is gravely implicated.

The sharpest lines of division are drawn between an evangelical theological conception of salvation and other religious and philosophical traditions. Some evangelical writers are of the view that an explicit profession of faith in the Lord Jesus Christ, as God, and his atoning work on the cross on behalf of humanity, dying on the cross in their place as sinners, accompanied by repentance of sin, is imperative to receive the gift of salvation as understood in Christian terms (Rom 10:9). This, as far as these writers are concerned, effectively leaves the rest of the religious world out of consideration for the possibility of divine salvation.

PART 1: CREATION'S IMAGING OF THE DIVINE

Is divine revelation confined to the Christian church? Is the right and true conception of God and God's revelation and action restricted to Christian theology?[46] To answer these related questions, it is necessary to address the pertinent issue of the meaning and signification of the Christian conception of salvation. From what are people saved through Christ? There appear to be at least two major categories of problems which the salvation of Christ decisively addresses. One, the salvation of Christ removes guilt and condemnation that separate human individuals relationally from God; two, the salvation of Christ overcomes the power of sin that separates human individuals morally from God through creating a division between the way in which they conduct themselves and that in which God conducts Godself, or God's approved pattern of human conduct.

To the extent that relationality with the divine or ultimate and morality are centrally concerned in the Christian conception of salvation, these facets and elements are recognizable in other religious and philosophical traditions as well. Buddhist bodhisattvas, full of compassion as they are, by their very essence and character narrow the relational gap between divine and human. They also model an image of human compassion and mercy which is essential in ideal and ethical human conduct in Christian terms. In Hinduism, the *telos* of human existence is to unite again with the impersonal supreme ultimate, Brahman, and the religious tradition, comprising multiple versions each touching on the nature of the world and the human soul in relation to Brahman, affords specific and attainable ways of achieving this unity, along with much ethical and moral guidance.

Does it matter that there is less of an emphasis in these religious traditions upon the phenomena of human guilt and the possibility of divine condemnation and a divine atoning act which accomplishes their repudiation? Does it matter that these traditions do not mention the name of Christ as the subject and object of atonement, or embrace the notion of God as a single personal being?

The truth of the matter is that guilt is a right and healthy response to a willing act of transgression, in which a person has caused harm to another person for no justifiable reason (such as in the course of medical treatment) when they could well have chosen otherwise, and divine condemnation is a right and healthy expectation to have of God or the divine

---

46. This is a highly problematic affirmation, seeing that another religious tradition might make the same claim (e.g., Q ʿImrān 3:19).

in such an instance. Any human individual with a proper conscience would experience these feelings and reactions to the wrong that they have done or participated in, not just Christians. Acceptable and reasonable ideas of moral right and wrong exist across religious and philosophical traditions. There is not always a single personal God, yet the conception of human morality is remarkably similar across these traditions.

This leaves us to suppose that the fundamentally non-contradictory visions of human morality and ethics that span religious and philosophical traditions, leaving aside for now the salient fact that apart from essential values, these traditions may contend against another for what represents, for instance, modesty in terms of the way a woman ought to dress in public, are a crucial component of a universal divine revelation. They are crucial because what really matters for any religious or philosophical tradition is how a person behaves, both internally and externally, in relation to the divine or ultimate, one another, and the rest of the natural order. No religious or philosophical tradition excludes any of the dimensions of the ultimate, humanity, and the rest of the natural world. There may be disparate names and conceptions for each of these, but they are nevertheless very much present in each.

What of conceptions in Christian (i.e., progressive and heterodox theologies) and non-Christian religious and philosophical traditions in which Jesus, the Trinity, sin and salvation, and other key tenets of traditional Christian theology are differently conceived? Some specific examples are in order. In Islam, Jesus is regarded as a remarkable prophet, even without moral blemish, and a worker of miracles yet not of the same ontological standing as Allāh or God.[47] Progressive Christianity conceives Jesus as a mere human being, albeit one exceptionally spiritual and inspiring. In the Hindu religion, the supreme ultimate is depicted in terms of an impersonal divine ground and source of all existence, seemingly coming into conflict with a Christian vision of a single personal deity. Atheists see no reason for espousing faith in the existence of any divine being.

What are we to make of these theological, religious, and philosophical disagreements? One will do well to attend individually to each of these cases and inquire as to the reasons for the clear difference in viewpoint. Antecedently, it is vital to leave room for misperception emerging from misunderstanding.

---

47. Yaqeen Institute, "Who is Jesus in Islam?"

PART 1: CREATION'S IMAGING OF THE DIVINE

The Islamic conception of Jesus' non-divinity, it seems, is rooted in a fear of violating the monotheistic attribute of the vision of the divine in Islam by splitting Allāh apart into two Gods. This, in turn, is precipitated by a misconception pertaining to the Trinity in which the Christian godhead is wrongly conceptualized in terms of a divine being who physically begets, through a human woman Mary, a son, Jesus, who is accorded divine status.

This conception of the Trinity arose possibly on account of the Prophet Muhammad's sustained reception of Christian beliefs through his Ebionite Christian cousin Waraqa Ibn Nawfal, with whom he discussed the Gospel according to the Hebrews, an Ebionite interpretation of the Gospel of Matthew which Waraqa further interpreted in his Arabic translation, over a period of 44 years.[48]

As an Ebionite, Waraqa deemed the Gospel according to the Hebrews a purer version of the gospel and held that Jesus is not divine but a mere human being, divinely commissioned to fulfill the Mosaic law. Viewed through the lens of Ebionite Christianity, orthodox Christian belief in the divinity of Jesus seems a wrongheaded attempt to deify a human being. As for the Marian inclusion, this may have come about through mainstream Christian veneration of Mary as the mother of God. Such a materialist grasp of the Christian doctrine of God, as the Qur'ān rightly rejects, does not belong to biblical teaching.

Regarding the mere humanness of Jesus in progressive Christianity, it is imperative to attain an appreciation of the aversion of this modern theological approach to, especially, the idea of a penal substitutionary atonement in relation to a decolonial mentality, divine omnipotence in light of human evil and injustice, among other things, and recognize the progressive Christian endeavor to formulate a more reasonable expression of Christian theology. What will prove helpful in this context is for conservative Christian theologians to seriously engage the concerns of their progressive Christian counterparts and attempt to reach a mutual landing point of some sort, in which the traditional theologian can put forward their arguments for a divine status for Jesus which address decolonial and theodictic concerns.

Where classical Hindu theology depicts the supreme ultimate as an impersonal being as opposed to the single personal divine being in Christian theology, it will serve us well to acknowledge the debt a Christian theologian owes to Hindu theologians for articulating a robust doctrine

---

48. Azzi, *Priest & Prophet*, 3, 4, 23–24, 41–50.

of the divine as a source of the possibility of the existence and flourishing of what is phenomenally other than the divine ultimate. In Christian theology as well, the divine is depicted as a root of non-divine existence, creating the possibility for free and independent creaturely movement and achievement, guided, aided, and sustained by the divine power.

Although classical Christian theology may disagree with Hinduism that human beings and other animate and inanimate entities in the world are divine in nature and to be reunited with a divine being, ontologically united and only phenomenally different and disparate, the former can affirm in common with Hinduism an inseparability of God and creation and a fundamental dependence of the created order upon the divine being, while expanding upon the personality of such a deity. The differences between Hinduism and Christianity in this regard are capable of being bridged to a significant extent.

Lastly, where the atheistic vision of the universe imagines no divine reality whatsoever, in stark contrast to a Christian vision of God, an aversion to a personal deity on the part of certain individuals may be due to a theodictic lack of justification for an omnipotent God in the face of evil and innocent or gratuitous suffering.[49] A Christian theologian may find it in themselves to commend to an atheist interlocutor a conception of a personal God in which the latter's fundamental disagreement on theodictic grounds is properly addressed.

For the reason that an ostensible overt incongruity between religious and philosophical traditions may well be due to misperception on the part of other groups, and all religious and philosophical traditions in mainstream society attempt to promote the flourishing of relationships between and among God, humanity, and the rest of the natural world, as well as elevate the spiritual, affective, social-relational, and physical dimensions of human existence, an attitude and culture of self-isolation or separatism, mutual suspicion or hostility will not be eminently helpful; indeed, it will stand in the way of human development as a whole.

In light of the foregoing, we can have the confidence that God redeems time in conferring a sense of purpose and blessing people with a sincere and unconditional love in which God endues each person with a moral-centered identity that draws unending fulfillment with (accompanied by God), from (given by God), through (modeled by God), and in God (existing in God).

---

49. The Epicurean dilemma often comes to the fore in such objections. For a summary of the problem of evil, see Sherry, "Problem of Evil."

2

The Christian Doctrine of Divine Transcendence

The Experience of God in the Freedom of Space and Trust

CHRISTIANITY IS NOT A pantheistic religion, if the Christian tradition is to be adhered to. Rather than God being us and we being God, in Christianity, there is an ontological distinction between God and the creaturely other. That being the case, it is not sufficient that human beings look inward to uncover truths about God, even discover God and perhaps establish God's nature, but it takes a revelatory framework to justify and vindicate all that we suppose we may say about God, including God's nature, purpose, and activity. This is a step we can take in view of the fact that we have laid the foundations for a Christian doctrine of divine revelation.

Our subject matter for this chapter is traditionally designated the Christian doctrine of divine attributes. The existential turn in Christian dogmatics apparent in theologians of the neo-orthodox movement such as Karl Barth reminds us, however, that God cannot quite be treated as an object of investigation, description, and analysis, as may have been done in previous centuries, but that whatever is actually known about God by us is mediated by God alone, apart from whose self-disclosure, the thick darkness that lies beyond the limits of human experience will forever persist, instead of giving way to a scintillating and sublime light of divine self-correspondence.

Some are of the view that God cannot actually be spoken of in any meaningful way, that all that we can ever grasp of God is a shapeless divine infinitude, always eluding the grasp of human knowledge and conception. Among these theologians, there are those who hold to the continued usefulness of abstract concepts including divine simplicity and perfection, concepts which express God's eternal being and attributes in a rational but incommensurable manner (radical transcendence: analogical access).[1] There are also those who espouse the perspective that God's transcendent nature exceeds all human capacity, including analogical ones, leaving us with only the possibility of pure symbols as ways of describing a particular human experience of God which do not actually touch on, represent, or reflect the divine being in any correspondent way (radical transcendence: symbolic access).[2]

Theologians who believe that God's being is not radically transcendent but transcendent in a manner open to human understanding may hold that God does not exist only in an eternal domain, hermetically sealed from human reality, existence, experience, and conception, but rather that God truly makes Godself known in a spatio-temporal realm of human existence and experience (dual transcendence).[3] Another group of theologians may propose that God had a former existence in an eternal realm, but with the event of creation, God's nature was changed when God became intertwined with the spatio-temporal domain of the universe, in that way becoming accessible to human perception and understanding (former transcendence).[4] Still others conceive of God fully in terms of immanence (non-transcendence).[5]

The limitations of existing perspectives of divine transcendence consist in the manner in which they draw too sharp a distinction between God's transcendence or surpassing of human conception and experience and God's immanence or actual presence within worldly reality and accessibility to human conception and experience. As much as God exceeds human capacities for conception and perception, there is also a

---

1. This is the classical Christian view. See Chua, *ECRST*, chapter 3.

2. This is a pluralistic view of God. See Hedges, *Controversies in Interreligious Dialogue*, 113–15.

3. This view is also known as the economic assumption of the godhead. See Chua, *STEA*, 78.

4. This view is otherwise known as pandeism. See Lane, "Pandeism," 566.

5. An example is the perspective of Jung Young Lee. See Chua, *STEA*/"Biblical-Cultural Trinity," chapter 3.

persistent impression from Scripture which affords a sense in which God is truly known in human experience and rightly spoken of in human ideas and words. While certain views of divine transcendence attempt to capture this tension and reflect a balance between the poles of God's surpassing and accessible reality, there remains an unbridgeable gulf of some sort in these interpretations, not to mention a certain inconsistency with other Christian doctrines such as theodicy.

For reasons such as these, it is perhaps best to conceive God's being not as radically transcendent, but only transcendent in quality, such that God is better thought of as immanent in the cosmos, existing and actual alongside human beings and the rest of the universe. In spite of this, there remains a necessity of positing a framework which serves to account for the reality, nature, and experience of all things, including the Trinity, which cannot serve as the fount of its own reality, nature, and experience.[6]

Such a framework must be supposed to be devoid of all personality, so as to preclude any conflict with the existent Trinity and justify the attribute of God as love in the midst of gratuitous evil and tragic suffering. To avoid any infinite regress of reasons underlying the existence of ever earlier predecessors, it is necessary to conceive of such a framework in an elegant way, as accounting, either directly or indirectly, for all the principles of reality and existence. Such a framework, which we may elect to designate a Divine Nature, is to be inseparably linked with the Trinity as its most critical expression (transcendence: formal and qualitative).

In what follows, we will articulate an epistemology and doctrinal formulation of a Christian doctrine of divine transcendence, grounded in the experience of God in the freedom of space. In so doing, we will consider the way in which God identifies with and distinguishes Godself from the rest of existence in such a way that that self-identification and self-distinction bear perfect and integrous witness to God's very nature, being, personality, character, and existence.

Epistemology

According to an analogical interpretation of radical transcendence, God properly exists in a vastly and infinitely different realm, one without a

---

6. For such a statement of trinitarian doctrine, see Chua, *STEA*/"Biblical-Cultural Trinity," particularly chapters 2, 3, 5, and 6; Chua, *GGG*; and Chua, *ECRST*, especially chapters 5 and 7.

succession of past, present, and future moments, but rather one in which all these moments in history exist simultaneously in the mind of God, who decrees all events. Even in God's internal relationships among the Father, Son, and Holy Spirit, there is non-succession in eternal, perfect, blissful, and sublime loving communion between the divine persons.

On the premises of this scheme, the revelatory actions of God in history, while belonging in the mind of God in eternity, as well as disclosing some facet or facets of the divine nature in an analogical way, can never fully or even adequately communicate what it means for the triune godhead to exist in an eternal and non-successive manner in divine simplicity and perfection. There are simply no analogues or parallels in human experience or the world. At the very most, a person can imagine what it would be like for the divine persons to exist in the way they do in eternity without any possibility of approximating that experience or even the abstract conception of that experience.

Furthermore, if God were to be indeed as far removed from human experience as is thought, with the understanding that God not just exists in a different realm but decrees all that transpires in the earthly or cosmic domain, then this would strongly imply God's absolute control over all events.[7] Yet, one often experiences a profound sense of loss and despair dwelling in a world riddled with chaotic evil and tragic suffering. At times, there are no words even to begin to express the degree of pain and agony felt by a sufferer. An eschatological promise of better things seems woefully inadequate in the midst of tremendous anguish and the notion of an omnipotent and eternal divine decree ordaining all events in history provokes a feeling of betrayal and ineffable disbelief: how could a divine drama which orchestrates such pain ever be justified on any grounds, ever be thought beautiful or righteous?

Ultimately, whether classical Christian theology is correct in averring that God ordains and orchestrates all events, be it good or ill, will be predicated on the question of the necessity of divinely-ordained human evil and tragedy as a precondition for the ideal state of affairs; namely, the glorification of God's power through a humiliation of wicked humankind and of God's justice through the judgment of evil,[8] a chastening of

---

7. "There is a human tendency to ask why God does not remove the evil in the world, or perhaps even to blame him for it. The knowledge that God is great and all-sufficient leads us in this direction and also to the assumption that God cannot suffer, being infinite and unchangeable." Erickson, *Christian Theology*, 720.

8. Zeeb, "Edwards' Method Concerning Reprobation," 269–70.

human persons as to the vanity of their self-dependence and the critical need for them, rather, to turn their reliance upon God alone, to seek God's glory as an end goal rather than their own glory.

Under this scheme, human beings are thought to be incapable of attaining to such an epiphany in the absence of a divine intervention both behind and above, within and apart of human factors in which the situations and modes of morality through which the human existence passes in an individual, who fully participates and is immersed in each of these moral modes, right down to the level of personal desire, will, and purpose, constitute critical sources of enlightenment.

In relation to a human participation in sin, this is deemed necessary as a prerequisite for the atoning sacrifice of the Lord Jesus Christ, for without it that atonement would have no place whatsoever in the God-directed economy of the cosmos. The fall and the disobedience of humankind serve both as a locus in which God is able to reveal God's salvific mercy as well as God's righteous judgment. This may be a direct or indirect revelation, a work performed by God either in an individual or through an individual. A divine will to disclose the full extent of God's mercy and righteousness may necessitate that some experience the full effect of God's mercy while others undergo the full brunt of God's righteous judgment. All this is in order that the human person might live as a God-centered and God-dependent being rather than one existing in moral and spiritual independence from God, for salvation is of the Lord alone, not of humankind.

To this we respond that there is no inescapable necessity for God to display the full extent of divine righteousness through orchestrating and foreordaining events of human evil and tragedy, or demonstrate the weakness and vulnerability of humankind through the same. Much as we believe that God's revelation is crucial for our relationship with God, we also hold reservations about a hypothesis which fails to give sufficient assent to the idea that God does not delight in human suffering or in punishing evildoers. It does not bring God any pleasure that the wicked should die rather than live, Ezekiel testifies (Ezek 18:23, 32).

That being the case, it is inconsistent to conceive of such a compassionate God as a first cause of human evil and tragedy. For to the extent that God brings it about that evildoers exist, God is thereby compelled to execute justice upon their evil acts, and yet, the Old Testament attests that God takes no delight in the death of the wicked. In classical theology, there is no obligation for God to create the world in a certain way;

consequently, it was in God's design that God created a world in which human beings would become wicked. God had full control over the type of world God would bring about, and to the degree that God does not take joy in seeing evildoers walk a path to destruction, God would not design a world in such a way that evil and tragedy would predominate, not even for a higher or nobler purpose.

Furthermore, God does not delight in human suffering. When Hagar was driven out of Abraham's household by Sarah's harsh treatment or in accordance to Sarah's will due to Hagar's demonstrated contempt of Sarah and Isaac, and left to die in the wilderness, God reached out to her in divine sympathy (Genesis 16 and 21). Similarly, we are informed in 2 Pet 3:9 that it is not God's will that any person should perish, but that all should repent and thereby receive salvation. God is patient with the sinner. The three parables of the lost things (Luke 15) lay bare the value of the sinner in God's eyes and God's deep hope for their repentance. In the parable of the lost son, specifically in the account of the older son, we encounter the fact that compassion and love arise—or ought to arise—in a father's heart toward their son, and that seeing a sinful person as having an earthly father and heavenly Father, and seeing them from their father's or Father's perspective, will enable us to love or pity them.

God does not need to reveal the full glory of divine righteousness or expose the weakness of humankind. Divine justice is meted out in situations which call for it as a response to human evil and the evil of other moral agents in the universe. It is also gratuitous to think that God's glory is fully displayed only in the humiliation of humankind. The human person is made in the image of God, to reveal God's glory in just functioning as a human being according to divine design. It is true that being human involves participating in the mandates of procreation and stewardship of the world, yet, even more fundamentally, to be human is to reflect the character of God. While human beings were only created *in* the image of God, Jesus just *is* the image of God as one whose being and character perfectly correspond to those of God (2 Cor 4:4, Heb 1:3).[9]

To the degree that that is indeed the case, the human being already possesses, essentially, the capacity for an imaging of the divine,

---

9. In Barth's understanding, Jesus is the one in whom God elected Godself as God of humanity and humanity as God's possession; the one in whom, in connection with whom, in line with whose image, God made the universe and humankind; and the one in whom God cut the eternal covenant of grace with humankind. Barth, *KD* IV.1, §61.2 (ET, Bromiley, p. 564).

in moral-spiritual, psychological, social-relational terms, precisely in the way Jesus modeled the divine nature, being, personality, character, and existence.[10] Such divine imaging in humanity, of course, owes very much to the way human beings originate from the Divine Nature, to the nature they have been given. The expression of such divine imaging will be indebted to the consistent guidance of the Holy Spirit of God in the human individual, calling attention to the teachings of Jesus, which, in turn, elucidate those of the Father, all of which represent the moral character of the Trinity.

In this way, salvation is no less of the Lord; it may not be construed in a purely instrumental and external sense in terms exclusively of the atoning sacrifice on the cross and a supernatural regenerative work on the human heart to cause it to respond in repentance and faith to the gift of salvation, yet it is nevertheless completely of the Lord, in which the human person is posited in the first place, with their nature, personality, character, desires, will, purpose, existence, guided by the Holy Spirit as to the teachings of Jesus and the Father as expressions of their moral being, human entities designed in such a way as to find their fullest and greatest self-fulfillment and liberty in imaging the divine. Salvation is of the Lord, and it is a salvation which invites and carries along the human person who discovers themselves in that salvific design and purpose. It is not something done *to* the individual, but something done *in* and *through* the individual, involving an authentic and free human response as a *yielding to* what the divine has willed for the human person.

More than what the cross of Jesus may have achieved in a transactional or instrumental sense in turning away God's wrath or displeasure of concern over human flouting of the moral laws of the universe through a propitiatory sacrifice, there is need to underscore that the human nature has never been so defaced by the onslaught of sinfulness that it has lost all trace of the divine image in which it has been created.

Human autonomy is not antithetical to God's utterly gracious initiative in salvation. Biblical writers such as St. Paul were never too concerned over reducing the role of the human person in decision-making in matters of faith and obedience; instead, they emphasized the unconditional premise of the divine approach in and through the person of Jesus Christ.

John made known that being adopted into the family of God as believers is not a process that takes place as a result of biological parentage,

---

10. Barth, *KD* IV.1, §63.1 (ET, Bromiley, pp. 743–44).

human striving or determination, only the free decision of God, made on the basis of God's goodwill rather than the meeting of any stipulated preconditions on the part of human individuals (John 1:12–13). Paul was emphatic that the Holy Spirit was given to the believers in Galatia not by the good works they had performed in accordance to the law, but purely through the hearing of the gospel in a posture of faith (Gal 3:1–6).

Neither does God so draw a believer toward Godself that there is no possibility at all of the believer resisting that approach, nor does God so shun another person that there is no possibility of that person ever finding God. The thirty-seventh and forty-fourth verses of the sixth chapter of John lend themselves to be cited in this connection.[11]

Although Jesus does observe, "All that the Father gives me will come to me, and whoever comes to me I will never cast out" (John 6:37 ESV) and "no one can come to me unless the Father who sent me draws him. And I will raise him up on the last day" (John 6:44 ESV), we do well to appreciate that these statements occur in the context of an attempt by Jesus to persuade the Jewish crowd to believe that he is indeed the Son of God come from heaven.

They originally sought Jesus out only for the physical sustenance he had proven to be able to provide in a miraculous way and, if they were to believe in Jesus as something more than a miracle-worker, they needed a further demonstration, a sign of some sort, perhaps one as tremendous as the one Moses performed in prophesying that and being the conduit through whom God would provide manna for the entire community of Israel during her wilderness trek (John 6:25–34; cf. Exodus 16).

To this end, Jesus endeavored to establish in the people's minds a clear connection between him and the Father in whom they believed as the God of Israel. In John 6:44, Jesus was highlighting that the Father was very much a part of his own work of calling and teaching his followers and disciples, that the only reason his disciples followed him was that the Father had first drawn them to Jesus; in John 6:37, Jesus expresses that those who follow the teachings of the Father, who already belong to the Father so that they are able to be subsequently given by the Father to Jesus, will certainly go to Jesus, that is, become his disciple or follower. This interpretation is supported by John 6:45: "It is written in the Prophets, 'And they will all be taught by God.' Everyone who has heard and learned from the Father comes to me—" (ESV) For this reason, it is best to expound

---

11. Calvin, *Commentary on John*, 1:256–57.

John 6:37 and John 6:44 in terms of Jesus' teaching that those who truly listen to and heed the teachings of the Father will be naturally drawn also to Jesus, rather than offended by him and his own teachings.

Therefore, what is solely of God in biblical teaching are the sacrifices made on the part of the Trinity in permitting Jesus to die an unjust death through public execution on the cross of Calvary, on charges of blasphemy and rebellion. Jesus' crucifixion is presented in Scripture as an event foreordained of God to transpire, foreknown and planned indeed by God (Acts 2:23), yet not so much as a historical necessity, but rather a locus for God's redemptive activity within the context of human sin and disobedience; what evildoers did in opposition to God's good purposes by nailing God's Son on a cross, God rehabilitated, imparting wonderful new meaning to an unjust public execution of an innocent man (cf. Gen 50:20).

Having conferred divine purpose upon the crucifixion of Christ, it has become possible and desirable for believers of Christ to look upon the cross as a means by which they may see themselves—and God regards them as legally—judged as sinners on that instrument of torture and punishment in the person of their representative, Christ, by the execution of which penalty God's wrath is averted as by a propitiatory sacrifice.[12] Furthermore, when Christ was raised on the third day, more than the Son of God was resurrected and vindicated before the world; all who trust in him may see themselves favored and indeed resurrected by God in the person of their representative, the resurrected Lord, whose glorified physical human body points powerfully toward believers' own glorious future as persons physically resurrected, raised in incorruptible bodies (1 Cor 15:20–23; 2 Cor 4:14).[13]

God is ready to forgive every sinner who comes to God with a humble heart, sorrowful over their sins, asking for God's forgiveness, and resolving not to do the same thing again. Whenever we ask God to

---

12. Cf. Barth, *KD* IV.1, §59.2 (ET, Bromiley, pp. 211–83). The penitent sinner who entrusts themselves to Christ is not literally crucified, and this is not the way in which God understands the spiritual action of the cross. Furthermore, the sinful nature is not done away with completely, such that it is surprising that the believer should still be able to sin; rather, the penitent sinner is encouraged to make a new start with faith in the crucified Lord and consciously and voluntarily choose to serve God in rectitude instead of persist in sinful conduct (Rom 6:1—7:6). Cf. Barth, *KD* IV.1, §60.3 (ET, Bromiley, pp. 502–503).

13. Cf. Barth, *KD* IV.1, §61.2 (ET, Bromiley, pp. 555–56); Barth, *KD* IV.2, §64.4 (ET, Bromiley, pp. 316–18).

forgive us for our sins with a commitment to repent, what happens is that God regards those very sins as having already been punished on the cross that Jesus died on two thousand years ago. But we need to keep going to God for forgiveness. We should not assume that God ought to forgive us or that our forgiveness is automatic.

Barth writes that Christ to every human person is "their Judge as the One who was judged in their place—delivered up in His death, and reinstated in His resurrection from the dead."[14] We find this assertion to be overdrawn insofar as it is intended as a literal description of the spiritual situation of humankind. We have not been delivered up in any way; it is only as though we had been delivered up, this deliverance has happened only in a legal sense. Paul is more circumspect (Rom 4:25), speaking only of Christ's being given over to death in God's way of addressing our transgressions against God.

By the same token, have we been primarily elected in Christ rather than as individuals before God? According to Barth, there is only one decision of eternal divine election; that of Jesus Christ, who is electing God, as elected man. Jesus Christ is not simply one among many elected persons, such that those not so elected are rejected individuals, given that the object of divine election is, at least "properly" and "originally", not each human individual but only one human individual—Christ himself, "the Elect". In virtue of Jesus being also electing God, the source of human election, therefore Jesus constitutes the Lord and head of all elect persons, who are elected indirectly *in* him and not simply *with*—in his presence—or *through*—by means of what he can accomplish for them—him, that is, in all that Christ is and does before God for them, an event which has already taken place for all believers so that all they need to do to be assured of their election is to believe in Christ, receive his Word, and rely on his decision to elect believers on the basis of his fulfillment of the requirements for God's election of such human persons.[15]

In fact, our election before God is individual rather than collective; it is for that reason that we will be individually accountable to God for our unrepented transgressions at the final judgment (Cf. Ezek 18; Rom 2:6–11). What of specific passages (Rom 6:6, 8, 11) which seem to employ such language as Barth utilizes? We note that even in the case of those verses, in which the Christian is spoken of as having been crucified

---

14. Barth, KD IV.1, §61.2 (ET, Bromiley, p. 550).
15. Barth, *KD* II.2, §33.1 (ET, Bromiley, pp. 115–17).

or died with Christ, Paul speaks only of the identity and identification of the believer with the cross of Christ in such a way that they are to regard themselves as having been crucified or died with him, not that they have been literally crucified or died.[16]

It is a moot question whether Christ represents all people as a whole, such that each person has only a part of his total sacrifice, or each individual, since in representing each person, he represents the whole, made up as it is of every individual person represented. The principle of representation is one where by an agreement or buy-in, in which a person agrees to have Christ as their representative, it is accepted that what Christ does, he is doing on the person's behalf such that it is as though Christ did not just have the identity of Christ in performing the act but also that of the person being represented instead.

A concurrence and coextensivity of the identities of every person represented in Christ means that a duplication of effort is unnecessary; a politician can sign an agreement once, on behalf of one million residents, without having to do so one million times, yet it is understood that when the politician signed the agreement, each resident represented by the politician individually signed it at the same time, at least in a legal and formal sense, whether or not an individual in question is in favor of the agreement or would have desired that such an agreement be ratified. In the same way, Christ died once, for each, and therefore for all who will buy in to his representation for them; he also rose and ascended once, for each, and therefore for all who will buy in to his representation for them.[17]

The divine-human exchange is comprehensive: When Christ died, God regarded believers in Christ as having died with Christ, that is, having paid for their sins; when Christ was resurrected, God regarded believers in Christ as having resurrected with Christ, that is, having been received back by God into God's family; when Christ ascended to the

---

16. See Barth, *KD* IV.1, §61.3 (ET, Bromiley, p. 582).

17. For a defense of penal substitutionary atonement in relation to whether it is possible to punish an innocent party (it is, and can be immoral), a related conception of a transfer of punishment (possible, since this is the prerogative of the victim; that is, God, so long as the substitute has the mental capacity to understand what the punishment and substitution for it involves and voluntarily accepts both), as well as the manner in which penal substitution does not preclude the principle of desert (while the offender is not actually punished, and therefore personal desert is not fulfilled, yet an efficacious representative takes the rap, thereby satisfying a key requirement for "*representative*" desert), see Labooy and Wisse, "Equivocal Penal Substitution," 228–33.

right hand of the Father, God regarded believers in Christ as having been raised to sit with Christ at the right hand of the Father, that is, having received a favored position beside God (Eph 2:4–7).

An adoption into the family of God and outpouring and indwelling of the Holy Spirit are experiences of faith with an objective element in a spiritual dimension into which the believer is brought through the knowledge and acceptance of Christ's salvific work on behalf of them. God does not hold back on demonstrating God's love, guidance, compassion, and forgiveness; at the same time, God does not usurp the role of the human person in actualizing the divine image in which they are posited and exist. To affirm that God genuinely expects each person to actualize their moral capacities without intervening in some utterly determinative way is not to undermine God's role as the source of salvation, understood as God's unremittingly loving relationship to and moral guidance of the human person.

Unfortunately, observations in Scripture of the prevalence of human sinfulness and transgression, intended only to turn people away from their wickedness, have been translated out of a paraenetic context into one of sterile scientific description, transmuted from speech act into dogmatic proposition. When a mother tells a child that the room is very messy, the goal is not to inform the child of what they may very well already know for a fact, but to urge them to clean up.[18] The case is similar with the numerous passages in Scripture denouncing human moral conduct. Even if we assume, for the sake of argument, that such passages are to be read clinically and scientifically, it makes little sense to decry all of humanity as sinful on the one hand, and concurrently hold up certain figures as morally virtuous persons to be emulated.

Consequently, it is not imperative that the human element be subdued in favor of a divine self-presentation. God's power is indeed revealed in moments of human weakness, whether due to finitude or sin, yet this is not the only or even profoundest way in which God's glory can be made known. On the contrary, there is no necessity that human beings exist in finitude or sin. That they do so is a result of limitation and disobedience rather than divine decree, decision, design, desire, will, or purpose. And it is God's merciful good pleasure to attend to each of these situations as they may arise and bring about an overcoming of such human finitude and sin.

---

18. This is an example of a locutionary act with an illocutionary force. See Austin, *How to Do Things with Words*, 98–99.

PART 1: CREATION'S IMAGING OF THE DIVINE

In view of the foregoing considerations of traditional Christian doctrines of transcendence, theodicy, predestination, Christology, and salvation, divine transcendence is ideally construed through the grid of a formal and qualitative dimensionality.

Doctrinal Formulation: Formal and Qualitative Divine Transcendence

God's transcendence is to be understood, formally, through the freedom of space, in terms of how the Divine Nature grounds and makes possible all of existence, its attributes, activity, and interactions, and, qualitatively, through the mode of trust, in terms of how the trinitarian entitative God exists in a loving relationship and serves as a moral guide to humankind individually and collectively.

Discussion

God's transcendence is to be understood, formally, through the freedom of space, in terms of how the Divine Nature grounds and makes possible all of existence, its attributes, activity, and interactions.

Transcendence as a concept presupposes distinction and differentiation, a duality of some sort and at some level as opposed to a nonduality; as a matter of fact, transcendence constitutes an extreme pole in a scheme of differentiation and distinction. Yet the formal transcendence of God as we may designate it should not be thought of as being of a radical or exclusive nature. In contrast to classical Christian theological conceptions of divine transcendence in terms of how God stands completely apart and separate from humankind not just in a moral but even ontological sense, we propose to interpret divine transcendence in formal terms as a complementary inclusive category, akin to the spatial dimension, which while being real does not quite exist in the way concrete entities do.

Even though things exist in space, which acts as a medium through which movement and activity is possible, space itself is not a thing like the concrete objects and entities we observe around ourselves, including we ourselves. Instead, space is what makes the existence and activity of all these things possible. Without the dimension of space, could any object exist which occupies space? In the absence of space, would it be possible for an entity to move, act, interact, and communicate with other entities? The answer is in the negative. For this reason, the Divine Nature like space acts as a presupposition and framework allowing for the being, existence, and activity of all entities and objects in the cosmos.[19]

Not being an object or entity like objects and entities observable in the universe does not render the Divine Nature a non-reality, in the same way that our inability to perceive space in itself does not detract from its reality—it just exists on a different level and dimension, one which we cannot directly perceive with any of our senses. This is not to say, of course, that the Divine Nature just is space and vice versa. Space itself is a reality generated and sustained in its reality by the Divine Nature, as is time, and as is every object and entity in existence.

Although the Divine Nature cannot be directly sensed, it is everywhere present, by definition. It is the *what* that makes the *where, when, what, who, how,* and *why* possible. As such, all of existence bears indirect and persistent witness to the reality of the Divine Nature. In spite of this, it is impossible that any entity or object function as a substantive witness to the substance of the Divine Nature, given that there is no such substance within what is really an ontological and existential framework.

It is possible, however, for an entity to be thought of as more or less critical to the ontological and existential framework that is the Divine Nature. What determines the degree to which an entity may be assessed to be more or less critical to the Divine Nature? The entity which makes the greatest contribution toward the Divine Nature is the entity which best facilitates and promotes the Divine Nature's *telos*, its goal or end for the entities and objects it posits. Among all entities posited into existence by the Divine Nature, the Trinity stands out as the entitative reality which most fully supports the goals of the Divine Nature for each of its entities and objects. Not only does the Trinity serve a critical function in the economy generated by the Divine Nature, but the Trinity is the concrete and entitative actualization of the Divine Nature with its ubiquitous processes of moral direction.

Some specific examples are in order. Along with the possibility of being, existence, activity, and fulfillment, the Divine Nature also

---

19. Seventeenth-century theologian and philosopher Henry More has drawn an analogy and connection between God and space, arguing that space has the same attributes as God and can be regarded as an "extension" of God, while Lyonhart holds out the possibility that space may be conceived as a dimension of the godhead. See Lyonhart, *Space God*, 165, 177.

supplies moral exhortation in the direction of encouraging a higher and deeper degree of love, compassion, empathy, righteousness, goodness, patience, gentleness, self-discipline, joy, peacefulness, holiness, solidarity, respect, ingenuousness, resilience, sincerity, passion, resolve, forbearance, forgiveness, longsuffering, equanimity, faith, hope, honor, kindness, responsibility, integrity, truthfulness, generosity, selflessness. Despite this moral guidance, so vital and beneficial to the sociality of all entities in the world, the Divine Nature remains but a locus of such being, existence, and activity. It is not in itself an entity, and therefore it is devoid of rationality, intellect, reason, affect, will, purpose, desire, consciousness, personality.

The Trinity, on the other hand, being an entity is capable of and only ever and most fully expresses the moral attributes promoted and encouraged in moral agents by the Divine Nature, doing its part, through its many angelic representatives, to promote and encourage those very attributes among all moral agents in the universe. For that reason alone, the Trinity most properly constitutes the entitative complement to the Divine Nature and the Divine Nature, the structural complement to the Trinity.

Alongside its moral guidance of all entities, the Divine Nature also directs the rational, philosophical, theological, and scientific development of humankind but only ever in a progressive and successive way, such that not even the Trinity itself is aware of stages of medical and scientific knowledge that have not been attained as yet.

God's transcendence is to be understood, qualitatively, through the mode of trust, in terms of how the trinitarian entitative God exists in a loving relationship and serves as a moral guide to humankind individually and collectively.

In some ways, it is difficult for the Christian tradition to affirm that God exists in a loving relationship with all humankind, God's love seeming to stand in contrast to God's holiness and righteousness. The latter attribute of God necessitates a forceful, negative, and punitive reaction to human transgression and, insofar as it is in operation, apparently obscures God's positive affections toward humankind.

In some theological traditions and interpretations, fallen humanity post-Eden is dimly viewed as deserving, as worthy, of nothing save divine judgment and destruction.[20] For the vast majority of humankind, seeing as such a situation obtained very early on, within the lifetime of one believed to have been among the first human beings, the experience of the human nature into which they were born has been nothing other than an object of divine displeasure, given the corruption with which Adam's own nature underwent by reason of his act of disobedience in the garden of Eden, in which he violated God's express command for him not to eat the fruit of the tree of the knowledge of good and evil.

Persuaded by the crafty serpent, Eve, his wife, was made to abandon her scruples. Her cunning interlocutor first attempted to have her question the transgressive nature of an act of eating such a fruit. When the woman crossed this hurdle by holding fast to the truth that God had indeed forbidden its consumption, the serpent proceeded to introduce an element of doubt and suspicion in her relationship with God, by suggesting that, just perhaps, God was not to be so fully trusted and that the only purpose for God's promulgating such a law was to protect God's own private interests rather than to promote the wellbeing and interests of the human couple. Indeed, the serpent went as far as to propose that not only was the fruit not harmful for consumption, but it could well bring wonderful benefits of giving them access to divine knowledge, by which they could fathom all things and become competent arbiters of morality in their own right, not having, therefore, to depend any longer on the divine judge.

The ruse evidently succeeded with Eve taken in and sharing the fruit with her husband. They discovered, only too late, that they had been deceived by the serpent into transgressing the divine commandment. Although Scripture uses a wordplay to imply that they had obtained what they had sought in the first place, that is, for their eyes to be opened in a figurative sense, in order to know secrets so far kept from them, including the way to divinity, it is clear that the biblical author intends their hearers and readers to understand from the narration that the couple had been plunged by their act of disobedience into an inferior state, for in being so presumptuous as to break the command of God, they had alienated themselves from the Creator and Lord of their lives, the one who posits their reality and constructed their material bodies, essentially, the reality and being to whom they owe everything.

---

20. Barth, *KD* IV.1, §60.1 (ET, Bromiley, p. 405).

They did not merely break a command by accident, mistake, or out of ignorance. It was not as though they stumbled upon a fruit as they were walking through the garden in the late afternoon, hungered, and so took a bite from the fruit, oblivious to the fact that it was literally forbidden to them to consume. The woman knew full well what the fruit was which she was considering, that it was forbidden to her; in spite of that, she believed the serpent's protestations that the fruit was in actual fact salutary as a source of food, her eyes were drawn to its beauty, and she accepted the notion that the tree had the power to usher her into a place of divine wisdom.

In one fell swoop, she went from a state of innocence into one of guilt. In questioning the rightness and goodness of God's commandment, in challenging in herself the incorruptible and ineffable virtue and purity of God's motives for handing down the command, she made herself a rebel against God, and the one posited and shaped by the Creator and Lord became estranged from the source of her own existence, life, and fulfillment. God had nothing to do with her putting herself away from God; it was not some dearth of a gift of perseverance by which she found herself having to succumb to the temptation of the evil serpent. Rather, she made the choice she did as an expression of her self-will, her desire to dethrone God and rule in her own right. The result of her choice, and that of her husband, was that instead of gaining divine wisdom, they discovered themselves to be naked, bereft of all joy and hope in the world, having distrusted the only one they ought fully to trust.

The human couple did not show themselves to be repentant or contrite, seeing as they immediately ran away from God, concealing themselves and affording for posterity a poignant pictorial depiction of the true crisis of humanity; namely, the incurable distrust of God's sublime goodness and unimpeachable purity and virtue. Each person, post-Eden, has existed in this relationship with their Creator and Lord, individually and collectively.[21] And yet, in spite of God's gracious outreach, as early as the time of Adam and Eve, there is an endemic failure to believe that God is anything but wrathful, hateful, bitter, and resentful at humankind for some inherent lack or deficiency over which many feel they have little if any control.

In the theology of John Calvin and the Reformed church, the efficient cause of Adam's fall consisted in his not receiving the will to

---

21. Cf. Erickson, *Christian Theology*, 719.

persevere against the seductions of the serpent. God did not deign to arm him with such a persevering will to serve divine glory—God desired to bring humankind first into a state of depravity in order that God might subsequently deliver them from that depravity into a state of salvation through the atoning act of Christ.[22]

How is it justifiable for God under a Calvinistic scheme to orchestrate the fall of humankind through the sin of Adam? While God predetermined Adam's disobedience and violation of God's command not to consume the fruit of the tree of the knowledge of good and evil, Adam acted of his own volition in that matter. The question of fairness and justice does not thereby properly arise since Adam was neither robbed of any possession rightly belonging to him, injured or harmed physically, psychologically, or spiritually, nor confined or compelled to act against his own wishes; rather, in eating the fruit, Adam only did what he most desired, thus bearing full responsibility for his action.

Adam's reproach is on account of the unity between his sinful intent and action, such intent being powerful and persistent enough to completely drive the subsequent sinful action, rather than the fact that he failed to choose otherwise, regardless of the fact that he was unable to have chosen otherwise. Likewise, even if all human actions have been dictated by God in eternity, it remains the case that human beings can be said to possess freewill insofar as their actions are wholly impelled by their personal intent, albeit there be no other recourse at a particular point in time, inasmuch as freedom under a compatibilist understanding is defined as the ability to act in accordance to one's desire.

Given that in the Calvinistic conception of total depravity, human beings are corrupt at the level of desire and will, always only loving and seeking to commit sin rather than glorifying God, all that is meted out to the non-elect in the form of divine judgment is justified and well-deserved, and the Calvinist cannot be charged with propagating a doctrine of a God who deals unfairly and unjustly with people. At the very most, one can express personal discomfort with a Calvinistic view of divine predestination and wonder why God is most glorified only in a context in which human suffering and evil exists alongside their beatitude and righteousness.

No individual person can charge God with unfairness for being non-elect, because in the case of any individual, nobody really knows

---

22. Calvin, *Inst.*, 1.15.8, 3.23.8; Anderson, "Why Did God Allow the Fall?"

whether they are elect or reprobate, at least not before the end of their lives. Should they seek God's salvation, asking that they might not be among the non-elect, this by itself already demonstrates that they are members of the elect. In the case that by God's decree not to regenerate them they do not actually seek the Lord throughout their lives, never having any real fear of God, always only using God's name to further their own agendas or pursue personal profit, these alone are rightly condemned for their disinterest in knowing and obeying God; all the non-elect are as such.

Anything that leads to a deeper understanding of God's grace through the cross of Christ glorifies God: the spiritual helplessness, hopelessness, and wickedness of unregenerate human beings through their inability to do anything but love and commit sin and face judgment in the non-elect, attesting to the human need for God's utterly gracious action at the cross for our salvation; the mercy of God in electing some to experience regeneration, justification, and glorification in spite of their helplessness, hopelessness, and wickedness. Why is it necessary to portray human helplessness, hopelessness, and wickedness through the non-election of actual individuals?[23] Until a person who has a particular illness succumbs to it, few will fully appreciate the direness of the state of health of those suffering from such a malady, and through that the wonderful nature of the treatment and medications that are capable of curing that disease. So it is with the spiritual disease that original sin is and the spiritual cure that God's salvation through Christ is.[24]

Beginning with Augustine of Hippo, it is possible to trace the development of a theology postulating a corruption of the human nature and will arising from the Edenic act of disobedience, comparable to a

---

23. From a Reformed point of view, a passage such as 2 Pet 3:9 which proclaims the divine will for all to repent and none to perish might be handled by recourse to the contention that here the writer is speaking to believers and therefore those who should repent rather than perish, and if anybody turns out to be unregenerate, they will perish. Hence, this exhortation functions as a warning to those in the church who may perceive themselves to be lacking in regeneration, to seek this grace of God, in so beginning to seek which, of course, they already show themselves to be regenerated. John Calvin interprets this passage as indicating God's revealed as opposed to hidden will. Calvin, *Commentaries on Catholic Epistles*, 419–20. Concerning 1 Tim 2:4, which is to the effect that God desires all people to be saved, this may be understood by Reformed Christians as referring to the way in which God wills even that some among rulers and princes might be saved, as the context bears out (1 Tim 2:1–2). Calvin, *Commentaries on Timothy, Titus, and Philemon*, 54–55.

24. Cf. Barth, *KD* IV.1, §61.2 (ET, Bromiley, p. 566).

spiritual sickness, so viral it is able to infect every member of Adam's progeny, in as thoroughgoing a manner as it has infected Adam himself. The Protestant and Reformed doctrine of total depravity speculates that the universal spiritual corruption in which humankind has involved itself in the person and by the wrong choice of Adam is a moral and spiritual disease from which no human person is capable of extricating themselves, not to mention all humankind.

The only recourse, in a happy tragedy made available by God through God's Son, is to look to the Lord Jesus Christ, crucified on the cross of Calvary for the sins of those atoned for, identify themselves in him as their representatives in being subjected to divine judgment for their sins, and receive divine pardon as mirrored in the divine favor which raised the same Jesus from the dead, a symbol of the fact that the believer has been justified before God, with all their sins having been wiped from their record so that it is as though they were a defendant standing trial and declared by the judge to be guiltless on the basis of the bearing by a substitute of penalties falling to them—a special arrangement made by God on the premise that otherwise no person could be acquitted from the divine trial, assessed to be sufficient to avert disorder in the heavenly court and the rest of the universe, for the pardon of sinners—and a foretaste of the believer's own future resurrection in a body incorruptible and immortal.

It is believed to be necessary strongly to assert an inseparable and inextricable relation between the sinful nature of humankind as a universal problem of cosmic proportions and the atoning sacrifice of the Lord Jesus as the sole solution. Accordingly, exponents of a Reformed doctrine surmise that human spiritual corruption entails that no positive moral inclination any longer exists in a human person (Gen 6:5), that God's wrath and hatred rest upon all members of humankind in consequence of the thoroughly ruined, transgressive, and rebellious moral nature and will of the human being, and that the single pathway away from alienation from God back to divine favor is through the way of the cross of Calvary, walked already by Jesus, on behalf of humanity, for the benefit of those who would receive God's offer of salvation and reconciliation. A clear distinction is struck between the non-believer, whose decisions and actions are completely driven by their sinful desires, arising from the corruption caused by the disobedience of Adam, and the believer, whose decisions and actions are increasingly and to be completely driven by their godly desires, which are birthed by the Holy Spirit on the basis of the substitutionary and propitiatory atoning work of Christ.[25]

These proponents of dogma fail to recognize that God does not relate with human individuals first and foremost as a judge. Adam and Eve perceived God in this light, and fled from the divine presence. They missed the note of friendship and solidarity even in the midst of transgression, with which God approached them in the garden. God did not thunder down majestically with a heavenly host or bear down upon the couple with terrifying and great hostility. Instead, God walked toward them, and sensing that they were in hiding, called out to the man. They did not perceive that in spite of necessary discipline, God remained very much in fellowship with them, even making for them garments out of skin.

The character of God's interaction with humankind is consistent throughout history, marked by inevitable consequences for transgression but at the same time always bathed in the warm glow of God's compassionate love, a love which disciplines and sets boundaries only to protect humankind from their rebellious nature and facilitate their highest wellbeing in obedience, and is ready to pardon and deliver, even such a one as Cain, who murdered his own brother, whom God chose to protect from those who would make an attempt on his life. At times, the discipline of God called for death and destruction, of individuals as well as ethnic groups, and yet Scripture informs us that God does not take any pleasure in the death of any person, including the evildoer.

There is a lack of appreciation for how God communicates with members of humankind, with whom God is in an eternal and loving relationship. Theologians are often too hasty in ascribing to God, on the basis of divine rebuke and condemnation, a negative and critical disposition wont to laying down difficult, even impossible, rules and making terminal assessments of human nature and conduct, leaving not a person with a glimmer of hope. We are quick to conclude that divine evaluations of human sinfulness in Scripture are to be treated as definitive and final, without hope of correction or for appeal. To support a sterile and clinical interpretation of such divine assessment, we devise

---

25. There is a place for human freewill in Reformed theology, as formulated and developed by John Calvin and his followers, yet only to the extent that such freewill is understood in a subjective sense: a person is deemed to be free insofar as they voluntarily engage in an action as opposed to being compelled to be so engaged. As such, it is possible for a person to both experience themselves as free moral agents and concurrently have all their actions fundamentally determined by the desires of their heart.

theories pertaining to how God eternally predestines our moral and spiritual situation of hopelessness for the express purpose of causing us to yield our self-confidence, abandon our pretensions, and desperately fling ourselves upon Christ alone.

Contrary to these expectations, however, God has always been accessible to humankind, both individually and collectively, in a relationship and communion of love. Always, even in the darkest periods of human history, there have been individuals who responded to the voice of deep spiritual intuition, calling them out of self-absorption into a life of faith in God. These were not often the rich or powerful of their day, merely human persons bold enough to embrace and chase the conviction that God might be good and trustworthy after all. Trust is the gateway to a genuine personal relationship with God, simply because love is founded on a willingness to suspend one's disbelief, cynicism, and suspicion and give oneself fully and wholeheartedly to another. Trust is an internal decision of the will marked by a desire to take what a person says at face value, seriously entertain the possibility in times of conflict that one may have misunderstood the intentions and actions of the other person, and ever pursue a still fuller apprehension of the character and personality of the one in whom one hopes to trust, and such trust should not be bestowed on just anyone, yet it ought to be bestowed on God, for God is trustworthy and has proven to be so in the course of centuries of history. No accusation laid at God's door has ever stood the test of honest and reasoned scrutiny, while so many have benefited from what they can only describe as God's perfect and affectionate love which draws them into a state of blissful contentment.

Without trust, it is not possible to truly know God, who is love (1 John 4:8, 16), because love is received in the context of a mutually-believing relationship. In the absence of trust, one stands outside the personal relationship without which knowing God becomes an impossibility and perceives but an external appearance of God open to all manner of distortion and misinterpretation, more often than not a projection onto God of our own fears and insecurities.

Therefore those who fail to trust in God irrevocably contrive a picture of God as a tyrant, a divine dictator (thought to be more or less benevolent in wielding the sway God holds over all of reality apart from Godself) who organizes all of reality external to God in such a way that everything must exist and inevitably does exist to bring Godself glory. While proponents of such a view demur that God's glory constitutes a greatest good in light that God is the greatest good, yet there is a very fine line between contending for a self-glorification of God at the expense of humankind, not quite a selfless act, and a glorification of God through a self-giving on the part of God to humankind, comprising a demonstration of affection toward and a conferment of moral guidance upon a beloved child.

God does not need to exact agony and frustration from human beings just in order to bolster God's glorification and draw them onto Godself. God's glory consists in nurturing the human person in affectionate love and guidance so that they rise eventually to God's level of concern for all entities and objects in the universe, for the order and integrity within the cosmos. God's highest glory reposes in all things attaining their *telos* in becoming like God in goodness, love, empathy, and righteousness, in a manner appropriate to their respective stations, a state attained by mirroring God as archetype and exemplar.[26]

It lies not in their becoming weak and humiliated that God alone might be strong and glorious. God does not need to drive humankind into a lowly state to secure their destiny as God's creatures and servants. A relationship established by force, power, and compulsion cannot truly last, and it is not the case that human beings left to their own devices will surely rebel. God in actual fact cedes control to human beings while maintaining affection for and kinship toward them, knowing that the first step in a loving relationship, such as God maintains with human beings, is to recognize and accord autonomy and independence within a framework of guidance and discipline.

As human persons grow in knowledge of and relationship with God, more space and freedom are accorded to empower the maturing person to voluntarily express love and concern and extend assistance to any as may be in need. God's kingdom is a sphere in which many become children who love and worship God through acts of goodness,

---

26. Cf. Barth, *KD* IV.2, §64.4 (ET, Bromiley, p. 269). The distinction between divine and human morality is not one of categorical difference. Although one would not expect a person to give up their life for an enemy as Jesus did at the cross, this is an act that represents a higher intensity of love rather than being utterly different from any self-sacrificial act of human love, such as someone choosing to die for a good or righteous person (Rom 5:6–8). Jesus' love for his enemies does not contradict human reason or conscience, at least not reason or conscience as freed from the dominion of sin, but stands as an impossibility for most and therefore an inspiration to do as he has done through remembering, in a conscious and intentional way, that we have already received such love and seeking to reciprocate it by doing likewise. Cf. González, *Reformation to Present*, 50.

love, kindness, and empathy for one another out of a sincere heart, rather than a place of indentured, fearful, or terrified servants whose only reason for drawing near to God is that there is simply no other option; it is either God or spiritual death. With children, love for a divine Father comes spontaneously and naturally, not as a product of threat, terror, fear, or worry (1 John 4:18).

As a case in point, consider the awe-inspiring and stunning vision the prophet Isaiah had of the Lord in the sixth chapter of the book named for him. When he felt and expressed deep anxiety over the fact that, as a sinful and guilty man of unclean lips, he has come face-to-face with the holy Lord of all, the first response of God was not to reinforce the sense of alarm and fear in the prophet, but rather have one of the seraphim expunge his sense of sinfulness and guilt by bringing a piece of burning coal from the altar to his lips. While some may see in this an allegory or figure pointing toward a future propitiatory sacrifice on the part of the Lord Jesus Christ, without which all the descendants of Adam will be rightly struck with terror at the thought of facing the Lord, whatever the mechanism, method, or process by which God brings it about that the sinner is cleansed of their sin and guilt, the fact remains that it is God's will to clear a person of their guilt and bear away their sense of sinfulness.[27]

Just as God does not desire that any person should perish, so God does not take any pleasure in leaving a person to wallow in their sin and guilt. Regardless of the manner in which a person may have alienated themselves from God, or grown up with such a sense of alienation coupled with a rebellious streak, each person, Jew, Christian, or other, will have an awareness that they have become estranged from God, since the law of God is written on every human heart and God has provided each person with a conscience to guide their own steps (Rom 2:1–16). In pictorial terms, it was the prodigal or lost son himself who "came to himself" (Luke 15:17) in the much-repeated parable of the Lord, there being no mention of any external influence in the form of an internal regenerative work or effectual calling, though the man was clearly persuaded by

---

27. Guilt should not constitute more of a problem than what the individual suffers as a result of their current inadequate level of understanding, since God is not a punitive judge who deems fit to pay meticulous attention to every slight infraction so as to mete out punishment (Job 35:5–8). A major theme of Job is that there is no necessary relationship between suffering and sin as well as between prosperity and righteousness, given that the righteous do suffer and the wicked do prosper.

the negative consequences he experienced in terms of a privation of food arising from his decision to separate from his father.

God, like the father in the story, waits for a person to recognize their need for God, never compelling them to understand this need.[28] As soon as they come to a recognition that they would be far better off in the presence of God, being found in a loving relationship with God, and make an emotional, intellectual, and spiritual return journey to the origin of their being and existence, God does not cast any of them away, as Jesus assures the crowd that he would not drive away any whom the Father gives to him (John 6:37), but will have compassion on them, display passionate affection toward them, bestow on them honor and dignity in spite that they come back filthy and unwashed, with no other motivation to show for their repentance than to be delivered from physical deprivation.

Jesus told the parable of the lost son, along with two other parables, in response to criticism of his ministry on the part of certain Pharisees and scribes for associating with people they deemed sinful by welcoming them and eating with them (Luke 15:1–2). Far from being insouciant as to the basic needs of human persons, be this physical, emotional, intellectual, or spiritual lack, God is anxious that all these needs are met in each person. Hence, that his followers might appreciate the pro-social, hospitable, and inclusive nature of his work, Jesus proclaimed early on that any lack a person might experience in their spirit, referring to their inner self and personality and all that makes them the individual they are, will be met in the kingdom of heaven (Matt 5:3). It is God's will only to build up, to edify a person, whoever it may be, reputable or disputable, rather than tear them down, for whatever reason.

Even in the case of the Babylonian king Nebuchadnezzar, whose cycle of pride, humiliation, and restoration are often adduced in support of a divine will that does as it pleases, including putting down kings for the sake of exalting the divine majesty, it was Nebuchadnezzar himself who boasted that he was solely to be credited for his ability to erect his royal palace and establish the kingdom so that nations and peoples might glorify him (Dan 4:29–30), with no mention of any secret divine decree ordaining that he do so. Indeed, it was only in order to learn the very lesson that he was not the source of his regal majesty and dominion that he was made to go through a period of humiliation (Dan 4:31–32).

---

28. As the Father of Jesus and in Jesus, the Father is "the Father of us all, the Father *par excellence*, the one true Father." Barth, *KD* IV.1, §61.2 (ET, Bromiley, p. 565).

There is no suggestion here that God had orchestrated these events, including his pride, in order to humiliate him so that the king might embrace his utter dependence on God as a weak and loyal vassal; the goal of the experience of humiliation was for Nebuchadnezzar to learn that he was not the source of royal power, rather than to be broken down himself before the divine majesty. If it was ingrained in the king's mind that the divine sway cannot be refused or resisted by any power in the world (Dan 4:35), the narrative makes clear that this was not the main lesson of the experience, but a reflection of the king regarding God's ability to humble God's servants, not so that they might worship God in a state of lowliness, but only in order that they might see that pride and conceit lead nowhere (Dan 4:37).

Pride is an evil that God successfully contained in this story, not an instrument by which God accomplished some greater or higher good. If God so detests pride and contempt that God opposes (Jas 4:6) and hates it (Prov 6:16–17; 8:13), why would God, who cannot bring Godself to look idly and indifferently at acts of evil (Hab 1:13), use it for any purpose, no matter how purportedly great, glorious, or necessary? God does not orchestrate trials in order that people might fall into sin on account of the fact that God is completely good and acts always only for the good of humankind (Jas 1:12–17).

In the theology of John Calvin, the "cause" and "occasion" of the "perdition" of Adam and his posterity are "found in themselves." This is not in consequence of a cleft between God's will and divine permission, as though there were a potential for that which God has willed to not be fulfilled or actualized.[29] Although Calvin allows that, at least in a hypothetical sense, Adam "could have stood if he wished, seeing that he fell solely by his own will," he very quickly diverts attention to the nature of Adam's will, in terms of its resilience and power to bear with temptation until it blows and breaks over, highlighting how Adam's will, though without being predetermined to choose good or evil yet with a mental apprehension of the benefits of obedience and the negative consequences of disobedience and an inclination of the will toward obedience, was liable to pledge its allegiance to either God or disobedience, and not endued with the ability to outlast temptation.

In addition, Calvin points out that Adam's fall was due to his lack of a persevering will that should have been able to see him safely through

---

29. Calvin, *Inst.*, 3.23.8 (ET, Battles, p. 957).

the storms of temptation; God withheld such a "virtue of perseverance," and how God's goodness can be reconciled with such a decision "lies hidden in his plan" and it is not meet for mere human beings to raise any doubts in relation to this. Still, it is not reasonable to exculpate Adam on account of this state of affairs, on the ground that Adam was under no compulsion to perform the evil in which he involved himself, but found his desire, will, and purpose in alignment and harmony with it. Furthermore, there was no obligation on God's part to provide Adam with anything more than "a mediocre and even transitory will, that from man's Fall he might gather occasion for his own glory."[30]

We have seen how there is no strong and incontestable scriptural evidence for espousing such a view of human freewill in terms of a compatibilist conception, wielded by God to serve the divine glory through orchestrating and ordaining a fall and redemption, but that people, beginning with Adam and Eve, sin when they choose mistrust and suspicion over entrustment and commitment of a human self to a divine inclusive and all-encompassing other.

Such theology as we find in Calvin is possible only through a formalistic and descriptive reading of Scripture which disregards intention and context, applying an overly literal and empirical hermeneutic to passages that address the sinfulness of humanity. A crucial passage frequently quoted in support of a doctrine of divine predestination in which the emotional and spiritual wellbeing of human individuals is subordinated to the divine will and glory is Rom 9:6–24. This passage and the way it has been interpreted by Reformed theologians present another opportunity to understand the nature and implications of a formalistic and empirical reading of Scripture.

In this connection, Reformed theologians are of the view that the passage affords an example of a biblical affirmation to the effect that all who are saved are saved only through the mercy and compassion of God, rather than their own merit, and those who are passed over for salvation are passed over because it pleases God to do this to creatures and, indeed, sinful ones to whom God has no moral obligation to preserve from certain destruction.

Yet, the references in the text to the twin brothers Jacob and Esau as well as Moses and Pharaoh do not quite give credence to the theory that God predestines some to salvation and leaves the rest to perdition,

---

30. Calvin, *Inst.*, 1.15.8 (ET, Battles, p. 196).

irrespective of their moral merits. Rom 9:6–9 introduce the theme of how adoption into God's family takes place on the basis of divine election and promise, that is, God does not make adoption possible for human persons on the premise of some accomplishment, whether it be Abraham's success in begetting a child such as Ishmael in testimony to his virility and the fertility of his servant-wife Hagar or some other person's similar qualities.

Rom 9:10–13 take up the subject of divine election by citing the cases of Isaac and Rebekah, parents to Jacob and Esau, children born in close succession with the latter coming forth first. While this set of references is often adduced in support of a doctrine of divine predestination, in which the observations that God had elected the older to serve the younger and favored Jacob above Esau, whom God hated, even before the children were born, serve as building blocks for a theory that God chooses whom to save and whom to reject, in actual fact, the passage does not go quite this far.

The only assertion being made is that God originally appointed Esau, the elder brother, to serve his younger brother, Jacob, and this was not in view of Esau's moral inferiority, since the children were not yet born. Although the mandate to service is often taken in a negative sense, as a sign of rejection or reprobation on the part of God, this interpretation is overdrawn, misinformed, and overly influenced by a secular mode of thinking, in which service of another is frequently viewed in terms of subordination to be avoided rather than a way of moral leadership and truth to be eagerly pursued. Jesus corrected this error, endemic among people of his time, by emphasizing his own commission to service (i.e., Mark 10:45; Luke 22:24–27). In fact, the election to serve was an election of divine approval bestowed on Esau at first. This reading is more in line with how Scripture depicts Esau as beginning with a birthright, which he regarded with contempt, rather than having lost it before he was born (Gen 25:29–34).[31]

31. An alternate reading inspired by Thomas Aquinas that preserves a traditional interpretation concerning a purported prophesied servanthood or subordination of Esau in relation to Jacob might contend that God did not predetermine the destinies of each child but that God conferred a subordinate role on Esau in view of God's foreknowledge that Esau, in spite of receiving divine grace that equips him both to know and fulfill the divine calling in his life, would reject the divine mandate. Neither this alternate view nor a traditional one based on the usual understanding of a call to service as inferior to a call to be served, synonymous with a divinely-conferred birthright of the chosen child, can avoid the fact that Esau had had his birthright, given that Scripture describes him as despising his birthright (Gen 25:29–34), implying that it was not

If it is objected that the election for the older to serve the younger is to be taken in a negative way because it makes more sense for Esau, who as the older brother has seniority to his credit, to be served by rather than to serve Jacob, hence showing God's favoring of Jacob as a sign of how election is based not on works but God's unconditional mercies, we respond that Scripture itself leaves no room for such an interpretation, since it refers specifically to the deeds of the brothers and how these have no bearing on God's election for one to serve the other, rather than physical seniority as such, which can hardly be accounted as a "work": "though they [Jacob and Esau] were not yet born and had done nothing either good or bad—in order that God's purpose of election might continue, not because of works but because of him who calls—she was told, 'The older will serve the younger.'" (Rom 9:11–12 ESV)

As such, Esau was initially favored by God with a mandate to serve his younger brother, though he had done nothing to merit this election; it is not usual for an older brother to serve his younger brother, indeed, the opposite is typically the case. In the story of the way in which Esau treated his birthright with contempt, apart from how the narrative seems to depict Jacob as a schemer who manipulates his brother into selling his birthright to him for a bowl of lentil stew, the story itself subtly shows Jacob at work in serving his older brother, a task for Esau which he abandoned for his hunting interest. As a result, God came to

---

something God did not confer on him, and Isaac having the power and authority to confer the blessings due to a firstborn upon Esau (regardless that Rebekah intervened and had Jacob deceive his father into thinking that he was Esau, thus receiving the blessings meant for the firstborn); hence, Esau was not eternally mandated to serve Jacob based on supposed divine foreknowledge that Esau would reject the calling of God. Furthermore, if God truly intended to assess each child on the basis of their response to a divine calling, there would have been no need to disclose this information to Rebekah, whose differential affection toward her two children, culminating in her ploy to deceive her husband into granting the birthright to her favored son Jacob, must have been influenced by the revelation. At the very least, the customary view of the mandate to service suffers from the deficient and highly problematic premise that God needs to employ or at least allows deception to achieve and actualize God's wishes and purposes among God's people. The perspective on the matter we are propounding avoids this complication because God is not responsible in any way, not even in giving permission, for the deception perpetrated by mother and son. In our view, Rebekah, influenced as she was by worldly ideas of greatness, interpreted God's revelation to her that the older child would serve the younger as giving her sanction to act deceitfully to dispossess her older son, Esau, of his birthright, not recognizing that there is no antithesis between the birthright and service and that indeed the birthright involves humble service, thus precipitating an unnecessary family feud in which one son experienced murderous urges toward the other. See Aquinas, *Summa* 1a, Q. 23, Art. 5, co.

favor Jacob and allow for the transfer of the election, with Esau as the original object, to Jacob at the death of his father Isaac. The descendants of Jacob, that is, Israel, similarly dwelled under the blessing of God, while Esau's posterity lived away from Israel.

Rom 9:13 cites Mal 1:2–3, concerning the way in which the Edomites became hostile and violent towards the Israelites, joining hands with the Babylonians in sacking Jerusalem (Obad 1:10–14); earlier in history, the Edomites refused safe passage to the weary Israelites as they were making their way through the wilderness after fleeing Egypt (Num 20:14–21). Not only did Esau betray God's election for him to serve his brother Jacob, but his descendants did the same as well. On account of the violence of the Edomites towards Israel, divine judgment fell on the former, and it is in view of this historical context that God speaks of divine hatred towards Esau and favor towards Jacob.

There is no suggestion in the passage that God specially favored and elected Jacob and his descendants from the beginning, before the brothers were born, and rejected Esau and his descendants, or that Jacob and Esau are to be regarded as archetypes for the elect believer predestined for salvation and the reprobate predestined for damnation or at least passed over for salvation, irrespective of their deeds. Rather, there is only the idea of a mandate of service bestowed upon Esau out of God's pure and unconditional grace, though none of the brothers had done anything to merit it, which Esau rejected and Jacob assumed.

It is not unjust for God to favor Jacob over Esau in this way (Rom 9:14). The question arises in the context of the change of dispensation; whereas God initially conferred the divine mandate on Esau, this was subsequently displaced from the original recipient, though not revoked or withdrawn, and transferred to Jacob.[32] After all, the election belongs to God and it is God's prerogative on whom to bestow it, based on human receptivity (Rom 9:15–16). God's election is an expression of divine mercy, given that there is completely no obligation on God's part to welcome any human person into a fellowship of the divine life, calling, mission, and a mutual sharing in all that is good that belongs to God.

To draw attention to a strictness in God's mercy, St. Paul segues into the story of Moses' encounter with Pharaoh. The citation of Exod

---

32. The divine calling cannot be revoked (Rom 11:29); it was only displaced, that is, handed to another person to fulfill without the original recipient losing their mandate. It is simply because Esau and the Edomites still had the mandate of God that they were penalized for their obstinacy in violating its requirements.

9:16 in Rom 9:17 has been interpreted as asserting God's indomitable will over Pharaoh, through whom God will do according to the divine good pleasure, raising Pharaoh up to show God's destructive power in order that God's name might be carried far and wide across the world. God does predict Pharaoh's arrogant stubbornness (Exod 3:19–20). At what point, however, does God begin to harden Pharaoh's heart against submitting to the Lord (Exod 4:21–23)? Narratively, Pharaoh had at least one opportunity to heed God's summons through Moses and Aaron to free the Israelites, which he rejected (Exod 5:1–9); at the next encounter recorded, God says God will harden Pharaoh's heart that God might display many signs of wonderful power (Exod 7:3–5). We see here an illustration of the way in which God gives a person an opportunity to do what is right, and if they persist in evildoing, while God may not be able to take control of their freewill, yet God may choose in certain instances to cause a hardening or even deception of a person's heart by withdrawing God's spiritual support to achieve some objective, in which case it is fitting that it be said that God hardened or deceived a person's heart since God intends that it be hardened or deceived by way of punishment and promotes such hardening or deception (e.g., Ezek 14:6–11) through retracting God's timely spiritual guidance.[33]

This reading is in line with the previous reference to Jacob and Esau in that in both the instances involving Jacob and Esau and Pharaoh, there is an election of God to serve the people of God which is rejected, in the first example, by Esau, and in the second, by Pharaoh. In these cases, the divine commission and mandate was given by unconditional mercy, not in consideration of the moral merit of the recipients, that these might share in God's ministry and mission of service within the context of a personal relationship with and knowledge of God. In both cases, judgment was meted out by God for a refusal to obey the divine call; in the

---

33. Cf. the discussion about how God's hardening of Pharaoh's heart is to be seen as a punishment for a prior transgression rather than an unprovoked act on the part of God, in Augustine, Gla, §41 (ET, Holmes, pp. 461–62). See also Augustine, Gla, §45 (ET, Holmes, p. 464). Can God's promotion of a hardening or deception be considered an act of temptation or even a full-blown and irresistible attempt to have a person succumb to temptation, contrary to Jas 1:13? Not so, since no temptation is involved; only the well-deserved punishment of a sinner, rendered in perfect proportion to the transgression. Is God unmerciful to assist the hardening of Pharaoh's heart in this way simply because the latter failed to respond on one occasion? Not so, given that Pharaoh practically brutalized the people of Israel by committing them to harsh slavery (Exod 1:13–14).

case of Esau, this involved the destruction of the Edomites, while in Pharaoh's case, it entailed a hardening of his heart.

Rom 9:19 continues with a critique of God's rebuke of those who fail to obey or submit to the divine election: if God is able even to marshal the disobedient and insubordinate toward accomplishing God's purposes, then why does God see fit to reproach anyone? To this, Paul replies that the work of God above the actions of these disobedient persons toward bringing about God's purpose is not to the credit of those persons themselves, for they contributed nothing willingly toward the divine cause, but, if anything, did their utmost to betray the divine election and foil the divine purpose; they cannot therefore take issue with God's condemnation of their actions on the ground that they did, in fact, contribute unwittingly, even against their own will, to the divine cause (Rom 9:20).

Paul addresses another complaint on the part of the objector, to the effect that it is unfair for God to use a person against their own will. He responds with the reminder that God as the Creator and Lord is above human persons, and therefore within rights to employ them to serve the divine purpose and mission in whatever way seems best and most appropriate in the circumstances (Rom 9:20–21). As a matter of fact, it is God's prerogative even to do what God did in the case of Pharaoh, whose insubordination provided an opportunity for God to pursue a course of hardening his heart, rather than destroying him at once, in order to have reason to reveal progressively more destructive and mighty acts of divine power (Rom 9:22–24). God demonstrates mercy even in Pharaoh's case; whilst there was every reason and capacity for God to put a complete end to Pharaoh himself and his nation (Exod 9:15), God ultimately spared Pharaoh himself and the entire nation, though the firstborn of each family was taken.

Is God's ostensible relegation of numerous Jews in Paul's time to a state of spiritual hardening and reprobation sufficient to establish a theology of lapsarian predestination? In Rom 11:32, God is said to have situated many individuals in Israel in a category of disobedience. Rom 11:20 specifies that the rejection of these persons was due to their inability to exercise faith in God. The literary context suggests that this incapacity was neither involuntary nor beyond their personal control, but very much voluntary and within the scope of their freedom of will, as far as even the Gentile elect believers were sternly urged not to become complacent concerning their election; rather, they were to continue in a sober awareness that they were neither better than nor superior to those who were rejected, having merely accepted God's kindness instead of showing contempt for it (Rom 11:20–24).

Moreover, the only reason many individuals in Israel at the time were unable to repose their faith in God was that they pursued self-righteousness rather than God's righteousness (Rom 10:2–4). How was it that they were ignorant of God's righteousness? Was this God's doing? Rom 11:7–10 appears to suggest this notion, in that it seems that God constituted the source of the spiritual blindness and deafness of these individuals. Be that as it may, a careful reading of the Old Testament texts adduced from the Septuagint (Isa 29:10, Ps 69:22–23) reveals that God's withdrawal of the gift and blessing of spiritual sight and hearing was not the fundamental cause of disobedience but merely a response to a preexisting disobedience. Consider Isa 29:13–14, where God declares a removal of wisdom and discernment from Judah's sages in consequence of their insincerity and lack of authentic relationship with and understanding of God, whereas Ps 69:22–23 comprises an imprecatory prayer on the part of David against those who actively sought his downfall in which he pleads for their retribution (see Ps 69:1–28).

A theology of predestination to sin and suffering is ultimately utilitarian. Typically, when moral responsibility is assessed, one looks at whether harm is caused and whether there was intent to cause such harm. A person who causes emotional harm through their actions without intending to do harm to another person, for instance, is still morally responsible since harm was caused,[34] while a person who only intends to cause harm but does not actually carry out the act or was prevented from doing so is still culpable for the duration of holding that intent.

A theory of lapsarian predestination violates the principle governing moral accountability by holding that God is justified in orchestrating spiritual harm on human beings (decreeing the events that take place in the fall without approving of them)[35] as a result of the fact that human beings belong to God and are at God's disposal[36]; that

---

34. Reflecting this is a concept in jurisprudence known as negligent infliction of emotional distress, where if it can be established that "the defendant's actions were reasonably foreseeable to cause the emotional distress," a claim can be made on this ground. Legal Information Institute, "Negligent Infliction of Emotional Distress."

35. Cf. Barth KD IV.1, §60.1 (ET, Bromiley, p. 409).

36. This is not supported by scriptural teaching, least of all the passage (Rom 9:6–29) where St. Paul speaks of the divine potter having the right to do as the potter wishes with the potter's creation, the intended signification of which, based on the source

when human beings are ordained to fall into sin, they will the sin that they commit and so they are morally accountable (rather than being accountable for not knowing better than to sin, something of which they are incapable), and the virtue of salvation involving human persons being brought from pride, independence, and self-glorification to humility, God-reliance, and God-glorification is so critical and of such infinite value that any harm that might have to be caused so as to effect that transformation is judged to be worthwhile.[37]

The obedience of God through keeping God's law is intrinsically expressed in the mode of trusting in God's goodness, a mode which is open to people of all cultures and religious traditions. According to Barth, "The Jews not only start like all the heathen with the presence and revelation of the gracious God which is objectively real from the very first."[38] This implies that Rom 1:19-20, on which Barth is commenting, teaches that members of other religious groups have access to God's accompaniment and the knowledge of the divine as God of grace.

Furthermore, "The Law of which Paul speaks in Rom. 2-3 is the Law of God, which, as the Law of His covenant of grace, calls man away from any attainment of his own righteousness to repentance and obedience in the form of trust in God's goodness."[39] Quite clearly, Barth makes of this passage that the role urged of humankind in relation to the self-revealing God is only a willingness to entrust and commit their whole being and confidence to this very God, relying on God's

---

passage in Jer 18:1-11, concerns God's compassion toward those who repent and wrath toward those who choose and persist in evil as illustrated in the cases of Esau and Pharaoh, both of whom rejected God's mandate for them to serve the household and community of faith prior to being consigned to judgment or a hardening of the heart.

37. Is it so impossible to conceive of a person who reveres God without the need to undergo sin and suffering due to sin? Is the experience of sin truly imperative for the consummation of God's purpose for humanity? Does God really need to create an at-first non-existent problem so as to orchestrate the occasion for its solution in a bid to bring about the greater good of humanity's dependence on God? Is it not enough for God to be glorified through the things God has created and not also by means of a startling liberation from sin? In any human person, the attempt to create dependence on oneself would qualify to be regarded as perversely manipulative. Although God is indeed the supreme and greatest good, the reception of such a good should not be impeded by a violation of one of the aspects of that good; namely, a kindness that would never seek to harm or manipulate an innocent or guiltless person (as Adam and Eve were at the point of creation, prior to which God had allegedly already eternally decreed their fall) no matter what the justification.

38. Barth, *KD* IV.1, §60.1 (ET, Bromiley, p. 395).

39. Barth, *KD* IV.1, §60.1 (ET, Bromiley, p. 395).

benevolence, purity, and alacrity to act on their behalf and always only, and most mercifully, in their favor.

Why is it imperative that we do not seek our own righteousness in our works but only through the goodness of God? Imagine if divine benevolence, care, support, and provision were secured solely on the premise of what we did for God or how we satisfied some requirement, and that God's friendly approach were to vanish as soon as we fall short of God's preconditions for experiencing divine kindness. What would the outcome of such a state of affairs be?

First, those who do manage to meet those prerequisites would be encouraged in arrogance, considering that they do merit God's benevolent approach on those terms. Second, people would subsist in a state of unremitting uncertainty, never being quite sure of God's continued good relationship with them given the worry that they themselves might someday slip from their current good and meritorious standing before God. Such ambiguity is ultimately an ambiguity concerning the persistence of their own well-doing and to the extent that this is so, the spiritual relationship with the divine becomes a treadmill on which they have to endlessly run.

All this is different from the loving relationship God already maintains with each person out of God's own goodwill and good pleasure, not on account of any satisfaction or meeting of requirements, in the context of which God expects at least some moral correspondence to God's moral character and expression, seeing that the moral relationship presupposes already a preexisting and unshakeable bond of love with God, in which all that is asked of the human counterpart is simply reciprocity and mutuality, a giving and reflecting back to God, in terms of one's trust, in God's goodness, and goodwill expressed in intent, emotion, will, and action, what God already does in relation to the individual.

The worship of idols is proscribed because they represent a transactional interaction with the divine; in fact, they misrepresent the relationship with God in this way. Dealing with idols demands interacting with them in a certain set of ways, meeting specific requirements of ritual obligation. Once those conditions are met, a worshipper can expect, even clamor, to receive the blessing of the idol, which becomes a symbol not only of the worshipper's merit in the realm of divinity, but of their claim to divine favor. The conversion of object to subject of the actual subject and of subject to object of the actual object is complete, in which process God is made subservient to humankind and humankind superior to God.

Instead of this, biblical teaching commends the worldview of a God who stands always in moral judgment against humankind, meting out penalties for disobedience and rewards—encouragements rather than obligations—for obedience. Unlike the idolater, the moral person cannot boast that they are virtuous, since the very capacity to act virtuously comes from the Divine Nature, which posits humankind in this way as fully actualized only in virtue; the desire to act virtuously comes from the Trinity, whose own virtuous presence and being are burned into the early ontological experience of each human person while existing as angelic beings; and the encouragement to act virtuously comes from the Divine Nature and the Trinity, so that the only contribution of the moral person is the decision to flee a burning house for their own safety (Jude 1:23), hardly a meritorious deed.[40] In contrast to the idolater, the moral person is assured of God's everlasting relationship of affectionate love, which does not end with sin and punishment but is rather manifest even then in the form of God's continued concern for the individual such that God refuses to abandon them in indifference or utterly destroy them in wrath, but pleads with them through chiding and tears to turn back for their own sakes and holistic and eternal wellbeing.

God's wrath has been misconstrued as an irrational or inordinate anger on the part of God against actions regarded by a pedantic and irrelevant God as sinful but by modern society as rather acceptable. In reality, it is the effect and product of God's affectionate love. Anger is certainly involved, not for private or petty reasons, but only because God knows that the sinner may be blind or insensitive to their own sin and needs to be jolted back to an awareness of who they are and how they ought to live.

Divine wrath is averted not by the sacrifice of Jesus, but by repentance. This is because wrath is due to sin and the problem of sin can only be resolved with the repentance of the one who committed sin; the natural consequences of sin cannot be transferred from one person to another (Ezek 18:4, 20).[41] Be that as it may, there is certainly a sense in which God does not mete out the punishment that a person deserves for their transgressions—recognizing that God does still mete out punishment post-crucifixion and reserves the right to do so, in cases involving the substitution of God among non-believers or spurning of God's

---

40. Cf. Barth, *KD* IV.1, §60.2 (ET, Bromiley, p. 459).

41. This is akin to Hugo Grotius's view on the matter as outlined in Erickson, *Christian Theology*, 721–22.

grace among believers (Acts 5:1–11; Rom 1:18–32; Gal 6:7–8; Heb 6:4–8; 10:26–31), even while permitting that the punishment for other sins fall on the crucified Christ (Rom 3:23–26).[42]

To avoid a scenario in which the human consciousness is incapable of living with a disparity between one's conviction that even sins repented of should be punished, and God's choice not to punish them, eventuating in guilt, and nurse the conscience back to health and wholeness, God has provided Christ crucified as a means by which a person who senses this disparity can look to the cross and project their need for a fuller penalty onto Jesus, seeing themselves as having been more fully penalized in him, having died and resurrected in him as a symbol of God's favor and a guarantee of hope in a future resurrection.

Martin Luther reckoned that the human will is in bondage to sin in consequence of Adam's disobedience. In this connection, passages like Gen 6:5 and, in the case of the Christian, to testify to the continual effects of sin, Rom 7:13–25 may be cited.[43] Yet it is crucial to understand that even at the time during which God found it necessary to send a deluge to wipe out creation, God at that very juncture found in Noah a blameless and righteous man; even in the case of the person of whom Paul spoke in Romans 7, whether this be himself or some other, not all is lost with that individual, given that there is at least still an "agreement" with God's law (Rom 7:16), a "desire to do what is right" (Rom 7:18), one of whom it can be said that they "delight in the law of God, in my inner being" (Rom 7:22), a "law of my mind" that makes war against "the law of sin that dwells in my members." (Rom 7:23)

As a matter of fact, in the case of the referent of Paul's painfully poignant descriptions, the inner being, the actual personality and true self, of the individual in question appears to be good rather than evil. While both godly and sinful desires coexist, he grieves his sinful desires

---

42. Penalizing sin is one of the ways in which God keeps immorality in check (1 Tim 1:8–11), another being the emphasis on good works as a testimony of an internal faith (Matt 25:31–46; James 2). How does it happen that a believer in Christ will engage in acts availing others in regard to some need? The passage in Matthew 25 limns two interrelated truths: first, the true followers of Christ are apt to serve the practical needs of the destitute and it is unbecoming of such a disciple not to do so; second, Christ suffers alongside those who suffer in any practical way and, whether or not they are cognizant of it, those followers of his who take it upon themselves to minister to the practical needs of the poor and needy minister ultimately to their Lord.

43. Luther, *Dsa*, 6.2, 7.17 (ET, Packer and Johnston, 6.2, 7.17, pp. 242–43, 313).

and actions while he does not grieve his godly desires and actions; on this basis, he identifies with his godly desires and actions.[44]

The intent, at least, is without reproach, albeit there is a constant struggle to prevent a manifestation of evil which often fails (Rom 7:15, 19, 23). It is the action rather than the will that is held captive by the principle of sin dwelling in the flesh, and in such a person, the desire not to commit wrongdoing does not coincide with but precedes or follows the perpetration of sinful action, for the very fact that one is able to participate in sin already presupposes that they do not at that point in time view the area in which they choose to direct their attention and energy as sinful, suggesting a need for further introspection involving a personal recognition of, penitence toward, and confession of sin, a determination to continue in such wrongful ways of thinking, feeling, desiring, and behaving no longer but rather embrace new and rightful ways of thinking, feeling, desiring, and behaving.[45]

The presence of these diametrically opposed mindsets implies the existence of two separate and distinct sources of self-assessment and moral agency; one, a principle from God and of humanity and, two, a principle not from God and against humanity, ensconced in a stronghold of captivity to sin due to psychological dysfunction conspiring with compulsive evil, one in need of tearing down and capable of being dismantled.

Along a specific line of interpretation, one is reminded of the insidious operations of sinfulness observed by Karl Barth, concealing itself as it does under the cloak of necessity of circumstance, purported nobility of intent, appearance of goodness, or utilitarian usefulness.[46] No Christian enters into an act of sin thinking that what they are about

---

44. A temptation is to be distinguished from a sinful desire by the fact that it does not resonate to any degree with the person in question as to their conation; that is, they do not feel the desire that the temptation suggests in a mental picture. According to Jas 1:13–15, no person succumbs to temptation without their own desire being implicated or involved in some way in being drawn to the temptation.

45. Chua, ECRST, 150.

46. Barth, KD IV.1, §60.1 (ET, Bromiley, p. 398): "It belongs to the very nature of evil that it is equivocal in its appearance. Where, then, do we see it otherwise than—if not in the lustrous garment of the good (as may happen)—at any rate with an admixture of the good, to some extent covered over and adorned and excused by all kinds of historical circumstances which have to be taken into account, by the praiseworthy aims and intentions of the human misdoer, or by the happy accompaniments or its indisputable appearances to the contrary or its undeniably positive results? Such a good case can be made out for the theory that evil is always in and for the good." Also, Barth, KD IV.1, §60.2 (ET, Bromiley, pp. 434–35).

to do is an act of depravity. As a matter of fact, there will always be some justification given by the sinner, whether this be that circumstances forced their hand (e.g., a busy minister who indulges in sexual sin might attempt to excuse that behavior by appealing to his fatigue and telling himself that it is only right that he experiences some "enjoyment" between ministry trips, not realizing or conceding that perhaps his tiredness and exhaustion is an indication to him that he should dial back on his ministry activity); that a sinful act is not actually sinful (e.g., one who consumes pornography might justify their behavior by recourse to the supposition that his action of indulging in or refraining from porn consumption does not really affect the porn industry as a whole, positively or negatively, not recognizing that he has a personal relationship with God and that God is grieved whenever he engages in porn consumption); or that one's sin brings about a higher good (e.g., the leader of a nation who takes it upon himself to wage war against surrounding nations to "reclaim" what "rightfully belongs" to his nation, not understanding that such an act of national glorification will only serve to destroy the lives of many innocents).[47] All it takes for such a person to break free from this state of captivity is to beseech God for wisdom through Jesus Christ (Rom 7:25; Jas 1:5).

Aside from moral lapses precipitated and facilitated by ignorance, there will also be instances of psychological disorder conspiring with moral evil of a compulsive nature in which a person becomes completely blind to the harm they are causing such that the person's conscience and moral structures fail to register the immoral act as wrong or unethical (1 Tim 4:2). In this case, immersed as they are in dysfunctional and immoral ways of thinking, an individual may be in a constant position of having to turn aside from thoughts of temptation before they lodge in the heart and become more difficult to manage (Gen 4:1–8).

In both the cases of sinning intentionally and partially as a result of ignorance or mental disorder, the individual, who only has good ethical goals, is temporarily misled or driven towards sinful behavior, which they come to express remorse for after the act and when confronted by the Word of God, the spiritual community, or even wider society, because these will appeal, through collective social persuasion, to an unconscious inner moral self that knows better and that is not satisfied with a person's unrighteous self-justifications even at the point of committing

---

47. Cf. Barth, *KD* IV.1, §61.3 (ET, Bromiley, pp. 584–85), in which he refers to a "right of wrong."

the transgression, knowing that there can be no justification for sin. Until they understand and address the root causes of their behavior, they will go through ceaseless cycles of commission and remorse.

For Barth, sin has the nature of pride, whereby one created by God to fully obey God's laws governing right and wrong, good and evil decides instead to play the judge of morality and truth, fancying themselves to be in a position to distinguish and choose between good and evil and, furthermore, to commit to its own choice of what is good as opposed to evil by way of coming into their own supposed maturity. The person who acts in this manner makes themselves "impossible", by which Barth means that the individual deludes themselves into thinking that they are judge of truth and arbiter of morality, a God and a Lord, when all that they really are amounts to nothing more than a child on a stool, a mere human and servant—there is no explanation or justification for such presumptuousness, and it represents nothing save a dangerous threat to the divine order which safeguards human wellbeing.

The assumed status has no basis in reality; all the same, such a person's self-delusion will have practical consequences upon their relationship with God, self, and other people (who may well entertain the same false view of themselves). For instance, they will reject God's principles and suppose that it is wise, prudent, and even necessary for them to do so, and they will be constantly at odds and in rivalry with their fellows who hold similar views about what is morally best for themselves, on the basis of what they themselves imagine to be true, correct, and good, based on their personal interpretations of Scripture or religious or non-religious traditions, their logical theories, and the experience of their conscience.[48]

It hardly stands the test of scrutiny for Barth to contend that the reactions and responses surrounding the passion of Jesus proved beyond a shadow of doubt the universally wicked character of the human heart in "rebellion against God, enmity with one's neighbor and sin against oneself," seeing that for every Judas Iscariot or high or chief priest, there were the disciples and followers of Christ whose fear or inability to confront the religious or political authorities cannot be held against them as symptoms of a primal human wickedness acquired from the time of Adam, for if they were truly filled with malice, they would not even have accepted the great risks of being in the presence of

---

48. Barth, *KD* IV.1, §60.2 (ET, Bromiley, pp. 445–51).

potential opponents, or wrestled with their conscience, as Peter and the women who followed Jesus clearly did.[49]

For this reason, it is quite unnecessary to propose on the basis of scanty scriptural evidence that the human heart is so trapped in wickedness and rebelliousness, the divine majesty so offended and enraged by it, the moral government of God so threatened, that the only destiny for such individuals is hellish eternal suffering, which can only and must be put away and resolved through a decisive turn to the atoning sacrifice of Christ. Such a theory tends to obfuscate the role of the regulation of moral behavior by divine judgment (Gal 6:7-8; 1 Tim 1:8-11) as well as any other way to enforce consequences for one's evildoing.[50] Furthermore, the limitation of a theory of atonement based on the idea of satisfaction (Anselm of Canterbury, 1033/34-1109) consists in the attempt to conceive of God on the analogy of a feudal lord, that is, as a divine overlord who views violations of God's law not simply as acts of immorality or those which destabilize the moral order but, indeed, as an injury to God's personal honor and dignity which God feels an ineradicable need to avenge.[51]

While God may very well feel a sense of dishonor at the commission of moral transgressions proscribed under God's laws, it is quite a different matter to suggest that the feudal ruler in the medieval age functions as such a felicitous analogue for God's relationship to those God governs that fundamentally the same system of punishment obtains in God's treatment of human persons who do not abide by divinely-ordained religious and moral regulations for human conduct. If the medieval criminal justice system performed a useful role in maintaining sociopolitical order through shoring up monarchical authority, it is also clear that there is no commensurability between a feudal penal process to which the insubordinate

---

49. Barth, *KD* IV.1, §60.1 (ET, Bromiley, pp. 398-99).

50. What does it mean to "sow" to one's "flesh" (ESV)? Earlier in Gal 5:19-21, St. Paul highlights a catalogue of sins that touch on sexual excesses and antisocial behaviors including hostility, jealousy, raging anger, and divisiveness. 1 Tim 1:8-11 stresses the function of God's law in regulating the conduct of the profane, those who raise their hand against their parents, those involved in murder or sexual excess, in the slave trade, and in giving false witness.

51. Cf. Erickson, *Christian Theology*, 728: "God being God, he not only may act to preserve his own honor; he must do so. He cannot simply disregard it." See also the wider context of the discussion of the satisfaction theory of the atonement in Erickson, *Christian Theology*, 727-29.

are subject for the stability of the kingdom[52] and God's patient disposition and posture toward sinners, which can only be reminiscent of the lavish and extravagant mercy, compassion, and paternal affection of the father toward his returning lost son in the famous parable. The theocratic system of Israel in the Old Testament period cannot serve as any inspiration or model for a conception of God as foundationally punitive in relation to sinners seeing as the Old Testament moral code is interested only in behavior rather than the internal movements of desire and intent, and so life in biblical Israel would have been livable for most.

Why did God command the erection of the tabernacle and the temple? What were their functions? God certainly did not need these to be enriched in any way. Therefore, God provided these centers of ritual sacrifice for the Israelites and Jews themselves, to furnish a way for them to be restored to God after committing transgression, by offering a sin offering, typically a sacrifice of a bull, goat, lamb, turtledove or pigeon, but possibly also fine flour for the less privileged, or a guilt offering, involving a ram, to atone for their sins and by which to assuage their guilt by receiving God's forgiveness (Lev 4:1—6:7).

Burned, grain, and peace offerings were made to mark devotion to the Lord, express thankfulness for God's provision, or share in one's good things with one's neighbors. Once a year, a ceremony was convened on the day of atonement to atone for the sins of the community as a whole by the high priest's act of imputing the "iniquities", "transgressions", and "sins" on a scapegoat and sending it into the wilderness, thus having their sins borne away by the goat (Lev 16:20–22 ESV).

We see then that the tabernacle and temple were a means by which God establishes and maintains a personal relationship with the community of faith and its members. The principle undergirding the Old Testament sacrificial system was atonement, forgiveness, and reconciliation rather than a sense of wounded honor or dignity, or private offense, and

---

52. God is not running an earthly political kingdom in which we are all God's subjects whom God would need to constantly turn away from all potential rebellious thought, desire, and action through implementing maximal deterrent punishment on us as individuals, unless we are already believers, in which case our sins will have been penalized on the cross of Christ, and it is enough to have the revelation and reminder of the extent of our sinfulness (that is, as people filled with desire, intent, and behavior worthy of death on the cross) as well as the efficacious work of the Holy Spirit in converting our human heart; indeed, so apolitical is the kingdom of heaven that Jesus did not even expect his followers to fight for him, as in John 18:36.

satisfaction. Jesus, who modeled his ministry after this system, expressed the same content of divine revelation.

Why, then, was God so strict with rules governing the sacrificial system, such as in the case of Uzzah, who took hold of the ark of the covenant after the oxen pulling the cart on which the ark was being transported stumbled (2 Sam 6:6–7)? Much like Jesus, the ark represented God's presence on earth in a physical way. Unlike Jesus, however, the ark symbolized God as a king and judge,[53] on the basis of which role God is able to prescribe atonement and declare forgiveness, lending shape and form to the reality or identity of God as the subject of all creation, regarded as the object of God's action and approach. Whereas Jesus could be touched without much peril, this was on account of his ministry as a servant of the Lord, come to earth to be among people as much as he remained God, while the ark pointed to an impenetrable glory and ineffable mystery of God, before which the entire world must submit in complete obedience.

Without God assuming such an identity shrouded in holy, inexpressible awe, the Almighty will become as other entities in the world and thereby be profaned, a friendly companion or even overfamiliar ruler, perhaps, but not a being to whom a place in the human heart reserved only for deity belongs. A person with the profession of a judge may be a most jovial and amiable man or woman among their family and friends, and yet there is a place, and there must be a place, for this person to behave exactly as a judge, and no less, while presiding over a court trial, setting aside all their usual social traits and adopting the phlegmatic demeanor of an officer authorized to render a binding verdict. A judge who is unable to comport themselves in a manner appropriate to the officer of the court that they are would be derelict in their very important professional duty, responsibility to the state, and moral obligation to society.

A passage cited in support of the idea that God is in complete control over all circumstances and that even in suffering God has a special purpose for the believer is Matt 10:26–31.[54] Proponents of such a view

---

53. See Exod 25:22 where God refers to the mercy seat as the place above which, between the cherubim, God will promulgate divine commandments through Moses to the people of Israel. Judges in certain jurisdictions do have a hand in passing laws. In the context of Singapore, judges may pass laws of a kind that constitutes an "expansion or elaboration of existing legal principles" when a decision of a case calls for it. Such common law cannot be in conflict with parliamentary- or government-enacted legislation or statutes. Singapore Courts, "Legal System."

54. That no sparrow will fall to the ground without (*aneu*) the Father is merely

place a premium on the guarantee of a positive eternal destiny even if this may come at the cost of much adversity and suffering, whereas those who do not hold such a view of divine providence espouse a view of God's love in which God will not allow any harm to befall a believer whom God loves, and instead fights endlessly for their protection and salvation. There will still be much suffering and adversity to endure in this life but God affords the comfort of God's love, and still brings all into God's eternal presence in perfect peace at the end of their earthly sojourn by promising a day on which angels will be obedient to God's calling to effect a day of judgment.[55]

Evil does not have eternal perseverance, and this not because God controls the will of evil moral agents, but rather on account of the fact that all things being posited by the Divine Nature and morally inspired and guided both by the Trinity and the Divine Nature, everything finds its highest actualization and fulfillment in corresponding to their good moral nature as posited and morally inspired and guided by the Divine Nature and the Trinity. Therefore, none of these theories changes the reality of divine and eternal comfort; the only distinction lies in how and the extent to which they explain the suffering the believer goes through, its relationship to divine providence, and the nature and scope of divine providence.

In our discussion of soteriology, we have not strayed from our intended focus upon divine transcendence, but have primarily engaged that key dimension of Christian theology even at this early point only as far as it was deemed necessary to do so in order to clarify the manner in which it may be said that God maintains and exists in a loving relationship with humankind. The reason for the depth of the discussion is that much of what appears in a classical theology of salvation makes very fundamental claims about God's disposal of and purpose for humankind which exposes itself to questions about the extent to which it remains meaningful to assert God's love for humankind. Along the way, we have seen a need to address the biblical basis of the doctrine of original sin, a major fixture of a classical doctrine of God.

---

indicative that the Father will know even when each of those little creatures expires, just as God is aware of the number of hair strands on a person's head.

55. Eternal peace does not begin at the point of death for those martyred continue to experience the pain of anguish; see Rev 6:9–11.

3

The Christian Doctrine of Divine Identity

The Experience of God in the Plurality of Encounter

IN VIEW OF ITS object of naming the definitive essence of the divine being or at least the definitive essence of God's activity in relation to the world or humankind, the Christian doctrine of the divine identity is entrusted with a most complex brief.

The Swiss neo-orthodox theologian Karl Barth is of the view that God's name as revealed in Exod 3:14 may be expounded through what he sees as a parallel passage in Exod 33:19. Barth believes that God names Godself in accordance to God's freely dispensed grace and mercy as conferred on humankind.[1] This is to be contrasted with the various pairing of the divine name in Exodus 3 with notions of God's self-existence and self-expression, through the tetragrammaton, as a warrior, desert, wind, and storm God.[2]

The proper identification of God is thought by the Lutheran theologian, Robert W. Jenson (1930–2017) to have become a pressing need in view of the rise and prevalence of religious pluralism in many societies around the world, including those formerly predominantly Christian,

---

1. On Barth's understanding of God's name, see Barth, *KD* IV.2, §68.2 (ET, Bromiley, p. 770).

2. On *ehyeh asher ehyeh* as inferring God's self-subsistence, see Enns, *MHT*, 194, 200; on YHWH as implying a warrior God of the desert, wind, and storm, see Römer, *Invention of God*, 32–34.

such that the doctrine of the Trinity, as a device which aids in such identification, has been given added importance in this regard.[3] Jenson identifies "Yahweh" and "Father, Son, and Holy Spirit" as God's proper names in the Old and New Testaments respectively.[4]

Theologians like Jenson take their cue from the historical action of the divine operations, and so identify God as the one who brought Israel out of slavery in Egypt, or as the one who raised Jesus from the dead.[5] It is important to these theologians that the God witnessed to in the Christian faith is clearly differentiated from the object of worship in other religious traditions (Divine Identity as Exclusive). Other theologians, among them, Choan-Seng Song or C.S. Song, hold that Jesus, and therefore God, is to be identified as the divine power of empathy and transformation in the lives of those who experience oppression or marginalization of some kind (Divine Identity as Pro-Social).[6] A third perspective, enshrined in the theology of Friedrich Schleiermacher, holds that God is the correlate of the human self-consciousness characterized by a feeling of absolute dependence from which human individuals wholly receive the receptive dimension of their existence and are able to actualize their active existence (Divine Identity as Focus of Absolute Dependence).[7]

In contrast to these views, we contend that God's identity is to be construed in a manner inclusive of all human experience, appropriating what is true, good, and beautiful in the experience of an individual person, cultural group, or religious tradition (Divine Identity as Established in the Plurality of Encounter).

Epistemology

One of the key processes in the development of a healthy self-identity and relationships with others is that of individuation. As a person identifies and asserts their individuality, they avoid an existential crisis in which they may discover that their identity has been subsumed under the preferences or wishes of influential persons in their lives.[8]

---

3. Jenson, *Triune Identity*, ix, xi.
4. Jenson, *Triune Identity*, xii-xiii, 3, 5, 9–10.
5. Jenson, *Triune Identity*, 7–8.
6. Song, *Jesus, the Crucified People*, 10–14.
7. Schleiermacher, *CG* §4.1–4 (ET, Tice, Kelsey, and Lawler, pp. 18–27).
8. Fraser-Thill, "What Is Individuation?"

God appears under the sign of concrete reality. This has to be case, for without this principle being true, there would be no possibility of truly knowing God. Hence, experience is a key source for Christian theology. A theology in which Scripture is interpreted only by appeal to tradition and reason but without the contribution of experience is necessarily deficient. As a matter of fact, all theology arises from experience, better, encounter; that is, the meeting by a person of reality as it presents itself and is itself presented to that person.

As human beings, for the most part, none of us is in a position to choose the way in which reality presents itself or is presented, through an external cause, to us. Only in the case of an object designed by a person is that person able in some way to shape the reality presented to them. Even then, that creator or designer has already been presented the form of their thoughts or ideas inspired by myriad preexisting ones, by which that object was designed and, beneath that, if they reflect more deeply, the mental framework by which those thoughts or ideas have arisen and are able to arise in the first place. Life is therefore encounter.

Scripture itself, which arises from the experiences of God's presence and activity by the biblical prophets and apostles, rendered in the form of testimony by inspired editors and writers, is a record of human-divine encounter, in which human individuals perceive God through faculties such as sense-perception, inner voice, and spiritual vision, made possible by a divine approach to the human person.

Whereas we do not shape much of the reality presented to us, including our physical appearance or personality, though we do shape part of that presented to others through our expressions of ourselves in our body language, speech, and action, God takes on physical forms in accordance to God's good pleasure and in actualization of God's wise counsel, having no real physical form of God's own. One of these physical expressions of divine reality was the burning bush which Moses encountered, while another is the incarnate person of Jesus Christ.

God therefore shapes God's physical manifestation, speech, and action in relation to the human recipient of divine self-revelation. Often, God chooses to hide Godself and appear in processes of seeming randomness and coincidence, only because God wishes not to coerce us but allow us to make our own decisions and even offer our own interpretations of events in which God may be acting; the apostles themselves believed God to work in processes of randomness such as the casting of lots to decide Judas' replacement as an apostle (Acts 1:24–26). Above

THE CHRISTIAN DOCTRINE OF DIVINE IDENTITY

and beyond God's direct self-revelation, the Divine Nature chooses also to reveal itself by means of the nature of the reality it posits, including the formal nature of the freewill of moral agents, but not the actual expressions of that freewill.

One should be careful not to convert human freewill and moral agency into a pretext on the part of God to allow suffering and evil. God does not permit myriad tragedies and gross injustices to befall the human species on account of God's wish to enable human beings to take full accountability for all their moral decisions and actions; such a justification does not explain the predicament of persons born with a monogenic genetic disorder such as sickle cell disease, given that the condition itself arises from a single gene mutation which, in turn, can be caused either by errors in DNA replication or exposure to chemicals and radiation, rather than an abuse of human autonomy.[9] Nor is suffering, as a consequence of misdeed, calculated to remind us of the wrongdoing of our first ancestor so that we may be driven to Christ, but simply the upshot of natural processes, occasionally impacted by unwitting or deliberate human action, which result in natural disasters, diseases, accidents, or mishaps—this entire realm of possibilities is opened up by a consideration of God as a divine being not in meticulous control of all that betides.[10]

The susceptibility of the human body to physical disorders is not to be thought of as a function of God's permissive will or an imagined supremacy of the devil but rather the limitations of a finite mortal physical human body, which God, working through God's angels, cannot overcome in the creation of the human body. The devil is not immensely powerful in any admirable way; much of the devil's sway is proportionate to selfish persons' abuse of their moral autonomy to commit evil and wickedness. Were the world to be filled with morally responsible and ethical persons, as it could well be, the devil would have no influence to speak of. Evil is brought about by God's inability to control the decisions of moral agents, whether angelic or human, in the context of God's desire to redeem as many as possible rather than bring an end to transgressors.

Something of the Divine Nature can be seen in every living and non-living thing in the universe which attains to our sense-perception. Abstract principles of logic applied to conceptions based on reality, such

---

9. Cleveland Clinic, "Genetic Disorders"; Brown, "Mutation, Repair and Recombination," chapter 14.

10. Even cancer is caused by natural processes; in this case, regular genetic mutation that goes uncorrected by cells. Mayo Clinic Staff, "Cancer."

as in the study of general features or characteristics of a group of living or non-living things, supply some notion of the structure of the underlying reality that is the Divine Nature.

When one looks at the frog and considers its amphibious capacity and character, one is drawn almost immediately to the versatility that marks the Divine Nature, while the human being as moral agent illuminates the entitative form of the Divine Nature that is the Trinity, with its own superior moral attributes. The expression of the moral will, however, along with certain flaws or defects of nature, such as harmful parasitic organisms, reflect not so much the Divine Nature or Trinity as they do an unholy or demonic principle operative in the world. The principle for determining which is which is solely the question of whether something or some feature of things symbolizes gratuitous harm or points to some moral evil or defect.

Insofar as the Divine Nature or Trinity is mirrored in concrete reality as encounter, it is mirrored as well in diverse cultures and even religious traditions. It is impossible, unrealistic, or untruthful for a religious tradition to discount cultural or religious diversity. If a tradition does so, it may be on account of a fixation on itself as tradition as a sole theological interpreter of Scripture or on excluding experience as a reliable and crucial interpreter—alongside tradition and reason—of Scripture.

One does well to realize that such a posture, of appealing to tradition as source of theology to the exclusion of experience, is an *a priori* decision, a point of departure, and a governing assumption or principle. It is not subject in itself to critique because it posits itself or, rather, it is posited quite arbitrarily, in that those who posit it as their approach to theological construction insist on excluding experience not on any reasonable or falsifiable grounds.

Some will object that experience makes for a poor theological interpretive source, since it is subjective, differing from person to person, culture to culture, and religion to religion. They fear that theology, if it depends on experience, will be left rootless or subject to continuous change, losing its original character or essence.

This concern is not entirely invalid. Yet it fails to address two issues. One, the question of whether everything in an individual, culture, or religious tradition's subjective experience belongs to what is good in that individual, culture, or religious tradition. Every individual, culture, and religious tradition comes with its own excesses, but do these define them in their essence? Two, the question of whether tradition is indeed diametrically opposed to experience. Was not tradition itself experience once upon a time? Did Scripture itself not arise from encounters that compose experience, and by extension, tradition as well, based as it is on Scripture? How much of tradition can be said to be divorced from experience? Did not the authoritative interpreters of Scripture themselves interpret Scripture with an eye to their own spiritual experience and encounter with God?[11]

Pertaining to the first query, not every expression of an individual, culture, or religious tradition is proper or appropriate to the essence of that individual, culture, or religious tradition. Under a system of libertarian freedom where, in contrast to a compatibilist conception, moral agents are believed to have autonomous decision-making powers not in any way influenced or determined by an external moral agent, that is, God, the moral actions of the human individual do not express either the divine nature or decree.[12]

When a man under the influence of alcohol chooses to shoot his family, this act does not reflect the character of God, which is good and will not stand for innocent human persons being harmed.[13] It is not an actualization of a prior eternal divine will, purpose, or decree which orchestrates events and circumstances to display the glory of God by leaving no doubt as to the thoroughgoing nature of original sin, which so twists the will of the corrupted individual that no responsibility can be attributed to God for orchestrating these actions in which the individual is fully implicated by their strong and incriminating desire to do harm to others.

Although it is believed, under Calvinist compatibilism, that God's benevolent nature can be acquitted by the nature of the divine will and the manner in which it successfully implicates the evildoer in their own sinful actions, it belongs to God alone to determine the nature of human freewill and the extent to which they will commit evil or suffer harm and injustice. God is under no obligation or necessity, not even to Godself, to design and bring into being a world in which humankind possesses

11. Consider Augustine of Hippo, whose doctrine of original sin owes much to his personal experience of sensuality.

12. Under the Arminian (libertarian) system, willful or intentional sin is still possible for Christians since conversion does not remove all possibility of willful sin so that only sin committed out of ignorance or being deceived as to the immorality of the transgression or the rightness of pursuing evil means to achieve a higher, good end remains possible (as in the Calvinistic system, which is compatibilist).

13. *Contra* Clark, *Religion, Reason, and Revelation*, 222.

compatibilist freedom, has their will corrupted by the disobedience and fall of Adam in which original sin replaces the original moral nature of the human being, has to manifest sinful deeds and be held to account for each of those, finds only some among them being saved and liberated from original sin, with the rest being consigned to perdition.

There is no need for God to write such a tragic script for humankind. It is possible, conceivable, and desirable that God's relationship to sin and suffering in the world and the human being and existence be conceived of in such a way as to completely detach and decouple God's will from the presence and activity of human evil.

Aside from some passages we have already considered, Eccl 7:13–14 and Isa 45:7 are appealed to in support of a viewpoint that God foreordains or predestines evil in the world. Eccl 7:13, "Consider the work of God: who can make straight what he has made crooked?" (ESV), given that God cannot be regarded as the author of evil or violate human freewill (Jas 1:13–18), is best taken as a general, phenomenological observation concerning how it often seems that the disposition and conduct of certain wicked individuals are well-nigh irreformable, to the point that it almost looks as though their evil is innate. As the saying goes, a leopard can't change its spots.

The following verse, Eccl 7:14, "In the day of prosperity be joyful, and in the day of adversity consider: God has made the one as well as the other, so that man may not find out anything that will be after him" (ESV), appears to offer hard advice for the prosperous person who is likely to think that their prosperity will ever continue, and consolation for the sullen person who is just as likely to envision that their adversity will never end, that nobody should be so presumptuous as to make these assumptions.[14]

Isa 45:7, "I form light and create darkness; I make well-being and create calamity; I am the Lord, who does all these things" (ESV), occurs in the context of a message from the Lord to King Cyrus, whom God has

---

14. In this regard, the Scripture finds resonance with the Taoist parable about a poor Chinese farmer who loses his horse and undergoes a series of fortunes and misfortunes. The instructive and rather surprising aspect of the story is that at no point does the farmer give an expected response to the good or bad things that happen in his life. Whenever he experiences blessing and is congratulated, the farmer shrugs off the idea that his good fortune would last; similarly, when he goes through setback and his neighbors commiserate with him, he again dismisses the belief that his misfortune will be a permanent one. This story is reproduced in Lee, *Theology of Change*, 59, and Smith, *Religions of Man*, 212.

appointed to defeat nations as well as allow the Jewish exiles to return to the land of Israel, rather than an indication that God meticulously predetermines all that takes place, whether good or evil, salutary or harmful.

Similar to the human individual, each culture or religious tradition will possess particular traits or features that are not helpful. One thinks of the charge of hypocrisy often leveled against the Christian church.

If so, the defects of an individual person, a distinct cultural group, or a specific religious tradition cannot be fairly ascribed to the will of God or interpreted as in some way characteristic of God's own nature and character. It is necessary to discern what is good, true, and beautiful in each person, culture, and religion to determine what is of God, and what is not, in each of these loci, if one is to appeal to experience as a reliable and credible source for the theological interpretation and systematization of the teachings of Scripture.

Scripture itself arises from the human experience on the part of certain individuals of God. The Pentateuch is to a significant extent the record of what Moses heard from God, laws delivered from on high, in an almost direct, personal encounter with the divine being, beginning with the encounter with God in a burning bush.

Other parts of Scripture chronicle the lives of remarkable ancestors of the Jewish and Christian faith such as Noah, Abraham, Isaac, Jacob, and Joseph, the careers of Moses and Joshua as military leaders of Israel, as well as the rise and decline of the Israelite monarchies, detailed in the way they are with the purpose of describing the divine encounter with human individuals for the benefit of their future or present communities.

Prophecies and wisdom literature take up a large portion of the Old Testament or Hebrew Bible; again, these exist and have been transmitted through the generations and centuries to serve as an attestation to human-divine encounter. Canonical history proceeds with the first advent of Jesus, the appointment of apostles, and the founding of the apostolic church, bearing witness to the self-revelation of God through God's beloved Son, the content of divine self-disclosure as to God's nature, character, and conduct in relation to humankind and the world.[15]

Not all that is in Scripture testifies to attitude or conduct that mirror those of God; in many instances, people fall short of the moral requirements of God's law or biblical writers express anguish at a perceived failure on the part of God to deliver from collective injustice or personal

---

15. See Barth, *KD* IV.2, §64.2 (ET, Bromiley, p. 119).

suffering. These are left in the divine self-witness only because God respects and underscores the importance of human freedom and experience. It is not enough that God lays down laws or delivers clear teaching as to what human persons ought to believe or do, but God is interested in the process by which a person arrives at the right decisions.

Hence, the negative examples of individuals who have fallen short are supplied, along with the consequences for their wrongdoing, in order to serve as a deterrent against moral transgression, while poets are permitted to express a sense of woe and lamentation to highlight a common human condition of wretchedness in a world riddled with evil and suffering, thereby establishing Scripture's awareness of such a state as well as God's capacity to minister into these painful moods, emotions, and states of mind.

Much like their spiritual predecessors whose encounters with God and experiences of faith were recorded in the Bible, the authoritative interpreters whose work came to constitute Christian tradition did not put aside their personal experience of God in writing or speaking about God. Augustine of Hippo's experience of God as the lover of his soul in spite of the perceived corruption of his will and desire colored many of his writings and doctrinal treatises, whereas Martin Luther did not fail to write and speak with great conviction regarding his fresh new understanding of Christian salvation, clearly a personal experience of liberation from a previous, difficult mode of relating with God in which he was unable to overcome a sense of personal sinfulness, unworthiness, and guilt.

Doctrinal Formulation: Divine Identity Established through Plurality of Encounter

God establishes God's identity through plural forms of encounter by human beings with God, whether this be the Divine Nature or the Trinity. As Divine Nature, God exists uncaused in a certain manner of reality, as a specific non-conscious and non-personal structure of ontology and morality to which no change or alteration can be made, not even by God, yet such change or alteration is essentially unnecessary, given that the structure that constitutes the Divine Nature is already perfect as a supreme ontological and moral framework, there being no possibility of adding to its glory. As Divine Nature, God is encountered through higher-level reflection on the possibility of existence, activity, and fulfillment, and a discernment of what is true, good, and beautiful in things which exist, in a broad-ranging sense on the basis of a long-term observation of reality in its concreteness, as well as the moral guidance such a Nature affords a person as a moral agent. In this way, people encounter God as Divine Nature through the structure of reality, including their own existence, as well as the inner voice of morality or conscience. As Trinity, God is encountered through God's self-distinguishing religion-specific manifestations as figures of biblical history encountered and as attested in Scripture for the benefit of posterity, as well as inner moral guidance, particularly that which alludes directly to the message of Christianity.

Discussion

God establishes God's identity through plural forms of encounter by human beings with God, whether this be the Divine Nature or the Trinity. As Divine Nature, God exists uncaused in a certain manner of reality, as a specific non-conscious and non-personal structure of ontology and morality to which no change or alteration can be made, not even by God, yet such change or alteration is essentially unnecessary, given that the structure that constitutes the Divine Nature is already perfect as a supreme ontological and moral framework, there being no possibility of adding to its glory.

Although God is the ultimate and supreme being, it is impossible and illogical to assert that God brings Godself into existence, causes or posits Godself, for the reason that the cause of the existence of God as for any other thing has to preexist God or the thing that is caused or brought into being, yet if God is the cause of God, God already exists and so does not need to bring Godself into existence.[16] This dilemma will remain so long as we attempt to discuss God as the cause of God. However, it is not proper to speak of a cause for God since God is the first and ultimate cause and source of being and existence. If God is not the cause of God, God is not in fact self-caused. Moreover God does not have a cause since God is necessarily the first cause.

How then is it possible to account for the being and reality of God as opposed to God's non-reality or absence? In short, why does God

---

16. Thomas Aquinas uses the analogy of a heated object to express that God cannot be both the cause of all things as well as the cause of Godself, given that a heated object is actually hot and potentially cold but not potentially hot, or actually cold, at one and the same time. Aquinas, *Summa* 1a, Q. 2, Art. 3, co.

exist rather than fail to exist? Philosophically, God is necessary being.[17] God's existence is the presupposition of reality. It is inconceivable that the world should exist without God being real or present. This is a metaphysical assumption determined by the belief in God as the first and ultimate cause. A philosopher is free to postulate God as other than the first cause, but then logic would demand that something else be defined or established as the true first cause.

To avoid unproductive wrangling, we choose to define God as the first cause and the first cause as God. This necessarily differs from a system in which it is not God, understood in an explicitly Christian sense,[18] but some entity or object in the universe or beneath the universe that is defined as the first cause. It differs from a system in which the Big Bang, some metaphysical but non-personal origin of reality, a permutation of a universe among millions of others in a multiverse existing as a result of pure chance and the expression of chance, or some primitive state of the world is defined as the first cause.

Given that our chosen framework is Christian, we will proceed with and build on the notion of God defined as the first cause. God as first cause can only exist as a given, as necessary. To the extent that God cannot be self-caused, God has no say in whether or not God exists or even the manner in which God exists.[19] Being and reality in a particular shape of existence is a brute fact that even God (as Trinity) has to and does accept.[20] We have previously excluded the possibility of a personality as belonging to the ontological and existential framework that undergirds all entities and objects in the universe, allowing them both to be and to function in the way they do, in pursuit of their respective visions of fulfillment. This we asserted on grounds of the equally critical tenets of divine goodness, power, and the presence of evil, injustice, and innocent suffering. A divine personal being existing as an ontological and existential framework cannot adequately address the theodictic dilemma concerning why an all-powerful and good God fails to prevent human evil and suffering.

---

17. Aquinas, *Summa* 1a, Q. 2, Art. 3, co.

18. It may be highlighted that the idea of an ontological and moral basis of all existence is necessary and universal which, in the Christian understanding, is named God and, in our interpretation, the Divine Nature.

19. Aquinas, *Summa* 1a, Q. 2, Art. 3, co.

20. This is akin to how God is in a position where God has to accept God's own forgiving nature. See Williams, *Being Disciples*, 40–41.

If God as ontological and existential framework, as Divine Nature, is non-personal and structural, God as entity or the Trinity is both personal and communal, one God in three persons. God as Trinity finds its ontological and existential origin and source in the Divine Nature. It is not a shame or limitation that God has no control over the shape of the nature, being, existence, and purpose of God, given that God is perfect in God's nature, being, existence, and purpose, in the things that pertain to God's essence, personality, disposition, character, morality.

With the proposed doctrine of God as Divine Nature and Trinity, there is a unity of moral vision and teleological purpose between God and the non-God other as well as the idea of God as a presupposition for the being, existence, activity, and fulfillment of all entities and objects akin to a Hindu conception of Brahman as ultimate reality unifying and objectively grounding all individual consciousness and entities conceived as separate through ignorance and confusion.

As ultimate reality unifying all individual consciousness and entities, Brahman is the true nature of all entities and objects, the human conscious mind and moral agent being no exception. The only reason people perceive and experience themselves as individual persons is that they are under a collective mental imagination characterized by unknowing and misperception. If they knew any better, they would better appreciate how their limiting self-perceptions are inaccurate and how they are truly one with Brahman. Although this will not necessitate any radical transition into a different mode of human existence, given that life continues after receiving and embracing such an epiphany, the life of the sagely person will acquire a decided sense of freedom from the preoccupations and encumbrances of worldly life.[21]

A Christian vision of the Divine Nature and the Trinity as we have outlined it is similar to the conception of Brahman as ultimate reality unifying all individual consciousness and entities in that a unity exists between God and the non-God other of a moral vision and teleological purpose. Within the Hindu understanding, Brahman is regarded as fundamentally incapable—without grave inaccuracy and misrepresentation—of being differentiated from any entity and object in the mental and material universe. Our doctrinal proposition may not give literal assent to such a viewpoint, in that we aver that, even ultimately, there is a real distinction to be made between God and the non-God other, yet

---

21. Dhavamony, *Classical Hinduism*, 22–25.

all things are truly inseparable as plural and diverse realities blossoming, in receiving reality, powers, and inclinations pertaining to their being, existence, activity, and fulfillment, on the bed of a framework of presupposition in the Divine Nature, and moral agents are united with the Trinity in their moral inclinations and goals and receive their material existence from its authoritative command.

As objective ground of all individual consciousness and entities, Brahman accounts for the very shape and character of the nature, being, attributes, existence, and activity of all things which have been, are, and will be. Although in Advaita Vedānta, Brahman is described as pure being, pure consciousness, and pure bliss, in no way does this suggest that Brahman itself is conscious, since all that it means to say that Brahman is pure consciousness is simply that Brahman constitutes the very possibility or ableness of consciousness as a quality in thinking and self-perceiving entities, and brings this very quality of consciousness into existence as an attribute of a thinking and self-perceiving entity, of which Brahman is not one.[22]

In relation to the notion of Brahman as objective ground of all individual consciousness and entities, our conception of the Divine Nature bears a native resemblance to that notion, in that all entities and objects are regarded as resulting, in their receiving reality, powers, and inclinations pertaining to their being, existence, activity, and fulfillment, from the Divine Nature as an impersonal framework which constitutes a presupposition of their reception of that reality, those powers and inclinations pertaining to their being, existence, activity, and fulfillment, be this of a physical, emotional, intellectual, relational, ethical, or spiritual nature.[23]

We have been expatiating on the manner in which the Divine Nature posits the existence of all things as presupposition of their being, existence, activity, and fulfillment. What does it actually mean to describe the Divine Nature in this way? As presupposition of existence for all entities and objects in the universe, the Divine Nature accounts for the reason that entities and objects in the world exist in the first place and for their various specific attributes, both the collection of qualities attached to their nature, as well as the freewill of moral agents.

---

22. Menon, "Advaita Vedanta."
23. Cf. John of Damascus, *Fid. orth.* 1.12 (Chase, ET, p. 193).

The Divine Nature is itself the unanswerable question and factor behind the immediate query as to why something is or is the way it is; that is, the Divine Nature supplies the percipient with a satisfactory reason that something exists or exists the way it does, without quite being able to offer an explanation as to why or how the Divine Nature itself exists or exists in the way it does. That the Divine Nature exists and that it exists in the way it does are simply assumed to be the case, as a logical necessity, no less, in order that we do not keep having to go behind something to establish that thing's source of existence and reality, *ad infinitum*. In spite that the existence of the Divine Nature cannot be accounted for, it is a necessary factor purely because entities in the cosmos do not exist in and of themselves—in contradistinction to these, the Divine Nature exists in and of itself.

Accordingly, the Divine Nature functions as an explanatory framework as much as it does an ontological and moral one. It is an invisible and imperceptible structure, to be sure, one which cannot actually or perhaps ever be directly observed, though its effects are copious, ubiquitous, visible, perceptible, sensible, palpable, and tangible in a manner appropriate to the specific effect. Such an explanatory framework is attested in Scripture, in passages such as Acts 17:28, in which St. Paul describes God as a reality in which all human persons have their vitality, their activity, and their being and existence, and Ps 139:7-12, where David confesses that there is no place to which he could go to depart from God's spiritual presence, which secures him and directs his path.

As an explanatory principle, the Divine Nature is conceived in as elegant a manner as possible, as non-personal so that it is precluded from any interference with external reality, which would make it difficult to validate any fully coherent and cogent doctrine of divine goodness, and yet it remains very much a dimension of God, in that the Divine Nature accounts for the existence and moral nature and character and undergirds the moral vision of the entitative dimension of God, the Trinity, which, with the freewill that it receives from the Divine Nature, pursues all moral goodness, so that it is no mistake to honor the Trinity as the true owner of the Divine Nature. The Trinity is the only being in the entire universe which perfectly actualizes and concretizes the didactic moral vision of the Divine Nature, the only being which is capable of so doing because the internal structures of its morality, its conscience, mirror the moral framework that the Divine Nature is, into which God shapes the internal structures of human morality for each individual, through the

PART 1: CREATION'S IMAGING OF THE DIVINE

Trinity's mirroring and concretization of the moral framework of the Divine Nature (the Divine Nature positing the human capacity to develop the ability to recognize and actualize the various attributes of morality and the Trinity stimulating the development of this ability), concomitant with the constant moral guidance on the part of both the Divine Nature (general) and the Trinity (Christian-specific).

God establishes God's identity through plural forms of encounter by human beings with God, whether this be the Divine Nature or the Trinity. As Divine Nature, God is encountered through higher-level reflection on the possibility of existence, activity, and fulfillment, and a discernment of what is true, good, and beautiful in things which exist, in a broad-ranging sense on the basis of a long-term observation of reality in its concreteness, as well as the moral guidance such a Nature affords a person as a moral agent. In this way, people encounter God as Divine Nature through the structure of reality, including their own existence, as well as the inner voice of morality or conscience. As Trinity, God is encountered through God's self-distinguishing religion-specific manifestations as figures of biblical history encountered and as attested in Scripture for the benefit of posterity, as well as inner moral guidance, particularly that which alludes directly to the message of Christianity.

How do we properly exercise discernment of the true, good, and beautiful in an individual, culture, or religious tradition in such a way that we can be confident that we do not miss the mark in all our identifications? It may be necessary to give greater credence to the fundamental intuitions of the human conscience, arising as it does from the operations of the Divine Nature, which promotes universal moral values that, in turn, have been imprinted, through a pre-terrestrial encounter with the Trinity in its moral glory and splendor, upon the internal structures of the human heart, including an awareness of right and wrong and an ineradicable desire and will to pursue right rather than wrong (cf. Rom 2:15), governing and regulating moral attitude and behavior.[24]

On account of that moral shaping by the Trinity and the continuous moral guidance of the Divine Nature and the Trinity, all human beings possess the moral image of God, giving them an intuitive ability to assess what is moral or immoral, good or evil, righteous or unrighteous.

---

24. See Chua, *ECRST*, 203–208.

This faculty of discernment is not a social construct; it is reinforced by parental upbringing. In the final analysis, however, moral discrimination resides in each human person as an innate capacity. Without the presupposition that morality constitutes an innate phenomenon in humankind, there will be no justification for holding any individual to a moral accountability; they may be held to account for being socially disruptive, but nothing more.

Furthermore, if morality were socially constructed, and only regulated in scenarios where social functioning is disrupted, there should be no outrage at the following hypothetical event: two adults consent to an arrangement where one murders the other, the one carrying out the murder to satisfy his need to kill, and the other fulfilling his desire to experience fear, pain, and death. In this hypothetical scenario, there is no disruption or interruption to the functioning of society or continuance of social relations; as a matter of fact, it is an arrangement that promotes efficiency, given that the two individuals involved find that they are quite unable to fulfill the expectations society places on them: the one in the position of carrying out the murder holds a day job and provides for his wife and children, yet the strong urge to kill distracts him from his marital, familial, professional, and societal obligations and saps his determination and sense of commitment to attend to these obligations, while the one in the position of being subject, in the near future, to the act of murder finds himself to be completely detached from the processes of social obligations and responsibility, desiring and willing all the time only to put himself or to be put out of existence. The thought of dying or being killed instils him with a sublime frisson that he has never known before.

Even in such a scenario of apparent complete mutual benefit, in which both individuals perceive themselves as standing to gain and to gain greatly from their arrangement, society and the individual members that compose it will not all sit—indeed, few would—easily with the plan of murder being executed by these two persons, though society as such will not stand to lose anything; indeed, it will only benefit from the arrangement, in a sense abstracted from any idea of an intrinsic or inviolable humanity or morality.

Nonetheless, in view that warped mindsets and value systems exist in which antisocial persons entertain strong desires to harm others, it is crucial to recognize the psychological disorders complicit with the sinful patterns of thinking and feeling with which these persons are afflicted, and to firmly and decisively acknowledge the innate nature of human morality, that is, an ineradicable and intrinsic tissue of seminal inclinations and predispositions which require parental or proxy-parental reinforcement, acts of moral discernment on the part of the individual and, if available, communal encouragement, the content of which project is provided by the moral paradigms and archetypes in religious tradition—in the case of Christianity, by the moral example and teaching of Jesus—in order to build increasingly toward a true, good, and beautiful vision for human morality entailing such areas as love, compassion, empathy, righteousness, goodness, patience, gentleness, self-discipline, joy, peacefulness, holiness, solidarity, respect, ingenuousness, resilience, sincerity, passion, resolve, forbearance, forgiveness, longsuffering, equanimity, faith, hope, honor, kindness, responsibility, integrity, truthfulness, generosity, selflessness.

Innate human morality entails more than just an intrinsic driving need to avoid actions which result in harm but also disrespect and disgust. Like the former intuition, the latter two intuitions are by no means learned.[25] Arising as they do from a divine love-shaped morality native to humankind, these intuitions are expressed differently across societies, cultures, and historical time only because a culture is an integrated whole with its own set of meanings that would be alien to those from other communities and societies until they decide to spend time in the former community. It is only as a person is integrated in a particular culture that they are able to see the natural, understandable, even sensible and needful reason why a member of the culture reacts as they do against specific behaviors which signify acts of disrespect or evoke personal disgust.

The one who professes to be Christian has to be willing to allow the moral example and teaching of the Lord Jesus to redirect them to the unchangeable essence of who they are as moral-ethical existents. We will now consider each of the traits previously listed in terms of how Jesus reveals their definition and therefore how we are to emulate him in each of those areas.

Love

More than romantic sentiment, love is defined in the Bible as the commitment a person makes to place the wellbeing and highest interests

---

25. *Contra* Haidt, *Righteous Mind*, chapters 1 and 3, eBook.

of another before their own, to allow the other to co-occupy a space in one's heart customarily reserved for oneself.[26] One who loves in this way does not do so out of a masochist or self-destructive tendency, in which a person does not value themselves but only values others. The second foundational commandment, after the Great Commandment, sets out the mutuality and reciprocity involved in any loving relationship; the one who seeks to love another person does so out of a place of self-care, which differs from a narcissistic love of self or a self-destructive love of other. In the love a person has for another person in the context of a proper care for themselves, the same principle is operative by which one loves and cares for oneself—a disposition and attitude of desiring and willing the highest good for the object of love, whether this be self or other.

When a person who practices love is presented with two contrasting alternatives, one being to care for oneself at the expense of caring for another, the other alternative being to care for another at one's own expense, and when the same person chooses to love the other person at the expense of caring for oneself, this decision is normally not made except in a situation of absolute necessity and emergency. For a preference for the needs of others to take precedence over one's own needs even in trivial circumstances is to make of oneself a slave or servant to another, and to create a relationship of indolent dependence on the part of the other person upon oneself.

However, when it is a matter of choosing to suffer lack or harm rather than allowing another person to face that lack or harm, such as in a case where a person is willing to give up one's food for the emergency sustenance of another, or suffer harm or death so that they do not need to suffer that, this is a noble and righteous expression of love for another person.

The moral requirement to love oneself in the right manner and to an appropriate degree deserves to be highlighted in a day and age where many fail to recognize their own inherent value independent of social approval, including self-approval. Unlike narcissistic self-love, in which a person may hold an inflated perception of their self-worth and trample on the basic rights of others, which is therefore excessive and selfishly directed toward a self-aggrandizement in terms of approval and resources, a healthy love of self involves no egoism, greed, jealousy, and competition, which is ultimately rooted in a personal insecurity, but rather finds

---

26. Cf. Hector, *Christianity as Way of Life*, 2; cf. Barth, *KD* IV.2, §68.1 (ET, Bromiley, p. 733).

contentment and value in being the person one is, without feeling a need to enlarge or extend their selfhood in a manner that asserts itself against and encroaches upon the selfhoods of others.[27]

Just as a person finds contentment in themselves, they also find contentment in others, not desiring that they be something other than they are, in the case of the expectations parents or relatives may have of their child or junior. The ability to find contentment in self and others leads naturally to a kinder disposition towards those who may be different or perceived to be lesser than oneself in respect to some capacity, ability, talent, or gift.

Self-love of a wholesome variety is paramount for any individual given that the moment a person renounces the pursuit of their own survival and wellbeing, it is very likely that they will take actions that refuse their bodies the nourishment it needs on a daily and regular basis, give out too much of themselves to others, or fail to safeguard themselves against potential oncoming threats.

What of a person who experiences a more or less intense self-rejection, self-dislike, or even self-hatred? Scripture is clear that God has created all humankind in the image of Godself, which is love (1 John 4:8, 16). An inability to love oneself in a proper manner is therefore a deficiency in personhood, in a self-relational sense. It will be imperative for such a person to explore the question as to whether there might be any dysfunctional emotional roots underlying their self-opposition.

Self-opposition may arise in a context where a trusting young mind is curious not just about the world but about who they are, observes the way people they have come to trust due to biological relation or familiarity treat them, and form a judgment about their own sense of personal worth and the treatment they perceive that they deserve from others. Being in a vulnerable state as a child, the impact of well-treatment or mistreatment is greater, serving to form either a human person who is secure in who they are and their self-value or one with a low self-esteem or bullying tendencies.

In one particular instance, an individual who was emotionally and sexually abused as a young child by two men became a person so lacking

27. True love, be it for self or others, begins at the point where a person resolves to regard the recipient of love as a person worth loving just for being the moral agent God as Divine Nature posited them to be; that is, acting in a manner that is geared toward promoting their welfare, wellness, and self-actualization, regardless of how one or others might feel about their value. Cf. Donald Hagner's commentary on the Great Commandment in Matt 22:34–40 in Hagner, *Matthew 14–28*, 648.

in self-confidence and self-value that whatever others might say in the way of how competent or gifted the individual in question is, he would shrug off all these positive appraisals as if they were absurd, in a similar way to how water will not be absorbed by a thick plastic film but flow right across the surface to the ground.

Indeed, so convinced was he by the physical and emotional abuse he endured at the hands of its perpetrators, the only ones who conveyed any form of physical touch to him as a child, a form of interaction he very much desired but in a sincerely rather than perversely affectionate way, that he was a person of no self-value who deserves maltreatment, that he became an individual who identifies himself with a certain personal identity and role in which he perceives himself to be more likely to be victimized by sexual predators.

Such tragic examples are exceptions and very far from what the Bible intends by the exhortation to love one's neighbor as oneself in what Jesus christened a second foundational commandment; here it is the intrinsic sense of one's love for God, self, human other, and the rest of the world that is in view, one that may be temporarily suppressed beneath layers of deception regarding oneself. This person has found it salutary to detach himself from images of the deceitful self-identity he has adopted over the years, as well as recognize the psychological foundations in childhood trauma of his feelings of low self-esteem and address them through encouraging himself to find his self-value not any longer in the way he was mistreated by the two individuals concerned but rather the way he is properly, respectfully, and lovingly treated by God and all who take God's relational path in their interactions with him.

Emotions do matter, and all emotions we experience should be acknowledged as what we truly feel rather than denied. Yet not all emotions should be affirmed. There are unwholesome emotions, such as arrogance, hatred, envy, and greed which we have to acknowledge as what we feel but at the same time not affirm but rather confess them to God and oneself, seek to understand their emotional roots, and regularly challenge these false notions in pursuit of emotional healing.[28]

In what way did Jesus demonstrate the attribute of love? Although it was the Father's will that he suffers and dies on a cross in redemption of humankind, the choice of whether to go this way was ultimately in Jesus' own hands, and the fact that he committed himself to take the

---

28. See Chua, *ECRST*, 146–51, 265–74.

path of the cross and made good on his commitment spoke and still speaks eloquently of the greatness of the love with which he loved and still loves humankind (Rom 5:6–8).

Few, if any, of us will be called to take the path of a cross, though martyrdom may remain a possibility, if not a reality, for others. Even so, personal and social situations will call for some degree of sacrifice, none of which should be devalued simply on the ground that they do not involve a transition from physical life to physical death.

In a time of significant and increasing polarization, the person who advocates a middle way between contrasting extremes may be misunderstood, even vilified, and is nourished daily not only by a commitment to represent the truth more accurately but, more importantly, out of love for humankind, which deserves to know the fuller truth and find a greater and deeper measure of liberty in thus knowing. A person that crosses social boundaries to associate with the marginalized person with no other intention than to express their equality with them is a practitioner of love. The one who elects to relinquish social validation and rather to love themselves, as well as others, in who they actually are will suffer certain social consequences, yet it constitutes an expression of love in personal sacrifice.

Compassion

An attitude of being attuned to the difficulty and suffering of others, compassion does not regard what the other person might have done in the past, their social background, or personal qualities, in the succor they might bring in relief of difficulty or suffering. The only operative consideration, aside from regard for the person as a human being and therefore of inestimable worth, is the practical need of the other person.[29] It is possible and necessary to show compassion or mercy to oneself, as when, for instance, one is riddled with guilt over some past act. In this case, what is already done cannot be undone, and there is little good in clutching tightly onto a sense of personal unworthiness, albeit it will be constructive to offer personal apologies and demonstrate a

---

29. Religious devotion and piety, at least in a Jewish-Christian context, is inextricable from deeds which express that faith in a benevolent God who sincerely cares that people, especially the destitute and vulnerable, are not oppressed and bullied in the mistaken belief that all that counts is for believers to participate punctiliously in rituals. See Douglas Stuart's commentary on Hos 6:6 in Stuart, *Hosea–Jonah*, 110.

commitment to change wherever possible and to direct one's attention to the lessons that might be learned from the incident, whether about oneself, others, or the situation at hand.

One of the prime qualities evinced not just in the life of Jesus but also the action of the Father in the world, mercy describes Christ's overall approach to his ministry among Jews as well as Gentiles during his earthly existence. It was clear that Jesus gave himself to the work of helping others, including freeing some from demonic oppression (Acts 10:38). Jesus assumed the mantle about which Isaiah prophesied, in which God's Spirit has anointed him to declare good news to the destitute, freedom for those in bondage, sight for the blind, liberty for the burdened, and God's grace for all humankind (Luke 4:18–19).

Indeed, it was the Father's merciful will that the Son enter Israel to bring the gospel of peace and reconciliation between God and humankind (Acts 10:36). The Father responded in mercy to the news that the Israelites were oppressed and enslaved by the Egyptians (Exod 2:23–25). In this regard, the Son mirrors the compassionate disposition of the Father, and believers in Christ, who have been adopted into God's household through God's Son, by faith rather than nature, have this quality to emulate.

Empathy

The one who is inclined to suspend judgment and make an earnest attempt to understand the circumstances in which a person has or had been caught, particularly one whom people tend to mock or criticize, is a person who practices empathy. Such an attitude should not be equated with moral approval of a person's actions or a failure to denounce evil as evil. Instead, the empathetic observer or listener is a person who strongly believes in making fair assessments and evaluations, whether this be internal or external. They are reluctant to settle for facile classifications of individuals, convicted that, in a fundamental sense, every human person is capable of moral reasoning, even if sinful impulse or ignorance might lead to immoral action.[30]

---

30. Ignorance is employed here in the sense of a dearth of a full realization of the consequences of one's actions rather than a failure of the conscience to alert to the wrongfulness of an action. Such an ignorant person remains accountable for their actions in view that they hold the freedom to have made a different choice.

Jesus demonstrated empathy when he prayed to the Father, as he hung on the cross, that the Father might pardon those who contributed directly or indirectly toward his crucifixion, seeing that, at some level and in some way, it is not inaccurate to assert that many of these actors were not fully aware, whether because of self-justification or ignorance, of the immoral nature of their actions, for if they had such awareness, they would not have crucified the Lord in the first place (1 Cor 2:8), though they remain accountable for their actions insofar as they had the awareness that it was wrong to have actually acted on their sinful instincts and the ability to have done otherwise.[31]

The challenge for the believer is to seek to fathom the anatomy of wickedness or immorality without countenancing that wickedness. They do this in order both to understand their neighbor better, as well as to inform a wider public discourse in such a way that, it is hoped, eventually one or more persons caught in immoral actions in which they justify themselves or of which immorality they are partially ignorant might come to a more radical personal realization of their spiritual and moral blindness, and mend their ways.[32]

---

31. Religious leaders involved in abetting the crucifixion of Jesus owed it to themselves to pay greater attention to the voice of their conscience, however soft or small, that told them they could not commit gross injustice simply to protect their social and financial status. Chua, *ECRST*, 133–34.

32. In what does repentance consist and why is it critical? Repentance is constituted by a change of mind about one's attitudes and actions. For this reason it involves a process of self-doubt, self-questioning and, ideally, some form of self-denial and self-transformation. To repent is to choose to take a closer and second look at the way in which one has thought, felt, desired, and acted; to open one's mind to the possibility that one may have been wrong about one's feelings and perceptions about and decisions made in relation to oneself, other people, the world. Repentance will feel unnatural and uncomfortable because the mind is a self-justifying system; it will feel as if one is going against the grain, and it has the potential to increase the space for new thoughts, feelings, commitments, and actions. Following Jesus as a Christian believer certainly entails a quantum of such introspective reconsideration, only because the moral truth of God comes into conflict with the dysfunctional ways in which many people think, feel, or act. Hence, Jesus' requirement for his followers to deny themselves and take up their crosses, amounting not merely to the literal process which Jesus suffered and underwent, which some of his followers also went through, but also an analogue by which his self-professed disciples are to pattern their attitudes and actions.

Righteousness

On the presupposition that God's moral laws do and should exist in that they correspond to ways a person should behave for the good of self, other, and the wider community and world, the quality of righteousness exists as a descriptor for the person whose attitudes and actions conform to these laws. Adherence to a divine or natural law should not be conceived in overly restrictive or casuistic terms, for in doing so one simply erects a set of rules and regulations governing specific circumstances, thereby giving rise to a form of legalism vulnerable to clever and calculated attempts at circumvention.

Casuistry does not provide a holistic and comprehensive framework which equips a person to adapt to changing circumstances and respond moderately to differing scenarios. What is needed is a desire to grasp and adhere to the spirit of God's laws rather than the mere letter of the same (2 Cor 3:6). The spirit and intent behind God's laws is always only to foster love between God and humankind and among human persons (Matt 22:37–40; John 13:34).

Jesus disclosed a profound understanding of righteousness by choosing to heal the infirm on the Sabbath and driving sacrificial animal traders and moneychangers from the temple grounds, knowing full well that the Sabbath law was not given in order that those who need practical help might be prevented from receiving it on the premise that it is not lawful to work on the Sabbath, and that more important than ensuring the convenience of Jewish worshippers in making it easy for them to obtain sacrificial animals and pay the temple tax, it was critical that the place of worship for Gentiles, the Court of the Gentiles, the outermost court where the animal sellers put up their stalls, be preserved in its sanctity and solemnity.[33]

Goodness

The sum total of the divine attributes, goodness designates the spotless, unblemished, and perfect nature of God's love manifested in unceasing, selfless, and timely practical action on behalf of those who suffer for any reason, as well as a strong, ceaseless, and pure desire for all, whether presently in suffering or not, to reach or maintain complete and holistic

---

33. Carson, *John*, 178–79.

wellbeing. Goodness forbears and absorbs the ill-will of animosity, without ever seeking private vengeance, upholding equality for closest friend as well as bitterest opponent.

Goodness is the internal and external expression of love in the face of need but also and especially moral evil and threat, displaying the quality of a refusal to allow evil and depravity, hardship and adversity, to turn the good person into one resentful and rancorous. It is a comprehensive character of all the divine attributes that draws them into a coherent and integrated whole, setting the tone and pace for every dimension of divine existence, so that in anything and everything that God does, goodness—the pure desire to come to the aid of those in need, the clean heart which refuses to be besmirched by evil—forms the motive, texture, and stimulation. In consequence that God and God alone is good (Mark 10:18), God is holy and set apart.

The believer and follower of Christ is implored to imitate the goodness of God in Christ, seeing to it that none of the corruption that is so prevalent in the world succeeds in overwhelming the good that remains in them. Light, true radiance, shines in the darkness which flees from it (John 1:5; Eph 5:13–14); where darkness overcomes the human heart, it is only because true light, as gloriously revealed in and through Christ, did not exist there in the first place. Even though the world is perverse and corrupt, the believer finds strength in their fellowship with the Trinity, who fills their spiritual and ethical vision, inspiring them to strive to escape and protect themselves against inner darkness by guarding their spiritual eyes from the seductions of the world (Matt 6:22–23), spurning these allurements by attending to the restoration of their souls from compulsive evil and, knowing they remain weak, consciously keeping thoughts, feelings, and images from the world from seeping into their heart.

Patience

The virtue of making room for moral repentance is an attribute proper to God, who understands the frailty and weakness to which human individuals often subject themselves in their ethical decisions.

As such, God chooses to make provision for sacrificial offerings as a means by which to atone for one's sins, satisfy the divine wrath, and receive divine forgiveness. Though God already provides opportunities for each individual, caught as they may be in sin, to repent, desiring not that anybody should perish, even then, though God should make an end of those who ultimately fail to turn from their wicked ways, God does not completely abandon humankind as a whole, but time and again offers a recourse by which they may yet redeem themselves.[34] The obverse of the teaching that God forgives those who repent of their sin is that God will ultimately judge all unrepented transgression and depravity.

The human person is similarly called to extend patience, particularly for moral transgressions, toward those who may have sinned against them, above and beyond the patience they ought to display in less serious circumstances such as a professional working environment. Sufficient opportunity should be furnished for a wrongdoer to come to a knowledge of their error, wherever this is possible, but always only through gentle direction (Gal 6:1).

There is no need to be so filled with anger and bitterness that one runs the risk of destroying an individual's self-worth or at least the relationship one may share with the person in question. Likewise, it is unnecessary to be so controlled by fear of losing a relationship that a person fails to mention in any way their misgivings about another person's behavior in as winsome and subtle a manner as they can muster.

The practitioner of patience will recognize that the lifeblood of any relationship is a second chance and that the gentle word of correction is delivered, prayerfully, only to help the person avoid future anguish under similar circumstances, so long as no grave offense and significant possibility of personal danger is involved, in which case the appropriate boundaries need to be quickly drawn and kept.

Jesus demonstrated patience of posture in his ministry. Although he encountered resistance and opposition in his work, Jesus did not see fit to assemble a crowd of supporters to put to shame, intimidate, or even take up arms against those who opposed him, but he only ever offered a response to objections and accusations in the form of reasoned arguments (Matt 12:1–21).

God models a patience that comprehends fortitude and resilience. No situation is so trying that God has to capitulate to it. Although God may grieve the loss of an intimate relationship with a person who has embraced corruption, God bounces back from such setbacks and

---

34. Cf. Barth, *KD* IV.1, §61.2 (ET, Bromiley, p. 566).

persists in God's mission to bring healing, wholeness, and peace to humankind as a whole.

Gentleness

The purpose of physical might or force is not to intimidate a weaker party into doing one's bidding, overpower those who fail to submit to one's wishes, or harm persons who may have wronged or even just triggered one. Power is given to protect those who are vulnerable, weak, or powerless from any who might seek to physically abuse or harm another person; it exists as a means of self-defense and, even then, only when physical safety is clearly threatened and on the verge of being compromised.

No one should suppose that it were permissible to use force against another party, whether an individual, community, or nation, to avenge a personal vendetta or attain some higher, noble objective of recovering territory that is thought to rightly belong to the potential aggressor. Criminal laws exist and function to prosecute acts that brought about loss or injury, while an attempt to "rectify" a territorial change of hands usually entails acts of aggression against innocent parties of all age groups, ranging from the very young to the very senior.

Similarly, people are not endowed with a measure of shrewdness so that they might manipulate certain parties for reasons of self-interest to the detriment of other individuals in various settings, whether it be at the workplace, school, or at home. On the contrary, the gift of strategic intelligence is bestowed with the purpose of enabling individuals so gifted to come to the aid of individuals and groups caught in situations, often not of their own making, of economic poverty, social disadvantage or discrimination.

We are not to go the way of the serpent of the second creation narrative, which was remarked to have been "more crafty than any other beast of the field" (Gen 3:1 ESV) and used its cleverness to harm the relationship between God and the human couple God created by sowing seeds of distrust, but rather emulate God in plying our greatest powers and wonderful faculties towards bringing a blessing to others. In the case of God, the greatness of divine power was wielded to actualize a material human existence capable of tending to the needs of their fellow human beings, other living entities, and the rest of the natural world, surrounded as they are by physical entities and objects symbolizing various attributes of the godhead and its moral vision, direction, and inspiration for humankind.[35]

Gentleness is an attribute which characterizes God's own and prescribed treatment of sinners (Gal 6:1). God does not bear down upon the sinner immediately, but gives them numerous chances to repent (John 8:1–11). As God does this, God urges and exhorts the sinner with great meekness to turn from their wicked ways. Jesus himself modeled the way of God through his own meekness (Matt 5:5; 12:15–21). None should think to condemn another person; none, all being sinful, is qualified to do so (Matt 7:1; John 8:1–11). The object of discipline is not to destroy the sinner but to rehabilitate them (1 Cor 5:1; 2 Cor 2:5–11).

Although accountability structures are necessary in a church among believers, and this simply because the believer has already come to a personal understanding of and commitment to the structures of God's grace, apprehending the threefold basis of the Christian life in terms of God's forgiveness for those who sincerely and contritely repent, an awareness of the moral life to which God calls a person, and an anticipation and therefore hope in a glorious and eternal future communion with God characterized by insuperable joy, peace, and love, this is not the case with non-Christians and non-members (1 Corinthians 5; Matt 18:15–17). Given their lack of vested interest in obeying and commitment to the church, it is unlikely that any chastisement will be taken well. It is possible, and far better, for a church to be clear about its stance on sinful behavior without being unfriendly or inhospitable toward non-Christians or non-members. A church can afford to be as friendly as it wishes to visitors through actions and micro-actions without compromising its position on sin through occasional and indirect verbal references to its definition of sinful conduct.

As much as one may desire to help spiritually/philosophically uncommitted people toward a Christian vision of salvation, very few are brought to the faith through direct threats of being consigned to hell for continued engagement in sinful behavior. More come to faith through the friendly relationships they have with Christians, especially when they experience setback. Without the conviction of the Holy Spirit, few will respond to preaching about the sinfulness of their behavior. It is therefore more productive and fruitful, rather than confronting people about

---

35. Cf. Barth, *KD* IV.1, §60.2 (ET, Bromiley, pp. 436–37).

Self-discipline

To exist healthily as a human person requires avoiding physical excesses of all sorts, running the gamut of the consumption of food, the search for personal entertainment, the pursuit of success and social approval, the quest for monetary gain, and the satisfaction of physical lusts. It is unbecoming for a human person, posited by the Divine Nature and materially created as we are in God's image, to allow ourselves to be enslaved by our physical and psychological appetites. Such insatiable thirst is often symptomatic of a deeper underlying mental disorder.

As far as this is the case, one should make every effort to address these issues while establishing mentally salutary routines such as the reading and meditation of Scripture, a prayerful personal relationship with God, the reading of beneficial theological and spiritual works, spiritually and psychologically conducive activities including spiritual support and other accountability groups, therapeutic care if needed, and physical exercise.

The Lord Jesus modeled a prayerful relationship with God in the course of his earthly ministry, taking care never to neglect this important dimension of his life despite his busyness.[36] One of the things a Christian in this day and age should especially guard against is a tendency to leave societal blind spots undiscerned, unchallenged, uncritiqued, and unaddressed.

Each community and society has their own undetected and unquestioned deficiencies; one of these is, perhaps, an inordinate emphasis on professional success and social approval. In certain societies, to their own

---

36. How is God the source of our faith, hope, and love? Can God have faith or hope the way we are summoned to put our trust in God and look forward to better things in God's future? The faith that God reposes in us is not equivalent to that which we are to repose in God, and yet there is a sense in which God trusts us to responsibly use rather than selfishly and gratuitously abuse or exploit our freewill, and also a sense in which God hopes for the redemption, through self-determined and self-chosen repentance, of every sinner, and the continuance of every righteous person in the good that they are doing. Few biblical passages attest more affirmatively to divine joy over the repentance of a sinner than the Lucan parables of the lost sheep, coin, and son. See John Nolland's commentary on the parables of the lost sheep and coin in Nolland, *Luke 9:21—18:34*, 773–74, 776.

hurt, many Christians have not developed the ability to detach themselves from and critique the standards society places on them as a whole. Instead of living in a way that discloses a relationship of faith, trust, and commitment in a personal God who grants them a self-identity of infinite value, many believers continue to look for a sense of self-worth in their professional competence and achievement, or social popularity.

Joy

Happiness for the Christian believer is not contingent upon attaining one's every desire for an earthly existence. Rather, its source lies in the purpose of God for humankind being achieved. When the disciples of Jesus were enthralled by the way in which demons submitted to them when they were sent out to preach and to heal, Jesus redirected them toward a worthier reason for joy: that their names were written in heaven (Luke 10:17–20).

God is not devoid of joy; indeed, the Bible begins with the joy of the Lord in the work of creation, implicitly, for while Scripture does not directly indicate God's happiness, it does affirm and attest that God saw that what God had made was good. Believers are entreated not only to know God as a personal being so that they might be enriched in their knowledge and guided in their conduct to emulate the one deserving of all emulation, but also in order that they might understand God's character and purpose, what brings God joy and, corresponding to God's character and purpose, take joy in those very things as well—and sorrow for what hinders those things from being brought into effect.

A related notion is freedom, which is found wherever the Lord is (2 Cor 3:17). The experience of freedom in the Lord is characterized by the awareness that in any situation, the goodness and purpose of the Lord are present for the believer to tap. Even if a person may be emotionally or physically confined, miserable as they may be, they can nonetheless know that God makes a space in which they can still enjoy God's presence and take heart in God's purpose.[37] God, therefore, constitutes society and acceptance where there is none.

---

37. Paul himself wrote some of his epistles from prison, declaring God's mercies and glorious power therefrom. Cf. Eph 3:1; 6:18–20; Phil 1:12–14; Col 4:3, 18; Phlm 1:9–10.

PART 1: CREATION'S IMAGING OF THE DIVINE

PEACEFULNESS

It is not God's purpose to stir up dissension and conflict among people to achieve some higher goal. Rather, God's ultimate aim is that God's children should make peace with one another (Matt 5:9). As a matter of fact, the followers of Jesus ought to be proactive in suing for peace with those with whom they may be in conflict, reaching out to any who might bear any sort of enmity to resolve the lingering bitterness and rancor; this will foreclose an escalation of the conflict (Matt 5:23–26).

Was this not the illustrious and magnificent example God showed in converting the evil and tragic event of the crucifixion of the Son of God into a timeless occasion for the guilt-stricken to return to the Lord with a clean conscience, cleared of a sense of unforgiveness by a dimension of atonement, satisfaction, and substitution with which the cross is imbued for the sake of the reconciliation of many human souls with God?[38]

One of the attributes of God's wisdom, as it is intended by God to be practiced among human persons, is that of peaceability. Such wisdom is marked also by its unblemished quality, tenderness, non-excessiveness, mercifulness, virtuous deeds, fairness, and sincerity, bringing about an emulation of these righteous qualities in others (Jas 3:17–18). In contrast, those who practice envy and an aggressive desire to succeed at all costs are in fact children of an ungodly wisdom, given to chaos and depravity (Jas 3:13–16).

HOLINESS

It is not a purported transcendence of earthly affairs and limitations that makes God holy; rather, it is God's transcendence of sinful attitudes and actions which qualifies God to be designated the holy one, who is in no way besmirched by the corruptions and depravity of humankind. Given that sin is an act of the conscious will, it is not possible to make a person commit sin. Similarly, righteousness is a matter of personal choice, arising from desire, sometimes against conflicting feelings and desires, confirmed by an agreement of the personal will with a righteous desire, which takes it upon itself to carry out the selfsame desire

---

38. Chua, *ECRST*, 133–37.

through birthing an internal commitment, plan, and purpose, which is executed in the form of physical actions.

Solidarity

Human persons are bound together by more than just taxonomy; that is, their biological classification as a species. They have the capacity to enter into relationships with one another which are characterized by a respect for mutual similarities and differences, an appreciation of the many ways in which a human person is really embedded in a social-relational plexus of interdependence, such that no single individual can function with respect to their various roles apart from the existence and functioning of others.

This is the case in any given context, be it familial, social, or professional. Without the human other to interact with, there can be no family, friendship, society, or livelihood. The roles associated with these spheres of activity are not optional elements which an individual can do without, being intimately connected with their self-perception and habitus.

On the premise of the importance of their more or less personal relationships with the closer and more remote other, human persons understand the need for community and society to be sustained and continue in the manner in which they have. Consequently, they agree to a social compact not often fully spelled out which governs all relationships within a society, especially the civil obligation to do everything in one's power to avoid disrupting the social order.[39]

Out of the social compact, the sense that each person belongs within a given society vested with obligations and rights, there emerges a communion of human beings, an emotional and psychological solidarity in which a person is inclined to feel for another person when they experience adversity of some sort, whether it be personal violence, economic poverty, or a natural disaster. On many occasions, an individual may discover a capacity to feel for another person living in a different part of the world who may be undergoing adverse circumstances.

Human solidarity does not provide an invincible safeguard against a potential deterioration of relations between individuals, groups, communities, and even whole nations, due to intentional sin working hand in hand with unrighteous justifications and mental disorders. This does

---

39. Cherry, "Kohlberg's Theory of Moral Development."

not detract from the fact that it is a good thing that God has posited human persons as interdependent entities, in the image of the Trinity as a community, in a single being, of three divine persons. As a matter of fact, it only serves to underscore the importance for human persons to find their way in the example, purpose, and wisdom of God and the truth of who they are as human persons.

God's example is that of a community of entities, the Father, the Son, and the Holy Spirit, who do not make selfish decisions to harm one another, much less attempt to justify sinful conduct, or suffer from mental disorder. The Trinity is psychologically sound and emotionally stable; indeed, the Divine Nature is the source of our psychological wellbeing, and the Trinity as the foremost and eminent disciple of the Divine Nature is of the utmost psychological wellness.[40] Not even God's wrath as displayed or threatened in Scripture is of an excessive nature, since the anger of God arises solely on account of and in perfectly proportionate response to moral injustice and human evil.[41]

God implants moral laws in human persons and makes them known to these persons. Being patient and benevolent, God chooses to overlook certain cases of moral transgression, not in such a way as to be complicit with a victimizer and unjust toward a victim, but only in the hope that the former might have and use the opportunity afforded to them to come to their senses, change their minds about their wicked conduct, and turn to the moral pathway laid out for them as human persons.

The concern, therefore, is for both victimizer as well as victim, for the victimizer because it is better for a depraved person to repent than to be punished with death, and also for the victim, since the depraved person who repents enacts part of the justice that is due to the victim for the mistreatment they have suffered. Moreover, repentance serves as the best antidote, by means of moral example and inspiration, to moral evil in society.

---

40. Baldwin, *Trauma-Sensitive* Theology, 110.

41. It may be wondered whether Jesus in assembling a whip out of cords and driving animal merchants and moneychangers from the temple in Jerusalem during Passover had acted overly violently (John 2:12–17). Donald Carson remarks that this may have been necessary to achieve the stated aim of forcing the sheep and oxen from the temple along with their sellers. Furthermore, had Jesus truly acted in manner that could only be described as brutal, this would have drawn a rapid reaction from the Roman garrison stationed at the nearby Fortress of Antonia, from which part of the temple complex was visible. Carson, *John*, 179.

Respect

Objectification is written into the Bible as a type of interaction between people that is proscribed implicitly, indirectly, and by implication as a result of the axiom that all people are of equal worth. Even slaves in the Old Testament were treated with regard for their dignity as human persons, in that there were laws specifically banning the physical abuse of slaves (Exod 21:26-27), including murder of slaves (Exod 21:20).

In the New Testament, Jesus exhorted his disciples to model a love for one another in the manner that he himself loved them, and this was not to be limited to the community of the followers of Jesus, but fully intended to provide moral and ethical inspiration for the wider community and world, within the context of a faith that God as Father sent the Son into the world in demonstration of God's love for the world through enabling people in the world not only to learn of the good deeds the Son performed during the Son's earthly ministry in the person of Jesus, but also come to grips with the truth that this Son was sent by God the Father to reveal Godself to the world. This is a revelation and self-disclosure of the Father's perfect love for the Son and the Son's perfect love for the Father, a divine glory which God means to share with the world through Jesus the Son, to the end that the world might not merely wonder in amazement at the sublime affection between the Father and the Son in their complete unity, but be inspired to share something of the same love with one another (John 13:34-35; 17:20-23).[42]

The fact that God did all this for the world evidences that God treats human persons with the highest degree of dignity and value, entrusting to us God's personal revelation of God's loving nature, character, and attitudes within the triune godhead and with respect to the human community. God's self-revelation constitutes God's greatest gift and treasure; it bespeaks divine hospitality and generosity, and encourages human persons to do the same one for another in entrusting their valuable treasures and gifts, even themselves, to one another, never stooping to violate the code of honor and generosity obtaining between

---

42. Jesus indicates in John 17:21 his desire that his disciples practice unity in the manner of the Father and the Son, a unity in a communion of love, in order that these followers might thereby also be found in the loving fellowship of the Father and the Son, and that the witnessing world might place their faith in the claim that it was God as Father and none other who sent Jesus into the world. In v. 23, Jesus suggests that the Father loves the people in the world to the extent that the Father is willing to send the Son to them. Cf. Barth, *KD* IV.2, §68.3 (ET, Bromiley, pp. 814-15).

host and guest, in which each person sees themselves as a host to the other person as guest in a dynamic mutual circle.

In this connection, it may be asked why God does not reveal Godself more directly, perhaps spectacularly, to people so that they might have greater reason to believe in God? This is on account that God does not favor an initial approach that is compelling or confrontational, preferring to reserve that for the last, and allows people to reach their own decision of faith in their own time.

Ingenuousness

When Jesus met Nathanael, he described him as "an Israelite indeed, in whom there is no deceit!" (John 1:47 ESV) These are words of commendation uttered toward a person whom he saw beneath a fig tree, presumably seeking God there, or even receiving a revelation of the Messiah or awaiting him, given that the Messiah is connected with the symbol of the fig tree as a deliverer who brings about such an idyllic world that Jews are able to find restful shelter under a fig tree (Mic 4:4; Zech 3:10).

A person without deceit is one who is ingenuous, who does not only appear to fear, obey, and serve God but in actual fact does so only for self-glorification, respectability, or some other personal benefit; instead, the guileless person is without pretensions, sincerely submitted under God's rule simply because they are well aware that God alone is worthy of their honor, worship, adoration, and adulation, that all they have that is good they really owe to God, and that God alone is able to provide a sufficient moral example for them to emulate.

No ingenuous person worships God in appearance while really worshipping themselves; they are truly and fully subservient to the one from whom they have their very being. In becoming human and appearing in the role of a servant, Jesus demonstrated the obeisance, dedication, and commitment that a human person ought to display with respect to God (Heb 5:7–10). Although he had the option and freedom to implore the Father to dispatch more than twelve legions of angels to remove him from a situation of imminent arrest and public execution (Matt 26:53), Jesus chose instead to confirm and wholly obey the Father's will, whatever it might be, whether for him to be crucified or to be saved from crucifixion. Here is an illustrative example for the believer in Christ; to seek the Father's will and to obey it rather than ignore that will and assert one's own self-will as the will of the Father, hoping that nobody will notice their spiritual duplicity, hypocrisy, or lack of integrity.

Resilience

The ability to endure adversity emerges from an abiding capacity to understand how difficulties shape personal growth and how it is quite impossible to predict the final outcome to which changing circumstances lead. An undesirable situation such as discrimination on the part of a relative on account of something that was done or experienced by an individual is not necessarily a hopelessly negative event for, at the very least, the person who experiences discrimination is positioned at a crossroads where they are to decide how they would respond to the unhelpful reaction on the part of their relative, whether to accept the other person's valuation of themselves, to treat others the way that other person has treated them, or to shrug off what is in all probability an inaccurate and unfair assessment driven more by subjective prejudice than objective factors, and to resolve not to behave or treat others in like manner.

The episode of discrimination, unpleasant as it is, then becomes an occasion for the resilient individual to shape their personhood through their response to mistreatment, whether it be for the worse, by allowing false ideas to infiltrate their soul and cause them to be vitiated or learn the ways of aggression and start trampling on others, or for the better, by repudiating those harmful, unjust, and chauvinistic notions, and making a stronger determination not to succumb to the seductions of emotional power-mongering—where people ever seek only to gain an advantage over others, identifying themselves with some group in opposition to other groups, which are written off as inferior to their own group in various ways, often relating to different facets of socio-economic status—but choosing to define themselves in accordance with meekness, empathy, sensibility, and justice.

The resilient person understands that it is always too early to decide if a personal situation is more deserving of optimism or pessimism. This principle is illustrated in a well-known Chinese parable of a farmer, whose fortunes seemed to have taken a turn for the worse when he lost his horse. His neighbors sympathized with him on his personal loss, yet the farmer was sober-minded enough to recognize that the situation he encountered was not the last word on the question of his success or prosperity. Indeed, even as the story appears to end on a positive note, with his son being spared military conscription for a war during which many died or were crippled, on account of hurting his leg while attempting to tame a horse, the farmer at the center of the parable remains unconvinced that there will be no further development of his personal circumstances, for better or worse.[43]

Consequently, the practitioner of resilience grasps that trying or even miserable circumstances do not hold sway over their personal success or failure, that a situation of apparent failure can always birth subsequent success and a situation of apparent success can also engender future decline. The moral of the story is that it is wise to refuse to be overly preoccupied with the external circumstances and changes of one's life, to hold lightly things, even people, over which one has little if any control.

There is an anti-consumerist and anti-worldly dimension to this message, a clarion call not to run on the treadmill of wealth, popularity, and power as a means to attain a sense of self, personhood, and dignity, but to renounce a war on the world in a wrongheaded bid to find one's true self, rejecting self-aggrandizement in pursuit of self-value, self-identity, and self-worth, and rather to embrace peace with and value in oneself.

We know from the biblical testimony that Jesus did not allow the ways of the world to corrupt his own ways, his own attitudes towards God, self, others, and the natural world. Although depraved persons employed violence against him, Jesus never retaliated (1 Pet 2:19–23), for it is unjust even to return evil for evil, given that evil has no justification.

Despite the recurrent disobedience and idolatry of Israel and the Gentile nations, God did not utterly abandon them; even though God did indeed give up transgressors for a time to their sinful acts, what this meant was that the individuals concerned were unrepentant and left to experience the fruit of their deeds and not that God had completely withdrawn from them the seeds of morality that had been implanted in them from the very beginning, or the moral guidance with which God constantly urged and admonished them. There is no suggestion or

---

43. This parable is from the second-century BC Chinese classic, the *huainanzi* and provides the source for the Chinese proverb, *saiweng shima* or *saiweng shima, yanzhi feifu*, which refers to a blessing in disguise. Editors of Encyclopaedia Britannica, "Huainanzi." The story is cited in Lee, *Theology of Change*, 59, and Smith, *Religions of Man*, 212.

implication in Scripture that Jesus or God ever permitted themselves to become somewhat like the wicked and faithless human persons with whom they dealt.

Sincerity

Not very unlike ingenuousness, sincerity is the quality of a person whose speech and profession match their inner intention and external activity. The sincere person can be trusted to deliver on what they have promised to do or claimed about themselves. In addition, there is a certain purity of intensity in their commitment to attend to some task, issue, or concern. The work of the sincere is never halfhearted but always persevering, pulling through to the very end of the task or obligation; if this is not possible, individuals characterized by such an attribute take it upon themselves to assume personal responsibility for an inability to perform what was originally promised, even if the fault is not technically their own, and make any amends as necessary or appropriate, if only on account of the earnestness with which they take on any obligation or duty.

Jesus clearly evinced the attribute of sincerity, in that he resolved to tread a road that led toward his being nailed to a cross in suffering and humiliation (Luke 9:51). What makes Jesus' resolution to enter Jerusalem especially remarkable is the fact that he knew full well what it would mean for him to go into that city, that he would suffer abuse at the hands of religious leaders and consequently be made to give up his own life (Luke 9:21–22).

Jesus went to Jerusalem in spite of the risk to his personal life because he was true to his own crucial teaching about God's agents being salt and a light to the world, witnessing to his commission as Messiah, that is, the anointed of God sent to declare and bring ultimate and eternal liberation both to Jews and Gentiles. Neither can a city standing atop a hill be concealed, nor Jesus as the light of the world and King not only of Jewish people but all creation hide himself from the very people to whom he came through his incarnation.[44]

---

44. In Chalcedonian theology, while Christ *truly* and *fully* became human as we are, in that Christ experiences the limitations, weaknesses, and even pains of human existence, he did not become *merely* human the way we are human; that is, our experience of being human is not definitive of Christ's own experience, in that, most importantly, in the case of Christ, as single personal subject, he had the experience of either a divine or human nature, yet not both at once, and even then in his human mode of personal experience, he was not completely like us in that while being human, at the same time

Even if he is finally rejected and repudiated by his own people, as God is rejected, he will not resort to the use of physical force or compulsion, because his nature and rule are not violent but meek.[45] God may visit judgment on the wicked and immoral, yet for the Son, being God as well in a godhead which comprises three persons in one divine being, an exception is made to demonstrate the prodigious pardon of God, in which the Trinity agree eternally that the cross of Christ should be converted into a propitiatory and substitutionary atoning sacrifice for the sins of humankind against God as yet unpunished, providing a second chance in a new lease on life through a conscience cleansed of its guilt and remorse but only for those who choose to repent; for the unrepentant person, final judgment is certain for participation in the crucifixion of Christ as well as any other sin. The question is apt at this juncture concerning whether sin eventuates in the destruction of the world for the individual in focus. In a manner of speaking the matter is still more severe, considering that the act of sin constitutes an existential crisis for the perpetrator in that in committing a sin, they expose themselves quite possibly to the judgment of the Lord, should it become a pattern of their lives of which they never come to ultimately repent.

Passion

Characteristic of God and the faithful follower of Christ is the strong and firm personal belief and conviction in the project of bringing about the greatest degree of mutual human flourishing. God gave God's only Son and this Son went the way of humiliation and death through flagellation and a crucifixion all to achieve a higher level of actualization of the full potential of human existence by Jesus' presenting himself as a propitiatory and substitutionary atoning sacrifice in satisfaction of divine wrath against sin, through which the contrite and penitent believer may find reconciliation and forgiveness with God.

God and the obedient believer's consuming personal desire are diametrically opposed to what is observed in mainstream modern society, particularly in the West or of a Western bent, with its extreme emphasis on feminine physical appearance. Research has revealed a greater degree

---

he possessed a divine nature suppressed in his humanity. For a summary and critical discussion of Chalcedonian Christology, see Chua, *ECRST*, 188–211.

45. Cf. Barth, *KD* IV.2, §64.3 (ET, Bromiley, pp. 167–69).

of satisfaction with one's physical body in women as compared to men, and an inverse relation between a person's contentment with their bodies and their usage of Western media and media that focus on physical appearance as well as their adoption of sociocultural standards.[46] The idolization of feminine beauty is somewhat farcical. It draws attention to what is undeniably a good and attractive asset, yet only at the expense of other equally or perhaps more valuable facts which are also good and attractive among people and in the world.

When websites, social media, and advertisements are replete with images of beautiful and desirable women, where in many modern societies there is an expectation that women should look good with the help of makeup and even a noticeable trend towards cosmetic surgery, this may be a sign that these communities have come to idolize feminine beauty restrictively understood, in complete alignment with the visceral and unrealistic dictates of male sexual pleasure, not that women make themselves appear more beautiful solely to satisfy men—there will be women who do this for themselves—but that their particular ideals of beauty, intentionally or not, often appeal to male sensibilities. Self-comparison among women results, with the effect that too many women feel dissatisfied—perhaps even disgusted—with their outer appearance.

This need not be so; humanity is not one big collection of male sexual organs or an endless catwalk and a self-examination in front of a mirror to ensure or maximize internal and external approval. Physical looks do not a person make; they are just one minor aspect of who we are as human persons, yet pulchritude has almost become a be-all and end-all in some places. Beauty will fade and, if youthful feminine physical beauty is all that matters for a woman—and this appears to be the case for too many individuals—there remains nothing attractive or valuable about an individual in a matter of years, so that the only consolation, so one thinks, is that one may reminisce that they were once beautiful.[47] For all its focus on physical beauty, the clueless world has forgotten that true human beauty reposes in those moral virtues that arise intrinsically in the human person through the Divine Nature and Trinity and stand in complete conformity with the example of the Trinity.

46. Quittkat et al., "Body Dissatisfaction," 864.

47. These observations about numerous women are not intended to be sexist; the author recognizes the equality between the sexes and genders. Men will struggle with other issues, perhaps the same number or more, but those are not the particular interest of this section.

PART 1: CREATION'S IMAGING OF THE DIVINE

Resolve

The virtue of resolve relates to the willingness to grit one's teeth and persevere through many difficulties. In that regard, we have considered Jesus' determination to tread the path leading to his crucifixion. This is a good place to discuss the dimension of human resolve pertaining to charting a straight and consistent path assessed to be prudent and astute.

In some ways, wars and conflicts transpire as a result of oppression and marginalization of particular groups, imprudent executive decisions taken to please others, whether colleagues in government or the general population, unsuitable or disproportionate means to address the sources of conflict, resentment, irredentism, expansionism, fear of potential future threats, an inability to more fully appreciate the severe negative consequences of military conflict upon civilian lives, isolationism as opposed to international cooperation to stem geopolitical conflict. Had these principles been adopted and operative, perhaps we would not have had to see the devastation of such conflicts as the two world wars.[48]

Those who presume to draw upon their scriptures to justify terrorism and war in effect abuse and exploit their own traditions. From the perspective of the Christian Scriptures, God does not endorse war except in historically momentous circumstances, at various watersheds of the history of God's salvation of humankind. When God sent a great flood during the time of Noah which eliminated most of humanity, this was only in order to give Noah and his descendants a fighting chance to establish a community of faith as a blameless man in a world of prevalent wickedness as well as to punish the wickedness of the world (Gen 6:1–13; 9:1–17).

A divine assurance regarding not ever making another end of humankind is possible in light of the fact that God has raised from an untarnished man a new generation from the ruins of an older, so that there is no longer any danger of a cataclysmic apostasy, not because people have been permanently reformed—in Gen 6:5, human wickedness is said to be grave, total, and persistent in the many individuals in whom it was present, whereas in Gen 8:21, human sinfulness is said to begin from the time of youth (Gen 6:5; 8:21)—but simply because the new patriarch of humankind, Noah, was a righteous example whom posterity could

---

48. Norwich University, "Six Causes of World War I"; World101, "Why Did World War II Happen?"

emulate, in contradistinction to Adam, who is not recorded to have performed any major righteous deed of obedience before God.

God's reason for authorizing a later invasion of Canaan by the Israelites under the rule of Joshua was similar: that Israel might smoothly transition from a nomadic to a national phase without the significant risk that its worship might be corrupted by the perverse cult of surrounding nations and that these peoples might themselves be judged for their spiritual depravities (Deut 20:16–18).[49]

These circumstances do not any longer obtain, for the reason that Israel was successfully established for a time as a kingdom and forever as a people, through whom God would send God's Son, Jesus Christ, God become human being, after a period of preparation through the Mosaic law and Aaronic cult to ensure that those to whom the Son came would fully and clearly fathom the Son's sinless nature, identity as God's only Son, mandate as anointed great high priest, prophet, and king, and work to provide in the Son's own person a propitiatory and substitutionary atoning sacrifice.[50]

God's role as territorial commander ceased with the inauguration of Israel as a national community capable of outlasting its dire straits in a physical region during a period of exile until its restoration, so that God the Son could appear in Jesus as a moral guide with the Holy Spirit coming after his ascension functioning in much the same role.

The virtue of resolve is one which is continually invested in safeguarding peace. It has inestimable regard and respect for the human individual, particularly those in more vulnerable positions. The resolute person considers that no better deed can be done than to protect and care for innocent lives with no recourse in a time of conflict and war, and no more heinous deed than to toy with the selfsame and exchange them for the slimmer or higher possibility of greater national glory.

Is the ascendency of a nation well worth the going to destruction, in many cases, involuntary, of many innocent lives? Can any war be won without numerous casualties and deaths? Scripture is unequivocal

---

49. The Amorites are singled out in Gen 15:16 presumably because they were major residents of the geographical region of Palestine which God had promised to give Israel; cf. Josh 24:15, in which "Amorites" as a category may be shorthand for all the Canaanite peoples, including the Canaanites, the Hittites, the Amorites, the Perizzites, the Hivites, and the Jebusites (Exod 3:8). Howard, "Who were the Amorites?"

50. This is without detriment to an Orthodox Jewish view of the sacrificial cult as being no indicator of the Messiah, for the sacrificial system is very well treated only as an expression of religious commitment. See Rich, "Qorbanot."

that God supports peace, not an unjust peace where the wicked are allowed to run amok (1 Tim 1:8–11), nor an ideological peace where wickedness has overtaken the highest echelons, the corridors of power, and oppresses and persecutes the weaker or displeasing on any pretext at all (Jas 3:13—4:2).

Sin is ultimately self-centered and self-serving; the human being is *homo incurvatus in se* ("man turned in on himself"), as Augustine of Hippo understood them. Contrary to the disposition of robbing others of their inner peace, joy, and possessions in a bid to enrich oneself, Jesus pursued the gift of eternal and abundant life for one and all (John 10:10). The Christian as the follower of Christ lives to do the same.

It is to be noted that Jesus is sinless in the sense that he is innocent and devoid of any entrapments of the flesh in which the transgressor inwardly already desires to do wrongful things on top of the temptation of seeing opportunities to do them present themselves. God, after all, which Jesus is, "cannot be tempted with evil" (Jas 1:13 ESV). Even though Hebrews adds the observation that Jesus was "one who in every respect has been tempted as we are, yet without sin" (Heb 4:15 ESV) as a matter of comfort, these temptations pertain to the way in which Jesus being authentically human (yet without a sinful nature) was in a position during his earthly ministry to be presented with the whole spectrum of wrongful options, such as to satiate his physical hunger after committing to a fast, confirm God's calling to and for him through flinging himself from the apex of the temple to compel God to rescue him, receive worldly authority, and avoid death by crucifixion.

These are options which may appeal even to an innocent mind rather than one riddled with godless, self-centered, and malicious intention (any of the temptations Jesus confronted may be recast as efficacious and expeditious ways to attain the goal of his ministry), options which Jesus nevertheless rejected in view that he came as a humble servant bringing God's Word to people and setting a godly, faithful, and selfless example for them to emulate, instead of a superhuman and powerful political figure.[51]

---

51. *Contra* Barth, *KD* IV.2, §64.2 (ET, Bromiley, pp. 92–93).

Forbearance

Why is it thought necessary in biblical ethics to eschew retaliation of any sort and, in lieu of that, help a person to repent, as far as this is possible, and relate to them socially and physically as if they had not done any wrong, even if we may feel unresolved anger towards them in our hearts? Part of the reason is that people tend to be immoderate when it comes to avenging themselves or others. We tend to go too far in exacting vengeance, thereby revealing as the root of vengeance something more than a thirst for justice; it is better to leave judgment to God and the criminal justice system, understanding that a person's sinful act is already their greatest punishment in that it represents a failure of one's raison d'être as a person created as a moral agent.

Knowing that our enemies are in God's good hands for judgment, who alone is able to mete out punishment proportionate to the transgression rather than insufficient or excessive in view of God's unimpeachable fairness and who alone furnishes adequate and even generous opportunity for repentance because God is perfectly patient, we are to love rather than hate our enemies, praying for them, that we might be like God who cares for and blesses even those who are ungrateful, hostile towards God, and disobedient to God's moral vision for relationships between people (Matt 5:43–48).

While it may not be possible to forgive a person who does not even seek it in the first place, a Christian can practice a forbearing love toward their unrepentant opponents, desiring not to exact vengeance but only the wellbeing of the person on every level.

Kevin Hector espouses the view that forgiveness constitutes just that which we define as forbearance, the reason for our definition being that forgiveness, as a bilateral process, amounts to an act of releasing from guilt a perpetrator of wrong, only on the part of the one wronged and not a representative, exclusively when requested to do so by the wrongdoer who has acknowledged and taken personal responsibility for their wrongdoing.[52] Should any of these two elements be absent, whether this be a desire on the part of the wronged to release from guilt the wrongdoer, or a desire on the part of the wrongdoer, having acknowledged their wrongdoing and being willing to take personal responsibility for it,

---

52. See Matt 18:21–35, in which, in both cases, the wrongdoer seeks patience and mercy on the part of the wronged, suggesting that forgiveness, like a financial debt, involves repayment or change of some sort.

to be released from guilt by the one who has been wronged, forgiveness will neither be possible nor enacted. It is critical that this process, specifically the dimension comprising the willingness and decision on the part of the wronged to release from guilt the wrongdoer, not be truncated by the presumption that such a prerogative may be delegated to a figure of moral authority such as God.

Although God does release a perpetrator of sin from guilt and punishment (though not from civil punishment which might justifiably include imprisonment though not corporal punishment let alone a death sentence), that is the case only in relation to God, against whom all sin is committed, and not the wronged, who retains the right to choose whether to release the wrongdoer from guilt and even propose a specific restitution. Insofar as it is within one's power to satisfy a demand to be forgiven, and the demand does not bring about that any form of psychological or physical harm befall the person from whom restitution is demanded, this ought to be pursued by the one who is in a position to make restitution to the best of one's ability. In the event that a person wronged steadfastly refuses to forgive one who has wronged them, the latter will have to be content with living with a sense of unforgiveness though this will not mean that they will have to feel bad about themselves in a crushing manner but only as a memory to learn from. Needless to say, a Christian who is wronged should always be ready to extend forgiveness toward those who plead for it, as in the parable of the unmerciful servant the Lord exhorted his followers always to be willing to forgive one another.[53]

We are to pray for the moral wellbeing of our opponents, in which we entreat God to guide them to reflect on the evil nature of their actions in order that they might repent and put an end to the hurt they cause to others, rather than offering hate-filled prayers for their destruction which, if actually answered, will bring some kind of psychological, relational, or physical harm upon the innocent lives around them (can anyone really say that the lives of innocent persons related to the wicked are less precious than those of their innocent victims, or that it is better to save ten lives at the cost of one?) and guilt upon the one who made such a prayer, even if it was not God's doing, but that of a wicked spiritual being or a pure coincidence, not to mention that the one who made such a request of God could only expect to be punished in the same way when they sin.

---

53. See Hector, *Christianity as Way of Life*, 3, 109–113, 217–25.

Imprecatory prayers, such as found in Ps 137:8–9, do not express hatred so much as the incisive observation, in ironic style, that the way Babylon was behaving as an imperial power, sacking and destroying the Judahite capital of Jerusalem, deporting most of its inhabitants (2 Chr 36:17–21), the Babylonians should live in fear that the same might be done to them by a ruler with a similar disposition.[54]

Second, those with whom we are at enmity, whoever is really at fault, are all too often apt to return evil for perceived evil, even if they have a greater responsibility for the trajectory of the interpersonal conflict. Whatever the personal consequences they may have to face, they will do their utmost to ensure that they inflict maximal damage upon the reputation of the person with whom they are at odds. Many people are far too vindictive.

As such, the Lord may very well be referring to a single scenario in his teaching on immoderate anger (Matt 5:21–26) in which he admonishes a person not to allow into their heart an anger which has a propensity to vilify another member of the community, goes on to speak on the clamant need for a believer to pursue reconciliation with another believer, and then how there is one final opportunity for a person subject to accusation on the part of another to reach a compromise with an accuser who is taking them to court.

If indeed the Lord had in mind just one person, this implies that both persons who are caught in conflict have reason for their mutual anger, and yet the Lord puts it to them that they are to restrain themselves from committing social—patently, a potential for the physical is included therein—violence against their opponents.

Rather than conducting themselves in such a way that the relationship is likely to worsen, and tensions escalate, they are to be proactive on their part in reaching out to the offended (and offending?) party, deferring whatever else they may be doing upon becoming aware, again, that they have offended somebody, even if it is a case of bringing a sacrificial gift to a priest at the temple, and do whatever may be necessary to make peace with the hostile party.

---

54. A distinction has to be made, and is in traditional theology made, between a hatred divinely and, in many cases, humanly demonstrated. God hates sin rather than the sinner, whereas sinful and immoderate human persons tend to hate the sinner and not so much the sin in and of itself, as evident from the fact that they do not often sincerely desire the rehabilitation of the sinner. Indeed, they tend to hate neither the sinner nor the sin, but rather the outrage and damage done by a person against their personal interests.

This includes taking personal responsibility for the hurt one may have caused to the other, offering a sincere apology, and making a promise of commitment not to repeat the offense, perchance without bringing up what that other person might have done, since the intention is only reconciliation.

In the event that they prove unsuccessful in this endeavor and the accuser has decided to haul the person in question to court, then they are to make a last-ditch effort to reach terms of peace, and this may necessitate some degree of self-humbling and a change of personal perspective, realizing that they have very much to lose should they come up against an opponent whose mind is set on putting them behind bars. The situation will not always play out in this way, and the Lord's discussion is meant to shed light on the uncontrollable implications of interpersonal conflict.

On the basis of the two reasons highlighted, an act of personal vengeance may well lead to innocent persons being harmed, usually and especially the loved ones of the offending party, who may have done nothing to deserve the injury that they suffer as a result of internecine conflict between two parties.

Accordingly, Jesus was and remains opposed to the application of the lex talionis in personal relations (Matt 5:38–42). As a principle of retributive justice and proportionate penalty in a criminal justice system, this is not to be transposed onto the private interactions between any two people, such that a person has always to put up a fight at an insult, accusation, humiliation; on the contrary, each person ought to be forbearing in all these cases.[55]

---

55. The law of talion as articulated in the Torah in Lev 24:17–22 and Deut 19:21 is to be appreciated in its proper literary contexts as furnishing a legal rationale for dealing with offenses involving some desire to subject another person or an animal to physical harm. In the case of Leviticus 24, the son of an Egyptian man and an Israelite woman was embroiled in a fight with an Israelite man and in the heat of the moment blasphemed God's name in cursing his opponent, the assumption being that he verbally expressed a wish that God physically harm the other person by striking him down. This interpretation is warranted by the fact that the decision was laid down by God through Moses that such an action (comprising the act of impugning and misrepresenting God as one who would bring about unjustified harm to a person, even death) deserved the death penalty by stoning (the very outcome he desired and falsely represented God as desiring for his opponent) and the community proceeded to do so. With regard to Deuteronomy 19, Moses is functioning as a divinely commissioned lawgiver, articulating the penalty due a person who acts as a false witness against another person, in the wish that the latter might suffer some physical harm. In this instance, judges are to conduct an investigation into whether false witness has been borne, and reach a decision that applies to the false witness the very penalty they sought to have the other party subject

The juxtaposition of the teaching of non-retaliation to a counsel to give generously to those who implore one for contributions and be ready to provide a loan points in the direction of the psychological need of the offending party; the one who perpetrates an insult, accusation, or humiliation is clearly one who has unresolved emotions vis-à-vis the individual in question; whether justifiable or not, they feel that the person concerned is indebted to them in some way, and that that debt can only be repaid through what they do to that person.

The key is not to indulge a person who may be mentally disordered and particularly and hostilely reactive toward another person, but to understand that the best bet is to pull away from such a person, choosing against aggravating a state of conflict, to the point of being willing not only to accept any degree of retaliatory action or demand but to invite a further demand, to the extent that the demand is within the means of the subject of retaliation to accede to and does not place them in a position of physical or psychological danger, if only just so the fateful relationship of bitterness can be ended.[56]

Although Jesus was not silent in face of his opponents' accusations respecting his own and his disciples' actions, this was not a matter of retaliation, but rather one of communicating truth and teaching from God. When it was time for him to endure the passion, Jesus did not obfuscate the truth of who he is by repudiating the politicized charges brought against him by his enemies, whether the question by the high priest as to whether he was the Christ (Matt 26:57–68; Mark 14:53–65; cf. Luke 22:66–71) or that by Pilate as to whether he was the King of the Jews (Matt 27:11–14; Mark 15:1–5; Luke 23:1–5; John 18:33–38).

Aside from being a sign of Jesus' truthfulness, his gentle and non-evasive responses reveal him to be above personal vendetta and how he continues to care for the spiritual wellbeing of his opponents. Jesus could very well have intentionally ignored his interrogators, fully aware of their machinations, or he could have reacted with great hostility. Yet, in his greatest danger, cognizant that his enemies were looking for a way to put him to death, Jesus did not refuse his opponents' insincere request to know the truth behind his person and mission, ever hoping that they might someday repent.

---

to. In both instances, it is Israelite criminal law in view rather than the institution of any license for individuals who feel aggrieved to retaliate to the desired degree against those whom they perceived to have harmed them. Cf. Hartley, *Leviticus*, 408–414.

56. Morris, *Matthew*, 128.

He testified not only before the relatively more politically neutral Pilate, but even the high priest, chief priests, and the Sanhedrin, all of whom were seeking witnesses who could facilitate a death penalty. Truly, in order to testify to the truth not only in word but deed as well, Jesus turned his other cheek to his enemies when they slapped him, gave them his cloak when they sued him for his tunic, and walked with them two miles when they demanded that he walk one mile, metaphorically speaking, all in the hope that they might come to see the error of their ways, repent, and place their faith and trust in him. Christians everywhere, too, are called to be as generously forbearing as Jesus was and is.[57]

Forgiveness

If there is one quality that defines Christianity as a religion, it is the idea that God forgives sinners. By this is meant that God does not consign a transgressor immediately to damnation, but provides an opportunity, at God's own expense through the atonement, for the sinner to repent and turn their lives around. It is not God's desire or will that a sinner should perish, because God is not susceptible to petty or private vengeance (Ezek 18; 2 Pet 3:9).

Scripture does portray God as angered by sin, but this is not an irrational and explosive rage, a self-centered emotion committed to the harm or complete destruction of the object of fury, as it were; as opposed to this, the unchanging attitude and disposition of God toward the human person, even the wicked and depraved, is to be understood in terms of God's loving solicitude. There is no human being that has put themselves so remote from God's purpose that they leave the fold of God's providential care.

There will be those who were and still remain "by nature children of wrath" (Eph 2:3 ESV), yet it is one thing to be under divine wrath and quite another to be one to whom God is indifferent. The context, the circumstances under which an evildoer comes to stand under the anger

---

57. Words can hurt, yet one who resents another for certain infelicitous or insensitive remarks evidences an enslavement to the approval of the latter. Actions done against oneself may not be capable of being undone, and the most that one might be able to hope for, absent the recognition and repentance of the other party, is to erect proper and sufficient psychological and perhaps even physical boundaries to obviate future recurrences of the action.

of God relate to the individual in question being a creation of God in the first instance.

All human individuals arise in and through God, and exist in covenant with God after the pattern of the triune godhead marked as it is by eternal and sublime loving communion. It is as the transgressor consciously and voluntarily departs from this design that they are subject to God's wrath. They may imagine themselves, and may well be appropriately described as, enemies of God or the gospel; even if this is so, they are not opponents of God in the sense of being God's rivals or competitors whom God seeks to undermine and terminate for self-interested reasons.

Rather, they are God's children and companions who have betrayed God's cause and that of one another, and need to be reined in and judged to preserve the moral order both externally in the universe and internally in their souls, that they might not instigate others to sin as they do, or be emboldened to continue in or exacerbate their sinful ways.[58]

God is saddened that this has to happen, on account of the sinner; God certainly does not wish for the transgressor to suffer grievous pain, much less delight in that anguish. Anger is that mode of God's love that is expressed in the context of a moral transgression. For this reason alone, divine wrath is not subject to the ills of private vengefulness; God remains loving even as God is angry with a sinner, God pines for the sinner to return to God, is always ready to pardon the contrite, and is willing to offer second chances in the interim.[59]

Christian theologians and ministers have to be careful not to afford the impression that God is concerned—and God's people should

---

58. A person is a child of God on the basis of at least three conditions: first, they are made by God (Eph 4:6); second, they are moral agents akin to God; and, third, they are able to, so long as they are willing, have a relationship with God as Father, if they do not already have one. It is not exclusively, or only in a loose way, on account of God being the origin of a human father's existence and his ability to beget a child that God is thereby to be considered Father to each and to all, given that God is also source of existence for all other things in the universe, whether a rock, plant, or animal, yet God is not said to exist in a paternal relationship to these things. Furthermore, the bestowal upon a man of the ability to generate a child does not automatically involve God in a paternal association with those granted such an ability or with those whose existence result from the granting of such an ability. A function has to be separated from the origin of that which performs the function; a jeweler crafts a diamond-studded wedding ring, intended for a man to propose to his to-be wife with, yet this action of originating the ring in no way involves the former in a marital relationship. Cf. John of Damascus, *Fid. orth.* 1.12 (ET, Chase, p. 193).

59. Cf. Lee, *TAP*, 93.

be concerned—only with the existential problem of guilt, as though this were the only crisis to overcome. Jesus did not come as the atonement for disobedient humankind simply to expunge a sense of remorse; important as this might be, the sole purport and object of divine atonement and the assurance of forgiveness that arises on its ground is that human persons might not be forever encumbered by their past, but ushered into a new day of hope in which they might at last exercise their due responsibility towards God in their covenant with God as children and partners with God in a loving communion mirroring that in the Trinity (Col 1:21–23).[60]

Less emphasized but perhaps just as important is the scriptural encouragement and prescription to seek forgiveness of God for sins committed, forgive as God is always willing to forgive one, and to seek forgiveness of others for wrongs done to them.

Longsuffering

The capacity and willingness to endure relational wounds is one which characterizes God in God's interactions with human beings. If it were not for God's longsuffering, and if God so took offense at something done against God by human individuals or communities, such that God finally decided to throw in the towel and abandon God's relationship with humankind, we would have been by far the poorer, denied the divine self-revelation in the person of Jesus or the presence of the Holy Spirit through whom alone we are able to rightly interpret Scripture by virtue of the Spirit's guidance of our thoughts concerning Scripture by means of confirming a certain view or position on a biblical passage.

Assuming that divine revelation was denied all religious groups as a whole, in consequence of God's renunciation of ties with humanity at some earlier point, we should not be able to appreciate God's compassion or mercy as much as we do through the complete or more complete

---

60. God's forgiveness does not depend on an act of atonement (Mark 2:1–12); atonement is made purely to enable human persons to remove their psychological burden of guilt due to past transgressions. A person thus forgiven by God should never presume that those whom they have sinned against have no further claim on them, since the forgiveness of God extends only to sins as committed against God. Each person can only atone for sins committed against them, through electing to suffer the hurt done against themselves without desire for retaliation. The distinction the cross bears is that it constitutes not simply a one-time atonement for a specific act but an atonement for all time, for any sin committed against God that God chooses to leave unpunished.

revelation or enlightenment. It is only as God proclaims and displays God's forgiveness that we are able to have confidence that we are pardoned upon our repentance.

Even if the non-theist or agnostic espouses views that do not admit of the existence of God, we believe that their intrinsic sense concerning their own right to exist, the dignity of their existence, and the sense that they ought to and are able to forgive themselves and others when they do wrong—in many cases—in spite of how the experience of guilt presupposes the psychological necessity of punishment in a normal person, emanates from a pre-terrestrial encounter with God in their former angelic modes in which they become convicted for the first time of divine love and forgiveness on the basis of a propitiatory and substitutionary atoning conception.[61] In this way also the religious person who does not admit of propitiation or substitution as a form of divine atonement for human sin is first introduced to the intuition and its tacit concept.

Equanimity

Despite the challenges on multiple fronts, God is not stirred up by the disobedience and rebellion of humankind and angelic beings to the extent that God is unable to function in light of surprise, anxiety, panic, or terror. Even though God experiences moments of strong emotion, such as we observe at the garden of Gethsemane as the most paradigmatic example, in which we propose that the horror felt by Christ was felt not just in his human nature but divine, given that impassibility is not a necessary attribute of divinity as a classical Greek philosophical construct, yet these emotional experiences are temporary and do not disrupt or alter God's essential relational nature.[62] Therefore, as much as Christ was initially affected by the prospect of going towards the cross, he held fast to God's

---

61. Barth has it right when he points out that the fact that God's forgiveness of sinners is not promulgated except upon satisfaction of divine wrath does not suggest a mercy that is less than free, unconditional, absolute, or unadulterated or that it is unsatisfactory to say that such mercy depends on a standard external to God in that it is bestowed on account of God's need to meet some requirement, on the part of the divine nature, of practicality, propriety, or fittingness. To this I add by way of explication that God's mercy based on satisfaction and substitution is nothing other than free, unconditional, absolute, and pure in view that it fully addresses, rather than glossing over, the psychological necessity in the event of the commission of sin for a human person to know that they have in some way been penalized for their sinful deed. Barth, *KD* IV.1, §60.3 (ET, Bromiley, pp. 486–87).

62. Cf. Chua, *ECRST*, chapter 3.

purpose for his earthly ministry and gave himself adequate time through prayer to recover from his personal anguish.

It is worth noting at this juncture that Christ did not lay aside his divine authority, to command angels to perform mighty works, at his incarnation in order to depend on the Holy Spirit for all his miraculous acts since, if this were the case, these mighty works would be, at best, the works of an anointed believer, like those performed by a biblical prophet, and fail to point to his divinity; yet, they did (see, for instance, Matt 14:22–33, in which the disciples worshipped Jesus as the divine son of God). The reason Jesus was anointed with the Holy Spirit for his ministry was to give glory to the Spirit (John 16:7) and as a model for the Spirit-empowered believer, so that the works that Jesus did by the authority of the Spirit are those that believers may emulate, yet the unique works that Jesus did by his own divine authority remain his own, which point to his divine nature. Jesus highlighted that believers will do greater works than he did because he was going to the Father (John 14:12), by which he means that because he was going to the cross to offer himself an atoning sacrifice and the way to God's forgiveness would be more fully disclosed, believers at that time would be able to exercise greater works of ministry. In drawing a comparison between himself and believers, Jesus is showing that in being anointed with the authority of the Spirit by which he did good works and healed from demonic oppression (Acts 10:38), he was setting an example for believers (Mark 16:15–18), especially in terms of helping those in need. As to the reason Jesus went to John the Baptist for baptism, this was to "fulfill all righteousness" (Matt 3:15 ESV), that is, to exercise his inherent humility (Matt 11:29) through exalting John.

Faith

One of the distinctive characteristics of the Christian faith, in contradistinction to a non-religious mindset, is a disposition in which an adherent of their own volition depends, not merely on another person, but on the personal and relationally self-giving nature of a gracious Creator and Lord. A prominent manner in which such reliance is demonstrated towards the Lord is in the practice of prayer.

The one who displays a dependence on the Lord in prayer will see the protection and blessing of the Lord; this, of course, for all its effects, is not a human work for which credit should be given to the one who intercedes.[63] Rather, God of God's own goodwill alone rather than human merit focuses God's attention and concerned interest on the practical needs of people, distributing God's resources through spiritual intermediaries to those who have need of them.

The one who seeks personal or practical assistance of God should not imagine that God permits the difficult circumstances that may have come into the life of the person. It is not God's will that Jesus should be tempted in the wilderness, but that in sending Jesus into the wilderness through the Holy Spirit, Jesus should resist the devil's wiles, none of which exist by God's intention. To assume that God is in some way responsible for the troubles we experience hinders optimism that the situation will change for the better and saps the motivation to pray for such change (since on this presupposition, God may not be quite done with the believer or the people being prayed for); and places a cloud of mystification between God and the one who prays given that God may have intentions the believer may not be privy to, and the believer is simply expected to trust that God knows what God is doing. The one who believes God is always on their side and seeking an improvement to their personal situations and those for which they pray will never lose heart in their intercession, for they trust that God wills only good in the specific situation. While they still may not see much of an amelioration of circumstances, at the very least none will charge God with wrongdoing, lack of empathy, or cruelty, and the believer's faith will be sustained by the hope that God, who already wields inalienable moral influence over the lives of all moral agents, will yet preside over a final judgment in which evildoers will be completely and forever isolated from the rest of creation.

---

63. The lesson of the parable of the persistent widow is that the one whose prayer is to be effective must be continually dissatisfied with their present situation characterized by a particular need for which they commit themselves to prayer, yet do so in a way that minimizes any disruption to their reasonable familial and functional responsibilities and that avoids perpetration of harm to self and others. The petitioner should implore that God convince them of the right, wise, or best decision they may make in the given circumstances, and open their minds to every possible option, especially those to which they are not partial. They are to ask not so much that God would perform a supernatural act to compel them to see and do what God desires but rather that God might lead them step by step into a clearer understanding of the demands and needs of the situation in which they may find themselves in relation to their own need for their prayer to be affirmatively answered, recognizing that God will not expect a person to do anything against their own rationally-ordered and intuitively-guided choice.

PART 1: CREATION'S IMAGING OF THE DIVINE

Within the triune godhead, faith is a property not only of the Son in incarnate form but even of the divine persons among one another, insofar as faith is defined as a mutual interdependence between two or more persons in a communal relationship which entails trust, self-surrender, and personal commitment. Although in classical Christian theology, there is a heavy emphasis on the aseity of God, in which God is said to exist of Godself, without need to depend on any entity, object, or power in the universe beyond the godhead for God's continued and perfect existence and reality, the three persons of the Trinity very much, indeed, most fundamentally and most radically, depend on one another, so much so that any one divine person cannot be conceived as existent and real, as the complete persons they are, in the absence of any or both of the other divine persons.[64]

Hope

Indubitably, God has hope, a better and ideal outcome towards which God strains all God's powers and energies. God's hope in and for humanity and the world is not isolated from God's eternal being construed as static, but very much an object of God's own personal existence. Why does the Spirit of God intercede to God on behalf of the believers with sounds of agony if it is not because the liberation of the children of God, the consummation of the foreknowledge and predestination of humankind to congruence with the image of God in and as the Son, is that which God eagerly awaits, along with humankind and all creation (Rom 8:19-30)?

Honor

Although all humanity arises from God, God treats humankind with respect and dignity. There is not the slightest tinge of utilitarianism in God's dealings with humankind. God's assessment of humanity and the rest of creation is that they are very good and pleasing in themselves and as a whole, rather than having value only as a result of a particular set of

---

64. Athanasius of Alexandria depicts God as the fount of God's Word, God's wisdom, God's brilliant light, and God's water spring, immediately drawing an eternal and ontological relationship between God and God's Word, wisdom, light, and spring, without which God would not be the origin of that which constitutes all these; namely, God's Son. Athanasius, *Contr. Ar.*, 1.5.14 (ET, Newman and Robertson, pp. 314-15).

functions they are able to perform for the benefit of some external entity to achieve a specific set of goals.

The profoundest way in which God demonstrates the fact that God honors humankind lies in how God did not spare God's Son the possibility and risk of suffering humiliation on earth and Godself the risk of having to grieve the death of God's Son but dispatched the Son into the world as a human being, being willing even to permit the Son to suffer torture and execution at the hands of cruel opponents and wicked conspirators (Rom 8:32), all because it is in God's very nature to suffer for others, including the human other, for the sake of redemptive love, to display and reveal this love, and thereby bring people back into the fold of divine goodness.[65]

Kindness

God's kindness designates God's conscientious sensitivity to the subtle needs of people, especially those which tend to be missed or ignored. It is on full display in the context of God's compassionate mercy held out towards those who transgress God's moral laws, extending new opportunities to make amends for past errors in the hope that God might see the fruit of repentance (Rom 2:4). In this respect, kindness is said to be shown by God in view that God sees beyond what most people are able to perceive; God understands that people are prone to evil, and if any good is to emerge from the human community, it is imperative that they be dealt with in a manner that bespeaks a certain breadth of latitude and a willingness to be quiescent and wait rather than only act.

God alone possesses the wisdom to know how much latitude will be salutary, without which all can only live in despair, beyond which point humankind will only be emboldened in their wrongdoing. Giving latitude is not an easy decision; kindness extended to a perpetrator may be injustice prolonged against the victims of depravity. God alone will know how much more these victims must be allowed to suffer and how much more time the perpetrator can be given to repent, based on the degree of emotional effort taken in attempts to arrive at a place of contrition, before God acts decisively in the role of judge.

---

65. Moltmann, *Crucified God*, 192, 203, 214, 216–18, 227, 229–30, 243, 245, 247–49, 252–56, 267–78.

PART 1: CREATION'S IMAGING OF THE DIVINE

Responsibility

There is no greater exemplar of the attribute of responsibility than God, whose inextinguishable sense of duty is manifest in the way in which Jesus descended to the lowest depths of service in order to cleanse, sanctify, and redeem humankind from sin (John 13:1). In electing to enter Jerusalem, he effectively played into the hands of those who plotted to kill him, all to attest to the truth of who God is as merciful guardian rather than shirk his responsibility as the foremost witness to God's truth, on account of the fact that such action, such a disposition and attitude of loving benevolence, defines him as a personal being. Jesus saw himself as one who surrendered his very life for those he considered his friends; that is, his disciples, as well as anyone else in the world who would appreciate his teaching and ministry (John 15:12–17).

Integrity

The quality of being self-consistent in one's words and deeds is seen in how Jesus did not hesitate to declare the error of the ways of Jewish teachers who had gone astray. Even when he did so, he was clear about his objective: to remonstrate with these figures of authority so that they might experience a change of attitude and heart in the understanding of and approach to religious ministry, and not rather to shame, ridicule, or undermine them.

If it is supposed that Jesus in fact was culpable of shaming his opponents in the accusations of hypocrisy he leveled against the scribes and Pharisees as attested in Matthew 23, he clarified his motive in the very emotional note he sounded in Matt 23:37–39, where he rued the way in which Jerusalem, that great city of God's people, repeatedly declined God's gracious invitation to enter into fellowship and communion with God.

Moreover, Jesus did not say or do anything in private that he was ashamed of, as he taught (Luke 12:2–3). Indeed, the Lord made good his commitment to suffer the fateful events of the passion (Luke 9:22, 51). He did not renege on his promises because the people to whom he made them, as well as everyone else included within the ambit of his address, matter to him.

TRUTHFULNESS

The attribute of being truthful designates not just the habit of abstaining from deception or false witness, neither orchestrating machinations to lure and entrammel people in a situation of exploitation nor acting as a false representative of things which did not actually transpire.[66] More importantly, it has to do with having a sensible estimation of one's value, motives, and contributions (Cf. Rom 12:3).

No person in the community of faith is to, as a case in point, imagine that they alone are indispensable and vital while their fellow believers are perhaps slightly less to be esteemed; in truth, all are just as necessary and thereby equal in worth (Rom 12:4-5); different persons perform differing functions in the community that upholds the faith and values of Christ and no single person is equal to the task of doing duty for all the members at once, and no single group can actualize all the functions required in the body of Christ.[67]

A sense of interdependence, in which each member appreciates the value that others have towards themselves, being "members one of

---

66. Was it righteous for Rahab to lie to preserve the lives of the Israelite spies in fear of and obedience to God (Joshua 2)? Yes, since if she had not done so, she would have become accessory to murder or at least the imprisonment of God's servants, leading to the destruction of Israel; in her context, it was more righteous to lie and save a life than to tell the truth and cause death to the Israelites, given that murder is a more serious sin than lying and saving a life is a greater righteousness than bearing true witness, for truth-telling is an expression of respect for the other person, while saving a life concerns the very viability of the other person. Cf. Butler, *Joshua 1-12*, 258.

67. As Christ is in each believer in the Holy Spirit, so each believer is in Christ, in that each is part of the interdependent body of Christ, ultimately dependent on Christ as head, into whose fullness of character each Christian seeks or should seek to grow through knowing and imitating Christ's character with the help of ministers commissioned and equipped for edification (Eph 4:1-16). Edification designates a process beginning with God the Trinity, involving a taking of another person into one's own heart; that is, making a conscious and conscientious decision to take on their social and personal habitus, allowing ourselves to experience what we know of their lives, observing their decisions, good or bad, and supporting rather than tearing down the other person, seeing them as capable of becoming enlightened and reformed, and helping them along that pathway, with the humble recognition that we, too, do not know everything or do everything right or might be wrong in our beliefs and actions, and might fall into the same or similar sins. Each divine person perfectly takes one another into their own heart; God takes and has taken us into God's heart; and God calls us to take each other into our own hearts. Hence, Jesus' emphasis on his unity with the Father in the context of his farewell sermon (John 17) highlighting as well the believers' oneness in being filled with Christ and the love of the Father for the Son. See Volf, "Trinity Is Our Social Program," 412-13.

another" (ESV), should define the relationships within the Christian community of faith. The equivalent in modern parlance of truthfulness is the virtue of humility, which refers not so much to an inclination to make oneself of no account even if we may have been contributing in the most significant of ways, for that would really be to misrepresent the factuality of the scope of our service, but rather to take a fair view of one's role and place within a community, giving honor, dignity, and respect where this is due (Rom 12:3, 10).[68]

Whereas God is said to possess the attribute of aseity or independent being and existence in relation to the created order, this is not the case within the godhead itself, within which the equally fully divine members recognize each other's critical role in the fellowship and communion of perfect and eternal love that is the Trinity. As a matter of fact, God, we propose, relates in like manner to the created order, coworking with angelic messengers and agents as well as human persons to steward God's mysteries and the rest of creation.

Generosity

God's abundant giving is powerfully expressed in the numerous miracles of providence God worked among the Israelites during their wilderness trek. Furthermore, God sent God's only Son, rather than an angel, to proclaim and concretely manifest the gospel, giving no less than the Holy Spirit to indwell each believer.

Selflessness

There is perhaps no more felicitous and accurate way to describe the nature of God in relation to humankind and the rest of the created order than the idea of selflessness. Jesus the Son of God gave his very life to accomplish the salvation of humankind and their liberation from guilt and condemnation, that those like the woman caught in adultery in a story recorded in John 8:2–11, we imagine, might find relief and solace in the fact that Jesus died on the cross not for his own sins but as a propitiatory substitutionary atoning sacrifice by which any residual divine wrath for sins against God left unpunished is satisfied (2 Cor 8:9).

---

68. Conversely, the arrogant are those who show contempt, not recognizing the value of the person they disdain, a function of their ignorance and self-deception.

THE CHRISTIAN DOCTRINE OF DIVINE IDENTITY

A Christian Formulation of Divine Identity

It is well to end off with a construal of divine identity that is peculiarly Christian in character. We pose ourselves two critical existential questions: Does God exist? Does God care?

Does God exist? God is whatever makes a person possible and real in the present time. God is whatever holds all things together (Col 1:17), whatever gives reality its wonderful design (Col 1:15–16). Christ is firstborn of all creation as its prototype, seeing that all things were created *in* Christ. Faith is not the absence of doubt but flourishes only in the context of possible doubt. A person who is unable to doubt can hardly be said to have faith. It is one who in spite of a capacity for doubt chooses to trust wholly in God who truly exercises faith.

The mind entertains possibilities however outlandish or improbable while the heart exercises faith even seemingly against all odds. Faith is the heart's believing against the mind's inveterate scepticism and unbelief. *Fides quaerens intellectum*. It is faith seeking understanding, in Anselm's idiom. What are we to believe against all doubt? God's love and righteousness, that God sent God's Son into the world to atone for our sins, that we have the Holy Spirit, that Christ will return. We are to believe in God's positive will and favorable disposition towards us, that God is indeed for us. We are to believe things that can only be believed about God, not analyzed. We cannot believe mathematics or scientific theory or analyze and test God's love. We can only analyze mathematics or test scientific theory and believe in God's love. As Graham Ward observes in his discussion of British psychiatrist Iain McGilchrist's work, *The Master and His Emissary*, "*credo* ["I believe"] is no longer linked to a calculus of probabilities, but to categories like trust, loyalty, and empathy."[69]

Does God care? When do we ask such a question? Typically when we lose someone dear to us or something that matters to us, when we are disappointed, when we or others suffer, when we see evil and injustice in the world. But theodicy is not quite an affair of the analytical mind but one of the committed heart. Theodicy is all about faith and trust rather than the realm of possibility. Theodicy is about trusting that in spite of my emotions and circumstances, God still loves me, provides for me, protects me, and is working out God's plan in my life. It is very hard for a grieving person, for someone scarred by great tragedy, to open their heart to a loving God. We give ourselves time but we keep this roadmap

69. Ward, *How the Light Gets In*, 257–58.

before us. In this connection, it may not be helpful to think, as some do, in terms of a connection building or soul-making theodicy, that all evil and suffering have been orchestrated by God in order that a person, who survives or witnesses a tragedy, might repent, live more soberly, or draw closer to God and others. Such a suggestion leaves open the question of the immoderate cost at which such benefits are accomplished.

How will we know we believe in God unless we lose what is valuable to us and are confronted with the choice either to renounce God in view that we value something else more than God and we find God not or no longer useful in enabling us to secure that more precious thing, or to hold on to God as supremely valuable, capable of restoring to us a hundredfold and worthy of being trusted that God will do so on God's own word? The disciples left their physical families and homes to follow Christ (e.g., Matt 19:27, 29). Some will do that even today, yet for all Christians the call is to emotionally subordinate the things we care most about beneath God as the highest value and greatest treasure in our lives.

4

The Christian Doctrine of Divine Immanence

The Experience of God in World Religions

It may be thought to be more intuitive to place a chapter on divine immanence immediately following one on divine transcendence, seeing as the two concepts form a natural pair. Yet without first identifying the divine being, it is futile to go into any greater detail regarding the scope of the action and activity of this divine being in the world.

More than anything else, the doctrine of divine immanence relates to the relationship between the biblical God and divinity or ultimate principles in the world religions. It is upon this that we will concentrate. The usual taxonomy is along the lines of exclusivism, inclusivism, and pluralism.

Within exclusivism, the biblical God is thought to be present and active as a revelatory source of salvific wisdom only in the Christian religion, so that other religions are thought to have no more than the name of religion without actually bearing any revelatory content or holding any salvific possibility.[1]

A modern interpretation of an exclusivist Christian theology of religions may be found in Gavin D'Costa as a "universal access exclusivist" who holds out the possibility that all who have had no opportunity,

---

1. Cf. Hedges, *Controversies in Interreligious Dialogue*, 20–23.

by no fault of their own, to hear and receive the gospel will be presented with it in the afterlife.[2]

It is worth mentioning at this point that a major attraction of exclusivism is that it promotes the notion of an inherent superiority; members are drawn to a religious or intra-religious group that purports to possess the unadulterated truth or version of the truth. Such groups tend to boast comprehensive and rigorous dogmatic arguments that make an extensive attempt to critique variant points of view and claim to do so most successfully and effectively. They only do this to varying degrees, of course, in light that the worldviews championed by each of these groups tend either to appeal to a literal interpretation of a passage that supports their point of view without recourse to a thorough contextual analysis; consider only their own Scripture or texts as deserving of serious consideration as possessing the truth; or, even if other worldviews are discussed, do this but in a superficial or unappreciative manner.

Inclusivism marks a shift from exclusivism toward pluralism, characterized as it is by a genuine openness toward the revelatory and salvific potential of other religious traditions, in which something morally good and anticipatory of real salvation is assessed to be present in world religions, yet only in such a way that the Christian religion remains the culmination of religious evolution and spiritual development, bringing together diverse threads found only fragmentarily in non-Christian religious traditions in a perfect and purified whole.[3]

In Barth, as a case in point, revelation, faith, knowledge of salvation, sanctification (inasmuch as the church is grounded in the revelation, knowledge, faith, and proclamation of Christ), rather than salvation, are situated in the church as a medium through Christ. Salvation itself is situated in Christ, and Christ is able to reveal himself to people beyond the proclamation of the church.[4]

A Vatican II-understanding of whether a person can be saved apart from a direct exposure to the gospel and explicit profession of faith in Christ emphasizes the possible activity of the Holy Spirit among non-Christian religions and cultures to bring to salvation those who have not refused the presentation of the gospel, who walk in accordance with the truth of God as revealed through natural law and the dictates of the

---

2. Thatamanil, *Circling the Elephant*, 51–55.
3. Hedges, *Controversies in Interreligious Dialogue*, 23–26.
4. Barth, *KD* IV.1, §62.2 (ET, Bromiley, pp. 688–89).

conscience, and whose hearts and minds are prepared and ready to receive the gospel when the opportunity arises.[5]

In the case of the German Catholic theologian Karl Rahner (1904–1984), non-Christian religion construed as "lawful" is explicitly regarded as a possible locus for the salvific work of the Holy Spirit through revelatory principles and even religious saviors. This is made possible by the fact that human nature is a "graced nature" capable of accepting and responding to divine grace, which may or may not be only an implicit acceptance by means of conformity of action with the truth of the gospel accompanied by a false profession of faith.

In intellectual terms, there is a certain precognition of the reality of God in which phenomenologists believe that human beings are able to grasp particular forms of knowledge only by demarcation and delimitation from an infinite knowing by God. The practical equivalent of this *Vorgriff* ("supernatural existential"), the ability for human nature to approach the supernatural divine by God's grace and access a "transcendent revelation", is an innate pursuit of what is true, good, beautiful, selfless, trusting, and hopeful in the "categorial" or historical experience. Rahner declares a proviso, that these "anonymous Christians", that is, people who by their graced nature seek after God in their intellect and actions, have to accept the gospel as and when it is presented to them in its full clarity.[6]

After Rahner, the Belgian Jesuit priest Jacques Dupuis (1923–2004) extends the inclusivist theology of world religions by suggesting that other religious traditions are pressed by God into service as instruments of divine self-disclosure and salvation, along with Christianity, though not to the same degree of excellence or completeness, through the mediatorship of Christ as a secondary form of the mediation of divine revelation and salvation. For Dupuis, Christ, and together with Christ, the Father and the Holy Spirit, remains central to the disposition of salvation history, with other religious traditions being brought into some proximity of relationship or degree of knowledge of the same God in Christ.[7] In spite of his concessions of religious plurality, Dupuis remains rigorously Christian-centric without reaching a hand to other religious groups to come to the table on equal terms. Another Christian-centric, inclusive

---

5. D'Costa, *Meeting of Religions*, 99–171.

6. D'Costa, *Theology and Religious Pluralism*, 81–82, 85–87, 92, 96–99, 103, 110–11.

7. Dupuis, *Christian Theology of Religious Pluralism*. See Mong, "In Many and Diverse Ways," 71–85.

model of religious pluralism, one keyed to the differing desirable yet ultimately inferior temporal and eschatological outcomes of the various world religions, is developed by S. Mark Heim.[8]

With pluralism, the transition to an equality of all world religions, including Christianity, is complete, typically in the form of a conception of religion-specific content regarding the nature and will of God as attempts at the comprehension of the same within specific cultural contexts and in such a manner that religious revelation pertaining to God in any one religious group cannot be said to be indicative of the nature of God in any universal or spiritually objective way.[9]

A fourth theology of religions, enunciated in the methodological volume of this systematic theological work, is distinguished by the terms integrative and pluriform, and has to do with a number of central claims.[10]

One, every world religious tradition, Christian or non-Christian, is on par with one another in terms of spiritual and moral value. It cannot be said of any one religious tradition, including Christianity, that it is superior to other traditions. Two, each religious tradition has to be understood and permitted to be understood on its own terms, within its specific theological framework. It is inadvisable to postulate a single religious tradition, including Christianity, as a completion or fulfillment of some sort of other religious traditions, satisfactorily bringing together partial truths situated in other religious theologies in a fuller and more complete manner.

In the claims advanced in this systematic theological work, especially in the light of its effort to establish a theological network of individual doctrines which profits from a discussion of facets of doctrine found in non-Christian religious traditions, there is no attempt whatsoever to suggest that Christian theology constitutes a fulfillment of world religions. The labor of theological construction and systematization is done purely with reference to the object of enunciating a more coherent and viable theology of the Christian faith for the modern century in which we live and write.

Similar efforts done within non-Christian religious traditions, in which an attempt will be made in theological construction and systematization but from a non-Christian religious standpoint, whether it be

---

8. Heim, *Depth of the Riches*; see Hick, review of Heim, *Depth of the Riches*.
9. Hedges, *Controversies in Interreligious Dialogue*, 113–15.
10. Chua, *ECRST*.

Hindu, Islamic, Buddhist, are certainly welcomed and encouraged as work that will only contribute toward a richer understanding of individual religious traditions in constructive and productive dialogue with other religious traditions, promoting a greater measure of harmony and solidarity between religious groups in the world by means of spurring an appreciative self-initiated exposure to the doctrine and teachings of other religious traditions with the aim of learning from and incorporating some of these doctrines and teachings within the specific religious tradition of the systematic theologian.[11]

Epistemology

Acts 10:34–35 suggests that people everywhere are able to honor and obey God and do what ought to be done as a person who intrinsically believes in God and exists in community and in the world: "So Peter opened his mouth and said: 'Truly I understand that God shows no partiality, but in every nation anyone who fears him and does what is right is acceptable to him . . .'" (ESV) For how is God able to declare acceptance of anyone on the basis of fearing God and doing what is right unless God is able to assess each person, whether Jew or Gentile, Christian or non-Christian, in terms of whether they fear God or do what is right in God's eyes; how is God able to render such an assessment, with the consequence that those who are assessed to fear God and be doing what is right are accepted and those not assessed to be doing so are not accepted, unless it is within each person's power to fear God and act righteously? Hence, we conclude that each person in every land has capacity to respond to God with fear and lead a life replete with righteous works.

As to the processes by which such an attitude and actions are made possible, some observations in Acts 17:22–31 bear these out, expressing how, contrary to God being nothing more than a physical object of idolatry crafted by the human hand, God is Creator of humankind (having posited the human soul in the Divine Nature and constructed the material human body through ages of evolution by a creative command of the Trinity delivered to angels), and contrary to God having to be waited upon by human persons, God is one who provides for the needs of all humankind, including physical life and sustenance.

---

11. The need for an appreciation of other religious traditions is paramount in multireligious settings, as a head of state has observed. Tan, "New Anglican Archbishop."

PART 1: CREATION'S IMAGING OF THE DIVINE

As a matter of fact, God raised the society of human beings from one human person, Adam, possibly the first example of a human person to attain to a knowledge, worship of, and fellowship with Yahweh, and guided them to populate different parts of the world only in order that in their respective differing historical and cultural contexts, they might lay hold of a knowledge of God made accessible to them in relevant historical and cultural ways by none other than God: "And he made from one man every nation of mankind to live on all the face of the earth, having determined allotted periods and the boundaries of their dwelling place, that they should seek God, and perhaps feel their way toward him and find him . . . " (Acts 17:26–27 ESV)

The knowledge of God is not a prize that God puts far out of human reach, as though God desired to toy with human feelings the way a school bully would dispossess a physically weaker student of a belonging only to dangle it before the latter, engendering anxiety in the student who makes every effort to reclaim his possession, never to any avail. Paul informs the Athenian men of the Areopagus: "Yet he [God] is actually not far from each one of us, for "In him we live and move and have our being"; as even some of your own poets have said, "For we are indeed his offspring." (Acts 17:27–28 ESV)

God has given access to knowledge about God and is constantly drawing people everywhere and in every time period toward Godself, in whom they live, move, and have their being, or, in short, in whom they not only exist and have the specific shape of their being and nature, but in whom also they may actualize the teleological purpose of their very nature and existence in their proper activity and functions, thus bringing fulfillment both to themselves and to those to whose lives they contribute, as the offspring of God who, by definition, enjoy a special closeness and affinity with God, a personal relationship with God which God establishes and maintains with each human person as a being posited by God in the Divine Nature and materially enfleshed by God in the Trinity.

It is for the reason alone that all human persons have access to knowledge of the divine that Paul is able to deprive of any justification and excuse those who would feign ignorance of God: "For what can be known about God is plain to them, because God has shown it to them. For his invisible attributes, namely, his eternal power and divine nature, have been clearly perceived, ever since the creation of the world, in the things that have been made. So they are without excuse . . . " (Rom 1:19–20 ESV)[12]

Religious traditions around the world reflect on the possibility of the existence of the human being and the physical world as grounded in the nature or/and will of the divine. As such, to return to Acts 10:34–35, all may know and fear God and do what is right, including those who do not believe there is just one God, those who believe that God is impersonal rather than personal, or those who do not believe a God even exists, since the fear of God referred to in the passage is simply the internal personal recognition of a reality beyond the observing and reflecting human self, one which posits the person and all other contingent reality, for one cannot claim to posit oneself; no one is conscious of so doing. If some person suggests that such self-positing might be unconscious or effected by a non-conscious part of the individual's nature, then that nature should not be subject to decay and corruption, and yet it is.[13]

Consequently, the referent for the recipient of human honor in Acts 10:34–35 is the source of the being and existence of humankind. Whether this is conceived as a single personal God, a pantheon of multiple deities, an impersonal unity, or the principle of a material universe in an atheistic worldview, God alone, without necessarily being so named, is made the object of reference. To the extent that people accord to something other than themselves the bringing into being or positing of the world, what Paul means by the knowledge of God that is "plain" and "shown" by God to all and the knowledge of God's "invisible attributes", namely, God's "eternal power and divine nature", that is "clearly perceived, ever since the creation of the world, in the things that have been made" (Rom 1:19–20 ESV), these individuals possess an intrinsic knowledge of God (cf. Ps 19:3–4).

Should they, on the basis of that ineluctable knowledge of God and their moral purpose, posited by the Divine Nature and imprinted by a pre-terrestrial encounter with the Trinity on their minds and the internal structures of their morality, reinforced by the general moral guidance of the Divine Nature and the religion-specific guidance of the Trinity, choose to act in accordance to natural and universal laws enunciating the basic rights of humanity which prescribe empathy, respect, harmony, and solidarity between people, they may be said to, in effect,

12. Cf. Calvin, *Inst.*, 1.3, 1.4.1.

13. See Thomas Aquinas' epistemological way via possibility/necessity. Aquinas, *Summa* 1a, Q. 2, Art. 3, co.

be demonstrating a fear of God and engaging in right action which win acceptance from God.[14]

To argue that it is not sufficient for faith in God just to believe that something other than oneself posits all reality since the first chapter of Romans presumes a system of conviction in the majestic personality of God is essentially to nullify Paul's entire thesis concerning a universal scope of the knowledge of God. This is because we need to give credence to the worldview of the atheist person, who genuinely does not hold any supernatural divine reality to exist beyond or within the world and who only recognizes that some principle outside of themselves accounts for the textures of reality part of which comprises their own being, out of which their being arises, and in which their being participates.

The modern theologian cannot possibly maintain that such an individual is only being deceitful about their own authentic spiritual understanding in order to defend the absolute necessity for a theistic conception of the relationship between an individual and God (or, in the case of the atheist, the ultimate material and moral principle).

As such, they are left in a quandary: do we deny the atheist's experience of the world just to assert the theological absolutism of Christianity, running the risk of our theological constructions and systematizations becoming obsolete and irrelevant, or do we deny that Paul was right in observing that the knowledge of God has a universal scope? As opposed to undermining the testimony of an atheist or Paul, it is more ideal to hold both in tension, and revise our understanding of what it means to say that all individuals know God.

Acts 17:22–31 and Rom 1:19–20 furnish telling complementary depictions of universal human access to the adequate knowledge of God and of God's moral purpose for humankind, in which the danger of idolatry is underscored.[15]

---

14. For this reason, Rom 2:14–15, 26 speaks of Gentiles without the written law of God being able to "by nature do what the law requires" as "a law to themselves, even though they do not have the law" as those for whom "the work of the law is written on their hearts, while their conscience also bears witness, and their conflicting thoughts accuse or even excuse them" and contends, "if a man who is uncircumcised keeps the precepts of the law, will not his uncircumcision be regarded as circumcision?" (ESV) The benefit of being a Jewish person consists in how they received the written revelation of God as well as the rite of circumcision, both of which testify to the life of obedience and good works they are to live (Rom 3:1–2).

15. Cf. Barth, *KD* IV.1, §60.1 (ET, Bromiley, p. 395).

THE CHRISTIAN DOCTRINE OF DIVINE IMMANENCE

Whereas traditional theology assumes that human communities and societies removed from the Jewish and Christian commonwealth begin with an insufficient or even defective knowledge of God,[16] the picture painted of the human engagement in idolatry is one in which diverse human communities begin with a universal and adequate knowledge of God and of God's moral vision, which is lamentably truncated and reduced to an affair of the service of physical objects accorded sacred, even divine status, to the exclusion of any higher and superior divine reality undergirding all being and existence and gracing all moral agents with salutary guidance in virtue and attitude from which they can only benefit.

It is not that non-Jewish and non-Christian communities begin with a lesser or defective knowledge of God and God conceals Godself from these societies, choosing only Israel and the church as sources of reliable knowledge of God, but rather that all communities begin with a universal and adequate knowledge of God, yet some individuals choose to reduce God to physical objects of idolatry out of an inappropriate desire to manipulate and control the divine for their purposes. Lending credence to this view is Hos 2:16, which suggests that all worship is directed toward God, and that therefore all religious traditions are duty-bound to ensure that they speak truthfully about God as, at the very minimum, a divine or universal principle constituting the source of ontology and morality, rather than misrepresenting divinity.

There are strong hints in Christian Scripture that those who do not willfully set their faces against God will not be excluded from salvation. Consider Jesus' reference to an unforgivable sin, which entails impugning the Holy Spirit of God by equating the Spirit, in the Spirit's work among people of driving out demons, with Satan (Matt 12:22–32; Mark 3:22–30; Luke 12:10). In this context, Jesus highlighted that all sins, all blasphemies, including those against the Son, may be forgiven people except for this blasphemy against the Holy Spirit, who constitutes not just the love between the Father and the Son but also that between God and the world as demonstrated in the divinely-ordained processes of creation, reconciliation, and redemption.[17] This is clearly suggestive of the way in which unless a person sins against God in this deliberate, malicious, and unchangingly persistent manner, all will be forgiven those

---

16. Calvin, *Inst.*, 1.4.1.
17. Barth, *KD* IV.2, §64.2 (ET, Bromiley, p. 43).

who face God in the afterlife so long as they ask God's pardon, even if they may not have explicitly professed their faith in Christ, or perhaps even consciously rejected God due to some misunderstanding or even willfulness during their earthly lives.

Furthermore, this declaration of Jesus concerning the unforgivable sin implies that one should be extremely cautious not to flippantly indict the good spiritual works done in other religious traditions as being of the devil, for to the extent that it is good work, it is to be encouraged, and indeed of the God who alone is good (Mark 9:38–41; 10:18). Any charitable and kind deed done toward the poor and needy is done as to the Lord himself; therefore the devil and the devil's agents are incapable of performing these kind acts (Matt 25:31–46). We know that the parable of the sheep and the goats speaks of the treatment or neglect of any poor or needy person, not just the followers of Christ, since the Lord spoke of strangers among those being served or neglected, people unknown to the community of faith.[18]

Heb 9:27, a passage typically cited in support of the contention that there is no opportunity for repentance after death, does not indicate that divine judgment directly follows death, while the parable of the rich man and Lazarus in Luke 16:19–31 in no way precludes the possibility that the rich man, while enduring torment in Hades, might, if he so chose, have called out to God in penitence and repentance and received salvation; instead, he showed no awareness of or reverence toward God, desiring only that Lazarus cross over to offer him some water or that he be permitted to return to the world to warn his brothers of certain judgment.

In regard to the creation by God of humankind, this refers naturally not to all human beings who have ever existed, since the method by which people come into being is via the route of biological procreation and reproduction, in most cases involving the sexual relations of a man and a woman.

In traditional Christian theology, it is thought that Adam and Eve constitute the very first human couple, before which there were no human beings, and furthermore that they were brought into being not through reproduction, since there were no human beings before them, but by a direct divine act of creation through which God, by an eternal decree, willed into existence the being of Adam and Eve on the sixth day of creation.

---

18. Cf. Barth, *KD* IV.2, §64.3 (ET, Bromiley, p. 170).

God is indeed the source of human existence in the view we propose, the Divine Nature positing the spiritual essence of the individual human person as angelic beings, with the Trinity directing their angels to construct a material embodiment for the human person, through many ages of evolutionary processes.

On this view, Adam and Eve were not the first human beings to come into existence, but the first worshippers of Yahweh. Adam and Eve were brought by God through the power of angels into material existence by means of an evolutionary creation of their material form and the inspiriting of that material form. In no way is this intended to suggest that no other human person already existed at that point in time, since apart from Adam's family, we see the appearance of Cain's wife and the other people to whom Cain referred whom he feared were inclined to take his life on account of the fact that he had murdered his brother, Abel.

As such, a human community already existed, and they attained their physical forms through a long process of evolution, by which animals evolved to become primates and humans, after which the processes of procreation and reproduction functioned to ensure the continuity of the human community.

The process by which Adam and Eve were inspirited is as follows: an angelic spirit was infused with a physical body to form a human individual. In the case of the true first human person, whose material body was shaped through the process of evolution, the angelic spirit was infused with that physical body when it was shaped into its particular and distinctive substance; in the case of members of a preexisting human species, the angelic spirit is embedded in a physical body produced through a natural process of conception.[19]

For this reason, the account of God's creation of humankind in the first creation narrative has a different referent for the object of this creative act (humanity as a whole rather than a specific individual) from that in the account of God's creation of Adam, and later, Eve, in the second creation narrative. Whereas the former account bespeaks the creation of a human species in general, the latter addresses that of the first fully functioning religious human person.

---

19. See Chua, *ECRST*, 203–208.

PART 1: CREATION'S IMAGING OF THE DIVINE

Doctrinal Formulation: Divine Immanence Expressed in World Religions

God is immanent in all world religions, a truth borne out in human religious experience. There is no contradiction between major religious and philosophical traditions in terms of their moral vision for humanity as responsible, caring, and compassionate toward God (or gods, the divine, or ultimately significant), self, and other, traits often mirrored in divine or human religious figures in many of these traditions. The very fact that a system of beliefs and practices exists as a religion or metaphysical philosophy suggests that some foundational claims are made about how a person should lead their lives in a way that will be most meaningful and beneficial to themselves and others. This implies that morality is at the heart of every religious or metaphysical philosophical tradition. A prescription for the way in which people ought to conduct themselves such that they do not cause harm to self, others, and the world around them but contribute towards the flourishing of each person lies at the center of every tradition. Some degree of harmony can be striven for between religious and philosophical traditions through discussing differences which are non-opposed and accessible to introduction, focused and accessible to extension, and polemical and accessible to functional equivalence, yet what ultimately matters is that all religious and philosophical traditions already promote and advance moral inspiration and support in the context of a human community. That they do this constitutes the quintessence of religion and metaphysical philosophy.

It has been observed that the myriad religious traditions of the world lack a common and essential core by which they may be unified as a single world religious tradition, and that insofar as a scholar, theorist, or theologian embarks on such an endeavor, they may justifiably be said to be joining what ought rather to be left asunder.

Without a doubt, varying theological claims with different degrees of emphasis are advanced in each religious system. Nevertheless, it remains potentially fruitful and promising to pursue a surer understanding of the fundamental elements that seem to divide one religion from another. I propose that the differences, so far as the doctrine of God or the ultimate principle is concerned, comprise those that are non-opposed and accessible to introduction, focused and accessible to extension, and polemical and accessible to functional equivalence.

THE CHRISTIAN DOCTRINE OF DIVINE IMMANENCE

On the compatibility of interreligious doctrinal differences

INTERRELIGIOUS DOCTRINAL DIFFERENCES NON-OPPOSED AND ACCESSIBLE TO INTRODUCTION

As an example of a difference between religious conceptions of God that is non-opposed and capable of introduction, Buddhism as an agnostic religion does not strictly foreclose the possibility of the existence of a divine being deserving of the title of God.

The Buddhist religion simply chooses to focus on the central existential concern that human suffering presents, attempting to rectify the error into which many have fallen as a result of displacing the object of personal psychological stability from self to people, things, and situations, imploring instead a recentering of self-worth in the personal self, an abstinence from attitudes and actions which reflect a search for the self beyond the self and an encouragement of attitudes and actions which reflect a self-valuing which chooses to value others and the world as a sign of one's gratitude and appreciation of the interconnectedness of all reality—an ultimate moral principle.[20]

Buddhism, as such, is not opposed to the notion of a God as source of the wisdom of placing value in oneself, exhibiting gratitude, and recognizing the interconnectedness of all things. Therefore, the belief that God exists can profitably be introduced as a new idea which may add—as a difference which is focused and accessible to extension—to the richness of a Buddhist system for those willing to go so far and, on the other hand, the Christian system can consider incorporating such Buddhist emphases as self-value, gratitude, and recognition of the interconnectedness of all things to strengthen its own core moral principles.

INTERRELIGIOUS DOCTRINAL DIFFERENCES FOCUSED AND ACCESSIBLE TO EXTENSION

What may be a source of conflict between Christianity and Buddhism is the idea in the latter tradition of a karmic law of the universe which constitutes a difference that is focused and accessible to extension. It is

---

20. The notion that all things exist only in relation rather than some or all things existing in and of themselves, without antecedent factors that account for or shape their being; that "everything is empty of self-existence", is an insight from the Madhyamaka philosophical tradition in Buddhism. Thatamanil, *Circling the Elephant*, 135–37.

sometimes argued that Christian theology stands in direct contrast to a Buddhist view of karma in light that divine grace permeates the Christian worldview and religious experience, whereas karma dictates that people receive what they deserve on account of their good or bad actions.

While God does indeed extend grace according to the Bible, there remains judgment for moral transgressions, so that divine grace should be conceived in terms of an aid in the development of morality over the course of an individual's life rather than a license to commit sin. God grants pardon and forgiveness in the form of a second chance for the transgressor, a withholding of rightful and just punishment for sin against God in the hope that the individual might use the opportunity for repentance. Beyond all doubt, the Bible proclaims a divine judgment for all who refuse the second chances from God to mend their ways (Rom 2:1–11). Likewise, Christian theology holds that believers who engage in good works are rewarded (Rom 2:6–7, 10), yet they do this not out of any fear of divine judgment (1 John 4:18) but out of gratitude to God for the greatness of their salvation, a desire for eternal reward (Matt 6:19–21), and a solicitude for the at times dire needs of others. In this regard, there is no real quarrel between a Christian and Buddhist theological system, and a Buddhist idea can again be extended to incorporate the idea of God as the source of universal karma, given the name of divine judgment in Christian theology, either for reincorporation in Buddhism or incorporation in Christianity.

A potential source of tension might reside in the Buddhist conception of endless cycles of reincarnation, whereby the quality of a subsequent mode of existence of the individual is based on their moral performance in the present life. There does not seem to be any indication in Christian Scripture concerning unending cycles of reincarnation, yet this is a relatively minor doctrinal point, not very different from doctrinal differences between Christian confessions such as whether the final judgment will involve an eternal conscious suffering or an annihilation of the soul.

THE CHRISTIAN DOCTRINE OF DIVINE IMMANENCE

INTERRELIGIOUS DOCTRINAL DIFFERENCES POLEMICAL AND ACCESSIBLE TO FUNCTIONAL EQUIVALENCE

Religious differences which are polemical and accessible to functional equivalence encompass areas of doctrines where a religious tradition either indirectly or openly contradicts another religious tradition.

As an example of an indirect interreligious opposition without explicit reference to the other religion, Hinduism posits that Brahman, the supreme ultimate, is an impersonal reality, defined not by sharing in properties of being, consciousness, and bliss, even while constituting pure being, pure consciousness, and pure bliss as the source of these attributes in living and non-living entities rather than possessing those attributes as a living entity itself. In contrast, Christian theology holds God to be a personal being rather than an impersonal ground of being, indeed, the true reality of all things itself.

In Hindu theology, the claim is that Brahman alone is true and real, eternal and permanent, as opposed to the plural entities in the world which constitute mere phenomenal modes of manifestation of Brahman, more or less real, in a fleeting or mentally constructed world.[21] A hearty attempt, therefore, is made to see beyond the physical manifestations of things in the world, to transcend the outward world as it appears to us, and to attain to a deeper underlying unity in Brahman. This is a project that is able to attract Christian sympathies, inasmuch as Christian theology, as well, envisions a faith that passes through and beyond external appearances to a deeper unity in Christ and in God as the source of all things.

Yet, the impersonality of the Hindu conception of Brahman and the identity of the Hindu understanding of the human person, along with all things, with Brahman, remain doctrines irreconcilable with the pertinent tenets of Christian theology, where God is personal and God and human person are non-identical.

---

21. The 11th- to 12th-century Hindu theologian and philosopher, Ramanuja, regarded Brahman not just as the efficient but also the material cause of the universe, which formed the universe as a form of spontaneous recreational self-expression without any grand purpose, while Shankara, the eighth-century Hindu theologian and philosopher, regarded Brahman as the only true reality, the experience of the world itself, with its visible parts, the individualistic self, change, evil, a personal Brahman and a Brahman with attributes being an illusion of the highest order eventuating from "ignorance" or "misperception" as karmic consequences. Tennent, *Christianity at the Religious Roundtable*, 67–69.

PART 1: CREATION'S IMAGING OF THE DIVINE

In this regard, one can opt for one of two pathways: first, the way of extension can be taken, in which the Hindu decides to embrace the personality of God and non-identity of God and human person or the Christian takes on such revised Hindu doctrine; second, the way of preservation can be opted for, where the Hindu decides that they do not wish to pursue a modification of their doctrine of Brahman. Even in the latter case, nothing of any critical importance is jettisoned, since Hinduism is robust enough to incorporate the idea of Vishnu as a personal manifestation of Brahman, this being a functional equivalent to the Christian doctrine of God as personal.

A case of a direct contradiction of a Christian doctrine as an example of a theological difference that is polemical yet accessible to functional equivalence is attested in the Islamic prohibition against seeing Jesus as the Son of Allāh and therefore Allāh as a Trinity.[22]

Quite apart from the materialist connotations entailed in the Islamic view of the Christian conception of the Trinity, it is crucial to pursue the question of the extent to which Islamic theology has a functional equivalent for the Trinity. The answer is in the affirmative, seeing that the major role of the Trinity in Christian theology is to inculcate a vision of God as relational and capable of being approached. Islam, as well as many other major religious traditions, incorporates some personal dimension or representation for a divine being or reality,[23] along with lesser intermediaries such as angels or minor deities; these often play an important role in bridging the metaphysical remove between divinity and the believer.

What can be said in this connection regarding metaphysical philosophies which posit the non-existence of God or any divine being? In an atheistic worldview, it is not enough that there remains a recognition of an other which gives rise to all of reality, including the human observer, given that this other, usually a principle and origin of material and moral reality, is not typically conceived in personal, much less interpersonal, terms.

Does anything at all in an atheistic worldview do the duty that the Trinity does in a Christian theological system? In fact, the material and moral principle is concretized or incarnated here in the human person as moral agent, emerging in the context of a community of material entities guided by moral standards. The human individual as moral agent

22. E.g., the *Sūrah al-Ikhlāṣ*.

23. This includes the idea that God is closer to a person than their jugular vein (Qurʾān 50:16).

is more than merely a puppet whose actions are dictated by an external party, but a conscious entity with the freedom and capacity to make decisions based on an intrinsic and inalienable sense of what is good, ethical, and right.

Within an atheistic conception of ultimate reality, the moral nature of the human person governs the actions of individuals, providing necessary ethical direction for human existence, while the human other, guided by the same universal human morality, serves as an exemplification of human virtues in which the practitioner of these virtues is actualized as a human person, models these good and ethical values to another human person, and allows that other person to benefit from the practical succor and emotional support and solidarity displayed by the practitioner of moral virtues. The personal convictions of an atheist will prevent them from embracing the central claims of specific religious figures, yet these convictions do not preclude a recognition of the humaneness evinced in the lives of both these historical figures as well as many other religious and non-religious persons who have lived in the course of human history up to the present time.

In the final analysis, the functional equivalent for the Trinity in Christian theology is constituted by the ubiquitous and universal presence of a community of human persons which supplies inspiration toward the actualization of intrinsic moral virtues as well as emotional solidarity and practical support.

Another possible difficulty involves Judaism and Islam's emphasis that Jesus is not to be thought of as God. None of these religions reject what Jesus stands for—a compassionate and forgiving God. They simply repudiate Jesus' divinity either on account of a hermeneutical inflexibility or due to some misconceived theological presupposition. The objection arises either from the sense that Jesus does not fit the mold of the Messianic ruler of Judaism—a consummate human political leader descended of the line of David who will govern Israel, enact an influx of Jews into Israel from around the world, bring it about that all Jews conscientiously observe the Torah, and herald a period of world peace[24]—or God cannot procreate and produce a son through biological sex with a virgin woman (Islam).

24. Telushkin, "Messiah." Orthodox Jews do not accept the Messianic claims of Jesus because he did not usher in a time of global peace. The influential commentary by Rabbi Solomon ben Isaac (1040–1106) interprets the vision involving a Son of Man in Dan 7:13–14 in terms of a symbol for the state of Israel rather than an anticipation of

PART 1: CREATION'S IMAGING OF THE DIVINE

If the various religious and non-religious traditions suggest different accounts of phenomena such as the creation or non-creation of the world (universe), this is no impediment to a broad-view unity of religious and non-religious traditions since each account encapsulates one or more critical aspects of a divine or ultimate ontological basis, so that all these accounts are capable of being harmonized in the direction of a metaphorical compatibility. In this regard, each account of creation or non-creation may be read not so much as one of literal or physical occurrences, but rather metaphorical depictions expressing various dimensions of the power, intention, and beauty associated with how all things came to be, written from an imaginative and poetic human point of view using analogies found in the world.[25]

A word is in order about different religious practices such as the Islamic prohibition against pork consumption, a proscription not found in other religions like Christianity, for instance. These religiously peculiar practices can be viewed as operative purely within the sphere of the religion in question; it would be odd for an adherent of a religion which does not consume pork to attempt to compel members of another faith, specifically one which does not proscribe the eating of pork, not to consume pork.

A BROAD-VIEW UNITY OF RELIGIOUS AND NON-RELIGIOUS TRADITIONS

The particular claims of various religious traditions concerning a transcendent or supernatural origin and source for all existence proffer alternative etiologies for the shape of the human experience of realities in the world, which the atheist will find difficult to accept, and there is no real need to foist a peculiarly Christian conception of ultimate being and reality upon an atheist. What truly matters—and what is worth celebrating—is that no religious or philosophical tradition is opposed to the vision and project of human flourishing, with a system of inherent moral virtues at the core of such an actualization and fulfillment of the human purpose, but all equally seek the betterment and welfare of the human person and of human community as a whole in providing

---

an eternal God-man, in line with the prior vision of the four beasts each representing a different kingdom or political power. See "Daniel: Chapter 7"; Sefaria, "Rashi."

25. Chua, *ECRST*, 50–55.

moral inspiration and support—the quintessence of any religious and metaphysical philosophical tradition.[26]

The very fact that each religion or metaphysical philosophy does not assume that humanity created the universe and seeks what is essentially the same moral good, wanting what is best for self and other in such a way that the majority will agree regarding serious violations of human rights and the need for better protection of these rights, infers the belief in one ontological and moral source, a single system from which being originates, or one set of laws in accordance to which all things exist rather than different sets of laws, and one version of morality, that is, one morally legitimate desire, which is to seek the wellbeing of oneself and others rather than different types of essential morality. Each religious tradition or metaphysical philosophy will have its unique way of identifying this multifaceted ultimate reality, whether by holding an agnostic, reticent, or underdeveloped view regarding the ontological source and focusing on the great practical benefit of universal moral laws or espousing some conception regarding both dimensions of ultimate reality. Therefore, God can be said to be immanent in all world religions and metaphysical philosophies.[27]

---

26. Differences in doctrinal ideas between religious traditions may be ascribed to variations in context, to which God as the Holy Spirit accommodates the truth about Godself and human purpose for the benefit of humankind. As some cases in point, Indian religion, Judeo-Christianity, Islam, and Buddhism may owe the distinct shapes of their religious teachings to circumstances in which occupying Aryan forces sought to control a diverse population in a large area, giving rise to an assimilative religion featuring the articulation of a universal moral law of consequences for human actions juxtaposed to an inward spiritual ethic promoting a detached and enlightened contentment, in the case of Hinduism; to a mighty divine liberation from a situation of oppressive servitude, into which religious teachings concerning a powerful, wise, and devoted divine champion and protector readily distinguishable as a single being from the polytheisms of hostile neighboring Egyptian and Canaanite nations with their unethical practices of child sacrifice, incest, and bestiality (Leviticus 18), in the case of Judeo-Christianity; to an urgent need to counter Arab polytheistic systems which encouraged child sacrifice, resulting in an emphasis on a divine being opposed to such unethical practices and easily differentiable as a single being as opposed to one having to share power with other divine entities, in the case of Islam; and to a crisis of moral-social rigidity and an excessive humanization of divinity in Indian society, justifying a radical movement away from personal divinity entirely into a non-theism which underscores a self-realization relating to how existential struggles begin at the point of an inability to separate one's self-value from other people, objects, and the changing circumstances of life, in the case of Buddhism. Ward, *Religion and Revelation*, 134–38, 172; Q Anʿām 6:137; Mawdūdī, *Understanding the Qurʾān*, 278–79.

27. Richard Dawkins highlights four possible reasons for observed altruism and generosity among human persons. All four theories (altruism as arising from a genetic

PART 1: CREATION'S IMAGING OF THE DIVINE

An additional support for the idea that God is present in all religions and philosophies that make metaphysical claims such as atheism and agnosticism lies in the manner in which no human person is ever completely devoid of goodness. Insofar as God is conceived as the source of human goodness, this suggests that God is immanent and operative in every human person, including individuals typically thought of as archetypally evil or depraved, such as Adolf Hitler.

Even in the case of the German dictator, incontrovertibly an example of a person overtaken by depraved desire and actions, the influence of evil is not total, utter, and absolute; if it were, Hitler would not have sought at least the wellbeing, in economic and political terms, of his own people, a commitment for which he became a source of hope amid crippling despair for many Germans.[28]

Furthermore, it beggars belief to presume, from a specific religious point of view, that God is absent in other religions or that some counterfeit, at most, is present therein, given that the sustainability and persistence of the major religious systems that have been preserved until now, some of which have lasted many centuries, infers that these traditions and communities of historical patrimony have adequately served the spiritual, psychological, social, and cultic needs of large sections of the global population, even if this influence has occasionally been imperfect.

To the extent that God is immanent in world religions, agnosticism, and atheism, it is ill-advised for the church to regard its faith as the only true religion, or fulfillment of other religious traditions. Pluralism contends that nothing adequate can be said about the divine being or ultimate reality as it is. Such a philosophical premise is partially a function of what

---

predisposition to ensure the transmission of the same genes within a species; altruism as arising from reciprocity; altruism as arising from the benefits of having a reputation for being altruistic; and altruism as arising from the impression of superiority and dominance afforded by altruistic behavior) are invariably contingent on an inclination or assumption relating to the protecting and advancement of either one's individual self-interests or those of the group to which one is biologically related. Aside from tarring all altruistic individuals with the brush of the supposition that they did what they did only to benefit themselves (what about those who act generously without drawing attention to the fact, even spontaneously; i.e., not in order that people or even God should reward them?), why should self-interest matter and from where does the related inclination arise? Insofar as God is the source of moral inclination, which includes the impetus to protect and love oneself as a foundation for loving one's neighbor, God is necessarily the ground of a reasonable and genuinely altruistic self-interest capable of self-sacrifice to varying degrees, even one that is complete, as the situation may call for it. See Dawkins, *God Delusion*, 214–20.

28. Rees, "Dark Charisma."

are perceived to be irreconcilable differences between religious traditions concerning the nature, purpose, and activity of the divine being or ultimate reality. Yet we have seen that these differences may be reconciled; hence it is conceivable that the divine being or ultimate reality may be known through a deep study of the various religious traditions and humanism. A particularist option, whereby a religious system is true, meaningful, or relevant strictly within a particular sociocultural and linguistic context, leading to the result that religious traditions are incommensurable, highlights the importance of considering each religious system on its own terms. At the same time, it veers to the extreme of disallowing any meaningful dialogue between these systems.

In an integrative and pluriform approach, Christianity is not only true without being exclusive of other religious traditions or of atheism but the same God and divine truth is expressed in all these traditions, the most crucial part of ultimate truth being an implicit acceptance of the existence of an ontological and moral source of the universe and a common desire to pursue human flourishing. Such a perspective encompasses both non-exclusivism and exclusivism; there is no exclusivism in relation to other religious/metaphysical traditions as they have one source of morality and it is vain to pit one religion/metaphysical tradition against another (religious/metaphysical non-exclusivism); at the same time, there is an exclusivism of that source in relation to the created order as the ontological and moral source of all creation (divine-creature exclusivism).

By way of a succinct summary of my position, based on a literalist interpretation of Scripture and biblical teaching, concomitant with a rational analysis of the Christian tradition which takes account of the human experience of psychological issues and cultural and religious diversity, on the mutual standing of Christianity and other religious traditions, all religions and humanism are equal in dignity and truth value. Although there may be clear differences between traditions in the conception of God, the gods, the divine, or the ultimately significant, each religious and non-religious conception registers a nonnegotiable, irreducible, and indispensable aspect of the divine reality. Furthermore, each religious and non-religious group is able to affirm that the human self is not the source of its own physical, psychological, spiritual, and moral reality and agency and that of the world, and so at least negatively and indirectly allows that the source of physical, psychological, spiritual, and moral reality and agency is external to oneself, and that it is single and the very reality recognized as divine in the various religious traditions. Each tradition is also able to promote a view of human morality that requires and encourages responsibility, respect, empathy, compassion, and care toward and for God, the divine, or the ultimately significant, self, others, and the world, universal values which all sensible individuals practice in their relationships with those whom they value.[29]

Divine grace and human repentance

This is a good place to expand on our consideration of divine grace in Christian theology as opportunity for repentance rather than a carte blanche to live in sin.

The cross is the clearest example available of God's grace construed as second chance. Although what Christ's opponents did in leveling false accusations and charges against him and conspiring to crucify him was deserving of the harshest divine judgment, God let these people off as it were, not by pretending they did not do what they had done or by treating what they did as less serious than it actually was, but allowing the events of the passion to take their course, yet at the same time testifying through the resurrection that Jesus is who he always claimed to be, so that every mouth might be stopped and transgressors against Christ begin to recognize the patient and merciful face of God who is not willing that any should perish but that all should reach repentance, bewailing their sin of crucifying the Lord, something none of them should ever have done, realizing that the atonement, satisfaction, and substitution of the Lord consist only in this: that when evil was perpetrated against the Lord, Christ did not return their unjust blows or their evil, but voluntarily received them all from their hand, withholding divine judgment which he could have meted out at any point during the passion, choosing to suffer injustice so that his enemies might clearly see that God is merciful and patient to them, not desiring that they should perish but only that they repent even until the very last moment before any sin is committed, for if he had had it any other way, the effect of that message would not be present.

If Christ fled those who had come to arrest him, some might imagine that God was intending to come back at some later point to enact judgment. If Christ judged them there and then, obviously the message of

---

29. Chua, "Religions as Path to God," 263.

grace and patience would have been obscured. And if he defended himself against all their accusations, in the way a most effective barrister would, he would not have been heeded since the powers that be had already predetermined that he should die for the peace of the whole nation. The atonement therefore consisted not in some requirement of the expression of God's holy wrath, given that God can overlook and has overlooked—in hope of repentance—past sins,[30] but rather the fact that the only way divine mercy that challenges if not leading to repentance can be demonstrated is by Christ suffering the unjust blows of evildoers to the point of death instead of avoiding or preventing them in any way.[31]

The passion of Christ is an atonement because he sacrificed his life just to reveal the merciful face of God to evildoers, that they might repent of their evil, including their crucifixion of Christ (thus the apostles called adherents of the Jewish faith to repentance for their role in the crucifixion in Acts 2:36–38), an evil deed which God has chosen not to punish as a sign of atonement, in the case of those who believe. To further glorify Godself in the crucified Lord, God has accepted the cross as a penal substitutionary act of atoning sacrifice and satisfaction brought to God when Jesus ascended to heaven to sit at the right hand of God, in which all transgressors may see themselves vicariously penalized for all the sins they committed for which they were never or never duly punished (Rom 3:22–26), in expiation of their personal guilt, that they might dwell always with God in a perfect and blameless conscience, honoring God with a life marked by penitence for past sins, true and heartfelt repentance, and abundant good works of life and service toward God, one another, and the world.

It is important to bear in mind that the overlooking by God of sins is not an exculpation, for all the sins of a transgressor are always remembered; divine pardon only comes into effect and its effect is only sustained through repentance. Should an evildoer decide not to repent, all their sins will be punished and their blood will be on their heads; hence the statement in Rom 2:5 that evildoers are piling up their sins to the day of God's wrath.

Repentance is clearly not beyond the possibility and capacity of a human person, according to a sober understanding of biblical theology.

30. Acts 17:22–30.

31. Not a hint of a divine child abuse may be found in an adequately biblical theology of the cross. On the idea of a cosmic child abuse, see Chalke and Mann, *Lost Message of Jesus*, 182–183.

The Scripture would not be as replete with moral directives as it is if repentance were impossible for human persons. The typical Augustinian theory that God's moral requirements are beyond human ability and that one should pray that God would so sovereignly transform the human heart that it is made capable of a moral correspondence to God's laws presupposes that the human will is ruled by desires of a certain negative moral quality.

The assumption is that human nature is simply characterized by a set of incorrigible evil urges, whether to kill, steal, or destroy, instead of being a complex of conflicting inclinations. Moreover, even if such a state of affairs is admissible, the theory imposes another layer of assumption, whereby the human will is effectively deprived of its independence from the desires of a human person. An Augustinian theology of the human will suggests that people's desires are only sinful and that they act only in accordance to their sinful desires, the path to justification and sanctification being rooted always and only in the regenerative and renewing work of the Holy Spirit.

Human existence, however, is not always only riddled with sinful and evil desires or consigned to express these desires and urges. There are numerous instantiations in Scripture of human persons who have demonstrated righteous attitudes and performed righteous actions pleasing to God, attitudes and actions which reflect a fear or reverence of the Lord, a disposition and desire to honor God as the highest reality and existence, worthy of all adoration, worship, and obedience. We observe such pious respect and submission in the cases of figures including Seth, Noah, Abraham, Isaac, Jacob, Joseph, Moses, Joshua, Samuel, and David.

How can St. Paul declare: "For by works of the law no human being will be justified in his sight, since through the law comes knowledge of sin" (Rom 3:20 ESV)? Does this Scripture not end all debate on whether human beings are only capable of sinning in favor of the affirmative position? It is true that works of the law do not serve to justify any human person in God's sight, since justification refers to the declaration of God as a heavenly judge to the effect that a defendant who stands trial in the heavenly court is an innocent and blameless person who cannot be held guilty. If the intention of a human individual is to exalt oneself as a model and exemplar of moral excellence and righteousness for others (Rom 3:27), a foil against which those who do not share one's religious beliefs are shown to be unworthy and wicked persons, as certain Jewish persons did in respect to non-Jewish persons toward whom the former felt a certain sense of moral superiority, then there will surely be nothing of which to boast, given that no human individual is immune to spiritual and moral decline and deterioration, the great figures of faith included.

In a writing displaying great discernment, judiciousness, and perspicacity, Augustine of Hippo identifies two opposing yet erroneous tendencies among Christian believers; namely, on the one hand, those who hold that the believer does not need to engage in any form of good works since faith alone is sufficient for salvation and, on the other, those who suppose that they may embrace some sense of moral or spiritual superiority on account of their assumed good works, imagining that they actualized them completely of their own choice and effort.[32] They fail to comprehend, in the first case, that faith designates an experience in which a human person becomes aware of Christ's atoning act to purchase assurance of God's forgiveness for those who are penitent and repent and that therefore it is indeed exclusively necessary for salvation conceived in these or similar terms, including an atheist understanding that there is something in the ultimate that permits them to forgive themselves, but without implying that faith assumes a broader definition as well of a mode of thinking, feeling, desiring, acting, and therefore being in which a person chooses to live in the presence of and in relationship to God, actualizing God's moral commands, especially those which enjoin on one a need to love God, self, and others. In this context, salvation takes on the meaning of the actualization of human existence in these terms; hence, equally here, salvation is exclusively conditioned on faith.

What is more apposite in connection to the foregoing is the way in which Augustine of Hippo strikes a careful yet clear distinction between the type of works that have their exclusive source in a person; that is, those works that a person imagines they are completely creditable for, and the type for which God has molded; that is, created or formed a person (Eph 2:10 ESV). The bishop of Hippo interprets this in terms of a new creative working within the human heart to turn the will completely unto God.[33] We do not go quite as far, simply averring that God has already created every human person with a moral orientation for works that please God, albeit in numerous cases, owing to the experience of a psychologically dysfunctional upbringing or other traumatic

---

32. Augustine, Gla, §20 (ET, Holmes, pp. 451–52).
33. Augustine, Gla, §33 (ET, Holmes, pp. 457–58).

experiences, there will appear to be an orientation, stronger or weaker, away from and even against moral good.

Ps 51:10 simply reveals David's perfervid desire, in wondrously poetic diction, for God to burn away the impurities of his heart and enable him to think, feel, and desire more righteously. The verse partakes in Hebrew parallelism and appears to involve an intensification of meaning from the first to second part. Inasmuch as this is so, and David continues his plea in the second part by asking for a restoration of a steadfast or right spirit before God, to bring him back to the disposition he had when he was a faithful shepherd boy and pious king-in-waiting. Accordingly the whole poem reads like a petition for God to grant the contrite king a second chance by restoring God's relationship with him. The passage in 2 Cor 5:17–18 stresses that the one who sincerely follows Christ's example and obeys his commands will be a completely changed person to the extent that they have not previously walked in righteousness.

Nobody is immune to sin or transgression. As a matter of fact, righteousness is not a game where a person may seek to surpass another person to express personal superiority. More than anything else, righteousness is the act of the will in which a person attunes themselves to their inner moral convictions already implanted by God in their souls, shakes off the contrarian voices, and chooses to carry out and express their noble desires. To the extent that righteousness becomes a game of personal superiority, it is lost and can never be recovered; indeed, it can never be attained in this way.

If this essential principle is well and properly conceived and understood, then it becomes evident that all personal boasting is excluded, as each individual turns inward to the fundamental moral convictions that mark out each person as human and outwardly expresses the marks of their individual and distinctive humanity by an act of the will. As they strive to be in touch with and express their moral human excellences as implanted in their innermost parts by God alone, and as they ought so to do, they will inevitably stray or fall from their intended purpose through an abuse of their freedom of will, and they will need and appreciate a means by which to get back on track. Such second chances are amply provided by divine grace, where God chooses not to immediately punish a transgression, but is patient with the wrongdoer through not one, two, but possibly multiple episodes of transgression, patient over the shorter or longer term, guiding, motivating, and inspiring human persons by divine kindness unto repentance (Rom 2:4).

The biblical figures of faith were not celebrated on account of the fact that they committed no sin, that their sins were completely forgiven and they lived in no fear of God's wrath or they understood that forgiveness so utterly as to be remarkable in that respect, or that their hearts and wills were so transformed that they could be capable of committing no more sin upon their conversion to faith in the Lord. David stands out among biblical figures as a possible anomaly in that, in contrast to his predecessor Saul, he committed more heinous sin, and yet he, not Saul, was feted as one who pursued God's heart.

Was David's heart so completely transformed through his relationship with God that he became incapable of sin? In point of fact, the Davidic narratives are filled with consistent examples of moral and spiritual failure. Was David then such a notable and God-pleasing person because, among other people, he most fully grasped the gift of divine pardon? David, of all people, would readily acknowledge that the faith, service, and obedience of God does not come without tangible and severe consequences for its abjuration. David knew God's pardon, but he also lived under the lucid awareness of God's wrath and anger toward the possibility and actuality of his transgression and sin, losing a child and many citizens through direct divine judgment as a result of his wrongdoings.

What David deeply understood was not that God had bestowed upon him an armor of divine righteousness in consequence of which he cannot be seen by God to do any wrong, or that God had so changed his heart, supernaturally of course, that he became powerless to stray from the moral vision and direction of God. David's occasional moral lapses and experiences of divine judgment were sufficient to disabuse him of these false and idealistic notions if he ever entertained any of them.

What David really discovered was the way in which God had implanted in him good and moral desires and an independent personal will to elect to express these good and moral desires in opposition to dysfunctional and wicked ones, that he is responsible for his moral as well as immoral expressions, to which different consequences are attached, and that God provides opportunities for him to repent when he falls, though he may still suffer irreversible consequences as a result of his actions.

PART 1: CREATION'S IMAGING OF THE DIVINE

Survey of the Biblical Narrative

This section will proceed to assess the scriptural viability of a conception of divine immanence as expressed in world religions through a broad sweep of the history depicted in the biblical narrative. To a significant degree, it may be said that the whole of Scripture limns the relationship between God and humankind in terms of a series of salvations, liberations, or deliverances.

God "liberates" humankind from nothingness/chaos

When God created or posited humankind, this was as a species imbued with a certain moral dignity, corresponding analogically to that which God possesses, hence, the idea that humankind was created in the image of God, communicating the fact that the antecedent moral nature and subsequent material embodiment of human beings indicate their internal moral dignity. Such dignity is not shared by sentient animals, as a result of which we are justified in slaying animals for our food, but not fellow human beings (Gen 9:1–7).[34]

Human dignity entails that we treat one another with the highest degree of concern, respect, gentleness, empathy, kindness, and generosity—a complex of attributes summed up in the word, love or benevolence. In so giving rise to the human species, God liberated us from nothingness. In one sense, this may appear to be a loose application of the idea of liberation in that liberation involves bringing a moral agent that already exists out of a place of captivity; in this case, human beings did not yet exist when they were said to have been brought out of a situation of confinement or limitation; namely, nothingness.

In another respect, however, specifically that of the perspective that an angelic insurrection preceded the creation of a world ruled or overseen by human beings, God did in fact spare humankind the need to dwell in a cosmos ruined by a fallen Lucifer and other disobedient angels by recreating the face of the world. In this sense, it is not inaccurate to say that God liberated humankind from the barrenness of the previous world by recreating the earth.[35]

---

34. The function of the animals consumed by human beings is just that, a Roman Catholic cardinal pointed out during a public lecture. Goh, "Culture of Death."

35. Did these fallen angels take material embodiment at some point in the past, akin to humankind, only to fail their earthly vocation due to the pride and arrogance

God liberates humankind from moral lawlessness

When God created and placed the man in the garden of Eden, appointing him to manage the garden, God laid down a rule that while he was free to consume the produce of any tree in the garden, he was not to eat the fruit of the tree of the knowledge of good and evil, an act that would usher death into human existence rather than imparting nourishment and life (Gen 2:15–17). The tree of the knowledge of good and evil is clearly a metaphor for moral authority, the power to decide what is good, right, and worthy for a human person to do. Far from bringing humankind under enslavement or restriction through promulgating this commandment, God safeguards the human person and human society from certain and inevitable anomie in the actual or perceived absence of such moral dictates. People would do as they wish and society would be in disarray. Instead God, both as Divine Nature and Trinity, posits and reinforces the moral values that undergird human being, existence, community, and flourishing. The regulation concerning the tree of the knowledge of good and evil, whatever the concrete form it took, did not bring about a moral nature in humankind but merely attested to what was already present, precluding or dispelling any latent or actual ambiguity and self-justification.

God liberates a human family from idolatry

In the sixth-century talmudic-era Jewish midrash and commentary on the Book of Genesis, *Bereshit Rabbah*, Abraham's ancestry is traced through Terah conceived as a worshipper and purveyor of idols (chapter 38).[36] To the extent that Abraham as a historical figure may be situated in the early second millennium BC in Sumer, he lived in a religious context in which idols were treated as receptables housing the spirit of gods and therefore living beings, regularly served by professional priests in large

---

of desiring prerogatives which belong only to God, as a result of which their world was destroyed and ruined by divine judgment, their sonship with God severed, and their spiritual forms consigned completely to earth with attenuated status, intended to be ruled over by human beings or a second batch of human beings, the new vicegerents? Such a theory is certainly suggested by a trajectory found in Anselm's *Cur Deus homo* (1.19), in which he discourses about the way in which it may be that God created human beings to replace those angels which disobeyed and fell, and how human persons are intended to be equal in status to good and obedient angels.

36. Bereshit Rabbah 38 (ET, Schreier).

temples.[37] By revealing Godself to Abraham and his successors and, through them, the community that will be called Israel, God brought the family of Abraham out of idolatry and into a worship of the true God.

God liberates a human family from famine

As much as God settled Abraham and his descendants temporarily in Canaan, God also saw to it that these people called by God's name would survive a famine by orchestrating Joseph's migration to Egypt initially as a slave and facilitating his promotion to premiership, setting the stage for the mass migration of the entire family of Jacob to Egypt to avert certain disaster.

God liberates a human community from slavery

During Israel's sojourn in Egypt, the day came when the incumbent Pharaoh stopped showing favor to the people and decided to oppress them. The plight of the Israelites moved God to compassion, and God commissioned Moses to deliver the Israelites from slavery in the land of Egypt through mighty acts of divine power including ten plagues and a miraculous crossing of the Red Sea in which a dry path was created for the people to cross the body of water.

God liberates a human community from structural chaos

Jurisprudence is imperative for the normal and proper functioning of a national community. The system of law exists to deter criminal wrongdoing and threats to collective and personal wellbeing and safety, as Paul observes in 1 Tim 1:8–11, and a society that lacks these binding rules that regulate human conduct through an efficient criminal justice system is likely to experience increased violence and social unrest.

When God brought the community of the Israelites out of Egypt, freeing them from a situation of enslavement, laws by which the nascent nation were to be governed were delivered through the hand of Moses, the leader of Israel. As a matter of fact, the first five books of the biblical canon are known as the Torah, or the law of God, as well as

---

37. Stark, *Discovering God*, 64–72.

the Pentateuch, acknowledging the presence of its large swathes of legal sections.

The Mosaic code, with its comprehensive scope encompassing moral, civil, and ceremonial regulations, was not simply intended to achieve a healthy and viable form of domestic and international functioning, but aimed, ultimately, at human beatitude through a proper collective religious relationship with God (Deut 30:11–20). The laws promulgated by Moses were to be conscientiously and consistently observed in order that the nation might experience prosperity in its natural environment both domestically and internationally rather than epidemic, disaster, siege, and deportation, which would undo its nationhood and lead the people back to their original circumstances in Egyptian slavery (Deuteronomy 28).

God liberates a human community from landlessness

After freeing Israel from her Egyptian captivity, God led the community through the wilderness for a period of 40 years, providing for them and protecting them against hostile opponents, even giving them victory over stronger enemies, until the time came for them to occupy Canaan in addition to the land east of the Jordan which they took from the Amorite kings, Sihon and Og.

God liberates a kingdom from instability (Judges)

Even as Israel was settled in Canaan, it remained for the fledgling nation to stay true to her piety and the accompanying laws; this proved a difficult feat. Therefore God sent judges to rule Israel through what was to become a transitional period prior to the monarchical era.

God liberates a kingdom from insecurity (Monarchy)

Although it was not God's initial intention for Israel to be constituted a monarchy in view that God alone was to be its king and lord, even then the Israelites worried that their lack of a king would put them at a disadvantage in relation to surrounding nations. God honored the people's wishes and ordained good men to serve as kings, though some fell as a result of their contempt for God's rule and laws.

PART 1: CREATION'S IMAGING OF THE DIVINE

God liberates a kingdom from idolatry (Divided kingdoms and exile)

When the kingdom of Israel was divided in the time of Rehoboam, in consequence of the impiety of Solomon his father and the previous king in worshipping the gods of other kingdoms, including those whose cult involved child sacrifice (that is, Milcom/Molech, a Canaanite and Phoenician god worshipped by the Ammonites),[38] at a time when the military power of a kingdom was defined by its cult (1 Sam 4:1–9; 2 Kgs 3:26–27), and assumed the form of a northern kingdom of Israel and a southern kingdom of Judah, the people fell into the worship of idols, including engaging in child sacrifice (2 Kgs 17:7–23). For a time, God watched over the kingdoms even in their moral and spiritual darkness, disciplining kings, when necessary, in the hope that they might repent and turn back to the Lord (cf. 2 Pet 3:9).

God liberates a nation from landlessness and structural chaos (Ezra-Nehemiah)

The discipline of the Lord led to the sacking and deportation first of Israel then Judah. When the time was ripe, God orchestrated the return of Jewish exiles during the reign of Persian kings favorable to their cause to rebuild the temple and city of Jerusalem and to reinhabit the city.

God liberates a people from religious burden and existential guilt (Gospels and the New Testament as a whole)

When Jesus came to Israel to preach and teach, it was as a religious reformer within Judaism. Jesus saw that many Jews were entrapped in a legalistic system of religion and acted to counter oppressive and hypocritical tendencies among religious authority figures who downplayed the importance of just, merciful, and faithful conduct in favor of strict religious rules while being concerned solely for their own interests and always only indulging their desire for praise and admiration (Matt

---

38. Attestation to child sacrificial practices has been uncovered in Phoenician sites in Carthage and Sardinia; child sacrifice was also practiced in Syria and Mesopotamia in the eighth and seventh centuries BC, in Assyria. Child sacrifice has been justified as a way to secure a military victory (Judg 11:29–40) or fertility for the land (Mic 6:6–7). See the commentary on Lev 18:21 in Walton, Matthews, and Chavalas, *IVP Background Commentary: Old Testament*, 132–33.

23:1–36).³⁹ He also imparted a new understanding of a personal relationship with God whereby one could come to God as a child through accepting the propitiatory and substitutionary atoning sacrifice of Christ on the cross with a penitent, grateful, and devoted posture of the heart through which one could receive God's forgiveness of sins against God left unpunished and discover an energizing new impetus to live one's life abounding in good works for the glory of God.

God liberates many peoples from idolatry (Acts)

The remarkable fact about the apostles' preaching to Gentiles or non-Jews is the way in which they focused on idolatry and its moral implications. Preaching in Athens, St. Paul targeted the error of worshipping and serving physical objects crafted in the form of divine beings (Acts 17:22–31) and in his epistle to the church in Rome, he highlighted how such idolatry bred immorality (Rom 1:18–32).

Ancient Near Eastern religion provides an intimation as to how Paul was able to comment on the manner in which adherents of Greek religion paid obeisance to gods in the form of physical objects, namely, idols; in the former cult, belief in the existence and activity of deities included the notion that these deities manifested themselves in physical effigies without limiting themselves to any one specific concrete idol.⁴⁰

Indeed, in ancient Greek cult itself, aside from being made and adorned in lifelike ways, statues of gods were believed to be a medium of their action in response to prayers, to prevent evil, afford healing, punish, execute, and a receptacle they visited and even inhabited on occasion.⁴¹ In contrast, the religion of Yahweh and the way of Jesus Christ was emphatic that God is not to be identified with physical images which had to be conscientiously served by human individuals.

Compared with Yahweh, who laid down universal and immutable moral laws and acted in line with a certain moral rationality, the gods of Greek religion did not promulgate any such binding laws but rather

---

39. Consequently, the lost sheep of Israel of which Jesus spoke is not to be identified with being a Jew who does not accept the claims of Jesus but rather those who feel harassed and helpless as a result of the pastoral negligence and theological excesses of religious leaders (Matt 9:35–38; 10:6).

40. Jewish Virtual Library, "Idolatry."

41. Chaniotis, "Statues of Gods in Greek World," *Kernos* 30 (2017): 2, 8–11, paragraphs 6, 28–45.

acted only in their own self-interest as elite members of a social hierarchy which unified the gods and human beings on different social strata. Situated at the apex of the social pyramid, the gods commanded unchallenged authority and unparalleled rights, including the freedom to choose a particular human woman of their preference with whom to copulate.[42]

Without moral guidance of a religious nature, adherents of a Greek cult were left to their own devices and arbitrary desires of a sensual nature, seeking different forms of exotic sexual entertainment, frisson, indulgence, and behaving in the most immoral and depraved of ways. As such, the identification of the divine not only with human vulnerability but excesses such as deception, theft, betrayal, murder, jealousy, hatred, torture, lust, adultery, rape, coupled with supernatural prowess and immortality, served to reduce the noble and admirable essence of divinity to a pale and unworthy image to avoid the demands of morality and intellectual complexity albeit God has already revealed to humankind universally the positing power and moral nature of the godhead (Cf. Rom 1:18–23).[43]

In point of fact, idolatry consists in any form of a reduction of the reality of God, including ideas of God which simply magnify human fears towards certain groups of other people and insecurities, relishing and trafficking in controversies as a way by which to consolidate an in-group's sense of moral superiority and righteousness, always only reacting to current events with a word of criticism of what some other group is doing, and how the beliefs and actions of these groups are contrary to the in-group's and therefore heretical or sinful. Such xenophobia allied with contempt of others, in which God is conceived as the embodiment of these sentiments writ large, constitutes a form of idolatry that dishonors the God such theological notions claim to represent, divides people, and discriminates against the weak and vulnerable. This tendency is found in all manner of orthodoxy, a system which claims a monopoly on the truth or its fullness to which no other system is privy.

---

42. Merrick, "Greek Gods and Yahweh," 17–23.

43. Cf. Stark, *Discovering God*, 77, 96–97, 130; when Scripture says that the god of this world has blinded the minds of unbelievers (2 Cor 4:4), this is simply a figure-of-speech shedding light on how those who worship idols reject the gospel because it is morally and intellectually demanding. The role of the devil lies in how the devil influences them to think this way, yet this does not negate their decision to accept that suggestion, which remains theirs alone.

Much to be preferred is a soft or egalitarian confessionalism, a commitment to one's particular beliefs and practices as true and beneficial yet without the added implication that those of other groups are thereby false or harmful—a false dichotomy rooted in hubris more than scriptural data, which is certainly open to and more congruent with a non-exclusivist interpretation—instead recognizing the value these groups bring with their distinctive and distinct ways of understanding and practising, their habitus, acknowledging the equality of the status of one's own confessionalism with that of other confessionalisms and affirming that it is possible to hold all these confessionalisms together in some coherent fashion, respecting different ways of doing so based on different confessional structures and approaches.[44]

To believe in Jesus as the only way to God the Father is not to exclude other religious traditions with their own concepts of revelation in certain traditions since Jesus as divine revelation never taught the truth he preaches as exclusive of other religions but rather only as truly declarative of divine truth without being exhaustive in such a way as to deny and contradict all other religious expressions of God or the divine since they attest to aspects of the same divine truth in their own inimitable way.

All religions and atheism are united in that all attest with different names and emphases that we are assured of forgiveness by the divine good when we repent (either a tradition directly speaks of a forgiving God or it is open to the idea of self-forgiveness which is ultimately possible only through a prior experience of divine atonement; guilt shows that we know that we need atonement and satisfaction for our sins and the only reason we are able to overcome this hurdle is by knowing our sins have been atoned for on an intuitive level) and we are called to be moral people by the power of God (either a tradition directly speaks of how God created and empowers humankind as moral and morally capable, that is, able to tell the difference between right and wrong and choose to do what is right rather than wrong, or it acknowledges that

---

44. As an example of a confessional hierarchy, I may not hold the view that Jesus is to be conceived as a mere human being, devoid of any divine ontology, with special religious insight into the nature of humankind as an instrument of divine love and an incarnation of the God of love in the same way that any enlightened human being may be. In place of that, I may espouse the view that Jesus is to be thought of as ontologically divine as well as human, fully God and fully human, yet I respect and appreciate the progressive Christian view of Christ as an inspired religious figure and will not speak against it, given that it attests to the authentic humanity of Christ, an aspect which tends to be sidelined in a traditional Christology.

PART 1: CREATION'S IMAGING OF THE DIVINE

all things exist apart from their own will and work with human beings as moral and morally capable persons, ultimately possible only through a prior experience of divine encounter). The Christian can say with the utmost integrity that Christianity is not very different from any other religion and atheism, that Jesus the sole savior is present in every other religion and atheism though under a different name or names.

There is no condemnation in Scripture of world religions as they are expressed today and as they have been expressed in centuries past, on account of the fact that in none of these venerable religious traditions, as well as atheism and agnosticism, is God, the gods, or ultimate reality reduced to a physical object or a set of physical objects which have to be served by religious worshippers, and personal and collective human morality glossed over.

A cursory survey of the moral teachings of a number of religious traditions will be cogent and suffice to demonstrate the spiritual and ethical nature of major world religions.

From the viewpoint of a Buddhist ethics, it is critical for individuals to cultivate a right or salutary understanding (*samma ditthi*): having a veracious conception of the nature of life in the world, that it is replete with suffering due to craving and aversion (*dukkha*), of the fleeting character of all things in the world (*anicca*), and of the transience of the human soul (*anatta*); right thought (*samma sankappa*): neither hating nor desiring to harm another being but rather being compassionate, tender, and considerate towards others (*metta*); right speech (*samma vaca*): refraining from spreading falsehood and verbal abuse but rather valuing others; right action (*samma kammanta*): refraining from causing harm to others, stealing from others, and sexual misconduct but rather practising contentment; right livelihood (*samma ajiva*): engaging in occupations that do not bring about or contribute to harm of others such as the arms or slave trade, raising animals for slaughter, and trading in alcoholic beverages, drugs, and poison, taking up a profession not out of greed but a desire to provide for oneself and one's family; along with the meditation-related aspects of right effort (*samma vayama*), right mindfulness (*samma sati*), and right concentration (*samma samadhi*), in what is known as the Noble Eightfold Path.[45] Five major sins or transgressions

---

45. London Buddhist Vihara, "Noble Eightfold Path."

are highlighted; namely, killing, theft, sexual misdemeanor, lying, and consumption of alcohol or drugs.[46]

In Hinduism, the universe itself is suffused by an ethical quality which determines its very nature and shape; this is a value of life known as *dharma*.[47] Universal duties encompass steadfastness, forgiveness, self-discipline, non-appropriation, cleanliness, repression of sensuous appetites, wisdom, learning, veracity, restraint of anger, refraining from causing injury to living creatures, and pursuing the good of all creatures.[48]

There are three kinds of virtues and vices, virtues being those of the body, namely, service to the needy; virtues of speech, namely, truth-telling, benevolence, gentleness, and the recitation of the sacred books; virtues of the mind, namely, kindness, religiosity, and unworldliness; whereas vices are those of the body, namely, callousness, stealing, sexual indulgence; vices of the speech, namely, lying or deception, severity, scandalous behavior; and vices of the mind, namely, enmity, greed, and unbelief.[49]

Five cardinal principles which guide most Hindu sects are purity (both ritual and spiritual), self-control (asceticism as well as balance in life), detachment (ethical action that veers between the extremes of world-renunciation and world-affirmation), truthfulness, and nonviolence (*ahimsā*, the commitment not to harm or hate any living being).[50] Gandhi is reported to have said that the ethic of nonviolence is shared by all religions.[51]

A Taoist ethics emphasizes the centrality of spontaneity (*ziran*) and flexibility (*wuwei*) in moral decision-making and action, in which a moral agent, vested with a portion of the universal Tao, the ontological principle, expressed in the form of its individual character and traits (*de*), does not engage in moral action simply on account of laws or rules but autonomously, guided by its own internal moral principles. Such a moral agent is capable of perceiving its interdependence and oneness with all other moral agents, entities, and objects and, to that extent, able to make the most prudent and fair decisions which benefit not

---

46. Wongsakon, "Buddhism 101."
47. Crawford, *Hindu Bioethics*, 14.
48. Crawford, *Hindu Bioethics*, 18–19.
49. Crawford, *Hindu Bioethics*, 20.
50. Crawford, *Hindu Bioethics*, 22–25.
51. Srinivas, "Gandhi's Religion," 1489, citing B. R. Nanda, *Gandhi and Religion* (New Delhi: Gandhi Smriti and Darshan Samiti, 1990), 12.

only themselves but people and the world around them. Taoist ethics underscores the traits of "gentleness", "non-assertiveness", "fragility", and "quietude", which allow a person to be attuned and adaptable in their dealings with others.[52]

An Islamic ethical system is closely allied to a Platonic conception of human morality in terms of the three parts of the human soul; namely, the rational, the irascive, and the appetitive, engendering the associated and respective virtues that are wisdom, courage, temperance, with justice summing up the character of the virtue of the soul, along with theological virtues including reverence, credence, love, and entrustment.[53]

The Sikh religious tradition values the five virtues of sexual self-restraint, contentment, compassion, patience, and humility, proscribing the five related vices of sexual immorality and indulgence, irrational anger, greed, excessive familial attachment, and conceit.[54]

Zoroastrian ethics places a premium on good and virtuous as opposed to evil, destructive, and immoral thoughts, words, and deeds.[55] Virtues extolled in the practice of adherents include religious commitment and conscientious observance; truthfulness in speech and delivering on promises; moderation in the use of food and sex; affection for and solidarity with all human persons, which may entail the charitable use of wealth and affluence; industriousness and ethical work; the pursuit of wisdom; respect for seniors, whether in age or rank; refraining from deception and hypocrisy; a willingness to forgive, showing kindness towards enemies by seeking to make them one's friends, sanctifying the transgressor, being tolerant towards personal offenses, and educating the uninformed; as well as sincerity in making amends for and accepting the consequences of one's sins. Zoroastrians are to avoid anger, envy, covetousness, sloth, conceit, vulgar and hurtful speech, bickering and fighting over trivial matters, corrupting company and content, as well as a desire to do harm to another or avenge wrongs.[56]

A Confucian ethic, indicated in the teachings of Confucius himself as well as Mencius and Xunzi, presupposes an orientation toward morality and justice as the basic distinction between humankind and animals, prescribing mutual respect and concern for those in need

52. Kamamoto, "Dao as Basis for Morality."
53. Ansari, "Islamic Ethics," 84–86.
54. Sacha, *Sikhs and Their Way of Life*, chapter 8.
55. Buch, *Zoroastrian Ethics*, 60–62.
56. Dadrawala, "Zoroastrian Ethics and Morals."

as indispensable for building a society marked by cooperation, order, and peace. In this respect, Confucianism advocates five virtues associated with the noble person (*junzi*), regarded as one to be emulated for their moral excellence, who is characterized by the five virtues of "benevolence/humaneness" (*ren*), including being considerate, sympathetic, compassionate toward others, displaying loving concern for humankind as a whole, and fostering virtue in others; "righteousness/appropriateness" (*yi*), which encompasses preferring rectitude to personal advantage; "propriety/harmonious differentiation" (*li*), which is related to conscientiousness in adhering to social rules and mores as well as procedures so as to promote collective harmony and oneness and minimize situations of conflict; "wisdom/knowledge management" (*zhi*), whereby a person develops an ability to accurately and sensibly assess and respond to the needs of a particular situation in an effective and fitting manner; "trustworthiness/integrity" (*xin*), in which a person has dealings with others which are sincere rather than duplicitous, and practices faithfulness and honesty.[57]

In the Bahá'í Faith, the following attributes are extolled as virtues: recognition of the common humanity of all people, which ought to engender a sense of solidarity and an inclination to overlook offenses; love for the human other and the rest of creation; charity in refraining from criticizing others for their inadequacies, choosing instead to pray for their change or gently nudge them towards it, focusing on the good that is in others; humility in keeping one's eyes on correcting one's own imperfections rather than those of others and eschewing drawing attention to one's experiences of suffering or being wronged; and a continuous pursuit of relationships between people characterized by mutual help and coworking.[58]

Within the religious system of Jainism, there is an emphasis on seeking the correct faith or vision (*Samyak Darshana*); the correct knowledge or understanding (*Samyak Jnana*); and the correct conduct (*Samyak Charitra*), known as the "Three Jewels", through fulfilling five fundamental vows: nonviolence (*ahimsa*), entailing vegetarianism; truth (*satya*), necessitating the responsible use of speech in the knowledge that the abuse of speech can cause harm; non-stealing (*asteya*), involving not claiming anything except what is freely offered and the pursuit of economic justice;

---

57. Snell et al., "Junzi Virtues," 183–84, 187–88.
58. Langness, "5 Baha'i Ethics."

chastity (*brahmacharya*), whereby monastics embrace celibacy while the laity practice moderation and faithfulness in marriage; and non-attachment or non-possession (*aparigraha*), entailing the surrender of any attachment to people or things, for worldly attachment tends to result in covetousness, envy, self-centeredness, and harm.[59]

In a contemporary iteration of paganism or neo-paganism, such aspects of human existence in the world are underlined as respect for diversity and plurality among people, a focus on harmonious co-participation rather than domination, a role for women in religion, a recognition of the natural world as a divine gift and abode, juxtaposed to emphases on democracy, humanism, the arts, and the natural sciences. Magick in paganism is not to be equated with an unhealthy desire to control supernatural forces for one's personal gain or as a means to harm others, but is more akin to prayer.[60]

In an atheistic framework, an ethical system is predicated upon the human need for happiness and the concomitant necessity to honor this desire in any individual in a manner that ensures each person's maximal access to opportunities for the actualization of their happiness. The moral requirement that opportunities for happiness should be distributed as fairly and equally as possible among all individuals is itself predicated on a recognition of the legitimacy of the pursuit of happiness on one's own part and, therefore, by implication through the law of fairness and empathy, on the part of each human person, engendering a desire to promote these opportunities in the most practicable way. Core to such a collective and universally acceptable moral framework are the three values of bravery, rationality, and concern as well as kindness, considerateness, honesty, and truthfulness. Atheism allows for the promotion of learning from not just the natural and social sciences, but religion and the arts as well.[61]

From the foregoing, which necessarily excludes some religious traditions for reason of space constraints, it can be observed that those

59. The Pluralism Project, "Jainism."

60. Jones, "Introduction to Paganism"; The Pluralism Project, "What Do Pagans Do?"

61. Walters, *Atheism*, 131–34. An atheist morality need not be thought of purely in terms of an enlightened self-interest, which is a form of consequentialism in that seemingly altruistic action is guided by potential negative repercussions of behaving in a manner that is antisocial, as opposed to reciprocity, on which an atheist morality is based, which revolves around fairness and justice grounded in empathy. Such rationalizations serve to justify rather than explain reciprocal human behavior.

religious traditions which we have discussed along with atheism teach and promote a valuing of the human other, mutual respect and kindness, as well as responsibility. In this way, it can be observed that the ethical desire for human flourishing is common to religious and philosophical traditions.

God liberates a church from persecution (Revelation)

Much of Jesus' final counsel to his disciples (John 15:18—16:4, 32–33) is taken up with the subject of persecution against the Christian church. As a matter of fact, some of the most grievous troubles which confronted the church in the first century had their origin in a state persecution of the Christian community. Revelation 13 describes the adversity as owing to the emergence of two terrible beasts, cryptic symbols for the Roman imperial state where emperors such as Nero (AD 54–68) and Domitian (AD 81–96) pinned the responsibility for national crises on Christians, compelling all residents to make offerings to the gods of the Roman cult on pain of death for refusal.[62]

---

62. Southern Adventist University, "Roman Persecution."

5

The Christian Doctrine of Divine Creation

The Experience of God in Self-Acceptance

AMONG THE MOST CONTESTED areas of Christian doctrine is the manner in which God created the world or the universe, along with all that they encompass. In this regard, there are a number of differing positions.

One group is of the view that God created the world out of no preexisting matter by fiat alone (*creatio ex nihilo*), a stance belonging to conservative evangelical theologians.[1] Others espouse a view in which God is responsible for creating the preexisting matter on which the same God works in reshaping it into the current fundamental state of the universe (creation as re-creation). Such a viewpoint is aligned with a speculative theory concerning the way in which upon the completion of God's initial creative work, a group of angels rebelled against God's rule, resulting in divine judgment and the destruction of the universe, and it is out of this state of ruination and devastation that God brings about a second creation or recreation of the universe.[2]

These two perspectives can be incorporated in a literal six-day framework of creation. This is not the case with the succeeding group of positions.

A third group embraces ideas popularized in Darwinian evolutionary theory and attempts to reconcile them with a biblical doctrine of

---

1. Erickson, *Christian Theology*, 340–42.
2. Erickson, *Christian Theology*, 350.

creation, proposing that God did not create the universe in essentially finished form, that is, the way in which they exist in the present time, but that God adopted a series of processes in engendering the present state of creation, including the macro-evolution of different species, over immensely long periods of time such as proposed in a modern scientific theory of the origins of the universe (creation by theistic evolution). According to this perspective, God remains the fount of all existence through instituting alone or both instituting and shepherding the development of the universe from its earliest days during the big bang through the emergence of the very first lifeforms, the appearance of increasingly complex organisms, followed by plants and animals, including primates, of which human beings constitute a species.[3]

The fourth perspective combines fiat creationism with theistic evolution in what is called progressive creationism, conceptualizing God as creating the first members of each genus and species and leaving these to evolve through natural processes instituted and overseen by God.[4]

In our position, the notion, common to the earlier four, that God as an active agent intentionally brings about and shapes a universe into being and existence is renounced in favor of a spontaneous appearance of diverse forms of spiritual existence in the context of a divine ontological and moral framework; these spiritual beings are given material embodiment through a long evolutionary process by divine decree, the process being enacted by the power of angels, in accordance to the basic truths of the first creation narrative in Genesis 1 (two-stage creation of spiritual beings and material bodies).

Epistemology

One of the ills of modern society consists in its harsh and brutal beauty standards which it relentlessly advertises in various ways. Contrary to popular perception, the perception of physical attractiveness is no subjective affair, people generally agreeing on whom is to be considered attractive, and the perception of facial attractiveness, specifically, has been tied to indications of fertility, health, and good genes.

Femininity in female faces and masculinity in male faces have been connected with fertility and health, while the averageness (closeness of

---

3. Erickson, *Christian Theology*, 445–46.
4. Erickson, *Christian Theology*, 446–47.

proportions of facial features to the mean of a population) of a female or male face is linked to more genetically diverse genes translating to better health and the absence of parasites and diseases, which render a potential mate more attractive in themselves and for the genes they can pass on to offspring.[5] A study by the University of Aberdeen shows that the contemporary fascination with female slimness is tied to perceptions of thin women as being more youthful and therefore more fertile and hardier.[6]

Unfortunately, the attribution of greater worth to individuals considered more attractive leads to many persons feeling devalued. This is a deplorable development, in view of the fact that societal beauty standards are not at all indicative of the value of a person. Instead, these norms arise from a biological instinct so ingrained it can be difficult to perceive that physical beauty or attractiveness has little to do with the inherent value of the individual, no more than an evolutionary code written into the human psyche and body to promote the proliferation of the species.

Nonetheless, many individuals feel pressured to adopt beauty norms tied to the survival and reproduction of the species rather than to individual self-worth and, sadly, judge themselves and are judged, and rewarded or penalized, in accordance to such standards. Dysfunction so arising is exacerbated by an inclination in many modern societies to valorize facial and bodily femininity and masculinity on popular and widely-used traditional and social media platforms. In this context, a social hierarchy emerges in which people are judged, and judge themselves, by norms, ideals, and standards of the physical female as well as male form epitomized in celebrities and supermodels, creating a self-justifying and self-selecting system of personal validation based on the possession of physical attributes which are often beyond a person's control.

The chaos brought upon humanity by social hierarchies, the very existence of, inclination to establish, and desire to advance in such systems of ranking, communicate the human need for social validation. If social validation were not a human need, no individual would be psychologically affected by an uneven distribution of the attributes of physical attractiveness among people, with the accompanying social advantages; construct such hierarchies; or seek to rise within them. Social hierarchies tend to be exclusive and favor only a small number of individuals; even so, they are accepted almost universally on account of some commonly

---

5. Little, Jones, and DeBruine, "Facial Attractiveness," 1640–42.
6. BBC, "Female Attractiveness."

agreed norm, standard, or principle; in this instance, the biologically-oriented esthetic instinct is at play.

In becoming individualistic and self-centered, human persons leave the psychological moorings of a relationship with the divine or an actualization of a moral principle from which they are to draw their sense of personal value and self-esteem. Instead of discerning the immutable ground of their personal worth, these persons establish and entrench alien systems of hierarchy by which they suppose to assess and confirm the value they possess or lack. Like biblical Israel during the time of Moses, they have their high priests, like Aaron, set up new gods (Exod 32:1-6), new sources in which to find their value, as a deplorable indication of how far they have strayed from their destined paths, and as a result, depend so little on their true source of value and so much on what does not indicate their value.

Akin to the Israelites who abandoned God, who supplies the water of life, and turned instead to self-made vessels which leaked water (Jer 2:13), are those who valorize the world's standards of physical attractiveness as a measure of personal worth, forgetting the invisible God or more distant actualizations of an ultimate moral principle, simply because the true source of human value, that is, God, is not something to hand, immediate, instantaneous, physical, obtrusively direct, but rather invisible, seemingly distant (like Moses in the incident of the golden calf), ostensibly insensitive or irrelevant to actual human need, even seemingly self-interested at the expense of human beings (like the serpent made God out to be to Eve in tempting her to eat the fruit of the tree of the knowledge of good and evil). In actual fact, God only seems remote because of naivete and intellectual indolence, leading to an ignorance of God's true vision of good and evil, that is, of what the goodness of God consists in and what the evils warned against; instinctual feelings allowed to rule the mind and tell it what to believe not just about the world but even itself; and an identification of social validation with true value and benefit.

While social validation is, in truth, a legitimate human need, this has to be in keeping, first and foremost, with an adequate and proper moral vision of human identity, value, role, and responsibility. In this respect, social validation functions as a means by which a morally-oriented community alerts its members to the risk of actual transgressions perpetrated by these members by expressing approval for moral obedience and concern or rebuke for moral disobedience.

PART 1: CREATION'S IMAGING OF THE DIVINE

Lamentably, social validation has attained a status in modern society that is without any anchoring in a moral vision. Instead, it has become inseparably attached to primal instincts relating to physical attraction, in such a way that people do not any longer consider how their inner feelings pertaining to the physical attractiveness or lack thereof of a person may influence not just their perception of the suitability of the physically attractive or less attractive person as a mating partner, but even their sense of dignity and value as human persons. Discrimination along these lines is rampant in the widespread phenomenon that is "pretty privilege", where individuals benefit merely from being physically attractive, though even this is not without its disadvantages.[7]

Pressures to become more beautiful are never too explicit or blatant; hardly any advertisement, celebrity, television show, or magazine openly discusses the benefits of being physically attractive and the disadvantages of being less attractive with a view to exalting the conventionally attractive and shaming the less. Furthermore, the individual is not physically compelled to attain higher degrees of physical beauty, on pain of direct punishment. Yet a person would have to be utterly blind or insensitive to fail to notice the tremendous emphasis laid by social messaging on the importance of physical beauty in the sheer amount of attention given to celebrities who fit the conventional mold of physical attractiveness, not just in blockbuster movies and popular television dramas in which they star, the mega concerts they hold, but the coverage they are given in traditional and social media through endorsements, advertisements, news articles, short videos, interviews, and television programs.

It is well-nigh impossible to be an internet user in a modern society and have no constant contact with these images, nolens volens. The subtle message underlying all these media is that being physically attractive is a supreme good, engendering popularity and social approval. More than that, leading film and television actors are often cast in the roles of protagonists who display some form of heroism, courage, fortitude, resilience, innocence, righteousness or other good qualities, effectively coupling physical appearance with morality and reinforcing the halo effect where individuals with positive traits such as symmetrical faces are perceived to be more healthy or have more wholesome personalities, leading to the development of confidence which affords an impression of competence,

---

7. Travers, "Pretty Privilege."

charisma, and likableness.[8] There will be exceptions, yet these serve to prove the rule rather than undermine the general trend.

It is easy, and commercially profitable, to capitalize on primal human instincts, but given the proliferation of social messaging that proves reductive and even harmful for many, it is unethical to continue to participate in such an enterprise with little regard for the psychological well-being of television viewers and internet users around the world.

Biological instincts are very strong, yet they cannot be allowed to occupy a space that does not belong to them; they should not be permitted to tell a person about their true worth. This will be very difficult to achieve in a world which commercializes physical beauty, yet it is not impossible. Some of the things people can try to do for their mental health include consciously decoupling in their minds the equation between social validation on the one hand and true identity and benefit on the other. What is popular is not necessarily good for the individual, and a person with less popularity, if any, is not less valuable than a celebrity, influencer, or some other public figure. Above all, individuals would do well to inculcate a deeper understanding of the true vision of good and evil in their respective religious and philosophical traditions so as to apprehend what truly matters in an ultimate sense and bring sobriety and clarity into their lives.

By singling out physical beauty as a trigger for a biological instinct as an asset to be admired and desired on the mass scale, popular media fosters a culture of sensuality, expanding the role of physical appearance far beyond the biological objective of mating, so that beauty becomes a focus of global attention and celebration, a cause of pride for a very few, and a source of insecurity and unhappiness for the great majority. The inordinate emphasis on physical pulchritude instigates immense discontent as the human individual's attention is diverted away from the numerous wonderful attributes each person possesses toward a single, immutable set of traits which most persons do not possess to an advantageous degree. The conscious and subconscious are tripped up and deluded into believing that physical beauty, along with a few other external characteristics, is a true measure of the value of a person.

Quite apart from the hierarchy of physical attractiveness, there exist other social hierarchies revolving around personal wealth and affluence, professional success, social status and reputation, family-related

---

8. Travers, "Pretty Privilege."

accomplishments.⁹ A world delinked from religious tradition and human morality erects a false social hierarchy which fails to accord due recognition to the inherent value that resides in all human persons, regardless of physical and social variables. It operates within a climate of hostile competition, promoting the idea that the individual deserves everything that they can potentially own, and that all other individuals constitute rivals to be undermined, removed, or overcome.

The advocacy of this deleterious philosophy and worldview is the reason that few people are satisfied with their place in society. Prescinding from the stations and conditions of those who truly do not have enough, people who lead reasonably comfortable and smooth lives, holding jobs by which they secure a livelihood, while there may be challenges on different fronts, frequently do not experience contentment with what they already have.[10] Instead, they seek to advance in various domains, and the pursuit of self-enhancement does not ever seem to end—all because they have been told, and they have accepted without question, that in actual fact the world belongs to them, and their task is to remove all obstacles to their personal success, including people who stand in their way.[11]

The root of envy and jealousy is not simply that one might have enough or even enjoy a comfortable existence, fully actualizing one's personal capacities; the root of jealousy is enmity with the person who seems to enjoy greater success in addition to the wish that they might be equal to those persons. They feel that they deserve everything other people possess, and they are suspicious that the persons they envy are somehow holding them back from attaining their deserved success, simply by enjoying successes they wish they enjoyed.

---

9. It is claimed that a society is meritocratic in which human worth is judged by how much one has or earns. Yet what decides how much a person is paid or possesses? The laws of demand and supply in the first case, and the good fortune of being a descendant of wealth or having the right opportunities in the second. And what determines the laws of demand and supply? Simply put, the values of a society which influence the desires, interests, and inclinations, not necessarily wholesome or salutary ones, of a population. A society with lopsided values cannot obviously be counted on to properly reward people according to the good that they do for their community rather than the size of the role they play in an economy dictated by uncontrolled wants, often revolving around status symbols and entertainment.

10. Our relationship to our responsibilities will benefit from our choosing to enjoy what we do whether in terms of our interactions with or actions for the sake of others or the work in which we engage (Eccl 8:15).

11. An all-too-common modern expression of this kind of uncaring and competitive self-centeredness may be found in office politics, often linked to territorial fear and self-aggrandizement. Richards, "Office Politics."

As a case in point, Cain did not murder his brother because there was indeed no way for him to enjoy the approval his brother received from God in making a pleasing offering; God informed him that if only Cain would do well, he would receive favor and that there was no reason for him to be angry with God or his brother (Gen 4:6–7).

For what reason then was Cain angry with Abel, enough to deprive him of his very life? Cain was enraged with Abel on account of the fact that he believed, wrongly, that Abel's very existence and success constituted a limitation and curtailment of his own success, that so long as Abel lived and thrived, there was no way he could ever actualize his full potential. He was certain that he deserved everything Abel possessed in the way of God's favor; that Abel stood in the way of his success; and that there was no way he could ever obtain success except by removing Abel (cf. Jas 4:2), though Abel received favor only because he did what was right, and Cain had every opportunity to experience the same favor by making a proper offering to God.

In other words, Cain was blinded by his jealousy toward Abel. Rather than considering and deliberating on what he could do to change God's response to his act of offering by learning from Abel, instead of looking at the value that remained at his own disposal, that is, the ability to change the course of his own life by altering his conduct, Cain concluded that God was unfair and practiced favoritism.[12]

Likewise, the reason Eve and Adam decided to violate God's command for them to abstain from eating the fruit of the tree of the knowledge of good and evil was that they believed the lie of the serpent that God deliberately withheld from them the fruit because God knew its consumption would make them as wise as God. They became distrustful of God, fancying that God had something to gain from keeping the fruit from them, falsely and presumptuously imagining that God was a competitor and rival with them in a world with limited resources, and that were God to give them access to a fruit that could grant them the same level of wisdom that God enjoyed, perhaps then God would lose God's unique status.[13]

---

12. Jealousy as the root of personal unhappiness is exposed and cured by a personal realization that one would not feel quite so miserable on account of what another person has so long as they are able to imagine that that person does not exist. The fact that one would not feel unhappy if the envied other person does not exist suggests that one is not deficient in any way.

13. To regard the Bible as the divinely-originated inscripturated Word of God is not to aver an ahistoricity, aculturality, asociality, or apersonality of the texts that constitute

These lies are just the things that facilitate chaos and disorder in the world today with its social hierarchies. Instead of taking pleasure in the diverse and valuable things a person is able to relish in their lives, including their family, work, friends, and pastimes, just as the primal couple did not care to enjoy the lavish supply of food in the garden of Eden, many people today choose to pursue things that do not quite belong to them, much as the woman desired the fruit of the tree of the knowledge of good and evil which was alone kept from her.

The reason for this is that such people are not able to find the validation of their self-worth in God, the divine, or the actualization of the ultimate moral principle, but seek it in lesser things such as social approval, admiration, or popularity.

Presumption is the root of envy. The one who envies feels that way only because they suppose they not only deserve what they have but also to have it all, preferably more than any other person. Objectively, the possession by another person of some trait to a superior degree, attainable or not, does not in any way harm us or decrease the worth of our own attributes. Yet if we find ourselves disturbed by this state of affairs, it is only on account that we desire admiration that is now apportioned more greatly to the person more well-endowed than we are, and this only for the reason that we place our self-value in external qualities rather than who we inherently are as moral beings.

It is critical to recognize that fairness does not consist so much in all people being equal in every way as in the fact that no unreasonable expectations are heaped on a person, that no person is blamed for what they have no responsibility for, and that no person is regarded as being of lesser worth than another. We ought instead to be thankful for what we already have, not taking it for granted.

The very fact that human persons subsist in need of a permanent self-legitimation that emanates only from God, the divine, or the actualization of an ultimate moral principle, discloses the truth of the existence

---

the Bible which thereby enjoins a need to interrogate textual authorial motives or agendas as in some recent historical-critical approaches including feminist and postcolonial scholarship. Instead, God mediates divine revelation through a sociohistorical and personal-authorial matrix. In opposition to the view that the biblical text needs to be critiqued as to its authorial or editorial agenda, we respond that this is a form of distrust in the divine origin of the text, and that it is preferable to accept the divine voice in Scripture, which is to be understood in its proper sociohistorical, political, authorial, and literary context rather than questioned as to its underlying motives. Collins, "Historical-Critical Methods," 129, 133–35.

of the divine and the ultimate in entitative form with God conceived as a Trinity of love in Christian theology.

Doctrinal Formulation: Two-Stage Creation of Spiritual Beings and Material Bodies

God is revealed as a divine community of love through the sober acceptance that all entities and things are of equal value and worth, both within a species and across species, and the survival instinct and structure of living beings and plant life. The destructive capacities of those who envision human and material reality in a fissiparous way make evident that all of existence, regardless of social messaging, personal opinion, and against the strongest convictions to the contrary, is indebted to and obligated under the truth that all things are of equal worth. This state of affairs, along with a human need for respect, discloses the universal value God places on each entity and object, in which each entity or object is designed to have and display its intended creational value through its individual function, and intimates an ultimate desire, through an ultimate valorization, attesting to the existence, personhood, and agency of a Creator. The human capacity for compassion discloses the reality of an atoning higher power. Similarly, the survival instinct and structure of living beings and plant life point to a principle of vitality, the possibility of each entity and object's being, nature, existence, activity, and flourishing indicate an ontological principle, and the moral consciousness, inclination, and agency of entities so endued suggest a moral principle, making for a common witness of moral agents, living beings, and plant life to an ontological and moral principle which gives vitality. A biblical doctrine of creation is capable of harmonization with biological evolutionary theory. Direct creation and a unity of ontological principle and entitative divinity cannot be admitted on account of logical and theodictic considerations.

God and creation

Generally speaking, Christian theology has had a fraught relationship with scientific theory; specifically, theories which attempt to explain the origins of the universe, the world, and the various species of the world. Disagreement arises from the way in which the Bible in the first creation narrative appears to depict a chronological sequence of God's direct

PART 1: CREATION'S IMAGING OF THE DIVINE

creative acts, through authoritative divine decree or speech, which does not quite cohere with current scientific theories concerning the age of the universe and the world, the time as well as the order of the emergence of the myriad species of living things and creatures. For instance, cosmological theory places the beginning of the universe through a big bang at around 13.7 billion years ago, whilst Genesis 1 seems to affirm a six-day creation of the universe or the solar system.[14]

Yet, one does well to observe several things about the first creation story. First, the account of creation contains apparent inconsistencies. As a case in point, God is said to have brought light into existence on the first day of creation, but then God only created the sun, the source of light, on the fourth day. Moreover, the second creation narrative in Genesis 2 (beginning at the fifth verse) contains a sequence that is in conflict with that in the first creation story. Although God creates plants and animals before humankind in the first story, God brings into existence the first human person before creating plants and possibly animals in the second story. Third, not all entities and objects are included in the first creation story, amphibians, microbes, and galaxies among these. Fourth, if the first creation story is a literal account, what was God doing before the first day? If God has existed eternally, why did God wait as long as God did before creating the world? Fifth, there is in the book of Job what appears to be an alternative account of divine creation with a variant sequence of creation; for example, here, the making of earth through the division of land from sea (Job 38:4–11) is antecedent to the creation of light (Job 38:12–15).

In fact, the law of the Sabbath in the Decalogue (Exod 20:8–11) determines the nature and function of the first creation story; the Israelites were to do no work but rest on the seventh day because God rested on the seventh day. Were the Sabbath law to be interpreted as affirming that God had created everything in six solar days and rested on the seventh and that therefore the Israelites were to work for six days and rest on the seventh as well, this reading of the first creation story would make very little sense as a foundation for a regular rhythm of life, given that the Israelites were instructed to mirror God's activity in their activity, yet God ceased all work on the seventh day. This day, if it was literal, has long since ended, and yet God's rest from creative activity

---

14. The Imagine Team, "Age of the Universe."

continues to the present time, so there is no basis for the Israelites to work beyond one week of activity as well.

A number of further considerations are notable in this regard. First, in Exod 20:11 (ESV), we find the following affirmation: "For in six days Yahweh made heaven and earth, the sea, and all that is in them, and rested on the seventh day." This statement appears to decide the issue of whether God made the world in six days, except that God does not quite rest for just one day, the seventh, but for every other day after the sixth given that God's work of creation has been completed. Second, the refrain at the end of each day of creation in Genesis 1 (ESV), "And there was evening and there was morning, the [ordinal] day", hearkens to the exhortation in various psalms to meditate on the law of God, the Torah, "day and night" (Ps 1:2). The person who does this is likened to a healthy and flourishing tree that provides abundant fruit at the right time, reminding us of the tree of life in the garden of Eden in contrast to the tree of the knowledge of good and evil which only brings eternal death (Gen 2:9, 16–17), suggesting that this is the kind of person Adam and Eve were designed to be and affording confirmation that the first creation story is to be read as a daily meditative resource.

Third, the psalmist in Ps 19:2 observes that the creative work of God in the skies, especially the sun (Ps 19:4–6), readily furnishes knowledge and reminders of how God made all these things: "Day to day pours out speech, and night to night reveals knowledge" (ESV). A bare observation of a wondrous sunrise and sunset may be impressive, yet it is only when the Torah enters the mind that the human heart is fully awakened to consider the marvels of God's action in creation (Ps 19:7–14). Fourth, the entire book of Job constitutes a powerful justification for the need for a proper meditation on God's work in creation (the denouement being in Job 38–42), an activity that enabled Job to overcome a crippling sense of injustice over his many personal griefs and losses, and remain in an intimate relationship with God.

Fifth, a parallel may be found in Psalm 136, a prayer of gratitude to God sung de rigueur at the end of the Passover which recounts the history of God's providence and salvation in relation to the people of Israel beginning with a recollection of God's acts of creation.[15] As the Israelites and then the Jews repeated the refrains concerning God's everlasting love as they called to mind the wonderful acts of God's providence and

---

15. Pope Benedict XVI, *General Audience*.

redemption, they would have not only reinforced their memory of God's benevolent deeds, but they would also have unconsciously associated God's love, etched as a prominent leitmotif in their minds, with those deeds and the elements in creation they produced, ready to call them forth as an answer in time of trouble to the nagging question regarding whether God is indeed good or loving. Likewise, as the Israelites and Jews went over the first creation story in Gen 1:1—2:3, the literary trope here being the days of the week, tied with the divine acts of creation, they would have been guided to link each of the days of the week with a particular work of God in making the world. In the Genesis 1 creation account, the first through to the sixth day of the week is precisely named, while the name for the seventh day, the Sabbath, is directly derived from *shavat*, the Hebrew verb rendered as God's act of resting on the seventh day (Gen 2:2–3).[16] The reason English speakers may not feel the same way about the creation account is that unlike Hebrew the English translation does not render each day of creation in Gen 1:1—2:3 in terms of the name of the day of the week, while in the Hebrew Bible, the Israelites and Jews hear of how God created the sky on, in our language, Monday; the land, seas, and flora on Tuesday; the sun, moon, and stars on Wednesday; marine creatures and birds on Thursday; livestock, large land animals, and crawling creatures on Friday. It would have been very natural for Israelites and Jews raised in a culture of Torah teaching to connect any day of the week with an act of creation, thus being reminded of God's creation and perhaps even defining a specific day by the creative act tethered verbally to it.

In light of these considerations, it may be preferable to read the first creation story as a basis and foundation for the meditative activity of the Israelites week after week. That is, the first creation account was written and handed down in the way it was in order to provide a framework, a devotional resource, through which the Israelites could remember God's gracious activity on their behalf each day of the week, recalling, on the first day of the week, God's creation of light, of day and night; on the second day of the week, God's creation of the sky; on the third day of the week, God's creation of the land and seas; on the fourth day of the week, God's creation of the sun, moon, and stars; on the fifth day of the week, God's creation of the birds and fishes; on the sixth day of the week, God's creation of land animals and humankind; and on the seventh day of the

---

16. Ivritalk, "Hebrew Days."

week, God's rest from God's work of creation.[17] The first creation story was given as a spiritual resource in the form of a daily meditation for the week, as well as a mnemonic device.[18]

On the first day of the week, therefore, Jews and their spiritual successors were encouraged to consider the manner in which God brings about light and, in this way, day and night. In bringing forth the diurnal cycle, God creates the rhythm of work and rest, urging responsible work routines and timely self-care, proscribing both indolence and workaholism. The meditation of day one revolves around time as God's gift of purpose.

On the second day, the people of God have their attention turned toward God's creation of the sky through a process of division. In so doing, God creates the space for creatures to be, gives them freedoms to exist, move, interact, and thrive, standing against any form of compulsion and abuse of freedom, given that freedom itself is a gift from God and hence to be used only as God dictates. In creating the domain of the birds, God also provides habitation, securing a safe space in which the birds can flourish. The creation of the sky sheds light on the need to attend to emotional safety, thereby discouraging infringements against personal, communal, organizational, territorial boundaries. War occurs as a result of a people's inability to put national pride and vengeance beneath their commitment not to disrupt and harm innocent lives. The message of day two is that space constitutes God's gift of identity.

On the third day, we are directed to meditate on God's creation of earth and sea and of plants and trees. God provides habitation for land and marine creatures, offering a safe space for these creatures to thrive. Emphasized again is the importance of attending to emotional safety

---

17. What we mean when we speak of God's creation of different parts of the universe is simply that God as Trinity commissions angelic forces to use both creative powers and natural and evolutionary processes to bring about these things in response to changing circumstances as a means of adaptation, God as Divine Nature setting the initial conditions and laws of the universe involving particles with their forces and interactions.

18. According to Gordon Wenham, the six days of creation in Genesis 1 function to infer the relationship between God's work and rest and human work and rest in the framework of a week. Wenham, *Genesis 1–15*, 40. We are not suggesting specifically that the Israelites came together as a social-religious community or as families singing or meditating collectively on an item in God's work of creation designated for each particular day, only that as the Torah was taught by the priests and elders to the people and by parents to children, there would have been a clear memory of the association between each day and a creative work of God, enabling individual and quiet meditation of some sort.

PART 1: CREATION'S IMAGING OF THE DIVINE

and refraining from violations of personal, communal, organizational, and territorial boundaries. God furnishes food for all land creatures; this bespeaks the necessity of attending to the needs of those who have less than enough, forbidding insouciance toward the lack of others. Consequently, day three reminds us of how food lies at the center of God's test of our humanity.

On the fourth day of creation in the weekly meditative system found in the first creation story, God creates the sun, moon, and stars, forming these intermediaries to give guidance through natural seasons and underscore the rhythm of work and rest. Similarly, God supplies agents of wisdom and instruction to exhort people through natural and personal phases, encouraging vigorous living and restful leisure. The fourth day, then, discloses knowledge as an instrument in God's test of wisdom.

The fifth day brings forth a meditation based on God's creation of marine and aerial creatures. These are made by God and worthy of respect and protection. In this manner, the meditation underscores the importance of ecological limits to industrial development and modernization, cautioning against an unbridled expansion of the human civilization, highlighting the way in which God places nature at the very center of God's test of respect.

The sixth day of the week corresponds to a reflection on God's creation of land and human creatures. All human beings have been made in God's image, that is, to adopt God's values, attitudes, and practices toward creation.[19] They are made male and female, so women are to be accorded equal respect. They are to have dominion over the animals, to use them to perform some forms of labor but without ill-treatment. The biblical exhortation in this regard is for human persons to carry on a harmonious coexistence with the animal world, eschewing the exploitation of animals. Human beings are given food from plants and trees, as are animals. This bears witness to a parity between human beings and animals, in which human beings are not superior to animals.

People are to recognize that land is given for food, not accumulation; therefore territorial conflicts are ruled out, and each is to look to the

---

19. The equality of all human persons is not anything that can be taken for granted. For centuries, the overly-enduring institution of slavery has enshrined a belief diametrically opposed to the idea that all human persons are of equal and inalienable worth, and that institution was an evil to which professed Christians fell prey such as Christopher Columbus, whose Spanish expeditions saw the enslavement of Native Americans, and the Christian English people who bought slaves in large numbers from West Africa in late seventeenth-century America. Kidd, "Slavery."

interests of other groups, to ensure that they have an equal share in the land and its resources, all of which are provided by God. To the extent that God furnishes food for human beings, the world's resources are sufficient for each person and group, and nobody should have to starve, provided there is an equitable distribution. For this reason, it is plausible that the divine gift of humanity stands in the middle of a test of peace.

On the seventh and last day of the week, reflection is lodged in the idea of God's rest from all God's labors. It is a day that awaits the future and which is achieved only by a constant struggle against greed, violence, indolence, indifference, injustice, unfairness, and discrimination. Day seven is all about how rest is constituted only by God's vision for justice.

In our view, the first creation story is not intended to be interpreted as a scientific description of the time God took to create the world with its various aspects or the sequence in which God created the various species; on the contrary, one of the purposes of the account is to attest to the way in which it was indeed God who brought order out of chaotic matter. This matter itself was originally created in an orderly way by God, but it became disorderly as a result of an angelic rebellion, taking place sometime during the history of the present universe, and the divine judgment which ensued.

As for the second creation story, God did indeed create a human being prior to bringing about plants and possibly animals as well, yet there is nothing in either this story or the first to suggest that evolutionary processes were not employed to engender all of material existence, or to indicate that the human being in the second story did not emerge from a process of evolution whereby God through the angels formed a physical human body out of a more primitive body into which a human soul (formerly integrated in an angelic body) was placed,[20] or that the plants or animals God created in the second story were not restricted to Eden, and they did not already exist elsewhere according to an evolutionary scheme. Adam and Eve were the first religious people among hominids, not the first human beings.

---

20. In Gen 2:7, the word *yāṣar*, used in reference to God's molding of the "dust" or the matter from which Adam was made, takes on the meaning of "to fashion" as used in Isa 44:9 in reference to the making of an idol. In turn, *'āpār* ("dust") designates the evolutionary predecessor of the human being as a material being; this semantic choice is appropriate in view that *'āpār* occurs in Gen 3:19 in a context in which it is used in two different senses; to signify the mortality (and materiality) of human beings, on the one hand, and the physical composition of the human body, on the other.

PART 1: CREATION'S IMAGING OF THE DIVINE

Apart from communicating the importance of reflecting on the world as the creative product of God as a means of centering one's emotions in moments of frustration due to injustice, the book of Job shows that God is responsible for order while the disobedient angels of God are accountable for chaos. Job 38–42 has a glaring omission of a theodicy when this is most to be anticipated, only because God was not responsible for the woes Job suffered. Rather, Satan held God to ransom by casting doubt on Job's blamelessness.

At issue was Job's motivation for his piety, whether he served God purely on the basis of his material blessings and the gift of physical health. With the devil's challenge, it became necessary for God to allow the devil to prove the devil's point and put Job through a gauntlet of tests accordingly. This was imperative if God's honor was to be upheld and God's wisdom rightly and justifiably prevail in the presence of the heavenly council, if Satan was to be proven wrong and shamed, thereby deterring other like-minded angels, potentially or in actuality, from engaging in the same conduct and, more importantly, if Job was to know in his heart why he worshipped God, as Abraham discovered in the course of his attempted sacrifice of Isaac.

Can God be charged with cruelty and injustice for permitting the devil to go out to harm Job? Could God not have simply declared to the devil that God's word concerning Job's piety was final and definitive and that the devil had no right to harm an innocent person just to prove a point? If God had chosen the easy route, the devil would have triumphed, God's wisdom would have been impugned since some might wonder if the reason God was insistent that Satan should not touch Job was that Job was perhaps not as pure a person as God was making him out to be, whatever the justification offered for preventing the devil from carrying out the devil's wishes; other angels would be emboldened to speak or revolt against God on the basis that God's honor and wisdom could not be upheld, and Job himself would not have been able to fend off the devil's accusations to the same effect.

To ward off these accusations and avert cosmic instability, God adjudged, certainly with great empathy and sorrow, that it was better for Job to undergo the trials brought by the accusing angel, while holding out a final day on which that very same disobedient angel would be properly punished for occasioning such discord in heaven and suffering on earth. In a very real sense, then, even God's hands are bound—God is not able to work directly in the human realm and has to depend on the obedience of angels and for this reason God has to appear with a heavenly host even at the final judgment (e.g., 2 Thess 1:7-9; Rev 19:11-16);[21] God has to permit angels to do their work, for good or ill. Furthermore, God's position in heaven is always precarious (by divine permission and necessary will) and has to be firmly and rigorously maintained against all and any decisive accusations for the sake of cosmic order.

As a matter of fact, God would not have allowed Satan to do anything to Job if Satan was not in a strong and nearly insurmountable position to do as Satan wished to Job and his family—it is inconceivable that, given the opportunity, a loving and fatherly God would not preclude events that visit harm on people, all of whom God loves without exception.

The nature of God is reflected in the diverse forms of both living and non-living things. It is revealed in the possibility and the actuality of the existence of entities and objects in the universe. Axiomatically, there is an unchanging ontological basis for the possibility and existence of each thing and all things. Behind and beneath the initial conditions, laws, and evolutionary processes of the universe, determining the particles and the forces and interactions between them, is an invisible framework and structure which can only be felt in its effects but not directly perceived in its actual reality.[22] It forms the explanation for the reality and existence of each thing and all things, for why it exists, the particular shape it takes in its existence, its capacities, its functions, and its activities, and

---

21. It may appear from these very texts that God possesses the ability to execute divine judgment rather than leaving this in the hands of angels. Nonetheless, we need to bear in mind that other passages provide alternative depictions of the manner and agents by which divine judgment will be carried out. Consider the dominical exposition of the Lord's own parable of the weeds in Matt 13:36-43. In the interpretation of the parable, the role of the Son of Man, that is, of the Lord himself, is to command his angels to identify and put together all who have transgressed for consignment to a burning furnace (vv. 41-42). Moreover, the seven trumpets, plagues, and bowls of divine wrath in Rev 8:6—9:21; 11:15-19; 15; and 16 are unleashed by angels. The cumulative evidence in this connection suggests that whenever God is said to be personally involved in discharging punishment upon sinners, whether it be in terms of "inflicting vengeance" (2 Thess 1:8 ESV), "strik[ing] down" nations with a keen sword from the Lord's own mouth or "tread[ing] the winepress of the fury of the wrath of God" (Rev 19:15 ESV), this is to be understood in terms of the Lord visiting judgment by delivering rather than directly executing a just judicial sentence. See Beale, *Revelation*, 961-63. The passage in 2 Thess 2:8 concerning how the returning Christ will destroy the antichrist is to be interpreted as a summary of a future event more carefully detailed in Revelation 19. Indeed, the Book of Jude (1:14-15) cites 1 Enoch to the effect that the Lord will return with ten thousands of the Lord's holy ones to execute the final judgment against sinners.

22. Siegel, "Fundamental Constants."

its implanted goals.[23] This includes the survival instinct of living things and the realm of human and angelic morality, encompassing moral consciousness, inclination, and agency.

Biological evolutionary theory in which species adapt to their natural environment through processes of mutation and natural selection is supported both by genetics and molecular biology[24] as well as the first creation story in that even there, God created the various domains of inhabitation and movement first; namely, the sky, seas, and land, prior to creating any plant or animal. According to evolutionary theory, life was brought about through some process by which carbon-based molecules and water combined with an energy supply came together,[25] the survival instinct drove the transition from aquatic single-celled organisms to multicellular animals (in the search for more efficient ways of hunting bacteria),[26] from aquatic animals to land animals (in pursuit of more abundant sources of food through the greater vision afforded on land),[27] and from tree-dwelling animals to hominids (through the expansion of the savannah which engendered adaptation to upright movement on the ground).[28] At every turn, the evolutionary course of the universe was guided by angelic intervention ordained by God in response to changing circumstances as a means of adaptation; these angelic forces provide entities with the means to endure and adapt to changing circumstances by enabling them to develop new features and attributes tailored to adaptation.

If direct divine creation cannot be admitted for theodictic (a God powerful enough to bring the universe into existence would be able to prevent evil and injustice) and logical (if God created everything directly, what was God doing before the advent of creation?) reasons, how does our theory cohere with passages such as Ps 104:27–30? Does God literally produce food for all living things as and when they need and receive it?

---

23. This is so in spite that the shape of the universe is determined by the voluntary and obedient action of God as Trinity and the angels of the Trinity in yielding the materiality of God's creatures, since the Divine Nature posits the Trinity and angels with their character, personality, and ability, thereby indirectly engendering even material bodies through guided evolutionary processes. The Divine Nature is neither directly nor indirectly responsible for sin, which marks a departure from its guidance.

24. National Academy of Sciences, *Science and Creationism*, 9–14.

25. CNEOS, "Life on Earth."

26. McGowan, "Where Animals Come From."

27. Ouellette, "Why Did Life Move to Land?"

28. Maslin et al., "Early Human Evolution."

Are the lives of these creatures subject to the will of God, who decides at what point they are to expire (Cf. Job 34:14–15)? Does God create each creature when they come into being by bestowing God's Spirit? One must realize that these are metaphorical descriptions of the way in which all being and existence emerges from God conceived as the Divine Nature, the ontological framework underlying the possibility and actuality of the nature, being, existence, activity, and fulfillment of all things.

God and human morality

The Bible depicts human action as ordered by God as the expression of a saving faith in God. Yet, is salvation by faith alone such that our good works are the product or effects of our salvific faith? Scripture certainly suggests this (Jas 2:14–26). At the same time, there is an implication that faith may not be genuine and the proof of true faith rests in whether a life is marked by good works arising from faith.

In what, then, does faith consist? We have considered how all people have faith, regardless of whether they adhere to a religious tradition, and this faith consists in their inherent belief and personal conviction that something external to them, whether a personal moral agent or ultimate principle, is the source of their existence and moral orientation, and the actions arising from the latter. The reason for this complementary and asymmetrical relationship between faith and good works is that faith places us in Christ and Christ in us. If we are in Christ, we are nourished by him and empowered to live the way he does, and if Christ is in us, then he guides the way we think, feel, and act, enabling us to become like him in his attitudes and actions.

Moreover, salvation and the faith that mediates it are said to be entirely the gift of God (Eph 2:8–9). Our works do not save us, including good works based on faith in Christ.[29] Christ did not come to earth and atone for our sins because we are deserving; he did so when we were ungodly (Rom 5:6). If we were virtuous persons, he would not need to die for each and every person, on account of their sins. Is it the case, therefore, that the faith itself that we repose in God; that is, our wholehearted, single-minded, needy, and grateful acceptance and reception of all that God presents to us as the most precious treasure of God's, namely, Jesus Christ

---

29. Cf. Barth, *KD* IV.1, §63.1 (ET, Bromiley, p. 752); Barth, *KD* IV.2, §64.1 (ET, Bromiley, p. 18).

and his moral demonstration and example of perfect love for sinners, is something which we have completely no responsibility for as moral agents vested with personal autonomy? Is it impossible, is it inconceivable for us to assert that when the gift of Christ is borne to us, we accept it by an act of our conscious volition, independent of any supernatural action in us specially enabling us to make such a choice though not in the absence of moral values and inclinations implanted by the Divine Nature and in pre-terrestrial encounter with the Trinity from birth, moral or religious teachings from Christ, and moral guidance by the Holy Spirit; that we, indeed, chose Christ even as he first chose us?

A classical Reformed theology would appear to preclude any such notion, preferring instead to speak of God's election of human persons to obedient faith in God in and through Christ for fear that to speak of a human choice of God in Christ would risk undermining a doctrine of the utter corruption of the human will as well as God's sovereignty even over the human will, preceding this will in such a way that all good effects that may arise from a reformed, converted, or regenerated human will must be seen to result solely from God's gracious work in the life of the believer.[30]

There is little scriptural support for the doctrine of original sin conceived in a biological rather than psychodynamic sense. The *locus classicus* of the doctrine, namely, Rom 5:12, "Therefore, just as sin came into the world through one man, and death through sin, and so death spread to all men because all sinned—", (ESV) simply affirms that death afflicted all people through their own sinful acts which in turn affected others, not that they become sinners through biological processes via being physically, psychologically, and spiritually present in seed form in Adam when he committed the sin of eating the fruit of the tree of the knowledge of good and evil[31] or are altogether regarded as sinners on account of some legal representation in Adam, but that those who uncritically accept the false ideas and feelings pertaining to self, others, and God suggested by parental neglect, abuse, and negative influence undergo a dysfunctional affective process, drawing a compulsive evil into their soul, a state of affairs from which it seems nobody is exempt

---

30. Cf. Barth, *KD* IV.2, §66.5 (ET, Bromiley, pp. 590–95).

31. Erickson, *Christian Theology*, 578. Cf. the description of the theology of original sin in the early church in Barth, *KD* IV.1, §60.3 (ET, Bromiley, pp. 500–501).

by reason of the prevalence, even ubiquity, of domination and concomitant trauma, a situation that is very much like death.[32]

As for Ps 51:5, the meaning is that David recognized that the circumstances in which he received life from his mother were those marked by evil thoughts and feelings in the woman, thoughts and feelings which would have affected his psychological wellbeing even in utero. This interpretation is supported by the following verse in which David reflects on the way in which God guides him along the right path even in his innermost thoughts and feelings, suggesting a certain freedom of will on the part of the fetus to accept or reject sinful or righteous thoughts or feelings.[33]

Does God, then, command sovereignty over the human will? In the case of Abimelech, king of Gerar, where Abraham sojourned for a period, it is recorded that God prevented Abimelech from sinning against God by having relations with Sarah on the presumption, incited by Abraham himself, that she was merely his sister (Gen 20:1–7). Now it is clear that in preventing Abimelech from touching Sarah, God did not manipulate or alter Abimelech's will in such a way that the king did not desire sexual relations with Sarah, for if that were the case, God would not have had to urgently visit Abimelech in a dream, disclose to him the truth about the relationship between Abraham and Sarah, and warn him to release her back to Abraham. As to how God might have stopped Abimelech from sinning against God by God's preventing Abimelech from being physically intimate with Sarah even after having taken her as a partner (as stated in v. 7), we propound that God generated in his mind images

---

32. Adam did not die, though he committed a sin that God had said he would die committing. The signification of death as a consequence of consuming fruit of the tree of the knowledge of good and evil, then, does not have physical expiration as a referent, but rather a complete deterioration of human existence in its spiritual and psychological dimensions. Such an interpretation is supported by a passage like 1 Cor 15:56, where Paul speaks of sin being the "sting" (ESV) or weapon of death and of the law as "the power of sin", implying that death in that context indicates a power of sin which drags all into slavery before itself through the instrumentality of the law by which sin is exposed and a person is tempted to fall into and remain in a state of condemnation and helplessness (Rom 7:7—8:1).

33. Thomas Verny believes that it is possible for a fetus to learn, feel, and respond to their environment, including the ways their parents interact with and care for them, and that these perceptions of the fetus' environment influence their lifelong emotional and physical wellbeing. Whilst still in the womb, the fetus receives messages about themselves and the world which can either result in the child feeling happy or unhappy, wanted or rejected, and living in a safe or unsafe world. Orlans, "Fetuses Are Aware."

of himself and Sarah engaging in non-sexual relational activity which served to temporarily curb his sexual desire.[34]

As such, there is no warrant for holding that God is sovereign over the human will. Even in the case of Pharaoh, God did not harden his heart in such a way that he was unable to exercise his own freewill; Pharaoh hardened his own heart because he was fundamentally bent on keeping the Israelites in captivity, and jumped at every opportunity to continue holding them in slavery, such as when Moses ended the plague of frogs (Exod 8:15), of flies (Exod 8:32), and of hail (Exod 9:34). It is likely that when Scripture depicts God as hardening Pharaoh's heart, it was not that Pharaoh had no wicked inclination at the outset, but that God merely gave Pharaoh up in those instances to his evil tendencies (cf. Gen 8:21).

Returning to our discussion of Ephesians 2, considering the wider context constituted by Eph 2:8–10, it is reasonable to propose that it is not the faith of the individual believer that is in view when the passage refers to God's gift, but rather the mercy of God displayed in and through Christ in relation to sinners, recognizing their inalienable worth as human beings, on the basis of which believers are to consciously choose to emulate Christ's loving and forgiving attitudes and ways, which are in accord with the moral values and inclinations implanted by the Divine Nature and in pre-terrestrial encounter with the Trinity, these attitudes and

---

34. The devil and the devil's agents are capable of doing something similar, in the direction of immorality and sin, as transpired in the course of the temptations Jesus endured while fasting in the wilderness, where the devil placed in the Lord's mind visualizations of scenarios through which the Lord might have seen himself standing before a pile or area of stones, urged to turn them into bread to prematurely satisfy his hunger after forty days and nights (the implication being that he had committed to go on for longer), effectively going back on his commitment to devote an unspecified period of time to the Lord, based on the command of the Holy Spirit (consequently, the quotation by Jesus from Deut 8:3, by way of a response to the devil, to the effect that human beings do not subsist strictly on physical sustenance but, more importantly and above and beyond that, the spoken words of God); on the pinnacle of the temple in Jerusalem and told to cast himself down in full view of the public that he might attract a great and eager crowd by forcing God to deliver a miracle of catching him; and on a towering mountain from which he was able to see all the kingdoms of the world and directed to prostrate himself before the devil so as to gain control of those dominions (Matt 4:1–11). By way of a piece of anecdotal evidence for the devil's direct or delegated intervention in the life of a human person, a Christian experienced on numerous occasions two disquieting phenomena: one, the hearing of a crude four-letter word often when encountering the personal name of God during a regular sequential reading of the Old Testament in an English translation; and, two, hearing an inner voice, to be distinguished from his thoughts, telling him a number that does not reflect something in reality that he has to remember.

ways being commended to us in our hearts by the Holy Spirit. Indeed, this is the most plausible reading in light of the fact that the tenth verse explicitly commends a vision of humankind as having been prepared by God from the beginning to perform the good works that God has in mind through their being posited by the Divine Nature, encountered by the Trinity, and endued with the moral consciousness, inclination, and agency necessary to do these works.

In 2 Pet 1:3–4, the ability to lead a life of vitality and godliness is given through God's power by means not of the sovereign activity of God but the knowledge of God who summons humankind to emulate God's own glory and virtue. If God were fully responsible for causing believers to perform these good works of godliness, it would not be necessary for God to work in the believer primarily through the knowledge of God's own virtue, which serves as a vision, path, and direction for them to consciously, intentionally, and deliberately follow from faith, through probity, knowledge, self-control, steadfastness, godliness, brotherly affection, to love (2 Pet 1:5–7 ESV). In truth, this is the process which God has entrusted to believers by which they are able to confirm their own calling and entry into God's kingdom (2 Pet 1:8–11).[35]

How may a person commit to a life of good works without falling into the twin dangers of legalism and self-promotion?

Legalism is the mindset that the good works we perform make us worthy of God's providence and salvation. Yet, our obedience is what we always already owe to God as the Creator and Lord, rather than a favor we do for God (Luke 17:7–10).[36] It is the outworking of the good nature God has implanted in us, and our only role is to nurture and carry to fruition our good desires in the form of good works by allowing these desires to take root and bear fruit, in a sort of positive analogue to Jas 1:13–15. For this reason, whenever we find ourselves experiencing good desires, or engaging in good works, we are obliged to give glory to God, understanding, however, that it is our responsibility to nurture our good desires into good works.[37]

---

35. See also Acts 5:32, in which the Holy Spirit is said by the apostles to be conferred on those who obey God, implying a volitional decision to accept Christ's atonement, divine forgiveness, and the Spirit.

36. Cf. Barth, *KD* IV.2, §68.3 (ET, Bromiley, p. 784).

37. On a Calvinistic outlook, this good nature is something worked into the very core of one's being through a process of regeneration in such a way that good actions inevitably and infallibly result, for which therefore the believer owes God entire and lifelong thanks. As for the sinful nature from Adam, one cannot blame Adam for one's

As for the inclination to impress others by our good works, the antidote to this tendency is the recognition that humility constitutes an integral dimension, a fundamentum, as it were, which guides all our good action, and that to the extent that humility is absent, none of our works can be properly designated good.[38] Hence, Jesus taught his disciples that they were not to perform any good works, whether it be in terms of prayer or almsgiving, to be seen, for though they might be praised by people for such actions, God, who knows all things including the intent of the heart, will not be able to bestow a reward for such ostensibly good but in reality false actions (Matt 6:1–6).

Is it true that a person who has accepted the message of the gospel is saved in such a way that they can never lose that salvation? It is generally risky to proclaim a Christian message that does not strike a fine balance between God's grace and human responsibility. Those who have majored on God's grace have run the risk of doing away with moral responsibility while those who place a premium on human moral duty tend to neglect the primary and central role of divine grace. Among Protestants, especially of a hyper-grace persuasion, there is a certain susceptibility and partiality to a deficient doctrine in which the role of Jesus is so emphasized that it appears that there is little if any role left to the believer in God's work of grace in the Christian life.

Particularly detrimental is the idea that Jesus does all that is necessary for a believer to be saved, guaranteeing that salvation in such a way that there is no possibility of one accepting the gospel and not finding themselves in heaven at the end of their earthly lives. If such a guarantee were given by the Lord, it would not have been possible for St. John to speak of false believers who were so convincing that they seemed for all intents and purposes to be no different from any Christian (1 John 2:19).

---

sins, since in sinning, one only acts according to one's sinful desires. This does not equate to a person being able to credit themselves for voluntarily carrying out God's desires out of a reformed nature, because these are the works that are required of a creature. See Barth, KD IV.1, §62.1 (ET, Bromiley, pp. 645–50). An effective way to nurture one's capacity for engagement in good works is by becoming conscious that one is doing something praiseworthy, not so as to become conceited, but in order that one might derive from it the intrinsic reward of self-satisfaction in the grateful knowledge that the desire and ability to engage in good works originate ultimately in God, and in which one begins to identify oneself as a person who engages in specific good works, in contrast to those who live irresponsibly. Cf. Clear, *Atomic Habits*, 29–41.

38. The truly humble person will not even make a boast of their confession of sin. See Barth, *KD* IV.1, §61.3 (ET, Bromiley, p. 594); Barth, *KD* IV.1, §61.4 (ET, Bromiley, pp. 635–36).

In all probability, they showed their true colors at some point in their time with the respective Christian community to which they belonged. Perhaps they denied the place of repentance in the Christian life (cf. 1 John 1:5—2:11; 3:4-10; 4:7—5:5) along with a repudiation of the doctrine of Christ's physical incarnation, salvific mediatorship, and divine nature (e.g., 1 John 2:22; 4:1-3; 5:1, 10).

Repentance is a necessary prerequisite for receiving God's gift of forgiveness and salvation through Christ.[39] Faith is more than a matter of mental or intellectual assent to a set of doctrinal statements of orthodox belief; a living and authentic faith is alive rather than dead, that is, it produces good works as evidence of its authenticity. It includes mental assent but transcends it, encompassing personal conviction that bears moral fruit.

Although salvation is a gift of God, it inaugurates a lifelong process beginning with a recognition that God forgives us our sins on account of Jesus' propitiatory and substitutionary atoning sacrifice on the cross of Calvary; our unpunished sins against God are forgiven on his account. The proper response to such an astounding and lavish act of personal sacrifice is a penitent attitude and inner disposition. Should we think to accept God's gift of forgiveness and salvation with an air of complacency or indifference instead of gratitude toward God for reaching out to us despite our sinfulness, eventuating in a desire to live rightly for God, we cannot be said to have actually received the gift of salvation; no, we have rather despised and effectively rejected it (see Luke 18:9-14).

In a Christian understanding, the state of salvation consists in remaining in or returning to such a disposition in relation to the grace of forgiveness through the propitiatory and substitutionary atoning act of Jesus Christ.[40] The parallel to this in other religious traditions as well as atheism is any disposition of gratitude or thankfulness towards a positing other based on an unarticulated but certainly universally

---

39. See Barth, *KD* IV.1, §61.3 (ET, Bromiley, p. 596).

40. Those who fail to remain in Christ, instead forsaking the moral virtues of the Christian faith which are really virtues of humankind as posited by the Divine Nature, shaped by the Trinity, and guided by both, place themselves in danger of divine judgment (Heb 6:4-8). In the Reformed theological perspective, such a passage as Heb 6:4-8 is interpreted in terms of a person who embraced faith in Christ either in a strictly intellectual fashion or merely pledged allegiance to God for utilitarian reasons; that is, so that one might be relieved of some adversity, as we see in the case of Pharaoh, so that it is possible for a person who has embraced Christianity, but not in a fully authentic manner, to revert to a former lifestyle of immorality and self-centeredness. Cf. Got Questions, "Does Hebrews 6:4-6 Mean We Can Lose Our Salvation?"

experienced sense that atonement has been made for one's sins and one is therefore pardonable. From a secular point of view, and therefore for the atheist, self-forgiveness is rooted in the compassion that one is able to feel towards another person in similar straits, and human compassion, whether for self or other, is in turn grounded in an overwhelming sense of being treated mercifully by a higher, atoning power.[41] The evidence of right faith is good works; conversely, we know our faith is neither true nor bona fide by the observation that it produces or facilitates nothing morally good in and out of us, whether this be an internal revulsion or guilt for morally evil thoughts or actions in our lives, or external works of compassion and love.

Since the Christian life is a lifelong process that incorporates many facets such as the reception of divine forgiveness and a life lived in gratitude toward and glorification of God, it cannot be said with any integrity that the Christian life does not involve any notion of good works or moral responsibility. At the very most, we can aver that God's everlasting and impartial commitment to love, forgive, guide, and care for us is not predicated on our personal moral merits.

Salvation engenders good works, produced by a true and living faith, and the goal of the Christian life is to seek consistently to confirm our election and calling through the good works we allow God to perform through us as we agree with and nourish the good desires of our hearts, allowing them to bear fruit in our lives, renouncing sinful desires (2 Pet 1:10). Growth is expected in the Christian life. As such the believer is advised not to quench the Holy Spirit (1 Thess 5:19), by which it is inferred that the purpose of the Christian's life is for us to progress in godliness. In two of Jesus' parables, servants were entrusted with sums of money, with minas (Luke 19:11–27) and talents (Matt 25:14–30), and expected to grow the sum. We note that the servants were provided with all the resources needed to succeed. All they had to do was put the money to good use by making wise investments in business and trading—they were rewarded accordingly in the parable of the minas. Similarly, God has provided us with all that is necessary to grow in godly character (2 Pet 1:3–4). The penitent thief should not be thought of as an exception, since he did what he could with his limited time to serve the Lord, and he would surely have done more if he were not sentenced to death. God calls us to serve God

---

41. Cherry, "How to Forgive Yourself."

with the time we have on earth, through growing in godly character and expressing our godliness in worship and service.

There is therefore no ticket to heaven one can hope to obtain from receiving the Christian message.[42] It is not possible for a person to be saved in the absence of a proper reception of divine forgiveness involving a recognition of personal sinfulness and a gratitude toward God which leads them to desire to glorify God for the rest of their existence. Jesus does not depose or displace us from our morally responsible roles before God; he comes both as sacrifice and moral example, and it is as we emulate Christ's example that we become perfect and reach the goal of the process of salvation.

It is crucial to bear in mind that the idea of salvation (*sōzō*) in the New Testament carries both a sense of Jesus' atoning sacrifice, which involves no human contribution, and of preservation from the judgment of God for sinful acts through engaging in actions or interceding for situations that facilitate avoiding sin and abounding in good works as the goal of the Christian life, certainly involving a human contribution.[43] Those who commit such sins may turn out not to be among the elect of God, though they professed faith in Christ; therefore, it is important always to confirm our calling and election through repentance of sin and good works.

Within a classical Reformed scheme, human striving to allow God to perform good works through them is part and parcel of God's sovereign control over their lives. Such striving is to be differentiated from a self-righteous type by the motive undergirding the determination to lead a godly life; whereas the self-righteous person exerts themselves in godly acts with a view to making a good impression on others, the truly righteous person does so only in grateful response to God and with the intention of confirming their calling and election, of assuring themselves that they are truly saved, through the godly attributes they see in themselves and the godly life they are able to lead, a life driven by a will to lead a godly life, recognizing that God's vision for human existence is one in which we choose to and willingly take up our rightful responsibilities (Matt 11:29).

This constant seeking of assurance is not self-serving, but rather part of our Christian responsibility and a way by which we demonstrate

---

42. Barth, *KD* IV.1, §62.2 (ET, Bromiley, p. 701).

43. For the former sense, see Eph 2:1-9; for the latter, see 1 Cor 3:10-15; 1 Tim 2:1-4; 2:8-15; 4:16; Jas 1:19-21; 1 Pet 3:8-22; 4:12-19.

the extent to which we cherish God's gift of salvation in us. It is not an expression of doubt that God has actually saved us since we engage in striving for good works in positive anticipation that we will see God accomplish much in our lives, but a legitimate means God furnishes us to rejoice in God's work in our lives. We are, indeed, called to strive after good works (Phil 2:12–13; Titus 2:14; 1 Pet 3:13). Of special note is the idea in Phil 2:12–13 of "working out" one's salvation (*katergazomai*, used also in 1 Pet 4:3 with reference to a carrying out of immoral intentions), recognizing that God is the ultimate actor in effectuating the good will and therefore actions of the believers.

The idea here is that believers, infused as they are with certain godly desires through a process of regeneration, are entreated and exhorted to confirm and carry out these desires, renouncing sinful ones, appreciating that as they engage in birthing good actions from good desires, God is with them to guide and encourage them.

In the Reformed tradition, the Christian believer does not gain possession of a set of godly attributes (fundamentally, a love for God's law and righteousness in which a person recognizes their wickedness and misery rather than being self-assured in and pleased with their perceived spirituality and righteousness and contemptuous towards those regarded as less spiritual or righteous)[44] but bears them only insofar as the Lord is in them and they in the Lord as *simul peccator et iustus* (simultaneously a sinner and righteous, adapted from Luther's *simul iustus est et peccat*).[45] In Luther, the believer is permitted by God to exist in a dual state of sinfulness and imputed righteousness so as to bring the believer to humble dependence on God for daily or regular forgiveness, God's empowerment against sin, and to curb their arrogance and pride.[46]

This implies the conviction that the believer experiences two distinct states of spirituality and morality, in one of which they experience themselves, though having godly desires (through the Spirit's indwelling), as incapable of actually doing the will of God with which they agree, and thereby lamenting and seeking God's grace, and in the other

---

44. Luther, *Röm*, 7 (ET, Mueller, pp. 112, 114–15).

45. Barth, *KD* IV.1, §61.3 (ET, Bromiley, pp. 573–96); Barth, *KD* IV.2, §66.4 (ET, Bromiley, pp. 566–74, 579). In the second reference, Barth elucidates conversion as a radical and persistent act of God in the believer throughout their lifetime and in every dimension which brings forth acts for God.

46. Luther, *Röm*, 7 (ET, Mueller, p. 116); cf. Barth, *KD* IV.2, §68.3 (ET, Bromiley, p. 818).

of which they perceive a congruence between their godly will and their actual actions, which are consonant with the will of God of which they have always approved from the time of their regeneration, through both the Spirit's indwelling and operation in the life of the believer.

Furthermore, the believer is to mark that their dual status is attested by the way in which, though sinful, they yet recognize their own sinfulness through which they understand their need to depend on Christ's atoning work alone for forgiveness and redemption from sin.[47]

Luther's line of thinking is one where Christian repentance will be characterized by sorrow for one's sin (the sorrowful recognition that sin displeases and saddens God, that sin is not God's design for our lives, and that sin destroys our lives and harms those around us), a turning to or pleading with God for forgiveness and redemption from sin through Christ's atoning sacrifice (the recognition that though we do not deserve God's forgiveness and God does not need to forgive us, yet through Christ's sacrifice, God always forgives us whenever we seek God's forgiveness; the attitude and posture of humility in pleading for God's forgiveness; the recognition that Christ has died in our place for our sins and that only Christ can save us from our sins), and a hope that someday, sooner rather than later, we will be relieved by God of our burden of sin, whether by the power of the Holy Spirit or at the return of Christ when we will receive glorified bodies with which to worship and serve God forever.[48] Repentance is not the less bona fide simply because the same sin recurs in a Christian's life almost without relenting, given that repentance is a process and we should not despise small beginnings. It is not a strictly intellectual change from knowing God as an angry judge to knowing God as a merciful Father to whom, as proponents of universal reconciliation appear to suggest, all are already reconciled through the

---

47. Luther, *Gal.*, 3.6 (ET, Middleton, pp. 130-33).

48. Cf. Barth, *KD* IV.1, §61.3 (ET, Bromiley, p. 598). There is a marked change in the sinful desires the regenerate Christian believer experiences in that whereas formerly these were desires which refused faith in Christ (John 16:9) and rejected the need to honor Christ in their lives, yet now they have become limited to the desire to succumb to temptations constituting a failure to fulfill a concrete and specific act of obedience of thought, desire, and action, which can be shown to be required of the love each Christian owes God and their neighbor from thorough and reasonable exegetical investigation of Scripture, excluding belief in God as triune Creator and the general recognition and conviction that before justification one is a helpless sinner in need of the gift of grace of salvation of Christ's atoning sacrifice, appropriated through the Holy Spirit by faith, and after justification one is to regularly resist temptation, repent of one's sins, and seek the forgiveness of Christ and empowerment of the Spirit to live a godly life.

work of Christ on the cross, regardless of their spiritual or moral state.[49] Life transformation is not guaranteed by such knowledge. Can a person who takes God's love for granted and continues living in sin be said to have been reconciled to God?

In a Reformed conception, regeneration evokes a change of spiritual disposition, such that whereas a person used to be opposed to the knowledge and obedience of God, now as a regenerate believer, they are gladly desirous of gaining an ever-clearer knowledge of God's nature, will and purposes, and of doing that will, regardless of fits and starts, or occasional departures.

It is futile for an indolent person to think, "given that God is sovereign, God will do whatever God wants irrespective of my effort, thus I do not need to make any effort whatsoever," since it is God's perfect and self-determined will for all creation that elect persons strive for good works through personal and voluntary choices and commitment; moreover, it is best and most in conformity to and harmony with our God-given, good inner nature that we do so. In the domain of primary causes, it is God who brings about circumstances, creates motivations, and engenders decisions, while in the domain of secondary causes, it appears that we are the main actors, acting in response to circumstances on the ground of specific motives.

Does a Christian person with sinful desires and actions need to doubt their salvation? No, on the contrary, they like Paul should identify only with their godly desires (Rom 7:13–25), bemoaning their sinful desires, constantly seeking God's undeserved, non-obligatory, yet always only assured forgiveness, trusting that the battle will ultimately be won by God, and doing everything necessary (including availing of proper and suitable therapeutic assistance) to grow their good desires and bring them to birth in good actions. According to Barth, God the Father has caused human beings not only to belong to God, who is indispensable to them, but God has also caused Godself to belong to human beings and made them indispensable to Godself, so that God cannot be God apart from human beings: "If God is his [humankind's] Father, and he is the child of this Father, God is as little God without him as he is man without God."[50]

---

49. Erickson, *Christian Theology*, 942.
50. Barth, *KD* IV.1, §61.3 (ET, Bromiley, pp. 600–601).

Barth is of the view that the true Christian is the person who sees and comports themselves as part of an assembly of other Christians for the purpose of worship, with a sense that God has elected them and by the Word of God called them to, and by the Holy Spirit made them part of the body of Christ, the church. Therefore God knows and desires them, brings them into existence by God's good pleasure, and keeps them from corruption.[51] Furthermore, the Christian is one who exercises at least a modicum of love for God and others, which engenders gratitude for the much that they have already received from God, such love entailing the giving of one's material resources and time as well as one's very self, Barth believes, a statement which I take to mean being personally available for the other person in a safe, accepting, non-judgmental, non-dismissive, non-minimizing, non-coercive, non-manipulative, empathetic, sensitive, attentive, receptive, and other-centered way, allowing for hard conversations and intense emotional expression, and being truly concerned about their fragility, wellbeing, sensitivity, need for patient and persevering care and forgiveness.[52]

God's sovereignty

What is the nature of God's sovereignty? God can be said to be sovereign insofar as God has a *legal claim* on human and angelic obedience, the enactment of which actualizes God's effective rule (Rev 4:11). God's rightful claim to sovereignty over all existence is validated and legitimated, *existentially*, by the fact that it is only as all creatures obey God's will for their existence that they find harmony with their inner natures (Psalm 1). Divine sovereignty is vested, *deterrently*, in God's ability to bring an end to all existence or forever isolate recalcitrant evildoers in a place of punishment as and when God so desires, through summoning all God's angels to judge the world (2 Sam 24:15–16; Job 34:14–15). That God's will, actions (e.g., investigation, rescue, hearing of prayers, judgment), and communication (human beings cannot communicate directly with God because they do not exist in angelic bodies), including God's powerful interventions in the created order, are *delegative* and *dependent* on angelic representatives is inferred from passages of Scripture including Gen

---

51. Barth, *KD* IV.1, §62.2 (ET, Bromiley, pp. 687–88, 696).

52. Barth, *KD* IV.2, §68.3 (ET, Bromiley, pp. 783–88); Epstein, "What Does It Mean to Hold Space?"

18:20–21 (cf. Heb 13:2, attesting to the angelic, rather than divine, nature of the three men who visited Abraham); Acts 12:1–17; Exod 2:23–25 (cf. Rev 8:1–5, attesting to how the angels are responsible to bring prayers before God); 2 Sam 24:15–16; Dan 9:3–23; 10:2–14.[53] Such destructive power is withheld *forbearingly* and only on account of God's desire to see actualized the potential for repentance on the part of evildoers (Ezekiel 18; 1 Tim 2:3–4; 2 Pet 3:9). God's power over creation is *general*, not meticulous or rigorous—God does not have the ability at any point in time to determine the choices of a moral agent or alter circumstances.

God is not the source of evil or our suffering but Satan and his fallen angels, along with all other moral agents, that is, human beings, who willfully choose to pursue a selfish course of action at the expense of others. Suffering often continues at the hands of these selfish individuals because God mercifully and patiently wishes to give them time to repent without condoning their wickedness, yet there is a limit even to God's patience. We may not see justice, peace, and comfort in our lives, but we will finally see them when we meet God, because God holds the power of final judgment, which God will mete out at the right time through the power of God's angels.

God calls Christians to patience amid tribulation (Rom 12:12), offering Godself as a source of comfort rather than direct intervention and immediate restoration (2 Cor 1:3–4). Jesus models the ideal pious disposition in moments of suffering in choosing to trust in and commit himself to God in spite of feeling rejected by God (Matt 27:46; Luke 23:46), believing God to be one who does God's best for him. An episode in the life of Abraham bears witness to the importance of perseverance in trusting God as love; namely, the incident in which he heard God instruct him to sacrifice his son, Isaac, for a burned offering (Gen 22:1–14).

Contrary to a superficial reading, the crucial test does not lie in whether Abraham would positively respond to a request or command on God's part to sacrifice his son, given that God did not ultimately require the sacrifice of Abraham. It was not even a test of whether Abraham would be willing to sacrifice his son upon God's command, for Abraham could have decided, in view of the nature of the command, that it was not actually the God he worshipped who delivered the command, but quite another being.[54]

---

53. Enns, *MHT*, 305.

54. That Abraham was able to discern that it was God rather than another being who commanded him to sacrifice Isaac is proof positive not of the patriarch's presumed

This leaves the reader with a third option: God summoned Abraham to decide if he would continue trusting in God, that is, continue believing in and obeying God, in spite that God appears to be acting in a cruel manner towards him. God's callousness is always only ostensible, for in Abraham's case, God did not require the sacrifice of him. Similarly, in the instance of Job's trials, it was not God who subjected Job to his grievous suffering; rather, to all intents and purposes it seemed God was compelled to permit Satan to put Job to the test.

Did God not in a sense orchestrate Abraham's temporary unease in the matter of the command to sacrifice his son? We have to answer in the affirmative, yet given that God's substantive revelation in Scripture is complete, there is no need to expect that God would once again subject a believer to such an experience; instead, as believers we can afford to turn to the account of Abraham in question as an encouragement to continue to trust in God's loving nature despite seeming evidence to the contrary. We may not be called upon to sacrifice our children, but we may very well undergo personal tragedy. At that time, will we continue to believe God is love, accepting that certain things cannot be restored or recovered, and wait patiently for an answer from God, whether in this life or the next, whether that answer is one of strength for endurance or of miraculous intervention?

Both Hagar and Abraham encountered God as one who sees. What does it mean to live under God's sight? One who exists in the consciousness that God will see (Gen 22:8, 14) or sees (Gen 16:13) recognizes that God is not ignorant or indifferent in relation to one's anguish, but concerned about one's suffering, and always ready to learn and empathize (as seen in God's concern to learn about what was transpiring in Sodom and Gomorrah and in Egypt during the slavery of Israel) and intervene wherever possible, though sometimes that intervention might be delayed due to angelic opposition as Gabriel was held up by his battle

---

credulity (of which there is no scriptural record) but that believers experience varying degrees of relational intimacy with the Lord. Those who know the Lord as purely good, recognize that the Lord is not to be held accountable for their suffering or that in the world, loving God with all their heart, soul, mind, and strength, being drawn to do so the more amidst the direst straits, hence fulfilling the meaning of being of a beatific poverty of spirit (Matt 5:3), seeking always only to obey God in every particular circumstance and aspect of life, command a refulgent and infinitely enviable relationship with the Lord in which God will do God's utmost to preserve and protect them above all others.

with the prince of Persia in bringing Gabriel's message to Daniel (possibly till death) or a heavenly contestation.

The meaning of Paul's self-confessed struggle with a "thorn" (2 Cor 12:1–10 ESV) is to be understood as an attack from Satan, yet converted by God into a limited yet "sufficient" form of grace, by which Paul could be restrained from conceit. There is no indication that God subjected Paul to suffering so that he might be humbled, still less that this passage could be extrapolated from to suggest that God regularly puts believers through diseases and tribulations to deal with their pride so that so long as a believer is suffering from some such ailment or condition, it may be presumed that they must have committed the sin of contempt.

There are two poles in God's being; one, an impersonal field of existence and being out of which all initial existents, including angels who as a whole are capable of astounding creative works, are posited (Acts 17:28) and, two, an entitative triune subsistence, separate from the impersonal field of existence and being (e.g., Matt 3:16–17). God in Godself is not powerful or sovereign in the way we typically think. God is not like a more powerful version of Superman. Instead, God has very limited power of intervention and is closer to the image of a king, surrounded by courtiers ready to do his will, and having command of a vast, strong, and powerful army. By the same token, it is possible for God's will to be resisted by God's creatures.

There are certain situations of unjust suffering, even that which is grievous, which it is beyond even God's ability to preclude, and this divine limitation accounts for God's inability to cause the Son not to feel forsaken as the Son hung on the cross (Matt 27:46).[55] Christ died painfully on the cross in order that the words of forgiveness which he uttered there might be an everlasting sign of God's unremitting mercy toward us sinners; in all this we see that God cannot manipulate our thoughts and emotions and cause us to know God's profound forgiveness apart from the cross.

The image of God as limited is more accurate in view of biblical passages which depict God as a master of a house whose tenants of his vineyard were in breach of their obligation to give him a portion of the

---

55. The sense of abandonment by the Father that Jesus experienced on the cross infers that Jesus had called out repeatedly to the Father yet seemingly to no avail though in fact he was heard by one whose emotional presence he could no longer feel in consequence of the Father's seeming non-response to the abject pleas of the Son for emergency succor (Heb 5:7). This contrasts with Jesus' confidence in the face of arrest, on account of an incalculably greater intensity of distress felt by Christ as he endured the full weight of crucifixion (Matt 26:52–56).

fruit harvest (Matt 21:33-41) and as a nobleman who traveled to a distant country to receive a kingdom whose servants either obeyed or disobeyed his orders for them to invest the capital they received from him (Luke 19:11-27). Although God has the power to completely wipe out God's disobedient servants as in the two parables, that of the tenants and of the minas, it appears that God has no power to violate their personal autonomy and freedom to make their own decisions.[56]

Therefore Scripture is replete with incidents where God strives in situations involving God's people in which we find God expressing a decision to destroy God's people only to withdraw the decision in view of a changed scenario of the rise of an intercessor, one who cares about God's glory and honor, thereby making it worthwhile for God to continue bearing and walking with the community (Exod 32:7-14; Num 14:11-20). As such, even God cannot know the decision a person would make before it is actually made.

Is God too weak on this count? No, because there is no failure on the part of God, only that of the angels who rebelled, and God only seems weak when a comparison is drawn between a preexisting, unnecessary, and unjustified view of God's power and the proposed conception.

Etymology-wise, the conception of divine sovereignty generally associated as it is with the title for God, "the Almighty", this term occurs 58 times in the English Standard Version translation of the Bible across both Testaments. In the Old Testament, "Almighty" translates the Hebrew *El Shaddai* while in the New Testament it renders the Greek *Pantokrator*. Taking these terms in turn, *El Shaddai* may indicate God's ability to actualize God's promises to the patriarchs concerning how God would grant Abraham, Isaac, and Jacob along with their descendants such a blessing of fertility, sustenance, wellbeing, and protection that they would be able to produce kings in their line of ancestry, occupy the land of Canaan at some future point with lasting rightful possession to it, and carry on an everlasting covenant with God (Genesis 17; 35:11-12; 48:3-4).[57] As for *Pantokrator*, this word is constituted by a combination of two separate words, *panto*, referring to "all", and *krator*, a ruler or monarch.[58] It is noteworthy that *Kurios Pantokrator* constitutes a translation in the Septuagint

---

56. Not even Jesus could do anything about people being doubtful of his power to perform miracles, at whose unbelief he "marveled"; indeed, he was prevented by unbelief from performing more miracles (Mark 6:5-6 ESV).

57. *NBD*, s.v. "God, Names of" (Manley and Bruce, pp. 420-22).

58. LSJ, s.v. *krator*.

for YHWH ṣᵉḇāʾôṯ, Lord of hosts, underscoring God's nature as a deity, akin to a supreme royal conqueror to whom all lands and peoples owe their obedience, who makes battle through commanding both earthly and heavenly armies including the stars, spirits, and angels.[59]

Taken together, both divine titles appear not to imply God's overriding, meticulous, and manipulative power over all reality but rather God's rightful claim to the rule of the universe and sovereign mandate through God's command of earthly and heavenly armies, as well as God's ability both to begin and maintain an interminable covenant with the elect people of God including long-lasting, even miraculous, blessings of fertility, sustenance, wellbeing, and protection upon large groups of people over long periods of time. As such, there is no suggestion, etymologically speaking, that God is to be conceived as an omnipotent ruler in the sense of one who holds the puppet strings behind all reality; instead, the preexisting meanings of words that compose divine titles as well as the literary contexts in which they are used strongly point toward God's capacity, through powerful angelic representatives and agents, to actualize God's plan for a people group much the way an earthly ruler could accomplish, with the important distinction that God is an eternal ruler and one with supernatural angelic forces at God's disposal.

There are some biblical passages that attest to God's ability to do all things (Gen 18:14; Job 42:2; Jer 32:17; Matt 19:26; Mark 14:36; Luke 1:37). God is able to make barren women and virgins procreate, form the world according to God's purposes, and punish those who disobey God. It is true that God can indeed do all things in both the shorter and longer term. However, God does not achieve these goals through the use of force, but takes time to work with moral agents, guiding, commanding, and inspiring them to do the right and good thing. Naturally, given the implications of freewill, not all will obey God in the end, yet God will still have God's way in holding the power to judge and destroy all who refuse to repent at the last judgment.

Our view of God, therefore, is that God is sovereign, though not omnipotent; divine sovereignty is *de jure*, legal and rightful; *de facto*, effective, through the obedient action of God's angels; *potentially destructive*, insofar as God reserves and wields the power at any point, through God's obedient angels, to bring the entire universe to nothing; *delayed*, giving opportunity to the utmost for all sinners to repent; and *diligent*,

---

59. *NIDNTT*, s.v. "God" (Brown, p. 69).

THE CHRISTIAN DOCTRINE OF DIVINE CREATION

in that God does God's best to serve the practical needs of people, but this help may not always come through on account that God's effective sovereign action *depends* on the obedience of angels.

In relation to the question of theodicy, God's sovereignty is tempered by the following factors: (i) the fact that God relies and must rely on angelic representatives to execute God's interventions in the world for the good and protection of humanity, representatives which are *limited* in their (a) *power* (it is easier for the devil's agents to destroy than for God's to create and restore)[60] and (b) *number*; (ii) representatives whose *loyalty* may be subject to tergiversation; (iii) the fact that loyal angelic representatives of God may face fierce *opposition* from the devil and the devil's agents; (iv) the fact that God wishes to extend patient *mercy* to wrongdoers in affording them ample opportunity for repentance (Gen 15:12–16; Rom 2:2–11);[61] and (v) the hesitation, arising from *compassion*, due to the manner in which evildoers, even those of the worst kind, are always surrounded by innocent parties who are likely to sustain some form of traumatic psychological, relational, or physical harm in the event that the wrongdoers in question are punished, given the way in which, in God's eyes, the wellbeing of a few guiltless persons matters more than the punishment of the many guilty and the value of all innocent persons is equal, whether associated with the guilty or not.[62] These constraints on

---

60. It is well to note that it is far easier to destroy than to create. A relatively very small amount of energy is needed to bring something to its existential end, such as through the bursting of an artery, compared to restorative work in the human body or the formation of an invisible protective shield around a person about to be harmed or killed which requires creation and therefore the use of significantly larger amounts of energy. As a guide, a single human body contains a vast amount of latent energy. As for the act of material creation, this was a delicate and long-drawn-out process involving numerous angelic forces working harmoniously to produce atoms with the qualities they possess and the ability to combine into various molecules which, in turn and in the case of living things, form cells and the organisms they constitute; at every stage of the evolutionary process, the angels invest energy into equipping organisms to adapt to thrive in their changing environments.

61. On this basis, God the Father did not extricate Jesus from his wrongful arrest, scourging, and crucifixion, seeing that the Father had hoped that at some point the transgressors might repent, as well as appreciating that, should the crucifixion indeed be precipitated, Christ's death might serve as a perfect atoning sacrifice that would remove the burden of guilt and condemnation from those who believe in Christ and enable them to continue striving after and pursuing a godly life.

62. Gen 18:22–33; Jonah 4:11, the 120,000 people who cannot distinguish their left hand from their right likely a hyperbole comparing a great number in Nineveh with infants by way of expressing their vulnerability and dependence on the continued existence and prosperity of a wicked society; and Matt 13:24–30, 36–43, in which

the part of God and the agents of God's will explains why God is able to help certain people or in certain situations but not others.[63]

Given the limitation of God's power as a divine sovereign, not powerful in Godself in terms of compulsive or manipulative ability, yet having rule over angelic hosts with great yet also limited supernatural ability to create and destroy, a rule conditional upon their obedience and ability to overcome demonic opposition which works in a manner much likelier to succeed than that in which God and God's angels work, that is, destructively, how may a believer have any confidence in the final judgment? The fact that God still commands two-thirds of the angelic forces (Revelation 12) means that while God's angels being restorative in their approach may not be able to fully or in most or many cases stop or restrain the work of the devil and the devil's agents—it is far easier to destroy than to create, as in the case of the relative ease and difficulty with which a person may destroy and create a work of art—yet in the final judgment when God summons God's angels to cast the wicked angels and people into the lake of fire, this will be effectively done since at that time God adopts a destructive approach with a greater host.[64]

---

parable Jesus describes the good children of God as being entangled with evil persons, the former designating the innocent and good persons surrounding evildoers who will undoubtedly be negatively affected when God judges them, so that both for the sake of these innocents as well as the possibility that wicked persons might repent given additional time, God delays the final judgment.

63. The limitation arising from God's reliance on the disposition of angels accounts for the reason there tends to be more reports of miracles and "power encounters" in contexts where witchcraft is still prevalent, in that there are more evil spiritual forces in these settings requiring more spiritual "backup" in the form of benevolent and obedient angelic forces. Miracles are given only for the purpose of attesting that God is to be worshipped and that people ought not to fear demons. To the extent that this is not the situation in a particular context, we can expect that there will not be as many miracles.

64. The lake of fire mentioned in Scripture is not to be conceived as a place of external captivity, almost a highly surveilled incarceration facility par excellence. Such a facility would by no means be able to address the problem of sinfulness, any more than an earthly prison facility could, in that its inmates could very well put on better behavior or actually improve morally, thereby increasing the justification for their eventual release, making nonsense of the idea of an eternal judgment, and impugning the unadulterated goodness of a God who rejects repentance after a certain point. On the contrary, those who find themselves in a proverbial lake of fire are simply—continually and more intensely—subject to the painful delusions of their contempt of God and goodness as they persist in the mistaken belief that actions taken to obtain the objects of their carnal desires yield for them the greatest degree of benefit. The difference is that this time, that is, having crossed the final judgment, most of them are unlikely ever to repent and pursue the good, since they have already seen the face of God as judge and Father, who simply and only passes a verdict on their eternal destinies based

At this juncture, it is important also to appreciate that God cannot communicate directly with human beings, this because God does not speak the same language as people; God's language is too wonderful. God cannot simply learn human language because God is a different kind of being. Therefore when it is said that Jesus grew in wisdom and stature, this refers in part to his development of human linguistic and social skills. On account that God cannot directly communicate with or understand us, God will not be aware of our needs even though the Holy Spirit is within us. The only way God can become cognizant of our needs is through angelic messengers. This is why we have to pray, for through the process of prayer we signal to one of these messengers to bring a message to God on our behalf so that God may dedicate some of God's limited resources to attend to our needs.

It is not the case that God cannot directly interact with human beings because God exists in a completely different dimension. Such a conception was formulated in an effort to attest to and emphasize God's transcendent and absolute, superior nature. While God is indeed transcendent in God's instrumental pole as the Divine Nature, God is not transcendent but indirectly relational in God's personal and entitative dimension as the Trinity.

---

on whether they fulfilled God's moral requirement to love others (Matt 25:31-46, a parable which provides support for the doctrine of the Trinity in representing a final judgment before God as that which takes place before the Son just as the description in Rev 20:11-15 has the final judgment occur before God the Father), and thereby rejected this God. The torments of the final judgment therefore consist in the inexorable anguish the unrepentant souls bring upon themselves continually by reason of their free decision to grasp at the things they desire to possess in the false conviction that in owning these status symbols or objects of pleasure they will reach the fulfillment of their happiness and potential, this time without any possibility of being restrained by a discovery or rather rediscovery of the knowledge of God. Hellfire, consequently, is nothing more and less than the self-imposed agonies of the world extended ad infinitum and immeasurably more intense. Their anguish (expressed in weeping and the gnashing or angry grinding of teeth; see Matt 13:36-43; 22:1-14; 24:36-51; 25:14-30) will be immense and everlasting because the destructiveness of the final judgment consists in their being forever separated from the righteous by a forced relocation beyond the massive and towering ramparts of a heavenly city that is to be established on earth (Rev 21:12) and being made to live among one another outside the city (Rev 22:15), hence being compelled to suffer injustice at the hands of one another without end, given that their resurrected bodies do not die.

PART 1: CREATION'S IMAGING OF THE DIVINE

God and human value

God's nature is mirrored in the very human need for an interpersonal relationship in which each person's dignity is respected and their value is recognized rather than dismissed. Such a psychological condition for human wellbeing reflects the fact that the godhead is itself such a community in which its distinct members are respected and valued. It is for the very reason that each human individual was formerly exposed to and nurtured by such a divine community, prior to these beings giving up their previous angelic bodies and incarnating in human ones, that human persons are intrinsically oriented towards love, concern, and care for self, the human and divine other which expresses these relational priorities of dignity and value, from which they can never depart in the interests of their ultimate and fundamental wellbeing since it is in such dignity and value that they have their possibility and actuality as existents; it lies in their very nature to be regarded and to regard one another with dignity and value.

Those who reduce human value to some restrictive set of qualities, thereby alienating an individual person from themselves, their true identity, and a veracious assessment of their value, act as spiritual thieves who come to rob, murder, and bring to ruin rather than impart life (John 10:10). The regnant regimes of sensual, material, political, and vainglorious obsessions, fixations, and preoccupations of the world—we will refer to this complex of pursuits as concupiscence, a lust for these things, or admiration-mania, that is, narcissism—requisition the approval that rightly belongs to each person on account of their individual virtues, merits, and advantages and redistribute it in accordance to a hierarchy of hard or soft dominance, by which measure only those individuals who attain certain levels of achievement, restrictively understood, or possess desirable traits lionized in these hierarchies are accounted sufficient as people.

Human value or self-worth existing as it does inherently in each person on the basis of who they are as persons of dignity, value, with their own sets of virtues, merits, and advantages, the value of each person never contingent on how they measure up on some scale but always only rooted in their uniqueness and individuality, their free nature as moral agents, can and should never be commandeered by any self-proclaimed authority and parceled out, as if these things belonged to these "authorities", more to those it deems deserving than those it deems less deserving on a mad sliding scale, with the consequence that nobody is ever liberated from their captivity to these systems of measurement of human value, since even those currently at the top of the pyramids live under the constant fear that they might someday be overthrown, outflanked, conquered, beaten, or surpassed. Hence, those who pride themselves on their physical beauty often find it difficult to gracefully accept the processes associated with aging, while people who enjoyed relatively significant professional successes may have to grapple with a sudden or increasing loss of personal significance through their retirement years. Another pitfall is that those who are possessed of certain external characteristics wrongly thought to confer human value will discriminate against or devalue those without the same characteristics.

Herein lies the limitation of the technocratic society, in which people are valued based on certain achievements, such attainment being regarded as a form of merit in justification of an axiological system. It is not the case, however, that being able to attain a certain high level of education inter alia, as opposed to not being able to acquire the selfsame, suggests a higher value of the one who attains as compared to the one who fails to attain it, for not every person receives the same opportunities.[65] We ought to add to our non-exhaustive list of external attributes which are far too often and erroneously thought to confer human value the religious identity. Many adherents of a particular faith tradition, including Christians, may be inordinately proud of their religious affiliation, believing that they stand in a more spiritually meritorious position than others. In this case as in all others, however, it is not an external characteristic, including some religious or spiritual belief or experience—such as in or of Christ as sole justifier of a sinful and depraved humanity, constituting an objectification of religiosity that has, very lamentably, done the Christian church much harm and too little good to even begin to compensate for the harm—that confers any value on the human person as such but only the internal moral capacity of a human person and their actualization of this capacity.

To all these lies, deceptions, and delusions of society, God, the divine, or the ultimate opposes a mighty reproach, promulgating the quintessential axiom that each person is indeed enough, sufficient, adequate, satisfactory, and that no more is needed in order to secure a greater and deeper sense of self-worth. There is no need to add to the perfection of

---

65. Cf. Markovits, "Meritocracy Debate."

what God has wrought in the creation of humankind.[66] By the nature which they possess by creation, human beings constitute the divine image which Christ reveals in his divine-humanness. We do not need to divorce divinity from humanity as the ancient Greeks did in their constant oppositions between divine immutability and human mutability, if only because an essential moral commensurability obtains between God as entity and the human being.

The image of God, let it be clear, as well as the ultimate human value—in which a person can and must take refuge if they seek to avoid begrudging others what they may possess which the person in question inordinately values—consists uppermost in the distinction human beings bear in knowing themselves as individual persons equipped with the desire and freedom and vested with the responsibility to comport themselves, both internally and externally, in a manner that is interpenetrated by love, kindness, compassion, mercy, gentleness, righteousness, justice, patience, hope, temperance, longsuffering, fortitude, resilience, integrity, truthfulness, prudence, benevolence, empathy, holiness among other qualities representative of God in the Bible, in all their relationships, whether towards oneself, the human other, or God, in the consciousness that they depend on the divine or ultimate and human other as much as the human other may depend on them. Due to a moral-psychological dysfunctionality, these attributes of one's relationship with God, others, and self will often only be actualized in relation to those whom one values.

If God confers no insufficient, inadequate, or unsatisfactory nature on humankind, the unequivocally positive divine assessments pronounced in the first creation narrative reinforce this truth. It is sometimes inferred that when God the Father expressed the Father's personal delight with Jesus during the event of his baptism, this was a special favor only God the Son could conceivably enjoy. Yet, this is to neglect the crucial fact that the Bible speaks of both Jesus, as human, and any other human being as the image of God itself and created in the image of God respectively, so that God's positive disposition toward Jesus at his baptism is in fact God's positive disposition toward any other human being as well.

---

66. As such, Jesus did not require anything of the penitent thief who hung on the cross beside his for entering paradise (Luke 23:42–43). In point of fact, God's unconditional mercy presupposes a recognition of an inalienable human value, modeling the way relationships should be.

To be sure, people will disappoint God and have always done so. Even then, such human actions as may incur divine wrath do not quite deplete the value with which they were created. We know for a fact that disobedient sinners do not decrease in value before God, whatever Scripture may say about their worthlessness, because of the character of God's response to human transgression.

If it were indeed the case that human beings lose their value in the context of sinful behavior, God's response should either be indifference toward those God ceases to care about, or to exact vengeance upon those who caused God to suffer some form of loss, given that these transgressors no longer matter to God. Nonetheless, the Bible does not depict God as apathetic toward sinners—as a matter of fact, it is precisely God's love that impels God to wrath, for a person without a relationship with another person would not bother being enraged over the manner of their conduct unless it affects them personally—or determined to bring about their utter destruction purely out of anger at suffering personal loss as a result of their actions rather than on account of their grave immorality.[67] We have already considered the manner in which God continually holds out hope that the sinner might repent and live, rather than cutting off ties with them completely and desiring only their death (Cf. Ezekiel 18 and 2 Pet 3:9). For this reason, in God's encounter with human sinfulness in the instantiation that the kingdom of Judah was, Barth perceives God's suffering.[68]

God is indeed said to have given up certain groups of people, such as in Rom 1:18–32, but presumably only because they failed to repent and mend their ways, and also in order that their estrangement from God might facilitate their repentance (Cf. 1 Cor 5:1–5). It is simply because human beings were created with the dignity of being the image of God that they are expected to exercise moral responsibility for the way they live their lives, actualize their capacities, treat one another, and penalized for not living up to their vocation as human persons. The image of God, in this interpretation, consists in the human moral awareness, orientation, freedom, and responsibility; it cannot, consequently, be lost as a result of transgression, only betrayed with the promise that, with repentance and within the timeframe of one's human existence

---

67. Barth, *KD* IV.1, §61.2 (ET, Bromiley, p. 537).
68. Barth, *KD* IV.1, §60.2 (ET, Bromiley, pp. 477–78).

before the final judgment, though currently and for a long time left unactualized, it may yet be consummated.[69]

What is God's wrath save the perception of the human conscience that God's judgment is well-deserved in the event of transgression? This perception, good, natural, and right as it is, is rooted in the structure of the human soul and existence and is averted through faith in Christ's substitutionary and propitiatory atoning sacrifice.

In stark contrast to the world, God is not enamored of those with some advantage of physical attractiveness, material affluence, authoritative status, or achievements of some other sort. It was none other than the Lord Jesus himself who instructed the rich ruler to sell his many possessions, give the proceeds from them to the destitute, and follow him as a disciple (Luke 18:18–30), accounting obedience to God's call to participate in the mission of proclaiming divine compassion and ministering solicitude and empathy as supreme human ends.

The Son of God did not account tax collectors—who were regarded as traitors and exploitative—or prostitutes as unworthy of himself but dined with them (Matt 9:10–13; Luke 19:1–10). Jesus did not regard a woman with a reputation for being a sinner as less to be esteemed as a human person, going to the length of allowing her to demonstrate her affection and gratitude toward him for an act of forgiveness which he previously displayed toward her (Luke 7:36–50). Furthermore, he rendered a wise and compassionate verdict in relation to an adulterous woman brought by some scribes and Pharisees before him by drawing attention to how it is impossible for a sinner to condemn another sinner in a private capacity and exonerating the presumably contrite woman of her guilt (John 8:1–11).

The Lord taught his disciples to spend time with and express practical concern for those in physical need of any sort, whether it be on account of lacking the basic necessities of life or infirmity, or who are incarcerated; therefore, any who may be destitute and downtrodden or even morally disreputable, making known his personal identification with and concern for these and warning people who call themselves his disciples against neglecting such witness (Matt 25:31–46).

Jesus also forbore with those who were unreceptive towards him (Luke 9:51–56) or treated him cruelly, such as the disciple who betrayed him, soldiers who arrested him, mocked and beat him, and religious

---

69. Cf. Barth, *KD* IV.1, §60.3 (ET, Bromiley, p. 492).

leaders who falsely accused and humiliated him during the events of his passion. In all these respects, we see how Jesus extended forgiveness toward those who sought it and patience toward those who were not ready to admit their guilt and thereby surrender it for him to bear on their behalf, that they might receive true life.[70] He did not regard these persons, who for one reason or another had no cause to hold up their heads on account of their actions, as less worthy but deemed them persons of dignity and value equal to that of every other person. God considers all persons, regardless of what they may have done or what they do not have, as God's children.

So profoundly did Barth grasp divine love that he was able to discern in the Lord's three parables that the lost sheep, coin, and son remained well within the domain of the finder, who always only seeks and waits for them, as far as this immense patience will extend.[71] More recently, Pope Francis perceived God as a responsible paternal and maternal parent; like mothers who visit their children in prison, willingly bearing the social awkwardness of being seen in public lining up for their turn, because their tender affections and concern for the one they birthed move them so to do. Similarly, he says, God does not cease to hold out tender sentiments of love and expressions of solicitude for any who may stray, albeit the intimacy of relationship might be, one imagines, a cause of indignity or heartbreak for God, indefatigably awaiting the day of the sinner's repentance.[72] God's covenant with or commitment to each human person cannot be annulled, though people may fail to fulfill the obligations they owe to God.

The confiscation and unequal redistribution, the usurpation of human value began in the garden of Eden, where God instructed Adam not to consume the fruit of the tree of the knowledge of good and evil, a capacity and possibility, as we are later told by the devious serpent,

---

70. It is important at some point for a transgressor to allow themselves to experience the guilt of their conscience owing to their sinful deeds rather than suppress it, to own to the fact that they are truly sinners and in need of God's mercy of pardon and forgiveness (Prov 28:13). God's compassion cannot be construed in an instrumental way; while God desires to release the penitent sinner of their remorse, notwithstanding this, the precondition for this process of absolution is the very consciousness that one has sinned against God, others, and themselves. Accordingly those who seek to release themselves of guilt through denial of sin or complacency will not be justified by God (cf. Luke 18:9–14; Barth, *KD* IV.1, §60.2 [ET, Bromiley, pp. 445–46]; Barth, *KD* IV.1, §60.3 [ET, Bromiley, p. 478]).

71. Barth, *KD* IV.1, §60.3 (ET, Bromiley, pp. 480–83).

72. Pope Francis, *General Audience*.

reserved for God alone. It is God's sole prerogative to pronounce on the goodness or lack thereof of something, and it is instructive that the Hebrew adjective, *ṭôḇ*, used to indicate the nature of that which yields God's positive assessment, occurs, prior to the record of the command for Adam not to eat of the tree of the knowledge of good and evil, only in the context of God's delight over all the living and non-living things God had created in the first creation story.[73]

In short, human beings are to actualize and fulfill God's design for their existence, to work hand in hand one with another to fill the earth rather than divide and conquer, and to care for creation, rather than exploit it. This alternative and destructive vision of human existence is expressed in the term, *raʿ*, that which yields the opposite of God's positive assessment, that is, God's negative assessment, in its literary context.

In this sense, things which are adjudged by God not to be good but rather bad, fall beyond God's intended purpose for creation. This certainly encompasses that which departs from God's moral vision for humankind, as well as ideas which are diametrically opposed to God's apprehension of the nature of living and non-living things posited by God as their essence, including the conception of humankind as having been created in no less than the divine image, individually and collectively. There is no hint in the first creation story of some people being made "less equal" than others, as if lower equality were not an oxymoron, on account of what they possess in terms of physical, material, political, and productive assets. All are created in God's image and this image is internally and externally expressed in their interrelationships with self, the human other, creation, and God.

The tree of the knowledge of good, *ṭôḇ*, and evil, *raʿ*, represents the human will to depart from God's positive assessment of the created order, and embrace an ambiguous assessment in its place. It is noteworthy that prior to the first reference to the tree of the knowledge of good and evil in Gen 2:9, the word, *raʿ*, does not appear. Is this, then, to say

---

73. As a side note, humankind is pronounced "very good" (Gen 1:31 ESV), not in and of themselves, but only in the broader context in which as people made in the image of God and gendered, they are to procreate and steward all animals, whether it be the fishes of the sea, the birds of the air, or land creatures, to utilize plants and fruits for their food, and for the land animals and birds also to partake of plants. Human beings, therefore, have value indeed, but this is inseparable from their particular roles and functions, that is, the inward and outward expression of their inward nature as productive and protective entities, acting to the fullest extent of their individual personal capacities and potential.

that prior to the fall of humankind, God did not deem anything to be evil or bad? Perhaps the first occurrence of God's negative evaluation may be found in Gen 1:2, in which God observed that the world was formless, empty, and flooded with dark waters, a possible consequence of an earlier angelic rebellion.[74]

Reinforcing this interpretation is the way in which the story of Adam and Eve in Genesis 2 to 3 spotlights the question of nakedness and shame. At first, the couple were comfortable with their state of nudity (Gen 2:25). Subsequently, after consuming the fruit of the tree of the knowledge of good and evil, however, they developed a new and detrimental understanding of their nakedness, one coupled with a feeling of shame. Although in an English translation such as the ESV, it is odd that the pair should come to recognize their nudity only after eating the fruit of the tree, primarily because it translates two different Hebrew words identically, with one English word, "naked", rendering different Hebrew words in Gen 2:25 (ʿārôm) and Gen 3:7, 10, 11 (ʿêrōm), in which the latter word carries a negative connotation of privation and shame (cf. Deut 28:48; Ezek 16:7, 22, 39; 18:7, 16; 23:29), the fact is that, while Adam and Eve were not unaware from the beginning that they were unclothed, yet upon eating the fruit of the tree, they realized that they were naked in a different sense, in a sense in which they felt they were inadequate or deficient, such that they had to sew fig leaves with which to cover themselves, and unworthy of being in the presence of God, such that they had to attempt to evade God.

That they started feeling this way about themselves was a matter of great surprise for God who, on hearing from Adam that he hid from God because he was naked, asked him who informed him that he was naked in the sense in which he understood himself. In other words, Adam had begun feeling deficient and unworthy, that he was not enough in and of himself; physical nudity is used here as a trope to indicate that Adam did not accept the person that he was, but sought to make himself more adequate and worthy and less deficient and shameful in various ways. This is the dire situation in which sinful persons find themselves. They imagine that they could be more acceptable to God if they could clothe themselves more adequately; indeed, it is telling that Adam revealed his true

---

74. Barth, *KD* III.1, §41.2 (ET, Bussey, pp. 101–102). There need not be any reference to a gap between the opening two verses of Genesis 1, in the light of grammatical considerations, on which, see Fields, *Unformed and Unfilled*, 86. Gen 1:1 could very well be describing God's act of recreation.

motivation for hiding from God, not because he had sinned against God, but because he felt bare and naked, and this only because he had departed from God's valuation of him as good rather than evil or bad.

In a different era, Paul spoke of being overcome by covetousness when he learned that it was sinful to covet, and to such a degree that the sin of covetousness indwelled his person, causing him to commit sin against his conscience and fail to do the good that God requires and he agrees with (Rom 7:7–24). Paul found himself guided by a corrupt internal value system characterized by an obsessive pursuit of goods, be it material, social, or intellectual, ultimately, the pursuit of self-acceptance exclusively in and through the acceptance of others; this is an evil that can only be removed through being renewed in one's mind (Rom 12:2) in and through one's personal relationship with God in Jesus Christ (Rom 7:24–25), in which one returns to God's proper valuation of the human person, the human self, as adequate and worthy the way it has been made by God, with its moral faculty.[75] Adam's punishment by God in the garden of Eden was for hearkening to his wife's suggestion and encouragement to eat the fruit of the tree of the knowledge of good and evil; to this day, his descendants continue to eat from that tree. The only way to escape divine judgment is to return to God's positive valuation of our human dignity and worth, seeing ourselves once again as God's child, the way Adam was meant to live and Jesus lived (Luke 3:21–28).[76]

Regardless of whether one accepts our interpretation of the tree of the knowledge of good and evil, the truth remains that it is critical for humankind to accept God's axiological assessments. To usurp God's role of providing axiological standards and become an arbiter of them, as we see in a world riddled with social hierarchies fomenting narcissistic tendencies of all kinds, in which individuals begrudge other individuals who own physical, material, political, and productive assets their social advantages and pursue these very assets in order to secure a measure of social approval, is invariably to eat the fruit of the tree of the knowledge of good and evil, to thereby account oneself God rather than God—so the serpent had it right, in that in such axiological usurpation, human beings become not God in reality but something akin to God, a pseudo-divine

---

75. The very fact that such self-awareness and self-mentoring are possible implies not just a clear divide between God's moral ideals for humankind and an evil and disordered self, but also moral discernment as part of God's gift to humankind, posited in their nature and existence.

76. The human being is constituted by God's blessing (see Gen 5:2).

pretender—and suffer the severe consequences of abjuring God's assessment of good and bad; that is, humankind begins to create and accept an artificial form of shamefulness, of fear, insecurity, instability.

A shaping of human personality by abusive treatment during childhood discloses the reality of God as the source not just of human value but also human values. There are two sides to abusive and violent behavior experienced during the formative years of an individual: deep modeling and the personal experience of violation. When a child is treated in an abusive manner or witnesses a loved one being treated that way, their capacity to learn new attitudes and behaviors begins to incorporate abuse as a means by which to navigate an unknown world through an example set by an authority figure, along with their justifications, including the rationalization of one's abusive behavior on grounds that it was necessary for self-protection—to a person who has experienced abuse as a child, the world feels very unsafe and the perpetration of abuse seems to be the only answer—or that one cannot rein in one's aggressive urges; claiming the victim "deserved" the mistreatment; or due to fears of the consequences of non-conformity.[77]

Deep modeling of abusive and violent behavior leads to its psychological and behavioral normalization, disclosing the nature of human beings as image-bearers of some sort, as a malleable material capable of being molded under an engraving or embossing instrument. The term used for Jesus is that he is the *charaktēr* of God, that is, the impression made by the seal or molding instrument that is God the Father, metaphorically speaking, in the sense that Jesus as the Son is completely identical to the Father in the essence of the Son's being, nature, and character. This term referred to a Roman die used in minting coins in which images attached to the top and bottom surfaces were clamped in a hinged die and pounded to create identical impressions on the two faces of a coin.[78] In Philo, the term *charaktēr* is used to express the unique characteristics of a person such as their physical appearance or stature and psychological makeup, things which cannot really be modified and which have their origin in God's power.[79]

---

77. Gabbey and Raypole, "Aggressive Behavior"; Narvaez, "Child Humiliation and Mistreatment"; Gray, "Cycle of Abuse"; Dunlap et al., "Normalization of Violence," 1; Hartney, "Cycle of Abuse."

78. Lesso, "Ancient Roman Coins."

79. *NTDNTW*, s.v. "*charaktēr*" (transliterated), pp. 1329–30.

PART 1: CREATION'S IMAGING OF THE DIVINE

God, however, is not the sole embosser or minter of the human personality. God does emboss, mint, and mold in each human person the values worthy of God and humanity, through a pre-terrestrial encounter between God and these human persons, then existent as angelic beings, but God bears no responsibility for human dysfunctionality, which is developed especially during the formative years of a child through the uncritical acceptance by a child of abuse and violence as "normal", "right", or "sustainable" ways of thinking, feeling, or behaving. This dual polarity brings an individual into conflict within themselves, engendering internal anguish, as when a person awakens to their dysfunctionality and begins to rue their past conduct or struggles with present moral conduct on account of a clash between the awakened conscience and inconsistent behavior.

As for the personal experience of violation, as much as the normalization of abusive treatment rationalizes it, there will be a part of the person that feels aggrieved on account of mistreatment, which strongly violates internal sensibilities developed during a pre-terrestrial existence.

A man with a former experience of gender dysphoria, currently detransitioned, presents a curious case attesting to how self-aggression can be linked to a sense of insecurity and fear.[80]

Due to the etiology of his psychological condition, rooted as it is in his feeling of parental rejection coupled with the sense that if he were born a woman he would have been better accepted given his experience of physical, sexual, and psychological abuse by two men who treated and regarded him as a girl including in a context of bondage and domination, constituting his first experience of physical touch to which he grew accustomed and which he interpreted as affectionate, he came to develop two kingdoms in his life; one, a domain in which he struggles as a man and expresses himself in anxiety and self-directed aggression and, two, a domain in which he fantasizes that he is a girl or woman—for a time transitioning to fully identify as one—and is able to become vulnerable and gentle.

The very fact that he is emotionally and sexually turned on not by all situations of vulnerability or lack of control (indeed, he is repelled by most of such situations) but only those in which he is forced by a man to don skimpy and uncomfortable attire and thereby subject to a more

---

80. Examples of gender detransitioners should not be weaponized against transgender persons as "role models" imposed on them to emulate. Each person's gender identity is sacred to themselves.

powerful force and exposed to possible public objectification infers that his emotional and sexual fascinations are unnatural rather than inborn.

He understands his past experience of gender dysphoria in this way: a child with a normal and healthy upbringing receives physical affection from his parents; such affection is necessary for a child in the first year of life to develop a sense of safety and security which it will carry into its adult life. Not only was parental affection withheld in this way,[81] but the first remembered experience of physical affection took place in the context of emotional and sexual abuse as well as gender contestation.

Whereas physical affection on the part of parents is geared toward establishing resilience through recognizing the child's existence and affirming its value, the extraordinary circumstances in which it was mediated in this man's case served to introduce a condition for resilience: to be accepted and valued, he would have to become a woman. It did not help that he was conscious that in his social context girls and women were in a position, at least in a visible manner, to receive more affection from family, friends, and partners—a fact of life an emotionally healthy man would be able to comprehend and accept because they have no doubt they are truly loved, though in different ways.[82] He now recognizes his need to acknowledge that he is accepted as a man and can stand on his own feet as one.

A recollection of how as a child he felt that he was unloved and therefore unprotected as a boy, hence rejecting his male appearance as ugly—on some level even as a child he could appreciate the true offense of the acts of abuse to which he was subjected, and developed the opinion that had he been born a girl his parents might have done more to protect him from such encounters—has led to a considerable reduction of his need to visualize himself as a young woman subject to controlling behavior.

For this man, the past experience of rejection is confirmed and triggered by moments when family members raise their voices at him or misunderstand or distrust him, suggesting the presence of an unresolved

---

81. He was almost aborted by his mother, surviving only through the pleading of his father who, as he remembers, never displayed physical affection toward him.

82. He recalls feeling intensely envious when his father proudly showed him an old photograph of the former allowing his elder sister as a toddler to take a staged shot of her sitting in the driver's seat of his father's previous and much-beloved car, with his father standing beside the vehicle, because his father had never displayed a similar sign of affection for him. Moreover, he recollects that while he was still identifying and living as a woman, his mother showed him considerably more tenderness.

emotional wound. Dysfunctional behavior in the form of disproportionate emotional responses is facilitated by such emotional triggers in addition to false and unhelpful beliefs about oneself and others which were accepted as a child through defective reasoning in consequence of a conflation of emotional and sexual abuse with loving affection.

This situation can be helped by greater self-clarity and healing relationships, that is, a pattern of interactions with one or more persons in which the man in question is heard and empathized with as to his pain, and treated with fairness and kindness.[83] How can such a person be helped toward the knowledge that the world God created is not fundamentally unfair? They can understand that if it were not for the crippling envy they feel toward the other gender, if they were able to appreciate the beauty of the other gender without feeling saddened that they do not share it, then life would be actually not just bearable but even pleasant.

If unnatural patterns of self-feeling and thought can be developed in the context of abuse and neglect, then other unnatural patterns of self-feeling and thought can result from a posture of resignation as a means of coping with harsh circumstances. As a case in point, the same person developed a sense that unless he is exemplary in his physical appearance and intellect—for his parents praised his siblings for possessing those very qualities—he has little value, as another means by which his then maturing young mind sought to make sense of his rejection, an immature emotional response that has not been overcome.

Still on the subject of axiology, related to our need to eschew robbing God of God's role of providing axiological norms, the concept of heresy may no longer be a helpful category. The notion in specific religious traditions that certain beliefs are to be proscribed on the ground that they contradict core beliefs or are harmful in some way to their specific spirituality served a beneficial role in defining and distinguishing their most important and foundational ideas from those of other traditions, on occasion in contexts in which spiritual life and death may be decided.

Irrespective of this and even in the most fundamentalist milieux, it remains imperative for religious communities to maintain links with the wider world by refraining from denunciations of those with whom they may disagree. It is one thing for a religious group to define its particular beliefs; it is quite another for the same group to claim that those beliefs, in the substance and shape in which they are held, necessarily render

---

83. Cherry, "Erikson's Stages of Development."

the group superior to another religious group, to the extent that they are made preferable and perhaps even critical and obligatory, on the basis of some ultimate benefit reposing in espousing the beliefs of this group as opposed to some notion of ultimate harm or destructiveness residing in holding the beliefs of some or any other group, for members of that group to seek to prevail upon those holding other religious views to alter their views and bring them in conformity with those of the religious community in question.[84]

The net effect of strongly forbidding certain ideas from being held is twofold. First, authentic and abiding personal learning is hobbled, in which an individual is presented with or identifies a number of possible perspectives on an issue, marshals their own intellectual energies in considering the value of each option through deliberating on expert opinions defending different positions in the debate before arriving at a personal intuition and conviction regarding the preferred perspective. Second, restricting the flow of ideas within strict religious communities has the effect of writing off whole perspectives and approaches which have value in themselves in that most religious or intra-religious systems, barring those which advocate unethical psychological and social practices including brainwashing or isolationism, distrust of political or medical authority, or outright immoral behavior, are governed and regulated by principles which promote a lifestyle of balance between material and spiritual aspects, community and solidarity within a group, cooperation and goodwill beyond it.

---

84. Steven Nemes outlines five features of a theology "without anathemas". This involves drawing a careful distinction between an opposition of orthodoxy and heresy and the subject of truth. Nemes stresses that any language of orthodoxy is one that debates differing ideas about a referent, whereas truth as a subject concerns the relationship between an idea and the thing of which it is an idea. He contends that one does not need to define truth in the definite terms of precise statements of belief and interpretation, given that it is preferable to acknowledge that no group has a monopoly on the truth, but any group's ideas will be deficient in some way. According to Nemes, such a theological stance is capable of remaining confessional while recognizing that beliefs will always be contextually situated, that what ultimately matters is one's personal trust in Jesus and the salvation that he brings through his atoning death without claiming to know everything about God and God's purposes for humankind and the world. We have to demur on the point about religious knowledge being "fallible", emphasizing our view that each religious or non-religious tradition attests many things that are completely true and metaphorically harmonizable about the divine or ultimate and the fundamentum for mutual religious appreciation is solely the fact that all human persons are bound by a common, irreducible, and irreversible sense of morality. Nemes, *Orthodoxy and Heresy*, 54–57.

To sanction religious and intra-religious groups on the basis that they do not measure up to or harmonize with the doctrines of a religious group in question is to deprive members of the group of an opportunity to receive different perspectives on the common human concern that is morality and spirituality. A religious leader need not fear that exposure to different viewpoints would result in adherents of their group turning to other faiths or sects, since human persons are vested with personal autonomy and moral responsibility for identifying, committing to, and practising or being consistent in their attitudes and actions with the particular worldview they espouse. The sole obligation and contribution of the religious authority is to present confessional ideas in a cogent manner which facilitates personal learning while respecting the autonomy of the individual in having the freedom to explore alternatives beyond the religious community in question.

Instead of proscribing beliefs that are not beyond the pale of psychological, social, or moral ethics, it is more helpful to promote the practices of theological charity, where a professing Christian believer chooses to entertain the possibility that groups with alternative views sprout because they meet legitimate needs, thereby drawing attention to these needs and permitting a consideration of whether we might already be meeting them adequately and to ways in which these groups might be effective in ministering to those needs, which one might learn from. Also salutary is theological silence, in which a believer recognizes that it may not always be their place to dogmatically correct a person who appears to have developed fixed erroneous or distorted views on the Christian faith, given that the rejection of a fairer and more accurate conception might very well be on account of strong emotional experiences and interpretations, and an insistence on dogmatic rectitude can only lead to altercation, relational damage, and a further misperception of the Christian faith on the part of the person being corrected. In such a context, a person will be far better served through the Christian speaking less and praying more for the former, in their heart, both when they see the person and whenever they think of them (John 16:8–11).

Trinitarian doctrine

Our conception of the Trinity as community of love, in which a single divine being is perichoretically constituted by three equally and fully divine persons, differs broadly from Barth's understanding.[85] To be sure, Barth holds that the divine image in humankind consists in a relationality modeled ultimately after that of the triune fellowship, one which is intended to be lived out on the part of the human person in correspondence to the internal relationships of the godhead, the way God interacts with humankind in their covenantal relationship, and the way Jesus interacts with other human persons.[86] One of his entryways into his interpretation of the biblical teaching on God as Trinity which is more fruitful for formulating his doctrine resides in his discussion of the subordination of the Son.

As against subordinationism, which Barth defines as the Son as subordinate constituting a different heavenly or earthly entity from the Father, he contends that there are not two different beings between a commanding Father and an obedient Son, but one God in two modes of being as commanding (vs. obedient), disposing (vs. compliant), eternally begetting (vs. eternally begotten), originating (vs. consequential) Father, and obedient (vs. commanding), compliant (vs. disposing), eternally begotten (vs. eternally begetting), consequential (vs. originating) Son. Against modalism, which Barth defines as the Son as subordinate being conceived as an improper mode of appearance of God (the Father being proper and the Son a manifestation on earth), he holds that the commanding Father and the obedient Son represent the eternal godhead in which a commanding Father and an obedient Son eternally exist as two modes of one being.

In Barth's trinitarian doctrine, there is, in God, an above and a below, a first and a second, a *prius* and a *posterius*, both equal and immanent within the one God. The first mode of God's being commands, the second obeys, and the third (the Holy Spirit) unites the first two while keeping them intact. There is only one personality in God, one center of identity, consciousness, cognition, volition, activity, effects, revelation, and name, existing eternally in three modes of being, two self-repetitions of the one original: the Father of the Son, the Son of the Father, and the Spirit of the Father and the Son. The Father is not apart

---

85. For a statement and articulation of my understanding of the Trinity, see Chua, STEA/"Biblical-Cultural Trinity," particularly chapters 2, 3, 5, and 6; Chua, GGG; and Chua, ECRST, especially chapters 5 and 7.

86. Barth, KD III.2, §45.3 (ET, Bromiley, pp. 323–24).

from the Son and the Son, the Father; the Father needs the Son to be Father, and the Son, the Father, to be Son.[87]

In consequence, through a doctrine of the subordination of the Son, Barth articulates a doctrine of the Trinity that is synchronic modalistic. It is modalistic in that like Sabellianism or modalistic monarchianism Barth understands the Father, Son, and Holy Spirit as the three modes of the single person that God is. Unlike Sabellianism or modalistic monarchianism, which espouses the belief that the Father, Son, and Holy Spirit as the three modes of the single person that God is, are diachronic; that is to say, they do not exist simultaneously but the single person that God is takes up these different modes of God's being and personality as needed, Barth holds that the Father, Son, and Holy Spirit as the three modes of the single person that God is, do exist concurrently.

The Cappadocian Fathers with their conception of relations of origin in the triune godhead apprehended that the divine essence is not to be identified with any one divine person; for if to be God is to be, say, the Father, then the Son and the Holy Spirit would not be divine. Barth, however, takes this idea to the extreme, contending that the single divine essence does not belong to any one of the three persons, not even as a shared attribute, but only to the single divine personal consciousness, mind, and will, with the implication that the persons constitute mere modes of being, media, almost, through which the single divine consciousness is eternally expressed in three different ways, including the commanding mode of the Father, the obedient mode of the Son, and the mode of the Holy Spirit, expressive as it is of the love internal to the godhead and that between God and the created order. In speaking of the incarnation of Christ as reflective of the eternal subordinate relation of the Son to the Father, Barth appears to espouse the idea of an eternal functional subordination of God the Son to God the Father as modes of a single divine being.[88]

---

87. Barth, *KD* IV.1, §59.1 (ET, Bromiley, pp. 195–210). In Barth's apprehension, the eternal and divine Son exists in a relationship to the Son's subordinate role in a manner that is natural rather than foreign, and the Son carries out the Son's subservient role without any compulsion, pride, or demand. Barth, *KD* IV.1, §61.2 (ET, Bromiley, p. 564). Cf. Barth's definition of the Holy Spirit as Christ considered as all-efficacious agent of sanctification in revealing himself to humankind, subjecting them to his direction and claim on them as a mirror of his sanctity in *KD* IV.2, §66.2 (ET, Bromiley, p. 522).

88. *KD* IV.2, §64.2 (ET, Bromiley, pp. 42–44).

Karl Rahner's conception of the Trinity in its threeness and oneness is in many ways similar to Barth's construal, in that the former also conceives of the triune godhead as having but one self-consciousness rather than three: "But there exists in God only *one* power, *one* will, only one self-presence, a unique activity, a unique beatitude, and so forth."[89] As a matter of fact, as far as Rahner is concerned, there is no possibility of a triune person conferring with another triune person within the godhead. There is, therefore, only one divine consciousness, mind, and will, faculties ascribed exclusively to the one being of God itself; in this way, the divine persons function as modes or instruments through which the one divine consciousness and mind is revealed, manifested, and actual.

How can the idea that there is just one God be reconciled with the other idea that there are three fully divine persons, the Father, the Son, and the Holy Spirit, each of whom is not identical to any other?

The logical problem of the Trinity surfaces in consequence of a latent latency to conceive of the divine persons in formal opposition one to the other. In short, the doctrine of the Trinity represents an insoluble problem only to the extent that one defines the Father, and the Son, and the Holy Spirit as more or less separate entities, irrespective of any purported monotheistic affirmation, owing to an inordinate humanization or anthropomorphization of the triune persons. One is easily led to imagine that the Father's being is completely separate from that of the Son and the Holy Spirit. Such a logical process serves only to set the stage for the doctrine of the Trinity becoming a contradictory idea. In truth, each divine person has being only on the basis of the being of the other two persons.[90] As such, the Father is Father only if the Son also exists—the Father's very name implies this truth. It is impossible to be a father without having a child. Likewise, the Son cannot exist as the Son without the Father. A person who does not have a parent cannot truthfully refer to themselves as a child. If Father and Son are relational names, so is Holy Spirit. This is in view that the Holy Spirit is defined as the Spirit of the Father and the Spirit of the Son, intimating an irreducible closeness between the Spirit and the Father and the Spirit and the Son without suggesting that the Father and the Son do not exist as distinct spiritual entities.

---

89. Rahner, DG, 2.c.5.b (ET, Donceel, pp. 75–76).
90. Cf. Athanasius, *Contr. Ar.*, 1.5.14 (ET, Newman and Robertson, pp. 314–15).

Father, Son, and Holy Spirit are not to be conceived as separate as to their being, but always ontologically interdependent and mutually constitutive. The conception of the Father should always bring to mind also the Son and the Holy Spirit, who are integrated, incorporated, included, entailed, and encompassed in the Father's being. Similarly, the conception of the Son should always bring to mind also the Father and the Holy Spirit, who are integrated, incorporated, included, entailed, and encompassed in the being of the Son, and the conception of the Holy Spirit should always bring to mind also the Father and the Son, who are integrated, incorporated, included, entailed, and encompassed in the being of the Holy Spirit.[91] In this way, the coherent reality of the Trinity explodes the myth that the doctrine of the Trinity is self-contradictory, safeguarding the truth of an internal divine relationality among the three persons, who constitute one God both together and in each person considered individually.

The solution to the three-one problematic of the Trinity lies in the objective-subjective distinction. There is just one objective divine substance; three unique personal identities each subjectively encompass this one objective substance, so that three persons each lay claim, each as the one true God, to the whole substance as their own without competition or rivalry, and the being of the three persons is numerically identical as a concrete object, excepting only the personal identity, consciousness, and agency distinctive to each of the three persons.[92] In this way, the three divine persons share the one divine substance, in a numerically identical way, taking turns to use it in a seamless way.

Furthermore, each of the three persons is indispensable to the whole, objectively contributing a unique element to the divine substance (whether the faculty of wisdom, will, or agency of action and affect, as well as the structure and system of the person's unique personal essence), though not in such a way that the divine persons have ever preexisted, been apart from, or been out of complete integration with each other, each person subjectively defining and identifying themselves as a person for whom the entire objective divine substance constitutes that person's objective being.[93]

In concrete terms of identity, consciousness, and agency, the Father is primarily seated on the Father's throne in heaven, yet secondarily

---

91. Gregory of Nazianzus, *Or.* 40.41 (ET, Browne and Swallow, p. 375).
92. Cf. Barth, *KD* IV.2, §64.1 (ET, Bromiley, p. 5).
93. Chua, *GGG*, 83–93; Chua, *STEA*, 199–200.

present also in the Son and the Holy Spirit. The Son is primarily seated at the right hand of the Father, yet secondarily present in the Father and the Holy Spirit. The Holy Spirit exists wherever the Spirit is present in many places around the world, yet is also secondarily present in the Father and the Son. In terms, however, of being, the Father consists not just of the being that exists in the Father seated on the heavenly throne, but also of the being that exists in the Son and the Holy Spirit, though with only the identity, consciousness, and agency of the Father; the same principle applies to the Son and to the Holy Spirit, mutatis mutandis.[94]

Such a view coheres with a Cappadocian accent on the concrete nature of the single substance of the godhead, as well as their conception of the three divine persons as distinct "distributions" and "presentations", "modes of coming to be" or "a mode of existence or relation" (Amphilochius of Iconium), of the single and indivisible godhead, distinguished by their origin and their relation with respect to one another.[95]

There is no "transitivity of identity" in which the identity between a divine person and "God" leads to the divine persons being identical to each other.[96] There is no exhaustive and complete equivalence between "God" and any one divine person such that a divine person constitutes a static definition of "God", thus making it impossible for the divine persons to differ in any way if they are to be each equated with "God". This is a misconception of the category, "God", which is not exactly identical to a divine person.

How, then, is "God" to be defined? This may be done in one of three ways; the necessary and sufficient conditions for an entity to belong in the category, "God", are that it comprises the divine substance, as well as the personal identity, consciousness, and agency of any one of the three divine persons.

This is how Jesus can designate the Father the only true God without detracting from his own full divinity (John 17:3). That a divine person does not ontologically encompass the personal identity, consciousness, and agency of the other two divine persons is not to divide the divine being into parts, since identity is not a part of a being, but suffuses it entirely, and a being is complete with just one identity rather than all three at once. There are not three parts in the divine reality, but three subjects, three

---

94. Chua, ECRST, 173–187.
95. Kelly, Early Christian Doctrines, 265–66, 268.
96. Sijuwade, "Logical Problem of Trinity," p. 3 of article.

self-identifications within the divine reality, each encompassing the divine reality fully with the exception of the other two self-identifications.

Barth's conception of the local congregation as the fullness of the body of Christ or the gateway into the entire body of Christ which is contained within itself as well as his apprehension of the individual Christian as the fullness of the entire congregation and gateway into the whole local assembly of the saints is helpful in bringing us closer to an understanding of how the entire godhead is contained within each divine person as a gateway to its fullness, analogically, without any suggestion that the Trinity is to be thought of as akin to a congregation of three human individuals.[97]

Knowing about any one divine person ushers the knower into the knowledge of the fundamental moral essence that characterizes all three divine persons, as well as the identity and character of the specific divine person qua person in relation to the other divine persons, affording a glimpse into that of the other divine persons, seeing that all three persons are interdependent and each encompasses the others, save their personal identity and consciousness, in their being.

Similarly, given a trinitarian structure in a theology of religion, knowing about any one religion yields insight into the fundamental moral character of all religions and humanism, bolstering the understanding of that moral essence given the possibility of underemphasis of one or more aspects of the moral nature of religion in any one particular religious tradition.

All religious paths do lead to the knowledge of the same God, yet it would be inaccurate to suggest that therefore salvation can be discovered in all religious traditions, for the concept of salvation may not be found in other religions.

The distinctive Christian conception of salvation is to be interpreted in terms of God's forgiveness of our sins through the atoning act of Jesus Christ on our behalf which we can always access through repenting and appealing to God for God's pardon. Yet, this simply marks the beginning of the journey, for what ultimately matters is moral virtue, and whichever religion a person may pursue, or if a person is a humanist, their beliefs are fundamentally about pursuing moral good. Although there will be a concept of forgiveness in other religious traditions, including divine pardon, it may not be referred to as salvation.

97. Barth, *KD* IV.1, §62.2 (ET, Bromiley, p. 681); Barth, *KD* IV.1, §63.1 (ET, Bromiley, pp. 753–57).

Part 2: **Humanity's Imaging of the Divine**

Introduction

THE CENTRAL THESIS OF the second part is that the incarnation, far from being incidental to God's essence or purely instrumental in the divine economy of salvation, is the key to understanding the eternal nature of God.

God's very being, nature, and character is disclosed by the very humanity of the incarnation of Christ, not as a transformation underwent—incidental to God's essence—in order to fulfill purely instrumental ends that cannot be fulfilled by earlier prophets including exemplifying to human beings how they ought to live (on the assumption that people would not understand God in God's infinitude) and dying in atonement for human sin (on the Platonic assumption that God being immortal is not capable of undergoing death).

Contrary to being simple, immutable, impassible, and infallible, as well as seemingly unheeding toward numerous desperate human cries for succor, God's essence undergoes a complete transformation, relative to preexisting and older theologies, in the direction of humanity; God's moral sense is situated on the same plane as that of humankind, the only difference being that God's morality is unparalleled in degree.

By the lights of classical Hellenistic, specifically Platonic, thought forms, the divine stands in a stark antithesis to the human, God being seen not merely as the supreme source of all creation but also unchanging and simple as absolute being, who is, lives, and knows in an absolute sense; not merely as the origin of beings, but also the very fabric of reality that enables each thing to be and exist as what it is, inferior reality completely determined as to their fundamental nature by absolute reality with no possibility of in any way affecting and therefore relating to that absolute being.[1]

In Augustine's reading, Platonist philosophers ascribe to God the function of being the origin of the earth with its physical shape, attributes, and regular motion, as well as all things which exist within its sphere; of all living things, be it botanical, animal, human, or angelic existence.[2] As Augustine writes, "all can only *be* through Him who absolutely *is*."[3]

Augustine homologates what he perceives to be a right Platonist emphasis on divine simplicity and immutability. According to him, the Platonists do not hold God to be an inert magnitude, a transcendent source beyond having mind or consciousness, but a being that always has perfect life, understanding, and blessedness simply because God has these qualities, not as accidents but as complete dimensions of God's substance, as inalienable traits that define God as the being God is, permanent attributes from which God can never be divorced; God's simplicity dictates that God's being is identical to God's attributes and that, hence, God cannot gain or lose any of God's qualities in the course of God's existence. In this respect, one thinks of how a human spirit cannot be devoid of its self-identity, given that the ability to perceive oneself as self, formally differentiated from all other selves, is an essential sign that one has a spirit, and an essential capacity of the spirit.

God's immutability is an entailment, culmination, and conclusion of a Platonist theory of gradually ascending perfections in the created order, in which the differing beauty or perfection of a physical thing or the reliability of the assessments of the human mind which are enhanced by intelligence, skill, practice, and experience, point ultimately to a highest perfection, not subject to improvement or decline.

The fact that God is immutable perfection is essential to God's ability to consciously and intelligently intervene to produce or generate all things in the world; were God's perfection equal to or less than that in the world God created, were divine perfection capable of being lost or acquired, God could not create those things which possessed a higher degree of perfection, or maintain them when God became less perfect than them, if this could be so; it is important to aver that God cannot acquire perfection which God does not already have because if such perfection ever existed in the world, God could not have made its bearer.

1. Augustine, *Civ.*, 8.6 (ET, Dods, pp. 250-51).
2. Augustine, *Civ.*, 8.6 (ET, Dods, pp. 250-51).
3. Augustine, *Civ.*, 8.6 (ET, Dods, p. 251).

INTRODUCTION

As Augustine writes, the Platonists "have understood, from this unchangeableness [that is, the fact that God constitutes the highest and greatest perfection that stands at the apex of all lower degrees of perfection found in physical things and the human mind, making it possible for God to create everything in existence] and this simplicity [that is, the simplicity in which God's being is identical to God's life, understanding, and blessedness, in such a way that God cannot gain or lose any of these qualities], that all things must have been made by Him, and that He could Himself have been made by none."[4]

It is fair to say that in Augustine's interpretation the followers of Plato conceived of God as an intelligent maker of all things, seeing that Augustine ascribes to them the idea of God as having life, understanding, and blessedness as integral qualities of divine being and the notion of God's unchanging and supreme perfection, rather than merely God's power or natural properties, as a prerequisite for God's making of the world.

According to Augustine, the Platonists "saw that there is some existence in which is the first form, unchangeable, and therefore not admitting of degrees of comparison, and in that they most rightly believed was the first principle of things, which was not made, and by which all things were made."[5]

The idea of divine immutability supports the notion of divine transcendence. If God in Platonist thought cannot change, then God cannot possibly share the same realm of existence as the created order in a way that creatures could relate to God. For any divine-creaturely interaction would entail God doing something God had never done before, such as addressing a creature with a particular set of words at a particular point in time. To allow this would undermine the doctrine of God's radically unchanging nature in which God as pure act does not possess any unactualized potentiality.

Such was the physical or natural theology that undergirded the theological constructions of St. Augustine of Hippo and Christian theologians of earlier times who contributed during the christological controversy of the late fourth and early fifth centuries.

In Christ, it was adjudged paradoxical for one nature of his to be divine and another human. For though certain Christian theologians could admit of a divine nature, transcendent and inaccessible due to its

---

4. Augustine, *Civ.*, 8.6 (ET, Dods, p. 251).
5. Augustine, *Civ.*, 8.6 (ET, Dods, p. 251).

unchangeability though it be, becoming incarnate—in a secondary mode of existence without nullifying or undermining a primary while still faithfully communicating God's presence and intentions to humankind[6]—in such a way as to be capable of relating with contingent physical human beings, yet the notion of it as subject to growth, need, or suffering could not be countenanced because of its attributes of simplicity and indivisibility, which entail that God's existence be identical to God's possession of God's attributes and therefore that God always be in possession of these attributes; independence; and impassibility.

In Leo's interpretation, so decisive for subsequent theological understanding of the nature and personhood of Christ, the divine Word is capable of "performing" in time miracles just as the human nature of Christ stands subject to "injuries".

It was none other than the Word which multiplied the five loaves and two fish for the consumption of thousands, granted the Samaritan woman living water which eliminated all spiritual thirst, walked on water, and rebuked the winds to still the waves, yet the human nature which enabled Christ to suffer the need for food, water, and rest.

Similarly, though the human nature of the Lord made it possible for him to be moved at the death of his friend Lazarus, yet it was only his divine nature which allowed him to command Lazarus to return to earthly existence; though as human, Christ could but be confined to the cross to

---

6. As such, these patristic writers of theological orthodoxy do permit the possibility of God's assumption of a secondary mode of existence as doing no violence to the idea of God as immutable, seeing as that immutability may be conceived as applying specifically to divine existence in the transcendent domain and not also to God's additional existence in the contingent realm. In the view of Keith Ward, patristic theological orthodoxy, such as in the persons of Tertullian, Gregory of Nazianzus, and Cyril of Alexandria, opposes the idea of the divine Word as the psychological subject constituting the center of cognition, experience, and agency of Jesus of Nazareth. Ward, *Religion and Revelation*, 267–69. At one point, Ward avers that Christ is unique and distinctive in his association with God the Word only in a quantitative sense—Christ, like all other human beings, is dependent for his human existence on God; unlike all other human beings, there is no division between Christ the human being and the divine source on which he depends—and, consequently, to speak of a divine subject in Christ is simply to highlight a divine ground of Christ's existence: "It is because of this indivisible unity, and because every finite being receives its reality solely from God, that the Word can be termed the subject, the existential ground which supports and is unimpededly and creatively expressed in the human subjectivity of Jesus." Ward, *Religion and Revelation*, 269. This appears to run counter to the central motif in patristic orthodoxy, powerfully articulated by Athanasius in the heat of the Arian controversy, relating to how Christ is no mere creature (not even the only human being with whom God can be said to be in unimpeded union) but Godself in the flesh.

which he was pierced, yet as divine, he was able to cause darkness to envelope the land and create an earthquake; while Christ's human nature could not escape the cross, even so his divine nature enabled him to admit a thief to paradise; even though as a human person, Jesus could only concede that his Father exceeds him in greatness, yet as a divine person, the same could declare that he is one with the Father. Consequently, patristic Christology continued to require a means by which to reconcile the antitheses of divinity and humanity in the single person of Christ.[7]

As one can clearly see, Christian theologians such as Leo admitted the possibility of a person with a divine nature being embedded in the space-time continuum in which all human beings are situated. Concurrently, he continued to discern an antimony between that which is divine and human in Christ, clearly differentiating between the proper works of each nature: "For each form does what is proper to it with the co-operation of the other; that is the Word performing what appertains to the Word, and the flesh carrying out what appertains to the flesh. One of them sparkles with miracles, the other succumbs to injuries." Furthermore, "it is not part of the same nature" to perform miracles and sustain need and debilitation.[8]

There need, however, be no formal dichotomy between divinity and humanity. The very fact and possibility of Christ as both fully human and fully God at one and the same time attests to the inherent reconcilability of the divine with the human. Whilst Chalcedonian Christology proposed a synthesis between Platonic philosophy and the scriptural presentation of Christ as Son of God and Son of Man, in which the divine-human antithesis was carefully preserved, a more thoroughgoing construction is necessary, particularly in light of cultural mediation in Christian theology and how this has impacted orthodox doctrinal definitions such as the Chalcedonian doctrine of Christ.[9]

Humanity discloses God's actual nature rather than that nature merely in accommodated form on account of two data: Jesus perfectly reveals God as God's impress or *charaktēr* (Heb 1:3) and human beings have been made in the image of God. The analogical use of *charaktēr* in reference to the affinity of being between God and Jesus indicates their substantial unity not just with respect to the eternal being of God and the pre-incarnate eternal state in which God the Son is found but also

---

7. Leo, *Ep. XXVIII*, 4 (ET, Feltoe, pp. 40–41).
8. Leo, *Ep. XXVIII*, 4 (ET, Feltoe, pp. 40–41).
9. See the first three chapters in Chua, *ECRST*.

the incarnate Christ. No such distinction is struck in the Epistle to the Hebrews, where the reference is found, in which only the Son as eternal being constitutes the express representation of God's being and not also the incarnate Son, so there is no warrant to make one.

As for the reference to human beings as made in the divine image or *ṣelem* (Gen 1:26–27), the rendering of this Hebrew word as *eikōn* in the LXX is patient of an association with 2 Cor 4:4 in which Christ is directly designated God's *eikōn*, whereby the divine image in which human beings are said to have been made is nothing other than Christ. The fact that Christ was not yet incarnate at the point God created human beings in God's image poses no difficulty if, as we are arguing, there is no formal antithesis or logical mutual exclusion between divinity and humanity and therefore between the divine Son and the human Christ.

Perhaps one might then object that the very fact that Scripture attests to God's creation of humankind in the divine image prior to the incarnation of Christ infers that the reference in 2 Cor 4:4 to Christ as the image of God perforce designates the eternal being of Christ and not also Christ incarnate. Once again, the biblical writer makes no demarcation between the Son as eternal and the Son as human; indeed, St. Paul goes out of the way to specify that the Christ to whom he has referred is none other than Jesus Christ (2 Cor 4:5–6).

To the extent that the foregoing is plausible as a reasonable interpretation of the Christian Scriptures, we are able to contend for a view of the Lord Jesus Christ, the incarnate Son of God, as a veritable, non-accommodated revelation of God the Father, the two being essentially identical in their moral values, emotional stability, just and loving desires and will, relational disposition, and pattern of conduct, with the Father's operation and activity within a purely spiritual realm among angels and other spiritual beings and Jesus' operation and activity within a physical realm among human beings and other physical things as the sole difference.

Details of each chapter follow.

INTRODUCTION

Outline

Chapter 6: The Christian Doctrine of Humanity: Sociality as Essential to Divine and Human Personhood

The doctrine of humanity in Christian theology has been typically interested in the nature of human beings as made in the image of God, a discussion which usually touches on human faculty, gender, and role in the created order as well as the composition of the human individual.

Although it is customary in some theories of salvation, particularly an evangelical version which focuses on the individual as a self-contained object of salvation, to conceive of human persons as ontologically discrete and independent, psychological and medical studies have shown that social interactions, beginning most of all with parental upbringing, form a crucial part of the individual's psychological development and wellbeing as a person. It is quite unimaginable for a person to be left all on their own, literally.

This fundamental interdependence between human persons is reflective of that which obtains between the divine persons of the triune godhead, attesting to two things: first, the fact that God had indeed created all humankind in the divine image; and, second, the fact that our humanity presents us with a resource by which to attain to a reliable understanding of the divine nature.

Our doctrine of humanity as revealing God's radical sociality has the following content: Whereas classical theology has postulated an independent God with an absolute power of self-existence (aseity), a claim entirely true of the Divine Nature, biblical testimony suggests that, on the level of God as the entitative Trinity, there are two levels of divine interdependence. On an intra-trinitarian level, the divine persons while having no need of development (scil., physical and psychological maturation) are entirely dependent on one another for their ontology and fullness of personal being. On an extra-trinitarian level, the divine persons experience a qualified dependence on human beings. While human actions cannot endanger God's existence, yet human actions can cause sadness to God or bring God joy. Therefore God, while having ontological aseity in relation to the created order, is relationally and emotionally interlocked with human beings because God is emotionally invested in their wellbeing. Such emotional commitment leading to emotional care and solicitude is borne out in human relationship. In

PART 2: HUMANITY'S IMAGING OF THE DIVINE

turn, the profound depth of human emotionality in intimate relationship functions as a substantive symbol of God's emotional binding with the future and fate of humankind.

Chapter 7: The Christian Doctrine of Adoption: Divine-Human Communion as Imperative for Full Personhood

There are two major types of conception of the psychological necessity of religion for the human individual.

On the one hand, a secular perspective asserts that religious affiliation is not imperative for human self-actualization; an individual may very well be non-religious, not hold any theistic beliefs, and still thrive and flourish as an individual person as a productive part of an economy, an essential albeit small component of, in many cases, a large and diverse society, an indispensable member of a primary family system and a wider network of familial systems, as well as a contributor toward human solidarity and humanitarian aid in times of crisis. This viewpoint encompasses the many and diverse groups in society of individuals who believe that some form of transcendentality or spirituality, whether tied or not to an institutional religion, is helpful though not absolutely necessary for human self-actualization.

On the other, with respect to a religious perspective, in particular an evangelical Christian interpretation, religious-cultic faith is regarded as quintessential for human flourishing. A person is assessed to be in peril of damnation should reconciliation with God not be sought and secured on an individual basis through the Lord Jesus Christ.

The view I propose is dependent on an evangelical perspective; be that as it may, I do not aver that biblical teaching requires that all human persons be reconciled to God in a peculiarly Christian manner and context, only that a religious, spiritual, mystical, or transcendental dimension is integral to human nature and conducive to full personhood, and that human persons neglect this aspect to their own detriment.

Our doctrine of humanity as revealing the necessity of divine position has the following content: It is impossible, if one is to eschew the possibility of being disingenuous with oneself, to take leave of the question of God in any fundamental sense. A person may well decide, for differing sets of reasons, that a theistic conception does not agree with their chosen worldview and modus vivendi, yet theism, insofar as it entails an acknowledgment that humankind individually and as a whole does not arise except in connection with a supreme source of its spiritual, psychological, moral, and physical existence and faculties, best explains the situation in which human persons find themselves. All act is the result of natural, deliberate, or mechanical processes which presuppose a natural or designed configuration of nature and its interaction with its surroundings. God is not exempt from this condition for God's action, requiring that God be given a nature as entity and this nature of God's be situated in an environment where that nature may interact with its surroundings. This entitative nature of God's along with the initial milieu (of fundamental spiritual entities, some of which bring into existence all of material reality) with which it interacts are posited by the Divine Nature, which is an undergirding principle and force that begins at an earliest point in time known as the horizon of all possibility, antecedent to which nothing exists and is able to exist.

Chapter 8: The Christian Doctrine of Faith: Divine-Human Communion as Critical for Clear Knowledge of God

In classical theology, it is held that God's nature is, first of all, immutable, so that God does not experience any fundamental change even in the divine-human relationship. At the very most, God brings it about that God is re-presented in a limited spatio-temporal form with which human beings are able to relate, in such a way that the projection is accurate as far as representing how God would most conceivably relate and interact with human persons were God to be limited in a spatio-temporal domain without in any way altering the eternal divine nature, for which the created order exists merely as a thought without real or eternal ontological status. In process theology, God attempts to move the minds and hearts of human persons through appealing to their inherent wisdom, solidarity, and love.

In agreement with the classical theological conception, I propose that God is indeed a being with personal characteristics, yet the being of God in its reality is no different from the being of God in its dynamic interaction with humankind. On these terms, human persons as made in the image of God in their relational as well as moral nature constitute an ectype instrumental in our apprehension of the divine relational as well as moral nature. Furthermore, it is only in an authentic and actual personal relationship with God, rather than purely or mainly abstract theological endeavors to attain an accurate knowledge of God, that a human person is able to more fully know God in all the essential relationality of the divine being.

Our doctrine of the triune God who fills our lack has the following content: God as Trinity is revealed through the patriarchs to Moses for posterity in terms of being the God of Abraham, Isaac, and Jacob. God is the one who fills the lack in us which keeps us from attaining our wellbeing in multiple dimensions: physical, emotional, and spiritual.

Chapter 9: The Christian Doctrine of Incarnation: Jesus as Revelation of God's Eternal Humanity

A traditional conception of Christ's divine and human natures has not overcome a classical Hellenistic opposition between divinity and humanity. Progressive theological interpretations attempt to resolve the aporia by humanizing the idea of the divine as that which inspires human persons to a greater capacity for love, empathy, and compassion.

In my estimation, it is not necessary to turn God or the divine into human or creational aspects, as though divinity simply represented the highest moral and spiritual aspirations of human beings, expressing a deep understanding of our common humanity. Rather, God is ontologically real and distinct from a human conception of divinity. As a matter of fact, God has aseity indeed, having no fundamental need for human friendship or cooperation in both structural and entitative forms. Having formed those relationships with people out of its own free will, however, the Trinity comes to be so embedded in relationship as to form a spiritual and emotional bond with human persons.

Detaching the idea of God from a completely transcendent realm and departing from a classical Greek antithesis between divinity and humanity, I propose that we see Jesus as the true reflection of the eternal being of God, perfectly and completely representing God's spiritual being but in physical form, in such a way that Christ is substantially identical in his moral values, emotional stability, just and loving desires and will, relational disposition, and pattern of conduct to the Father in the Father's eternal being, the only difference being that Christ as a spirit-soul-body complex is able to interact with the physical beings that human persons are, whereas the Father, being spirit and soul as dimensions of the Father's being, interacts with spiritual beings such as angels. In Jesus, the divine moral nature is conceived as being in perfect agreement with ideal human moral nature—this being defined by the Divine Nature positing and operating in each human life—and humanity, in their identity, is restored to its proper position as an image of divinity in moral terms, a vocation to which each person, in their moral agency, should indefatigably aspire with the power afforded to them by God in the Divine Nature and the Trinity.

Such a proposal concerning Jesus' humanity as the reflection of God's humanity affirms the doctrine of divine self-revelation through Jesus rather than merely providing for a representation of God in an accommodated measure which does not and can never truly reveal the godhead, to the extent that the finite cannot touch the infinite, as classical theology categorizes humankind and therefore the veiled form of the Son, and God respectively.

Chapter 10: The Christian Doctrine of Perfection: Divine Work as Human Capacitation

What does it mean to be perfect in biblical and Christian terms? Many Christian traditions are of the view that to be perfect is to have one's moral values, emotional stability, just and loving desires and will, relational disposition, and pattern of conduct be in harmony with those of Jesus Christ. Where these differ may be in the aspect of whether such perfection is attainable on earth. Furthermore, traditional theologies divide neatly between divine and human desire, will, and action. We propose that perfection is achievable in earthly existence and argue for a concurrence between divine and human desire, will, and action. Furthermore, perfect and sinless humanity is expressed and actualized in Jesus both as a dimension of God's nature as well as an instrument revelatory of God's nature, particularly in the mercy which Christ extends to sinners.

Our doctrine of perfection through divine work as human capacitation has the following content: God guides humankind into moral and spiritual perfection and sinlessness through human moral proactivity rather than passivity. The scourge of ritualism in soteriology, in which a person erroneously espouses that ritual provides a shield by which to ward off divine wrath or attain divine good pleasure, is wholly overcome in a biblical conception of God's work in human perfection where solely the penitent and repentant sinner is forgiven through the blood of Christ and set free for a renewed life in imitation of Christ in which God accompanies the believer in investigating and treating the disorders of emotion and thought that result from past traumatic experiences of subjection to neglect or abuse. More than that, a second scourge, this time of an understanding of divine election which eventuates in othering, is surmounted in the enlightened grasp of the insincerity undergirding such ostensibly humble conceptions of one's self in light of the divine privilege and immunity that one stands to gain from them.

6

The Christian Doctrine of Humanity
Sociality as Essential to Divine and Human Personhood

AS ONE OF THE two main parties in the economy of salvation, humankind plays a prominent role in Scripture. From the very outset, the biblical reader's attention is directed to the manner in which God created all things in the world for human beings to use (heavenly bodies), consume (food), tend (animals), as well as enjoy and build a future together (each other).

Of especial note is the way in which Scripture declares God as having made humankind in the divine image. This image has been variously interpreted in terms of the human faculty of reason or freewill (substantive view), the relationship as experienced between God and the human individual (relational view), or the functional authority human beings are mandated to wield over the created order as caretakers of the natural world (functional view).[1]

Modern theology has also discussed the composition of the human being, variously asserting that people are constituted by one (an integrated self in monism), two (a material and an immaterial dimension in dichotomism), or three dimensions (a spirit, soul, and a body in trichotomism).[2]

Our purpose in the present discussion of the Christian doctrine of humanity is to throw light on the issue of the extent to which a human

1. Erickson, *Christian Theology*, 460–67.
2. Erickson, *Christian Theology*, 477–83.

person can be considered in isolation from their fellows in a comprehensive sense.

An evangelical turn has curtailed the emphasis on the church as a medium through which salvation is mediated by God in Christ. Whereas a Roman Catholic conception of salvation has encompassed Christian community as an essential factor in the processes of salvation (humanity as shaped by salvific liturgical processes)[3], an evangelical interpretation has customarily singled out the Christian individual, abstracted from the Christian community, as the primary object on whom God acts in bringing salvation (humanity as individual patient of salvation).[4]

In *Christian Theology*, an evangelical systematic theological text, the individual stands at the center of every stage of salvation, from justification, through adoption, regeneration, sanctification, perseverance, and glorification.[5] Indeed, Erickson goes as far as to write, in speaking of perseverance, of an "individual's maintaining faith and commitment to the very end through the grace of God".[6]

To what degree, however, is it accurate and realistic to speak of an individual believer apart from the Christian community of which they are part in addressing the subject of salvation? Apart from the Christian church, very few would have come to hear the gospel concerning Jesus Christ, of how the Lord Jesus came as a human being to save sinners.

Having heard and received the gospel with gladness, becoming a part of the church, is a believer now left to their own devices? Certainly not, considering that much of the Christian existence revolves around religious observances and social bonding among fellow believers, not to mention efforts by the Christian community to relieve the needs of other communities during humanitarian crises and bring the good news of Jesus to other places.

Christians participate in community not simply to engage in ritual observances but also to practice Christian love by emulating Christ in service of others and to be encouraged, empowered, and supported in

---

3. Erickson, *Christian Theology*, 837–39.

4. In Colin Gunton's nomenclature, this is related to an "individualistic [conception] of sin, encouraged by a certain kind of evangelistic strategy which seeks to impress on human individuals at almost any cost their need for salvation". Gunton, *CF*, 61.

5. Erickson, *Christian Theology*, 840.

6. Erickson, *Christian Theology*, 840. An individualist conception of salvation appears to have emerged during the mid-nineteenth century in America among traditional evangelicals, exemplified in the preaching and ministry of the revivalist preacher, Dwight L. Moody. Shelley, *Church History*, 392.

that practice as well as maintain their own mental wellbeing as a person in community rather than an isolated individual.[7]

Although it remains helpful to conceptualize humankind as distinct individuals even in the context of a discussion regarding salvation, such a conception has always to be paired with the idea of community, so that we conceive not of individuals per se but of individuals embedded in community.[8]

To a significant degree, the human individual does not truly possess their personhood in abstraction from the community of other individuals. In order to arrive at clarity on this point, it is necessary first to define the scope or limits of human personhood.

A human individual is said to be a person insofar as they are able to distinguish themselves from the rest of the world, including other individuals, as a physical, intellectual, and ethical subject as well as identify themselves as a physical, affective, and spiritual whole; that is, as an entity in their own right with a controlling influence over their physical bodies, their processes of reasoning, and their volition or decision-making capacity, concomitant with a persistent conscious awareness of selfhood in their particular unique physical bodies, with their specific psychological states of mind, and with an identity unique to themselves.

While all this seems structural and substantial, we can neither neglect the fact that personhood is developed only in the context of a nurturing and safe environment, nor that personhood is sustainable only within community. The centrality of relationship to personhood has led Barth to speak of the image of God in humanity as the relationality defined by God's relationships within Godself, with humankind as a covenant-partner, and by Jesus' relationship with humankind so that a human person in relation to God is to acknowledge and express their utter dependence on God for their preservation, along with a sense of gratitude, responsibility, obedience, and love that recognizes God's worthiness, renouncing any self-interested claim on God, others, or anything in creation, and the human person in relation to other persons is to embrace rather than ostracize, reject, or care nothing for them, exploit them or see them merely as a subject to whom one may be obligated, to value and be valued by them, hear and be heard by them, and help and be helped by them. The nineteenth-century English Christian Socialist Anglican theologian F. D.

---

7. Grenz, *TCG*, 424.
8. Cf. Grenz, *TCG*, 424–25.

Maurice spoke of the human being as fully actualized only in communal relations which bear witness to and exemplify the conviction regarding God as Father of all human beings as God's children and people as brothers in and through Jesus Christ. Neo-Confucianism defines the human person not as self-actualizing ego but a distinct self that is nevertheless imperatively embedded within a social group.[9]

Concerning how personhood develops within an interpersonal environment, the tragic case of Genie Wiley highlights social interaction as imperative for the psychological and social development of a human individual from childhood on. To abstract the human individual from the community in which they are necessarily embedded and alone viable is tantamount to capturing on camera that instantaneous moment in which a stick, having been held upright by a person's hand, is released by that hand, yet still upright, but only in that instant, immediately succeeding which the stick falls to the ground on account that it is fundamentally unable to maintain its position on its own.

As an example of the fact that personhood is sustainable only within community, a Christian person may very well attempt to leave a Christian community, yet without the spiritual environment in which they are able to practice and be encouraged in their faith, as well as have their need for sociality met, they will not last very long as a person. Their mental health will be compromised. Indeed, studies have revealed that when a person is removed from social bonding, the likelihood that they experience premature death is greatly heightened.[10]

As a clear sign of human interdependence, the human mind evinces a brittle quality. It is capable of being completely misled by those with malicious motives as well as being scarred. Consistent attempts to cause a person to doubt what they remember, feel, and sense or gaslighting have the potential to lead to a person's inability to trust themselves over the longer term or to their concern that they may be grappling with a mental health disorder.[11]

The human mind is capable of being scarred in a more permanent way. Even though a person may long have left a situation of great distress, trauma might still linger in them and, as it is triggered by personal traits or situations which bear some form of affinity with the traumatic

---

9. Barth, *KD* III.2, §45.3 (ET, Bromiley, pp. 323–24); Barth, *KD* IV.2, §68.1 (ET, Bromiley, pp. 743–46); Shelley, *Church History*, 412; Kim, *Theology of Dao*, 235.

10. Novotney, "Social Isolation," 32.

11. Nall, "What Are the Long-Term Effects of Gaslighting?"

experience and memory, occasionally take control of their emotions in the unconscious, retrojecting them back into a tumultuous past for a period of time, despite the mind's clear knowledge at other times that they are no longer in extremis.[12]

This is the mechanism operative in instances of prejudice toward a person for what they have done in the past but which they do no longer, in that the same feelings of bitterness and rancor may surface in the event of the approach of the person in question in view that the emotional memory or unconscious treats them as the person they were at the point at which they were perceived to have caused great discomfort.

In addition, a human mind which has been wounded through childhood abuse remains in a state of frailty and weakness in adulthood in spite that the adult self would go through the same oppressive circumstances and emerge with strength and resilience which at a younger age it proved quite unable to do.

As such, there is a man who underwent emotional and sexual abuse at an early age and interpreted the string of incidents as suggesting his rejection by his parents and society as a whole solely on the basis of his gender.[13] Even after receiving professional therapy and coming to himself regarding how the abuse was perpetrated against him not on account of what was wrong about him but rather in consequence of the willful and sinful choices of his abusers, he continues to struggle with feelings of abandonment that arise whenever he sees the image of an attractive woman wearing sensual attire such as celebrities don at a public event.

Having never developed a sufficient sense of self-acceptance during his early years of identity formation in view of rejection from both his parents in different ways, whilst having experienced something remotely close to physical intimacy only at the hands of his abusers, he is primed to perceive rejection in all situations which involve some disagreement, misunderstanding, or withdrawal. An emotional wound

---

12. Post-traumatic stress disorder in those who have been deployed in combat situations is a clear example of how the human mind is fragile and stays gravely impacted by severe stress and trauma experienced at some particular point or during a period in the past. Smith, Robinson, and Segal, "PTSD in Military Veterans." An anecdote may be proffered from the life of Edmund Smith, who struggled at first to relate romantically with his future wife because of abusive treatment perpetrated by his mother against him as a child when she forcibly attempted to compel him to cease his female gender identification. Chun, "I Knew I Wasn't a Mistake."

13. A similar dynamic was at play in the life of Edmund Smith, absent sexual abuse. Chun, "I Knew I Wasn't a Mistake."

engendered by a past traumatic incident of rejection can blind the patient to the situation in all its holism, causing them to forget the good that was actually done to them by the person in the present time who is perceived to be rejecting them.[14]

Such a feeling of rejection, in turn, drives him to seek acceptance (whether in an imaginary world or in reality) in conforming to the physical image into which he was shaped by his abusers; that of an attractive woman entrapped in a controlling relationship with a man, compelled to exhibit parts of her physical body through sensual clothes. While his conscious mind is generally aware of the origin of the dysfunctional processes and patterns of thought (e.g., thinking, "this celebrity is beautiful") and feeling (e.g., of envy toward a beautiful celebrity) he experiences—though not so much at the point of being overwhelmed by those thoughts and feelings—and he understands that nobody rejects him on the ground of his gender, the unconscious has not caught up and stands in need of further healing. All the same, he is so in need of validation that comes only through a feminine appearance that his mind constructs a self-image of himself with a feminine face and body projected from images of women to which he is attracted, a false self-image that can only be undone through conscious realization and a decision to see and embrace his actual physical appearance by focusing on men who look like him.

A fear of rejection has led the same individual to forbear to smile when he meets a person for the first or even a subsequent time or feel awkward when a stranger looks in his general direction in a manner that does not demand suspicion. Raised to think that a parent's approval may only be secured through performance, he grew to become a person who requires nothing less than perfection of himself and has found it difficult to concede his errors and therefore apologize to others. Psychological neglect and abuse have also fostered a dysfunctional and compulsive need for people to behave in a fair way, a stressful preoccupation that may be overcome through learning to embrace every possible outcome.

That the human mind is susceptible to being distorted or harmed through exposure to negligent or abusive actions attests to the manner in which we have been made by God in the divine image to receive just, fair, and dignified treatment, as well as to express the same toward others, seeing that like us, they too will be harmed by anything less than

---

14. This differs markedly from a blindness in relation to the virtues of others that owes itself to an arrogant presumption.

humane treatment and we ought only to do those things that we would desire for others to do unto us.

Less tragically, the mind proves that it needs sociality in that it tends to be deceived into thinking that it has a clear understanding of some issue. This is evident in the way that we often learn something new from the questions people ask us about a topic we have been analyzing and reflecting upon. In addition, the far-reaching epistemic implications of being in possession of a different cast of mind attests to our fundamental need as human persons for one another.

According to Barth, the human person who regards themselves as self-sufficient or against-others attempts the "impossible", by which he presumably means the irrational decision for an unsustainable state of affairs. In the final analysis, human beings are chosen, made, and shaped for sociality.[15]

Without properly and duly embracing ourselves as distinct individuals found and coexisting in integrated and relational community with other persons, we run an actual risk of obscuring for ourselves the true nature of God as one presiding over and concerned for a whole community as opposed to a single individual, and who summons us to love one another as much as we love ourselves.[16] We run the risk of doing to God what we do to other people.[17] Barth is emphatic in underscoring that those who permit themselves to slip into such a state may well be culpable of making an idol of God. Furthermore, apart from the personal other, there can be no external affirmation of the self so essential for healthy and vital selfhood.[18]

I may add that the social responsibility commanded and commended by the gospel makes perfect sense in light that the Lord feels exactly what the sufferer of need and oppression experiences (cf. Matt 25:31–46; Acts 9:1–9). Christ is empathetically connected to each of them primarily because the closest analogy to Christ's earthly sufferings, by

---

15. Barth, *KD* IV.2, §65.2 (ET, Bromiley, pp. 433–34). Another impossible or unviable scenario is sought by those who endeavor to become more than mortal. Barth, *KD* IV.2, §65.2 (ET, Bromiley, p. 469).

16. To love our neighbor as ourselves is to do this: just as we value our own selves and consider ourselves important, so we are to value others and consider them important, not in such a way as to seek to supplant their personal responsibilities but rather to show a genuine interest in their lives, their joys, hopes, struggles, and extend practical care and help wherever necessary and possible.

17. Barth, *KD* IV.2, §65.2 (ET, Bromiley, pp. 441–43).

18. Cf. Barth, *KD* IV.2, §65.2 (ET, Bromiley, p. 443).

PART 2: HUMANITY'S IMAGING OF THE DIVINE

implication of being a person who possesses traits wrongfully considered to be deserving of ridicule and abuse (in Christ's case, being sincerely but also out of a selfishness-driven presumptuous intellectual laziness viewed as a religious and political renegade, revealing not only the wickedness of those who conspired against Christ but also that of members of the population who rejected Christ without fair consideration), resides in the disgust, mockery, and discrimination endured by the destitute.[19]

For this reason, Christ taught his disciples that blessing consists in being poor in spirit or even simply poor, in that indigents experience—and those who empathize with them (the poor in spirit) vicariously experience—the manner of suffering and social affliction that would prove to be nothing less than a divinely precious treasure of the kingdom of heaven or of God (Matt 5:3; Luke 6:20), were it to be turned toward Christ as a hermeneutical resource by which to lay hold of the similar suffering he himself went through (in the imaginative posture that empathy is), and that he went through without harboring any resentment toward those who discriminated against him, but only the desire that they might repent so that they would not have to see eternal judgment, giving his own life in

---

19. Empathy is a prerequisite for loving action directed toward helping others flourish. Without feeling the need and legitimate desire of another person or being, even though we were surrounded by images or messages of the dire need and misery of the world, we should be pococurante regarding these matters. At the very least we would be simply unaware of the struggles faced by others in different places. Yet the one who is able to mentally connect with another person who is afflicted with a need in such a way as to imagine how it might feel to be in a similar situation, perhaps bringing to mind a time in their own lives when they experienced some more or less serious want, extrapolating from and adapting this memory as necessary, such a person would be poised to endeavor to do something to alleviate the deprivation of the one presently in need. For this reason, Jesus spoke of himself in the parable of the sheep and the goats as one to whom good or bad deeds are done as to a person in a moment of need precisely as and when someone relieves a needy person of their deprivation and privation, all and only because Jesus himself always connects himself mentally, imaginatively, self-relatedly, and therefore emotionally with the needy and destitute in a way that results in practical action. So intense and strong is this emotional connection that Jesus feels aggrieved when any needy person in the world with whom he empathizes fails to receive help from a person in a position to help them, and gratified when they do so. God does not need us in order to love and be loved but God's existence as the one whose being is identical with God's love is necessary for us to love, if only because God is the ground of our moral orientation and the one by whom our hearts have been fundamentally imprinted, in our primal and pre-human encounter with God in the very beginning, with a moral and loving nature. As such, the one who truly loves in that very act authenticates the knowledge of God in them. Barth, *KD* IV.2, §68.2 (ET, Bromiley, pp. 751–58).

excruciating agony at the cross that these might have a pledge by which to be assured of and receive God's forgiveness.

Another reason that those who are poor or poor in spirit are blessed is that gratitude is a direct function of our ability to empathize with the destitute. It is because we frequently imagine ourselves only in the place of the wealthy and powerful rather than that of the poor and vulnerable that we fail to see that we have much to be grateful for; were we caught in a situation of exigent need, many of the things we long for presently would not occupy our minds, and we would be happy with far less. Life is an exercise in learning to give up everything we have, one which Jesus underwent with success.[20]

The crucial requirement for sociality cannot be vitiated even by an appeal to apocalyptic prophecy, which has been looked to as a reason to cast off all restraints by abandoning social responsibility and simply awaiting an impending return of the Lord.

Certain groups of Christians may be mistaken in espousing the view that the dreadful final epoch which precedes the return of Christ, the so-called end times, is merely a calendrical event inevitably foreordained of God.

Such a supposition is put to rest by the Lord's clearly disapproving reference to the acts of moral turpitude which have led to his own arrest and crucifixion under false charges (Luke 23:28–31), acts committed during a time of relative peace which will only be escalated and exacerbated when disaster strikes as happened during the first Jewish revolt which ultimately engendered the fall of Jerusalem in AD 70.

Regardless of the reasons for the insurrection, in this case, socioeconomic inequality, bureaucratic corruption, and the Roman ruler's religious insensitivity, unnecessary conflict could have been avoided through accommodation or more creative and indirect protestation on the part of the Jewish population.

The ominous signs of the end highlighted in Matthew 24 were those that would have occurred by the time of the destruction of the city, including the entry of the abomination of desolation into the holy place within the temple, a reference to the desecration of the Jewish temple by Antiochus IV Epiphanes.

---

20. What is keeping a person from treating every moment as if it were their last, receiving each new moment as a gift of grace, and therefore ceasing to be as exercised as they might otherwise be about their successes or failures?

PART 2: HUMANITY'S IMAGING OF THE DIVINE

Antiochus sought to foster socioeconomic stability in his empire through cultural conformity in the form of adopting a Hellenistic lifestyle and worshipping the Greek pantheon, particularly Zeus, whose incarnate form he claimed to be. In reaction to Jewish resistance to his systematic efforts in this direction, he carried out a brutal policy of forced Hellenization of Jerusalem upon his return from Egypt in 167 BC, stripping the city of its privileges and garrisoning it whilst proscribing the worship of Yahweh and Jewish rites with a penalty of death imposed on those who violate the law. Antiochus set up an altar to Zeus Olympios in the temple, ordering that sacrifices be offered at the feet of an idol crafted in the likeness of the king.[21] These were acts of abomination, in that they promoted idolatry, bringing desolation into the land through profaning the holy place of the temple.[22]

In applying that past event to a future catastrophic event, the Lord meant to point to a subsequent incident in which the temple would again be profaned, this time through its plundering and the enforced polytheism in its surroundings. The fall of Jerusalem, however, was not willed or predestined of God, being the consequence of a Jewish revolt against their Roman rulers in what is known as the First Jewish Revolt (AD 66–70).[23]

This sets the stage for a presentation of a conception of the human person as fundamentally and radically dependent on the divine and human other, supplementing our apprehension of the human individual as made in God's image in terms of receiving their formal and substantive moral capacity from God.

Morality, after all, presupposes the existence of the divine and human other and relationship with them, defined as it is as the pursuit of fairness and justice in one's relationship with God and fellow human beings. The fact that we ourselves are made with dignity, with a need to be treated fairly and justly, is seen in how we cannot tolerate psychological indignity, which constitutes allowing others to abuse us with impunity.

Insofar as human beings have been created, posited, or inspired in God's image as morally obligated and morally responsible entities, just as the divine persons are toward one another as well as toward human beings and the rest of the created order, their interdependent existence can be said to attest to their being made in God's interdependent image.

21. Drummond, "Antiochus Epiphanes"; Volkmann, "Antiochus IV Epiphanes."
22. Doriani, "What Is the 'Abomination of Desolation'?"
23. Oates, "Great Jewish Revolt of 66 CE."

On this basis, the interdependence seen in human existence embedded in community discloses the very nature of the triune godhead as interdependent.

If this seems tautological, it is not in actuality. The reality of interdependence among human persons is not sufficient in itself for attaining to a knowledge of God; there is no logically necessary correlation between the godhead and humankind in this regard. The divine initiative is required, as a first step in the sequence, to proclaim the relational nature of the godhead as a clue, orientation, or direction for theologians to explore.

Even so, God would not be able to disclose the divine nature in this way to human recipients of that divine knowledge were there no analogue in human existence. As such, in positing human beings as interdependent entities, the Divine Nature graces, first, the Trinity with ability to convey knowledge about itself in a manner that human beings may comprehend and, second, human beings with the ability to comprehend the self-knowledge that the Trinity confers on humankind.

Having done so, all that is left for God to do is to declare the triune godhead as interdependent in nature, akin to the social character of humankind, as evidence that the latter has been created in the image of the former. This constitutes a formal analogy, revolving around the theme of interdependence, between the Trinity and humankind. Subsequently, our understanding of God's interdependent nature is fleshed out by observations of our sociality, in what constitutes a substantive analogy between the sociality of the triune godhead and that of humankind. To this doctrine of humanity I confer the name: humanity as revealing God's radical sociality.

Epistemology

The ancient Greco-Roman world found solace in the idea of God as a sovereign ruler. Seeking to avoid thinking about the endless march toward decay and death, philosophers took refuge in the notion of an immutable God for whom everything was under control.[24] In contrast to the fallible and flawed gods of the theater and the masses, the God of the philosophers was in no form of need. Divine strength and power were emphasized and this emphasis culminated in the doctrine of aseity, God's self-existence or independence of all that exists.

24. Sanders, "Historical Considerations," 68.

Christian theologians were careful not to attribute any form of weakness to God. If Christ's experience of agonizing suffering had to be noted, it was quickly relegated to the sphere of Christ's human nature rather than the divine nature per se, which could not experience weakness or undergo suffering.

Early Christian thinkers like St. Augustine of Hippo were not even certain that God could be spoken of as comprising three persons, underscoring that the idea of personhood was ascribed to the Father, Son, and Holy Spirit only because it had to be testified that there were three in God, and not because the nature of each of the three was exactly known, whether or not they could be said to be personal in their character in a similar way to how we may speak of a human individual as having a personal or social nature.[25]

Such concerns led to an unnecessary bifurcation between Christ's divine and human natures. Theologians tussled over the *communicatio idiomatum*, the question of the extent to which it was proper to say that Mary is the mother of the uncreated God, Christ being divine, and that therefore God was born; or that Christ's impassible and immortal divine nature suffered or even died. These were not just academic questions for theological interlocutors, given the tension between averring what is true of Christ (e.g., that he was born, suffered, and died) and the unity of his personhood (i.e., Christ cannot be thought of as divine without being human or human without being divine at any point in his incarnate life).

Nestorius, the fourth-century patriarch of Constantinople, was firmly opposed to the idea of designating Mary, the earthly mother of Jesus, *theotokos* or God-bearer because it carried the implication that the uncreated God was actually born from the womb of a human woman, suffered and died on the cross, and was buried.

The bishop of Constantinople believed that the term *theotokos* suggested that Christ was a divine-human mixture, similar to an Arian or Apollinarian christological conception, and that the resurrection constituted an event through which such a partially divine Christ became fully divine, having resonance with ideas associated with Paul of Samosata.

Instead, Nestorius contended for the usage of *Christotokos*, Christ-bearer, as a way of describing the role of Mary as the vessel through whom the human Jesus came into the world, being himself only the bearer of God but not divine.

---

25. Augustine, *Trin.*, 7.3.4.9, 7.3.6.11 (ET, Hill, pp. 229–34).

The patriarch of Alexandria, St. Cyril of Alexandria, Nestorius' chief opponent in this debate, set his face against solely referring to Mary as *Christotokos*.

Cyril feared that such a change of customary nomenclature, adopted by theologians of former generations such as St. Athanasius of Alexandria, would imply that at the incarnation God caused a human man, Jesus, to be born in and through Mary, who would be supposed on this view to have subsequently received the divine Word within himself.

This would jeopardize the clear conception of the redemption accomplished in and by Christ, seeing that the subject who went to the cross is no longer divine, but human, Christ being regarded as a mere human being accompanied or indwelled by God, just like any other saint.

In his bid to avoid mixing divinity with humanity, and insinuating that the divine could be subject to suffering, Nestorius argued that the divine and human natures in Christ were brought together in a union (*henosis*) or conjunction (*sunapheia*) of two free and spontaneous agents, juxtaposed rather than being further integrated in any way.

Cyril deprecated such a view of the unity of Christ's divine and human natures as akin to two persons of equal honor being united in some common purpose, as juxtaposed one to another, or as being brought together in a similar fashion to how a believer can be said to participate in the Lord, Christ's divine and human natures being brought together by the will and good pleasure of the Lord through the bringing forth and assumption and indwelling of a human being.

Instead, Cyril insisted that there was ever only one subject, God the Word, who took on human flesh through a miraculous conception involving Mary as an earthly mother, whereby God can indeed be said to have been born of a woman, but only so as to receive a human body with all its faculties, including the intellectual, psychological, and spiritual capacities of a human being, a conception of Christ's two natures as integrated in his single person or hypostatically united.[26]

According to later formulations, the divine (of the Word) and human capacities in the one Christ enable him to fully experience the existence of a divine and human person on different occasions, both natures working complementarily and harmoniously to allow Christ to fulfill his work of redemption through becoming capable of suffering (in his human

---

26. Artemi, "Cyril of Alexandria's Critique of Theotokos," 1–16.

PART 2: HUMANITY'S IMAGING OF THE DIVINE

identity and mode of existence or experience) and in his capacity as God (in his divine identity and mode of existence or experience).

These are questions that emerge from a philosophical framework ascribing two irreconcilable sets of qualities to divinity and humanity. In truth, if God is to be known in any way to human beings, there needs to be an analogue of some kind. To declare in advance, therefore, that nothing in the world bears adequate witness to divine reality in view that divinity and the world are diametrically opposed is to dispense with the possibility of divine revelation altogether.

Consequently, theologians tend to speak of some correspondent relationship between God's being and that of humankind, though only in a highly qualified way. What is flawed and defective in human existence is automatically excluded, while limitations and constraints experienced by all creatures that inhabit the world are removed.

Such a procedure is problematic at best, misleading at worst. On the one hand, sinfulness is not part of an authentic and full human existence as God has created it. As such, it is improper to contrast God and humankind as sinless and always only sinful, respectively. To the extent, therefore, that human beings do reflect, or come to reflect, the nature for which they have been created, then it should be fair to say that in so doing they accurately reflect the nature of God as beings made in the divine image.

On the other hand, concerning the issue of divinity lacking any limitations and constraints whatsoever such as experienced by human beings, it is rarely useful to promulgate an absolute principle that is to be applied across the board.

Although it remains accurate to speak of God as uncreated, unlike human beings and anything else in the world, as immortal in distinction from human individuals in their mortal physical bodies, or attribute power and authority to God as king such as no human person commands, has yet to command, or will ever command, yet it is quite another thing to contend for God as so entirely and utterly transcendent that nothing in this world may actually be said to be indicative of God's nature, which is conceived as technically inconceivable.[27]

---

27. On the question of whether it is possible that some political leader or leaders have had a hand in shaping or corrupting the content of the Bible in such a way that it serves primarily to defend their rule rather than communicating God's truth, this is unlikely. The Bible advocates piety above human rule and authority, depicting humankind in unflattering terms as being constantly in need of God's grace and liable to sin and wickedness.

In numerous ways, God may be said to be superior to humankind. Is this equivalent to the assertion that God is infinitely superior to them rather than merely superior in some quantitative way? To be sure, there will always be some element of mystery to the being of God, the ineluctable fact of God's unoriginated nature contributing much in the way of the distinction between God and humanity.

Even so, in many other ways, God is truly like humankind, only better or greater. As some cases in point, God has being as the Trinity, though not as the Divine Nature, being the structure of being itself.

The divine persons, the Father, the Son, and the Holy Spirit, exist in a mutually loving relationship in which they genuinely care for each other and treat one another with fairness and justice. This is evident in the manner in which the Son, incarnate as a human person, had regular moments of prayer with the Father (Luke 5:16). In addition, the Son maintained relationships with the apostles and disciples, caring that they obtain eternal life (Matt 19:16–30).

To the objection that there is no parity between the life of Jesus and the eternal existence of the Son, we may advance the prolepsis that the incarnation takes nothing away from the distinct subject that the Son constitutes, and to suggest that in the incarnation the godhead added to itself a distinct subject is to subscribe to a notion of an expanding economic Trinity not substantiated in the scriptural testimony, which bears witness only to a *withness* between God the Father and God the Word from the beginning (John 1:1), a Word distinguishable from God itself and therefore no mere internal component of its reason.

It is therefore the same divine subject, the same Christ, which relates with the other divine persons from the beginning and with the human persons with whom Christ came into contact. A Chalcedonian conception would postulate that the same subject fostered interpersonal relationships with human persons both in a divine mode as well as a human mode. As far as we are concerned, however, the humanity of Christ does not exclude the Son's experience as divine being, simply because God does not become any less divine in being subject to lack, suffering, and even death. It is God's character, role, identity, and authority that defines God as God rather than any incapacity as such, even if this be an incapacity to be "weak".[28]

---

28. Chua, *ECRST*, 208.

In point of fact, it is in God's capacity to endure human weakness characteristic of humankind that God is given the opportunity to demonstrate true courage and solidarity. It is possible for a divine person who was truly subject to dread (in Christ praying desperately in the garden of Gethsemane) to reveal uncommon courage but not an impassible and undaunted transcendent entity.[29] Likewise, it is only if a divine person truly stands to lose something, even momentarily, in the form of the Son's relationship with the Father (through the experience of abandonment on the cross) and the earthly life of the Son (through the Son's earthly death by crucifixion), that the boundless and sacrificial love of God can be seen. At the cross, where he eventually overcame the feeling of abandonment and yielded his spirit to the Father in a carefree way, Jesus demonstrated that no amount of temptation from the devil can cause him to stop trusting God's love.

God's undying affection toward humankind is also disclosed in God's very apparent frustration with and sorrow because of God's covenant people whenever they fall into a state of spiritual decline. Just as the unconditional and selfless love of a parent is evident during moments when they experience their children in recalcitrance or even rebellion, so the unconditional and selfless love of God was manifested in light of the rebellion of the Israelites during the different eras of the Old Testament.

The ability for God to be affected by the human response to God's invitation is not in itself a mark of weakness. This was in fact the crux of St. Paul's refutation of the accusation that the cross of Christ is a sign of weakness and foolishness (1 Cor 1:18–25). Around the turn of the third century, Minucius Felix wrote a dialogue, *Octavius*, in which he reproduces the views of Caecilius, a pagan, concerning Christianity as a religion lacking in wisdom on account that it promotes the worship of a crucified criminal and his instrument of execution (Book 9).[30] In point of fact, the divine Son's assumption of the frailty of the human nature as well as the Son's mission and mandate to suffer redemptively as a servant constitute the Son's claim to lordship so that it is impossible that the power and majesty of God should be divorced from human weakness and anguish.[31]

---

29. Edwards, Gabel, and Hosmer, "Physical Death of Jesus Christ," 1455–56.
30. Felix, *Octavius*, 9 (ET, Wallis, pp. 177–78).
31. Barth, *KD* IV.2, §64.4 (ET, Bromiley, pp. 264–65).

In truth, God confirms God's identity as divine through the love that God revealed in the crucified Christ.[32] At the cross, where he suffered most grievously unto death, Jesus extended forbearance toward his mockers, forgiveness toward those who nailed him to the cross, and mercy toward a sinful but penitent purloiner. While he felt an immense sense of abandonment from the Father, Christ continued trusting in the Father, committing himself to the Father at the point of death.

What did Christ's suffering on the cross involve? Prior to his crucifixion, he endured merciless scourging with a whip to which were attached small iron balls or sharp pieces of sheep bones and was made to carry the heavy crossbar of his cross (weighing between 34 and 57 kilograms) for about 4 kilometers from the city up the hill of Golgotha. In a state of fatigue and pain, Jesus had his wrists and feet nailed to the cross. In that upright position, he needed to lift his body upward in order to exhale, but this would cause burning pain to both his wrists and feet besides wearing him out and making each breath increasingly difficult.[33]

Although this was the state in which Christ found himself, he did not become resentful, despairing, or even self-absorbed, but continued to care for those around him and trust in the Father. Seeing the way he died, accompanied by the signs of three hours of darkness preceding Christ's death and after his death an earthquake, the centurion who was posted to ensure he was properly executed could not help but confess that Jesus was truly the Son of God (Mark 15:39).

By far the greatest expression of Christ's love consisted in how, in seeing his disciple betray him and religious leaders conspire against him with political authority to have him scourged and crucified, instead of fleeing from danger or enlisting the aid of an angelic army to put to death those who were making their way to arrest him and put him to death on false charges, Jesus elected to forgive his opponents and love all people to the very end (John 13:1). This he did by allowing himself to be taken and nailed to the cross, that through his death he might make atonement for their sins and through his resurrection be vindicated of the false and grievous indictments against him, giving endless hope to those who trusted and will trust in him through his ascension to sit at the right hand of the Father as glorified God-man. What was his dread in the garden in Gethsemane if not the dread that he might

---

32. Cf. Barth, *KD* IV.2, §68.2 (ET, Bromiley, pp. 756–58).
33. Edwards, Gabel, and Hosmer, "Physical Death of Jesus Christ," 1457–61.

choose to yield to the seductions of the devil and opt for avoidance or the vengeance of a majestic but forceful victory and, having made his momentous decision, the dread of the pain of dying on the cross?[34]

In being able to love in a manner in which only God can love, Jesus revealed his divinity in a manner that empirical investigation can never prove, being apparatuses to detect and measure only physical quantities with God being spiritual. His resurrection exploded false claims as to his being an enemy of religion and state. For this reason, St. Paul can say that salvation comes through confessing that Jesus is Lord and believing that God raised him from the dead (Rom 10:9).

One enters a personal relationship with God not through becoming worthy of it and thereby being conferred such a relationship. We can never be worthy of a relationship with God because we will make mistakes. The relationship each person has with God is analogous not so much to the relationship between an employee and their superior as that between an ideal loving parent and their child (Rom 10:5–13). The loving parent desires only the best for their child. They will never abandon the child even if it makes mistakes, but forgive and seek to guide it accordingly back to the right way. The child on their part will need to be willing to accept correction and seek to do what is right.

God loves us like such a parent, desiring that we let God love us, and that we know the love of God and how much God values us through learning about Jesus, that we love and value God, and understand, love, value, and care for ourselves and others the sincere and unconditional way God loves us, in a spiritual community that shares the love of God with others. In being able to save us in this way, given that salvation consists in having a personal relationship with God, Jesus demonstrates that he is God (Matt 11:27; John 1:18).

Hence, St. Paul describes the display of God's redemptive love on the cross in Rom 1:16–17 as the gospel, the power of God for salvation to all believers, and as the righteousness of God, as something we are to emulate in the way we are to serve others as well for their psychological

---

34. The Father, too, suffered with the Son on the cross, in Barth's conception, and not in a secondary but primary way. In keeping with his doctrine of the Trinity as the one God in self-repetition or one mind in three modes of being, the Swiss theologian is able to aver that the Father became brother of humankind and suffered for them in the Son. Barth, *KD* IV.1, §59.1 (ET, Bromiley, pp. 195–210); Barth, *KD* IV.1, §61.2 (ET, Bromiley, p. 564); Barth, *KD* IV.2, §64.4 (ET, Bromiley, p. 357); Barth, *KD* IV.2, §65.1 (ET, Bromiley, p. 384).

and moral wellbeing (therefore, righteousness, that is, providing the standard for a righteous life) as powerful for the redemption of many.

True strength, for God as well as humankind, is the ability to display humility in spite of one's greater learning or ability, to be gentle with the powerless and in a moment when vulnerability is shown, to be empathetic toward the afflicted, to endure adversity with fortitude, to bear patiently during periods of agony or oppression, and to refuse to exact vengeance against those who have hurt us. It is not the possession of superior physical or military might, having the authority or power to oppress others as one wishes, or the ability to dictate one's circumstances of life.

As we have already begun to observe, the divine persons experience many emotions with a human analogue. To what extent is it appropriate to speak of God as experiencing emotions, given that emotions are tied to the physical body? Emotions are associated with the physical body only because human beings have a physical dimension. People will not lose their affective capacity once they depart from the physical realm on the point of their demise. They continue to experience feelings of distress in the afterlife (e.g., Luke 16:19–31; Rev 6:9–11). That is because emotions do not in fact originate with the human brain, but with the spiritual personal being, in line with which the brain releases the chemicals associated with various states of emotion.[35]

The relationship between God, evil, and suffering is as such: God does not orchestrate or cause evil. It may well be that, in some instances, God permits or uses evil or suffering as an instrument of repentance, yet this is not to attribute any necessity to evil or suffering, since if ever a person, through the suffering they experience, recognizes and turns away from their arrogance, this will be on account of their own moral action, made possible by the Divine Nature and inspired by the Trinity.[36]

It is unconscionable to suggest that God may be behind every instance of evil or suffering, including that which results in the harm of those innocent of any unrepented wrongdoing. Is it possible that God might desire that human persons confront evil so that they might learn forbearance as well as forgiveness and face suffering so that they might nurture patience along with perseverance? This is plausible under circumstances whereby God wishes for the person to attain a greater

---

35. On the view of emotions as generated by the physical body, see Spencer, "What's the Difference between Emotions, Feelings, and Moods?"

36. Cf. Chua, *STEA*, 60.

measure of resilience so that they might be better able to handle the inescapable stresses of life.[37]

Appreciating the limits of God safeguards against an unnecessary and wrongheaded loss of faith as when a person prays and the prayer is not efficacious, not because God does not hear but because Satan and Satan's demons prevented communication with God or hindered timely intervention in the hope that this might lead the believer to suppose that God either does not hear or exist.

Doctrinal Formulation: Humanity as Revealing God's Radical Sociality

Whereas classical theology has postulated an independent God with an absolute power of self-existence (aseity), a claim entirely true of the Divine Nature, biblical testimony suggests that, on the level of God as the entitative Trinity, there are two levels of divine interdependence. On an intra-trinitarian level, the divine persons while having no need of development (scil., physical and psychological maturation) are entirely dependent on one another for their ontology and fullness of personal being. On an extra-trinitarian level, the divine persons experience a qualified dependence on human beings. While human actions cannot endanger God's existence, yet human actions can cause sadness to God or bring God joy. Therefore God, while having ontological aseity in relation to the created order, is relationally and emotionally interlocked with human beings because God is emotionally invested in their wellbeing. Such emotional commitment leading to emotional care and solicitude is borne out in human relationship. In turn, the profound depth of human emotionality in intimate relationship functions as a substantive symbol of God's emotional binding with the future and fate of humankind.

Discussion

Classical theology has postulated an independent God with an absolute power of self-existence (aseity), a claim entirely true of the Divine Nature

The idea of God as utterly self-existent or independent; that is, of having aseity, has been a conditio sine qua non of Christian theology from

---

37. Cf. Amaechina, "Why Mature Christians Rarely Experience Miracles."

the time of the scholastics of the medieval age.[38] Aseity is the claim that God is not dependent for being who or what God is upon some external source. This divine attribute is brought into stark relief against the contingency of created beings, who depend for their being and existence upon the creative activity of God. Moreover, the self-existent and independent God is in no need of growth or development but has perfection in Godself.

Aseity is not to be interpreted in terms of God having the source of God's existence in Godself—this would be to require the self-contradictory idea that God pre-exists Godself—but rather that God always already exists, always already *is*.[39] Being and existence are the natural state of God's nature, and no specific etiology is needed for God to exist. It is not natural or necessary for created beings to exist. For a created thing to have existence, it would need first to be created. In addition, certain conditions would need to be in place to mediate and maintain its physical form in the world. Take away the parents, the biological contributors, as well as physical sustenance and safety and there is no possibility for a human being to exist or continue to exist.

This is not so with God. Nothing first created God prior to God's existence. God has always existed. The Divine Nature as the structure of ontology is a given, a logical necessity. There is no specific set of environmental conditions that need to be in place for the Divine Nature to continue to exist.

Aseity as self-existence and independence is a crown of God's attributes and eventuates in the unchangeability of God as the Divine Nature. God's self-existence intrinsically excludes any idea of development in terms of physical or psychological maturation; a being that experiences growth has a beginning, a point antecedent to which it did not possess the power of its existence and was therefore brought into existence by an external factor rather than having its existence always only in itself. Immutability is also a source of other divine perfections in classical

---

38. Bavinck, *GD*, #192 (ET, Bolt, pp. 186-87). Even in the modern theological turn which he inaugurated, Friedrich Daniel Ernst Schleiermacher, the eighteenth- to nineteenth-century pastor and theologian, refused to countenance the notion of God as other than completely impervious to being affected in any way by anything in the created order, stiffly resisting any literal idea of God as personal and capable of being disclosed to sense perception as a "corruption" of doctrine. See his *CG* §4.4 (ET, Tice, Kelsey, and Lawler, p. 27).

39. Cf. Van Til, *Introduction to Systematic Theology*, 327-28.

theology, for it is as the Divine Nature is unchanging that the Divine Nature is impassible and eternal.

Biblical testimony suggests that, on the level of God as the entitative Trinity, there are two levels of divine interdependence. On an intra-trinitarian level, the divine persons while having no need of development (scil., physical and psychological maturation) are entirely dependent on one another for their ontology and fullness of personal being.

The fundamental interdependence within the godhead is indicated in the very names of the divine persons; that is, "Father", "Son", and "Holy Spirit". These divine personal names are not devoid of signification beyond inferring that three exist rather than any other number, within the single godhead.

As early as Justin Martyr, patristic writers applied preexisting terms with specific meanings to their understanding and articulation of the nature of the triune godhead. Justin employed the Greek word, *prosopon* (*persona* in Latin, to which the word "person" may be traced), which was used up to that time in the sense of dramatis personae to denote characters in dramas of classical antiquity, including divine figures, who were given lines to speak to enhance human interest.

As a matter of fact, *prosopon/persona* originally designated the mask worn by actors and acquired the wider definition of a role in the setting of a dialogue. Adapting the word and broadening its meaning to encompass not just a dramatic role but the social reality of a thinking and willing social being, Justin not only supposed that prophetic speech in the Bible was declaimed by actual persons, but that it was the divine *Logos* or Word who motivated both the act of speech and the content of that speech.[40]

Decades later, Tertullian outlined personal multiplicity within the godhead when attesting to how Scripture (in Gen 1:26; 3:22; Ps 110:1) alludes to God being in the company of God's Word and God's Spirit in God's Word.[41] Much later, Augustine of Hippo would suggest that the very use of the word, "I", presupposes the existence of a "you", an interlocutor.[42] Joseph Ratzinger, later Pope Benedict XVI, articulated a con-

---

40. Ratzinger, "Person in Theology," 441–43.
41. Ratzinger, "Person in Theology," 442–43.
42. Ratzinger, "Person in Theology," 446–47.

ception of human personhood in terms of fullness in self-transcendence, encompassing not just other human persons but, most of all, God.[43]

It is not possible to imagine the Father being without the Son, or the Father and Son being apart from the Holy Spirit, in virtue of their very names.

To the extent that fatherhood or paternity defines the being of the first person of the Trinity, this person cannot be conceptualized or even exist apart from the Son, the second person. To the extent that sonship or filiality determines the being of the second person of the Trinity, this person cannot be conceptualized or even exist apart from the Father, the first person. To the extent that spirituality defines the being of the third person of the Trinity, this person cannot be conceptualized or even exist apart from the Father and the Son, the first two persons, given the manner in which the Holy Spirit is defined in terms of the communion or spirit of love between these persons. After all, the Father is the Father of the Son, the Son the Son of the Father, and the Spirit the Spirit of Father and Son.[44]

Lest we misconceive the Father and Son as being somehow beholden to a third category, namely, the Holy Spirit, Barth makes it clear that the Spirit in proceeding from the Father and the Son is spirated by the Father and the Son and therefore that the bond of love between these two persons constitutes a relational act that is completely of their own desire and will.[45]

It was the significant error of theology to conceive of the divine persons as separate entities unified by a common nature, will, purpose, and action, a situation not ameliorated by the decision to adopt *hypostasis* as a category term for the Father, Son, and Holy Spirit which assumed, in post-Aristotelian classical Western philosophy, the signification of a thing that exists outside the mind or an individual thing. Origen melds both meanings in his description of the Trinity as comprising the three real individuals that are the Father, Son, and Holy Spirit.[46] In regarding the divine persons as real individuals, the interdependence among the divine persons is neglected.

It will not do either to view the Father, Son, and Holy Spirit as mere modes of manifestation on the part of one subject with its single

---

43. Ratzinger, "Person in Theology," 451–52.
44. Cf. Barth, *KD* IV.1, §58.4 (ET, Bromiley, p. 129).
45. Barth, *KD* IV.2, §64.4 (ET, Bromiley, p. 345).
46. Wolfson, *Faith, Trinity, Incarnation*, 318–20.

self-consciousness, will, power, and activity, as Karl Rahner does, given that this does away completely with even the presupposition of the possibility of mutual dependence, since there are now not even three personal subjects but just one and hence no possibility of interdependent subjects within the godhead.[47]

In truth, the divine persons are each triune persons, enveloping as each does in their ontology the being and experience of the other two persons though not the self-identity, consciousness, and agency of the other persons. We see this in the way Jesus depicts himself as the revealer and bearer of the Father's very presence, quite apart from his role as the Father's authorized representative. Jesus, for instance, does only the works that he sees the Father doing (John 5:17–30). Furthermore, Jesus constitutes the Father's very presence on earth among the disciples, so much so that when Philip requested the Lord to show him and the other disciples the Father, Jesus could respond by saying that whoever has seen him has already seen and met the Father in person (John 14:6–11).

As such, whenever God is spoken of in the context of this work, the referent is any one of the three divine persons, so that the word functions as a generic placeholder for the divine person. Consequently, Barth is well able to speak of God as knowing Godself; God as Father knowing Godself as Son and God as Son knowing Godself as Father.[48]

The ontological mutual indwelling of Father, Son, and Holy Spirit, in which each divine person contains already the other two divine persons as part of its own being, is represented in the depiction of Jesus as a man filled with the Holy Spirit as part of his own being, the Holy Spirit being his very spirit, a spirit which proceeds from him, witnesses to him, in whom we are afforded the knowledge of ourselves in Christ so that we may always be with Christ.[49]

The knowledge of God the Father is not attained through unaided human observation. If one person claims that they can see God's fatherly and munificent hand in the created order, another emphasizes instead the chaos and disruption that leaves many people suffering in privation. Instead, we clearly know the Trinity exists and that the first person of the triune godhead has the name of Father only through Jesus Christ himself.

One of the Lord's most memorable teachings which revealed the name of God the Father is the Lord's Prayer, by which he taught his

---

47. Rahner, DG, 2.c.5.b (ET, Donceel, pp. 75–76).
48. Barth, KD IV.2, §64.4 (ET, Bromiley, p. 344).
49. Barth, KD IV.2, §64.4 (ET, Bromiley, p. 347).

disciples and followers to invoke God as their heavenly Father. Classical theologians are quick to point out that the privilege of calling God our Father is conferred only upon the believers of Christ, not all individuals, seeing that Christ alone is Son by nature while the rest of humankind are, at most, children of God by grace through a process of adoption that takes place with a profession of faith in Christ as Lord and Savior.

The name of God the Father is therefore no abstract quantity removed from any relational signification, but permeated with the deep personal affection undergirding a profound and vital sense of duty shown by the Son toward the Father during the former's earthly life.

Whilst Father is not a nebulous concept far removed from concrete reality, the concrete reality of the Father is revealed only in relationship to the Son, Jesus, by whose life the concrete reality of the Son is at the same time made known.

With the exception of occasions on which the Father directly spoke with the Son in the hearing of others or of others through the testimony of the Son; namely, at the baptism of Jesus (Matt 3:13–17), the transfiguration (Matt 17:1–8), or at the request of the Son as religious leaders were plotting to kill him after he resurrected Lazarus from the dead (John 12:27–30), always in affirmation of the Son, the personality of the Father is disclosed only through the Son, Jesus Christ (John 1:18), by whose deeds the name of the Father, that is, the Father's identity and character, has been revealed (John 5:19–30; 17:4, 6).

Jesus so identified his works on earth with those of the Father, all done in the Father's name, that he could tell Philip his disciple that all who have seen him have effectively seen the Father, the Father being both in Jesus as well as acting through Jesus as the Father's perfect emissary, doing exactly as the Father does in all that Jesus does, so that the writer of the Epistle to the Hebrews can aver that Jesus is the exact representation of God's nature (John 14:6–14; Heb 1:3).

If Jesus manifested the Father by doing all his works in the name of the Father, as mirroring exactly the works that the Father does, the Father dwelling in Jesus in the first place, then Jesus also disclosed the concrete actuality of his own being and existence as the Son. During his human existence, Jesus vouchsafed a filial relationship marked by obedience and self-sacrifice along with a passionate love for God instantiated in his sensitivity towards God's will.

This was on full display at the garden of Gethsemane where Jesus made an earnest plea to the Father to relieve him of the cup of bitter and anguishing tribulation he had to bear, adding almost immediately an expression of his desire to do the Father's will alone rather than his own (Matt 26:36–39). It is clear from Jesus' subsequent statement to the effect that he could call on God and have twelve legions of angels sent to extricate him from the situation of danger if only he so desired that Jesus was under no compulsion from God the Father to act against his own will (Matt 26:47–54).

Ultimately, Jesus decided to obey the will of the Father; he willed the will of the Father, whatever it be, rather than seeking to be liberated from the clutches of a clear and present threat. Although his initial intuitions were to pursue self-preservation, yet he quickly composed himself, took command of his senses and, plumbing the depths of his soul, realized that what he truly wanted was only to submit to the purposes of the Father for his life.

In being so disposed toward the Father in an intimacy borne of an unbreakable communion of love such that he not only believed in the Father's goodness but trusted that the Father's intentions for his life were the best, fearing that his refusal to do the Father's will might disappoint the Father in some way, and in an undying and uncoerced loyalty to fulfill the desire of the Father characteristic typically of a slave or servant of a feudal lord, Jesus exhibited, disclosed, and modeled the perfect life of the Son of God the Father, thereby affording guidance for all who have believed and would come to believe in him in their own relationship to the Father (Heb 5:7–10).

If the impression that the Holy Spirit is a nebulous quantity is afforded to any person, this is premised on at least two reasons.

First, the Spirit being what it is cannot be naturally perceived by a human person in its personality. Second, the Spirit may have been decoupled in the minds of these individuals from its rightful connection with the Father and the Son.

In truth, knowledge of the Spirit, not as abstract quantity but as person, is accessible only through Jesus himself. It is Jesus who reveals the Spirit to be that which performs a role illuminating divine truth requiring intelligence, will, and emotional sensitivity such as that performed by a helper, counselor, or advocate, who takes up residence in the believer (John 14:16–17). The Spirit as *paraklētos* is one sent from a higher authority to bring timely assistance in the areas of encouragement, comfort, or intercession, a successor of Jesus in relation to his ministry on earth among the disciples and followers of Christ, the church.[50]

Akin to the Son, the Spirit arrives as an emissary to the Father, sent from the Father in the name of the Son or for the Son's sake; the Spirit is commissioned by the Father to be a tutor, dispensing the truth of God in particular situations as well as drawing out the memories in the disciples' minds of all that Christ had already taught them (John 14:26). The Spirit is the Spirit of truth who is requested by the Son of the Father, proceeding from the Father as the ultimate authority, so that it may be said that the Spirit proceeds from the Father and the Son in that order (John 15:26).

The Spirit comes in order to pick up the baton from Jesus in some of his roles as he had to return to the Father. The role of the Spirit entails working in the hearts of unbelievers and moving them towards a rightful recognition of their own sin of unbelief toward Christ, their misunderstanding concerning why Christ was executed and how they wrongly believed that he died because he had committed blasphemy and sedition, and the fugitive nature of the reign of Satan, the *de facto* ruler of the world.[51]

Jesus exercises a continued ministry of teaching through the Holy Spirit among the disciples, teaching which originates ultimately in God the Father. The Spirit informs the believers of things that are to take place in the future (John 16:7-15). Furthermore, the Spirit guides the believers as to what they ought to say when they are hauled in by authorities (Luke 12:11-12).

As such, the cognition of the personal reality of the Father, Son, and Holy Spirit is not precluded or evacuated of its meaning through rendering God as so wholly transcendent as to have no tellurian analogue, static and immovable perfection characterizing God's being and even the internal relations between the divine persons to such an extent that it is impossible to express what it means for the first person to be

---

50. Mounce, "Paraklētos."

51. Cf. Barth, *KD* IV.2, §64.3 (ET, Bromiley, p. 260). Barth underscores the fact that apart from the historical event of the crucifixion and the spiritual acceptance of the revelation by God of our true relationship to the cause of the death of the Son of God there as those whose sinfulness might very well move us to commit the same injustices against Christ—whose sins he therefore bore along with those of others—and of the fact that we are compared in moral terms with nobody else but Christ as perfect and proper human and always found completely wanting, there is no authentic recognition of the real and full measure of our sinfulness. Barth, *KD* IV.2, §65.1 (ET, Bromiley, pp. 381-91).

named Father, the second, Son, and the third, the Holy Spirit, apart from the fact that these names constitute markers distinguishing the respective persons as distinct one from another rather than coalescing to form an indistinguishable whole.

To the extent that God is conceived as supreme perfection that does not admit of dynamic change, including that associated with interpersonal relationships, for to speak of change within the godhead would be, so Plato thought, to introduce the possibility of a loss of or transition toward divine perfection, the divine names communicate very little, in spite of sounding relational.[52]

To put this simply, relationships presuppose some gain and loss in respect to knowledge and experience of the other person. The bond between two persons necessarily begins with a set of circumstances that bring them together, whether in a common household or a situation of friendship, in which a person gradually glimpses the personality and disposition of other persons, be this a child growing accustomed to the ways of a parent, vice versa, or two persons in a deepening friendship.

Under a Platonic philosophical framework, it is inconceivable that the divine persons of the godhead experience such a growth in an interpersonal relationship marked by a developing knowledge and experience of the other person on all sides. Yet this is just what characterizes the relationship between God and the human persons with whom God comes into contact.

Was it not said that God came to grasp Abraham's fear of God after the former put the latter to the test (Gen 22:12)? Or that God reacted to changing situations after Adam's disobedience in barring the human couple from access to the tree of life (Gen 3:22–24), that God decided to confound the builders of the city and tower of Babel because they had arrogated to themselves the place of God (Gen 11:1–9), or any other situation of divine intervention?

Especially remarkable were the two occasions on which God threatened to make an end of Israel because of their apostasy and install Moses as the founder of a new people and eventually relented because of Moses' intercession on behalf of Israel (Exod 32:1–14; Num 14:1–24). The biblical narrative presents God as a divine being who adapts to the changing behavior of the people of Israel. And what of Jesus' experience of resolute betrayal at the hands of his disciple and apostle, whom he

---

52. Sanders, "Historical Considerations," 62–64.

tried to turn back to the path of righteousness by giving an object lesson of servanthood, warning against betrayal, and offering him a piece of bread as a token of friendship and final plea to come back to his senses (John 13:21–30)?[53]

Is it inconceivable to postulate that Jesus' experience of dread in the face of the cross, in reaction to which he pleaded with the Father that he be permitted not to undergo the process of criminal execution, as well as his torrential emotions of being forsaken by God the Father, were genuine experiences at the conclusion of which the Son came to terms with the Son's role as the servant of God in the former incident and overcame the insurmountable temptation to renounce the Son's trust in the Father's goodness as the reason for hoping against all hope in the latter? This seems to be the clear signification of the witness in Heb 5:7–8 to the effect that the Son "learned obedience" (ESV) through his suffering.

Another argument in support of the thesis that God exists essentially in dynamic relationship with humankind with whom God, as well as human persons, grows in the understanding of and trust in the other person consists in the manner in which God's most perfect act—that is, the incarnation and atonement of Jesus as the revelation of the love of God—is given possibility and actualization exclusively in the movement and passage of time rather than an unchanging eternity.[54] There is nothing for a divine person to give to another divine person in eternity, under a classical schema, since no need or sin and therefore no redemption is involved.

Furthermore, it is not demeaning for God to exist in dynamic reality because relationality is superior to any form of impersonality, even if this is construed in terms of a transcendence whereby God is said to exist in an inaccessible dimension in unchanging perfection, as per classical theology. Although the eternal, transcendent, sovereign, omnipotent, immutable, and impassible God of classical Christian theology is often touted for its unparalleled and incommensurable sublimity, the one thing that cannot be said of such a deity is that it is eminently relational, a divine attribute very much integral to the scriptural presentation and depiction of God.

Instead, we see influential theologians such as Augustine of Hippo attempting to circumvent the clear testimony of the Bible to the humanity of God. Augustine contends that God did not actually acquire any new

---

53. Carson, *John*, 474.
54. González, *Reformation to Present*, 48.

knowledge regarding Abraham's faith when the latter passed a test involving an initially required sacrifice of Isaac, but that the verse (Gen 22:12), in which God appears to inform Abraham that God has witnessed his fear of God in his willingness even to offer his only son, miraculously conceived by Sarah when Abraham was one hundred and his wife ninety, as a burned offering, is to be understood in terms of God having caused Abraham's reverence of God to be known both to Abraham himself and all who will be exposed to the tradition of Scripture. Augustine's rationale for the gloss is that God was not oblivious of Abraham's fear of God.[55]

Similarly, the bishop of Hippo Regius reinterprets the descent of God mentioned in the narrative of the confounding of the builders of a city and tower at Babel in Gen 11:1–9 as, not so much designating a literal movement of God from heaven down to earth, but rather that God, in being said to descend, brings it about that people experience God's presence through localized supernatural occurrences and, in being said to see the city and tower at Babel, brings it about that people perceive and understand the builders of Babel in a new light, in all its obnoxiousness to God.

Moreover, Augustine apprehends of the various references to God going down to Babel and some others to go down there with God a summons to the angels of God to engage in those activities as divine representatives. Once again, the reason the theologian proffers for his reconceptualization of critical elements in the narrative is simply that God being omnipresent cannot be said to move from locality to locality without involving contradiction, nor can God being omniscient be said to see and understand what God had not formerly understood.[56]

In these two cases, Augustine presupposes God to be omniscient and omnipresent, allowing those presuppositions to drive and control his interpretation of the Bible. "God, who is always wholly everywhere, does not move locally" and "He does not by "seeing" learn some new thing, for He cannot ever be ignorant of anything".[57] In this, we see Augustine applying a Platonic conception of God as all-determining absolute reality to his reading of Scripture.

In Platonism, God is set infinitely and forever above created and contingent reality as the Good and Beautiful, constituting the source of the good and beautiful in creation; God or the Good and Beautiful

---

55. Augustine, *Civ.*, 16.32.
56. Augustine, *Civ.*, 16.5.
57. Augustine, *Civ.*, 16.5 (ET, Dods, p. 528).

comprises a divine Mind or Reason; a divine craftsman that is the Demiurge; the Absolute Living Creature, the Form of good and beauty itself to which other forms are attached, which constitutes the archetype of all things in creation; and the source of the animating principle that is the World-Soul.

The Absolute Living Creature, as the concrete expression of the divine Mind or Reason which exists mediately in all creatures as the source of their goodness and beauty, is the basis on which the Demiurge creates all things in the world, including living things through the World-Soul. The divine Form explains the reason human beings constantly seek the good that is in God alone, in perfection. Given Plotinus' pantheistic and rationalistic conception of the divine which does not admit of any direct creative activity on the part of the divine resulting in the created order, Augustine in his doctrine of divine ontology followed classical Platonism rather than Neoplatonism.[58]

Neoplatonism posits a series of gradations of divinity and creation involving a movement from oneness to plurality through processes of self-analysis and reasoning, eventuating in the creation of the cosmos, in which the purpose of human existence is to come to reflect the divine unity through enlightened contemplation. The hierarchy begins with the One, an indescribable reality exclusively occupied in thinking about itself. Out of the One proceeds a power (*dunamis*) which comprises the Intellect (*nous*) and its object of thought (*theōria*).

In objectifying itself in its contemplation about itself, that is, by conceptualizing itself as separate from the One, the Intellect, the true divine principle of all creation, gives rise to the Forms (*eidē*), constituting separate thoughts, having their own existence, analyzing the *dunamis*. Out of these Forms, a Soul emerges which is occupied with further analysis and the bringing into being of actual and living manifestations of the divine Intellect; namely, individual souls. These souls are concrete and living realizations of the potentialities of the Forms. As for the Cosmos or Nature, this is engendered by way of self-expression by the Soul's self-differentiation through thought and action.[59]

The goal of humanity is to merge with the One, possibly through ecstatic and mystical practices. The World-Soul as active spiritual energy is seen as inferior to the Intellect or Mind, which indulges in analytical and

---

58. Morley, "Western Concepts of God," 427–31.
59. Moore, "Neo-Platonism."

critical mental activity; the Intellect, in turn, is inferior to the One, where there is no longer any separation between self and other in a contemplation so profound that self-awareness simply disappears; it is to such a state of self-forgetful contemplation, where there is no more division between self and the rest of the world, that the human being is to aspire.[60]

The idea of transcendent divinity owes much to Plato, who conceives of God as the supreme and most sublime entity in all reality who is directly responsible for the form and shape of the contingent dimension of things, crafting (as demiurge) the whole and each thing in the whole out of matter, conceived as uncreated and eternal, in keeping with forms or archetypes tied to God as, in one aspect, the impersonal Form of the Good and Beautiful. Matter, while not being evil, is regarded as inferior to the invisible world of the forms, to which it can ever only be an imperfect copy through imitation and participation.[61]

To the extent that God transcends all created reality as its ultimate source and fount, no depiction of divinity is plausible other than that which presents God in omnipresence (being fount of all existence), omniscience (being the one who shapes all things), and omnipotence (being the creator and mover of all things).

God cannot be completely excised of the concurrent reality of the Father, Son, and Holy Spirit, God not being a fourth person or abstract nature, but divinity as concretely existent only in Father, Son, and Holy Spirit. Just as the divine persons considered distinctly do not exist in themselves but only in one another, and just as they do not exist as a whole in themselves but only in the divine substance, so the divine substance does not exist in itself but only in the divine persons.[62]

60. Brown, "Platonism," 427–31.

61. Chua, *ECRST*, 142; Morley, "Western Concepts of God"; Brown, "Platonism," 427–31. David Brown gives the examples of how a perfect knife or circle (perfection being defined according to the end for which a thing exists; cutting well in the case of a knife and having points on the circumference at the same distance from the center in the case of a circle) do not exist in practice or reality, pointing to the existence of a form of a knife, which is able to slice perfectly, and of a circle, where every point on its circumference is equidistant from the center.

62. That the divine persons are ontologically dependent is laid bare through a description such as we find in Col 1:16 whereby the same Christ is said to be the agent, instrument, as well as reason of and for creation. This can only be so if it is grasped that, when all things were brought into material existence over a long period of time, both Christ and the Father authorized or decreed the angels to execute this work, in such a way that it is veracious to affirm that the Father enacted the decree of creation through the Son in that the Son is a passive dimension of the Father's being, both Christ and the Father issuing the command to create the material universe for the sake of Christ.

The concrete existence of God in the Father, Son, and Holy Spirit is required for God to be more than a supreme being whose character as loving, peaceful, and unifying is nothing other than the result of God's relationship with the created order but very much expressed internally in inner relationships of love, peace, and unity between the divine persons from the beginning. Such concrete existence is also required for God to be able to create and maintain relationships of these kinds among people, and not out of a need of any sort to have a partner to love.[63]

Aside from an ontological interdependence, we may speak also of a relational dependence among the members of the divine Trinity.

In an example of the relational need of Father, Son, and Holy Spirit for one another, we may adduce the fact that at the crucifixion the Father may be said to have grieved the loss of the Son of the Father; that the Son receives all things from the Father during the Son's earthly ministry; and the Holy Spirit has its identity defined for itself as one sent by the Father at the Son's request to carry on the earthly ministry of Christ as helper, counselor, and advocate.

In view of the scriptural testimony, it is almost axiomatic that the Father, and not just the Son, suffered when Jesus died on the cross.[64] When the Gospel of John witnesses that the manner in which God demonstrated love for humankind has lain in the form of the Father giving the Father's only Son for the sake of bringing eternal life to the world, these words are pregnant with meaning.

It behooves us to consider whether it is at all possible that God the Father displayed no emotion whatsoever in that great display of love for humanity, whether it is conceivable that the Father regarded the giving of the Son merely in a transactional or mechanical way as an act that ought necessarily to be done in accord with the divine nature. This may be an option if divine love were radically redefined in opposition to the love experienced and given among human beings, and yet this cannot be the case, considering that divine love is to be the model and paradigm for human love (1 John 4:7-21).

It is not that the divine love which we are to emulate is to be restricted exclusively to that which Jesus showed to us, leaving a possibility for us to continue to think of the Father's love as transcendent and therefore without any emotionality. For almost immediately after

---

63. Cf. Barth, *KD* IV.2, §64.4 (ET, Bromiley, pp. 341-42, 345-46).
64. Lee, *TAP*, 82, 91-94.

PART 2: HUMANITY'S IMAGING OF THE DIVINE

John exhorts believers to have their interactions marked by love one for another, seeing that love originates from God and those who display the character of love are born of God and have knowledge of God (v. 7), John goes on to specify in the course of what he is saying that the referent of "God" has been the Father all along, since God is the one who sent God's Son into the world (see v. 9).

A second way in which relational interdependence among the Trinity can be seen is how the Son receives all things from the Father during the earthly ministry of the Son.

Therefore, Jesus speaks of how he as the Son makes a point of only engaging in such activity as he sees the Father involved in, works which the Father shows the Son that the Father does (John 5:19). In short, the Son follows the lead of the Father in the nature of the works that the Son does. As a matter of fact, the very teaching in which Jesus engages is only that which the Father delivers (John 7:16).

According to Christ, the work of the Father which he emulates includes the breathing of new life into dead persons (John 5:21), presumably referring to events which transpired in the time of Elijah and Elisha, where Yahweh raised the son of the widow of Zarephath (1 Kgs 17:17–24; the resurrection happened through Elijah's prayer, as per vv. 21–22), the son of the Shunammite woman (2 Kgs 4:18–37; the resurrection took place by means of Elisha's prayer, as per v. 33), and a man whose corpse touched Elisha's bones while being buried (2 Kgs 13:20–21; Elisha was obviously already dead so he had no part in the resurrection, which God performed directly). These events took place during the era of the divided Israelite monarchy, in the northern kingdom of Israel.

Similarly, Jesus performs three resurrections during his earthly existence, raising Jairus' daughter (Mark 5:21–24, 35–43), a young man, the son of a widow in Nain (Luke 7:11–17), and his friend Lazarus (John 11:1–44). In the third instance alone, Jesus is witnessed as having spoken to God about something he had said that God had certainly heard (vv. 41–42). This might have been a reference to a private prayer on the part of Jesus for God to raise Lazarus from the dead, given what Martha said about God being inclined to hear Jesus' prayer even after Lazarus had died (v. 22). Even if this was the case, Jesus clearly participated in the raising of Lazarus, as it was by his command that Lazarus was revived and walked out of the tomb (vv. 43–44).

Furthermore, the Father grants the Son the prerogative to judge all people, whether living or dead, according to whether they have been receptive to the word of Christ and exercised their faith in the Father or done good, in which case they have crossed from death to life and will enter into eternal life at the resurrection, or done wickedly, in which case they will enter into judgment at the resurrection (John 5:22–29).

Curiously, Jesus points out in John 5:26 that the Father, who has life inherent, has granted the Son to also possess life inherent. While the verse may relate to the authority of the Son granted by the Father to pronounce a decree of life on human souls dead or alive, it may also bolster the perspective that the Son has authority to do so by virtue of the fact that the Father ontologically dwells in the Son and allows the Son to carry out the Father's wishes in relation to the ultimate judgment of humankind.[65] This interpretation would be more consistent with the earlier pattern in which the Son emulates the Father, instead of one in which the Son acts on the Son's own initiative in executing divine judgment, doing so apart from the Father.

A third way in which we can detect interdependence within the triune community based on relationship is that the Holy Spirit has the identity of the Spirit defined for itself as one sent by the Father at the Son's request to carry on Christ's earthly ministry as helper, counselor, and advocate.

In spite of their ontological and relational interdependence, the divine persons are not subject to growth or development whether in physicality or psychology.

On an extra-trinitarian level, the divine persons experience a qualified dependence on human beings. While human actions cannot endanger God's existence, yet human actions can cause sadness to God or bring God joy. Therefore God, while having ontological aseity in relation to the created order, is relationally and emotionally interlocked with human beings because God is emotionally invested in their wellbeing. Such emotional commitment leading to emotional care and solicitude is borne out in human

---

65. If the Son is judge of all humankind on the basis of the Father being in the Son, will the rule of the Son during the millennium be theocratic in its character? This need not be the sole supposition, since all things are to be subjected to the Son for the purpose of the final judgment, after which the kingdom will pass back to the Father (1 Cor 15:20–28). What, then, will be the tenor of the eternal reign of the Father? It will be a rule of love and non-compulsion rather than of violence and compulsion, not so much a theocracy as a fair rule of human beings among themselves which takes into account the needs and concerns of the populace whilst constantly looking to God as Trinity for wisdom and help to analyze, critique, and implement the policies of just and compassionate elected leaders.

relationship. In turn, the profound depth of human emotionality in intimate relationship functions as a substantive symbol of God's emotional binding with the future and fate of humankind.

At this juncture, the question is to the fore of the extent to which we may speak of God as Trinity, while ontologically independent of humankind, as being dependent on humankind. Classical and Reformed theologians have been reticent to speak of God as capable of being characterized by any manner of emotionality.

And yet, Scripture is replete with references and a witness to the myriad ways in which God was affected with sorrow and joy at the commission of particular human actions which called for those emotions. In a striking example, the biblical prophet Zephaniah highlighted the way in which God would express joy over the restoration of Israel, comforting the nation as though it were a terrified infant as a tender parent would do, serenading the child with a loud song (Zeph 3:17). In another, very different, case, God's formerly enraged heart swelled with compassion at the thought of a disobedient nation, the northern kingdom of Israel, whom God could not bear to punish yet again (Hos 11:8–9).

God is emotionally invested in God's human creation, a fact borne out in the story of Cain and Abel in Gen 4:1–8. Cain was the older son born to the first couple, Adam and Eve. After Cain, the couple had another son, Abel. The two sons worked in different professions, Cain being a farmer and Abel a shepherd. One day Cain decided to bring to God an offering of plants while Abel his brother brought the firstborn of his flock of sheep with their fat portions.

God was pleased with Abel's offering of the animal sacrifices though not with Cain's offering of plants, for Abel gave God the first and best of the fruit of his labor, whereas Cain only gave God a random part of his produce. Abel believed that giving God his most precious possessions was the best investment of his life, because God knows how to reward God's servants with eternal rewards. Not that Abel necessarily thought he should serve God just because there are rewards in store, but that he likely knew he did not have to fear that he would be shortchanged in his dedication to God, apprehending that God would surely properly compensate him for his service for God. On the other hand, Cain did not exercise such faith toward God, leading him to make an offering out of a random part of what he had rather than giving his first and best.

If Abel's giving his first and best to God has any application at all to our own lives, this lies in its highlighting the importance of prioritizing God. One who puts God first naturally serves God rather than their ambitions or personal goals. Whatever they do, whether at work, play, home, or in their social lives, they do it mindful of God's presence in their lives, thanking God, communing with God, obeying God, and serving God. God becomes the center of their lives rather than simply the source of a set of obligations they satisfy grudgingly or mindlessly.

It is well to focus our attention on Cain's anger toward God in response to God's acceptance of Abel's offering but not his own. God asked Cain why he was angry. This may have been due to Cain's sense that he was entitled to the favor of God. Those fall into this trap who blame God for not protecting or blessing them the way they see God protect and bless others. The truth is that God is not obligated to do anything for us. Even then, God is most gracious and generous toward us. God is not behind any injustice, real or merely perceived. Sometimes, we compare ourselves with others and become envious of others. Yet that is the problem of the value system of society. Society values certain things rather than other things and so we follow the lead of the prevailing culture and end up thinking we are worth less or even worth nothing, compared to other people.

We see that God was concerned about Cain's emotional state because God asked Cain why he was angry. And so we need not feel that God stands aloof from us. We may freely pour out our concerns to God, and refrain from grumbling and complaining against God, the church, or Christians, which inevitably put us far away from God, given that God is concerned about our emotional state. We can trust that God means only well toward us and we can even ask God to show us why we are angry, and help us to untangle the knots of our anger.

Many Asians were brought up in such a way that they were taught not to ask too many questions, challenge authority, or be too emotional.[66] As a result, these persons came to mirror the advice they were given and neglected their own emotions. Instead of dealing with those powerful inner torrents which they were told to fear and which they did not try to understand, they focus on academic and professional success, becoming very pragmatic people who want to have something to show for their success in life.

66. Louie, "Asian Parenting."

PART 2: HUMANITY'S IMAGING OF THE DIVINE

It can be hard therefore to come to terms with God's emotional concern, to understand why God would ask anyone the question God asked Cain, "Why are you angry, and why has your face fallen?" (Gen 4:6 ESV) This, however, is a liberating question, simply because it conveys that God is not afraid of or offended by our emotions, including negative emotions we may nurse towards another person. God was not too terrified of Cain's anger towards his brother Abel, only deeply concerned for Cain. Similarly, God is also deeply concerned for our emotional states. Whatever emotions we may be currently caught up in, God is concerned for us, and wants to guide us to understand our own emotions. We can afford to give God and ourselves a chance to understand our emotional life. Reading books or articles on emotions will also be helpful.

Another question God asked Cain was a rhetorical one. God asked: "If you do well, will you not be accepted?" (Gen 4:7 ESV) If we have ever looked at the lives of the saints or other giants of faith, figures in church or Christian history, or godly Christians around us, and wondered why they seem to have a more intimate relationship with God than we do, then we need not be overly concerned. It is not because we are a particularly secular person or that these others were or are particularly saintly. It is simply that they have discovered the way to intimacy with God. Abel found the way to be accepted by God. Cain did not. And God was imploring Cain not to fret, despair, or feel hopeless, but learn from godly example. In Cain's case, he could have learned from Abel. Instead, he allowed his envy toward his younger brother to take over himself.

Envy is typically the product of narrow societal ideals and values. Cain may have felt consumed with envy towards his brother perhaps because being spiritual was held up as a high ideal in his time. Perhaps his parents had high hopes for him as an older son after the couple was thrust out from the garden of Eden. Perhaps his parents had raised him with very conditional affection, ingraining in him the idea that he could only be accepted if he were a spiritual person.

In Cain's mind, there was no room for failure. Therefore, when he was not accepted by God the first time, he was devastated. The very same thing happens in modern society when we brand certain people failures for not having achieved certain academic grades, holding certain jobs, or attaining a certain standard of living.[67] When we impose such narrow

---

67. In a Singaporean context, the professions of doctor and lawyer are often placed on a pedestal in a culture that sets great store by earning power, social standing, and social impact. See Chong, "Why Are Law and Medicine So Popular in Singapore?"

ideals across the board, favoring only certain attributes and disparaging others, it is little wonder that so much envy is bred among people.

In God's economy, there are no such invidious or lopsided norms, values, and ideals. The very fact that the question begins, "if you do well," demonstrates that God is asking for something that anyone can do. God is not simply interested in the hyper wealthy, the hyper luxurious, the hyper famous, the hyper successful. God is interested in everyone, interested that they are willing to take up God's invitation to do what is needed, to do well, so that they can be accepted by God.

Furthermore, God said to Cain, "And if you do not do well, sin is crouching at the door. Its desire is contrary to you, but you must rule over it." (Gen 4:7 ESV) This is a warning to Cain that if he does not do anything to curb his strong emotional torrents, they will eventually overcome him and cause him to do something he will regret.

This is a cascading process. The fact that sin had entered Cain's heart showed that he did not do what God had instructed him to do. Now that it had entered, Cain still had a responsibility to do whatever it takes to keep his emotional situation under control. This is a reminder that we cannot ever give up the struggle against sin. We cannot give up letting God come into our emotional lives to heal us. We cannot give up finding out more about our emotional responses and their undercurrents. And we cannot be resigned to always allowing our emotions to dictate our actions. We have to take responsibility for our actions, pick ourselves up each time we fall, knowing God will forgive us, and try again. And we keep putting up a good fight, without ever losing hope.

If God is concerned about our emotional state with its undercurrents and that we keep our emotional state under proper reins, God's gentle and loving presence penetrates the human psyche, and the Christian faith can hardly be regarded as a superficial and shallow religion that only expects its adherents to fulfill certain religious obligations. It is rightly said that Christianity is a personal relationship with God. To the extent that that is true, then we need to let God invite us away from the narrow standards of success in the world, follow God's fair standards, and do well according to those standards so we can be accepted by God. These standards include love, forgiveness, compassion, empathy, patience, gentleness, kindness, goodness, truthfulness, justice.

Human experience, if one is sufficiently fortunate, encompasses expressions of commitment to the emotional wellbeing of one another. These profound expressions in human relationship constitute a substantive symbol of God's emotional commitment to see humankind through to its future.

Strangely enough, emotional investment between human individuals is bound up with the idea of authority. That the divine mandate for humankind entails having dominion over all of creation (Gen 1:26, 28) symbolizes the human duty to use their authority in ways that reflect the image and likeness of God. In truth, each human being carries authority and influence in some specific sphere of life over which others do not exercise that same primary degree of influence. This is the case with regard to a father in a modern nuclear family, who has authority over his household, over which not even a prime minister, president, or king has a comparable degree of influence.

Even a person in a seemingly subordinate position such as a child or a wife in a non-egalitarian marital relationship commands influence, given that the child would have friends over whom they exercise more influence than their own parents in the sense that their peers are more willing to divulge their true feelings to them more readily than to any adult. Moreover, when the child grows to become an adult and starts to lead his own family and the father moves in to live with the child's family, the authority of the child's father diminishes even as the father remains de jure the head of the family of which his son is and will always be a member.[68] Similarly, a wife in a modern home is typically equal in authority to the husband, though even if she is not accorded that equality, she continues to exercise a significant degree of influence over her husband, children, close friends, and in the realm of domestic administration.[69]

---

68. Cf. Lee, *TAP*, 169–70.
69. Cf. Lee, *TAP*, 155, 161–62.

7

The Christian Doctrine of Adoption

Divine-Human Communion as Imperative for Full Personhood

THE QUESTION OF THE degree to which relationship with a divine reality and presence is requisite for full humanity is tethered to that of whether God is necessary in the first place. While death of God theologians had contended that the divine is not in fact needed as an explanation for the condition of the world and developments that take place within it, and this in view of naturalistic cosmological theory, the need for human beings to assume moral responsibility in such a way as to not be impeded by the mythos of a determinative divine influence, as well as the worst terrors and traumas of disasters such as the Holocaust, a contestation continued beyond the death of the movement, in truth it is an untenable affirmation.[1]

Much depends on how one defines "God". If deity is to be identified as a supernatural causative agent whose actions are conceived as occupying the very roles that natural causation fills in a naturalistic apprehension of causal processes hypothesized as bringing the universe into existence and accounting for its entire course of development, where either God or natural conditions must explain the growth of a beansprout, and God is taken to be the real explanation, then there is little basis for faith in God.

Yet if God were defined in the sense of an ultimate and essential source of existence and morality, such as determines human reality, in which belief in God consists in one's grasp of the fact that neither did

1. Fiddes, *Creative Suffering of God*, 174–77.

they wish or will themselves into existence—a meaningless statement, because illogical, anyway—nor wish or will themselves into existence as moral agents consistently under inward desire and pressure to be respectful, responsible, caring, empathetic, and honest, at least in relationship to those they value, then one has to admit that the cumulative evidence on a universal scale of a human morality, though limited in many ways, in and of itself attests to the existence and reality of God.[2]

Accordingly, all already know God, regardless of their explicit religious or non-religious profession. Barth does not err in spelling out the ways in which an ignorance of God foments a lack of true equality and solidarity in relationship to others, given that apart from recognizing God as Father, it is improbable that one will recognize the other as their fellow sibling; an inability to recognize the superiority of spirit over body and yet the need to not neglect either; as well as an incapacity to know one's true origin and destination.[3]

Yet if all already exist in relationship with God by virtue of being human, then the nonexistence of such a relationship is impossible, and all that matters is the degree to which a person probes their inner ontological and moral nature and surfaces with insight as to what the answers they discover mean for their relationship with others and with themselves.[4] Seeing, for instance, that they did not generate their own existence or shape the persons that they are, some form of gratitude or at least relief is owed to that factor which ought to impel the soberness of a life of self-giving and self-loving.

Just as an awareness of the finitude of a human lifespan is almost certain to herald a sense of purpose and social calling according to Paul Tillich, so the recognition that none could be or be as they currently are in the absence of an ontological and moral source is sure to guide a person into a sober responsibility in life toward self and the other.[5]

The argument is untenable that God does not exist just because God cannot be empirically measured and therefore have God's existence proven in any conclusive manner. This is for the reason that God cannot be empirically detected and measured by any scientific instrument

---

2. Chua, "Religions as Path to God," 263.
3. Barth, *KD* IV.2, §65.2 (ET, Bromiley, pp. 420–24).
4. In the estimation of Pope Francis, there is "divine inspiration" in all religious traditions, not just Christianity. We would add that such an influence is present even among humanists. Cf. Pope Francis, *Message to International Meeting for Peace*.
5. Fiddes, *Creative Suffering of God*, 195.

or apparatus. In turn, the explanation for this inability to be scientifically detected and measured is not due to a limitation on the part of these instruments, but rather the nature of those attributes and qualities that have most to do with God, that is, with God's essential character.

Specifically, qualities such as faith, hope, and love concern an expression of a moral personality toward another moral personality. Only a subject with a self-identity and self-consciousness (so that self and other may be differentiated), along with a faculty and alacrity for believing something about another subject with a self-identity and self-consciousness which is not empirically provable, can exercise faith (nearly identifiable with trust) in another subject, which also has a faculty and alacrity for believing things of the same nature about other subjects. It is the same for hope, which entails a capacity and readiness to be disposed toward a future possibility that may differ from the current state of affairs in which the subject in whom hope is reposed finds itself; and for love, involving a faculty and alacrity to empty and completely give of oneself to another.

These qualities are imperceptible and uncertain in the absence of personal intuition and trust. God as a spiritual being is approached in the same way faith, hope, and love are demonstrated toward other persons and cherished from them to us. It is completely possible for two persons to be in some form of physical proximity to one another, bear some relationship to one another, and yet have no trust in each other's faith, hope, and love, or even be without faith, hope, and love, on the part of one party if not both. If that is the case, however, the relationship is unlikely to last very long.

A person who calls himself the friend of another is not likely to be appreciated in the long run if he begins to question and doubt what his friend says, perhaps even suspect the latter's motives for initiating any conversation or activity. A biological relationship might be inerasable on a physical level, yet a lack of trust, or faith, hope, and love, is a recipe for lasting estrangement. Suspicion misjudges an authentic companion and prevents their faith, hope, and love from reaching one, while an inability to exercise faith, hope, and love toward another person makes a relationship one-sided.

Contrary to the supposition of Reformed theology, true conversion and regeneration is not evinced by anything approaching theological rectitude or a mystical and profound experience of one's utter sinfulness, but rather the ability to love, to give of oneself to another person.

Consider 1 John 4:7–8, 12, in which St. John exhorts believers to love one another, for the very reason that love has its origin in God and therefore that those alone who display love for others can rightly affirm that they have been born of God and that they truly know God. The person who does not practice love cannot be said to know God, since God is love. As a matter of fact, despite the dictum that no person has visibly encountered God, it remains true that believers who love one another show by that very fact that God dwells in them and that God's love is made complete in them. Indeed, those who live in love and obey and practice God's commandments dwell in God, and God in them (1 John 3:24; 4:16); those alone who practice righteousness are righteous, in the same manner that the Son is righteous (1 John 3:7).

One should not entertain false beliefs about Christ as an adherent of the Christian faith, such as the view that Jesus Christ is a purely spiritual being who has not taken on a material human body (1 John 4:1–6), and this because it harms and undermines God's revelation to humankind, obstructing belief in a divine Christ who alone can be wholeheartedly worshipped, worthily emulated, and fully obeyed, as the perfect revelation of the Father's love for us.[6]

In 1 John 4:9–11, we find an apostolic witness to the fact that God's love for us was made apparent in the midst of believers in that God sent God's only Son into the world, with the object of enabling and empowering us to live through the Son. The coming of the Son into the world exposes our lack of love and reveals and extols God's love for us, love enough that God should send God's Son to be the atoning sacrifice for our sins. St. John concludes with the exhortation for believers to meditate on God's love for them, and find in that divine love an impetus to love one another.

If love is the manifestation of the knowledge and indwelling of God in an individual person, it seems disingenuous to restrict these statements to Christians alone and leave out adherents of other religious faiths or even non-religious persons, among whom genuine love may just as frequently be found.

Consequently, it may be asserted that by the very fact that a human person may repose faith, hope, and love in another person and that other person may entrust themselves to the faith, hope, and love of the first individual, God's existence may be sensibly assumed as a given.

---

6. For an outline of Docetism, see Erickson, *Christian Theology*, 650–51.

The same faculties expressed in showing and receiving faith, hope, and love to and from another person are entailed in believing in God. Indeed, God is the material cause of faith, hope, and love among human persons, as St. John understood, through displaying faith, hope, and love to human beings in their pre-incarnate angelic forms.

This faith on the part of God toward humankind is manifested in the manner in which God sent God's Son into the world, an act that reveals God's trust that humankind would respectfully and reverently receive God's Son (Matt 21:33–44), but even prior to that in the manner in which God as Trinity does not simply do away with us in one fell swoop but gives us space and room to be whom God has called us to be.

Divine hope is reposed in human beings in the fact that God gives us time to actualize our moral capacities rather than penalizing us at the first opportunity, trusting that we will come to be contrite, repent, and make amends for our errors.

As for love, this is most evident in the manner in which in spite of humankind's depravity and sinfulness in oppressing, persecuting, abusing, and murdering the Son of God, neither the Father nor the Son gave in to resentment and rancor, but always practiced only forbearance, forgiveness, mercy, grace, and compassion. Given their centrality in legitimating and constituting the content of belief in God, it is little wonder that St. Paul declares faith, hope, and love to be abiding qualities, of which the greatest, of course, is love (1 Cor 13:13).

The crucifixion is in and of itself a mirror of the world's inner state of morality that unblushingly discloses the human abuse of religion, insofar as Jesus the Son of God was conspired against and led to his unjust execution not by those who might be described as profane but religionists, those with a zeal to execute what they believe to be the divine will in the concrete situation in which they find themselves.

With these remarks and considerations in place, there is occasion now to delineate the central features of a secular and religious perspective of the psychological necessity of religion for the human individual.

In an atheistic view, the fullness of human personhood is not linked to the acceptance of tenets of a religious tradition. A person can do very well without religion. As a matter of fact, a person can do without religion very well. Some atheists are of the opinion that people acting out of religious conviction, misguided ones to be sure, have engendered much harm. It is quite easy to pinpoint historical events such as the Christian crusades of the eleventh to the thirteenth centuries to make a case for an ethical dilemma brought about by religious zeal arising from ignorance.

More than constituting an individual in the fullness of human personhood, it occasionally seems to critics as though religion served to undermine humanness, eradicating the respectful tolerance and mutual concern that should characterize all interactions between people, including groups that seem different to one another. There will be others, still within the same classification, who do not see any absolute necessity, though according clear benefit for those so disposed, in terms of psychological wholeness for having a religious affiliation or identity, whether this be in an institutional religion or more a form of personal transcendentality and spirituality (Religious cult as unnecessary for human personhood).[7]

Within a religious perspective of human personhood, religion is regarded as a central component or dimension of human existence. This leads to varying degrees of commitment to a religious tradition, ranging from occasional exposure to some form of religious teaching or practice to a lifelong dedication within a monastic or ascetical community.

In an evangelical Christian conception of the role of religious faith in the fullness of human personhood, it is proposed that the human being was created for relationship with God. The Swiss psychiatrist Paul Tournier observes that the Bible makes an assertion about the nature of human personhood, that it consists in the fact that the human individual is an entity whom God addresses in speech, with whom God maintains an interpersonal relationship.[8]

As a matter of fact, in Tournier's estimation, for Scripture to claim humankind as having been crafted in the divine similitude is shorthand for expressing human social capacity and sociality, with the freedom that that capacity entails.[9] It may even be suggested that a person stands in danger of damnation unless they accept reconciliation with God

---

7. Richard Dawkins expresses the view that the existence of God may not be necessary for human morality. Dawkins, *God Delusion*, 227.

8. As to how one differentiates between God's actual speech and a symptom of psychosis, one is able to do so by the fact that God's speech always only counsels moral responsibility and urges against sin. Although God did make something of an exception in instructing Abraham to sacrifice his son Isaac as a burned offering (Gen 22:1–2), yet by the intimacy of relationship he enjoyed with God, Abraham was able to rightly recognize the voice that commanded him to do so as God's own.

9. Tournier, *Meaning of Persons*, 163

through explicit profession of belief in Christ (Religious cult as necessary for human personhood).

In my estimation, the Bible does not dictate that all human individuals profess explicit faith in Jesus Christ, but simply and merely indicates that a religious, spiritual, mystical, or transcendental dimension is so central to human nature as to facilitate full personhood (Spiritual-transcendent as necessary for human personhood).

Epistemology

It is worth pursuing the question as to the reason some are able to interpret Scripture in such a way as to promote a form of religio-social exclusivism. Wide divergences in interpretation of Scripture tend to arise by reason of either focusing on one's duty, responsibility, or obligation before God as a legal authority or on one's relationship to God as a being of all-embracing goodness intuitively and emotively approached.

The possibility of theological contention between persons of a legalistic mental tendency on the one hand and a relational one on the other is copiously illustrated in the confrontations Jesus had with the scribes and Pharisees who, insisting that Jesus had taken leave of cherished Jewish customs such as the Sabbatical laws, were met instead with the counterresponse on his part as to how they had twisted the Mosaic law into a legalistic, ritualistic, and reductionistic system which hindered the sick from accessing the healing they needed and the hungry from having their hunger satisfied while allowing its strictest adherents who ignored important moral commandments such as filial piety and love for one's neighbor to vaunt their piety in keeping religious rules in a punctilious manner.

More critical for our purposes, the legalistic bent of mind as contrasted with a relational bent accounts for the inability to accept a literalist interpretation of Scripture's teaching on the truth of salvation in Christ in a manner that eschews exclusivism. Such a cast of mind may well be due to an individual having been brought up and shaped in such a way as to value more highly than anything else their attention to conformity whether as a means of finding safety and security in an inner and outer world riddled with danger and insecurity, as a means of personal fulfillment, having been a reliable condition for parental approval a person may have counted on since their formative years, or as a means of satisfying one's need for power and control over others.

Some form of tribalism may be at work in groups of individuals who tend to play up differences between people. The Christian church evinces such tribalism when it comes away from its reading of Scripture and of how it teaches Jesus as the only way to the Father, the only one by whose name (in the sense of the identity and character of the person) God bestows salvation, the one at whose name every knee shall bow and every tongue confess that Jesus is Lord, with the mindset and conviction that it alone, among and in stark contrast to all other religious communities, teaches, points, and leads to the way of spiritual life and vitality in a manner that no other faith tradition does or can do, not recognizing that Christ is the same source of deepening spirituality and humanity at work in other religious and non-religious traditions.[10]

This is not the teaching of Scripture, however, seeing as it asserts one's community as superior to or more important than all others. Such parochialism is based on a Platonic conception of God as absolute subject, interpreted through the grid of the teaching of St. Augustine of Hippo and Martin Luther, both of whom grappled with different forms of psychological dysfunctionality which were misunderstood as symptoms of a controlling power of sin, passed down through the generations from Adam, over the human heart, mind, will, and behavior.[11]

---

10. Religious exclusivism may be an epiphenomenon of some form of social prejudice. Consider the attitude of James and John toward the Samaritan village which rejected Jesus because they were making their way to Jerusalem on a pilgrimage and there was historical enmity between Jews and Samaritans (Luke 9:51–56), where they asked if the Lord would like them [making it look as if it was the Lord's will instead of blatantly asking permission to do so] to call down fire from heaven, some manuscripts add, in the manner of Elijah in face of two armed detachments sent by King Ahaziah of the northern kingdom of Israel to arrest him (2 Kings 1). The nub of the problem, of course, is how they went ahead of the Lord in presuming that he would approve of their brutal designs for the villagers. Moreover, they were completely unaware of the underlying prejudices they held as Jews against the Samaritan people, enmity between the two groups due to the Samaritans organizing their religious cult around a different temple, Samaritan assimilation of Greek paganism during the rule of Antiochus IV Epiphanes, a Jewish invasion, and a Samaritan religious harassment and massacre in the first century AD. This is a psychological phenomenon known as projection, whereby a person finds it difficult to acknowledge troubling feelings (in this case, social prejudice) and unconsciously gives these feelings a more acceptable spin, perhaps with the help of religious language. *NBD*, s.v. "Samaritans" (Williamson, pp. 1052–53).

11. See Chua, *ECRST*, 20, 47–50, 77–80, 248–79.

When Aurelius Augustinus interpreted his intense psychological struggle with an uncontrollable desire to seek and obtain sexual self-gratification and continuously satisfy an insatiable appetite for food in terms of a swingeing hold that sin had over his soul which he experienced himself as incapable of loosening by his own strength and for deliverance from which he was convicted he had to turn solely to Christ, the great bishop of Hippo Regius in Numidia, Roman North Africa, set the tone for Western Christianity as its most influential theologian.

It cannot be maintained that St. Augustine was completely wrong about his spiritual self-diagnosis and assessment of the spiritual state of all of humanity. An obsessive preoccupation with sexual activity, regardless of whether any legal immorality is involved, necessarily detracts from one's properly focused engagement in the many areas of human life as a whole. To the extent that sexual behavior or an eating pattern is compulsive, it is dysfunctional; that is, it serves to impede an individual's psychological, social, and professional functioning in comprehensive aspects. For one, it is challenging for such a person to concentrate on what they are compensated to do at work, carry out their duties at home, or pay the necessary attention to their physical and mental wellbeing. Insofar as Augustine's feelings, thoughts, and actions relating to sex or food affected his ability to discharge his different responsibilities as a human person, they can be justifiably described as problematic from a functional point of view.

Is it fair, however, for the same bishop to declare himself, and by extension all of humankind, as being under the thrall of a principle of sin for the very reason that he suffers these afflictions of his mind and for no other? In the first place, does Augustine make such a pronouncement in any way? It is evident from his self-testimony that the bishop of Hippo considered his excessive consumption of food and drink, and for that matter, of anything else, to be sin.

Speaking of his constant watchfulness against slipping into a boundless desire to satisfy his physical appetite for food and drink, Augustine first contrasted his battle with food against that with fornication, having previously highlighted that food being required for sustenance cannot be completely avoided (the implication being that sexual sin can be more easily avoided in Augustine's case), remarking that he had made a nearly complete end of his sex addiction (except in dreams) but not his addiction to food. Subsequently, the bishop assesses himself to be unlike the person who is able to exercise self-control over their physical appetite:

"Who is the person, Lord, who is never carried a little beyond the limits of necessity? Whoever this may be is great and will magnify your name . . . I am not like that, for I am a sinful man."[12]

Whatever the church might make of addictions to sex or food, with the benefit of modern scientific studies, we now know that certain individuals are more predisposed than others to specific forms of addiction and we have discovered ways of helping individuals to manage their addictions. Contrary to the pious supposition of the great Latin theologian presently in our focus, suffering from compulsive sexual behavior or binge-eating disorder does not single out a person as being especially sinful, nor is it symptomatic of an insuperable power of sin biologically transmitted and operative in the lives of every human being post-Adam.[13] Instead, it is facilitated by the higher risk to which individuals in certain formative life situations are exposed, particularly those involving some form of abuse. For every excessive desire, there is an underlying psychological entanglement that can be unraveled and there is a psyche that can be put back in order with the right individual spiritual-moral and professional-therapeutic approach.

The appeal to Augustine of a Platonic conception of God may very well have been due to its emphasis on an unhindered divine determination of worldly reality, a theory which would have held especial relevance and breathed hope for a person suffering from crippling mental health conditions. We suggest that Augustine ontologized his sexual urges as a form of condition of sin, ineradicable but by the supernatural hand of God, to displace some of the guilt he may have experienced in relation to his seemingly uncontrollable sexual experiences. That was one of the peculiar possibilities he found in his reading of certain passages in Scripture, by no means one that can stand the scrutiny of comparison with the rest of Scripture.

To the extent that Augustine came to recognize the deleterious effects of his harsh schooling which he critiqued in the *Confessiones*, he was able to process some key traumatic experiences that would have

---

12. Augustine, *Conf.*, 10.30.41 (ET, Chadwick, p. 203); Augustine, *Conf.*, 10.31.44, 47 (ET, Chadwick, pp. 204, 207).

13. Augustine appears to hold that the lustfulness of the sexual act serves to morally corrupt the fetus ("bind" by original sin) and render it guilty. *De nuptiis et concupiscentia*, 1.24 (ET, Holmes, pp. 274-75).

contributed toward his addiction to sexual behavior and find some measure of relief.[14]

The Protestant Reformer Martin Luther gives insight, as well, into the development of an exclusivist interpretation of the Christian faith vis-à-vis other religious traditions.[15]

Erik Erikson has reason to believe that Luther's formative years, brought up as he was by authoritarian parents who like many others at the time saw fit to resort to draconian methods of discipline, came to have a considerable impact on his intuitions relating to the lovingness of God the Father.

Hans Luder was an ambitious miner who like other miners in the area was given to superstition. Moreover he was burdened by the arrival of his younger brother known for being a drunkard and having possibly killed a person and by rumors that he himself had slain a shepherd before moving to Mansfeld. Luder hoped that his oldest son, who was Luther, would be able to lift the family economically through becoming a lawyer; he was also adamant that his son would be nothing like his tumultuous and violent uncle and even himself. Luder thought of himself as an exemplar of righteousness and justice, maintaining a flawless public image while expressing his anger at the world toward his family.

To that end, Luder, who like any other father in his social milieu thought of his children as his property, dealt mechanically rather than emotional-sensitively with Luther as any good father should. Without reflecting on the moral example he was presenting to his son, Luder, who never quite addressed his own propensity to succumb to abusive outbursts of anger, treated the child harshly, holding the latter up to standards of moderate temperament he himself could not meet.

Such "fateful two-facedness" would be instrumental in cultivating in Luther a conception of the Father in heaven, imagined as a transcendent and more powerful version of an earthly father, characterized by actual capriciousness and ill-will underlying an external display of love and justice, both of whom he hated. In these early experiences we find already the lineaments of the reformer's later articulation of a *deus absconditus*, a hidden God, a God who controls all reality including dictating the good and evil that is to transpire while, on a different external

---

14. Augustine, *Conf.*, 1.9.14-15 (ET, Chadwick, pp. 11-12); Mayo Clinic Staff, "Compulsive Sexual Behaviour."

15. This section benefits from the study of Luther's youth by Erik Erikson in *Young Man Luther*, 50, 57-76, 139-40, 155-58, 163-64.

level, commanding that people are to obey divine dictates to practice good and punishing those who participate in wickedness.

Given his superstitious worldview in which he regarded a thunderstorm as God's way of warning him against taking a contrary path, inevitably nurtured by his father's consciousness that death could strike at any moment—held in common with other miners in Thuringia— Luther lived in a constant fear of God's judgment and could not but turn to a form of hyper-religiosity in the hope of escaping the brutal penalty he expected from God. Even then, he constantly doubted his good works as a potential mirage from the devil and questioned his desire and role in experiences he had during less than conscious states such as in a dream. He hated God because he experienced his anguished existence as arising by an arbitrary divine will and this served only to exacerbated Luther's anxiety that, having committed such a mortal sin, there may be no hope for him after all.[16]

In the context of Luther's existential situation, however he arrived at his hatred of God, whether via his upbringing or the culture or theology of his age (more likely through a combination of all these factors),[17] incapable of directly resolving his dysfunctional state of mind, considering he could not cope with any theology of divine command whatsoever, the reformer's inner intuitions led him to take a peculiar reading of Rom 1:16–17, not so much as a statement to the effect that God's moral character is disclosed to human persons through the act of faith, that is, trust that all that is revealed in Scripture of the subject originates in God, for a consolidation of faith through emulating God's character, but rather that an external righteousness is conferred on the believer as an inward operation in a supernatural act of the Holy Spirit attested to outwardly by a person's willingness to repent and turn to the Lord in faith.[18]

---

16. John Montag assesses that the reason Luther could not be sure of the affirmations in Scripture of God's love and God's ability to save the believer was partly due to the fact that he lived after the turn away from an ascending ladder of being to the conception, through John Duns Scotus, of the created order as univocal to the being of God concomitant with the relegation of language to the philosophically realist role of representation (as opposed to a direct indication of the thing being represented or referent, hence necessitating evidence either from God or reason so as to avoid deception) rather than a manifestation or structure of divine revelation. Montag, "Revelation," 50–52.

17. Cf. Johnson, *Psychohistory and Religion*; Marius, review of Johnson, *Psychohistory and Religion*, 463.

18. Cf. Barth, *KD* IV.2, §66.1 (ET, Bromiley, pp. 507–508). In Barth's view, the forgiveness of sins and adoption into God's household of the believer logically precedes

In the two possible arrangements of the latter part of Rom 1:17, "the righteous shall live by faith" (ESV), being a righteous person is connected to living by faith; alternatively, faith is itself a mark of a righteousness that leads to life. The source passage (Hab 2:4) suggests a reference to a need to exercise humility and obedience in a time of moral crisis, remembering that God is the source of our moral capacity and desire which we must obey at all times. Given this literary context and the intertextual reference, it is best to interpret Rom 1:16–17 as a call to recognize and obey God as the source of our moral capacity and desire as opposed to viewing it as a declaration that God bestows an alien righteousness on believers in Christ.[19]

In any event, Luther read the text the way he fatefully, for all Protestant history, did, and it completely transformed his perception of God into one of a loving being. No longer, because there were no more laws to keep to assure God's favor, did Luther have to labor in obedience to God's laws under the grudging feeling that God is a capricious and wrathful being who takes pleasure in punishing him.

Both Augustine and Luther experienced an irruptive supernatural intervention, the former in a series of serendipitous incidents where the future bishop faced a challenge to his sense of honor when he realized that people who lacked his understanding of the classics as an imperial professor of rhetoric at the Roman capital of Milan were advancing ahead of him into the kingdom of heaven.[20]

Augustine may have had in mind the two Roman soldiers spoken of by Ponticianus, a high official who paid Augustine and Alypius a visit. According to Ponticianus, these off-duty soldiers stumbled upon a biography of St. Anthony, the founder of Christian monasticism, and decided to serve God by joining the monastery where they found the book, leaving behind their fiancées who also became celibate servants of God.

The retelling shattered Augustine's illusion of comfort, presumably the psychological sense that he had justification for behaving the way he

---

their calling, inclination toward living as a disciple of Christ, conversion to faith, good works, and cross-bearing.

19. Luther, *Heid. Disp.*, §26, in which the Protestant reformer enunciates his belief that all God's laws have been fulfilled in the believer on account that Christ, who alone has fulfilled all these commands, has become their possession through faith. Even so, Christ stirs believers to good works by imitation of the Lord through their perception and recognition of the wonderful works that Christ does (*Heid. Disp.*, §27).

20. The *indocti* (sing. *indoctus*): untaught, unlearned, ignorant, or untrained. Augustine, *Conf.*, 8.8.19 (LT, Hammond, p. 390).

did seeing that everyone was doing the same thing, and with that came the recognition that he was a wretched sinner attached to the evil, perverse, filthy, and sickly desires of the world. He eventually found relief in what seemed to be a supernatural turn of events where, completely devastated by his self-realization and left without hope except that God answered his desperate pleas for help, he was suddenly drawn to the voices of children urging to take up and read.

Interpreting the words as a command from God because he could not recall any children's game in which such a phrase was used, thinking that God might very well be speaking to him the way Anthony experienced God as speaking to him through the reading of Matt 19:21, asking him to sell his possessions, give them to the poor, and follow Christ, Augustine picked up the book of the Apostle Paul he had set down and read Rom 13:14, which exhorts against continuing in a lifestyle of drunkenness, sensual pleasures, and divisiveness, and felt his doubt and anxiety ebb away.[21]

In brief, Augustine was confronted by the stark consciousness of the gravity of his participation in sensual pleasures, learned the better way of the gospel, and discovered a new freedom from his former shameful preoccupations. In his reflections on his past manner of life, he noted that he had been incapable of escaping a situation in which his body was unwilling to obey the soul and its will.

In fact, the only reason Augustine was able to find release from his former attachments was because he saw the truth about the poor decisions he had allowed himself to make time and again (though without quite understanding the psychological impact his experiences of trauma during his formative years had had in facilitating what appears to be compulsive sexual behavior and binge-eating disorder) and came to a realization that he did not need to continue making those decisions.

Augustine could not be reasonably expected to have known the psychological dynamics that influenced his unwholesome habits, and he developed a theological perspective in which his addictions to food, drink, and sex were blatantly regarded as intentional acts of sin arising from an incorrigibly corrupt will. Given that his release from these evils came in the form of a sincere petitionary prayer to God for divine assistance, and he seemed to have received such assistance in a most miraculous way, Augustine became convinced that humankind is

---

21. Augustine, *Conf.*, 8.6.13–8.12.29 (ET, Chadwick, pp. 141–53).

encumbered by a flaw of their moral nature which cannot be addressed, corrected, and reformed apart from a complete dependence on God as conceived in the Christian tradition.

Similarly, Luther had an epiphany regarding the way certain Scripture passages were to be understood, and his novel interpretation—where God completely shields believers from God's wrath through conferring on them God's own righteousness, giving a false assurance that can only be had through proper moral living—liberated him from the terror and horror of living under a supreme being perceived to be capricious as a person fully aware of the degree to which they fall short of the divine moral standard for humanity, a tragic condition of faith fomented by his experience of dysfunctional, emotionally-neglectful, and physically abusive parenting. To confirm one's calling and election through good works is not tantamount to showing by one's character and conduct that one has indeed already received the righteousness of God through Christ, but simply to shore up one's confidence and that of others that one has truly been created for the purpose of good works.

To the extent that the theological interpretations of Augustine and Luther became paradigmatic for and definitive in evangelical theology, the way was paved toward an exclusive understanding of the Christian faith. The entrenched nature of religious exclusivism—which is not to be confused or conflated with a theological exclusivism where God is rightly regarded as the ontological and moral source of creation—evinces that evangelical theology is cautiously ectypal or imitative and based on foundational historical precedent; Christian theology is often as much a discipline of sacred texts as it is of significant historical personages.

This translates to a personalization of Christian theology, where the specific theological views and opinions of particular individuals of historical importance are elevated to a definitive and authoritative status. In this way, the exclusivist views of figures such as Augustine and Luther worked their way into evangelical Christian theology, accounting for the persistence and prevalence of religious exclusivism.[22]

One can only surmise the reasons that some might opt for an exclusivist reading of Scripture and its theology; certainly, a feeling of moral and spiritual superiority as well as an associated greater moral authority and prerogative on the part of a leadership of a community to instruct

---

22. On Augustine's religious exclusivism, see Grislis, "Martin Luther and World Religions," 143–54; on Luther's, see Kaljouw, "Christian Exclusivism and Violence," 284–88.

the latter just how to conduct themselves in a comprehensive sense. That Augustine's conversion had its turning point in his vexation at having been apparently bested by those he considered intellectually and socially inferior to himself supports the point.

Specific factors lend themselves more easily to the Christian members of a society having a predilection toward religious exclusivism; in the case of Singapore, given the rat race and competitiveness, in which self-value is often measured in terms of one's success incorporating indices such as social standing and power, it is inevitable that such a cultural value would spill over into a religious realm and adherents of the Christian church favor the idea that they are clearly special and superior (even by reason of grace) in relation to other groups not just in terms of their belief but their practice as well, and in a position to guide others to live a more spiritual or moral life.

Much like Augustine, Luther assumed that his compulsive thoughts, feelings, and desires—in Augustine's case, compulsive sexual behavior and binge-eating disorder and in Luther's, religious scrupulosity—were innate and indicative of his moral nature and status as an incorrigibly wretched and sinful individual.

The idea of being in thrall to the power of sin makes a good bedfellow to a religious-cultic rigidity bordering on superstition. Finding no relief whatsoever from a persistent experience of comprehensive and thoroughgoing sinfulness and wickedness, spiritually-minded individuals are wont to draw blood from stone and latch onto the very first sign of a possibility of salvation they can discover. The conception of God as Savior, Reconciler, and Redeemer in Christ presents itself very naturally in this connexion, given our evolutionary tendency to jump to conclusions without having first ensured we have secured all the facts of the matter as a means of survival.[23]

On account of its mystery, we turn to sacrament or religious rite which, as a source of unknown power, frees us from any need to explain its nature or process of operation whilst inviting us to find in it an inexplicable fount of divine assurance and reassurance. Calling entirely into question the human moral enterprise, a decisive and dramatic turn is made toward a cult which promises divine righteousness through a special, irruptive, and supernatural act of divine intervention, distinct from the divine act which formed human beings in their nature and existence.

---

23. Miller, "People Jump to Conclusions."

The localization of existential and spiritual-moral hope along with the cultic operationalization of right human interaction with the divine power of liberation sustain the communal impression that God is not without goodness, nor human beings left without a future, via the perfect and scintillating integration between divine grace for salvation or deliverance and the relatively straightforward requirements for religious profession and communal responsibilities prescribed by a religious cult.

These minor cultic requirements pertaining to what the believer is to hold to be true in terms of the transcendent and what they are to do in terms of practical acts of piety or communal gatherings perform the duty of providing a means of immanent participation prior to moral and spiritual actualization, a concrete type of guarantee or encouragement that a religious adherent is in good standing with the divine power of salvation and liberation.

Doctrinal Formulation: Humanity as Revealing the Necessity of Divine Position

It is impossible, if one is to eschew the possibility of being disingenuous with oneself, to take leave of the question of God in any fundamental sense. A person may well decide, for differing sets of reasons, that a theistic conception does not agree with their chosen worldview and modus vivendi, yet theism, insofar as it entails an acknowledgment that humankind individually and as a whole does not arise except in connection with a supreme source of its spiritual, psychological, moral, and physical existence and faculties, best explains the situation in which human persons find themselves. All act is the result of natural, deliberate, or mechanical processes which presuppose a natural or designed configuration of nature and its interaction with its surroundings. God is not exempt from this condition for God's action, requiring that God be given a nature as entity and this nature of God's be situated in an environment where that nature may interact with its surroundings. This entitative nature of God's along with the initial milieu (of fundamental spiritual entities, some of which bring into existence all of material reality) with which it interacts are posited by the Divine Nature, which is an undergirding principle and force that begins at an earliest point in time known as the horizon of all possibility, antecedent to which nothing exists and is able to exist.

PART 2: HUMANITY'S IMAGING OF THE DIVINE

Discussion

It is impossible, if one is to eschew the possibility of being disingenuous with oneself, to take leave of the question of God in any fundamental sense. A person may well decide, for differing sets of reasons, that a theistic conception does not agree with their chosen worldview and modus vivendi, yet theism, insofar as it entails an acknowledgment that humankind individually and as a whole does not arise except in connection with a supreme source of its spiritual, psychological, moral, and physical existence and faculties, best explains the situation in which human persons find themselves.

The whole offense of theism consists in a reductionistic conception of divinity as some troublesome supernatural killjoy or interposer between our current situation in life and what we may believe is necessary for our personal flourishing or that of the world. As such, a person might fancy that God does not desire that a person be happy but only holy (not just in the sense that God does not homologate self-indulgence or hedonism but also that God forbids that people take pleasure even in the more honorable and commendable aspects of their lives), that those who believe in God are somehow involved in a dereliction of personal responsibility, or that the idea that there exists a transcendent and powerful being external to ourselves constitutes an indelible and insoluble scandal in face of the recurrence of personal as well as societal and even global tragedies on a smaller (but inexpressibly intense) or larger scale.[24]

Such criticisms of theism may not be entirely unwarranted, no thanks to professing Christian believers who intentionally or unintentionally afford an erroneous impression concerning God's nature, God's character, God's purpose, and God's relations with humankind. Some Christians espouse a dichotomy between the power and ability of God and that of the human person, experiencing a certain discomfort with speaking of a need to repose confidence in oneself vis-à-vis actualizing specific important tasks, opting instead to exercise faith in God alone, as though to be assured of one's ability automatically excludes a person from the possibility of trust in God's ability to empower or deliver people.

For the sake of convenience of discussion, let us name the idea of God as a supernatural force that is only external to humankind and constantly obtrudes and seeks to obtrude itself into human affairs, depending on one's disposition and response to God (whereby God

24. Fiddes, *Creative Suffering of God*, 174–77.

may grant a person the authority or ability to act according to God's will) a competitive or friendly, intervening or supportive deity; God Overbearing—in our view, an erroneous conception of God's nature, purpose, and relations with humankind.[25]

Such a conception of the divine being finds expression in the exclusively supernaturalist theology of divine revelation of Karl Barth, which is diametrically opposed to any form of natural theology or the idea that God may be revealed through the natural world or any capacity or act of the human being, apart from the incarnate Christ.[26]

The very fact that the world is so starkly distinguished from God betrays the presumption that God cannot be revealed through human capacity and effort. Understandably, Barth felt he needed to react to what was an abuse of natural theology to support political claims on the part of Nazi leadership, to preclude the theological option, adopted by the group known as the German Christians during the rise of National Socialism, that God may be acting in a manner that identifies God's presence and action with those of a racially-motivated German dictator, given a precedent of antisemitic theology in the writings of a key historical figure, Martin Luther, the exegetical and interpretative latitude afforded by liberal theology, along with the powerful directive influence of the National Socialists themselves on the Christian church in Nazi Germany.[27]

We are not suggesting, however, that all that people desire and do is necessarily a revelation of the will and character of God, only that which measures up to the will and character of the incarnate Christ as the supreme revelation of God. While human desire and action may appear to be external to God as the sole revealer of God's will and character and thereby seen to be competing and false sources of divine revelation, yet God's revelation in Christ is not restricted in the forms it can take in the world, and is able to employ human desire and action as a medium of its communication, insofar as human desire and action are in conformity to and agreement with those of Christ. Therefore Paul speaks of believers being a letter from Christ, implying that God in Christ is revealed through the capacity and actions of those who believe in Christ (2 Cor 3:3).

In a related area of discussion, Holder criticizes Barth for seeming to decouple God's self-revelation from the human rational ability to

---

25. Barth, *KD* IV.2, §66.4 (ET, Bromiley, pp. 578-79).
26. Holder, "Karl Barth and Natural Theology," 22-37.
27. Wilson, "The Orthodox Betrayal"; Gritsch, "Was Luther Anti-Semitic?"

consider and thereby confirm claims of divine revelation.[28] In fact, it is not human rationality per se but rather the moral critique, based on a principle of reciprocity in which a person is to treat another in the manner that the former would desire to be treated by another, that decides the question concerning whether a set of beliefs is indeed to be regarded as originating in a divine source—by adjudging whether a specific system of beliefs commends the devaluation or psychological or physical harm of God or the transcendent (sacrilege), self, or others (as appropriate).[29] Aside from beliefs that promote some form of ethical violation, all claims of divine revelation are to be regarded as equally true, originating in the one divine source that God is.

God Overbearing (designating not fact but theory) lends impetus to the fundamental protest and charge that theism is an outmoded system of belief and thought, given that such a divine authority can hardly ever be appeased, determines the scope of a person's moral and spiritual freedom, and constructs a version of reality in which all the pain and suffering endured in that version of the world is thought to redound most greatly to the divine glory often through fostering, facilitating, and even compelling humility and penitent and repentant obedience on a phenomenal level (and with the intention that human persons might attain to the realization, recognition, assessment, and conclusion that God is all in all and they are very small, even nothing at all) but, in truth, ordering all things, including human thought, emotions, feelings, desire, and action, on an ontological one.

The repudiation of God as an idea that has an objective basis in reality may therefore stem from a decisive and fundamental misconception concerning the nature, character, purpose, and relationality of God. A rejection of the divine as lacking objective reality is not itself rooted in fair and objective criteria guiding observation or experience toward an inevitable conclusion that God constitutes nothing more (in purportedly having no objectivity whatsoever) and nothing less (in purportedly having an imaginary existence) than a projection of our

---

28. Holder, "Karl Barth and Natural Theology," 36.

29. Devaluation is justified with respect to behavior that devalues or harms a person, human or divine, while harm itself may be justified only in rare and restricted situations such as a medical surgical operation performed in order to relieve a person of a physical ailment or even physically save an individual in terms of enabling them to function as a conscious person. In arriving at a judgment as to whether an action can be said to unjustifiably devalue or harm a person, the intention of the actor is primary but so is the general perception of the community that is affected by the action.

inherent attributes writ large onto an external divine being, the visualization of a collective humanity that has overcome its fundamental physical need for a refuge from a malignant world, emotional need for safety and stability, and spiritual need for meaning in life, conceived via a process of self-displacement, in terms of an external form that is God, to whom worship and obeisance is given (Feuerbach) or even the soothing idea of a benevolent and powerful father able to protect an anxious and fearful adult from harm (Freud).[30]

Abjuration of God is not based, first of all, on any hard proof that nothing of God has been detected in the universe. Although it is possible to continually expand the horizons of what we currently know of substances in the observable universe, given the scope of the size of the universe, it is unlikely that we will ever know everything about every part of the universe. Even if it were assumed to be possible to know everything about the observable universe, our scientific apparatuses can only ever measure physical quantities. This means that we will never be able to reach a point where we will be able to detect God, who is spirit (John 4:24).

How, then, is it that not just individual persons but entire groups are able to declare with any confidence that God does not exist? To be fair, we need to include the assertion that God does exist under the category of arguments that need to be demonstrated to be true. Neither statement can be proven empirically, using scientific instruments. Be that as it may, the affirmation to the effect that God exists may be indirectly, implicitly, and philosophically demonstrated by turning to universal subjective and objective categories of human experience; namely, the religious consciousness, human morality and conscience, and an idea of which we are more often than not persuaded by the bare fact of our existence, given the obvious temporal limits of our existence: that we do not exist in, of, and from ourselves.

Regarding the religious consciousness, innumerable individuals throughout human history have espoused some form of belief in a supernatural being, beings, or realm. Such belief has been tied to norms for human behavior which appear to be intrinsic qualities of the human soul, reacting as it does to any moral infringement. Occasionally, the two dimensions are brought together through a notion of divine wrath or even sorrow, whereby God or a god is thought to be angered, offended, or saddened at sinful acts, as defined within a religious tradition

---

30. Gooch, "Ludwig Andreas Feuerbach"; Michaud, "Ludwig Feuerbach"; Broussard, "Is God Just a Fantasy?"

or system in terms of some violation of a moral code. These notions of divine sorrow and anger may be combined progressively, as when God is said to be grieved at human transgression, which will be penalized in a final judgment during which God's wrath will be revealed toward perpetrators of evil and wickedness.

Religious morality is more than a matter of being encouraged to adhere to the laws of an external authority; it often entails emulating the positive moral example set by religious figures, including God incarnate, in the case of Christianity. In this connection, to what extent may the Christian message of Christ's servanthood be rightly glossed and presented in a hortatory way as an instance in which a godly, pious, righteous, and moral human person voluntarily commits an act of self-immolation for the betterment of others?

The nature of Jesus' decision in relation to his crucifixion has to be properly construed. In the first instance, Jesus did not consciously or systematically act to deprive himself of the essential elements that maintained his human existence. Rather than walking toward the Roman court and pleading that the governor execute him on a cross, Jesus was made the subject of a conspiracy leading to trumped-up charges of sedition and blasphemy which ultimately secured his execution by crucifixion. To be sure, Jesus did not resist his arrest the way he sounded as if he might have done, invoking the Father to dispatch more than twelve legions of angels to liberate him from those who would accost him and carry him to safety. Yet he did so only out of his concern that no blood would be shed that night, that neither he himself nor his disciples would be known as a people of violent resistance or, should they attempt to flee arrest on first suspicion of possible betrayal by one of his disciples, as an abortive religious movement that had to go into exile because of their enemies.

In short, Jesus' decision not to eschew his impending arrest constituted a principled stand based on his personal convictions regarding the nature of the movement he had started. It was not an instance of foolhardy bravado or a heedlessness toward one's own legitimate personal needs. The cross of Jesus cannot therefore be appropriately adduced in support of the view that a person should give beyond their means and abnegate their personal needs in the interests of others. Jesus did refrain from resisting his arrest out of his love and compassion for his disciples and other persons, yet what guaranteed that he would die was not purely his love but the specific circumstances under which he operated which required a choice of facing death in accordance with his philosophy of ministry. Jesus did not so much sacrifice himself as he died a casualty of his circumstances.

At the same time, Jesus having given up his life at the cross, God the Father turned the situation around by transforming a political execution and converting it into a great symbol and pledge of God's atonement on behalf of humankind for all their sins, so that were any individual to repent of their sins and turn to the cross in acceptance of what had already occurred there in terms of Jesus having received the penalty for their sins through his death, they may be fully assured of God's complete forgiveness.

If human morality and the faculty of conscience coexists with the idea that God definitely does not exist, the question needs to be pursued concerning the reason for the definiteness of a conclusion or judgment that is not based on any hard evidence warranting any such certainty of assessment of the question. It is well to ask whether such definiteness is due to an emotional reason as opposed to an intellectual one, or to a defective or inadequate intellectual reason, and whether the person who gives such an answer is ready to encounter a cognitive objection and fully-fledged counterproposal.

If the ubiquity of the religious consciousness of humankind, coupled with our morality and faculty of conscience, mutually attest to the existence of God as the source of such consciousness and of morality and conscience, then the undeniable datum of the human experience—namely, that we truly do exist, at least as a single individual, as excogitated by Augustine of Hippo and the French philosopher René Descartes[31]—considering the fact that we did not create ourselves or bring ourselves from a state of nonexistence into one of existence, and that we do not in that sense account in any way for our existent reality, serves as incontrovertible testimony that there is an external source of human existence, which theistic systems would recognize as and designate God.

As the source of morality and conscience, God is not simply a giver of an external law that is ancillary if at all related to God's own intrinsic ethical qualities. Instead, the laws promulgated in the Scriptures pertaining

---

31. Augustine, *Civ.*, 11.26 (ET, Dods, pp. 370–71). Descartes recognized in his *Second Meditations* that the one who doubts cannot have been deceived by the Creator into thinking that they exist when they do not since only one who exists is able to be deceived. Although it may be as an avatar or dreamer, the fact remains that a person who doubts exists in some capacity. See an English translation of Descartes, *Meditations*.

to how each person is to think, feel, desire, and comport themselves in relation to God, themselves, and others describe and depict the very ways God thinks, feels, desires, and comports Godself, in ways appropriate to the being and station of God, in relation to Godself (both the relationship to self of any divine person and the internal relationships between the divine persons) and humankind. Contrary to the scribes and the Pharisees, who do not practice what they preach (Matt 23:3), God does not ask anything of humankind in regard to ethical injunctions that does not already define the way God perceives and interacts within the godhead and with the created order.

One of the quintessential qualities of a person of God is to have the fear of the Lord, in which they have regard for the wise teachings that originate in God as a fount of life and blessing for themselves. Reverential fear of God entails a humility which predisposes to obedience in shunning evil and embracing good, including righteousness, truthfulness, faithfulness, love, and contentment,[32] a trait demonstrated by Jesus himself as the perfect and supreme revelation of God the Father.

Thus Jesus as God's prophesied servant did not assert his importance in any way or make much of his greatness (John 12:15–21), before or after public exposure in Jerusalem, but simply attended to the needs of those in some form of deficiency to which he ministered by his miraculous prowess, at first in the quiet and subsequently in the presence of crowds, after he had gathered and trained a number of disciples and was ready to encounter the religious establishment in the capital as a viable alternative, "saving the best for last" as per the allegorical symbolism introduced at the wedding at Cana (John 2:1–11), and appearing in public only after he had found the new wineskins of his community of followers (Matt 9:14–17).

That Jesus suffered as a model and paradigm for believers is crucial for a proper and adequate conception of Christian discipleship. It is only as Christians are taught that suffering, quite possibly even to a grievous extent, is their lot that they will be disabused of the illusion and myth that it is appropriate and felicitous for them to do everything in their power to avert inconvenience and suffering. This will only happen when Christians begin to grasp that carrying their cross in correspondence to Jesus' own but as disciples rather than the master in their respective stations

---

32. Prov 1:7, 29; 2:5; 8:13; 9:10; 10:27; 14:26–27; 15:16, 33; 16:6; 19:23; 22:4; 23:17.

and situations of life is the manner in which they will distinguish and exalt themselves as Christians.[33]

By no means does Jesus compel people to do radical things that are against their will. In the case of the rich young man, though the Lord urged the latter to sell the great and many possessions he had, this was not because possessions are evil in and of themselves, but simply for the reason that the man had not learned to make a proper use of the things he had received out of God's bounty (everything belongs to the Lord, so whether we have obtained money or other assets via ingenuity or have had the good fortune of inheriting great wealth from our ancestors, all that our money may be exchanged for and all that we have are the product of God's material creation).

In other words, the man hoarded his great wealth rather than thinking of using it for the benefit of the poor and destitute. In consequence, his handling of his money precluded his following of the Lord; hence, in order to follow him, the man had to dispose of his wealth in giving them to the poor, in order that his heart might be set free from his love of money and his mind finally turned toward the concerns of the Lord. Does this account in any way suggest that a Christian should renounce and part with all their wealth, leaving themselves with not a single cent to their name? Correspondingly, does it infer that it is wrong to hold a significant amount of money? That homespun lesson cannot be so readily drawn from the relevant passages in the synoptic Gospels.

It may well be possible for a wealthy person not to be so controlled by their assets that they are of no use to the Lord with their many possessions instead of using what they have for the Lord, more effectively by holding on to what they have. Nonetheless, it is the rare person that does this, since wealth is more often than not a temptation and snare for the vulnerable soul, and the principle of the Lord's teaching should be heeded that much wealth withheld from those who need it brings no ultimate good to the owner.

Moreover, in delivering such a surprising and startling exhortation to the rich young man and his disciples after the man departed in sorrow, Jesus may well have been seeking to make a point via hyperbole, enough to shake the rich person out of his self-assured state of religious piety, as well as comfort those among his disciples who left everything for the sake of the kingdom of heaven by drawing attention

---

33. Barth, KD IV.2, §66.6 (ET, Bromiley, pp. 598–601).

to the inverse relationship of the values of that kingdom to those of the world where, in the case of the kingdom of heaven, wealth possessed has no significance for salvation, unlike in the world, where it is often regarded as a key to happiness and success.

The effect of the message of Christ, as opposed to its literal meaning, may well have been sufficient for the rich young man to be obedient to the call of the Lord without his having to distribute all his possessions to charity, albeit some measure of material giving would have been entailed. Jesus' use of the fantastical analogy of a camel going through the eye of a needle to describe the difficulty for a rich person to enter the kingdom of heaven intimates that the Lord does not quite intend that his earlier instruction to the rich young man be taken literally, though if the latter went to that extent, as St. Anthony did, he would have found in him a valuable addition to his traveling entourage.[34]

While extreme to modern people, the Christian call to discipleship which in Jesus' days might well have involved martyrdom (Mark 8:34–38; John 12:24–26) remains valid and operative in the present age, not as an injunction to literally give up one's physical life for the sake of upholding their faith (bearing in mind that the early martyrs of the church did not generally seek out opportunities to be killed for their faith), and not therefore to seek ways to dispense with one's earthly existence whatever it might take, but on the contrary to be ready to die to oneself and rise anew in a selfless mode of existence. This entails being, among other things, loving, meek, and caring for the interests of others (Phil 2:2–4).

If God's ethical attributes are defined by the moral laws which God promulgates within the human world, then the human being is enjoined to be a mirror of God's loving character. In light that the world has been sullied by sin, myriad misrepresentations of God's character are generated, making it necessary to turn to the inscripturated Word of God to be afforded a glimpse of God's moral nature supremely revealed in Jesus Christ.

Moral norms cannot be coopted as a means to increase one's reputation among others. According to Barth, those who endeavor to think or speak of themselves as fulfilling their humanity when they have really failed to do so in light of their refusal to live as fellow human persons to those around them, that is, those who have chosen the path of hypocrisy, will inevitably find that they are only doing a disservice to their

---

34. Franciscan Media, "Saint Anthony of Egypt."

soul's intrinsic desire for humanity since they are not only impeding their moral development but effectively slipping into the inhumanity that they disavow because they do not confess their sin and, we would add, therefore adopt the posture of resolution, aided by moral insight, that is necessary to leave a life of sin.[35]

As the moral source of human existence, God is the reason that the greatest evildoer nevertheless possesses an inalienable human value, independent of their actions, desires, feelings, beliefs, and thoughts, that cannot be reduced in the slightest by any of those factors, elements, or skeins—any person is valuable because they did not have to exist and the fact that they do exist demonstrates that they have been posited by the Divine Nature and inspired by the entitative Trinity for an existence as a moral and social agent. In consequence of specific experiences of trauma during one's formative years, a person comes to develop a distinct dysfunctional self that stands over against their natural or authentic self. In view of this, it is necessary to engage in talk therapy, whether as facilitated by a professional or done on one's own but in a duly informed way. The premise underlying such a procedure is this: there are two selves in any person, a natural and a dysfunctional. The dysfunctional self does not adequately or fittingly love or value itself, while the natural self recognizes its own value. If there were only a dysfunctional self, one would immediately give up all hope of redeeming or renewing oneself and completely yield to different forms of self-destruction. If there were only a natural self, one would not doubt one's self-worth.

Having established the existence of a natural and dysfunctional self, one is in a position now to begin to appreciate the importance of self-talk. An adequate procedure consists of *acknowledgment, reminder, forgiveness,* and *self-acceptance* (ARFS). Acknowledgment comprises a personal recognition that one's actions are driven by a value system that is not in the least healthy, wholesome, or conducive to sustainable mental wellbeing. To the extent that one recognizes this, one is able to appreciate that there are two main approaches to dealing with sinful actions. The first is the way of condemnation, where criticism from society or self veers into imputations that undermine a sense of one's inherent worth or value. This route can lead only to further sinful deeds as self-esteem is continually and increasingly assailed by unending condemnation. The second way is that of criticism without condemnation,

---

35. Barth, *KD* IV.2, §65.2 (ET, Bromiley, pp. 437–38).

in which a person recognizes what is right or wrong and does their part in behaving in a morally and socially responsible way, without condemning themselves when they slip into error but picking themselves up each time. This way of criticism without condemnation and of attempting to do one's best while allowing for error is to be paired with an interrogation of one's unhealthy value system.

Such a value system is not innate or inborn. A man preoccupied with his work to the neglect of the urgent emotional and physical needs of his family members was not always committed to such a worldview but came to acquire it perhaps in the course of having been raised by his parents to believe that his self-worth resides solely in his material assets or professional success, and they did so only because they had a difficult financial situation and sought for their child not to endure the same scenario, little realizing that the child needs unconditional emotional acceptance from the parent and that, while financial literacy and even personal ambition may be inculcated in a child as positive traits, these should never be linked to self-worth, which should never be taught as predicated on the fulfillment of specific conditions. The man in the example is best served identifying and acknowledging his dysfunctional value system, reminding himself that he does not need to espouse a transactional or conditional belief regarding his self-worth, forgiving himself for having made his inherent worth a matter of satisfying specific requirements, and accepting himself.

Others may have cultivated a sense of fear of their social environment as a result of having been mistreated by their parents and others during their early years. In such a scenario, it would be salutary to recognize that they have physically moved on from the years of fear and danger and that the emotions can afford to catch up with the changed situation of life.[36] In an additional example, a person brought up in an unsafe environment could develop a sense of crippling worry and anxiety, in response to which they do well to return to the awareness that they are no longer in danger or exposed to any serious risk of harm (if this is indeed the case) and recognize also that, to counter worry, one takes things a step at a time, not focusing on the amount of work, suffering, or even time still to be endured, or negative possibilities (Matt 6:25–34).[37]

---

36. See Side Effects, "Childhood Trauma."

37. It is quite possible that one who has been nursing anxiety in the heart over a longer-term issue finds themselves more intensely affected by sources of worry from specific situations in view that those specific causes of worry unconsciously remind the

A sense of the world as unsafe being one of the two strongest driving forces underlying human behavior and most deeply hurtful feelings, a second is the perception, absorbed by a person in the course of their interactions with those who have called their worth into question typically on the basis of an inordinate emphasis on behavioral nonconformity, where approval and a lack thereof is always exclusively applied in a context of conformity without any acknowledgment of an individual's emotions[38] and affirmation of a person's inherent acceptability and worth, that one has no value and does not matter. This latter feeling undergirds a subsequent sense of rejection and therefore an unconscious or automatic aversion to rejection so as not to be reminded of the pain of the same, such that perfectionism is cultivated in order to avert a scenario in which they are cut off by others, and rigid expectations of others in view of the perspective instilled in them to the effect that behavior is an index of the value of a person. The wound of rejection also eventuates in people-pleasing, to foreclose the possibility of being cast aside. In the case of such an individual, it would be beneficial to reflect meta-cognitively on the fact that their former caregivers erred in assigning worth to them based on conformity and affirming their own inalienable and irrefragable self-value.

All act is the result of natural, deliberate, or mechanical processes which presuppose a natural or designed configuration of nature and its

---

person of their main anxiety, sapping their emotional strength and capacity to weather the stresses of life. Moreover, some of the most effective learning in relation to personal insight and growth comes about when one takes an affirmative interest in making sense of a particular subject or issue, guided by faithful and integrous mentors who are willing to stop at presenting the facts of a matter, conclusions arrived at through reasonable interpretation of those facts, premises and reasons for that interpretation, and a survey of alternative common points of view along with a statement and explication of their inadequacy, as opposed to being told what they need to know and how they ought to believe, feel, and think.

38. Such acknowledgment of emotion, which can also be that of one's own, is not tantamount to validating or approving of the affect, emotions, or feelings a person experiences whilst recognizing that the affect or emotions—but not feelings or conscious interpretations of the actions of others which a person is at liberty to restrain or change—that people involuntarily experience cannot be imputed to them, and being sure to identify the roots of unhealthy affect, emotions, and feelings. Although not every emotion can be approved of, each expression of pain is to be properly honoured with a recognition that justice is due the person, an attempt wherever possible to alleviate the suffering, and, as to the one who can be established to have caused the suffering, make a proper and—by reasonable standards—satisfactory repentance.

interaction with its surroundings. God is not exempt from this condition for God's action, requiring that God be given a nature as entity and this nature of God's be situated in an environment where that nature may interact with its surroundings. This entitative nature of God's along with the initial milieu (of fundamental spiritual entities, some of which bring into existence all of material reality) with which it interacts are posited by the Divine Nature, which is an undergirding principle and force that begins at an earliest point in time known as the horizon of all possibility, antecedent to which nothing exists and is able to exist.

All act is the result of natural, deliberate, or mechanical processes which presuppose a natural or designed configuration of nature and its surroundings. A breeze is able to move across the land or sea at a certain altitude because of temperature differences between the land and sea, which is in turn due to the differential ability of soil and water to retain heat. A human being engages in any action at all through a confluence of multiple factors, including an intellectual and emotional ability to perceive a need for such an action in view of specific and concrete circumstances, a desire to meet that perceived need through some form of action, and a will to engage in such an action, even if it is one that is only reluctant or lackadaisical.

A generator is able to run by virtue of the fact that it is designed to convert a certain input into an output; as a case in point, most of the electricity produced in a modern society like the United States is produced by steam turbines using electromagnetic generators that convert mechanical energy, in high-pressure steam produced by boilers, relying on fossil fuels, biomass, nuclear, solar, or geothermal energy as heat sources, to electricity by moving an electromagnetic shaft which redirects loose electrons in a uniform direction in wires coiled around it producing a strong current.[39]

God is not exempt from this condition even for God's action. Divine action requires that God be given a nature as entity and this nature of God's be situated in an environment where that nature may interact with its surroundings. Although we are able to speak of God in terms of being a Divine Nature which undergirds God as entity and the initial surroundings of fundamental spiritual entities (some of which are responsible for

---

39. U.S. Energy Information Administration, "Electricity in the United States"; U.S. Energy Information Administration, "How Electricity Is Generated"; "Magnets and Electricity"; Petrotech, "How Does a Steam Turbine Work?"

generating material reality) in which this entity interacts, this is not to defer the question of origin by assigning an ultimate status to the Divine Nature, since even this Divine Nature begins at the horizon of all possibility, so that it begins its existence at a point, before which nothing does or can exist, already equipped with its nature and capacity.

God as entity may very well elect to speak through the messengers of nature, as God has done in scriptural history. We think of Yahweh choosing to appear before the people of Israel in a fiery cloud and speak to Moses through thunder at Mount Sinai (Exodus 19) and of the Father who spoke to Jesus in a voice that sounded to those in close proximity like thunder (John 12:27–30). God may also decide to communicate with God's servants through other natural phenomena, as Elijah experienced, the pertinent passage seeming to indicate that the prophet was trying to listen for God's voice in the natural phenomena that occurred prior to the divine speech; namely, wind, earthquake, and a fire (1 Kgs 19:9–18). This implies the possibility that to all intents and purposes God may command nature spirits present in natural objects (as some are, others being in animal form or discarnate like the angels that did not become human) to impart a message through expressions natural to themselves that those who are spiritually attentive will be able to register.[40]

The line of enquiry may be pursued as to why, in the biblical testimony, God appears to conceal Godself from all but those with whom God shares an intimate personal relationship. One immediately thinks of Moses, who among all the people in the community of Israel was clearly taken into God's confidence (Exodus 19), of Peter, who among all the disciples was conferred the unshakable spiritual conviction that Jesus is the Christ, the Son of the living God (Matt 16:13–20), or the circle that comprised the disciples of Jesus, to whom he delivered and entrusted the truth about what he was going to endure at the hands of the religious leaders in Jerusalem, in terms of suffering and even death (Matt 16:21).

Why did God not reveal Godself to many more people through numerous and undeniable wondrous signs or perhaps one earth-shaking prodigy? The fact is that the sceptical and unbelieving are unlikely to change their posture in spite of the greatest wonders. Someone can see

---

40. That Rom 8:19–22 speaks of the subjection to futility of creation, that is, the entirety of the natural world, infers that nature is indwelled by spirits which the passage limns as compelled to witness and bear with the daily acts of sinfulness and wicked perversion committed by humankind and rebellious angels. See Edwards, "Sinners in the Hands of an Angry God," Application, 9.

a miracle worker and yet doubt that God has been acting in that person, choosing to attribute those miracles to the devil or some other ungodly source, as the Pharisees did in relation to Jesus' ability to drive out demons and deliver the spiritually oppressed (Matt 12:22–32). Furthermore, there were those who doubted that Christ had resurrected and stood before their very eyes (Matt 28:16–17). The fact is that unbelief is a personal decision and choice, an act of the most intense individual volition, rather than one that is considered or measured.

More often than not, it entails a willful willingness and resolve to hold on to one's personal opinions and beliefs with an unjustified and ironclad sense that a further search for the truth will be unfruitful, a sense that such a one wishes to maintain against all possible odds, constantly attempting to convince not only others but themselves that what they hold to be true is indeed the truth, and succumbing to the temptation to disguise spiritual indifference and indolence as spiritual wisdom, taking on a contrarious posture so as to intimidate those who would dare to challenge their worldview, mastering platitudes and marshaling typical arguments to deal with those who would think to tease out problems in their rhetoric without actually desiring to learn, and making groundless and blanket assertions with glee to shut down discourse.

The devil and the devil's agents tempt in such a manner that either a pleasant or unpleasant affect is instilled in the person being tempted. As a case in point, one may feel an inappropriate sense of delight regarding another person's suffering because it is beneficial to one. Thus, Christ was subject to an intense test when he was led into the wilderness to pray and fast, in which he might have been made by the devil to feel a sense of unhappiness over his situation of privation (in the case of the temptation to turn stones into bread to satisfy his hunger before reaching the end of the period he committed to prayer and fasting), difficulty (in the case of the temptation to fling himself from the pinnacle of the temple to compel God to deliver him miraculously before the crowd and gain an immediate following), and lack of external authority (in the case of the temptation to prostrate himself before the devil with the promise that all the kingdoms of the world will be handed over to him), and to feel a heightened agony over his impending death (while he prayed at the garden of Gethsemane).[41] In the event of temptation, it is imperative that one refrains from being too hard on oneself, recognizing that

---

41. See Matt 4:1–11.

what they might be feeling right now may be what all people go through under similar circumstances; that one confesses their sins and recommits themselves to the Lord who has mercy and will confer the Lord's grace on them; and that one carries on an ongoing and relentless internal dialogue disowning inappropriate pleasant or unpleasant affect.[42]

Perhaps even more insidious than typical temptation is the ease with which one can slip into a routineness of life in which we become indifferent to the needs of those around us. A person might hear of the suffering of a religious figure and feel no sympathy or concern for them, only coming to a realization of the insouciance to which they have succumbed while at a church service and thereby given an opportunity to reflect on their lives, at which point they begin to imagine the pain and discomfort the religious leader must be in and start to pray sincerely for him to recover quickly. The reason it comes about that we fail to exercise empathy is simply that we may be too stuck in our routines, too automatic and unconscious in our responses to developments in the day, so long as we are not directly impacted as to our survivability. We may have taken our lives and opportunities for granted, assuming that we own them rather than recognizing that they are gifts to us. The key then is to have a habit of breaking the routine of life by being mindful of the daily need to examine our lives and constantly returning to the mode of giving thanks for all that we have as things we have received without exception (1 Cor 4:7).

---

42. Lisa Feldman Barrett, *How Emotions Are Made: The Secret Life of the Brain* (Boston: Houghton Mifflin Harcourt, 2017), chapter 4, endnote 36, reproduced in Barrett, "Affect vs. Emotion."

8

The Christian Doctrine of Faith

Divine-Human Communion as Critical for
Clear Knowledge of God

A COMMON REFRAIN AMONG theological writers and pastors in the contemporary period, reflecting an observation apposite to an age with as many opinions as there are individuals, is that each person has a different view of God, some more favorable to the view that God does indeed exist and as a benevolent authority, others less.

The primary interest of the discussion in this chapter is to explore the extent to which it is fair to say that one's personal relationship with God, as opposed to a strictly academic grasp of God as a being, may be determinative for an accurate conception of God.

By and large, there are two major views governing the understanding of the direct authenticity of the knowledge of the divine. One sees God as a being that stands forever at a great distance from human intellectual access; that is, incognizable. If anything about God is known at all, it is registered only in the sense in which it is accommodated to our finite nature and limited mental capacities by an utterly transcendent divine source (Knowledge of God as Accommodated).[1]

Another perspective holds that God, though invisible, is capable of being apprehended as an empathetic being through dialogical processes in which God, as an outward-looking "physical"/"consequent" (other-centered) pole and unifier of all possibilities, giving them a value structure, works to persuade human beings to choose the best possibility

1. Chua, *STEA*, 67, 171n76.

among other possibilities (integrating the range of elements in the past ["subjective aim"] with comparable or integrative elements in the present ["concrescence" as describing a process moving from concrescent creativity through satisfaction into transitional creativity for each occasion], ad infinitum) so as to bring about some form of harmony with God's "primordial vision" (God's "mental"/"primordial pole") for the world (Knowledge of God through Supportive Divine Presence).[2]

In contrast to these views, we hold that God as entity is capable of being apprehended by human beings in relationship with God (Knowledge of God in Personal Relationship).[3]

Epistemology

The view that God is humanly conceivable only in virtue of God's making Godself known through an intermediary, such as an angel of the Lord, finds support in a passage like Exod 3:2, 4–22. Exponents can also adduce the cryptic line where St. Paul describes God as dwelling in unapproachable light which no human being has ever seen or can see, including Paul himself (1 Tim 6:13–16).

One way, therefore, of interpreting texts like the visions of God in Isaiah, Ezekiel, and Revelation is to assert that they are visions rather than direct encounters with God. Another line of interpretation highlights that the light that God inhabits is truly inaccessible and unseeable in the sense that the full glory of God is not something any person or creature can directly perceive. This is not simply because God dwells in a completely separate dimension—the visions of God may be taken literally in which a prophet sees God seated on a throne—but rather that no creature may take in or survey the infinite goodness of the light in which God lives, that is, the essence of God, described as light, that is the source of all life.

This designates the Divine Nature as the undergirding framework of all being and morality, which cannot itself be perceived. In substantiation of this perspective, to the extent that light is unseeable, that is, invisible, it is typically not said to also be something that cannot be approached. There are different kinds of light that we cannot perceive, such as radio waves, microwaves, X-rays, ultraviolet rays, infrared radiation, and

---

2. Suchocki, *God, Christ, Church*, 237–55.
3. Cf. Barth, *KD* IV.2, §68.2 (ET, Bromiley, pp. 756).

gamma rays.[4] These cannot be said to be unapproachable in the sense that we cannot be surrounded by these different forms of light which are invisible to the human eye.

Furthermore, to the extent that the visions of Ezekiel (1:26–28) and Revelation (4:2–3) describe a light visible from God, they do not depict the unapproachable and invisible light of 1 Timothy 6. As a matter of fact, in both visions in Ezekiel as well as Revelation, the light around the figure of God is visible, with both Ezekiel and Revelation describing it as a rainbow. No light emanating from God is mentioned in Isa 6:1–5; moreover, Isaiah attests to having seen the Lord with his own eyes.

It is meaningful to consider in this context whether anything may be made at all of an apparent affinity between the sociocultural and historical conditions of Greco-Roman Christendom with its monarchical political model, during which much that is still decisive in Christian theology was formulated, and a doctrine of God where a palpable sense of distance is experienced between a God who is supremely high and has the prerogative to make decisions for a multitude of other people on a macro-scale without having to engage very personally (or at the minimum in a way that can be personally felt) with the situations of the many individuals who grapple with the concrete difficulties of living in the world, including economic inequality, social discrimination, and political oppression, and the feelings these circumstances evoke.

The conception of divine immutability enunciated in classical theology as elicited from Platonic philosophy and implanted within a new Christian theological context is quite foreign to ideas about God in the biblical material. For one thing, nowhere does Scripture depict God as dwelling in a timeless domain. The saying about how to God a thousand years is as a day (2 Pet 3:8) simply attests to the fact that God has presided over all of time and so no duration experienced by humankind can possibly compare to God's length of existence.

Nor does the Bible speak of God as being so incapable of change that God is unable to experience any true sense of surprise, shock, disappointment, or sorrow given an unexpected, unfavorable, or unbefitting human response of distrust or disobedience. Where God is said to be unlike humankind in that God is unable to change God's mind, these were references to the manner in which God will not revoke God's good plan for the people of Israel made known by God in the context of Balak's request

---

4. NASA Hubble Space Telescope, "The Electromagnetic Spectrum."

for Balaam to curse Israel (Num 23:19); God's decided rejection of King Saul following his act of disobedience concerning the utter destruction of Amalek (1 Sam 15:29); and God's loving and merciful purpose to see to Israel's purification rather than its destruction (Mal 3:6).

God as entity, that is, God as Trinity is essentially invisible to the human eye. Even so, the voice of the Holy Spirit in the believer or toward the nonbeliever produces an impression which corresponds to the divine character. More importantly, the incarnation of the Lord establishes a basis upon which, through the physical embodiment and activity of Christ, those who receive the witness of the Lord, be it through the Scripture, the preaching of the same, or some other form of recollection of the coming of the Lord similar to that recounted in the Gospels, are given the privilege and pleasure of knowing the Trinity, whose moral attributes are perfectly revealed in the moral qualities disclosed in the life of Jesus through the way he cares for God and others and takes care of himself.

God is certainly concerned that humankind, created in the divine image with a moral awareness, orientation, freedom, and responsibility, embraces those very spiritual and moral values which have been demonstrated and evinced in the life of Christ and therefore the life of the Trinity itself. This fact is borne witness to in the manner in which Jesus cautioned his disciples against being deceived by the actions of false prophets, demon exorcists, and miracle-workers, who appear outwardly righteous and pious but whose nature is to exploit others for their own benefits.

These are those who being diseased trees do not and cannot bear good fruit but only bad fruit, as a sign and index of their unrighteousness, and will therefore be judged with death and fire, in stark contrast to the righteous who being healthy trees do not and cannot bear bad fruit but only good fruit, as a sign and index of their righteousness. These are those who do the will of the Father in heaven, that is, in sincerely caring about and attending to the welfare of others and taking responsible care of themselves (Matt 7:15–23).

A question arises at this point as to the manner in which one might know that a person bears bona fide good fruit rather than bad fruit that has the appearance of good fruit. The way to discern if this is the case differs between self and other. Where another person is concerned, deception may be involved and so it may not actually be possible to perceive their true nature unless one has the opportunity to observe the way in which they behave in settings where they know or feel that they have little if anything to gain from keeping up good conduct, such as the way they comport themselves in their dealings with those of lower social status or even of an out-group.

With respect to oneself, the matter is complicated by a very human predilection to think better of ourselves than we ought or deserve to think. At the same time, we are in a better position to judge our own morality in view that we have unimpeded access to our own thoughts, feelings, desires, and motivations underlying all our actions. In addition, we have lived with ourselves all our lives, through both the secretive and social or public moments of our lives, and we will know, in a way and to a degree that we cannot of another person, whether we have been respectful, responsible, integrous, empathetic, and solicitous in relation to God, other persons, and even ourselves.

If we find we have good cause to doubt our morality, that very judgment places us in a good stead to affirm the goodness that dwells in our minds and hearts, goodness which defines the person we are in the present moment, though not in the next, and to which we have to resolve to commit ourselves wholeheartedly and single-mindedly. The reason we cannot simply assert that we are and will be good for the rest of our lives in the light of the remorse, regret, and sorrow we experience toward all the evil or wickedness we have committed previously is that we are just as much constituted by our actual decisions as by the posthoc workings of the conscience in our souls.

The fact that we may very well betray our conscience and moral status at a later point in our lives does not give the lie to our present good moral standing as indicated by the posthoc workings of our conscience.[5] We should always do our utmost to remain within a good morality. That we will be given a second chance through the forgiveness that Christ affords and quite possibly even by those we may hurt or harm should not make us complacent or cause us to be indifferent to moral matters and the constant existential urgency of making the right moral decision. Those who slip into such indifference, nonchalance, and insouciance should worry or fear that they might well have fallen from grace even as they falsely imagine themselves to be godly persons who piously resort to what is seen to be the only basis for spiritual security that is Christ.

---

5. Barth, *KD* IV.2, §67.4 (ET, Bromiley, pp. 701–702): Barth assesses that knowledge of oneself and others as Christian can only be secured through "trust" alone, albeit there is an external indicator, by no means infallible, in the fact of baptism in the name of the Lord and profession of faith in salvation through his name.

The mistake lies in the failure to observe how the sealing of the believer with the Holy Spirit takes place not only through the hearing of the word of truth that is the gospel of salvation but also through subjective faith in that word and gospel (Eph 1:13). Yet faith is demonstrated not purely through one's words, claims, or affirmations, but by actions that back up those words (Jas 2:14–26). It has to be asked whether faith that exists in the complete absence of good actions is salutary and able to save the person who exercises such faith (Jas 2:14); that is, such faith is of no benefit to the fellow believer who lacks proper clothes and nourishment (Jas 2:15–16). Consequently, faith without works is to be considered as lifeless or dead (Jas 2:17).

It is impossible that faith and works should be separated one from the other, given that faith cannot exist without works but it can only be indicated through works (Jas 2:18). The one who seeks to exercise faith without works, thinking it sufficient to believe that God is one is no better than demons, who believe the very same thing (Jas 2:19). Faith apart from works is useless (Jas 2:20), since Abraham was justified by his act of offering his son Isaac on the altar (Jas 2:21), making his faith visible as the driving force behind his actions, and showing his actions as the consummation of his faith (Jas 2:22)—the very meaning of the testimony in the Old Testament to the effect that Abraham had faith in God and was therefore declared to be a friend of God (Jas 2:23).

In this way, James concludes that a believer is counted righteous not just through their claims but also through actions which attest to their faith as the impetus for those actions which complete their faith (Jas 2:24). Similar to Abraham, Rahab was counted righteous through her actions in welcoming the spies and seeing to it that they leave safely (Jas 2:25). The absence of a body from its spirit can be said to be dead, in the same way that what professes to be faith and yet lacks confirming and corroborating action is to be regarded as dead (Jas 2:26).

Doctrinal Formulation: The Triune God Who Fills Our Lack

God as Trinity is revealed through the patriarchs to Moses for posterity in terms of being the God of Abraham, Isaac, and Jacob. God is the one who fills the lack in us which keeps us from attaining our wellbeing in multiple dimensions: physical, emotional, and spiritual.

PART 2: HUMANITY'S IMAGING OF THE DIVINE

The triune God discloses Godself to Moses through the patriarchs for the sake of posterity in terms of being the God of Abraham, Isaac, and Jacob.

God the Father corresponds to the God of Abraham in that the Father made Abraham, as one who left his homeland in Mesopotamia, a symbol of the Father's own movement from the Father's glory in heaven to care about the creation. God the Father and God the Son correspond to the God of Abraham and Isaac in that the Father and Son made Abraham, as one who demonstrated willingness to sacrifice even his only son through Sarah, Isaac, and Isaac, as one who showed willingness to be sacrificed by his father Abraham, a symbol of the Father's own willingness to give up the Son to those who would crucify him and of the Son's own alacrity to be given up to his enemies.

God the Son corresponds to the God of Isaac in that the Son made Isaac, as one who was sent by his father Abraham to Mesopotamia (Paddan-Aram) to take a bride from among his own people, a symbol of the Son's own initiative to found and establish his church in a world originally far from the Son (Mesopotamia now standing for the remote world rather than one's own home).

God the Holy Spirit corresponds to the God of Jacob in that the Holy Spirit made Jacob, as one sent by his father Isaac to Mesopotamia (Paddan-Aram) to take a bride from among his own people, through whom the sons of Israel and therefore the foundation of the nation would be born, a symbol of the Holy Spirit's own procession from the Father through the Son in order to perform and continue the work of the Son in the world, through the empowerment of the apostles, through whom the church was to be born on Pentecost.[6]

God is the one who fills the lack in us which keeps us from attaining our wellbeing in multiple dimensions: physical, emotional, and spiritual.

Much as God revealed Godself to Moses through the patriarchs, God continually discloses Godself to people in the present age and will continue to do so into the future. The manner in which God apprises a person of the fact that God has been or is present in the life of the same person or in another is through an experience or testimony of having some helpful insight or impulse arise in their mind, in which an intervention on the part of God the Holy Spirit is presented in a manner indistinguishable

---

6. Jewish Virtual Library, "Paddan-Aram."

from one's own thoughts, and regardless of whether less helpful insights or impulses are also present at the same time since the products of disorder do not nullify the work of God in a person.

Such insights or impulses pertain to being in reality, becoming, or merely desiring—as a function of conscience which as the guide to right human behavior according to the law of God (Rom 2:12–16) is the operation of the Divine Nature in a human person—to be a person who is more respectful, responsible, integrous, empathetic, solicitous for another, hopeful amid difficulties, or trusting of God or those who have no reason to harm or betray them, or gaining deep personal insight into the nature of their physical, psychological, or spiritual struggles or those of others, or the character of the physical world as a realm upheld by God and created for humankind and other creatures or the spiritual world indwelled by God and other immaterial beings in a way that does not contradict a moral vision which values self as well as others.

Another way whereby one can know that God reveals or has revealed Godself to oneself or others is through the experience or testimony of seeing an unexpressed need met or explicit or implicit positive responses to their petitions for divine assistance. Implicit responses constitute those where a request was not granted, and yet the votary recognizes the potential good that resides in their not having been granted their request, the emotional or spiritual growth they underwent as a result of the whole experience, including the fact that their prayer was not directly answered in an affirmative way, or perhaps the sense of hope they have learned to cultivate in the midst of disappointment which they did not previously possess in the degree they now do, in the renewed knowledge, confidence, and conviction that God is not, in numerous cases, accountable for the fact that a prayer request has not been granted. On the contrary, personal petitions for the critical need of a person or that of a loved one, friend, or even people on the other side of the world, were incapable of being fulfilled as a result of limitations on God's ability to accomplish them as the entitative Trinity and the fact that the Divine Nature is but an undergirding structure of all reality rather than an entity with affirmative executive capacity.

Contrary to the belief of some, God does not reject some persons while accepting others exclusively on the basis of God's own personal choice, independent of the merits or demerits of an individual. Such a doctrine, concomitant with the notion of an insurmountable deceitfulness of the post-Adamic sinful human nature, has the potential to give rise to an equally insurmountable doubt that one has indeed received a divine gift of salvation. To absolutize in relation to what humankind is capable or incapable of perceiving or doing is to give a hostage to fortune, not just in the case of the purported complete deceitfulness of a sinful nature in humankind, but also a presumed inability on the part of a fallible person to do any good whatsoever, simply on account of the fact that they cannot produce an action that is completely devoid of self-interest.

We do well to realize that a personal desire in performing some action to benefit oneself in some way does not detract in any way from the fact that, parallel to the pursuit of self-benefit, there may be and there often is a concurrent desire, however impoverished it may seem relative to the motivation provided by the knowledge that one stands to gain something from the action, to also serve the needs of others or enrich their lives in some meaningful way.[7]

There is no person, Christian or not, who acts in line with a good moral law only to avoid punishment or receive a reward, without any willingness or desire to obey the moral law or love for the same but only unwillingness and a sense of compulsion, such that they would not keep the law if there were no consequences for disobeying it, as Luther believes,[8] since the conscience reminds even the wicked person of their failings, urging them toward repentance, and there will, at least in many instances, be not just a knowledge of what is right but a desire to be a good person as well as an inner delight—evincing an appreciation for and reverence of

---

7. The one important exception to this general observation is a scenario where a person intentionally commits a harmful or evil deed.

8. Luther, *Röm.*, *Praefatio* (ET, Mueller, pp. xiii–xix). One might add, from a Reformed viewpoint, that no human love, irrespective of its purity and altruism, such as the unconditional love of good parents or the heroism of specific historical figures, might pass muster in the eyes of God, who demands that all acts, in order to be considered truly good, should be directed toward the glory of God alone, not simply arising from parental instinct or motivated by love of another human person, the community at large, the natural world, by social approval, or self-gratification. Such a perspective is a function of a commitment to the view that Scripture teaches that human nature is incorrigibly and thoroughly corrupt, an interpretation of the biblical doctrine of original sin that is discussed, critiqued, and refined in a reinterpretation proffered in Chua, *ECRST*, 248–79. Indeed, nothing can be done except in such a way as redounds to divine glory, since all our moral, psychological, intellectual, spiritual, and physical capacities are endued of the Divine Nature, the ontological and moral source of our existence. As such, Paul's exhortation for Christians to do everything to the glory of God (1 Cor 10:31) urges that believers be conscious, rather than ignorant, of what is already happening in every deed they perform according to their natural capacities or even by the specific guidance of God.

the law as a proper authority in their lives—in being successful in heeding one's inner moral compass and choosing, for instance, to tell the truth even at one's personal expense or risk or to make some other personal sacrifice, a decision and action which will have been at least partly engendered by a desire to act according to the moral law.

Paul in Romans 2, on which Luther comments to the effect that no person exists who truly desires to obey God's law and loves it in their actions of obedience, does not make any such claim, only an affirmation that those who boast of their own righteousness in keeping God's laws while showing contempt for Gentiles and treating them judgmentally, as some religious people were culpable for doing at the time, were all too often also those who indulged some rather odious hypocrisy in their hearts.

Certain practices were begun as a matter of function. For instance, the steeple is prominent in Western church architecture as a result of an imitation of an original structural design to ensure that bells could be heard faraway.[9] Over time, this function was superseded by modern ways of gathering a community for important meetings and giving instructions during emergencies.

In the same way, religious beliefs are not to be essentialized or reified. The different texture of each religious tradition is due to differing sociohistorical contexts in which religious figures and communities lacked some essential ingredient for their wellbeing and had that lack met in God or the divine source manifesting itself, its connection with humankind, and its action in ways that serve to address that need. God is therefore the one who cares for and supports us to attain our holistic wellbeing. God desires that we be in good health, that we enjoy a healthy emotionality in terms of respecting, appreciating, and caring for one another, and that we know a relationship with the transcendent or spiritual that is wholesome in terms of respecting, appreciating, and caring for the transcendent or spiritual source.

Hence, God appeared to Abram the vulnerable migrant as a protector and patron; to Moses and his enslaved people as an independent sovereign and cosmic conqueror with the means to liberate, establish, and rule over the people; to the apostles who had the message of God's compassion distorted by religious leaders as a gentle and wise leader and elder brother; to Muhammad as one who rejected an immoral polytheism as

---

9. Wellman, "Why Do Churches Have Steeples?"

PART 2: HUMANITY'S IMAGING OF THE DIVINE

an anti-polytheistic monadic being; to the Hindu community as a diverse group in need of a unified religious tradition as an undergirding divine source encouraging both inner contentment and moral responsibility through a law of karma; and to the Buddhist community in its opposition to social-moral rigidity and an anthropomorphization of divinity as a source of guidance that draws attention to social and moral responsibility by minimizing the role of deity through an agnosticism.[10]

So beneficent is God that God does not restrict God's blessing of salvation from those beyond the Christian community but draws into God's personal-communal fold all who carry with themselves an "implicit faith" in divine providence as mediated by God (Aquinas), that is, the conviction that God alone can ultimately redeem and deliver (scil., as the ultimate cause of events that bring liberation in temporal matters as well as in the role of one who guarantees an individual's eternal beatitude through guiding them along good paths of thought, feeling, desire, will, and action), even if they do not possess an explicit faith in Jesus Christ.[11]

A conception of God as the fulfiller of bona fide human need brings us closer to the reason that the names and associations of God found in the biblical witness and text tend to be connected, in terms of gender, if at all, with masculinity. It is relevant, as a case in point, to wonder why God has been revealed as Father and Son, with the latter having elected to take on a male biological form as opposed to feminine names and a female form.

Concerning the divine names of the Father and the Son, God was revealed as Father on account of the role God sought to and would play vis-à-vis Israel and the way in which Israelite society, along with much of the ancient Near Eastern world, was not ready for full feminine inclusion in positions of military leadership (see Judg 4:1–10), and as the Son, especially from the days of the Son's incarnation as Jesus, in virtue of the fact that he endeavored to and did assume the role of a Jewish rabbi, a teaching function not open at the time to women.[12]

---

10. Ward, *Religion and Revelation*, 134–38, 172; Q Anʿām 6:137; Mawdūdī, *Towards Understanding the Qurʾān*, 278–79, https://www.kalamullah.com/Books/Towards%20Understanding%20the%20Quran%202.pdf.

11. Aquinas, *Summa* 2a-2æ, Q. 2, Art. 7, ad. 3.

12. As a matter of fact, Jewish women in the first century AD were not permitted to study religious texts, were segregated in religious spaces, not allowed to initiate divorce, and placed under male socioeconomic custodianship. Leonhard, "Jesus' Extraordinary Treatment of Women."

The age-old question of whether and, if so, how Christ the son of Mary may be said to be divine in such a way that it needs to be conceded that Mary is not only to be recognized as the mother of God but as one who carried God to term deserves proper and adequate treatment in this context of our discussion of the subject of the divine-human communion as critical for a clear knowledge of God.

With its Platonic slant, classical Christian theology has proposed that the divine and the human in Christ be clearly demarcated and distinguished one from the other. If the human in Christ is that by which the divine Son of God is able to experience weakness and frailty, including fatigue and death, then the divine in Christ is that by which the psychological subject that Christ truly is is able to know, desire, and will that which is in accordance to God's purpose and the Son in a human frame accomplish supernatural and miraculous deeds.

The divine subject that is Christ provides the human nature in him the time and space to express itself whilst maintaining its hold on his consciousness even during moments of the manifestation of the human nature with the freedom at any point to cause the human nature to shift into dormancy so that the divine nature might concurrently shift into active operation and actualization. What does it mean therefore to say that Christ feels tired or that he even dies? It would be nothing other than a description of the experience which the human nature causes the human body of Christ to undergo in a physical sense.

Christ's humanity in and of itself does not necessarily entail vulnerability to physical injury or mortality—when the divine nature is in operation, the human body of Christ is impervious to any form of physical harm and threat. It is the human nature in its active operation that exposes Christ's physical body to corporeal limitations and potential dangers. When Christ's material frame is so exposed, the divine subject in him suffers no physical injury—like any psychological subject, it is psychological and spiritual in nature—though the subject undergoes an emotional experience of physical pain, mediated as this is by signals from the central nervous system.[13]

Although God is omnipresent in a classical theology, nowhere is the divine nature physically embodied as it is in the human Christ. It is no detriment to divine immutability to assert that the divine became

---

13. Engel, "Psychogenic Pain," 899–918. The agony which the Father and Spirit underwent at the crucifixion arose from seeing one so beloved experience intense suffering.

embodied at a specific point in human history and the history of the universe, seeing that the principle of immutability is not applied in a thoroughgoing and rigid fashion to God's presence in the world, but only to the divine existence in eternity.

Two questions stand in need of being addressed in any theology of God. A first is how we may know that a spiritual domain actually exists without our having any empirical and falsifiable evidence of the same. The second is the question of how we may know that the universe is real rather than a pure, clever, and seamless simulation.

Concerning the query into whether a spiritual realm is an objective reality rather than a phantasy or figment of human imagination, there is in fact no method of proving empirically that God exists, that the nature of God is what the Scripture declares it to be, that Jesus is divine, that the Holy Spirit exists, and does so in a believer's heart, or that a person has been saved by God through Christ in the power of the Holy Spirit.[14]

There are ways of establishing the truth of the Christian faith in reliable historical testimony to the existence of Jesus of Nazareth, attested as it is in secular historical writings; in the divinity of Christ as self-attested in the gospels, and confirmed by the devotion of the apostles of Christ, most of whom were martyred for their faith; in the resurrection of Christ, showing the favor of God the Father despite his having claimed to be God the Son, which would be blasphemy were Christ not indeed God the Son;[15] the non-possibility that Christ died and had his

---

14. The limitation of closed philosophical systems developed by Immanuel Kant and Georg W. F. Hegel consists in the unquestioned assumption, which Kant adopted from Hume even in his reaction to Hume and Hegel from Kant in Hegel's reaction to Kant, that the criterion for true and certain knowledge is its capacity to be humanly observed and proven via empirical studies, through definition, or by logic. It is to elevate the human experience and reason to the status of an arbiter of truth. Such closed systems have a tendency to neglect or even undermine the possibility that God might well have the freedom to disclose God's nature and purpose for humanity through the human conscience or even supernatural occurrences that God has the power to cause to transpire alongside the regularities of nature. Olson notes that the extreme empiricism of David Hume would not be something that harmonizes with the way he would live; that is, Hume would conduct himself with the expectation and assumption that other people with whom he interacts are real thinking beings, for instance. Cf. Olson, *Journey of Modern Theology*, 72–98, 106, 108.

15. The surest evidence that Christ claimed to be the divine Son of God reposes in the manner in which religious Jews who encountered Jesus concluded that he was a blasphemer on the basis of his having referred to God as his Father in conjunction with his claims about being God's coworker and therefore justified in working even on the Sabbath through healing an invalid (for God, in permeating the entire world, in sustaining all of creation does not carry anything outside God's domain or lift anything

body hidden away by his disciples (given that the opponents of Christ and his followers could have sought to discover and produce his body and the fact that some of these opponents are recorded in the gospels as having engaged in subterfuge instigating the soldiers who guarded the tomb and found the body missing to tell people that the body was stolen by the disciples, in Matt 28:11–15); and the non-possibility that the disciples who encountered the risen Christ were subject to hallucination (group hallucination has never been reported, since a hallucination is a dysfunctional mental experience in the mind of a specific individual and has no basis in external reality; a group hallucination would not explain the disappearance of Christ's physical body).[16]

Even so, we can have certainty concerning what the Bible declares about God and Christ through deduction beginning with the observation that the conscious human self is able to know that it does not account for its own physical, psychological, spiritual, and moral existence.

That is to say, I as a human person am fully aware that I am not the cause of my own existence as a physical being with the ability to receive input through the five senses, move and use the limbs attached to my body; as a psychological being with the capacity to experience emotions and develop feelings or opinions regarding what I experience; as a spiritual being capable of discerning the presence of the spiritual and transcendent, whether this be some religious notion of a divine or spiritual presence or simply a sense that something exists outside myself that gives me my existence in every respect; and as a moral being with intuitions appertaining to what it means to value a person through respect, responsibility, empathy, compassion, and fairness, as well as a desire to do what is right in this regard by following those intuitions, with all these

---

above God's height), which for a conscientious religious Jew, as Jesus was, meant that Jesus was implying that he was equal to God (John 5:17–18), rather than bearing a generic signification of a human person being a creature made by God, as all human beings are. Although the Father and the Son have been working since creation (though not to create but to sustain all living things by deputing angels to grant to creatures a capacity to adapt or evolve), they have also been resting since that time (in the way of creation, though not of providence), for God's rest from creation does not consist in doing nothing, but in actively sustaining all of creation albeit with complete effortlessness, and without a sense of hard labor, agony, and exhaustion (see Philo, *De Cher.*, 2.26.87–90). Carson, *John*, 179–80, 246–49. Equally strong indications of Jesus' divinity consist of the witness to Jesus as the "exact imprint" of God's nature (Heb 1:3 ESV)—seeing as nothing except God could be identical to God in every attribute yet without being the same person—and his authority to forgive sins on behalf of God and abolish the Mosaic food laws instituted by God (Mark 2:1–12; 7:19).

16. Licona, "Jesus' Resurrection Appearances."

dimensions of our being completely integrated in one person such that messages can be sent between them allowing a person to function (e.g., to will through the spirit that the physical body engages in a specific movement or identifies and critiques a particular emotion of the mind) or sense or experience in a multifaceted way.[17]

On account of this manifold observation, it is possible to establish the existence of a spiritual realm. Yet, this is not to be equated to an all-powerful sovereign being which controls and directs the sequence of historical and personal events accounting for all that occurs in the universe, including the affairs of humankind. If it were the case that such a powerful supreme being did actually exist and causally and comprehensively influence the flow of all events, we would have to conclude that we were under the paramount rule of a rather malicious or arbitrary deity inclined to permitting the tragic agony of many innocent persons, including the very young and vulnerable.

As far as Jesus is concerned, God the Father is not a being that is willing that any of God's elect, who intercede for themselves, should suffer under conditions of injustice and oppression, but instead a divine being that will do everything in God's power to bring about justice expeditiously (Luke 18:7–8). The fact that many who call on God, including faithful Christians, continue to go through great suffering and anguish suggests that God is not all-powerful in a completely determinative way, but that while possessing the authority to judge the universe at the appointed time and punish all sinners, God does not have the means to control events that transpire in the world.

As such, we propound the existence of a non-personal divine undergirding framework which we have called the Divine Nature, distinct from the entitative divine being that the Trinity is. We ascribe to the Divine Nature the natural generation, at the horizon of all possibility, before which nothing can and does exist, of the initial spiritual reality including the Trinity, angels, and other spirits, antecedent to material creation. This two-tiered structure of the generation of all things is necessitated by

17. E.g., the physical impacts the psychological through the unpleasant sensation of pain whilst particular mental states may cause psychosomatic symptoms; the spiritual and moral are intertwined in that one's sense of God's friendship is tied to one's moral behavior while moral conduct is improved through religiosity; the moral aspect of human existence impacts the psychological when having a good conscience leads to better feelings about oneself and psychological dysfunctionality generates distortions of one's perception of the value of others which, unless willed against, brings about negative moral behavior.

our reluctance to ascribe to a personal divine being such as the Trinity the material creation of the universe, for if the Trinity were capable of bringing into existence a material realm, the Trinity would also be able to control events in the world. The existence of evil and injustice, however, implies that the Trinity is not in control of the world. Hence, the theory of a two-tiered structure of the generation of the universe stands as a viable conception. Instead of the Trinity, the angels are responsible for material creation; even then, only when they work together.

A conception of God in such terms is given shape and voice in the venerable Exodus tradition. Consider how the book curiously speaks of Moses taking a role akin to that of God in relation to Aaron, his older brother, on two occasions (Exod 4:16; 7:1).

The reference in the fourth chapter makes it clear that the signification of Moses assuming a role similar to that of God vis-à-vis Aaron consists in the fact that Moses shall command Aaron just what to say to the people of Israel, God promising additional support in the form of guiding both Moses and Aaron in what they are to say to their respective audiences.

In the seventh chapter, God informs Moses that God had appointed the latter to be in a position similar to that of God with respect to Pharaoh himself, while making Aaron something of a prophet to Moses as akin to God. The tradition proceeds to enunciate what it means that Moses assumes a similar role to that of God: that Moses will receive the command of the Lord that he is to pass on to Aaron; namely, that Pharaoh is to free the people of Israel (v. 2).

It is patent that the role that God assigns to Moses in connection with Aaron and Pharaoh that God compares to that of God intimates the position of God as one who commands that God's will and purpose be carried out by God's agents, rather than that God should be acting in God's own capacity.

A delegation of some kind can be discerned as early as Exod 3:2, where an angel of Yahweh manifests itself in a spectacle of an ever-burning bush to draw Moses' attention (vv. 2–3), before God, who seems to be separate from all that the angel is doing as a sovereign and commanding voice (v. 4 onwards). The power of God is never vested in Godself but in the agents and objects commissioned by God for special purposes, whether this be the angel of Yahweh or the specially empowered staff of Moses. Even if Moses, standing in a position akin to that of God, was able

PART 2: HUMANITY'S IMAGING OF THE DIVINE

to work the empowered staff, turning it into a serpent, yet he did so only by the power of the staff and not his own (Exod 4:17).

We go on now to consider the question regarding whether the universe is real rather than a pure simulation. We have already enunciated the elements that compose a human person as a physical, psychological, spiritual, and moral being. Although it may be speculated that an external force is responsible for running a massive simulation that constructs an impression, in an observer's mind, of human persons as real and distinct psychological, spiritual, and moral subjects, yet the human experience bears testimony to a profound degree of emotional sensitivity, sense of justice, of goodness, fairness, compassion, truthfulness, responsibility. This suggests some deep level of understanding of these human traits on the part of that which is purported to generate the simulation. Something that grasps the essentials of humanity is likely to possess humanity itself.

Think of the author of a psychologically sensitive novel; it would be reasonable to assume that such a writer would be in possession of the aforementioned attributes. The one who understands unconditional love is unlikely to be a loveless and malicious person, but rather draws on their own experience of being an unconditionally loving individual to construct a narrative involving fictional subjects that practice unconditional love. Such an author would not put their characters, though fictional, through pain and tragedy for their own sake. If they do design a character that endures tremendous suffering and injustice, this would only be out of an endeavor for their imaginative work to be as true to life in an experiential sense and therefore relatable to a real audience. If the author has determined that a character go through a crucible so as to emerge a stronger person, this again is not a type of scenario of the author's own making, but a recurrent human experience.

In contradistinction to an author of a fictional story who often has to adhere to the contours of human responses to differing situations and the typical reactions to those responses, God is free to construct a very different narrative of the world and each individual human life, where the characters in this real-life story are moral, virtuous, gentle, loving, and compassionate in and of themselves, without having first to face unspeakable evil and anguish. That good people frequently encounter injustice is no evidence that evil is necessary for the flourishing of good, that the Almighty God determined that some darkness and corruption would serve the moral advancement of humankind, and that there was no better way for God to design the moral capacities and limitations of the human soul.[18] The state of affairs suggests rather that God is in no position to design these capacities and limitations, that God did not orchestrate events that transpire in the world and each individual life, and that it is untrue that sin and evil can ever subserve human moral wellbeing. Far from predetermining people for moral growth through unjust suffering, God struggles with and even against angelic and human creaturedom in pursuit of justice and compassion for the weak and vulnerable, judgment for the unrepentant, rewards for the righteous, and the wellbeing and flourishing of all humankind.

Concerning the origin of cruelty, the excessive and gleeful desire to see another person or sentient being suffer arises from a sense of having one's genuine affection spurned by the one formerly beloved, though the fact that an erstwhile lover should be able to descend to such dark depths strongly suggests the immaturity of that love.

Violent malice among humankind was given an impetus when Lucifer out of a wish to retaliate to God's decision to evict Lucifer from heaven for having coveted God's throne deceived Adam and Eve into believing that God was to be viewed as their chief competitor, and as a pseudo-authority bent on keeping humankind under God's rule by enforcing their ignorance under the guise of caring for their wellbeing.

The sense of betrayal led the first couple to cast off all restraints in the supposition that they could trust no authority whatsoever. Their attempted autarchy was necessarily insecure, because it did not involve mutual trust but rather domination as a means to guarantee a desired outcome. Brutality of both physical and psychological, direct and indirect kinds became an instrument by which faithless and insecure human persons sought to consolidate their rule in various domains of influence so as to preserve some semblance of order (Rom 1:31).

Human authority thus assumed a cruel character, and successive generations were raised from the beginning in a climate of brutality and extreme distrust of authority begetting further brutality—parental, political, or religious. Even parents who thought or made it seem that they knew better resorted to various forms of discipline—cruelty, in essence—thinking to drive the foolishness out of their children.[19]

---

18. The set of assertions being opposed is a restatement of Leibnizian optimism. For an outline of this philosophical view, see Editors of Encyclopaedia Britannica, "Best of All Possible Worlds."

19. Erik Erikson considers a sin of the greatest magnitude any calculated effort on the part of a disciplinarian or self-indulgent parent which results in grievous emotional

PART 2: HUMANITY'S IMAGING OF THE DIVINE

In this psychological context, one could hardly conceive of a personal God in terms other than supremely brutal and brutally supreme. Trust is thereby imperative for developing a proper and healthy understanding of God, and such trust can only be nurtured in the context of a personal relationship with God.

Some might wonder if a conception of God as something other than imperious, forbidding, and unapproachable will be salutary given the human tendency to misuse the grace of God. If we suppose that God has forgiven all sins through faith in Jesus Christ, would it not, it is asked, be only too easy for the insincere and hypocritical to imagine that they could continue in their sin with the greatest degree of impunity? Since God has already designated me a righteous, even innocent, person, with a legal moral standing equivalent to that of a person who has never had the slightest wrongful thought or desire, what incentive is there for me to pursue or continue in the way of righteousness?

The idea of an imputed righteousness may not find a solid basis in Scripture. Although Romans 4 discusses a reckoning by God of Abraham, David, and the believers of Jesus as righteous on account of their faith in God, whether for the blessing of a child in the case of Abraham, or of forgiveness and mercy in that of David, or of the sure forgiveness of our sins through faith in Jesus Christ, this is not to be conflated with the speculative hypothesis in which we have not just had our sins borne by Jesus on the cross but we have had his righteousness conferred on us. On the contrary, the posture, the disposition, the habitus of a person who truly believes God has made promises of blessing and forgiveness which God is able to fulfill is in itself a good work deserving of the title of righteousness, whereas those who fail to trust in God for those things fall afoul of God's moral expectations.

What of the ways in which St. Paul speaks of believers as baptized into the death of Christ, thereby buried with him and having died with him (Rom 6:3–4, 8), of how, indeed, one has already been crucified with Christ (Gal 2:20), or of believers as having been raised with Christ, and of their lives as hidden with Christ in God (Col 2:12–13; 3:1, 3)? For a believer to recognize that they have died with Christ in his death is simply to acknowledge that Christ died for us, in atonement of our sins, which is as good as saying that we ourselves died on the cross on

---

harm to children. Erikson, *Young Man Luther*, 70; that Jesus values and protects children in a special way is evident in how he instructed his disciples not to prevent children from going to him (Matt 19:13–14).

which Christ died, rather than Christ himself, though he, and not we, died. To say of believers that they have been raised with Christ is simply to affirm that the spiritual and moral life of the believer is completely bound up with the life of Christ, predestined and destined to become increasingly like that of Christ, as they emulate his attitude, outlook, and desires in all that they do.

What, then, is the free gift of righteousness believers in Christ receive of which Paul speaks (Rom 5:17; 2 Cor 5:21)? This is none other than the power and guidance we have in God and in Christ to lead a spiritual and moral life that reflects the image of Christ. This inherent power in the Divine Nature and constant guidance in both the Divine Nature and the Trinity is not anything that we need to worry about paying for. If Rom 1:17 avers that the righteous shall live by faith, this designates the recognition and awareness of the believer that their inherent moral capacity is posited of God the Divine Nature, and their constant moral guidance is posited of God the Divine Nature in the form of the conscience and granted of God the Trinity in the form of the voice of the Holy Spirit.

In view of the foregoing, it is imperative to realize that while one has forgiveness through faith in Christ's atoning act, this is not a carte blanche—while God's love is unconditional, God's forgiveness is conditional upon authentic repentance and a commitment to a sincere life in the days that follow.[20] We are to engage in good works out of gratitude for God's good intentions and beneficial actions towards us, out of a desire to glorify God, out of a need to know that we are truly Christians from observing the sincere and praiseworthy works that we do, and out of a wish to positively influence our neighbors to admire or even consider Christ, and simply because it is the right thing to do.[21]

It is meet at the present juncture to pursue the question concerning the nature of the relationship between God and sin: is an action proscribed as sinful in biblical teaching in an external and incidental connection to the nature of God and divine action? That is, in regard

---

20. Barth recognizes that the nature of God's forgiveness, of the release from condemnation for our sins as a result of God's alacrity so to exonerate us in virtue of Christ's great atoning act, is such that one is not in a position to appreciate or avail of it except that one upholds their moral duty to the upbuilding of the community of Christian believers and lives in the awareness that judgment awaits all according to their obedient or disobedient deeds. Barth, KD IV.2, §67.1 (ET, Bromiley, p. 638).

21. Cf. Barth, KD IV.2, §66.5 (ET, Bromiley, p. 598); the idea that one is to do good simply because it is right is that of Samuel Wen-Sheng Chua.

to being an external factor, is sin unrelated to the being of God and the character of divine action; and, in regard to being an incidental element, is sin non-fundamental in a moral sense, such that the actions stipulated as sinful are not inherently immoral?

It is neither the case that sin constitutes action divinely ruled to be unrighteous and unlawful which is external nor incidental to the nature of God and of God's action. When an action is determined by Scripture to be sinful, it is so because determined to be in disharmony with and violation of the righteous character of God and dishonoring to the same as perpetrated by a creature of God's.

A few examples will suffice in this regard. When the Bible prohibits blasphemy, that is, any speech or action intended to mock God, this is done to protect God's name and person from being dishonored by God's creatures, presupposing that God cares about God's own dignity and honor.[22] When Scripture disallows any form of conduct that dishonors, manipulates, exploits, or otherwise harms a human person, this is done on the assumption that God so cares about the physical, psychological, and spiritual weal of God's human creatures that God will not countenance any mistreatment of an individual, whoever the object of such intended action might be, whatever their background and however they may have behaved in the past. In light of the same reason, biblical commandment does not brook any intention to harm oneself, including engaging in dishonoring behavior or casually or insouciantly allowing oneself to be dishonored, manipulated, exploited, and harmed.

In short, people have to answer to God, the divine, or the ultimately significant for anything they do to themselves, one another, or God, the divine, or the ultimately significant in their earthly course of existence (Rom 14:8). This dictum and requirement does not apply merely to those who believe in a personal God, but even those who hold that God is a ground of existence or that God does not actually exist.

---

22. On this definition, blasphemy does not include contesting the historicity, nature (divinity), character, meaning, or significance (as appropriate) of a religious conception of God, figure, or text, critiquing empty or formalistic worship, or criticizing those who hold religious office (though one should still refrain from mocking them, yet only on the grounds that one should not mock another human person). A religious community will differ from this minimalist definition and that is acceptable so long as it does not extend the application of these rules to those who do not hold the faith that stipulates them or apply them to members or adherents in such a way that these individuals are subject to psychological dysfunctionality or physical harm. This definition of blasphemy is consonant with that proffered in Demarest, *NDT* s.v. "Blasphemy". See also Barth, *KD* IV.2, §67.4 (ET, Bromiley, pp. 709–710).

Although in the latter cases there may be no personal God to hold them to account for how they have lived their lives, the very core structure of their personal morality, in which they value themselves and know that they are to be loved and cared for and they are to love and care for, a system of values from which they can never extricate themselves, will not permit them to pursue a self-destructive, destructive, or sacrilegious course of behavior.

While such individuals may consider themselves to be those who have to answer to themselves rather than to any God, in point of fact they are duty-bound to act morally by the ontological and moral source of their existence, which they believe to be impersonal but whose undeniable reality and inseparable relationship to them as existent beings and moral agents hold tremendous ramifications for the way they are to conduct themselves morally.

Among the first prohibitions of the Decalogue are those against worshipping other gods and idolatry. In connection with devotion to another divine being, this designates any notion that the object of one's worship is other than and different as well as disparate from the God who revealed Godself in Jesus Christ.

Idolatry stands for the act of substituting anything that is non-God in place of God. This includes a complete identification of a physical statue with the divine being it represents as well as an abolition of healthy relations in which one regards the divine with reverence and love or the ultimate with seriousness and thankfulness, human persons, including oneself, with respect, lovingkindness, empathy, and compassion, other living beings with respect, lovingkindness, and compassion, and all other things with care and respect, degenerating into a situation where one is devoid of these qualities and omits these practices in pursuit of an idée fixe concerning the accumulation of wealth, power and status, personal appeal, among other possible reductive and reductionistic preoccupations or even monomanias, perhaps even beginning to see or already seeing divine-human, human, and human-world relations in terms of what they can bring to the table.[23]

For this reason, Christians are given to excesses who espouse the conscious and conscientious avoidance of certain religious places or practices, given that only the choice to worship a God seen as other than

---

23. Pannenberg, *Syst. Theol.* 1, 3.4, (ET, Bromiley, pp. 178–87); Gunton, *CF*, 4.13, p. 61n2.

the triune God, irreverence, or inhumanity can lead a person down the path of turning away from God or turning to idolatry.

In Augustine's treatise, "De gratia et libero arbitrio" ("On Grace and Free Will"), the bishop of Hippo Regius defends his doctrine of the captivity of the will of the human being who is heir to Adam's fall and moral corruption, a volitional captivity in which nothing save the sudden and supernatural intervention of God will be of any avail for an individual who desires not to be so overwhelmed by a sinful will as to be able to perform no good deed.[24]

A summary statement of Augustine's doctrine of God's conversion of the human will may be found in the thirty-third chapter of his work: "He works in us that we may have the will, and in perfecting works with us when we have the will . . . He operates, therefore, without us, in order that we may will; but when we will, and so will that we may act, He co-operates with us. We can, however, ourselves do nothing to effect good works of piety without Him either working that we may will, or co-working when we will."[25]

A recapitulation is found in the forty-first chapter, where Augustine describes the grace of God as so operating in human individuals that "the human will is not taken away, but changed from bad to good, and assisted when it is good" and how "men's good wills" are objects of God's action in which "God Himself converts [them] from bad ones, and, when converted by Him, directs to good actions and eternal life".[26]

Both the good and evil wills of people are "so entirely at the disposal of God, that He turns them whithersoever He wills, and whensoever He wills,—to bestow kindness on some, and to heap punishment on others, as He Himself judges right by a counsel most secret to Himself, indeed, but beyond all doubt most righteous."[27]

---

24. Augustine, Gla, §5 (ET, Holmes, p. 446); Augustine, Gla, §45 (ET, Holmes, p. 464).

25. Augustine, Gla, §33 (ET, Holmes, pp. 457–58). Augustine considers that Phil 1:6 constitutes a basis for this theory, yet this verse only expresses St. Paul's confidence that God will ultimately consummate God's work in the lives of Christians at Philippi with whom he has been engaged in a missional partnership. The part about God cooperating with humankind to bring to actualization good works is true, though not that whereby it is supposed that God acts irruptively on the human will to turn it from evil to good.

26. Augustine, Gla, §41 (ET, Holmes, pp. 461–62).

27. Augustine, Gla, §41 (ET, Holmes, pp. 461–62).

Indeed, the bishop of Hippo thinks that God has the power to put hardness into Pharaoh's heart, fear into that of the Israelite soldiers when they attacked Ai without first taking stock of their standing before God; disrespect toward David in the heart of Shimei for the king's sin in the matter of Bathsheba all for David's own humbling, without violating Shimei's freewill but merely inclining his wickedness toward the disgraced king; betrayal in the heart of Judas to actualize the crucifixion of Christ; malice in the heart of the devil to prove the faith and devotion of the righteous unto God; foolishness in the mind of Absalom which led him to reject Ahithopel's expedient counsel, on account of David's prayer; folly in the mind of Rehoboam causing him to reject the good advice of his older counselors and so lose much of his kingdom, that the prophecy concerning the division of the kingdom might be fulfilled; a desire for war in the hearts of the Philistines and Arabians who attacked Judah; Amaziah's ill-advised decision to attack Joash, king of Israel; and a favorable inclination toward Esther in the heart of Ahasuerus.[28]

While all these examples, with the exception of that concerning Christ, are valid, it needs to be emphasized that God does not have complete control over the human will, given that each person has charge of their own decisions, though they may experience influences for better or worse, whether from God or some other source, and that when God is said to influence a person for ill, it is always only through a withdrawal of divine spiritual support rather than a direct instigation to do what is not good.

It is worthwhile taking a closer look at Augustine's scriptural support for his teaching and interpretation about God's conversion of the human will from evil to good. Augustine cites 1 Cor 15:56–57 in buttressing his major claim, contending that the passage indirectly implies that apart from God's gift of grace to assist the human being in the exercise of their freedom to perform the will of God in obedience to God's precepts, there is no possibility of a human actualization of the divine command.[29]

This is an ostensibly redoubtable argument, and the tenor and content of the verses is reflected in Rom 7:7–25, especially vv. 7–13, where St. Paul highlights the deceitful manner in which sin exploits the holy, righteous, and good law of God to bring death upon him. The keyword here is that Paul said he was "deceived" (v. 11; ESV) by sin. No doubt the

---

28. Augustine, Gla, §41-42 (ET, Holmes, pp. 461–63).
29. Augustine, Gla, §8 (ET, Holmes, p. 447).

apostle had in mind the fundamental seductiveness and deceptiveness of sin, whereby a person finds themselves "lured" and "enticed" by their own carnal desires (Jas 1:14; ESV), desires which promise happiness, fulfillment, and freedom to those who satiate them, such as for power, influence, possessions, or success beyond what one needs to maintain a healthy and sufficient livelihood.

There was an uncontrollable nature to Paul's internal struggle with his sinful behavior, more than warranted by a mere wish for power, influence, possessions, or success, such that it is plausible that the post-traumatic stress disorder he would have suffered as a result of his stoning and near death at Lystra in Asia Minor would in all probability have increased his aggressiveness in seeking to satisfy his craving for any one of the usual indices of worldly accomplishment.[30]

Another verse Augustine quotes in support of his thesis is John 6:65, which the bishop evidently believes reinforces the idea that the grace of God constitutes an irruptive element by which people are enabled to do God's bidding, as seen in the passages he cites; namely, Ps 80:7; 85:4, 6, which aver not so much that God abruptly "turns" the believer as that God is able to be invoked to restore the community of faith to its previous glory.[31] On the contrary, in John 6:65, the Lord explicated the expected outcome that not all of his followers would remain with him in due course by appealing to the fact that those who have accepted the words and testimony of the Son were only able to choose to do so because the Father had spoken and testified to them about the Christ (John 6:45). It is granted, however, that God is indeed able to see to the strengthening of the human will against temptation within God's limitations expressed in the finite power of God's angelic delegates (Matt 26:41; Luke 22:32).[32]

In the fifteenth chapter, Augustine proposes that the meaning of 1 Cor 4:7 validates his conjecture regarding the complete corruption of the human will which is said to be unable to help itself in spite of the moral faculty and resources provided it by God.[33] Here, Paul reminds Christians in Corinth that that which they have they received from God entirely, and so form no occasion for boasting. Augustine appears to believe that this verse supports his theological interpretation that the good works that are done by the believer unto eternal life are possible only because God had

---

30. Mayo Clinic Staff, "Post-Traumatic Stress Disorder."
31. Augustine, Gla, §10 (ET, Holmes, p. 448).
32. Augustine, Gla, §9 (ET, Holmes, p. 447).
33. Augustine, Gla, §15 (ET, Holmes, p. 450).

performed a prior work on the human will of the individual to expunge it of the corruption that prevents it from performing God's will.

The context of 1 Corinthians 4 suggests, however, that the things which Paul had in mind that the Corinthian believers had already been bestowed by God refer not so much to anything as specific as a converted or fully transformed freewill as to their wealth, influence, and honor in the sight of the onlooking world (vv. 8–13). Working backwards, these believers were exalted against each other (v. 6), some using the fact that they were partisans of a certain apostle or evangelist to incite envy among one another (1 Cor 1:12; 3:4), reveling in their purported greater wisdom (hence Paul's emphasis on true power and wisdom from God in the first two chapters). There was indeed some credence to the idea that the Corinthian believers had certain gifts in speech and knowledge (1 Cor 1:5). Yet they could hardly be said to have been walking in the love, faith, and hope of Christ, and hence the bishop of Hippo's use of this text to defend a notion of a human freewill that stands in need of complete conversion by God antecedent to the actualization of any good work at all seems to be all but illegitimate.

In the following chapter, Augustine marshals these passages: 2 Cor 3:5; Deut 8:17; Rom 8:37; and 9:16 to substantiate his point of view concerning the necessity for God's irruptive supernatural action on the human freewill to create and actualize the possibility of good works pleasing to God.[34] Yet the sufficiency of which Paul speaks in 2 Corinthians 3 has to do not with the fact that those thoughts that are virtuous and please God arise from God through a sudden irruption of divine power efficacious in the human will but instead that of being a minister of the gospel; the capacity to achieve desired ends to which the Mosaic tradition refers in Deuteronomy 8 is the opportunity and ability to acquire the wealth and stability into which the sojourning Israelites are destined to come, not so much again a sudden power from God that enables a person to will and perform good deeds; the conquering might of which Paul speaks in Romans 8 is that of abiding in the love of God in Christ in regard to remaining confident in and personally reflecting it in spite of trials and tribulations, not a sudden power of God operating in the will that is thereby primed to do good works; and the divine mercy which operates independently of human will and striving in Romans 9 points to the eternal truth that God's compassion for sinners cannot be restricted

---

34. Augustine, Gla, §16 (ET, Holmes, p. 450).

by human expectations, including the idea that God is duty-bound or obligated to show unchanging and unconditional favor toward Esau as the elder child despite the latter's dramatic failure—along with that of his biological descendants—to live up to God's appointment for him as the older brother who ought to serve the younger in the spirit of God's character as would be disclosed later in the gospel, and not any idea that God chooses on whom to work God's good will in utterly transforming a human will to desire and will the good.

Faith is indeed the gift of God, as Augustine asserts in the seventeenth chapter, yet not if it is propounded that this gift necessarily and always works separately from or even in opposition to the volitional nature which God has conferred on all humankind.[35] The bishop of Hippo veers from the literary context of Ezek 11:19–20 in suggesting that from these verses it is to be deduced that God holds the power to turn the "hardest" and an "absolutely inflexible [will] against God" toward God, for the promise to the returning Jewish exiles, deported following the Babylonian invasion of Jerusalem, is simply that those who are minded to give up their idolatry and wickedness will cleanse the land of idols and wickedness on their return, and to these God will grant a new, united, and obedient heart, whereas those who refuse to turn aside their idolatry and wickedness will be judged (v. 21).[36] The reference to a heart of stone being converted into a heart of flesh is to be understood in terms of the people of Israel choosing the decision of obedient faith according to the moral orientation posited in them by the Divine Nature and thereby properly receiving the gift of faithful obedience from God; in view is the nation of Israel ("the whole house of Israel") rather than the individual. Hence, this passage cannot be interpreted as a support for the theologoumenon regarding an individual conversion in which a human will is dramatically reshaped in goodness.

As for Ezek 36:22–27, on which Augustine also comments, mention is made of a sprinkling of clean water by God on Jewish returnees from exile (v. 25).[37] In Scripture, the sprinkling of fresh water or a solution containing water is performed in the event that someone dies in a tent, or a person touches someone who was killed by a sword or dies or human bones or a grave, and the tent as well as anybody who touched the corpse needs to be cleansed by that action. In this instance, the onus is

---

35. Augustine, Gla, §17 (ET, Holmes, pp. 450–51).
36. Augustine, Gla, §29 (ET, Holmes, pp. 455–56).
37. Augustine, Gla, §30 (ET, Holmes, p. 456).

on the unclean person to cleanse themselves (Num 19:14–20). Another occasion for the sprinkling of fresh water is in the context of the cleansing of a house with a mold problem that is under control (Lev 14:33–53). A stronger affinity is observed between the Ezekiel 36 cleansing and the ritual for the cleansing of the Levites for their service to the Lord on behalf of the firstborns of Israel in which the water of purification is sprinkled on them (Num 8:5–19).

In all these instances, the tacit presupposition or explicit indication is that an action of cleansing is performed, and if the object is a moral agent, then the latter willingly receives it and is aware of its implications rather than being compelled against their will to accept the action. It is unlikely that Ezek 36:25 involves a complex theological-philosophical conception in which the will of a moral agent is entirely renovated apart from its own intentions. Were that to be case, it would be completely surprising that it is only in the following verse (26), after the cleansing action by a sprinkling of clean water, that God speaks about a gift of a new heart, a new spirit, a heart of flesh, of God's own Spirit, and of an obedient life.

This suggests, again, that God strengthens the returning community of Jewish exiles in their decision of faith and obedience rather than controlling their wills; we observe once more that the object of God's action refers to the nation as a whole (the "house of Israel") rather than to individuals. The effect of the joint divine-human action, on account that the obedience of Israel is only possible and indeed natural through the moral orientation posited by the Divine Nature in the first place, is that, in a spiritual and metaphorical manner of speaking, the faith and obedience of the community of the people of God are a gift from God alone, accepted through an apposite human response. In substantiation of this argument, God urges Israel through Ezekiel (18:31) to repent of its transgressions, in other words, to make for themselves a new heart and a new spirit, strongly implying that the phraseology expresses a necessary act of penitence and repentance wholly driven by the will and decision of a sinner (with salutary encouragement from God based on an inherent moral orientation implanted in all human persons by the Divine Nature), rather than some divinely-initiated supernatural and irruptive action that alters the will of the transgressor.

Augustine references Ps 37:23 in support of his theory of a divine conversion of the human will from evil to good. Yet, set in its overall context, this is simply an affirmation that God will protect the righteous, provide for them so they can continue to be generous, and assure them of a future in the land, instead of suggesting that God controls the movements of all human beings.[38] As for Ps 141:3, which the bishop highlights, this verse is a prayer attributed to David for God to help guide him in his speech, reminding him of what is fitting and wise, concomitant with an associated plea in the following verse for God to guard his heart against slipping into a habit and routine of evil machinations.[39] There is no indication here that the psalmist wishes for God to take control of his speech and decisions, only a desire to be guided through remembrance of God's wise teachings and commandments.

A critical issue pertinent to a discussion of the doctrine of faith is the question why some people believe in Christ while others do not. The Christian faith is professed by those who fulfill two basic preconditions touching on knowledge and need. In order for a person to truly embrace Christ as their Lord and Savior, rather than a distorted perception of the same, it is necessary for them to possess an accurate knowledge of Christ, that they might not be beset by misconceptions that could either hinder their relationship with God in Christ or slowly and eventually turn them away from Christ. A second requirement for a person to have faith in Christ and to come to have faith in Christ, is for them, respectively, to possess a continual interest in that faith or sense a need for the same. This sense of a need for the Christian faith in replacement of their former beliefs might itself presuppose a misconception of their old religious or non-religious profession, arising from lack of knowledge on one's part or from doubts sown by interreligious polemics.

The be-all and end-all for a person's incapacity to believe the tenets of a religious tradition differing from their current belief system is no more and no less than their perception that they do not need anything that belief of the religious tradition can afford them. Accordingly, those who have become disaffected from the Christian faith or who entertain some form of misconception regarding the faith such as inaccurate thoughts about God's nature and purpose, or insurmountable self-doubt, find themselves completely unable to persuade or compel themselves to believe the Christian message, if only because they have become emotionally detached, whether because of a sense of God's unworthiness or self-unworthiness,

---

38. Augustine, Gla, §32 (ET, Holmes, p. 457).
39. Augustine, Gla, §32 (ET, Holmes, p. 457).

from answers and possibilities held out by Christianity, and have no more personal investment in any Christian tenet.[40]

For a religious belief to have any chance of being accepted, it has first to be acceptable, and if it is to be acceptable, it has to fall within the bounds of what is desirable, viable, actionable, practicable, attainable, and achievable. Should a person come to feel that God is unworthy, there goes the desirability of the faith, and in the event that they feel they are beyond redemption, there goes the viability of Christianity. Hence the acceptance of Christian religious belief becomes impossible, since personal faith is a matter closely tied to affect and emotionality as a subjective phenomenon involving the whole of a person's being. So long as the heart of a person cannot be won, faith is out of the question. The essence of Christian faith consists in personal trust in a living God. Much as one cannot be asked to simply trust another person whom they have just met or with whom they have only recently been acquainted, and any such request put to most people will almost certainly and forthwith meet with internal rejection if not also an external refusal, so also those whose trust and faith in God have been undermined by a sense of God's unworthiness or self-unworthiness will have no power whatsoever to embrace Christian beliefs about God's nature and purposes for humankind and the world.

Though doctrine may be somewhat abstract or at least susceptible of abstraction, yet the one of whom faith is requested interfaces not with a source of information but rather a living personal source of truth, wisdom, and redemption. Everything depends on what one feels about God, and if that falls apart, faith falls along with it. In this way, the nature of religious faith itself as a subjective phenomenon based on one's personal trust in God's character attests that God is personal in nature.

It is appropriate at this juncture to inquire into the criteria for an assurance of one's salvation; that is, one's true and actual communion with God which will see them through to an eternal afterlife. In this connexion, one observes first the traditional Christian theological understanding as encapsulated in classical evangelical theology. One can hardly do better than appeal to the revivalist theology of the eighteenth-century

---

40. As a case in point, YouTuber Kristi Burke shares that it was a Calvinist conception of God's sovereign and meticulous predetermination of some to salvation and others to damnation, which felt to her like a form of controlling behavior, that ultimately caused her to leave the Christian faith in which she was raised and to even be unable to re-embrace the faith. Burke, "From Holy to Heretic."

pastor-theologian Jonathan Edwards for an adequate articulation of an evangelical conception of Christian salvific assurance. In his famous 1741 sermon delivered to an initially spiritually complacent congregation at Enfield, Connecticut, "Sinners in the Hands of an Angry God," Edwards preached that it was not sufficient for a person to have all the outward signs of godliness, which at the time involved a change of behavior, personal and emotional investment in religiosity, leading one's family in pious habits, commitment to private prayer, and participation in the life of the church, even in a disciplined way; none of these things could possibly deliver a person from the fires of hell into which God, incensed with sinners, could at any moment justly and inexorably cast them.[41]

On the other hand, that which alone could salvage their lives from eternal destruction is a spiritual transformation of the human heart effected by the Holy Spirit unto rebirth, new creation, resurrection from death in sin to an unprecedented new condition of light and life. In his sermon, Edwards strikes no real distinction between the converted and the unconverted as far as personal desert and effort are concerned. Every human person is bound for eternal damnation, the only difference being that the converted have come to trust in Christ for deliverance from this abject state and are securely safeguarded, whereas the unconverted persist in seeking solutions outside of Christ and in themselves, in their own physical, affective, and spiritual resources, and only find themselves subject to eternal destruction.[42] All this suggests that for Edwards as a paradigmatic Calvinist evangelical theologian, the conditio sine qua non of salvific assurance resides in the knowledge of the profundity of the sinfulness of the human nature itself, human desert in being destined for eternal destruction in the wrath of God, and the plain truth that faith in Christ alone is capable of preserving a person against endless and irreversible misery. Even if the regenerate Christian continues to wrestle with a principle of sin within themselves as a justified believer, they need not fear that they have been mistaken as to the authenticity of their conversion, seeing that it is not possible for an accurate personal knowledge and understanding of one's despair in human sinfulness and need for Christ to be the result of the deceptive work of the devil, if only on account that such a person is stood in good stead for moral and spiritual

---

41. Edwards, "Sinners in the Hands of an Angry God," Application, 9–10; Moody, "Jonathan Edwards Preaches 'Sinners in the Hands of an Angry God.'"

42. Edwards, "Sinners in the Hands of an Angry God," Application, 9–12.

transformation.[43] As such, the believer with personal convictions that agree in the aforementioned way with the faith of Christ can be confident that God is working in their lives to bear good fruit in due course.

In contradistinction to the traditional evangelical conception of Christian assurance as expressed by Edwards, we propose that a person locate their sense of eternal security in the way in which they manifest the good nature with which they have been endowed through the creation or position of God the Divine Nature and imprinting by God the Trinity. This will require the profound self-honesty of intentionally, systematically, and consistently attending to all one's psychological disorders and pursuing decisive if not complete healing of the psyche and affect, to remove fundamental hurdles to living a morally good and virtuous life. One will need to find one's place in the world where they see themselves and others see them as making some contribution toward alleviating the physical, social, psychological, and spiritual problems endured by others or simply serving their immediate needs in these domains.

Adjourning to a related issue, what is the relationship between biblical teaching and the laws of a state; that is, should the laws of a country be shaped or determined by a biblical ethics? The Old Testament provides copious testimony of the way in which God established the statutes of a nation. Be that as it may, the political landscape in many countries in the present time is characterized by a secular democracy governed by common and statutory laws in which religious belonging does not in any way influence the way an individual is treated in regard to their legal rights and responsibilities. As such, it is salutary to propound that religious faith, including the Christian religion, should shape the individual conscience but not the laws of a state in any direct fashion. In biblical teaching, each person stands or falls before God alone (Rom 14:4); in other words, each Christian believer is accountable to God for the ways they have properly or improperly understood and responded or ignored God's guidance to and for them.

It is therefore difficult to assess if the German theologian Dietrich Bonhoeffer can be justified by God for having knowingly supported a planned assassination of Adolf Hitler, in spite that he did only what he felt was right and necessary in view of the enormities perpetrated by the Nazi regime against countless innocent people. What Christians may be

---

43. Edwards, "Marks of Work of True Spirit," 2.2, p. 267.

certain of is that God will surely make a perfect judgment and assessment of his actions (1 Sam 16:7; Rom 2:6–29; Heb 4:12–13).[44]

In any event, the singularity of the scenario in which Bonhoeffer was entangled has to be underscored if only so that Christian believers do not go away thinking that they can resist the laws and statutes of any government they subjectively consider oppressive. Believers are to remember that political authorities are ultimately instituted by God to maintain law and order and they are to conscientiously submit to the laws of the land (Rom 13:1–7), embracing other members of society of different religious traditions or of a humanist leaning as partners with whom to pursue a shared future in community, utilizing peaceful and not violent methods in their endeavors to bring social improvement (Rom 12:18).

44. Smith, "What Would Bonhoeffer Do?"

9

The Christian Doctrine of Incarnation

Jesus as Revelation of God's Eternal Humanity

CHRISTIAN THEOLOGY HAS BEEN, not always unfairly, subject to the criticism that it tends to be overly speculative and metaphysical, bearing little if any connection to a world with often more pressing and concrete human concerns.

Such critique will ever plague conceptions of God that attempt to put divinity and humanity at some unbridgeable remove from each other. This is typically done not out of any malicious intent to obscure the meaning and significance of the divine in the human domain but instead arises from a desire to give due respect to a transcendent power in which hopes for human liberation in the midst of the vicissitudes of existence are and are to be reposed.

It is imagined and averred that an unchanging and infinite Creator God alone is able to rescue and deliver mortal and finite human creatures. An immutable God may be conceived as being more perfect than a mutable one in light that should God be thought of as being capable of being subject to change, then God would necessarily become more or less perfect through that process of change and so either not previously perfect or less perfect than before and therefore not eternally perfect. Like any sentient entity in the world, a mutable God would be constantly in search of fulfilling some sense of need, be it a relational or political one.

As for the idea of God as infinite, this seems to be grounded not so much in the biblical witness as in theological implication. For instance, it is asserted that God thought of as being without limits ontologically and correspondence morally would serve as a powerful source of hope and practical support in a world full of need and suffering as well as stand as a bulwark against a constant human temptation to seek self-deification (Antithetical View of Divine-Human Moral Distinction).[1]

Theological progressives endeavor to humanize the message of Christianity and relate it to contemporary contexts of human need and aspiration by recourse to an envisioning of biblical teaching as the product of human reflections on diverse experiences of the divine and of Jesus as a particularly enlightened and spiritually-attuned individual rather than being of a different nature than any other human person in addition to the human nature he clearly possesses (Conflated View of Divine-Human Moral Distinction). Although Jesus, who is regarded as divine in nature in traditional Christian theology, may be de-absolutized in such a view, it may nevertheless leave room for a conception of God as mystery and beyond human comprehension. Hence, the conflation of the perspective consists not so much in its perception of God per se as in that of Jesus.[2]

In contrast to the forementioned conceptions of the divine-human distinction, we propose that the moral nature of God and humanity be thought of as formally correspondent (with a supreme quantitative moral difference between God and humankind) rather than antithetical or conflated; that is, that Christ reveals to us the humanity that exists in God as an essential quality of God's proper being (Correspondent View of Divine-Human Moral Distinction).

Epistemology

A theological response to the twin assertions of God as immutable and infinite is in order. In relation to the proposition that God is necessarily impervious to alteration for the fact that predicating God's ability to change is equivalent to predicating God as not being eternally perfect, we object to the supposition that God loses something of God's perfection by being conceived as capable of undergoing change such as in

---

1. Williams, "Theology of the Infinite," 114, 118–19.
2. See Chia, "Progressive Christianity."

being able to pursue relational desires and aims. Given a scenario in which a single individual or group of individuals is experiencing some form of privation, to use an extreme example, it would be infinitely more perfect—and indeed decent—for God to be able to respond to that need rather than be incapable of so doing.

To be sure, proponents of a classical theological conception of divine immutability do not espouse the view that God could ever be faced with a situation in which a human need exists to which God is unable to respond if and as God wishes. In the classical Christian system of belief, God is not only immutable, but eternal, omniscient, omnipotent, and omnipresent. Consequently, God is fully cognizant of any and every human need that could exist or develop, even from the beginning of creation, and being supreme God has already taken measures to ensure that God's providential will for the created order and therefore each human individual is and will be done.

That being the case, the question then becomes one of interpretation and the acceptability of an interpretation. If one suggests that all suffering, tragedy, and injustice that occur in the world do so under the providential hand of a completely benevolent God, and that justice is or will be done for those to whom some disservice has been done, then it is germane to ask whether such an interpretation may be accepted or received as an adequate explanation for human agony and justification for divine foreordination, permission, or even predestination of human perversion and depravity.

This is not a question that can be glibly answered or even dismissed out of hand, not least by the bien pensant with an interest to protect and, chances are, who have probably not suffered very much tragedy or injustice, or at least nothing comparable to those who impugn the usefulness of traditional conceptions of deity in direct consequence of their experience of tragedy and injustice.

Societies around the world are becoming increasingly aware of the need to acknowledge suffering and injustice that has been done to human individuals, especially members of a vulnerable demographic such as minorities of any kind. It is one thing to suppose or suggest that God gives a person a test of faith every now and then in order to strengthen the intimacy of their communion with God and depth of trust in the same; it is quite another to speculate that God intentionally causes or allows a person to be traumatized in such a way that they cease to function normally in their personal life or work, becoming socially withdrawn, painfully depressed, and completely without hope—all because they have committed some sin of which they have not repented or are continuing in some form of immorality or God wishes to purify them even of weaknesses that might lead to future sin;[3] because God desires to point them toward the truth that God alone is the source of human virtue;[4] because God desires to test the courage of the believer's faith and the selflessness of the believer's love for God;[5] because God wishes to purge the believer of their attachment to worldly good that they might long instead for that which is eternal.[6]

3. Augustine of Hippo cites as an example chaste Christian women, that is, the unmarried, the widowed, and the sexually-abstinent married, who were violated during the 410 sack of Rome, whom he contended were assaulted against their will and in spite of their integrity because God in God's profound and unsearchable providence desired to wean some of them of their pride in their sexual self-discipline, their wish for human commendation, envy of those who possess such self-control, or desire that few should exercise self-control the way they have so that they might receive higher praise; or, in the case of those who were not culpable of any sin, God wished to preserve them from any conceit that might arise from a weakness through allowing them to go through sexual abuse. Augustine, *Civ.*, 1.28 (ET, Dods, pp. 33–34). In another passage, Augustine suggests that God permitted both Christians and wicked people to suffer during the sack of Rome on account that the "weaker" believers—that is, those who marry and have children or desire these things, and who own houses and businesses as opposed to those who "live at a higher level" in that they have committed themselves to celibacy and poverty—neglect their spiritual and moral duty of admonishing or rebuking the wicked and immoral in view of the effort required, the fear of offending them or losing friendships, forgoing an advantageous relationship, or risking reprisal, whether out of a conscious desire for these things or because one has grown overly attached to them, and the "higher" believers as well are derelict in their moral responsibility to warn sinners out of a desire to protect their own reputation and personal safety arising not from a wish to have a better chance of admonishing sinners but because they love the praise of people, do not wish to offend anyone, and desire to avoid bringing trouble on themselves. Augustine, *Civ.*, 1.9 (ET, Dods, pp. 11–13).

4. Augustine gives as an example a chaste woman violated during the sack of Rome who may have been permitted by God to undergo such a horrific experience in order that she might recognize that her true chastity consisted not in her freedom from physical violation but in her constant sincere devotion and dedication to God, her steadfast conviction that God will not abandon those who have served God, her consistent petitions to God based on such conviction, and her recognition of the delight to God her chastity brings, all of which is possible and actual only by divine gift. Augustine, *Civ.*, 1.28 (ET, Dods, pp. 33–34).

5. This was Augustine's proposal for the reason God punished both Christians and the wicked during the sack of Rome. Augustine, *Civ.*, 1.8–9 (ET, Dods, pp. 10–13). He further opines that the righteous suffer so as to encourage others who are just as good to embrace the same suffering.

6. Hence, the fact that both good and wicked were assisted by the mercy shown by the victors of the sack of Rome to those who took refuge in churches was on account that God wanted them not to cleave to earthly goods with greed through observing

While some of these aims may be seen as noble, it beggars belief to the utmost to suppose that a God whom Scripture attests as a prodigally loving Father in heaven could be capable of putting people through situations that leave them permanently scarred. Should it be even remotely necessary for a person to go through trauma, surely a good God would see to it that they are endued with the strength to overcome or at least manage their distress.

Seeing that it is unconscionable to conjecture that a good God should be willing that people undergo extreme emotional distress for whatever noble reason there might be, and that to suggest such emotional distress could constitute a result of divine judgment would be to promote an unnecessarily punitive view of God's behavior, it may be best to conceive of God not as immutable but mutable, having the means to relate with human persons in pursuit of common relational and communal aims.

Concerning the assertion to the effect that God is to be thought of as infinite, this is conventionally tied to an appeal to scriptures such as 1 Kgs 8:27, Psalm 139, Isa 66:1, Jer 23:24, and Acts 7:49, it is helpful to note that none of these passages directly indicate that God is without limit, only that, respectively, God's presence cannot be confined to a single location such as the temple King Solomon had built, given that God could not even be contained by the highest heaven; that God's presence is always with David; that God has God's throne in heaven and God's footstool on earth and so the role of the temple Solomon constructed in mediating God's presence is not to be exaggerated; that God's presence fills heaven and earth as the Divine Nature and God's angelic messengers bring word of all that occurs in the world to God in heaven; and, again, that the temple of Solomon should not be made too much of in view that God rules from heaven and rests God's "foot" on earth.

Regarding David Williams' affirmation of divine infinity in the context of its theological usefulness in the areas of affording a greater sense of hope, practical assistance, and defense against temptation, we do well to observe that belief in an infinite God of classical theology may do little to assure those afflicted with grievous suffering of any hope.

At the very most, pious sufferers would more or less grudgingly accept their lot as from the Lord simply because they cannot do otherwise and to attempt to do so might yield divine judgment. Some might fancy

---

how even the wicked enjoy these goods but persevere for a heavenly reward. Augustine, *Civ.*, 1.8 (ET, Dods, pp. 10–11).

that being reduced to a state of rigid obedience and constant fear could do wonders for facilitating humility and meekness; there may be some value in learning from the mistakes a person commits in the course of their lives, yet to constantly live in terror of the divine and to become servile may not be beneficial for the development of a healthy and responsible sense of personal autonomy.

The New Testament undoubtedly extols the way of the servant of God in Christ, one modeled by the Son of God himself, yet we must not make too little of the fact that nobody was ever compelled to become a servant, but anyone who responded to the call of God did so always only of their own volition. It was of his own freewill that St. Paul lived as a bondservant for Christ, out of his love for his Lord.[7] The entire admonition in Romans 6 is one in which the apostle urges Christians in Rome to present themselves to God as servants; that is, offer themselves willingly for the ministry of God in the church.

If the classical conception of God assures of little hope, it does not afford much practical and concrete assistance, and we have already considered, in our discussion of how it is unhelpful for God to foreordain or predestine a person to severe emotional suffering, how that might prove to be the case. Third, relating to the view that divine infinity as a conception forestalls the vain human temptation to substitute idols for God, being compelled to recognize God's absolute and categorical superiority may not be quite the effective prophylactic it is touted to be. In the first place, it is unclear how an infinite being can truly communicate the truth about its nature and will to finite beings.

In the final analysis, it is not imperial majesty that will ensure the flourishing of a human community, but sober and sensible relationality and responsibility on the part of governors and leaders—this much we have gleaned from the demise of traditional absolutist monarchies. God can indeed lead more efficaciously, in terms of God's moral leadership being better respected, not as a supreme and utterly transcendent sovereign hidden in the mists of eternity, forever beyond human reach, but as a loving and compassionate shepherd among God's people and creatures. There need be no fear concerning human beings seeking to become identical to God, since God remains the presupposition for all existence, orientation, and capacity as the Divine Nature, a position and

---

7. Cf. Barth, *KD* IV.2, §66.5 (ET, Bromiley, p. 593).

role no creature as entailment of the Divine Nature can ever hope to arrogate to themselves.

While there are clear reasons why God has to be more than a mere human being in order to truly be able to bring an end to evil and injustice, this is a far cry from the assumption concerning God's universal and intricate ability to bring complete relief to a situation of need, choose to use means including evil and suffering to bring about a higher good, and predetermine, or at least foreordain, every historical occurrence, down to the level of the individual person and minutest organism and object, in such a manner that all events, little or great, in the world and wider universe bear testimony, at some level, to or in some other way serve the greatness, majesty, glory, goodness, wisdom, and righteousness of God.

In contradistinction to classical Christian theology, we propose that God's moral nature is formally correspondent to that of the human being. That is, we hold that there is nothing in the moral nature of the human being that prevents it from being like or even identical to the moral nature of divine being.

Doctrinal Formulation: Jesus' Humanity as the Reflection of God's Humanity

Jesus is the true reflection of the eternal being of God, perfectly and completely representing God's spiritual being but in physical form, in such a way that Christ is substantially identical in his moral values, emotional stability, just and loving desires and will, relational disposition, and pattern of conduct to the Father in the Father's eternal being, the only difference being that Christ as a spirit-soul-body complex is able to interact with the physical beings that human persons are, whereas the Father, being spirit and soul as dimensions of the Father's being, interacts with spiritual beings such as angels. In Jesus, the divine moral nature is conceived as being in perfect agreement with ideal human moral nature—this being defined by the Divine Nature positing and operating in each human life—and humanity, in their identity, is restored to its proper position as an image of divinity in moral terms, a vocation to which each person, in their moral agency, should indefatigably aspire with the power afforded to them by God in the Divine Nature and the Trinity.

PART 2: HUMANITY'S IMAGING OF THE DIVINE

Karl Barth is of the view that the incarnation of Christ discloses the formal possibility that a human person might function in their actions to reveal the very actions of God.[8]

When Jesus appeared, God showed God's true face in a human visage. There is no face of God more complete than that which is human in all its moral characteristics, and perfectly human at that. Jesus is the revelation of the intrinsic humanity of God—indeed, this is a misnomer, for God is the archetype rather than the ectype in relation to humanity, so that it would be more fitting to say, not that God is human, but rather that human persons are divine in their moral character, insofar as they live out the fullness of their humanity.

Far from concealing God's true deity, Jesus disclosed God's divinity in all its fullness. The light unapproachable in 1 Tim 6:16 refers not so much to God living in a transcendent sphere as that God's life, God being the source of all being, cannot be directly perceived. *Mystērion* ("mystery") is not used in the New Testament in the sense of something hidden about God relating to God's nature or character, but typically in reference to a revelation of God's plan of salvation for humankind, both Jews and Gentiles, a plan once concealed or only vaguely intimated but clearly revealed in the age of Christ and the apostles (e.g., Matt 13:11; Mark 4:11; Luke 8:10; Rom 11:25; 16:25–26; 1 Cor 2:1; 2:7; 4:1; 15:51; Eph 1:9; 3:3–4; 3:9; 5:32; 6:19; Col 1:26–27; 2:2; 4:3; 1 Tim 3:9, 16; Rev 1:20; 10:7). It is also utilized in coded language to identify great forces of darkness that are opposed to God and their character (2 Thess 2:1–12; Revelation 17).

God is identical to the divine-human Christ in God's moral values, emotional stability, just and loving desires and will, relational disposition, and pattern of conduct. The advent of Jesus Christ vouchsafes mightily the eternal verity that God and humanity are identical in moral terms. God is to be defined in terms of what an ideal human being is vis-à-vis morality, this idealization being informed in the first place by the positing and operation of the Divine Nature within each human individual. The opposite is also true: human beings are to be defined in regard to the degree to which, in doing everything in the power that they have been given by God in the Divine Nature and the Trinity, they measure up to God's righteous character as the image of God in a moral respect.

No more clearly can the essence of God's character be seen than in the act of Christ on behalf of sinful humankind. Christ died not for his

---

8. Barth, *KD* IV.2, §66.5 (ET, Bromiley, p. 589).

own sins, but for ours. We deserve to be punished for our sins, yet the punishment was not meted out against us but against him alone. As it was meted out on him, it was meted out on us. It was meted out on us only as it was meted out on him. Because what was meant for us was meted out against him, we are able to identify with the shame and disgrace he went through.[9] As soon as we approach God as a penitent, confessing that we have sinned and showing our willingness to make a clean break with our past sinful lives, God grants us forgiveness in Christ's name, through all that Christ has done in suffering and dying for us on the cross.

There are two themes concerning the crucifixion of Christ and its significance for humankind; namely, the crucifixion as an event planned, foreknown, foretold, and predestined of God (Acts 2:23; 3:18; 4:28) and the crucifixion as the result of acts of absolute wickedness on the part of those who conspired against Jesus and falsely accused him of blasphemy and sedition so as to have the Roman governor put him to death (Acts 3:13–15). These motifs have conventionally been brought together in some idea of compatibilist freedom.

Compatibilism is contrasted with libertarianism as varying conceptions of human freedom. In the case of the former, freedom consists in the ability to choose a particular action without constraint.[10] Libertarian freedom, on the other hand, entails that an agent be capable of choosing actions that violate our expectations for that agent's actions under given circumstances.[11]

In a compatibilist construal, the event of the crucifixion being desired both by God and the conspirators against Christ, in which God completely foreordained all circumstances in such a way that these circumstances would lead necessarily to the death of Christ by that manner of execution, including orchestrating the development of a sinful and wicked will by which these sinners are driven in such a way that they can do nothing to alter that will, not that they wish to in the first place, it can rightly be said that the crucifixion was both predetermined by God and yet at the same time that human beings who schemed against Christ to put him through that experience are to be held accountable for their wicked collusion against the Lord.

Aside from appeal to a compatibilist understanding of human freedom, the crucifixion of Christ as an event divinely predestined and yet

---

9. Cf. Barth, *KD* IV.2, §64.4 (ET, Bromiley, pp. 293–94).
10. Chua, *ECRST*, 217. Cf. Crisp, "On Barth's Denial of Universalism," 24.
11. Chua, *ECRST*, 219. Cf. Crisp, "On Barth's Denial of Universalism," 24.

also resulting from acts of human wickedness may be reconciled in this way: Jesus died as a result of being put to death by human conspiracy. God had nothing to do with Jesus' path to the cross, only human beings. Sinful people having brought it about that Jesus was nailed to the cross and thereby executed, God raised him from the dead on the third day and inspired biblical authors such as of the Epistle to the Hebrews to grasp God's amazing act of redemptive love in choosing against abandoning humankind after the event of the crucifixion of God's own Son. Instead of forsaking humanity, God the Father elected to regard and accept the cross as an act of propitiation by Jesus on behalf of humankind.

Like Joseph who decided not to count his brothers' sins against them but chose to focus on the good that came out of his personal betrayal through the faith that he exercised in God and the grace that God displayed toward him during his darkest hours (Gen 50:20), God chose to make something good out of the tragedy of the death of God's Son. In making of the cross a sin offering to assure us of forgiveness whenever we confess our sins before God and seek to lead a repentant life, God demonstrated the greatest degree of forgiveness—the desire not to take revenge on those who have hurt God. In choosing not to succumb to vengeful hatred as he hung on the cross, indeed, in praying to the Father that the Father not count the sins of those who mocked and hated him against them, Jesus displayed forgiveness to the highest degree.[12]

On the basis of this convertive view of the atonement, we do not have to be offended at God's ostensible need for a blood sacrifice to appease divine anger at our sins and reconcile an internal division within the godhead. For the cross was not predestined by God in such a way that nothing otherwise than the cross could have happened. Were all events predetermined in this way by God, we would have reason to ask why tragedy befell us when it does. Yet God is very powerful yet very weak at the same time, and tragedies only happen due to evil or natural causes or accidents, having nothing to do with God's intention or action. Therefore, God did not require a blood sacrifice from God's Son from the very beginning, but gave the greatest tragedy of the triune life a new meaning which draws from the Old Testament sacrificial cult. The atonement is a reframing of an event of unspeakable pain and betrayal

---

12. Do we really wish harm on those who have wronged us? A good test is to imagine whether if such harm does befall the person in question, we will truly be happy. Perhaps what we really desire is simply that the other person acknowledges and repents of the wrong that they have done to us.

in terms of a blood sacrifice for the forgiveness of sins, rather than an actual requirement on the part of God which Jesus fulfilled.

It is unconscionable to attempt to justify one's sinful acts or those of others on the purported basis that at times, as it may be argued, some acts of sin are said to create the conditions for righteousness to prevail. To offer an example, certain individuals had contended that were it not for the transgressions of those who conspired to put Christ to the death on the cross because they viewed him as a religious and political threat, there would not have been the occasion which presented itself for God to reveal God's redemptive grace toward sinful and errant humanity, a possible imagination and an immoral and irresponsible argument that St. Paul appeared to be anxious to forestall (Rom 5:12—6:1).

Even were the sacrifice of Christ necessary, God could well take a sacrifice without the participation of morally corrupt human persons. In addition, were a scenario conceivable in which a transgression shaped a situation in which some form of good could arise, such as that of repentance, even then that act of sin would be unwarranted, since sin is never justifiable as the ultimate anti-end and thus the supposed "benefits" of sinning cannot ever be weighed against its consequences and made the reason for opting in favor of committing transgression.

A further dimension of the correspondent humanity or humaneness bringing together God and humankind in a common category of moral being and existence is one to which the traditional Christian doctrine of divine aseity is germane. Numerous persons of means would have discovered subsequent to having spent a part of their lives enjoying their riches that wealth does not secure happiness.[13] As a matter of fact, biblical teaching speaks against avarice and lust for wealth as a fount of all kinds of evil (1 Tim 6:10). Although the context suggests that the writer has in mind a striving for riches, which might lead to theft and even betrayal (e.g., Judas Iscariot, who conspired with the chief priests of the time to deliver Jesus to them for thirty pieces of silver, in Matt 26:14-16), the general teaching could very well also encompass hoarding on the part of those who already own riches (e.g., those exemplified by the trope of the rich fool in Luke 12:13-21). Furthermore, Jesus himself cautioned his disciples after his interview

---

13. This differs from the sensible critique that a state of poverty can itself be a source of unhappiness and distress which can be alleviated by the influx of material income and hence that money can indeed contribute toward human happiness, yet only in situations of privation.

with a rich young ruler that the affluent face an immense obstacle in attempting to enter the kingdom of heaven, implying that they do not have true inner peace (Matt 19:16–30 and par.).

The primary and fundamental reason that material possessions cannot confer true happiness or beatitude is that those who have acquired or inherited them see the desideratum for what it is; not the pursuit of material goods in and of themselves, but the desire to be treated in a particular way by those who would be impressed by their material success. Nevertheless, the search for a secure place in the world, for the admiration of others, be it those near or far, in the form of material wealth is a wrongheaded approach to personal happiness and inner peace certain to lead to disappointment, disenchantment, and disillusionment. For the true desideratum, which one does not yet know or accept, may well be the overcoming of a socially inflicted sense of inferiority, an eminently sociopsychological issue. To the extent that that is the reality of the situation, more or even significant wealth will never be sufficient. Riches will not be able to erase the trauma of marginalization and rejection endured during one's formative years, or convert the world of one's relationships to a mode of obsequious submission and fawning that will appease an insatiable appetite for admiration. Philosophically and existentially, the human individual knows and is convicted that they cannot settle for living for the approval of others or predicate their inner composure and sense of wholeness on their response.

Part and parcel of Paul's forceful insistence that believers in Christ ought not to dally any longer with sin (Rom 6:15–16) consists in how the decision to partake in that which offends the conscience and God is never simply a possibility which remains fully within human control, but attracts psychological and even spiritual forces and powers that both seem and are actually eager to bring a perpetrator in thrall to itself and under subjection and captivity, much of the time through urging a person to put the satisfaction of their emotional, carnal, and sensual desires ahead of any moral considerations (e.g., Gen 4:6–7) or devise pretexts to support their chosen course of action.

The cunning of the principle of sin lies in the manner in which the transgressor is often themselves completely blind to the wrongfulness of acts in which they engage which they may think to be unharmful to others or themselves in a physical way but not necessarily an emotional one (i.e., taking sensual delight in self-bondage, which damages one's self-concept).

It is worthwhile pursuing the inquiry at this juncture as to whether and to what extent human beings are entrapped in sin. Jesus said in John 8:34, "everyone who practices sin is a slave to sin" (ESV). The meaning is not that human beings have no freedom not to sin and that there is no capacity in humankind for any form of moral good, as Luther supposed.[14]

This is in spite of the evaluative statements in Rom 3:10–12: "None is righteous, no, not one; no one understands; no one seeks for God. All have turned aside; together they have become worthless; no one does good, not even one" (ESV). These statements are based on Ps 14:1–3 and Ps 53:1–3, which do not constitute a categorical denunciation of human morality, since they recognize the presence of a godly people; namely, the ṣadîq in Ps 14:5, the ʿānî in Ps 14:6, and the ʿammi in Ps 53:4. This leads us to conclude that the statements in Psalm 14 and 53 which form the basis for the quotation in Rom 3:10–12, comprise a hyperbolic criticism of the conduct of a great many individuals.

Contrary to Luther's interpretation of John 8:34, the more plausible signification is that all who practice sin show that they are subjugated under the dominion of sin. Jesus had in mind the specific group of Jews who intended to make an attempt on his life, but could just as well have referred to anybody else for whom sinning had become habitual and hardly questioned or even just actual.

To sin requires decision, and to decide for sin requires intention. Those who have reached the point of committing sin show that they are entrapped in sin to the extent that they not only bore sinful intent but made a decision for sin and thereby served the master that sin is. The actual sinner (that is, the person who has carried out a sinful act rather than merely harboring sinful intent) cherished the seductions of sin to the extent of actually deciding in favor of sin rather than God's righteousness or the human conscience. That this is the likelier interpretation is substantiated by a parallel passage in Rom 6:12–16, where Paul speaks of the act of sin as, in effect, one of submission to the power of sin as one's master.

In addition, the exact phrase in John 8:34, "*ho poiōn tēn hamartian*" ("the one who practices sin") is found in 1 John 3:4 (where the act of sin is tied to that of anomie) and 1 John 3:8 (where the sinner's allegiance is exposed to be not to God but to the devil). In both contexts, the exhortation appears to be to the effect that the believer should be

---

14. Luther, *Heid. Disp.*, §13.

mindful of the moral quagmire in which they implicate themselves in simply choosing to commit an act of sin.

Another passage[15] which has been deployed in support of the view that human beings after the time of Adam are not possessed of both a good nature or will to pursue righteousness is Rom 3:9 where, however, the signification is not that all individuals are controlled by the power of sin but simply that Jews are not exempt from subjection to the dominion of sin. This is in light that earlier Paul highlights the cases of Gentiles (given Rom 2:12–16, 24, 27, holding out the actualized possibility of certain Gentiles being obedient to the internal moral law of God in the conscience and having the right to judge Jews who, though they had the law, did not obey it) as well as Jews (given the general thrust of the hortatory portions of Romans 2 addressed to Jews in which the apostle admonishes members of his ethnic community not to presumptuously and cavalierly indulge in sinful acts unaware that God uses a fair and impartial standard for both Jews and Gentiles, punishing all who sin, as well as Rom 3:3, where the mention of a scenario in which "some" were unfaithful implies that others were faithful) who uphold the moral laws of God.

Any who find themselves in such a situation are called to repentance, entailing confession or acknowledgment of their sin before God, self, and others (as appropriate), a rethinking of old ways of thinking, feeling, and behaving, and a commitment not to persist in sin, in order that sin's hold on them might be broken. Psychology cautions us against allowing others or our own minds to cause us to feel ashamed of our emotions and feelings. This is true, but only to a degree. Whereas a person ought not to feel guilty for experiencing emotional impulses, these being beyond one's immediate control, this is not equivalent to accepting those internal circumstances as normal or feeling no urge to help themselves get out of the rut. One will still need to attend to the resolution of those emotions, insofar as they are inordinate, such as explosive or excessive anger, lust, envy, or aversion or even hatred toward another person, in the manner highlighted in the foregoing, while knowing and remembering that God does not condemn them for experiencing emotional impulses per se (Rom 8:1; 1 John 3:11–21), and neither should anyone else, yet God desires that the person in question do that which is needful to tackle and address the internal problem.

---

15. Luther, *Heid. Disp.*, §18.

The Reformers were correct in underscoring that God's glory is the highest motivation and object of the human life, since all the good that we can do and all the beauty that is in the world come directly or emerge naturally by the power and nature that is of God.[16] Therefore Paul urges Christians at Philippi to work out their salvation (that is, do their part to respond to God's gracious invitation to live as God's children) in fear and trembling, since it is God who works in them, both to will and to work for God's pleasure (Phil 2:12–13).

All grievous sins, obsessions, and moral preoccupations are related to phantasies in which a person with some form of psychological need is willing to do everything in their capacity either to literally achieve their wildest dreams or, if these dreams seem unattainable, indulge in a make-believe in which they free themselves from the constraints of physical reality so as to embrace a different self-produced reality. This is possibly only because the mind affected in this way demolishes the barrier between what the person is and what they want to achieve, in such a manner that it is sufficient that these persons see themselves in the persons or objects they admire or in the latter's experiences.

As such, a person might lead their lives through the life a celebrity is perceived to live, reconstructed on the basis of numerous carefully curated images and content released about the idol, which more often than not do not present an accurate impression of the lives they actually lead. This is why many celebrity fans tend to be gravely offended at any negative opinion about their object of personal admiration or become unusually crestfallen in consequence of learning that the celebrity with whom they are enamored has fallen into some scandal, simply because their view of their own selves is inextricably tied to their view of their celebrity and of the lives they lead.

Idolization in this respect is unwise because it fixates on attributes that do not encompass the fullness of humanity, such as an attractive physical appearance, wealth, and fame (not all will be considered physically attractive, not all will be wealthy or influential, yet those perceived to be less attractive and those who are less wealthy and influential are no less human and so such thinking has no way of appreciating the fullness of humanity). Physical appearance, wealth, and fame constitute external and circumstantial attributes (wealth and influence may to a certain extent be contingent on specific character traits such as resilience and creativity yet

---

16. WSC Q. 1.

these very traits are present in all individuals to differing degrees) which do not touch on what is most significant in a human person; namely, their moral awareness, orientation, freedom, and responsibility.

Another person might link self-acceptance with some atypical experience of bondage and submission (perhaps as a result of having been abused in that way), in response to which situation they might focus their attention and energy on erecting and weaving an elaborate phantasy world in which they break the wall separating self from other and imagine and visualize themselves to be the same entity as the person they see in a pornographic image or video.

Accordingly, while these persons may not directly perpetrate sexual harassment or assault and may appear to be upstanding citizens, perhaps even feeling a sense of outrage at news concerning sexual assault on some member of the public, yet still they are able to bring themselves to participate as consumers in the continuance of the pornographic industry. This is for the reason that their sense of reality has become warped and they have come to lose sight, at least in the context of their satisfaction of personal indulgence, of the objective reality and rights of the persons assaulted in the videos they watch, of the fact that these individuals are actual human persons, with feelings, rights, dignity.

The need has become so great and in need of immediate satisfaction that once awakened it is all but impossible to resist. The solution therefore is for all persons given to such proclivities to take conscious and deliberate efforts to avoid images and experiences that might trigger a renewal of temptation.[17] If this cannot be done and temptation is about to strike, the individual should take it upon themselves to remove themselves physically and psychologically from any such compelling images, avoid even beginning to indulge their phantasy in the mistaken belief that innocuous participation is possible so long as one is creative and discerning enough to imagine such a possibility, and remind themselves of the fact that the value of their personhood resides not in becoming the person of their phantasy but the fact that they have been created by God as moral agents with a moral vision and are fully and unconditionally loved by God.

It is all too easy at this juncture to slip into a mood of guilt and remorse, even to spiral into a sense that one is only evil in their own

---

17. If personal effects that facilitate an experience of phantasy, and thereby demand that the desire for such an experience be satisfied, can be removed, that is for the best, given that one might have the moral strength to face life without such indulgence.

nature, hopeless, beyond redemption, a hypocrite through and through destined for eternal damnation. This is where the promise of divine forgiveness through the atonement of Christ on the cross on which he died comes into its own.

The same scenario can obtain among groups of persons, whether small or very large. Some group might repose their confidence in the fact that they perceive themselves to be different—in some positive way—from all other groups in society. Perhaps a religious or political group might imagine themselves to be superior in some way to all other religious groups or even fancy themselves custodian of public order, whether or not they actually articulate these feelings and sentiments. As soon as these aspects of their identity seem to be threatened by some perceived enemy, they strike back with a vengeance, not worrying about conscience, ethics, or humanity.

In view of the link between human salvific hope and ritualism promising moral transformation through supernatural assistance, some Christian groups envision themselves as a fundamentally evangelistic organization or custodians of social decency, propriety, and even morality. In relation to the former, they view all other religious traditions as essentially deficient as vehicles and instruments for the communication of divine salvation. Given this exigent state of affairs, they look past considerations of religious sensitivity and are impelled by a strong desire to share the teachings of the Christian faith and bring—or rather allow the Holy Spirit through their efforts to bring—a non-Christian person to faith in Christ.

However appropriately or felicitously they may comport themselves in the sight of those outside the Christian community, inwardly they are constantly praying for God to bring these non-Christian persons to Christ and seeking opportunities to put in a word for converting to Christianity. They may even internally ask God to bring it about that other religious groups do not prosper or flourish, that members of these religious traditions come to discern the supposed inconsistency of their own teachings and turn to Christ.

As to the groups which see themselves as guardians of social norms and morality, they may so disagree with the self-concept and behaviors of certain sexual minority groups that they imagine that the Scripture has only one—a predominantly negative—route for the interpretation of its teachings on these minority groups, assuming that

Scripture even does speak directly to the question of the morality of the actions of these very groups.

Presumption of another person's guilt, whatever amends they may have made or even in the event that their culpability cannot be solidly established with reasonable people may very well be symptomatic of a phenomenon where a person projects their inner frustrations and feelings of insecurity on one on whom they find they can situate the cause of their insoluble stresses and distresses. An individual gripped in the pall of powerlessness, fear, anxiety, or despair presents fertile ground for an unconscious psychological adjustment to alleviate their personal disquiet. This entails a shifting of the battlefield and warzone from where it is actually to be located, and where no victory lies in sight or can even be thought plausible even with tireless effort, to the disparate and new locale for a renewed fight; namely, the person or member of a group subject in some way to moral question, whether conclusively, decisively, convincingly, or not, if only so the agent of such a psychological acclimatization may feel that there is hope after all in life. In this way, their problems of survival can now be re-visualized as rooted in those subject to their moral aspersions, and the survival instinct which naturally produces fear and anxiety in a time and situation of threat can finally be cooled, and life may carry on as usual.

Typically, the more intensely alienation from society and loss of control over one's stability, security, and potential success are experienced, the greater the vindictiveness felt toward an individual or member of a group held to account for some moral flaw or infringement. The byword of such scapegoating consists in the way Adolf Hitler pinned responsibility for Germany's defeat during the Great War on Jews, as well as Social Democrats and Communists, all of whom were falsely alleged to have engaged in treasonous activity during the war. This was a time when many Germans were unable to come to terms with their national defeat.[18]

The ideal way to address a tendency to indulge in scapegoating is firstly to confess that one may have already committed it, and then to reflect on how it is unnecessary to continue doing so, and why one is so inclined to project their fears and insecurities on others, and it may be because they feel incapable of grappling with the stresses of their lives in view that they grasp their present possessions too tightly, on account that they

---

18. Smilde, "Hitler's Antisemitism."

may have spent their developing years in the thick of a constant struggle for survival, and cultivated a false sense that they have only themselves and what they own in which to trust. They have not learned to adopt an attitude of relationality, both towards themselves and others.

Not all of the aforementioned phenomena involve sinful action. In particular, an obsession or moral preoccupation in and of itself may not eventuate in behavior that violates moral laws. Moreover, not all the attitudes identified would be commonly recognized as sinful. Be that as it may, even if an attitude per se may not entail sin, yet the decisions that arise from that attitude and the fruit of those decisions might make the attitude deserving of the title of sin, as happens in the case of those who persecute or harm others for any reason (not for legitimate medical or judicial procedural reasons). In that context, it will be imperative for those so implicated to conscientiously and vigilantly seek to do away with any self-justification and repent of their sinful attitudes and decisions.

The limitation of a conservative Christian theology reposes in its frequent incapacity to differentiate between an interpretation of a biblical passage and the full signification of the passage itself. Believing itself to be in the right about what Scripture has to say about the disposition of the heavenly bodies in the solar system, the Roman Catholic Church tried the Italian polymath Galileo Galilei, found him guilty of being strongly suspicious of having committed heresy, and placed him under life imprisonment for propagating a heliocentric conception of the solar system.[19]

In point of fact, the case of Galileo suggests and underscores the need to attend sufficiently to context in any theological work. Astronomers and scientists in the seventeenth century believed that the earth and stars were stationary, while the sun, moon, and planets moved around the earth, basing their understanding on the evidence available at the time. Galileo himself was not able to fully prove his theory, as he would require more sensitive measuring apparatus to do so, such as was subsequently developed.[20]

In a second example, church authorities and figures, both Protestant and Catholic, who carried out some form of inquisition did so in the supposition that passages in Deut 13:12–18 and 17:2–7 sanction

---

19. Wolf, "Galileo and the Catholic Church"; Catholic Answers, "Galileo Controversy."

20. Catholic Answers, "Galileo Controversy."

such action.[21] This law, as well as Israel's theocratic system of governance, existed in all probability to preserve the integrity of Israel as a landless and vulnerable nation on the move toward a land of its possession, constantly subject to incursions by hostile neighbors. Whereas Israel's military direction came from God through Moses, it would be imperative for a unity that would enable the community to claim its territorial heritage for every member of the entire group to be fully committed to God. Those who turned to or promoted the worship of another God would have to be harshly penalized. By the advent of the Lord Jesus, long after the landed and territorial phase of God's economy of salvation in and through the physical community and nation of Israel, it was made known that the kingdom of God, now inaugurated and to be consummated in Jesus alone as its head and ruler, would not be political or militant in nature, but spiritual (John 18:36).

Deplorably, the popes and Catholic and Protestant figures who were involved in spearheading and implementing inquisitions were more interested in protecting their sense of total control by ruling through fear and terror instead of listening carefully to the voice of God in the biblical witness. In the modern day, with considerably more democratic access to biblical texts and to resources that equip one to interpret these texts in accordance with their context, it has become far easier to avoid the past error of misreading and misinterpreting Scripture.

In a more sinister respect, Christian theologians who supported some form of antisemitism, including John Chrysostom, Augustine of Hippo, and Martin Luther, instantiate the fact that there was far less clarity in their times, as compared to ours, regarding how an entire ethnic group cannot be blamed for the deeds of a few at one point in history.[22]

As such, the church of the contemporary age will benefit from attending to the indisputable fact that its received theology emerged out of very specific conditions in history, when our understanding of the natural and human sciences had not developed quite as much as they would in later periods, with more rigorous instruments and methods for measuring or surmising the ways the world and human beings behave and the conditions that shape them. A theological researcher living in the twenty-first century is far better poised than theologians

---

21. Catholic Answers, "What Is the Inquisition?"
22. Hedges, *Religious Hatred*, 55–56, 60–63.

who wrote great works of lasting historical and theological value in the fourth, fifth, or sixteenth centuries to formulate and enounce a modern systematic theology that gives rightful consideration to domains such as psychological wellbeing, cultural diversity, and the equal spiritual value of all religious traditions.

We ought not to neglect the very real possibility that sociocultural and political realities may well have shaped and influenced theologians' understanding of God, God's purposes for humankind, the nature and agency of human beings, and the place of the world itself. Embedded as the church fathers and Protestant reformers were in patriarchal societies variously committed to an absolute monarchy on the one hand and to an absolute monarchical papacy on the other, in a world abounding with constant threats to peace, stability, and livelihoods from potential invaders, there would have been a predilection for seeing God as an absolute monarch. Modeled after the ideal Roman emperor with near-unlimited force of violence at his disposal, capable of guaranteeing a true Roman peace, an eidolon baptized by the Emperor Constantine the Great in his transformation of Christianity into a state religion in which the Roman emperor became not just a sponsor and guardian of the church but more importantly its earthly representation of the heavenly Logos and Christ reigning above, the church leadership was brought into government administration, and the hierarchy of the Roman imperial state proved to be an exemplar worthy of the church's vaunting and admiring emulation.[23] Humankind was seen as controlled by such a divine monarch, and the world itself as a thing of which the monarch could easily dispose however the monarch wishes. It would have been far more difficult to view other religious traditions in a more appreciative light given the political threat with which they may have been identified, as in the case of Islam and its caliphates and empires.[24]

---

23. See Kee, *Constantine versus Christ*, 159–65.

24. The challenge from Islam to Christianity remains in the contemporary world in the form of polemics directed at cardinal Christian doctrine such as that of the death and therefore resurrection of Christ. Islam disputes that Christ died a physical death (Qur'ān 4:157–158), and the Gospel of Barnabas has been deployed by polemicists. Irrespective of the fact that the Gospel of Barnabas is almost certainly a medieval forgery, the idea that Christ was not actually put to death is inconsistent with the fact that Christ's death, if it was not actualized, would beggar belief. It is far easier to hold that a messenger from God like Jesus was divinely protected from harm than for him to have gone through an execution in the most ignominious way conceivable, not to mention the hindrance the latter notion would put in the way of others accepting the teaching about Christ's divinity due to dominant philosophical ideas about God as immutable

PART 2: HUMANITY'S IMAGING OF THE DIVINE

The higher level of political stability in monarchical England in the eleventh and twelfth centuries, through force of conquest (implying confidence in violent power to bring peace and order), may have inspired Anselm of Canterbury (1033/34–1109) to develop a stronger theory of God's sovereign rule over sinful humanity based on the penalization of sin as an injury to the divine honor. This was an idea which is by no means scriptural given the incomparability between feudal kingly rule over potentially rebellious subjects which constantly need to be deterred with sufficiently harsh penalties (a matter of political stability, which Jesus seemed to show little concern for in relation to the kingdom of heaven as in John 18:36) and God's personal relationship to the human person as defined by Jesus' teachings on the merciful, compassionate, and unconditionally loving nature of God the Father.[25] If God ruled biblical Israel in the Old Testament via a theocratic government, it was historically conditioned and did not penalize thoughts, desires, and intentions, and so was a socially sustainable model for that epoch where Israel battled socially detrimental and directly harmful religious systems (with which no world religious tradition today may be categorized).[26]

Given the emphasis in this chapter upon the humanity of God in Jesus, a subject intimately related to the question of the humane manner in which God treats humankind, it may be salutary at this juncture to consider how it is that the Apocalypse of John could discourse in its penultimate chapter regarding the termination of all earthly sorrow and agony (Rev 21:4) in the light of four challenging possibilities that emerge with the sinfulness of humankind; namely, the wrong that has been perpetrated against us especially by those who neither know nor truly repent of the fault, the residual and lingering regret that we may feel toward those we have wronged to a significant degree, that there will be some with whom we have a personal relationship who will refuse to repent and thereby fall to eternal damnation, and the general sadness that we endure as a result of personal tragedy?[27]

Is it possible ever to completely forget and satisfy the memory of the injustices which others have committed against us without

---

and impassible. See Sorensen, "Why the 'Gospel of Barnabas' Is a Medieval Fake."

25. Barr, "British History."

26. A strong theology of God is likely to impinge on the way people use the differential power they have at their disposal. Baldwin, *Trauma-Sensitive Theology*, 114.

27. A version of this problem has been formulated by Eric Reitan in *Troubled Paradise*, 1.

acknowledging or really repenting of the wrongdoing? We can heal from the emotional wounds we have suffered through basking in God's unconditional love, by which our pain is diminished and our joy increased. In addition, we can take comfort in the fact that God will hold every evildoer to account.

If we have gravely mistreated another in the course of our earthly existence, this too can be addressed at the final judgment, when God summons all to choose whether to forgive those who have wronged them, in view of the fact that God will show these victims of wrongdoing—if they do not already know it—that God has always only treated them forgivingly (Matt 6:14–15; 18:21–35) and sternly require that all who have done wrong to another truly repent of their unjust and unrighteous ways, failing which they will be consigned to eternal damnation.

Concerning those with whom we may have a personal relationship and who, in refusing to change their ways, are plunged into everlasting misery and despair, there will not be any sadness or pain over their fates since, by this point, those who continue in their unreformed attitudes and manners will be exclusively those who have no regard whatsoever for the wisdom and ways of God. In appearing before God, they will have access to more than a glimpse of a picture of what it means to be the human person they have been created to be. All who refuse God at this juncture will be akin to Lucifer, that bright angel which decided to usurp God's position in heaven, not out of any legitimate need or perception of the same, but simply because that angel desired to be higher than anyone or anything else, including God, in their disobeying God for no other reason than that they willfully—in deep ingratitude and with shocking insolence—choose to.

Finally, the pain owing to tragedy with which we have been afflicted will decrease through God showing us our need to forgive in light of God's own forgiveness—in the case of those who have severely hurt or harmed us—and through God restoring to us all that we have lost—in that of those who have been bereaved of a loved one. Moreover, we can expect that the comforting and daily presence of God who reveals and discloses to those who do not yet know it that God has always extended love and mercy toward each person will serve as an efficacious balm for the wounded soul.

In sum, the reason mourning, crying, and pain will fade away is that God will be present for people as their God, and God will personally wipe away every tear from each person's eyes as God reminds them of

God's love for them. Relief will not occur all at once but progressively, as people learn to live with the new normal that is life post-final judgment, in the illuminating and encouraging love of God.

Having considered various and not altogether unrelated facets of morality, serving as they do to illuminate the humanity of God either by affinity or contrast, to draw the discussion still closer to the leitmotif that is Jesus' humanity as a reflection of God's own humanity, we highlight a concern with Barth's conception of God's love as an "electing love", tying this to the idea of God's freedom in choosing to love Israel and the Gentiles all called ultimately into God's kingdom.[28] For there is no absolute freedom, not even on the part of God conceived as meticulously controlling all reality, seeing as God's loving and gracious character, which God will never and can never annul, prevents any divine choice other than that which reflects and mirrors perfect and unconditional love. What Barth seems to be desirous of safeguarding is instead the idea that God loves Israel or the Gentiles not on account of some inherent nature in God that is distinct and separate from the faculty of volition, or on the basis of some perfection or virtue discerned to reside in the object of divine affection, but purely because God chooses of God's own loving nature to shower God's affection and favor upon those objects of divine love.

We may be better served designating such a love of God not in terms of absolute freedom or even freedom in general but rather a divine loving willing which is contingent not on the attractiveness or beauty or virtue of the recipient but arises from the value which God chooses to ascribe to them as objects God considers worthy of God's time and faithful concern. This is in spite of their unlovability by the moral norms espoused by rational and sensible persons who are able to bring themselves to decide that another person is not or no longer deserving of their time and attention, because they have proven untrustworthy or insensible. Present-day society, shaped as it has been by frequent concerns for an individual's wellbeing and the need to practice self-care, will be of the estimation that some people are not worthy of one's solicitude. One can perceive more than a hint of self-interested volition in the call and urging toward such a possible decision.

This, however, is not the way God sees things and relates with people. With God, one can expect a different kind of volition and willing,

---

28. Barth, *KD* IV.2, §68.2 (ET, Bromiley, pp. 766–71).

one that is without any tinge of self-interest, one that is therefore completely unconditional, selfless, altruistic, and gratuitous. In contrast to a conception of God's love for the created order as a free and electing love, it is more accurate to suggest and canvass that God's love for God's creatures involves a personal commitment that is devoid of any self-interest; in short, a disinterested love. Such a love of God for the creature knows nothing of any moral transformation, unilaterally, supernaturally, irruptively, and even permanently and irreversibly effected by God in the creature apart from their consciousness and volition, attached to it as a precondition, given that God loves those who rebel as much as those who obey, just that that affection is accompanied in the one case by pain and punishment and in the other by bliss and reward.[29]

So great and bounteous indeed is God's love that the vilest forms of idolatry cannot put it to death. In Hos 2:16–17, the Scripture declares that the people of the northern kingdom of Israel who have worshipped physical statues of the Western-Semitic god Baal as though they were a living being, or the supernatural power represented in these statues which demanded immoral practices including sexual debauchery, unnatural sexual practices such as bestiality following in the footsteps of the god himself who had sexual relations with a heifer in a Ugaritic myth, and even child sacrifice (Isa 57:3–10; Hos 13:2), will no longer call Yahweh "Baal." This suggests that even when a devotee worships a false god (scil., entertaining a partially erroneous image of the divine and directing their religious attention to that which they suppose is accurately represented in their erroneous conception of the divine, or to an object that is other than God, such as a physical idol), they are in effect still worshipping God, in that as they participate in such religious activity, God sees and hears them in an immediate manner. This is akin to the way a person addressed by another hears the latter's voice and is drawn by the sound of their name being called, in a greeting, or a question or response in the context of an ongoing dialogue, though they direct their prayers to a being represented by an erroneous conception of God or an object that is not God.[30]

Quite apart from evincing the love of God, such a signification highlights the possibility that the same single God or godhead could be known and worshipped under different names in various world religious and non-religious traditions, with the proviso by way of a clarification that

---

29. Cf. Barth, *KD* IV.2, §68.2 (ET, Bromiley, pp. 771–76).
30. Pope, "Baal Worship."

PART 2: HUMANITY'S IMAGING OF THE DIVINE

as known in these other traditions, God is properly named, understood, and worshipped or given due place in word and deed, in ways felicitous to members of those traditions, particularly in view of the historical contexts in which the faith emerged and developed, in ways, that is, by which God may be accurately known in some number of facets of God's being, and in a manner that urges, challenges, inspires, and admonishes human individuals to pursue a humane way of life.

It is inexorable in any doctrinal engagement involving a discussion of tenets and belief systems in multiple religious traditions that the question will arise concerning the validity and value of a Christian doctrine of the Trinity. Islam in particular mounts a forceful and, in some instances, intransigent criticism of the conception of God in terms of three persons rather than a single person. The Qurʾān in 4:171 sternly warns believers of Scripture against attributing sonship of God to Jesus, who is to be regarded only as a messenger of Allāh; Jesus is constituted of a soul created by the speech of Allāh. The logic expressed in this verse is as follows: Allāh is a single divine being, whose oneness carries a sense which does not admit of Allāh's having a son, a circumstance and situation which is beneath Allāh's status and grandeur. As the creation of Allāh, Jesus belongs to Allāh, along with the rest of the created order, whether in heaven or on earth, and Allāh alone is adequate to preside over and rule the universe, so that it is taking matters too far to ascribe divine qualities to created beings or accord them more reverence than they deserve in light of their ontological standing.[31] In the qur'anic system, the one who claims that Allāh is the Christ, the son of Mary, is guilty of unbelief, given that Allāh, being other than Jesus, could destroy him, Mary, and every person in the world; Allāh is the ruler of the heavens and the earth, and that which is between them, and Allāh creates everything as Allāh pleases, and has the ability to independently and singlehandedly preside over all of creation.[32]

The reason it is tantamount to unbelief to affirm that Allāh is the Messiah, the son of Mary, is that Jesus himself has, according to the Qurʾān, set out his status as the mere messenger of Allāh, calling Jews to the worship of Allāh alone, who is both Jesus' Lord and the Lord of his people. For those who insist on associating a creature such as Jesus is or any others with Allāh the Creator, Allāh shuts to them the door to

---

31. Q Nisāʾ 4:171.
32. Q Māʾidah 5:17.

paradise and prepares for them hellfire instead, a torment from which none can deliver them. In truth, the one who declares that Allāh is one of three parts in God is nothing other than an unbeliever, for there is only one complete God, and an excruciating penalty awaits those who persist in their obstinacy. So grave and offensive to Allāh is this wrong-headed belief that those who espouse it ought to recant it and seek Allāh's forgiveness for having previously held it; these can be assured of Allāh's forgiveness and mercy based as these qualities are on Allāh's character. The Qurʾān is emphatic that Jesus is but a messenger of Allāh, one among others. Mary knew and advocated belief in the truth. The error of believing that Jesus is anything more than a messenger of Allāh is evident in the fact that both Jesus and his mother Mary had need of food, presupposing that a divine being would not need physical sustenance, and so, on the basis of this presupposition, Jesus cannot be divine.[33]

Those who hold that Jesus is God should be aware that there will come a day when Allāh will call them to account by having Jesus clarify whether he had exhorted Jews to worship him and his mother Mary as Gods, at which time he is certain to gainsay that he has taught anything like that, which he had no right to teach, and he would have only to appeal to Allāh's intimate knowledge both of his words and thoughts as the one who knows even what cannot be seen (in contrast to Jesus' ignorance of what is in Allāh) to be vindicated of this false charge. Jesus will highlight that he was faithful in discharging his duties as a messenger of God in summoning the people to worship Allāh and Allāh alone, Lord both of Jesus and of them. The people to whom Jesus preached were given ample warning by him against committing this transgression during his earthly ministry and by Allāh thereafter. While they are deserving of Allāh's judgment as the servants of the same, should Allāh elect to forgive them, this would be testament to Allāh's power and wisdom.[34]

To aver of Allāh that Allāh has received a son is to commit an enormity which pushes the heavens and earth toward splitting, and the mountains toward destruction. It is not fitting that Allāh should take a son, since all that exists in heaven and on earth is merely a servant of Allāh.[35] It is erroneous to state that Allāh has taken a son, or that Allāh coexists with another deity, for if that were indeed the case, these Gods could only divide the world between themselves and be in competition

33. Q 5:72–75.
34. Q 5:116–18.
35. Q Maryam 19:88–93.

and conflict with each other, a fanciful notion that is beneath Allāh.[36] In the prominent *Sūrah al-Ikhlās*, believers of Allāh are enjoined to affirm the oneness of Allāh; that is, Allāh's singleness, uniqueness, and indivisibility.[37] They are to confess that Allāh is the only one to whom they should flee for refuge for eternity, implying that Allāh is the need of every creature.[38] Allāh has neither begotten a son nor was Allāh given birth to; there is none that is equal to Allāh.[39]

The qur'anic criticism of the Christian doctrine of the Trinity may be summarized in the following tour d'horizon: 1) Allāh is merely a single being, indeed, a single person. As such, the suggestion that Jesus is divine as well as Allāh is equivalent to introducing a tritheist conception of the godhead; 2) this is impossible, because Allāh is uniquely superior to all else that exists, the latter having all received their being from Allāh, including Jesus and Mary, as evident from how both persons needed to rely on physical sustenance; 3) to speak of Jesus as the divine Son of God is also to introduce division into God, in such a way that instead of one complete divine being, there are now three parts to God: Allāh, Jesus, and Mary (who is presumably divine as the mother of God), and such partism can only undermine the uniqueness of Allāh, as well as create the possibility of an interdivine conflict; 4) the doctrine of Christ's divinity also embodies the error of identifying Allāh with the Messiah; 5) Jesus has never taught that he is anything more than a messenger of God, who called believers to worship Allāh alone, and for whom Allāh is Lord, as Allāh is Lord for all other people.

The fundamental theological conceptions undergirding these criticisms are interesting; nonetheless, they do not intersect in any way with Christian notions of God as Trinity. The Qurʾān is not reacting against the doctrine of the Trinity per se, but false permutations of the same; that is, the illogical and false ideas that God, conceived as a single person, should consist of two other persons or be identified with one of them (that is, Jesus); that Mary conceived Jesus in his divinity and thereby deserves a place in the divine pantheon; and that a human being can be completely identified with divinity.

In contradistinction to the view presented in the Qurʾān, the Christian doctrine of the Trinity posits God as a single divine being, comprising

36. Q Muʾminūn 23:91.
37. Saheeh International, *Qurʾān*, 658n1879.
38. Saheeh International, *Qurʾān*, 658n1880.
39. Q Ikhlāṣ 112:1–4.

three distinct persons; that is, three fundamentally spiritual agents each with the faculties of consciousness, identity, conation, and action, indwelled by the other two agents in such a way that each person in containing the other two as constitutive of the former's being is completely and uniquely divine, and can be said to be the one and only true God, the very things that can be properly spoken of the other two persons, since the same ontological state of affairs obtains with each of them. These three are coeternal, having existed from the beginning, at the horizon of all possibility from which time itself began. If it is said of the Father that the Father eternally begets the Son and the Son is eternally begotten of the Father, that the Father eternally spirates the Holy Spirit through the Son and that the Holy Spirit eternally proceeds from the Father through the Son, these things are not to be understood in a chronological and materialist fashion, but rather as different ways of describing the eternal relationships among the three divine persons, who have always coexisted, none of whom brought it about that another came into existence.

Moreover, in the incarnation of Christ, the divine Son, both by the will of the Father and the Son, became integrated with a physical human body at the point of the miraculous virginal conception by Mary of Christ, this transpiring as she was overshadowed by the Holy Spirit. The implication is that the divine status of God the Son is not transferred in any sense, except a highly metaphorical one, to the physical human body which the Son assumed. It does not belong to the divine to be in need of physical sustenance, and this statement was true of God the Son prior to the incarnation; having taken on a physical body, the Son, in becoming Jesus of Nazareth, came to require sustenance, yet without compromising or losing the Son's divine ontological standing, since the divinity of the Son, as also for the Father and the Holy Spirit, consists simply in the Son's divine identity, character, role, and authority.[40]

It is imperative to recognize that the doctrine of divine triunity best consolidates the aseity of the godhead in view of the defining characteristic of the divine nature as goodness and love (1 John 4:8, 16), so that apart from being a multiplicity of persons in one divine being, capable of loving internally, it would be necessary for God to create beings on whose existence God would be dependent for the exercise of that natural relational trait which is most proper to God, exclusive self-love, of which a single-personed God is capable, being deficient as a form of love absent the love

---

40. Chua, *ECRST*, 208, 210.

of another.[41] Furthermore, if the triunity of God is a conception that appears to differ markedly from the oneness of God affirmed in the teachings of the Old Testament, this is only because God's revelation of God's inner nature as three persons had to await the promulgation and acceptance of God's oneness, prior to a further revelation in which that unity is more clearly elucidated in all its simplicity yet also complexity.[42]

---

41. Cf. Richard of Saint Victor, *Trin.* 3.2 (ET, Angelici, pp. 116–17).
42. Gregory of Nazianzus, *Or.* 31.26 (ET, Wickham, pp. 137–38).

10

The Christian Doctrine of Perfection
Divine Work as Human Capacitation

THE QUESTION OF WHETHER it is at all possible that humankind attain sinlessness and perfection during earthly existence constitutes a major subject of this chapter.

Sin may be defined as any action that serves to take advantage of or devalue God; take advantage of, devalue, or indirectly or directly harm a human person, be it self or other; or exploit the natural environment, or abet or assist the same. Our responsibility in the world is the diametrical opposite of sin as earlier defined: to engage in action that serves to safeguard the genuine interests of God and value God; safeguard the genuine interests of a human person, be it self or other, and value and protect them; and protect the natural environment as well as indirectly or directly promote the same.

In Reformed theology, on the basis of passages such as Rom 7:7–25, Gal 5:16–24, and Phil 3:10–14, a dim view is taken of humanity's ability, even with the assistance of divine grace, to cast aside its sinful ways, a state it prefers to leave to the condition of glorification through the resurrection of the bodies of believers upon the return of Christ and the onset of the millennium, electing to speak instead of an *obedientia inchoata* ("inchoate obedience") or *sanctitas inchoata* ("inchoate sanctification"), in which a little beginning is made of constantly being repulsed by sin and taking joy in righteousness.[1]

---

1. Clark, "Brothers We Are Not Perfectionists."

In contrast, a Wesleyan conception postulates that Christian perfection, defined as a disposition of total love for God and one's neighbor, is very much attainable by sincere and obedient believers, through the empowerment of the Spirit of God, whether at the point of death or after a significant period of continuity in such a posture during one's earthly existence.[2]

Although disparate in their conceptualization of the question of perfection, these differing perspectives are allied to what amounts to nothing less than a clear and unmistakable division between what is seen to be the nature, disposition, and act of God and what is seen to be that of humankind.

Martin Luther is certain that Scripture teaches people can do no good works out of their own moral capacity, but have need of a special infusion of God's grace to create a heart of faith led by God-given stimulation by the good works of Christ, by which truly good works may be done;[3] that believers are to be content to seek such an infusion of God's grace, whether and whenever it comes, through being humbled by the message of the cross and by adversity (in which alone God can be found)[4] and not simply to exert themselves in good works by their own moral capacity.[5]

In the *Die Kirchliche Dogmatik*, Karl Barth contends for a strict dichotomy between divine and human understanding, desire, will, and action in the process of repentance from sin. As far as he is concerned, there is no possibility of attributing to any human capacity a heart that is open to turn away from its sinfulness. If it is completely determined by an external divine power in a "pure [human] act without the corresponding human potency", the converted Christian life is set on its path from beginning to end in an irresistible way.[6]

Barth's presentation, being neo-Reformed in nature, posits the human being as a creature riddled by sin and corruption, capable of nothing moral and good unless God first chooses to work and does work effectively in an individual.

In Barth's eyes as a Reformed theologian, there is no way for human beings to be so freed from their sin, not even temporarily, that they

2. See Lok, "Doctrine of Christian Perfection."
3. Luther, *Heid. Disp.*, §§25, 27.
4. Luther, *Heid. Disp.*, §21.
5. Luther, *Heid. Disp.*, §24.
6. Barth, *KD* IV.2, §64.4 (ET, Bromiley, pp. 308–309).

become capable of performing a good work by their own moral capacity. On the contrary, he is emphatic that if any good work is actually done among human persons, this must and can only be the result of a "special" work of God operating in the lives of specific individuals via a process of divine "illumination" whereby God's own good work is proclaimed to these individuals, identified, borne witness to, and presented to them, in such a way that those persons cannot stop thinking about how they might reflect the good work of God, that they are given a new capacity and confidence arising from a sense of divine authority to perform a good work—though still riddled by sin—that corresponds to God's own, and that they are supernaturally enabled to be volitionally and emotionally inclined to perform these good works.[7]

The Swiss theologian is able to bring himself to speak of the basis of human love in terms of God's "creative" love. Divine love does not operate strictly via rationality, in which a person receives God's command to love and comes round to obeying it as a sensible thing to do; morality, whereby the love of God becomes an example and standard for people to emulate; or a "quasi-physical" path, where a person is mechanically impacted by God's love and becomes loving. To love is not a "human possibility" which people are obligated to turn into practical action in the context of God's exhortation. It is completely a unilateral act on God's part so to remold a human heart as to make what was previously impossible on account of a sinful nature, that is, selfless love, now possible on the basis of the altruistic work of God in the life of an individual.

Barth leaves no room for any doubt that he firmly believes that the human being is completely powerless to enact a practical display of selfless love, whose only freedom is to pursue self-interest under the guise of love, virtue, and faithfulness: "The presupposition of genuine love is the existence of a man who is free for it, and therefore—since he is not and cannot be this of himself—freed for it. The love of God is this liberation of man for genuine love."[8]

So corrupt is humankind that they are exclusively and even necessarily filled with self-love, and love, though it be the fundamental determination of humankind to love God and one another, can hardly be expected of them, but only of God, since love among humankind is strictly founded on the new birth and new creation they are able to experience through

---

7. Barth, *KD* IV.2, §66.5 (ET, Bromiley, pp. 590, 592, 594–95).
8. Barth, *KD* IV.2, §68.2 (ET, Bromiley, p. 777).

the powerful working of the Holy Spirit alone, a supernatural event, discontinuous with all that precedes it, which is beyond the control of humankind, and which involves God becoming present in the very midst, psyche, spirit, and personhood of the believer:[9] "For a proper estimation of the greatly devalued term "love" it is as well to be clear that where love takes place, we have to do with nothing more nor less than a revelation of the real presence of God in Jesus Christ."[10]

God demonstrates love for a human person in giving of Godself to them, for their benefit, and in such a way that God personally enters the life of the individual and that person is altered beyond recognition as a human being who has now been brought into communion with God in all the person's wretchedness and sinfulness, revealing that God is the x-factor, the indispensable element, the conditio sine qua non for the positive, dramatic, and complete transformation of the conation of the individual.[11]

This process of change sees the human person receiving the gift of Godself in such a way that an imprint of God is left on the soul, the person becomes a child of God the Father, by grace and not by nature, and the individual receives the freedom to take after God in God's self-giving action. It is not as though the changed person, having been delivered by God, were wholly liberated from God subsequently, but that this self-giving nature is implanted in them by God alone, not just as a moral and relational exemplar but more importantly a fundamentum, the efficient cause for the possibility of even being able to love in a self-giving manner in the first place.

Although Barth is correct in observing that true love cannot be demanded, nor yet performed simply in response to a demand, this will only be the case if that demand is regarded as an external command, rather than an internal conation on the part of the individual who by virtue of having been posited to exist in a human way by the Divine Nature deeply desires, wills, and determines to fulfill this command, to love selflessly the way Christ has done, as an imperative, critical, and non-negotiable necessity, or at least desires to more deeply desire, will, and determine to do so as a function of having been made and shaped this way. The divine commandment to love, then, is not to be viewed as an imposition competing for human attention and acceptance of its

---

9. Barth, *KD* IV.2, §68.3 (ET, Bromiley, pp. 784–85).
10. Barth, *KD* IV.2, §68.3 (ET, Bromiley, p. 785).
11. Barth, *KD* IV.2, §68.2 (ET, Bromiley, pp. 777–78).

seriousness, but a codified expression of the inner mandate and law that defines an individual as human rather than anything else.[12]

Barth's need not be the only approach to biblical teaching concerning the Christian existence. One imposes unnecessary requirements in divorcing that which God engenders in the life of the Christian as to their obedience and that which the Christian has in themselves in terms of the capacity to obey and submit to God's moral principles and instructions.[13]

The very intuition concerning God in a human person, their very power to know, assess, and recognize what is moral and what is evil, the very inclination and resolve to pursue the path of moral good as opposed to moral evil, and their freedom to actualize those honorable desires and determinations in various situations, including the most trying circumstances—these are the very things provided by God, both as ontological-structural Divine Nature and entitative Trinity, from the beginning of the existence of the persons that would become human in the course of the development of creation under the wise and sovereign plan of God.

It is the Divine Nature which posits human persons as moral beings in a formal sense, with the capacity to develop the ability to recognize, desire, and actualize various attributes of morality, while the Trinity by means of a pre-incarnate experience of the triune godhead in all its awe-inspiring and indelibly remarkable moral excellences in splendid heaven which left their unmistakeable imprint on the human soul stimulates the development of the ability to recognize, desire, and actualize those various attributes of morality.[14]

---

12. Barth, *KD* IV.2, §68.2 (ET, Bromiley, pp. 781–83).

13. Indeed, Paul does not speak in vain of how believers are to build on the foundation that is Christ in ministering among believers and nonbelievers (1 Corinthians 3). That Christ's role is limited to laying a foundation for subsequent human participation in the ministry that reflects the character and action of Christ and that Christ does not usurp the place of the believer in building upon the foundation that he has laid infers that there is an unmistakable, irremovable, and ineffaceable role for the human person in responding to the enlightenment and encouragement of God as to moral action. Moreover, the Lord taught two parables (Matt 25:14–30; Luke 19:11–27) in which, within the parable, the objective is to take the money one has been entrusted and make more with it, this money constituting a metaphor for the moral capacity with which one has been vested (in the initial money) as well as the actualization of that moral capacity (in the money earned). Cf. Barth, *KD* IV.2, §67.1 (ET, Bromiley, p. 637).

14. This chimes with the way in which the divinely-ordained rest for the people of God is attested in Scripture to entail acting in a way that recognizes God's provision of moral capacity (alternatively designated the way of faith) and in accordance to God's specific dictates for moral behavior, as spelled out in the Decalogue. The Israelites in the wilderness did not trust in God's provision of strength to overcome their mightier

Such a conception of divine conferment of a human capacity for obedience is not to be confused with any notion of divine-human cooperation, so vehemently contradicted in Reformed theology, whereby a person is thought to have been freed from the captivity of Adamic sin and corruption and given an authentic opportunity to choose whether to respond positively or negatively to God's offer of salvation through Christ. Under an Arminian-libertarian framework like that, the antithesis between God's understanding, desire, will, and action and those of the human being is not overcome. The very use of the concept of cooperation infers the presence of more than one agent.

While there is indeed place, and a necessity, for speaking of a human response to God, this should not detract from the quintessential truth that everything that exists in the being and capacity of the human person originates from divine reality. For that reason alone, no person can legitimately lay claim to obligating or indebting God to perform any action in their behalf in return or compensation for what the human thinks they have done for God. In this connection, Scripture speaks of how everything belongs to God, and so it is inconceivable that a human being might have something to offer to God, connoting that the object of offering does not belong to God in the first place (Job 41:11). In addition to owning everything in creation, God does not need anything from the created order in the way of physical sustenance (Ps 50:10–13). Not only does God not need anything in a physical sense but God furnished humankind with all that is necessary and good for their specific mode of existence (Acts 17:24–25).

Shorn of the punitive connotations embedded in his thought, the theology of Anselm of Canterbury provides a reliable guide to the standing of humanity before God as the Creator and Sovereign—we owe God deference and honor, expressed in the obedience of our actions. Whenever a person obeys the principles and teachings of God, they most conform to the nature with which they were created; it is what ushers in the greatest and most sublime of delights in earthly existence. As such, the Lord advised his followers that they were not to attempt to obligate God to compensate them for their good moral actions but recognize always that all the good that they do they do in line with

---

enemies in the land of Canaan nor did they obey God's express command to take the land with the return of the twelve spies; hence, they were consigned to wander in the wilderness and had no power to claim the land of promise (Numbers 13–14; Heb 3:7—4:13).

their duty and responsibility as God's creatures (Luke 17:7–10); St. Paul, following the Lord's exhortation, argued that all that we have, including our good desires, comes from the Lord (1 Cor 4:7). St. Anselm of Canterbury reminds modern believers of what they might have forgotten: that all the worship and glorification they may offer to God is what they owe God in the first place.[15]

If we understand this passage metaphorically, what the Lord means to say is that we should serve God because that is the nature with which we have been made. We are happiest when we serve God on account of the fact that that is the purpose of our existence. Consequently, the opportunity and freedom to obey God's moral laws and teachings are a greatest gift from on high, rather than a task or worse yet a chore for which we presume we may claim some form of compensation from God, not realizing that an obedient life is the supreme good that God can allow and confer on us. If even the inclinations, ability, and opportunity to pursue those inclinations are endued by God, then what is left for us but to follow our God-given morally good intuitions and desires and communicate our gratitude day after day to the one who has so bountifully and munificently blessed us?[16]

Some contend for the position that solely human individuals who glorify God in the midst of their actions have performed those actions in the true and authentic faith of Christ and therefore not in their own strength but in the strength and power of the regenerating, converting, and sanctifying Holy Spirit of God alone. Are morally good actions done on the spur of the moment, yet without any prayer of praise to God for having granted such desire, ability, and opportunity, to be excluded from consideration? What ultimately matters is the view that we come to take of our positive or negative experience of serving God.

In this regard, the distinction that psychological studies make between feelings and emotions is salutary. An emotion is a physical sensation that transpires under a certain set of circumstances whereas a feeling is the name given by the patient to the entire experience. Different individuals may experience the same bodily emotion in a similar situation and yet label that experience differently, one expressing that the discomfort at attending a large social gathering indicates fear (on account of not

---

15. Anselm of Canterbury, *Cur Deus homo*, 1.20 (ET, Deane, p. 241).

16. Barth is right to highlight the point about our need to show our gratitude toward God as a key attribute of the Christian life. See Barth, *KD* IV.2, §64.4 (ET, Bromiley, pp. 308–309).

knowing many people at the party) and another calling it excitement (on account of being able to meet new people).[17]

Similarly, a person who has done a good deed, eventuating in a personal bodily emotion of the pleasure of self-fulfillment in one sense or the emotional numbness associated with having overworked oneself or faced an excessive degree of difficulty or both, might label that experience meaningful or dreadful or parts of both. The central question in the feeling associated with the experience of doing something morally good revolves around whether one is self-congratulatory about the good deed or something else, be it feeling nothing in particular at first or being thankful to God for the morally good desires, abilities, and opportunities that made that deed possible in the first place. If one is anything but grateful to God for providing everything that undergirded that good deed, one's role being limited to enjoying the use of those faculties, then it may be necessary to reconsider those particular feelings and come to embrace the truth about the root of one's good deeds and feel and express gratitude toward the divine alone.

To the extent that we do not feel that God's moral laws and teachings point and urge us toward the actualization of our inmost being, nature, and inclinations, in view that our desires, will, and actions seem to run contrary to the obedience of God, the primary reason is that some disordered way of thinking and feeling has entered in through an experience of subjection to neglect, domination, and abuse.

The Christian faith recognizes the observation in psychological studies that emotional dysfunction is engendered by an early experience of being neglected, dominated, or abused so that it is accurate to speak of emotional dysfunction as emotional immaturity, a stunting of psychological development on an unconscious level, coexisting with a normal or higher degree of functioning, which impinges on one's relationship to God, self, others, and the world in the way of promoting fearful or abusive behavior toward the other.

Emotional abuse brings it about that a person is put in a position of confronting a wider scope and higher intensity of temptation to sin. For this reason, the Lord curiously connects the rejection of a child with the result of causing that child to sin (Matt 18:5–6). "Whoever receives one such child in my name receives me, but whoever causes one of these little ones who believes in me to sin [or stumble] . . . " (ESV)

---

17. Allyn, "Difference Between Emotions and Feelings."

When the Lord expresses approval of an action which is done in his name, he means by this the form of acceptance, whether by a parent, guardian, educator, or short-term caregiver, in which the child is not devalued or diminished in any way, let alone neglected or maltreated, characterized by the understanding that those who care for a child do so on behalf of Christ, and in the very manner in which Christ himself would treat the child; that is, with loving affection, gentleness, and patience.

This very teaching discloses Christ's fundamental nature as a parent towards all human beings, caring for them with the sensitivity an ideal and perfectly loving parent would extend to a child throughout the entire course of the life of the latter, until the parent themselves is unable to provide that care by reason of mortality.[18] In turn, the exhortation of the Lord reveals both the highest vocation of humankind and the nature according to which they are to orientate their relational attitudes and behaviors.

That is to say, firstly, the human person corresponds the most to the divine design in properly and adequately nurturing, whether as parents, guardians, or caregivers over the longer or shorter term, the young lives in their care in physical, psychological, and spiritual ways. Secondly, the human person is to see to it that the tenor of their lives reflects the lovingkindness akin to that displayed by an ideal and perfectly loving parent toward their child. Not that we are all to treat one another as though we were children if we are not, but that we are to be patient, tender, and considerate toward one another even as adults, forbearing to resort to apathy, resentment, contempt, insensitivity, selfishness, exploitation, aggression, violence, or cruelty.

We are to regard each other as people on a journey toward personal and relational progress and wellbeing, this because we have been appointed by Christ to be the salt of the earth and the light of the world (Matt 5:13–16, defining our roles as human persons among other persons in terms of the nurturing, life-giving, enlightening, and inspiring influence we are to have on one another, akin to salt as a preservative in the ancient world and light as a means of navigating a dark place), to be as perfect as the perfect heavenly Father (Matt 5:48, a passage on loving our enemies), by which is intended that we are to take a sincere interest and concern in the personal and relational welfare and wellbeing of

---

18. Christ is prophesied as the everlasting Father (Isa 9:6), revealing the Father even as the Son.

other individuals, being slow to take offense and always ready to pray for them and guide them in all gentleness.

All this is and is to be anchored in the selfless and unconditional love which God has extended to each one of us, who in loving us inspires—indeed, commands—us also to love others in the same way that God has loved us (John 13:34; 1 John 4:19). The value of the human person reposes in the inalienable fact that each of us is posited by the Divine Nature as existents and as moral agents with psychological and social needs and that we are each called by God as Trinity to actualize our existence as moral agents seeking not only to fulfill our own psychological and social needs but to fulfill those of others as well, and in a way that recognizes the right of other creatures to exist in the same space as precious vegetative and animal companions, some of whom are given to serve human needs, without according to humankind the right to destroy the environments and ecologies in and by which these lifeforms live (Gen 1:28–29; Gen 9:1–4).[19]

A human person is to be defined as a moral agent posited and guided to know and display the selfless and unconditional lovingkindness of God for oneself toward God, self, other, and the world in a manner proper to humankind as revealed by Jesus in his earthly life as the image of God, a direct reflection of God's character, in which we have been created, constituting the capacity from the Divine Nature to develop the ability to recognize, desire, and actualize morality, the stimulation by God as Trinity of such development, and the actualization of our morality; that is, revealing fairness, justice, tenderness, compassion, and empathy in one's thought, feeling, desire, will, word, and action. As such, no physical disability disqualifies a person from being considered fully human. While our moral deficit may well endanger our humanity, this is only insofar as we fail to acknowledge and repent of our sinful attitudes and actions or find creative solutions to lift ourselves from the rut of indifference.

The height of sin is irresponsibility. For a person is always only obligated to discharge all their moral duties unceasingly towards God, self, others, and the world, whether or not there is a disordered pattern of thought, feeling, and even desire which will certainly make it more challenging to obey the dictates of morality considering that the temptation to sin becomes more frequent and even more intense. It is a person's responsibility to take the necessary and efficacious steps to attend to

---

19. Dicastery for the Doctrine of the Faith, *Dignitas Infinita*, paragraphs 7–8, 28.

their own psychological wellbeing and to make an end of their disorderly ways of thinking, feeling, and desiring, rather than using them as a pretext for an attempted extenuation of their depraved behaviors, since no evil thought can be manifested in concrete action without the consent, will, and direct personal involvement and execution of that act of the individual in question. If Lucifer and the first couple brought sin into the world through their inordinate desire to become first in importance, even ahead of God, how destructive is the sin of arrogance!

As to the seeming restriction in Matt 18:5-6 of such loving action to those children who believe in Christ, this need not occasion any supposition that preferential treatment ought to be accorded to Christian children. It is more a feature of the context in which Jesus was speaking, using the child in the midst of his disciples as an example for his teaching about humility, moral concern, and the love of the Father which is directed at the single person.

Biblical teaching attests to the relationship between emotional functionality and dysfunctionality and personal maturity in speaking of the goal of Christian existence in terms of a journey toward becoming a mature human person (Eph 4:13).

Psychological and emotional maturity can be attained through seeking clarity regarding the emotional reasons underlying our inappropriate, defective, or sinful thoughts, feelings, or desires and establishing their moral status; concession entailing an acceptance of these reasons and their respective positions on the moral spectrum, commitment not to continue in the volitional decisions spurred by those non-volitional ways of thinking, feeling, and desiring; a covenant to gently guide oneself away from those ways of thinking, feeling, and desiring by telling oneself that one does not have to persist in them; and professional or spiritual consultation.[20] This will lead to the actualization of our desire and will to do what is morally good as pertains to God, ourselves, one another, and the world.[21]

By far the most difficult people to relate with are those who refuse to concede their inner struggles with some form of past emotional wound because there is little possibility of change through the usual methods of resolution and self-control. Some may go as far as to insist that they are fully justified in all that they do in how they interact

---

20. Chua, *ECRST*, 150.
21. Cf. Barth, *KD* IV.2, §64.4 (ET, Bromiley, pp. 314-15).

with others, perhaps even if they rely mainly on the use of emotional violence to achieve their relational objectives, desiring to gain no new knowledge about the foundations of their emotional lives which powerfully shape the ways they treat other people.

Why do people avoid addressing the issues of their psychological wellness? They may not believe that the emotion plays any important part in their lives. They may consider themselves mentally strong and rational, so much so that they wrongly believe that they can overcome any challenge that rises over the horizon with bravado and that their ways are always only correct. There is very little in the way of sincere self-reflection and examination concerning the rightness, propriety, or long-term sustainability or effectiveness of their actions. It is almost as if they fear discovering the imperfection of their souls, that such insight would be a crushing blow to them for some reason. Perchance they were warned not to cry when they were very young by apathetic caregivers, or in some other way had their emotions suppressed through the neglectful and uncaring response of significant adults.

Taking their cue for how they should behave from these adults, they learned to ignore uncomfortable emotions and falsely labeled them as feelings of weakness to be dismissed as soon as they arose, or to be endured in the knowledge that they will settle down in time. They never cultivated the critical practice of listening to their psychosomatic responses to various adverse situations in life. Neglecting difficult emotions in both themselves and others may make for temporary relief, yet proves to be unviable in the long run, if only because the past experience of trauma due to neglect or abuse creates disorders in thinking, feeling, and desiring that, left unchecked, urge a person towards sinful actions against others, perpetuating a cycle of abuse leading to trauma leading back to abuse.

Recalling the experience of trauma that has been long suppressed can be a frightful thing. The mind knows this and chooses to hide the memory from the conscious mind until the person has come to such an understanding that the past no longer exists in the present that they are able to confront the entire truth. I know of an individual, emotionally and sexually abused in his childhood, for whom the memories of those incidents were kept from his conscious knowledge by his mind for the first few decades of his life. It was not until he evinced a very strong resolution to unearth the truth about his past and how it may have shaped his present self that he began seeing first bits and pieces then longer scenes as he put together consistent narratives while undergoing professional therapy.

Only after all this had transpired, and after another few years, did he experience a dream where he saw himself as a little boy speaking directly to him, perhaps representing his own mind, telling him, "Now you know everything." This was succeeded almost immediately by another voice—at first, he thought it was his own voice, seeing that he was facing the boy, whom he did not instantly identify as himself—which urged, "Don't be afraid." This was the voice of God, and it spoke to comfort his soul a little before he had another dream sequence where he was hyperventilating in a hospital ward. Perhaps this was where he was brought after having been abused. He also remembered a family trip to a nearby crockery shop which must have taken place around the time of the incident.

The fact is that trauma completely demolishes trust; in the weeks leading up to this revelation, he remembers nearly hyperventilating or clenching his jaw whenever in close physical proximity to an adult, including his own family members, suggesting that his mind had already begun releasing emotions pertaining to that scene in the hospital, in preparation for the visual revelation.

A person that is emotionally wounded can hardly see the truth beyond their passions. As a case in point, a woman may show that she is upset not so much with her husband as with the situation yet the latter might conclude that she is really upset with him. When he confronts her about his sense of injustice arising from the perceived mistreatment, she might protest that she was not actually targeting or criticizing him in any way. Even then, he would take in her words only cognitively at first, without quite learning anything about his spouse's pattern of reactions from that encounter until after some time has elapsed. An understanding based on personal knowledge of a person and trust in them may be delayed in its development.

In light of the foregoing, it seems that the unconscious dimension of a person is to all intents and purposes a self-functioning entity with its own thoughts and feelings which need constantly and consistently to be examined, critiqued and, where necessary, brought in line with proper moral conduct. Operating apart from the conscious awareness of an individual, it is easy to assume that the strongest passions which drive our inner and outer selves constitute mere instincts, even of an animal kind. If this were the case, there would be no possibility of maturation or development beyond a present psychological state, a supposition controverted by the personal testimony of many individuals who have experienced healing from brokenness.[22]

Regarding how it is possible for St. Paul to say in 1 Cor 5:7 that the believer is "really . . . unleavened" and yet to also "cleanse out the old leaven that you may be a new lump" (ESV), that those who have already died, with their life hidden in Christ, are called to put to death what is earthly in them (Col 3:3, 5), this is to be understood in the sense that the believer in their baptism has identified with Christ as having died with him on the cross, that is, having had all their sins punished in being regarded as having legally been crucified when Jesus was crucified and having the object of their existence secure in the vision with which Christ presents them as a man resurrected, ascended, and seated at the right hand of God, one completely attainable through his teaching and guidance via the Word and the Holy Spirit.[23]

To the extent that the nature, disposition, and action of God and humankind cannot be as cleanly differentiated as customarily held, God's work in human beings is equivalent to a capacitation of human understanding, desire, will, and action whereby human persons who have worked through their disorders of emotion and thought arising from past traumatic experiences of subjection to neglect or abuse are furnished with the inclination of mind, affection, resolve, and execution to simply decide on their freewill to act on these inclinations in such a way that proper accreditation is given to God for God's role in all their good action. On this view, a state of perfection and sinlessness is attainable by human beings on the terrestrial side of eternity (perfection through divine work as human capacitation).

Epistemology

There are, in general, five major approaches to or ways of attempting to deal with human sinfulness: alienation, extenuation, resignation or license, crusade, and mercy.

---

22. Cf. the conception of the shadow in Carl Jung's analytic psychological theory. See Diamond, "What Is the 'Shadow'?" If the unconscious has an instinctual dimension, perhaps this is that which experiences stressfulness in distressing situations in such a way that we may be completely oblivious to the tension we ourselves are under until we become indisposed and are informed by a doctor that we have been under considerable stress.

23. Cf. Barth, *KD* IV.2, §64.4 (ET, Bromiley, pp. 363–67).

An account, in different voices and from different perspectives, in the synoptic gospels of Jesus' meeting with tax collectors and others over a meal in which he responds to his Pharisaic objectors (Matt 9:9–13; Mark 2:14–17; Luke 5:27–32), alludes to the first way of handling sin while affording insight into the Lord's posture toward the one who takes a morally unacceptable path.

Research conducted among US college students in 2011 suggests that people tend to form friendships with those whose values, social outlook, and behaviors match their own. However, those with less of an option and who have to content themselves with making friends different from themselves tend to form closer friendships, yet this is probably only because they know they have less options and so they make more of an effort to deepen their friendships.[24]

The surprising thing about the account of Jesus' meal with tax collectors and others is that the Lord, who had a choice of befriending anybody at all, decided to make friends of people who were completely different from himself; namely, Matthew, as well as Matthew's friends. Matthew, also called Levi, was a tax collector before Jesus called him to be a disciple. When Jesus called him, Matthew left his tax booth and followed Jesus. He even held a feast among colleagues and friends to which he invited Jesus.

But not everybody was delighted with the fact that Jesus kept company with Matthew and his friends. The Pharisees, for one, were displeased and complained about Jesus to his disciples. "Why does your teacher eat with tax collectors and sinners?" they asked (Matt 9:11 ESV).

The Pharisees were a group of Jewish people who set themselves apart to strictly keep Moses' law down to very minute regulations, as worked out by the religious lawyers or scribes. They observed rigorous rules on ritual purity, including washing, eating, tithing, and Sabbath festival observance. The Pharisees figured prominently during Jesus' ministry, mainly as his critics, because they often felt that Jesus and his disciples were not keeping the religious laws as they should. Here they were in their element, criticizing Jesus, now, for dining with tax collectors and people they called "sinners".

Why did the Pharisees find fault with Jesus' eating with tax collectors and others? It probably had something to do with the fact that tax collectors in those days tended to collect far more taxes than reasonable. They

---

24. Groeger, "A Friend like Me."

collected more than they ought to. Aside from the moral issue, tax collectors also interacted with Gentiles or non-Jews among their colleagues. To the Pharisees, Gentiles were ritually unclean, so there was also an issue of ritual purity. These were the main problems the Pharisees found with the company Jesus kept at Matthew's dinner party.

The issue with Jesus' dining with tax collectors at Matthew's house was simply this, that Jesus as a Jewish religious teacher, a rabbi, ought not to be so cozy with them, lest they be emboldened to continue their lifestyles of immorality and lack of ritual observance. For it was a big thing in those days to share a table with somebody, as it implied a measure of solidarity. In fact, the Pharisees could not even be in the same house as a tax collector as they believed it would make them ceremonially unclean.[25]

We considered how the Pharisees were critical of Jesus throughout his ministry. Not once amid any of these criticisms did Jesus ever concede that he had made an error, simply because the Pharisees failed to understand the heart of Jesus' teachings and, for that matter, the heart of the Law of Moses they sought to honor and obey.

In the account of Jesus' meal with tax collectors and others, Jesus was yet again unfazed by the criticism of the Pharisees. He replied with three statements. "Those who are well have no need of a physician, but those who are sick." "Go and learn what this means: 'I desire mercy, and not sacrifice.'" "For I came not to call the righteous, but sinners." (Matt 9:12–13 ESV)

We learn from these three statements about the differences between religiosity and piety. In this context I define religiosity as an uncritical or mechanical observance of the practices of faith without real spiritual meaning or power, while piety refers to a faith-oriented observance of religious practices which is deep and transformative.

The first thing we notice is that religiosity gives up on people all too easily. The Pharisees took one look at the people Jesus ate with at Matthew's and decided that they were not worth their time of day and should not be worth Jesus' either. They fancied themselves upstanding people, the moral crowd, people who kept ritual laws and were purer than those who did not. Therefore, they even stooped to calling people "sinners".

Let us consider how the Pharisees reacted to people they consider less moral or ritually pure than themselves. The complaint of the

---

25. Morris, *Matthew*, 221n26.

Pharisees was not completely unjustified. As a case in point, they took exception to the exploitative conduct of tax collectors in those days. They rightly disapproved of such unethical behavior but they believed that the only way to deal with people like that was to completely avoid them, to ostracize them basically.

The only issue with ostracism is that it is not a viable solution over the longer term. Consider this: we are all imperfect people. If our attitude toward sin is one of alienation, then we are going to have to avoid not just the people we deem to be immoral, but we will also try to avoid what is sinful in our own hearts.

Those who practice alienation as a way of dealing with sin try not to think very much about the sins they have committed. They try to forget they did anything sinful. They may even deny that they are sinners in the first place. People who take this path must wish they had Chinese goddess of forgetfulness, *Meng Po*'s *mihun tang*, a soup which erases all memories a person has.[26] And if it is the case of the sins of others, we ostracize them, we wish to have nothing at all to do with them.

The Pharisees are the classic case of alienation. They were so alienated from themselves that they did not even see the sins they themselves were culpable of. The psychological defense or coping mechanism worked so well, was so ingrained in them, that they completely blotted out all memory of their own sins and lived their lives criticizing and condemning others.

To enable themselves to more effectively forget their sins and flaws, the Pharisees resorted to the psychological shield of religiosity. They took great pride in their religious practices. They made much of the fact that they were careful to observe these practices to a tee to keep themselves ritually clean.

Now rituals are not bad things in and of themselves. But, like all good things, they are susceptible to being perverted to become something they are not. For instance, a ritual does not make anyone righteous, nor does not participating in a specific ritual make a person sinful. The Pharisees perpetrated the terrible mistake of seeing God as a pedant, a higher authority solely concerned with correct ritual performance rather than a divine authority concerned to promote morality and humanity among people.

---

26. Colville, "Meng Po."

If the first way of dealing with sin is the way of alienation, the second way is that of extenuation. A person who practices extenuation gives themselves excuses for the sins they commit or that others commit. They tend to highlight that their personal circumstances make it difficult if not impossible for them to avoid sinning. An abusive person may point out that their inability to manage or hold down their anger is something that has become natural to them and so others should just accept it. Another example is an indulgent or permissive parent for whom a child can do no wrong.

A third way is that of resignation or license. Someone who takes this option tells themselves the struggle against sin is so hard that perhaps the best way to move forward is to simply accept that things will always remain this way. They give up the fight against sin. They might even claim that it is not necessary to try too hard since God forgives all sins, that it is alright to sin so long as one confesses in the end. Of course, this is a misrepresentation of God's grace. God is not looking for our confession per se. God is looking for a heart that sincerely desires to live righteously by confronting sin and doing something about it, on a consistent basis.

Unfortunately, the three methods of dealing with our sinful acts we have considered earlier do not actually work. Denial or ostracization does not remove sin, nor does extenuating our actions, or trying to live with them.

So how do we deal with sins, whether those in our own lives or those in the lives of others? Jesus said, "I [that is, God] desire mercy, and not sacrifice." (Matt 9:13 ESV) Mercy here is the English translation of a Greek word, *eleos*, which means mercy, clemency, compassion, or pity (Gingrich). This statement is a citation from the book of Hosea (6:6), which records prophecies made seven centuries before Jesus' birth.

Here, Jesus teaches us to extend mercy both to ourselves as well as others. Unlike the ways of alienation, extenuation, and resignation or license, the way of mercy does not try to deal with sin by avoiding it, excusing it, or letting it be. Mercy does not create a circle around our sinful acts or those of others which it allows us to leave untouched. It does not deprive us of our personal responsibility for our moral actions. It does not let us give up on ourselves as people meant to live a righteous and good life.

Even though mercy does not take the easy way out, it also does not beat ourselves or others up for not doing enough to combat sin. It does not adopt the approach characterizing the crusader, which is yet another harmful way of dealing with sin, where we attack ourselves or others for not being good enough.

Instead, mercy is patient with ourselves and patient with others.[27] Make no mistake. Patience is not an effort to skirt the issue of sin. It holds the problem before us, but it knows that we are frail and brittle beings who need time and lots of sensitive care before we are able to reach our moral goals. Nor does patience downplay our responsibility for our sins. It knows where it wants to go; it is clear and uncompromising about its moral objectives. So there is no watering down of sin here.

Nor does patience resign itself to sin or give itself license to sin. It does not accept the status quo or assume that things will always be the way they are, much less that God's grace gives us license to sin. On the contrary, it hopes in God's work through the support God gives us in various ways. It looks to the renewed self of a new creation and does not give up so easily on self or others.

A common misunderstanding is that by making it so easy for us to be forgiven, God does not really care about the way we lead our lives. God does care about our moral lives. The Father sent the Son, Jesus, to die on the cross just so we can be purchased by his blood to live in a way distinguished by our piety and morality.[28] Therefore, sin is an issue that we have to deal with continuously. We will fall at times, and when that happens, God provides a way for us to be forgiven through the cross. Even if we seem to be making little progress in our lives, even if people around us are caught in some sin, we should never give up praying and seeking solutions both for ourselves and others.

Prayer enables us to see new vistas of moral possibility whether for ourselves or those around us. It allows us to put aside our agony

---

27. The patience advocated here is worlds away from a brand of insecure impatience where a parent in playing an educational role treats a child in an instrumental way, as a means to advance or maintain their own success, assessed by the norms of society, in the eyes of others. Such a parent may embark on something as praiseworthy as spiritual or emotional guidance of the child with numerous expectations and neglect to observe that child's interest in the subject while dampening the latter's enthusiasm with those demands. This is a potent combination which leads to a vicious cycle where the parent experiences disappointment with the child and the latter resentment toward the former. It ought also to be mentioned that parents that seek to guide their children emotionally doom their efforts to failure by omitting to exemplify the calm and composure they desire of their children in the very tone and diction they use to correct their children. Cf. Arky, "Calm Voices, Calmer Kids."

28. That morally acceptable behavior is at the core of the Christian message can be gathered from the way in which Jesus was said to preach about repentance (Matt 4:17), as was John the Baptist (Matt 3:1–12), and St. Paul (Acts 26:19–20).

about our own sinfulness and bitterness regarding the sins of others, because we know that change is ultimately possible, because we are not in this alone; God is with us and we have God's help. It does not matter how long the struggle against sin finally takes; all that matters is that we do not ever give up and that we take the way of mercy and patience towards ourselves as well as others.

In our struggle against sin, it is crucial to secure clarity about why we think, believe, or behave in certain ways. Only when we understand the deep emotional roots of our thoughts, beliefs, and recurrent behaviors can we attain the freedom to think differently about ourselves and give up unhealthy patterns of thought, belief, and action, so as to embrace healthier ones. Ask God for revelation about yourself in these respects. By all means, avail also of professional counseling, which is very beneficial for bringing clarity.

We need to bear in mind that we are all sick in some way, and Jesus comes as our physician. We are sick as sinners, and God is in the business of making us healthy as righteous people. God desires not our ritual observances but our merciful attitude towards ourselves and one another as we struggle against the problem of sin. In conclusion, religiosity allows sin to hold sway by giving up the struggle, whereas piety faces sin with mercy, patiently making efforts, finding solutions, and committing the struggle into God's hands.

Is it possible to show that you do not accept a person's bad or harmful behavior (not amounting to a distinct threat to one's fundamental emotional wellbeing or physical safety) without being unwilling to forgive them, that is, choose not to hold any grudges toward them or bear any prejudice against them, even without ceasing to love them? Yes, we register our moral disapproval of their actions by verbally and clearly expressing our stand, regardless of how the other party receives the sharing of our perspective, whether they accept or reject it, attempt to exculpate themselves, or even minimize the harm they have done. While highlighting that we forgive them and choose not to hold any grudges or bear any prejudice against them, that we do or still love them and are concerned for their ultimate wellbeing, we do not slip into a gullible mode of trusting that they have truly repented when it is unclear that that has transpired, but discern how we should maintain a relationship of any sort with them.

Pity or compassion alone will enable us to put aside our grudges and resentment toward those whom we perceive to have hurt us in some way. It was on account that Jesus saw that the crowds that came toward him for ministry seemed to be harried, powerless, and without a gentle and caring fatherly protector that he had compassion on them and taught them, proclaimed the gospel to them, and cured their illnesses and encumbrances (Matt 9:35–38). Likewise, the Lord was able to extend forgiveness toward those who crucified him (Luke 23:34), whether this be the soldiers, religious leaders, or political authorities, simply because he saw that they were ignorant of the gravity of what they were doing to him, as a result of which they lived and languished in the darkness of their sinfulness, depravity, and wickedness (1 Cor 2:6–8; v. 6 highlighting that the authorities of the present age at the time were certain to cease to exist).

Doctrinal Formulation: Perfection through Divine Work as Human Capacitation

God guides humankind into moral and spiritual perfection and sinlessness through human moral proactivity rather than passivity. The scourge of ritualism in soteriology, in which a person erroneously espouses that ritual provides a shield by which to ward off divine wrath or attain divine good pleasure, is wholly overcome in a biblical conception of God's work in human perfection where solely the penitent and repentant sinner is forgiven through the blood of Christ and set free for a renewed life in imitation of Christ in which God accompanies the believer in investigating and treating the disorders of emotion and thought that result from past traumatic experiences of subjection to neglect or abuse. More than that, a second scourge, this time of an understanding of divine election which eventuates in othering, is surmounted in the enlightened grasp of the insincerity undergirding such ostensibly humble conceptions of one's self in light of the divine privilege and immunity that one stands to gain from them.

Ritualism in soteriology

Ritualism is defined as an excessive or extreme preoccupation with or dependence upon the punctilious or proper observance of religious ceremonies and practices; it is often allied to an erroneous conception of faith and God.

PART 2: HUMANITY'S IMAGING OF THE DIVINE

The sixteenth-century Protestant reformer Martin Luther is an instructive study in this regard. He came from a traumatic childhood during which he was repeatedly abused by his father and teachers. In consequence of his difficult formative years, he projected onto God the cruel and punitive nature of his father and teachers and felt that he was incapable of fully obeying God in a manner God would deem worthy and unable to love God from his heart.

Feeling inadequate, Luther turned to good works and penance, the latter entailing, during the late Middle Ages, a feeling of contrition or sorrow for one's sins, confession before a priest, and doing all that the priest required in the way of works of satisfaction or punishment as a means of purification. While minor sins could be purified in purgatory, Luther was especially scrupulous and sought to call to mind all his sins and make appropriate penance for them. This mentality left him feeling anxious whenever he recalled a sin he did not make penance for, not to mention his keen sense that sin was deeper than thought and action, touching on the condition of the human heart.[29]

What Luther did not recognize there and then was that God had no interest in menacing and punishing him for thoughts and feelings over which he had no control, sinful or wrong though they were, nor was God watching him like a hawk to see just where he would fail to catalogue some sin so that God could subject him to punishment. The idea of God as wrathful was encouraged by pre-scientific reflection on waves of plague that held Europe in their thrall during the late Middle Ages. Such a conception of God as an angry judge was exacerbated in Luther's mind and emotions by his unfortunate and tragic experiences under the draconian hands of his father and teachers.

Even in the case of a person like Luther, there may be observed a turn to ritualism. The doctrine for which Luther is known, justification by faith, is essentially a means by which to temporarily ignore or put aside the pressing issues of internal morality by recourse to the notion that God has conferred Christ's righteousness upon the believer along with the conviction that any sin that remains in a person will be gradually dealt with through the sanctifying action of the Holy Spirit as the believer cooperates with the Spirit in reverent obedience.

All this is believed to take place at the point of the sinner's prayer, where a person acknowledges themselves as sinners in need of God's

---

29. González, *Reformation to Present*, 22–24; Missouri State University, "Medieval Era."

grace, publicly professes their faith that Jesus died in atonement of their sins so that they may be adopted as God's children through being indwelled with the Holy Spirit, and identifies themselves as Christians, to be baptized at a later date. Notwithstanding the popularity of this view, salvation in biblical teaching is not synonymous with the observance of a religious ritual such as the sinner's prayer or with being part of a particular religious community or organization.

Salvation is an internal process by which we turn from a way of sin to the way of righteousness for which we are predestined. This process is ultimately possible only on the basis of the moral nature with which we have been created. It begins with our realization of wrongdoing which, if we are theists, may be accompanied by a confession of sin before God, is followed by our God-given ability to forgive ourselves on the basis of our pre-human experience of God's compassion and, if we are Christians, the atoning act of Christ on the cross as our substitute. The process is concluded and continued in a changed and transformed life, adhering to the good moral values inherent in our God-given human nature with its moral desires, though obscured at times by certain disordered ways of thinking, feeling, and acting or, if we are Christians, obeying the teachings of God and Christ as well as emulating their moral example. By its very nature, salvation as understood in these terms is open to Christians as well as people of other faith traditions and none.

For those without a clear foundation in broader doctrine, the doctrine of justification by faith constitutes a form of pseudo-pious procrastination that is more likely to engender indifference to one's habitual sins and condition of heart than cultivate an urgency to attend to these issues, given the constant temptation to be self-justifying. Despite the evangelical emphasis on the necessity of good works in the life of the believer in confirmation of their election by God, one may be easily deluded into imagining that Christ's sufficiency dictates that people do nothing at all requiring of their initiative and effort in terms of their sanctification.

As a matter of fact, the sinner's prayer has come to serve as an instrument affording false consolation and hope in a mistaken ritualistic understanding of faith. Instead of properly and rightfully examining our hearts, minds, and lives with the purpose of amending our way of living, we presume it suffices for us to think back to that one time in our lives when we prayed to receive Jesus as our Lord and Savior, assuming that

God will do everything necessary and effective to purify us and take us to our heavenly abode by the end of our lives.

While it is true that we can be assured of forgiveness in Christ when we come before God with penitent and repentant hearts (and of being indwelled by the Holy Spirit when we seek that indwelling for the very first time in the context of such a prayer of repentance), there is no scriptural support for the theory that the first time we did so, God has conferred on us an external and ironclad righteousness that we can never lose, even if it is supposed that this has to be confirmed by good works.[30]

This is a misunderstanding of the righteousness that God reveals in Christ which, as God's righteousness or righteous standard for our emulation, is God's potent display of compassion and grace toward sinners rather than simply punishing them (Rom 1:16–17; 3:21–28).

An idea of a conferred righteousness involves an inability to understand that those who choose to trust that God is able to freely justify the sinner through atoning for their sins can be said to be acting righteously or in line with what is moral or good (Rom 4:5).

It entails a failure to see how law and faith are constantly opposed in Paul's writings as referring, in the case of the former, to a life lived boasting of one's religious deeds apart from God's help and, in that of the latter, to a life lived in the clear knowledge that one is a moral being whose moral nature and desires are from God (they have God's law written upon their

---

30. In Barth, *KD* IV.2, §68.2 (ET, Bromiley, pp. 775-76) may be found a classical statement of such a theory of a divine shield afforded to those who entrust themselves in a believing fidelity defined primarily, essentially, and more by intellectual or cognitive assent and emotional affect than the conative result that concrete internal change and external action constitute, seeing that in numerous cases or even the paradigmatic instance, a person will seem helpless to be transformed, according to a misinterpretation of Rom 7:13-25, especially the last couple of verses. Here the Christian fights an endless battle against the sinful principle by which they do what they do not desire to perform in an almost passive way, simply holding the fort and doing their utmost to fend off the invasions by temptation of the soul which inevitably bring the psyche to near ruination, whilst awaiting the advent of the renewing and metamorphic power of the Lord. For how else are we to apprehend the Swiss theologian's assertion to the effect that the New Testament differs from the Old in that in the former God is said in the atonement of Jesus Christ to have already won the victory over human sin, that judgment will no longer follow grace; curse, blessing; abasing, lifting up; striking, restoring; and putting to death, raising to new life, where all the judgment that God might have reason to mete out upon humankind has been fully carried away by the Son through his death by crucifixion in satisfaction to God on behalf of transgressive humankind so that all that remains to be done in regard to resolving human sin is to proclaim this fact of the atonement of Christ and presumably the need to give assent and credence to it?

hearts as well as the faculty of a conscience) and that one is therefore to live for the glory of God in this sense (Rom 2:12–16; Phil 3:9).

Furthermore, the notion of a conferment of an external righteousness is tied to an inability to recognize that we will be made (Rom 5:19) or have the opportunity to become (2 Cor 5:21) righteous in or through Christ and that Christ is our righteousness (1 Cor 1:30) in the sense that Christ lived his life in such a way that it constitutes a moral example for us (as our righteousness or standard for a righteous life), which we will be able to emulate through sincere commitment in harnessing the good moral desires God has placed in each of us and identifying, understanding, and tending to the emotional roots of our disordered ways of thinking, feeling, and acting.

If the Pharisees, oblivious as they were to their internal and external sins in contrast to Luther, looked to the Mosaic law and the traditions of their elders as a ritualistic tool to assure themselves of deliverance in the afterlife through receiving circumcision (for males) and repenting of sinful actions through keeping various religious regulations and having resort to provisions for divine forgiveness through prayer, fasting, and giving of alms, evangelicals exalt their personal confession of faith in Christ, contingent on their continued or at least present believing, as the sufficient condition of their salvation in Christ.[31] The problem consists in a misunderstanding of God as a punitive judge, a divine being only too ready and quick to scrutinize the human heart, mind, and life for any failing so as to fling people into hellfire.

God is not our enemy but our chief ally when it comes to our attempts to mend our ways. This means that there is no need to fear divine disapproval at the early stage of finding out that we are caught in some condition of sin, but seek God for ways to address these internal issues.[32] If God is in the business of healing our souls, we can trust that God will come alongside us in our personal journey to unearth the reasons we feel or think a certain negative way about God, ourselves, or other persons rather than simplistically attributing our sinful condition

---

31. Morris, *Matthew*, 52n9; 59n35. The obverse of an excessive frightfulness of God in viewing God as a punitive authority is a presumptuous attitude, dictating that God is obliged to recognize and reward every pious act or good work, failing to understand that piety and goodness are part of who we are and what we do as human beings, rather than external favors we do for God.

32. In the case of non-theists, they have recourse to the study of human psychology from a holistic angle, taking into account the role of trauma in shaping the persons they have become.

to an act of disobedience on the part of Adam and thinking no further about the question.

As a matter of fact, God is ready to follow us as we search our lives, from the time of earliest childhood, for clues as to how the ways in which we may have been and felt dominated in the past led us to our present state of instinctively seeking to dominate others or be content with our being mistreated by others.[33] We need not discount the benefits of secular professional therapy in aiding efforts to arrive at greater self-clarity.

The major error lies in seeing Christ as a God-given shield against God's wrath. There is no scriptural warrant for such a viewpoint. In the two passages in the New Testament that directly link Jesus' work with averting the wrath of God, namely, Rom 5:9 and 1 Thess 1:10, the process of salvation from the coming divine wrath made possible through Jesus is given a future tense in the former (*sōthēsometha*, from *sōzō*) and his work of deliverance from the coming wrath is in the present tense in the latter (*rhuomenon*, from *rhuomai*), both instances indicating that the work of salvation and deliverance through Christ is not complete at the point of conversion.

While the passage in Romans (2:1–11) is the locus classicus for the perspective that God judges all who commit sin, believer or not, the Epistle to the Hebrews supports the same argument. The people of God are compared to the generation of Israel who made a habit of rebelling against God in the wilderness (Heb 3:7–19; see v. 8). Believers are to admonish each other on a daily basis not to be hardened in sin through the deceitfulness of the devil (v. 13).[34]

Similarly, believers who show contempt toward the atoning work of the Son of God by leading worthless rather than useful lives will be destroyed with fire (Heb 6:4–8; see v. 8). Christians are in no position to indulge in sin but should wait only for divine judgment if they continue in it (Heb 10:26–31). There is no sacrifice that avails for those who sin intentionally, given that Christ did not die in atonement so that people can sin with impunity (v. 26).

Christians are not to despise the correction of the Lord in their struggle against other sinners, seeing that Christ himself set them an

---

33. Chua, *ECRST*, 15.

34. The devil has the ability to completely lull a person into accommodating sin through a stepwise and gradual fashion, persuading them that no harm can be done. The devil can also foster unrealistic expectations about how a person can change their physical appearance and nurse in them a desperate desire to do so.

example in displaying forbearance towards those who opposed and persecuted him, even giving himself up to death at the hands of wicked people (Heb 12:2–17; see v. 3).

They are to bear in mind that when God fails to mollycoddle believers who are confronted with a situation in which they are mistreated by sinners but instead chides and even punishes them for holding grudges against others, sexual immorality, and unholiness (perhaps in a situation where one is tempted by one's opponents to barter one's position of faith for temporary pleasure as Esau was by Jacob; vv. 14–17), this is only because they are the legitimate children of God (vv. 5–11).[35]

In relation to the question of right and wrong feeling, attitude, and behavior, Christ gives us nothing more or less than the right teaching as to sin and righteousness, an inspiring personal example of righteousness, and an assurance that God forgives those among us who repent of our sins. Christ does not shield us from our path to moral reformation; on the contrary, his atoning act makes it possible for us to always pick ourselves up when we fall, knowing that with God it is never too late to make amends.

God is angered only to an understandable and reasonable degree. In other words, God does not subject us to wrath on account of things over which we have no control, such as sinful thoughts and feelings, though not intent. There is divine anger only for those who consciously and willfully choose the path of non-repentance after having come to a knowledge of their sin.

What, then, is salvation if it does not involve a believer being given some form of permanent protection against God's wrath through the atoning act of Christ? In the first place, salvation cannot consist in any defense against God, even from God, since God's character is completely expressed in that which salvation represents. There is no former or more primitive logical stage of God's relationship to humankind in which only divine wrath is manifested toward the latter. But when God forgives sins and chooses to always forgive them, it is akin to when Jesus publicly absolved the paralytic of sins (Mark 2:5)—that is, both the Father and the Son began always from a place and position of mercy and forgiveness, without any need to somehow metaphysically resolve an inherent wrath against sinners so as to thereby demonstrate compassion and love.

---

35. Cockerill, *Hebrews*, 638–39.

The reason why this is so is that there is not a metaphysical phenomenon that interposes itself between God and God's loving relationship with humankind. Original sin is not such a deep-seated and irremovable problem that it is impossible for God to reach out in any loving way toward humanity. There is not an utter corruption of the human will on the level of essential substance or nature which would validate complete divine repulsion. There is genuine evil, to be sure, that arises from wicked intent conspiring with some disordered way of thinking or feeling to bring about evil actions, that affects all human individuals to varying degrees. Be that as it may, God's grace is such that the human will has been preserved in its free character in spite of the abuse of freewill in intending, planning, and carrying out evil, despite its contortion and distortion through the traumatic experience of domination.[36]

As for the signification of salvation, this primarily indicates the certain assurance of divine forgiveness through the atoning act of Jesus Christ at his crucifixion. The locus of the Christian notion of salvation is not to be found on the existential level for the human individual, such that a person may be said to be saved either once for all time or on multiple occasions. Rather, salvation is the opportunity from God, made available once for all time through Christ, for each person to receive the certainty that God absolves them of all their sins, no matter how grievous, the unforgivable sin being what it is only on account that it removes every possibility of being assured of God's forgiveness through Christ. One may not be capable of receiving salvation on more than one occasion, but a person is able to be assured of the single act of salvation—performed as it is once for all time at Golgotha at one particular point

---

36. For a modern development of the classical doctrine of original sin, see Chua, *ECRST*, 248–74. It is well to observe that a Reformed conception of sinfulness lends impetus to a certain scepticism and pitilessness towards an individual in a time of internal struggle. Consider the following example: a person finds themselves unable to overcome a repetitive thought, feeling, and desire adjudged to be sinful and in consequence manifests that thought, feeling, and desire in the form of a corresponding action. Suppose the individual in question understands that that thought, feeling, desire, and action are wrong. Yet, in a classical Reformed view, it is common to assume that one who is unable to overcome sinful thought, feeling, desire, and action is nothing other than unregenerate and only Christian in name. Given the doctrine of original sin, it is asserted that an unregenerate individual is captive to sin in such a way that they wholly desire to sin and, even if they appear to be penitent, regret arises only on account of fear of continued social alienation or of professional consequences rather than on account of the sin itself. For this reason, the primary approach that might be taken by a Christian community based on such assumptions about the individual will be a punitive one.

in time in first-century Judea—and its singular or remarkable impact on their soul, at more than one time.

Salvation naturally results in good works, as the atonement of Christ removes the colossal obstacle of a sense of God's rejection in the mind of the person who, having been with all other individuals created in God's moral image, seeks to express the good desires of their heart in agreement with an implicit moral vision and goal. While faith as an internal personal decision to trust in God is to be distinguished from good works, it is never devoid of those works in the sense of being capable of existing in the absence of good works. This is for the very fact that faith is inseparable from the divine act of salvation, being trust that God has indeed counted Christ's crucifixion as a propitiatory sacrifice for the forgiveness of our sins as we seek it in penitence and repentance.

Rather than to provide a divine shield against God's wrath or enable us to have something about which to boast before God, rituals are given only to help us gain a glimpse of the character of God and express our heartfelt thanksgiving and praise unto God amid the many confusions and distractions of the world. For that reason, rituals can be abandoned in exceptional cases where to follow a particular ritual would violate God's desire for us based on our knowledge of God's character given through Jesus. Therefore Jesus approved of Sabbath laws being set aside to address issues of hunger or the need for healing.

According to Barth, Jesus did not simply die in our place, procuring from the Father a forgiving disposition toward and the Father's actual forgiveness of our sins, but he also rose, ascended, and sat down at the right hand of the Father in our place, presumably procuring from the Father an approving disposition toward and the Father's actual approval of us as our head and Lord, so that, seemingly, for all intents and purposes, all humankind, regardless of whether they know him and as low as they may be morally or spiritually speaking, are elected in him to certain salvation, reconciliation, and redemption.

As a matter of fact, Jesus' substitution of all humankind on the cross and in exaltation as the new man has engendered a state of affairs in which all human beings have already become regenerate and may know and declare themselves to be such, and all humankind has already been reconciled to God in a fixed manner and it is merely for all people to accept the message of themselves as sinners reconciled to God in Christ through the latter's atonement on behalf of their sins, and take comfort and joy in the fact that they have already been reconciled to

God, adopted as children of God's and sanctified, through the victory, substitution, and intervention of Christ.

Through formulating Barth's doctrine of the death and resurrection of Christ, we espy a certain asymmetry. Existentially, Christ is sinless though not in being without a sinful nature (which in fact he has assumed in his redemptive capacity) but in forbidding both the desire and act of sin; legally, he has taken on the guilt of the sins of the entire world as his own. Ontologically, we are sinful; legally, we died with Christ and we are exonerated of sin and regarded as having never sinned. Existentially, Christ condescended in taking on the status of a servant and was exalted upon offering a perfect atonement for humankind in receiving resurrection and the status of a glorified human being seated at the right hand of the Father. Ontologically, we remain on earth working out our salvation and sanctification with a certainty in Christ's resurrection and exaltation of hope of divine glory; legally, we have been resurrected, ascended, and are seated with Christ.[37]

Called as we are as believers to partake in the divine nature by embracing in our character God's glory and excellence or moral virtue, that is, God's being as truthfulness, irreproachability, righteousness, innocence, agreeableness, reputability, virtue, and every other praiseworthy quality (Phil 4:8) such as faith, wisdom, self-mastery, longsuffering, piety, kinship-like affection, and love (2 Pet 1:3–11), we are to pursue good works mirroring those attributes not out of a fear that if we fail to do so God would finally consign us to hell and damnation, but simply out of the awareness that we as God's children are summoned to lead lives that are worthy of our heavenly vocation and spiritual identity.

Doing so in increasing measure keeps us from being or becoming ineffective or unfruitful believers who have lost sight of the high goal for which we have been cleansed from our former sinful way of life, furnishes us with confirmation of our calling and election, keeps us from falling, and affords us a rich source of confidence that we will indeed be welcomed into the kingdom of our Lord and Savior Jesus Christ.[38]

---

37. Barth, *KD* IV.1, 61.2 (ET, Bromiley, pp. 555–56); Barth, *KD* IV.2, §64.2 (ET, Bromiley, pp. 92–93); Barth, *KD* IV.2, §64.4 (ET, Bromiley, pp. 316–18); Barth, *KD* IV.2, §65.1 (ET, Bromiley, pp. 379, 382–83, 395–97); Barth, *KD* IV.2, §66.6 (ET, Bromiley, p. 600).

38. It is possible that a person who has thought of themselves as a believer might discover that they have not actually been saved by divine grace in finding themselves falling (as in this passage) or, as in the parable of the wedding feast (Matt 22:1–14) or of the talents (Matt 25:14–30), being cast out into an outer darkness inhabited by those

Ultimately, therefore, according to biblical teaching, it appears that we are reconciled to God and redeemed through a self-identification that proves its authenticity by means of concrete attitudes and actions: our self-identification as sinners who died with Christ on the cross in his atoning act; our self-identification as children of God the Father adopted through our self-identification as sinners for whom Christ died; and our self-identification as those in whom God the Holy Spirit dwells akin to the way God inhabited Solomon's temple through our self-identification as children of God the Father adopted through our self-identification as sinners for whom Christ died.

No room is left with this threefold self-identification relating to each of the members of the Holy Trinity for spiritual complacency given the necessity for a self-identification to be matched with a corresponding attitude and behavior. The one who claims benefit from Christ's work of atonement cannot continue to live in sin since they are only reconciled to God through having died with him on the cross. This is a legal truth. It is also to be an existential truth, a truth that involves the entirety of the believer's being.

A person who truly believes that they have already died with Christ on the cross of Calvary simply cannot persist in the ways they used to live while they were still independent of and separate from Christ (Rom 6:1–14). Similarly, one truly of the conviction that they are adopted children of God the Father will not continue flagrantly in sinful acts but pursue a life full of righteousness and love for others (1 John 3:1–10). Finally, a person who sincerely believes that they have been indwelled by the Holy Spirit will not be able to bring themselves to foment or accept division in the church, which is commonly indwelled by the same one Holy Spirit, or engage in sexual immorality, seeing that they have become one spirit with the Lord and therefore received God's Spirit into their physical body (1 Corinthians 3; 6:12–20).

---

filled with the sadness or anger of regret, revealing that they have voided the calling and election which characterizes all believers and necessarily produces good moral fruit. Although many are called (that is, given an opportunity to be saved), few are chosen (that is, take up that opportunity), as per Matt 22:14. Consequently, believers are to concretize their salvation with God's hortatory help in the context of a deterrent consciousness of the frightful repercussions of not having done so, arising not from any desire to preclude God's anger but rather eschatological regret of not having harnessed earthly potentiality to lay hold of an eternal prize (Phil 2:12). Cf. Barth, *KD* IV.3.1, 69.2 (ET, Bromiley, pp. 72–79).

PART 2: HUMANITY'S IMAGING OF THE DIVINE

Karl Barth is of the view that sanctification is a process initiated and carried through by God that is efficacious in all people, not just elect Christian believers, one which will only be completed and manifest in the coming to faith of all people in the eschaton.[39] He draws an analogy between the idea of justification, as popularized by Martin Luther, as entailing God conferring an alien righteousness on the human being and that of sanctification, whereby, if we dare complete the analogy, God confers an alien holiness on the human being, a legal state which continues irrespective of their actual moral behavior, akin to how justification ensures that a person is declared to be without guilt. Barth may very well be thinking, in relation to both justification and sanctification, in terms of a permanent possession, granted by God's action through Jesus in atoning for our sins, of a legal positional and moral standing which can never be annulled and, therefore, of where the human being, post-crucifixion, stands vis-à-vis the possibility of the wrath of God.

This possibility may not exist in truth or reality, as far as God's economy is concerned, though it may absurdly persist in the realm of human subjectivity and human affairs, where a person may continue to fear the wrath of God on account of how their moral conduct may not hold up to divine scrutiny, or live in ignorance of what Christ has achieved for them and, consequently, with irreverence, ingratitude, disobedience, anger, jealousy, envy, covetousness, perversity, profligacy, dissolution, depravity and all manner of other sins, absurd perceptions and behaviors which have no ramifications, even while on earth, on God's favorable disposition toward all humankind, having been bought and atoned for by Christ, and which will slowly die and finally drop off in eternity.[40] In contrast to a universal effective predestination, Calvin's conception of a double predestination implies that God makes a choice of whom to elect and save in a manner that cannot be humanly comprehended and even one that may be described as not following any logical pattern.[41]

What sets God apart from mere human beings; that is, from individuals who conceive of themselves and who function in a purely or significantly individualistic, reductionistic, materialistic, jejune, and therefore

---

39. This concrete sanctification of Christians is already achieved by Christ though not as possessed by believers in the here and now but as yet hidden in Christ. *KD* IV.2, §67.2 (ET, Bromiley, pp. 647, 651–53).

40. *KD* IV.2, §67.1 (ET, Bromiley, p. 620). Barth holds that the sanctification of all has been assured by legal right through the work of Jesus Christ.

41. *KD* IV.2, §66.2 (ET, Bromiley, pp. 513–33).

inhuman (in the sense of non-human) way? The fact alone that God is no recluse in self-comfort and indifference toward the wider world beyond the self, but travels experientially without Godself, immigrating to the emotional, intellectual, conative, and social worlds especially of those caught in some form of dire need, whether it be economic destitution, physical or emotional oppression, social-based self-devaluation, or even psychological despair of hope in one's life. It is to this that every human person is called by God in harmony with the nature of their being.

Divine election and othering

In a Reformed theological system, humankind came to be rejected by God not because they have no inherent value but because the sinful nature they have inherited from Adam, consisting as it does in a constant desire to live in opposition to God and that which God desires for humankind, is something a just God can never accept. Humankind has become so utterly corrupted that they can desire nothing good. Under these circumstances, there is no injustice in divine rejection of any or even all persons, and the election of a limited number of individuals is rightly seen as a great bonus arising from God's tremendous benevolence.

While we do not gainsay that God rejects sinful behavior and judges those who do not ultimately repent of their wickedness, we maintain that humankind has not become so corrupted that they can make no right or virtuous choice. There is indeed a principle of corruption and wickedness in human beings, yet this is not some spiritual factor which can only be removed without our participation.

Instead, by reason of having experienced subjection to domination at some early stage in their lives, since the age of Adam, human beings have entered a state of psychological disorder in which violence and domination seems to them to be most necessary to protect themselves from further harm. So long as they fail to recognize their condition of psychological disorder, these individuals will ever encounter powerful temptations to sin against others by attempting to dominate or abuse them. Yet, even in such a situation, a person does not lose the ability to choose against following the tide of their passions.

Some may wonder if this constitutes a type of Pelagianism. It does not, on the ground that whereas Pelagianism contends for an inherent human ability to resist evil and choose the good, without necessity for the operation of divine grace, we maintain, however, that nothing within a human person that desires or enables them to choose the good is devoid of divine grace, the ability to recognize, desire, and actualize morality being posited by the Divine Nature and the development of this ability inspired or stimulated by the Trinity in the pre-incarnate state of humankind.

Those who hold that God sovereignly elects some to salvation and others to reprobation, not on the basis of any moral considerations in which only the unrepentant wicked are eventually judged and rejected but of God's inscrutable choice alone, are more likely to view those different from them (whether in terms of religious or even denominational affiliation) in stark and negative terms: the religious and denominational other is judged to be without any or real merit or virtue. They are wrong whereas the electionist Christian groups are right. They are blind while the electionist Christian groups alone have true sight.[42]

Such groups do this without realizing that all they have really been up to has been to draw hard lines and boundaries between themselves and others. The only thing that distinguishes such groups from others is the idea of distinction from all other groups, the belief that out of all people in the world, they alone have been selected by God. This is not a difficult doctrine to accept given that they are ultimately not the ones who are in danger of being damned.

To make such a discriminatory—not to mention invidious—view more acceptable, it is commonly allied with the notion that it is God alone who made the choice of selecting these groups rather than anyone else, and that it is not a question of what makes a person fit to be chosen but purely God's choice, based as it is not on one's merit but God's grace which confers God's virtues on people where they previously lacked any virtue.

They devise a self-validating theory of God's choice of them above others, and their acceptance of such divine choice, as a sign of God's favor and intervention in their lives since, as it is suggested, no sinful human being in their pridefulness could ever bring themselves to concede that they contribute nothing to their own salvation conceived in terms of an acceptance that all is from God and none from them.

This, in fact, is a very small price to pay for a badge of honor and privilege that sets them above the rest of the world as a specially favored people. It is a small expression of apparent humility in return

---

42. Barth, *KD* IV.2, §64.4 (ET, Bromiley, p. 313).

for permanent privilege and glory, having no connection whatsoever to their moral selves or status since it is false humility or humility resorted to as an instrument to gain great glory and exaltation.[43] And the sinful, calculating, and shrewd mind knows this.

Having spoken at length about the deficiencies of other systems, it is meet to discuss the question of the extent to which it is congruent with biblical counsel to assess other schools of thought in this way, given that the Lord himself explicitly instructed his disciples not to judge others (Matt 7:1–5). It is important to understand that the Lord was not asking that his followers do not exercise their ability to distinguish between morality and immorality (1 Cor 2:15) but rather that they are not to do this on the supposition that they are somehow morally better than others but with the humble apprehension that they, too, are subject to sin and moral corruption (Matt 7:5).[44]

Even if a person is indeed, in moral terms, ahead of another individual, this need not occasion arrogance, since each individual is created with the same moral capacity, albeit this might be temporarily obscured by some disorder of thinking or feeling; it is incumbent on each person to choose to obey God fully as their due so that the personal choice to abide by the commandments of God cannot be strictly considered as a meritorious act which God is bound to repay; and each individual receives their capacity to develop the ability to recognize, desire, and actualize various facets of morality from God alone, as well as has the development of that ability stimulated by God alone.

---

43. Humility has long been an issue in the Christian church. During the period of the Great Awakening in the 1730s and 1740s, radical revivalist preachers such as George Whitefield, Gilbert Tennent, and James Davenport took it upon themselves to raise doubts about the conversion status of established ministers, with Davenport going so far as to identify ministers he suspected of not being converted, provoking church splits and dividing revivalists and antirevivalists as a whole. If they had only pursued a more dialogical rather than antagonistic way of helping their ministerial colleagues or equivalents in the various churches grow deeper in their spirituality, if need be, the unfortunate situation could have been avoided. Kidd, *Great Awakening*, 14.

44. We tend to judge others because of a failure to understand their circumstances sufficiently so as to allow us to view their actions through a more gracious lens. In contrast, we tend to be far more lenient with ourselves, on account that we do grasp our personal situations rather well. The reason we fail to understand others is that we do not make an attempt to do so. This, in turn, may be due to our entertaining some prejudice towards them, which serves to reinforce the judgmentalism to which we subject others.

Works Cited

"Daniel: Chapter 7." *The Complete Jewish Bible with Rashi Commentary.* Chabad.org. https://www.chabad.org/library/bible_cdo/aid/16490/showrashi/true/jewish/Chapter-7.htm.

Allyn, Rachel. "The Important Difference between Emotions and Feelings." *Psychology Today.* February 23, 2022. Sussex Publishers. https://www.psychologytoday.com/sg/blog/the-pleasure-is-all-yours/202202/the-important-difference-between-emotions-and-feelings.

Amaechina, Oscar. "Why Mature Christians Rarely Experience Miracles." *The Christian Post.* July 25, 2024. https://www.christianpost.com/voices/why-mature-christians-rarely-experience-miracles.html.

American Psychiatric Association. "What Is Depression?" *American Psychiatric Association.* https://www.psychiatry.org/patients-families/depression/what-is-depression.

Amodeo, John. "A Sneaky Obstacle That Undermines Our Well-Being." *Psychology Today.* July 3, 2022. Sussex Publishers. https://www.psychologytoday.com/intl/blog/intimacy-path-toward-spirituality/202207/sneaky-obstacle-undermines-our-well-being.

Anderson, James N. "Why Did God Allow the Fall?" *The Gospel Coalition.* 27 June 2017. https://www.thegospelcoalition.org/article/why-did-god-allow-the-fall.

Andrews, Edward D. "Unveiling the Truth: The Authenticity of Codex Sinaiticus—A 19th Century Forgery?" *Christian Publishing House Blog.* Accessed February 18, 2025. https://christianpublishinghouse.co/2023/07/19/unveiling-the-truth-the-authenticity-of-codex-sinaiticus-a-19th-century-forgery.

Ansari, Abdul Haq. "Islamic Ethics: Concept and Prospect." *The American Journal of Islamic Social Sciences* 6, no. 1 (1989) 81–91. https://doi.org/10.35632/ajis.v6i1.2834.

Anselm of Canterbury. *Cur Deus homo.*
    Critical edition: In *S. Anselmi Cantuariensis archiepiscopi opera omnia,* vol. 2, edited by Franciscus Salesius Schmitt, 37–133 (Edinburgh: Thomas Nelson and Sons, 1951). Translation: "Anselm's Cur Deus Homo." Translated by S. N. Deane. In *St. Anselm Basic Writings,* 2nd ed., 191–302 (La Salle, Illinois: Open Court, 1962).

Aquinas, Thomas. *Summa theologiae.*
    Critical edition: In *Sancti Thomae Aquinatis doctoris angelici opera omnia editio Leonina,* 4–12 (Rome: Ex Typographia Polyglotta S.C. de Propaganda Fide,

WORKS CITED

1888-1906). Translations: *Summa Theologiae*, edited by Thomas Gilby and T. C. O'Brien, 60 vols (London: Blackfriars, 1964–76); *Summa Theologiae: A Concise Translation*, edited by Timothy McDermott (Allen, Texas: Christian Classics, 1989).

Arky, Beth. "Calm Voices, Calmer Kids." *Child Mind Institute*. Last modified February 5, 2025. The Child Mind Institute Family Resource Center. https://childmind.org/article/calm-voices-calmer-kids.

Armfield, Jason M., Emmanuel S. Gnanamanickam, David W. Johnston, David B. Preen, Derek S. Brown, Ha Nguyen, and Leonie Segal. "Intergenerational Transmission of Child Maltreatment in South Australia, 1986–2017: A Retrospective Cohort Study." *Lancet Public Health* 6, no. 7 (July 2021) e450–61. https://doi.org/10.1016/S2468-2667(21)00024-4.

Artemi, Eirini. "Cyril of Alexandria's Critique of the Term Theotokos by Nestorius Constantinople." *Acta Theologica* 32, no. 2 (December 2012) 1–16. https://www.scielo.org.za/scielo.php?script=sci_arttext&pid=S1015-87582012000200001#.

Athanasius of Alexandria, *Orationes contra Arianos*

    Critical edition: *Athanasius Alexandrinus Werke: Band I/Teil 1: Die Dogmatischen Schriften: Lfg 2: Orationes I et II contra Arianos*, edited by Karin Metzler, Dirk U. Hansen, and Kyriakos Savvidis, vols. 1–2 (Berlin: De Gruyter, 1998), https://doi.org/10.1515/9783110803297; *Athanasius Alexandrinus Werke: Band I/Teil 1: Die Dogmatischen Schriften: Lfg 3: Oratio III contra Arianos*, edited by Kyriakos Savvidis and Karin Metzler, vol. 3 (Berlin: De Gruyter, 2000), https://doi.org/10.1515/9783110829044. Translation: *Against the Arians*. Translated by John Henry Newman and Archibald Robertson. In *St. Athanasius: Select Works and Letters*, 303–447, A Select Library of Nicene and Post-Nicene Fathers of the Christian Church, Second Series, vol. 4 (New York: Christian Literature, 1892).

Augustine of Hippo. *De civitate Dei.*

    Critical edition: *De civitate Dei*. Edited by B. Dombart and A. Kalb. Corpus Christianorum Series Latina 47–48. Turnhout: Brepols, 2014. Translation: *The City of God*. Translated by Marcus Dods. New York: Modern Library, 1993.

———. *Confessiones.*

    Critical editions: *Sancti Augustini Confessionum libri XIII*, edited by L. Verheijen, Corpus Christianorum Series Latina 27 (Turnhout: Brepols, 1981); *Confessions, Volume I: Books 1–8*, Loeb Classical Library 26 (Cambridge, Massachusetts: Harvard University Press, 2014). Translations: *Confessions, Volume I: Books 1–8*, translated by Carolyn J.-B. Hammond, Loeb Classical Library 26 (Cambridge, Massachusetts: Harvard University Press, 2014); *Confessions*, translated by Henry Chadwick, Oxford World's Classics (Oxford: Oxford University Press, 1992).

———. "De gratia et libero arbitrio."

    Critical edition: "Ad Valentinum et cum illo monachos de gratia et libero arbitrio liber unus." In *Späte Schriften zur Gnadenlehre: De gratia et libero arbitrio. De praedestinatione sanctorum libri duo (olim: De praedestinatione sanctorum, De dono perseverantiae)*, edited by Volker Henning Drecoll and Christoph Scheerer, Corpus Scriptorum Ecclesiasticorum Latinorum 105 (Berlin: De Gruyter, 2019), 129–76, https://doi.org/10.1515/9783110607789. Translation: "On Grace and Free Will." Translated by Peter Holmes. In *A Select Library of the Nicene and Post-Nicene Fathers of the Christian Church*, First Series, vol. 5, edited by Philip Schaff, 443–65 (Grand Rapids, Michigan: Eerdmans, 1956).

———. *De nuptiis et concupiscentia*.
Latin text: https://catholiclibrary.org/library/view?docId=/Synchronized-EN/Augustine.MarriageConcupiscence.en.html;chunk.id=00000061. Translations: "On Marriage and Concupiscence," *The Catholic Library Project: Catholic Source Texts from Scripture, Tradition, Liturgy, and the Magisterium*, https://catholiclibrary.org/library/view?docId=/Synchronized-EN/Augustine.MarriageConcupiscence.en.html;chunk.id=00000061; "On Marriage and Concupiscence," translated by Peter Holmes, in *A Select Library of the Nicene and Post-Nicene Fathers of the Christian Church*, First Series, vol. 5, edited by Philip Schaff, 263–308 (Grand Rapids, Michigan: Eerdmans, 1956).

———. *De Trinitate*.
Critical edition: *De Trinitate libri XV*. Edited by W. J. Mountain and F. Glorie. Corpus Christianorum Series Latina, L. Turnhout: Brepols, 1968. Translation: *The Trinity*. Translated by Edmund Hill. 2nd ed. The Works of Saint Augustine: A Translation for the 21st Century, part 1, vol. 5. Hyde Park, New York: New City, 1990.

Austin, J. L. *How to Do Things with Words: The William James Lectures delivered at Harvard University in 1955*. Oxford: Clarendon, 1962.

Azzi, Joseph. *The Priest & the Prophet: The Christian Priest, Waraqa Ibn Nawfal's, Profound Influence Upon Muhammad, the Prophet of Islam*. Translated by Maurice Saliba. Los Angeles, California: The Pen, 2005.

Baldwin, Jennifer. *Trauma-Sensitive Theology: Thinking Theologically in the Era of Trauma*. Eugene, Oregon: Cascade, 2018.

Barr, Niall. "British History: The Threat of Invasion 1066–1789: An Overview." *BBC*. 17 February 2011. British Broadcasting Corporation. https://www.bbc.co.uk/history/british/normans/invasion_threat_01.shtml.

Barrett, Lisa Feldman. "Affect vs. Emotion." October 20, 2023. https://how-emotions-are-made.com/notes/Affect_vs._emotion.

Barth, K. *Die Kirchliche Dogmatik*. Zollikon, Switzerland: Verlag der Evangelischen Buchhandlung, 1932–67. Translations: *Church Dogmatics* 2.1, translated by T. H. L. Parker, W. B. Johnston, H. Knight, and J. L. M. Haire, edited by G. W. Bromiley and Thomas F. Torrance (Edinburgh: T&T Clark, 1957); *Church Dogmatics* 2.2, translated by G. W. Bromiley, J. C. Campbell, Iain Wilson, J. Strathearn McNab, H. Knight, and R. A. Stewart, edited by G. W. Bromiley and Thomas F. Torrance (Edinburgh: T&T Clark, 1957); *Church Dogmatics* 3.1, translated by J. W. Edwards, O. Bussey, and H. Knight, edited by G. W. Bromiley and Thomas F. Torrance (Edinburgh: T&T Clark, 1958); *Church Dogmatics* 3.2, translated by H. Knight, G. W. Bromiley, J. K. S. Reid, and R. H. Fuller, edited by G. W. Bromiley and Thomas F. Torrance (Edinburgh: T&T Clark, 1960); *Church Dogmatics* 4.1, translated by G. W. Bromiley, edited by G. W. Bromiley and Thomas F. Torrance (Edinburgh: T&T Clark, 1956); *Church Dogmatics* 4.2, translated by G. W. Bromiley, edited by G. W. Bromiley and Thomas F. Torrance (Edinburgh: T&T Clark, 1958); *Church Dogmatics* 4.3.1, translated by G. W. Bromiley, edited by G. W. Bromiley and Thomas F. Torrance (Edinburgh: T&T Clark, 1961).

———. *Die Menschlichkeit Gottes*.
Translation: "The Humanity of God." In *The Humanity of God*, translated by John Newton Thomas (London: Louisville, Westminster John Knox, 1996).

Bavinck, H. *Gereformeerde Dogmatiek*.
    Translation: *Reformed Dogmatics*. Edited by John Bolt. Grand Rapids, Michigan: Baker Academic, 2011.
Beale, G. K. *The Book of Revelation*. The New International Greek Testament Commentary. Grand Rapids, Michigan: Eerdmans, 1999.
Pope Benedict XVI. *General Audience*. The Holy See. October 19, 2011. https://www.vatican.va/content/benedict-xvi/en/audiences/2011/documents/hf_ben-xvi_aud_20111019.html.
Bernstein, Jeffrey. "4 Ways Parents Can Hurt Kids' Self-Esteem." *Psychology Today*. Last modified July 4, 2023. Sussex Publishers. https://www.psychologytoday.com/sg/blog/liking-the-child-you-love/202307/when-parents-hurt-their-childrens-self-esteem.
Bright, John. "Ezra." *Britannica*. Last modified 27 December 2024. Encyclopaedia Britannica. https://www.britannica.com/biography/Ezra-Hebrew-religious-leader.
British Broadcasting Corporation. "'Evolutionary Factors' in Female Attractiveness." *BBC*. 25 August 2015. British Broadcasting Corporation. https://www.bbc.com/news/uk-scotland-north-east-orkney-shetland-34050485.amp.
Broussard, Karlo. "Is God Just a Fantasy to Comfort Scared People?" *Catholic Answers*. March 16, 2021. https://www.catholic.com/magazine/online-edition/god-fantasy-comfort-scared.
Brown, Colin, ed. *The New International Dictionary of New Testament Theology*. 3 vols. Grand Rapids, Michigan: Zondervan, 1975.
Brown, David. "Platonism." In *The Dictionary of Historical Theology*, edited by Trevor A. Hart, 427–31. Grand Rapids, Michigan: Eerdmans, 2000.
Brown, Francis, S. R. Driver, and Charles A. Briggs, eds. *A Hebrew and English Lexicon of the Old Testament. With an Appendix Containing the Biblical Aramaic*. Oxford: Clarendon, 1907.
Brown, T. A. *Genomes*. 2nd ed. Oxford: Wiley-Liss, 2002. https://www.ncbi.nlm.nih.gov/books/NBK21114.
Burke, Kristi. "From Holy to Heretic: Why I Left Christianity." *YouTube*. July 1, 2022. https://www.youtube.com/watch?v=qaOkoJeDG-s&t=68s.
Calvin, John. *Institutio Christianae religionis*.
    Critical edition: In *Ioannis Calvini opera selecta*, vols. 3–5, edited by P. Barth and G. Niesel (Munich: Chr. Kaiser, 1926–52). Translation: *Institutes of the Christian Religion*. Edited by John T. McNeill. Translated by Ford Lewis Battles. 2 vols. The Library of Christian Classics. Louisville, Kentucky: Westminster John Knox, 2006.
———. *Ioannis Calvini opera exegetica et homiletica*.
    Critical edition: In *Ioannis Calvini opera quae supersunt omnia*, vols. 23–57. Edited by G. Baum, Ed Cunitz, Eduard Reuss, and Alfred Erichson. Brunswick, New Jersey: C. A. Schwetschke, 1863–. Translations: *Commentaries on the Epistles to Timothy, Titus, and Philemon*, translated by William Pringle, in Calvin's Commentaries 21 (Edinburgh: Calvin Translation Society, n.d.); *Commentary on the Gospel According to John*, vol. 1, translated by William Pringle, in Calvin's Commentaries 17 (Edinburgh: Calvin Translation Society, 1847); *Commentaries on the Catholic Epistles*, translated by John Owen, in Calvin's Commentaries 22 (Edinburgh: Calvin Translation Society, 1855).
Capua, Rebecca. "Papyrus-Making in Egypt." *The Met*. March 1, 2015. The Metropolitan Museum of Art. https://www.metmuseum.org/essays/papyrus-making-in-egypt.

Carson, Donald A. *The Gospel According to John*. The Pillar New Testament Commentary. Grand Rapids, Michigan: Eerdmans, 1991.
Catholic Answers. "The Galileo Controversy." *Catholic Answers*. August 10, 2004. https://www.catholic.com/tract/the-galileo-controversy.
———. "What is the Inquisition?" *Catholic Answers*. August 10, 2004. https://www.catholic.com/tract/the-inquisition.
Center for Near Earth Object Studies. "Life on Earth." *Center for Near Earth Object Studies*. California Institute of Technology. Accessed January 18, 2024. https://cneos.jpl.nasa.gov/about/life_on_earth.html.
Chalke, Steve, and Alan Mann. *The Lost Message of Jesus*. Grand Rapids, Michigan: Zondervan, 2004.
Chaniotis, Angelos. "The Life of Statues of Gods in the Greek World." *Kernos* 30 (2017) 1–20. https://doi.org/10.4000/kernos.2492.
Cherry, Kendra. "Erikson's Stages of Development: A Closer Look at the Eight Psychosocial Stages." *Verywell Mind*. Last modified August 3, 2022. Dotdash Meredith. https://www.verywellmind.com/erik-eriksons-stages-of-psychosocial-development-2795740.
———. "How to Forgive Yourself." *Verywell Mind*. Last modified December 5, 2023. Dotdash Meredith. https://www.verywellmind.com/how-to-forgive-yourself-4583819.
———. "Kohlberg's Theory of Moral Development." *Verywell Mind*. Last modified November 7, 2022. Dotdash Meredith. Accessed January 28, 2024. https://www.verywellmind.com/kohlbergs-theory-of-moral-development-2795071.
Chia, Roland. "Progressive Christianity: A Primer." *Ethos Institute for Public Christianity*. 17 October 2022. Ethos Institute for Public Christianity. https://ethosinstitute.sg/progressive-christianity-a-primer.
Chong, Claudia. "Why Are Law and Medicine So Popular in Singapore?" *Asian Scientist*. 17 June 2016. Asian Scientist Magazine. https://www.asianscientist.com/2016/06/academia/law-medicine-popular-degrees-in-singapore/2.
Chua, Edmond Zi-Kang. *Experience, Culture and Religion in Systematic Theology: An Integrative and Pluriform Methodology*. Cambridge: James Clarke, 2023.
———. *'God-ness', 'God-ity', and God: A Historical Study and Synthesis of the Christian Doctrine of the Divine Being*. 2nd ed. New Orleans, Louisiana: University Press of the South, 2022.
———. "Jung Young Lee's Biblical-Cultural Trinity: A Systematic Theology from East Asia." PhD diss., University of Otago, 2021.
———. "Pope Francis on the Religions as a Path to God." *Japan Mission Journal* 78, no. 4 (Winter 2024) 258–69.
———. *A Systematic Theology from East Asia: Jung Young Lee's Biblical-Cultural Trinity*. Eugene, Oregon: Pickwick, 2023.
Chun, Michelle. "For the First Time, I Knew I Wasn't a Mistake." *Salt&Light*. March 10, 2025. https://saltandlight.sg/profiles/for-the-first-time-i-knew-i-wasnt-a-mistake/?utm_campaign=feed&utm_medium=referral&utm_source=later-linkinbio.
Chung, Titus. "Jesus, the Glory of God." Dedication of the Nave and Christmas Eve Combined Service, sermon, St. Andrew's Cathedral, Singapore, 24 December 2023.
Clark, Gordon H. *Religion, Reason, and Revelation*. 2nd ed. Hobbes, New Mexico: Trinity Foundation, 1995.

WORKS CITED

Clark, R. Scott. "Brothers We Are Not Perfectionists." *The Heidelblog*. December 5, 2012. Heidelberg Reformation Association. https://heidelblog.net/2012/12/brothers-we-are-not-perfectionists.

Clear, James. *Atomic Habits: An Easy & Proven Way to Build Good Habits & Break Bad Ones*. New York: Avery, 2018.

Cleveland Clinic. "Genetic Disorders." *Cleveland Clinic*. Accessed March 8, 2024. https://my.clevelandclinic.org/health/diseases/21751-genetic-disorders.

Cockerill, Gareth Lee. *The Epistle to the Hebrews*. The New International Commentary on the New Testament. Grand Rapids, Michigan: Eerdmans, 2012.

Collins, John J. "Historical-Critical Methods." In *The Cambridge Companion to the Hebrew Bible/Old Testament*, edited by Stephen B. Chapman and Marvin A. Sweeney, 129–46 (Cambridge: Cambridge University Press, 2016).

Colville, Alex. "Hell's Bittersweet End: Meng Po, Goddess of Forgetfulness." *The China Project*. January 18, 2021. https://thechinaproject.com/2021/01/18/hells-bittersweet-end-meng-po-goddess-of-forgetfulness.

Crawford, S. Cromwell. *Hindu Bioethics for the Twenty-First Century*. Albany, New York: SUNY Press, 2003.

Crisp, Oliver D. "On Barth's Denial of Universalism." *Themelios* 29, issue 1 (Autumn 2003) 18–29. https://media.thegospelcoalition.org/documents/themelios/Themelios29.1.pdf.

D'Costa, Gavin. *The Meeting of Religions and the Trinity, Faith Meets Faith*. Maryknoll, New York: Orbis, 2000.

———. *Theology and Religious Pluralism: The Challenge of Other Religions*. Signposts in Theology. Oxford: Basil Blackwell, 1986.

Dadrawala, Noshir H. "Zoroastrian Ethics and Morals." *The Circle of Ancient Iranian Studies*. Accessed December 24, 2023. https://www.cais-soas.com/CAIS/Religions/iranian/Zarathushtrian/zoroastrian_ethics_morals.htm.

Dawkins, Richard. *The God Delusion*. Boston: Houghton Mifflin, 2006.

Demarest, B. "Blasphemy." In *New Dictionary of Theology*, ed. Sinclair B. Ferguson, David F. Wright, and J. I. Packer (Downers Grove, Illinois: IVP Academic, 1988).

Descartes, René. *Meditations*.
Translation: *The Philosophical Works of Descartes*. Translated by Elizabeth S. Haldane. Cambridge University Press, 1911. https://people.bu.edu/wwildman/courses/wphil/readings/wphil_rdg21_meditations_entire.htm.

Dhavamony, Mariasusai. *Classical Hinduism*. Documenta Missionalia 15. Rome: Gregorian University Press, 1982.

Diamond, Stephen A. "Essential Secrets of Psychotherapy: What Is the 'Shadow'?" *Psychology Today*. January 3, 2021. Sussex Publishers. https://www.psychologytoday.com/intl/blog/evil-deeds/202101/essential-secrets-of-psychotherapy-what-is-the-shadow.

Dicastery for the Doctrine of the Faith. *Dignitas Infinita*. April 8, 2024. The Holy See. https://press.vatican.va/content/salastampa/en/bollettino/pubblico/2024/04/08/240408c.html.

Dittmann, M. "Self-Esteem That's Based on External Sources Has Mental Health Consequences, Study Says." *Monitor on Psychology* 33, no. 11 (December 2002) 16. https://www.apa.org/monitor/dec02/selfesteem.

Doriani, Dan. "What Is the 'Abomination of Desolation'?" *The Gospel Coalition.* September 8, 2014. https://www.thegospelcoalition.org/article/what-is-the-abomination-of-desolation.

Drummond, John. "Antiochus Epiphanes—The Bible's Most Notoriously Forgotten Villain." *Biblical Archaeology Society.* November 24, 2023. https://www.biblicalarchaeology.org/daily/ancient-cultures/ancient-israel/antiochus-epiphanes-the-bibles-most-notoriously-forgotten-villain.

Dunlap, Eloise, Andrew Golub, Bruce D. Johnson, and Ellen Benoit. "Normalization of Violence: Experiences of Childhood Abuse by Inner-City Crack Users." *Journal of Ethnicity in Substance Abuse* 8, no. 1 (2009) 15–34. https://doi.org/10.1080/15332640802683359.

Dupuis, Jacques. *Toward a Christian Theology of Religious Pluralism.* Maryknoll, New York: Orbis, 1997.

The Editors of Encyclopaedia Britannica. "Best of All Possible Worlds." *Britannica.* Last modified 6 June 2017. Encyclopaedia Britannica. https://www.britannica.com/topic/best-of-all-possible-worlds.

———. "Huainanzi." *Britannica.* Last modified 1 July 2005. Encyclopaedia Britannica. https://www.britannica.com/topic/Huainanzi.

———. "Jehoshaphat." *Britannica.* 20 July 1998. Encyclopaedia Britannica. https://www.britannica.com/biography/Jehoshaphat.

———. "Josiah." *Britannica.* 10 June 2004. Encyclopaedia Britannica. https://www.britannica.com/biography/Josiah.

———. "Zechariah." *Britannica.* 20 July 1998. Encyclopaedia Britannica. https://www.britannica.com/biography/Zechariah.

Edwards, Jonathan. "The Marks of a Work of the True Spirit." Revised by Edward Hickman. In *The Works of Jonathan Edwards* 2 (Edinburgh: Banner of Truth, 1974).

———. "Sinners in the Hands of an Angry God." Revised by Edward Hickman. In *The Works of Jonathan Edwards* 2 (Edinburgh: Banner of Truth, 1974).

Edwards, William D., Wesley J. Gabel, and Floyd E. Hosmer. "On the Physical Death of Jesus Christ." *The Journal of the American Medical Association* 255, no. 11 (March 1986) 1455–63. https://doi.org/10.1001/jama.1986.03370110077025.

Engel, George L. "'Psychogenic' pain and the pain-prone patient." *The American Journal of Medicine* 26, issue 6 (1959) 899–918. https://doi.org/https://doi.org/10.1016/0002-9343(59)90212-8.

Enns, Paul. *The Moody Handbook of Theology.* Chicago: Moody, 2008.

Epstein, Sarah. "What Does It Mean to Hold Space?" *Psychology Today.* May 25, 2023. Sussex Publishers. https://www.psychologytoday.com/sg/blog/between-the-generations/202305/what-does-it-mean-to-hold-space.

Erickson, Millard J. *Christian Theology.* 3rd ed. Grand Rapids, Michigan: Baker Academic, 2013.

Erikson, Erik H. *Young Man Luther: A Study in Psychoanalysis and History.* New York: Norton Library, 1962.

Felix, Minucius. *Octavius.*

Translation: "Octavius." Translated by Robert Ernest Wallis. In *The Ante-Nicene Fathers* 4, edited by Alexander Roberts, James Donaldson, and A. Cleveland Coxe, 173–98 (Grand Rapids, Michigan: Eerdmans, 1885).

Fiddes, Paul S. *The Creative Suffering of God.* Oxford: Clarendon, 1988.

Fields, Weston W. *Unformed and Unfilled: A Critique of the Gap Theory*. Phillipsburg, New Jersey: Presbyterian and Reformed, 1976.

Pope Francis. *General Audience*. The Holy See. December 2, 2020. https://m.vatican.va/content/francescomobile/en/audiences/2020/documents/papa-francesco_20201202_udienza-generale.index.html.

———. *Message of the Holy Father Francis to Participants in the International Meeting for Peace Organized by the Community of Sant'Egidio*. The Holy See. September 17, 2024. https://www.vatican.va/content/francesco/en/messages/pont-messages/2024/documents/20240917-messaggio-pace-parigi.html.

Franciscan Media. "Saint Anthony of Egypt." *Franciscan Media*. Accessed November 9, 2024. https://www.franciscanmedia.org/saint-of-the-day/saint-anthony-of-egypt.

Fraser-Thill, Rebecca. "What Is Individuation?" *Verywell Mind*. Last modified October 7, 2021. Dotdash Meredith. https://www.verywellmind.com/individuation-3288007.

Gabbey, Amber Erickson, and Crystal Raypole. "Aggressive Behavior: Understanding Aggression and How to Treat It." *Healthline*. March 3, 2022. Healthline Media. https://www.healthline.com/health/aggressive-behavior#causes.

Gigot, Francis E. "Daniel." *Catholic Answers*. Accessed February 17, 2025, https://www.catholic.com/encyclopedia/daniel.

Gillis, Kaytee. "The Lasting Harm of Conditional Parental Love." *Psychology Today*. January 7, 2024. Sussex Publishers. https://www.psychologytoday.com/sg/blog/invisible-bruises/202310/the-negative-effects-of-conditional-love.

———. "Why Child Trauma Survivors Often Blame Themselves." *Psychology Today*. November 11, 2024. Sussex Publishers. https://www.psychologytoday.com/sg/blog/invisible-bruises/202411/why-child-trauma-survivors-often-blame-themselves.

Gingrich, F. Wilbur. *Shorter Lexicon of the Greek New Testament*. Revised by Frederick W. Danker. 2nd ed. Chicago: University of Chicago Press, 1983.

Goh, William S.-C. "The Culture of Death." Public lecture, Ethos Institute for Public Christianity, Singapore, 17 November 2023.

González, Justo L. *The Reformation to the Present Day*. The Story of Christianity 2. Rev. ed. New York: HarperOne, 2010.

Gooch, Todd. "Ludwig Andreas Feuerbach." *Stanford Encyclopedia of Philosophy* (Fall 2024). https://plato.stanford.edu/archives/fall2024/entries/ludwig-feuerbach.

Got Questions. "Does Hebrews 6:4–6 Mean We Can Lose Our Salvation?" *Got Questions*. Last modified January 4, 2022. Got Questions Ministries. https://www.gotquestions.org/Hebrews-6.html.

Gray, Brianna. "Cycle of Abuse: When Toxic Situations Become Normalized in the Family." *Peer Mental Health*. May 26, 2022. https://www.peermentalhealth.com/cycle-of-abuse-when-toxic-situations-become-normalized-in-the-family.

Gregory of Nazianzus. *Oratio XXXI*.

Critical edition: *Grégoire de Nazianze: Discours 27–31*. Edited by Paul Gallay and Maurice Jourjon. Sources Chrétiennes 250. Paris: Éditions du Cerf, 1978. Translation: "The Fifth Theological Oration." Translated by Lionel Wickham. In *On God and Christ: The Five Theological Orations and Two Letters to Cledonius*, 117–47 (Crestwood, New York: St. Vladimir's Seminary Press, 2002).

———. *Oratio XL*. Greek text: In *Patrologia Graeca* 36, cols. 359–428, edited by Jacques Paul Migne (Paris: J.-P. Migne, 1858). Translation: "Oration XL." Translated by Charles Gordon Browne and James Edward Swallow. In *A Select Library of the Nicene and Post-Nicene Fathers of the Christian Church*, Second Series, vol. 7, edited by Philip Schaff and Henry Wace, 360–77 (Grand Rapids, Michigan: Eerdmans, 1983).

Grenz, Stanley J. *Theology for the Community of God*. Grand Rapids, Michigan: Eerdmans, 2000.

Grislis, Egil. "Martin Luther and the World Religions." *Word & World* 18, no. 2 (Spring 1998) 143–54.

Gritsch, Eric W. "Was Luther Anti-Semitic?" *Christianity Today*. July 1993. Christianity Today International. https://www.christianitytoday.com/1993/07/was-luther-anti-semitic.

Groeger, Lena. "A Friend like Me: When Given More Choices, People Pick Friends Similar to Themselves." *Scientific American*. September 26, 2011. https://www.scientificamerican.com/article/a-friend-like-me.

Gunton, Colin E. *The Christian Faith: An Introduction to Christian Doctrine*. Malden, Massachusetts: Blackwell, 2002.

Hagner, Donald A. *Matthew 14–28*. Word Biblical Commentary 33B. Grand Rapids, Michigan: Zondervan, 2015.

Haidt, Jonathan. *The Righteous Mind: Why Good People are Divided by Politics and Religion*. New York: Vintage, 2012. eBook.

Hartley, John E. *Leviticus*. Word Biblical Commentary 4. Grand Rapids, Michigan: Zondervan, 2015.

Hartney, Elizabeth. "9 Reasons the Cycle of Abuse Continues: Why the Abused Sometimes Becomes the Abuser." *Verywell Mind*. Last modified January 4, 2024. Dotdash Meredith. Accessed January 17, 2024. https://www.verywellmind.com/the-cycle-of-sexual-abuse-22460.

Hébert, Martine, Andréanne Lapierre, Heather B. MacIntosh, and A. Dana Ménard. "A Review of Mediators in the Association between Child Sexual Abuse and Revictimization in Romantic Relationships." *Journal of Child Sexual Abuse* 30, no. 4 (2021) 385–406. https://doi.org/10.1080/10538712.2020.1801936.

Hector, Kevin W. *Christianity as a Way of Life: A Systematic Theology*. New Haven, Connecticut: Yale University Press, 2023.

Hedges, Paul. *Christian Polytheism? Polydox Theologies of Multi-Devotional and Decolonial Praxis*. London: Routledge, 2025.

———. *Controversies in Interreligious Dialogue and the Theology of Religions*. Controversies in Contextual Theology. London: SCM, 2010.

———. *Religious Hatred: Prejudice, Islamophobia, and Antisemitism in Global Context*. London: Bloomsbury Academic, 2021.

Heim, S. Mark. *The Depth of the Riches: A Trinitarian Theology of Religious Ends*. Grand Rapids, Michigan: Eerdmans, 2001.

Hick, John. Review of S. Mark Heim, *The Depth of the Riches: A Trinitarian Theology of Religious Ends* (Grand Rapids, Michigan: Eerdmans, 2001). *Reviews in Religion and Theology* 8, no. 4 (September 2001). http://www.johnhick.org.uk/articles.html. Accessed August 8, 2024.

Holden, Michael. "God Did Not Create the Universe, Says Hawking." *Reuters*. September 2, 2010. Thomson Reuters. https://www.reuters.com/article/lifestyle/god-did-not-create-the-universe-says-hawking-idUSTRE6811FN.

Holder, Rodney. "Karl Barth and the Legitimacy of Natural Theology." *Themelios* 26, no. 3 (2001) 22–37. https://www.thegospelcoalition.org/themelios/article/karl-barth-and-the-legitimacy-of-natural-theology.

Howard, J. Caleb. "Who Were the Amorites?" *Tyndale House*. December 9, 2022. https://tyndalehouse.com/explore/articles/who-were-the-amorites.

Huddleston, Jr., Tom. "Harvard-Trained Parenting Researcher: The Most Successful Kids Are 'Healthy Strivers'—Here's What Their Parents Always Do." *Make It*. October 15, 2023. CNBC. https://www.cnbc.com/2023/10/15/parenting-researcher-how-to-raise-successful-kids-healthy-strivers.html.

The Imagine Team. "Then vs. Now: The Age of the Universe." *Imagine the Universe!* May 2006. National Aeronautics and Space Administration. https://imagine.gsfc.nasa.gov/science/featured_science/tenyear/age.html.

Ivritalk. "Hebrew Days of the Week." *Ivritalk*. The Jerusalem Post. https://www.ivritalk.com/hebrew-days-of-the-week.

Janiak, Andrew. "Kant's Views on Space and Time." *The Stanford Encyclopedia of Philosophy* (Summer 2022). https://plato.stanford.edu/archives/sum2022/entries/kant-spacetime.

Jenson, Robert W. *The Triune Identity: God According to the Gospel*. Eugene, Oregon: Wipf and Stock, 2002.

Jewish Virtual Library. "Idolatry". *Jewish Virtual Library*. Accessed December 9, 2023. American-Israeli Cooperative Enterprise. https://jewishvirtuallibrary.org/idolatry.

———. "Paddan-Aram." *Jewish Virtual Library*. American-Israeli Cooperative Enterprise. https://www.jewishvirtuallibrary.org/paddan-aram.

John of Damascus. *Expositio accurata fidei orthodoxae*.
Greek text: In *Patrologia Graeca* 94, cols. 790–1228, edited by Jacques Paul Migne (Paris: J.-P. Migne, 1864). Translation: *An Exact Exposition of the Orthodox Faith*. In *Saint John of Damascus: Writings*, translated by Frederic H. Chase, Jr., The Fathers of the Church 37 (Washington DC: Catholic University of America Press, 1970).

Johnson, Roger A., ed. *Psychohistory and Religion: The Case of Young Man Luther*. Philadelphia, Pennsylvania: Fortress, 1977.

Jones, Prudence. "Introduction to Paganism." *The Pagan Federation*. Accessed February 19, 2024. https://www.paganfed.org/paganism.

Kalb, Claudia. "Learning Right from Wrong." *Newsweek*. March 12, 2000. Newsweek Digital. https://www.newsweek.com/learning-right-wrong-156391.

Kaljouw, Wil. "Christian Exclusivism and the Justification of Violence: A Case Study in Augustine." In *Christian Faith and Violence*, vol. 2, Studies in Reformed Theology 2, edited by Dirk van Keulen and Martien E. Brinkman, 284–95 (Zoetermeer, Netherlands: Meinema, 2005).

Kamamoto, Yuka. "Essay: Dao as the Basis for Morality." *The Nanyang Philosophy Review*. Accessed December 21, 2023. https://nyphilosophyreview.wordpress.com/2017/01/06/essay-dao-as-the-basis-for-morality.

Kee, Alistair. *Constantine versus Christ: The Triumph of Ideology*. Eugene, Oregon: Wipf and Stock, 2016.

Kelly, J. N. D. *Early Christian Doctrines*. 5th ed. London: Bloomsbury Academic, 1977.
Kidd, Thomas S. *The Great Awakening: A Brief History with Documents*. The Bedford Series in History and Culture. Boston: Bedford/St. Martin's, 2008.
———. "Slavery Old and New: Comparing Early America with Biblical Times." *Desiring God*. February 23, 2021. https://www.desiringgod.org/articles/slavery-old-and-new.
Kim, Heup Young. *A Theology of Dao*. Maryknoll, New York: Orbis, 2017.
Labooy, G. H., and P. M. Wisse. "The Coherence of Equivocal Penal Substitution: Modern and Scholastic Voices." *International Journal for Philosophy of Religion* 86, no. 3 (December 2019) 227–41. https://doi.org/10.1007/s11153-019-09709-y.
Lane, William C. "Living God Pandeism: Evidential Support." *Zygon* 56, no. 3 (September 2021) 566–90. https://doi.org/10.1111/zygo.12704.
Langness, David. "5 Baha'i Ethics: Oneness, Love, Kindness, Humility and Peace." *BahaiTeachings.org*. December 6, 2018. https://bahaiteachings.org/5-bahai-ethics-oneness-love-kindness-humility-peace.
Lee, Jung Young. *God Suffers for Us: A Systematic Inquiry into a Concept of Divine Passibility*. The Hague, Netherlands: Martinus Nijhoff, 1974.
———. *The Theology of Change: A Christian Concept of God in an Eastern Perspective*. Maryknoll, New York: Orbis, 1979.
———. *The Trinity in Asian Perspective*. Nashville, Tennessee: Abingdon, 1996.
Legal Information Institute. "Negligent Infliction of Emotional Distress." *Legal Information Institute*. Cornell Law School. Accessed January 23, 2024. https://www.law.cornell.edu/wex/negligent_infliction_of_emotional_distress.
Pope Leo I. *Ep. XXVIII*.
Translation: "Letter 28." In *A Select Library of the Nicene and Post-Nicene Fathers of the Christian Church*, Second Series, vol. 12, translated by Charles Lett Feltoe (Grand Rapids, Michigan: Eerdmans, 1894), 38–43.
Leonhard, Barbara. "Jesus' Extraordinary Treatment of Women." *St. Anthony Messenger*. November 2017. Franciscan Media. https://www.franciscanmedia.org/st-anthony-messenger/jesus-extraordinary-treatment-of-women.
Lesso, Rosie. "Ancient Roman Coins: How Were They Made?" *The Collector*. February 4, 2022. https://www.thecollector.com/ancient-roman-coins-how-were-they-made.
Licona, Michael. "Appearances of Mary and Jesus' Resurrection Appearances." *The Good Book Blog*. October 26, 2018. Biola University. https://www.biola.edu/blogs/good-book-blog/2018/appearances-of-mary-and-jesus-resurrection-appearances.
Liddell, Henry George, Robert Scott, and Henry Stuart Jones, eds. *A Greek-English Lexicon*. Rev. ed. Oxford: Clarendon, 1940. Perseus Digital Library Project. https://www.perseus.tufts.edu/hopper/text?doc=Perseus%3atext%3a1999.04.0057.
Little, Anthony C., Benedict C. Jones, and Lisa M. DeBruine. "Facial Attractiveness: Evolutionary Based Research." *Philosophical Transactions of the Royal Society B* 366, no. 1571 (12 June 2011) 1638–59. https://doi.org/10.1098/rstb.2010.0404.
Lloyd, Christopher E. M., Graham Reid, and Yasuhiro Kotera. "From Whence Cometh My Help? Psychological Distress and Help-Seeking in the Evangelical Christian Church." *Frontiers in Psychology* 12 (16 December 2021). https://doi.org/10.3389/fpsyg.2021.744432.
Lok, Gilbert. "The Doctrine of Christian Perfection." *Ethos Institute for Public Christianity*. 15 April 2024. Ethos Institute for Public Christianity. https://ethosinstitute.sg/the-doctrine-of-christian-perfection.

Loke, Andrew. *The Teleological and Kalām Cosmological Arguments Revisited*. Cham, Switzerland: Springer Nature, 2022.

London Buddhist Vihara. "The Noble Eightfold Path." *London Buddhist Vihara*. Accessed December 10, 2023. https://www.londonbuddhistvihara.org/teachings/the-noble-eightfold-path.

Louie, Sam. "Asian Parenting." *Psychology Today*. April 11, 2015. Sussex Publishers. https://www.psychologytoday.com/us/blog/minority-report/201504/asian-parenting.

Luther, Martin. *Galatervorlesung*.
Critical edition: *D. Martin Luthers Werke kritische Gesamtausgabe*, vol. 40, parts 1–2. Edited by Albert Freitag. Weimar: Hermann Böhlau, 1883–. Translation: *Commentary on Galatians*. Translated by Erasmus Middleton. Grand Rapids, Michigan: Kregel, 1978.

———. *Die Heidelberger Disputatio*.
Critical edition: *D. Martin Luthers Werke kritische Gesamtausgabe*, vol. 1, pp. 353–74. Edited by J. K. F. Knaake. Weimar: Hermann Böhlau, 1883–. Translation: "Heidelberg Disputation." In *Luther's Works* 31, translated by Harold J. Grimm, 35–70 (Philadelphia, Pennsylvania: Fortress, 1957).

———. *Römervorlesung*.
Critical edition: *D. Martin Luthers Werke kritische Gesamtausgabe*, vols. 56–57. Edited by Albert Freitag. Weimar: Hermann Böhlau, 1883–. Translation: *Commentary on Romans*. Translated by J. Theodore Mueller. Grand Rapids, Michigan: Kregel, 1976.

———. *De servo arbitrio*.
Critical edition: *D. Martin Luthers Werke kritische Gesamtausgabe*, vol. 18, pp. 597–. Edited by Albert Freitag. Weimar: Hermann Böhlau, 1883–. Translation: *The Bondage of the Will*. Translated by J. I. Packer and O. R. Johnston. Grand Rapids, Michigan: Revell, 1957.

Lyonhart, J. D. *Space God: Rejudging a Debate between More, Newton, and Einstein*. Studies in the Doctrine of God. Eugene, Oregon: Cascade, 2023.

Manley, G. T., and F. F. Bruce. "God, Names Of." In I. H. Marshall, A. R. Millard, J. I. Packer, and D. J. Wiseman, eds., *New Bible Dictionary*, 3rd ed., IVP Reference Collection (Downers Grove, Illinois: IVP Academic, 1996), pp. 420–22.

Marius, Richard. Review of Roger A. Johnson, ed., *Psychohistory and Religion: The Case of Young Man Luther* (Philadelphia, Pennsylvania: Fortress, 1977). In *The American Historical Review* 83, no. 2 (1978) 463.

Markovits, Daniel. "Meritocracy Debate." *Oxford Union*. January 30, 2022. https://www.youtube.com/watch?v=cn1_jhqqNQo.

Maslin, Mark A., Susanne Shultz, and Martin H. Trauth. "A Synthesis of the Theories and Concepts of Early Human Evolution." *Philosophical Transactions of the Royal Society B* 370, no. 1663 (March 2015) 20140064. https://doi.org/10.1098/rstb.2014.0064.

Mawdūdī, Sayyid Abul A'lā. *Towards Understanding the Qur'ān*. Translated by Zafar Ishaq Ansari. Leicester: Islamic Foundation, 1989. https://www.kalamullah.com/Books/Towards%20Understanding%20the%20Quran%202.pdf.

Maxouris, Christina. "23 Years Ago, Another 6-Year-Old Boy Fired a Gun in School. The Victim Was His Classmate." *CNN*. Last modified January 16, 2023. Cable News Network. https://edition.cnn.com/2023/01/16/us/virginia-6-year-old-shooting-michigan-kayla-rolland/index.html.

Mayo Clinic Staff. "Cancer: Symptoms & Causes." *Mayo Clinic*. November 19, 2024. Mayo Foundation for Medical Education and Research. https://www.mayoclinic.org/diseases-conditions/cancer/symptoms-causes/syc-20370588.

———. "Compulsive Sexual Behaviour: Symptoms & Causes." *Mayo Clinic*. April 19, 2023. Mayo Foundation for Medical Education and Research. https://www.mayoclinic.org/diseases-conditions/compulsive-sexual-behavior/symptoms-causes/syc-20360434.

———. "Post-Traumatic Stress Disorder (PTSD): Symptoms & causes." *Mayo Clinic*. August 16, 2024. Mayo Foundation for Medical Education and Research. https://www.mayoclinic.org/diseases-conditions/post-traumatic-stress-disorder/symptoms-causes/syc-20355967.

McGowan, Kat. "Where Animals Come From." *Quanta Magazine*. July 29, 2014. Simons Foundation. https://www.quantamagazine.org/did-bacteria-drive-the-origins-of-animals-20140729.

Menon, Sangeetha. "Advaita Vedanta." *Internet Encyclopedia of Philosophy*. Accessed November 22, 2023. https://iep.utm.edu/advaita-vedanta.

Merrick, Heather. "The Role of the Greek Gods and Yahweh: Emotions or Morals?". *Draftings In* 2, no. 2 (1987) 17–23. https://scholarworks.uni.edu/draftings/vol2/iss2/5.

Michaud, Derek (ed.), Xiang He, Richard Peters, and Kile Jones. "Ludwig Feuerbach (1804–1872)." *Boston Collaborative Encyclopedia of Western Theology*. https://people.bu.edu/wwildman/bce/feuerbach.htm.

Miller, Korin. "Surprise, Surprise: People Jump to Conclusions without Having All of the Information, New Study Finds." *yahoo!life*. October 10, 2024. https://www.aol.co.uk/lifestyle/surprise-surprise-people-jump-conclusions-180047067.html.

Missouri State University. "The Medieval Era." *Missouri State University*. Accessed August 8, 2024. https://www.missouristate.edu/Reformations/the-medieval-era.htm.

Moltmann, Jürgen. *The Crucified God: The Cross of Christ as the Foundation and Criticism of Christian Theology*. Translated by R. A. Wilson and John Bowden. London: SCM, 1974. Reprint, London: SCM, 2015.

Mong, Ambrose Ih-Ren. "In Many and Diverse Ways: Examining Jacques Dupuis' Theology of Religious Pluralism." *Dialogue & Alliance* 25, no. 2 (2011) 71–85. https://archive.upf.org/resources/speeches-and-articles/4092-a-mong-ih-ren-in-many-and-diverse-ways-examining-jacques-dupuis-theology-of-religious-pluralism.

Montag, John. "Revelation: The False Legacy of Suárez." In *Radical Orthodoxy: A New Theology*, edited by John Milbank, Catherine Pickstock, and Graham Ward (London: Routledge, 1999).

Moody, Josh. "This Day in History: Jonathan Edwards Preaches 'Sinners in the Hands of an Angry God.'" *Crossway*. July 8, 2018. https://www.crossway.org/articles/this-day-in-history-jonathan-edwards-preaches-sinners-in-the-hands-of-an-angry-god.

Moore, Edward. "Neo-Platonism." *Internet Encyclopedia of Philosophy*. Accessed August 8, 2024. https://iep.utm.edu/neoplato.

Morley, Brian. "Western Concepts of God." *Internet Encyclopedia of Philosophy*. https://iep.utm.edu/god-west.

Morris, Leon. *The Gospel according to Matthew*. The Pillar New Testament Commentary. Grand Rapids, Michigan: Eerdmans, 1992.

Mounce, William. "Paraklētos." *Bill Mounce*. https://www.billmounce.com/greek-dictionary/parakletos.

Nall, Rachel. "What Are the Long-Term Effects of Gaslighting?" *Medical News Today*. June 29, 2020. Healthline Media. https://www.medicalnewstoday.com/articles/long-term-effects-of-gaslighting.

Narvaez, Darcia F. "Adult Justification of Child Humiliation and Mistreatment." *Psychology Today*. March 20, 2016. Sussex Publishers. https://www.psychologytoday.com/us/blog/moral-landscapes/201603/adult-justification-child-humiliation-and-mistreatment?amp.

NASA Hubble Space Telescope. "The Electromagnetic Spectrum." *Hubblesite*. Last modified September 30, 2022. NASA Hubble Space Telescope. https://hubblesite.org/contents/articles/the-electromagnetic-spectrum.

National Academy of Sciences. *Science and Creationism: A View from the National Academy of Sciences*. Washington DC: National Academy Press, 1999.

Nelson, Janna, Anne Klumparendt, Philipp Doebler, and Thomas Ehring. "Childhood Maltreatment and Characteristics of Adult Depression: Meta-Analysis." *The British Journal of Psychiatry* 210, no. 2 (2017) 96–104. https://doi.org/10.1192/bjp.bp.115.180752.

Nemes, Steven. *Orthodoxy and Heresy*. Elements in the Problems of God. Cambridge: Cambridge University Press, 2022. https://doi.org/10.1017/9781009268189.

Nolland, John. *Luke 9:21—18:34*. Word Biblical Commentary 35B. Nashville, Tennessee: Thomas Nelson, 1993.

Norwich University. "Six Causes of World War I." *Norwich University*. Accessed December 6, 2023. https://online.norwich.edu/six-causes-world-war-i.

Novotney, Amy. "The Risks of Social Isolation." *Monitor on Psychology* 50, no. 5 (May 2019) 32. https://www.apa.org/monitor/2019/05/ce-corner-isolation.

O'Leary, Joseph S. "Demystifying the Trinity." *Archivio di Filosofia* 82, no. 1/2 (2014), "Il monoteismo come problema," pp. 229–242.

Oates, Harry. "The Great Jewish Revolt of 66 CE." *World History Encyclopedia*. August 28, 2015. World History Publishing. https://www.worldhistory.org/article/823/the-great-jewish-revolt-of-66-ce.

Olendzki, Andrew. "Practicing the Middle Way: Devadaha Sutta." *Insight* (Spring 1998) 1–40. https://www.buddhistinquiry.org/article/practicing-the-middle-way-devadaha-sutta.

Olson, Roger E. *The Journey of Modern Theology: From Reconstruction to Deconstruction*. Downers Grove, Illinois: IVP Academic, 2013.

Orlans, Michael. "Fetuses Are Aware." *Evergreen Psychotherapy Center*. May 4, 2015. https://evergreenpsychotherapycenter.com/fetuses-are-aware.

Ouellette, Jennifer. "Why Did Life Move to Land? For the View." *Quanta Magazine*. March 7, 2017. Simons Foundation. https://www.quantamagazine.org/why-did-life-move-to-land-for-the-view-20170307.

Pannenberg, Wolfhart. *Systematische Theologie*, 3 vols. Gottingen, Germany: Vandenhoeck & Ruprecht, 1988–93. Translation: *Systematic Theology*. 3 vols. Translated by Geoffrey W. Bromiley. Grand Rapids, Michigan: Eerdmans, 1991–98.

Petrotech. "How Does a Steam Turbine Work?" *Petrotech*. Accessed February 17, 2025. https://petrotechinc.com/how-does-a-steam-turbine-work.

Phan, Peter. *The Joy of Religious Pluralism: A Personal Journey*. Maryknoll, NY: Orbis, 2017.

Philo of Alexandria. *De Cherubim*.
Critical edition and translation: *On the Cherubim. The Sacrifices of Abel and Cain. The Worse Attacks the Better. On the Posterity and Exile of Cain. On the Giants*. Translated by F. H. Colson and G. H. Whitaker. Loeb Classical Library 227. Cambridge, Massachusetts: Harvard University Press, 1929.

The Pluralism Project. "Jainism: An Ethic for Living." *Harvard University*. Accessed December 24, 2023. https://pluralism.org/an-ethic-for-living.

———. "What Do Pagans Do?" *Harvard University*. Accessed February 19, 2024. https://pluralism.org/what-do-pagans-do.

Pope, Marvin H. "Baal Worship." *Jewish Virtual Library*. Accessed February 15, 2025. American-Israeli Cooperative Enterprise. https://www.jewishvirtuallibrary.org/baal-worship-jewish-virtual-library.

Pratt, Douglas. *Being Open, Being Faithful: The Journey of Interreligious Dialogue*. Geneva: World Council of Churches, 2014.

Quittkat Hannah L., Andrea S. Hartmann, Rainer Düsing, Ulrike Buhlmann, Silja Vocks. "Body Dissatisfaction, Importance of Appearance, and Body Appreciation in Men and Women over the Lifespan." *Frontiers in Psychiatry* 10 (December 2019) 864. https://doi.org/10.3389/fpsyt.2019.00864.

Rahner, Karl. "Der dreifaltige Gott als transzendeter Urgrund der Heilsgeschichte." In *Die Heilsgeschichte vor Christus*, Mysterium salutis, Grundriss heilsgeschichtlicher Dogmatik 2 (Einsiedeln, Switzerland: Benziger, 1967). Translation: *The Trinity*. Translated by Joseph Donceel. New York: Crossroad, 1997.

Ratzinger, Joseph. "Concerning the Notion of Person in Theology." *Communio* 17 (Fall 1990) 439–54.

Rees, Laurence. "Viewpoint: His Dark Charisma." *BBC News*. 7 November 2012. Last modified 12 November 2012. British Broadcasting Corporation. https://www.bbc.com/news/magazine-20237437.amp.

Rehm, Jeremy, and Ben Biggs. "The Four Fundamental Forces of Nature." *Space*. December 23, 2021. https://www.space.com/four-fundamental-forces.html.

Reitan, Eric. *Troubled Paradise: Limited Salvation & the Problem of Heavenly Grief*. Eugene, Oregon: Cascade, 2024.

Reynolds, Gabriel Said. "On the Qur'anic Accusation of Scriptural Falsification (*taḥrīf*) and Christian Anti-Jewish Polemic." *Journal of the American Oriental Society* 130, no. 2 (2010) 189–202. https://doi.org/10.2307/23044514.

Rich, Tracey R. "Qorbanot: Sacrifices and Offerings." *Judaism 101*. Accessed April 6, 2025. https://www.jewfaq.org/sacrifices_and_offerings.

Richard of Saint-Victor, *De Trinitate*.
Critical edition: *De Trinitate*. Edited by J. Ribaillier. Textes philosophiques du Moyen Age 6. Paris: J. Vrin, 1958. Translation: *On the Trinity: English Translation and Commentary*. Translated by Ruben Angelici. Eugene, Oregon: Cascade, 2011.

Richards, Laura. "Office Politics: How to Handle It." *Intelligent People*. January 9, 2024. https://www.intelligentpeople.co.uk/employer-advice/office-politics.

Römer, Thomas. *The Invention of God*. Translated by R. Geuss. Cambridge, Massachusetts: Harvard University Press, 2015.

Sacha, Gurinder Singh. *The Sikhs and Their Way of Life*. 2nd ed. Southall, United Kingdom: Sikh Missionary Society, 2003. https://www.sikhmissionarysociety.org/sms/smspublications/thesikhsandtheirwayoflife.

Sanders, John. "Historical Considerations." In Clark Pinnock, Richard Rice, John Sanders, William Hasker and David Basinger, *The Openness of God: A Biblical Challenge to the Traditional Understanding of God* (Downers Grove, Illinois: InterVarsity, 1994), 59–100.

Schleiermacher, Friedrich Daniel Ernst. *Der christliche Glaube nach den Grundsätzen der evangelischen Kirche im Zusammenhange dargestellt*.
Critical translation: *Christian Faith*. Translated by Terrence N. Tice, Catherine L. Kelsey, and Edwina Lawler. Edited by Catherine L. Kelsey and Terrence N. Tice. Louisville, Kentucky: Westminster John Knox, 2016.

Sefaria. "Rashi." *Sefaria*. Accessed March 2, 2025. https://www.sefaria.org/topics/rashi?tab=author-works-on-sefaria.

Shelley, Bruce L. *Church History in Plain Language*. 3rd ed. Nashville, Tennessee: Thomas Nelson, 2008.

Sherry, Patrick. "Problem of Evil." *Britannica*. Last modified 12 February 2025. https://www.britannica.com/topic/problem-of-evil.

Side Effects. "Childhood Trauma Leads to Brains Wired for Fear." *Side Effects*. February 3, 2015. https://www.sideeffectspublicmedia.org/community-health/2015-02-03/childhood-trauma-leads-to-brains-wired-for-fear.

Siegel, Ethan. "It Takes 26 Fundamental Constants to Give Us Our Universe, but They Still Don't Give Everything." *Forbes*. August 22, 2015. https://www.forbes.com/sites/ethansiegel/2015/08/22/it-takes-26-fundamental-constants-to-give-us-our-universe-but-they-still-dont-give-everything.

Sijuwade, Joshua Reginald. "The Logical Problem of the Trinity: A New Solution." *Religions* 13, no. 9 (31 August 2022) 809. https://doi.org/10.3390/rel13090809.

Singapore Courts. "About the Legal System." *SG Courts*. Government of Singapore. Accessed March 4, 2025. https://www.judiciary.gov.sg/who-we-are/about-legal-system.

Skariah, George. "The Biblical Doctrine of the Perfection Preservation of the Holy Scriptures." ThD diss., Far Eastern Bible College, 2005.

Smilde, Koen. "Hitler's Antisemitism: Why Did He Hate the Jews?." *Anne Frank House*. Accessed February 15, 2025. https://www.annefrank.org/en/anne-frank/go-in-depth/why-did-hitler-hate-jews.

Smith, Huston. *The Religions of Man*. Perennial Library. New York: Harper & Row, 1965.

Smith, Melinda, Lawrence Robinson, and Jeanne Segal. "PTSD in Military Veterans." *HelpGuide.org*. Last modified April 22, 2024. https://www.helpguide.org/articles/ptsd-trauma/ptsd-in-military-veterans.htm.

Smith, Peter. "What Would Bonhoeffer Do? Anti-Nazi Pastor's Legacy Claimed, Debated across Political Spectrum." *Associated Press*. January 7, 2025. The Associated Press. https://www.ap.org/news-highlights/spotlights/2025/what-would-bonhoeffer-do-anti-nazi-pastors-legacy-claimed-debated-across-political-spectrum.

Snell, Robin Stanley, Crystal Xinru Wu, and Hong Weng Lei. "Junzi Virtues: A Confucian Foundation for Harmony within Organizations." *Asian Journal of Business Ethics* 11, no. 1 (2022) 183–226. https://doi.org/10.1007/s13520-022-00146-1.

Song, C. S. *Jesus, the Crucified People*. The Cross in the Lotus World. Minneapolis, Minnesota: Fortress, 1996.

Sorensen, Jon. "Why the 'Gospel of Barnabas' is a Medieval Fake." *Catholic Answers*. June 30, 2014. https://www.catholic.com/magazine/online-edition/why-the-gospel-of-barnabas-is-a-medieval-fake.

Southern Adventist University. "History of the Christian Church: Roman Persecution." *Southern Adventist University*. Last modified July 12, 2023. https://southern.libguides.com/historyofchristianchurch/romanpersecution.

Spencer, Megan. "What's the Difference between Emotions, Feelings, and Moods?" *Dakota Family Services*. June 7, 2022. https://dakotafamilyservices.org/resources/blog/archive/moods-feelings-emotions.

Srinivas, M. N. "Gandhi's Religion." *Economic and Political Weekly* 30, no. 25 (June 1995) 1489–491. http://www.jstor.org/stable/4402906.

Stark, Rodney. *Discovering God: The Origins of the Great Religions and the Evolution of Belief*. New York: HarperOne, 2007.

Stuart, Douglas. *Hosea–Jonah*. Word Biblical Commentary 31. Grand Rapids, Michigan: Zondervan, 2014.

Suchocki, Marjorie Hewitt. *God, Christ, Church: A Practical Guide to Process Theology*. Rev. ed. New York: Crossroad, 1989.

Talmudic Israel. *Bereshit Rabbah*.
    Text and translation: "Bereshit Rabbah 38." Translated by Joshua Schreier. In *Sefaria Midrash Rabbah* (Brooklyn, New York: Sefaria, 2022), https://www.sefaria.org/sheets/256044.1?lang=bi&p2=Bereshit_Rabbah.38.13&lang2=bi.

Tan, Wei-Xuan. "Singaporean Named New Anglican Archbishop for South-East Asia." *The Straits Times*. Last modified 23 January 2024. SPH Media. https://www.straitstimes.com/singapore/singaporean-named-new-anglican-archbishop-for-south-east-asia.

Telushkin, Joseph. "Jewish Concepts: The Messiah." *Jewish Virtual Library*. American-Israeli Cooperative Enterprise. Accessed March 2, 2025. https://www.jewishvirtuallibrary.org/the-messiah.

Tennent, Timothy C. *Christianity at the Religious Roundtable: Evangelicalism in Conversation with Hinduism, Buddhism, and Islam*. Grand Rapids, Michigan: Baker Academic, 2002.

Thatamanil, John J. *Circling the Elephant: A Comparative Theology of Religious Diversity*. New York: Fordham University Press, 2020.

Thomasson, Amie. "Categories." *The Stanford Encyclopedia of Philosophy* (Winter 2022). https://plato.stanford.edu/archives/win2022/entries/categories.

Tournier, Paul. *The Meaning of Persons*. Translated by Edwin Hudson. London: SCM, 1957.

Travers, Mark. "A Psychologist Explains the 'Pretty Privilege' Paradox." *Forbes*. October 15, 2023. https://www.forbes.com/sites/traversmark/2023/10/15/a-psychologist-explains-the-pretty-privilege-paradox/?sh=4b9c545e45fc.

U.S. Energy Information Administration. "Electricity Explained: Electricity in the United States." *U.S. Energy Information Administration*. Last modified March 26, 2024. https://www.eia.gov/energyexplained/electricity/electricity-in-the-us.php.

———. "Electricity Explained: How Electricity Is Generated." *U.S. Energy Information Administration*. Last modified October 31, 2023. https://www.eia.gov/energyexplained/electricity/how-electricity-is-generated.php.

———. "Electricity Explained: Magnets and Electricity." *U.S. Energy Information Administration*. Reviewed November 19, 2022. https://www.eia.gov/energyexplained/electricity/magnets-and-electricity.php

Van Til, Cornelius. *An Introduction to Systematic Theology: Prolegomena and the Doctrines of Revelation, Scripture, and God*. Edited by Wiilliam Edgar. 2nd ed. Phillipsburg, New Jersey: P&R, 2007.

Verbrugge, Verlyn D., ed., *The NIV Theological Dictionary of New Testament Words*. Grand Rapids, Michigan: Zondervan, 2000.

Volf, Miroslav. "'The Trinity Is Our Social Program': The Doctrine of the Trinity and the Shape of Social Engagement." *Modern Theology* 14 (1998) 403–23.

Volkmann, Hans. "Antiochus IV Epiphanes." *Britannica*. Last modified 2 September 2024. Encyclopaedia Britannica. https://www.britannica.com/biography/Antiochus-IV-Epiphanes.

Walters, Kerry. *Atheism: A Guide for the Perplexed*. New York: Continuum, 2010.

Walton, John H., Victor H. Matthews, and Mark W. Chavalas. *The IVP Background Commentary: Old Testament*. Downers Grove, Illinois: IVP Academic, 2000.

Ward, Graham. *How the Light Gets In: Ethical Life I*. Oxford: Oxford University Press, 2016.

Ward, Keith. *Religion and Revelation: A Theology of Revelation in the World's Religions*. Oxford: Oxford University Press, 1994.

Wenham, Gordon J. *Genesis 1–15*. Word Biblical Commentary 1. Nashville, Tennessee: Thomas Nelson, 1987.

Westminster Divines. *Westminster Larger Catechism*. London: Westminster Assembly, 1647.

Williams, David T. "A Theology of the Infinite." *Koers* 60, no. 1 (1995) 103–120.

Williams, Rowan. *Being Disciples: Essentials of the Christian Life*. London: SPCK, 2016.

Williamson, H. G. M. "Samaritan". In *New Bible Dictionary*, edited by I. H. Marshall, A. R. Millard, J. I. Packer, and D. J. Wiseman, 3rd ed., IVP Reference Collection, 1052–53. Downers Grove, Illinois: IVP Academic, 1996.

Wilson, William D. "The Orthodox Betrayal: How German Christians Embraced and Taught Nazism and Sparked a Christian Battle." Honors thesis, Georgia Southern University, 2016. https://digitalcommons.georgiasouthern.edu/honors-theses/160.

Windle, Bryan. "The Three Oldest Biblical Texts." *Bible Archaeology Report*. February 6, 2019. https://biblearchaeologyreport.com/2019/02/06/the-three-oldest-biblical-texts.

Wolf, Jessica. "The Truth about Galileo and His Conflict with the Catholic Church." *UCLA*. December 22, 2016. Regents of University of California. https://newsroom.ucla.edu/releases/the-truth-about-galileo-and-his-conflict-with-the-catholic-church.

Wolfson, Harry Austryn. *Faith, Trinity, Incarnation*. 3rd ed. The Philosophy of the Church Fathers. Cambridge, Massachusetts: Harvard University Press, 1970.

Wongsakon, Acharavadee. "Buddhism 101." *Knowing Buddha*. Knowing Buddha Organization. Accessed December 10, 2023. https://www.knowingbuddha.org/home-en.

World101. "Why Did World War II Happen?" *Council on Foreign Relations*. Last modified July 25, 2023. https://world101.cfr.org/contemporary-history/world-war/why-did-world-war-ii-happen.

Yaqeen Institute. "Who Is Jesus in Islam?" *Yaqeen Institute*. December 22, 2022. Yaqeen Institute for Islamic Research. https://yaqeeninstitute.org/read/post/who-is-jesus-in-islam.

Zeeb, Janelle Louise. "An Examination of Jonathan Edwards' Theological Method Concerning the Problem of Reprobation." PhD diss., Wycliffe College and University of Toronto, 2022.

Subject Index

abuse
    importance of recognizing self-value in the context thereof, 24n15
    normalization thereof, 245–46
    roots thereof, 439
    sense of injustice in the context thereof, 246
adversity, epiphanic value thereof, 20n10
aggression, 38–39, 41, 120, 124, 129, 245–46, 368, 415
    self-aggression, 246
agnosticism, 145, 167, 173–74, 190, 354
    of Buddhism, 167
Anselm of Canterbury, 6, 90, 153, 183n35, 398, 412–13
Anthony of Egypt, 323–24, 336
Apollinarianism, 282
Aquinas, Thomas, 36, 77n31, 103n16, 161n13, 354
    salvation as mediated through "implicit faith", 354
Arianism, 262n6, 282
ark of the covenant, 15n2, 92
Arminianism, 99n12, 412
Athanasius of Alexandria, 148n64, 262n6, 283
atheism, 22, 35, 44, 47, 49, 161–62, 170–72, 174–75, 179, 189–90, 194–95, 221–22, 315
    critique of religion thereof, 315–16
    whether reciprocity or enlightened self-interest, 194n61

atonement, for sins against oneself, 144n60
autonomy, 19, 30, 38–39, 56, 72, 97, 99, 191, 215–16, 231, 250, 382
    in relation to divine grace, 55–58, 215–24

Baal, 401
Baháʼí Faith, 193
Barth, Karl
    synchronic modalism, 251–52
beauty standards, 197–201
Bible, revelatory nature thereof
    cognitive, 16
    non-revelation, 14
    non-revelation, comprehensive, 14
    non-revelation, corruptive, 14–15
    specific, conceptual/textual, 16
    specific, existential, 16
    theological-specific, 16
    universal, morality-centered, 16–49
biblical account of creation, first
    as Israelite devotional resource, 205–11
biblical account of creation, second
    interpretation thereof, 211
blasphemy, definition thereof, 364
Bonhoeffer, Dietrich, 375–76
Buddhism, 44n45, 46, 159, 167–68, 173n26, 190–91, 354

Calvin, John, 66, 68n23, 70n25, 75–76
Calvinism, 67, 99, 219n37, 373n40, 374

SUBJECT INDEX

Canaan, 135, 184–85, 231, 412n14
Canaanites, 135n49, 173n26, 186
Cappadocian Fathers, 252, 255
casuistry, 117
causes, primary and secondary, 226
celebrities, 198, 200, 275–76, 391
child sacrifice, 173n26, 186, 401
    justification for, 186n38
Christ's divinity, evidence thereof, 356n15
Christ's divine and human natures, paradox thereof, 40n41, 261–62
Christian perfection
    as attainable, 408
    as unattainable, 407
    through divine work as human capacitation, 408–41
Christian theology, influences thereof
    feudalism, 6, 90–91, 398
    monarchism, 346, 382, 397–98
    non-condemnation of other religions, 190
    theocracy, 91, 398
classical doctrine of God
    divine absoluteness, 259–60
    divine-human antithesis, with critique, 259–64, 284
    divine unknowability, 53
    scriptural incongruence thereof, 40n41, 299–300
communicatio idiomatum, 282
competition, as nurtured in childhood, 26–27
confession
    as worldview, 39
    of personal faith, 431
    of sin, 87, 220n38, 390, 424, 428–29
    religious/denominational, 4–5, 7, 168, 189, 249n84, 250
    soft/egalitarian approach to, 189
Confucianism, 192–93
    Neo-Confucianism, 274
conservative theology, 3, 48, 395
    vis-à-vis seeking help for mental health, 3n1
conversion
    Augustine's reason for, 323–24, 326
    of evil to good, 124, 230, 333

religious, 30, 393
spiritual, 3n1, 6, 56, 68, 73, 99n12, 178, 181, 216, 219n37, 224–26, 272, 313, 323n18, 326, 366–67, 369–71, 374, 408, 413, 432, 435, 441n43
simul iustus est et peccat, 224–25
cosmological development
    angels as responsible for material creation and evolution, 209n17, 359
    Divine Nature as establishing initial conditions and laws, 209n17
cosmological structure, 34n29
covenant, 8, 55n9, 83, 143–44, 231–32, 241, 251, 273, 417
creation, divine
    as re-creation, 196
    by theistic evolution, 196–97
    ex nihilo, 196
    progressive creationism, 197
    two-stage creation of spiritual beings and material bodies, 197–256
crucifixion, of Christ
    compatibilist view thereof, 385
    convertive view thereof, 58, 124, 233n61, 333, 385–87
    nature of Christ's feeling of abandonment in the context thereof, 230n55
    the Father's motivation for not extricating Christ from, 233n61
cruelty
    origin thereof, 361
    perception of God's, 361–62
Cyril of Alexandria, 262n6, 283

depression, as nurtured in childhood, 22–26
desire, as rooted in disorder, 320
dignity, as innate, 280
divine aseity, 148, 152, 265–66, 268, 281, 290–91, 305–6, 387, 405
    and interdependence, 148, 152, 265–66, 290, 305–6
    and Trinity, 405–6

SUBJECT INDEX

definition thereof, 148, 152, 265, 291
divine atonement
   as experienced in pre-terrestrial divine-human encounter, 145
   as instituted to remove guilt, 144n60, 145n61, 189
divine election
   and othering, 439–41
divine image, in humankind, definition thereof, 238
divine immutability
   and divine physical embodiment, 355–56
   as source of other divine perfections, 291–92
   definition thereof, 261
   of God, 6, 8, 40n41, 238, 259–61, 262n6, 291–92, 299, 346, 355–56, 377–79, 381, 397n24
   of God's laws, 187
   of social ideals for beauty, 201
   Platonic connection thereof to divine transcendence, 261
   Platonic connection thereof to God as Creator, 260
   Platonic connection thereof to perfection, 260, 298, 377
   Platonic connection thereof to salvation, 377
   scriptural incongruence thereof, 346–47
   untenability thereof in face of human suffering, 379–81
   vis-à-vis God's secondary mode of existence, 261–62
divine impassibility, 6, 40n41, 145, 259, 262, 286, 292, 299, 398n24
divine laws, effeteness thereof, 414
divine moral qualities, revelatory
   compassion, 114–15
   empathy, 115–16
   equanimity, 145–46
   faith, 146–48
   forbearance, 137–42
   forgiveness, 142–44
   generosity, 152
   gentleness, 120–22
   goodness, 117–18
   holiness, 124–25
   honor, 148–49
   hope, 148
   ingenuousness, 128–29
   integrity, 150
   joy, 123
   kindness, 149
   longsuffering, 144–45
   love, 110–14
   passion, 132–33
   patience, 118–20
   peacefulness, 124
   resilience, 129–31
   resolve, 134–36
   respect, 127–28
   responsibility, 150
   righteousness, 117
   self-discipline, 122–23
   selflessness, 152
   sincerity, 131–32
   solidarity, 125–26
   truthfulness, 151–52
Divine Nature
   as imperceptible, 345–46
   as impersonal, 52, 104–5
   as insubstantial, 63
   as ontological and moral source of existence, 4, 11, 32n27, 33–36, 52, 62–63, 96, 102–8, 161–62, 170, 173, 175, 189–90, 197, 205, 213–15, 312, 325, 345–46, 352n8, 358–59, 365
divine omnipotence, 12, 48–49, 53, 232, 302, 379
   untenability thereof in face of human suffering, 379–81
divine omnipresence, 300, 302, 355, 379
divine omniscience, 300, 379
divine simplicity, 6, 40n41, 51, 53, 259–62, 406
   definition thereof, 260–61
divine sovereignty, 4, 6, 216–17, 227–35
   tempering factors thereof, 233–34
   whether it controls human will, 217–18, 366–72
divine strength, signification thereof, 289

SUBJECT INDEX

divine Word, as psychological subject, 262n6
divine-human communication, 227, 235
divinity, marks thereof, 405
domination, roots thereof, 439
Dupuis, Jacques, 157–58

Ebionitism, 48
Edwards, Jonathan, 35n30, 373–75
emotions
    acknowledgement thereof, 113, 339n38, 390
    vs. feelings, 413–14
empathy, lack thereof, 343
end, as prophesied by Christ, 279–80
Enoch, Book of, 213n21
eternal security, criteria thereof, 373–75

faith
    as source of self-esteem, 199
    definition of salvific, 179, 218–19
    erroneous views thereof, 179
    why not all believe in Christ, 372
fall of humankind, efficient cause thereof, 66–67, 75–76
feelings
    godly, 414
    vs. emotions, 413–14
Feuerbach, Ludwig Andreas, 330–31
forgiveness
    as required from wronged in spite of God's, 138, 144n60
    God's as independent of atonement, 144n60
    impossibility thereof apart from repentance, 137–38, 363
freewill
    Adam's
        in biblical teaching, 65–66
        in Calvinism, 66–67, 75–76
    compatibilist, 67, 99–100, 70n25, 99–100, 385
    God's
        voluntas naturalis, 31
        voluntas necessaria, 31
    libertarian, 99, 385, 412
Freud, Sigmund, 330–31

Galileo Galilei, 395
gender dysphoria, 24, 246–48
God
    as Almighty, 92, 231–32, 360
    as *El Shaddai*, 231–32
    as *Kurios Pantokratōr* ("Lord of Hosts"), 231–32
    as ontological and moral source of existence, 4, 11, 32n27, 33–36, 52, 62–63, 96, 102–8, 161–62, 170, 173, 175, 189–90, 197, 205, 213–15, 312, 325, 345–46, 352n8, 358–59, 365
    as *Pantokratōr*, 231–32
    as peace, 39
    as pro-social, 439
    as source of universal duty, 365
    as spiritual, 331
    as total source of humanity, 10, 62, 267, 327
    as universal and necessary, 104n18, 312, 352n8
    vis-à-vis human value, 236–50
God primarily as judge, view thereof
    scriptural incongruence thereof, 61, 64–91, 397–98
good works, nature thereof, 352n8
    contra legalism, 219
    contra self-promotion, 220
goodness, as innate in humankind, 174
Gospel according to the Hebrews, 48
Gregory of Nazianzus, 262n6
group practices, unethical, 249

hermeneutics, 4, 5n4, 17, 278
    as based on legalistic motivations, 317–18
    as based on relational motivations, 317
    empirical, 76
    evangelical, 7, 9
    historical-grammatical, 4
    inflexibility thereof, 171
Hinduism, 34, 36, 44n45, 46–49, 105, 169–70, 173n26, 191, 354
human beings, calling thereof, 416
humanism, 175, 194, 256, 312n4, 376
humanity, doctrine thereof

SUBJECT INDEX

as individual patient of salvation, 272
as revealing God's radical sociality, 272–310
as shaped by salvific liturgical processes, 272
hypostatic union of Christ, 283

identity, divine
as established in the plurality of encounter, 95–154
as exclusive, 95
as focus of absolute dependence, 95
as pro-social, 95
idolatry, 35, 38, 84–85, 130, 133, 159, 162–63, 183–84, 186–88, 211n20, 277, 280, 365, 370, 382, 401
as contrasted with the moral, 84–85
as social competition, 38, 277, 365–66
as xenophobia, 188
error thereof, 84
of feminine beauty, 133
nature of ancient Near Eastern/Greek idolatry, 187
religious, 84, 130, 159, 162–63, 183–84, 186–95, 211n20, 280, 365–66, 370, 382, 401
definition thereof, 365
motivation thereof, 188n43
true recipient thereof, 401
insensibility, 400
intellectual censorship, 249
Islam, 15n2, 35n30, 47–48, 159, 170–72, 173n26, 192, 397, 402

Jainism, 193–94
Jesus of Nazareth
as only quantitatively distinctive from other human beings, 262n6
as present as sole savior in all religions/humanism, 189–90
as religious reformer, 186–87
psychological subject thereof as identical with the divine Word, 262n6

response to Jewish/Islamic rejection thereof, 171
justification by faith
scriptural incongruence thereof, 288–89, 362–63, 427–37
vis-à-vis Luther's mental health, 318, 321–23, 325
Justin Martyr, 292

knowledge, of God
as accommodated, 344
in personal relationship, 345–76
through supportive divine presence, 344–45

lake of fire, 234n64
laws, vis-à-vis biblical ethics, 375–76
legalism, 117, 186, 219, 317
Leo I, 262–63
love of money, root and futility thereof, 388

Mary, mother of Christ, 48, 282–83, 355, 403–5
as *Christotokos*, 282–83
as *theotokos*, 282–83, 355
virginal conception thereof, 171, 232, 405
mollycoddling, 38–39, 433
monarchism, 6, 90, 101, 185, 231, 304, 346
monotheism, use of terminology, 35n30
moral attributes, 39, 63–64, 72–73, 110, 129, 161, 176, 182, 238, 268, 309, 312, 348, 351, 357, 365, 416
moral change, in non-theism, 431n32
moral development
divine basis thereof, 56, 107–8, 145, 161–62, 216, 218–19, 236, 246, 315, 337, 411, 439–41
moral distinction, divine-human
antithetical view thereof, 377–78
conflated view thereof, 378
correspondent view thereof, 378–406

SUBJECT INDEX

morality
    as innate, 108–10
    as universal, 173, 249n84
    responsibility for the development thereof, 109–10
Muhammad, Prophet of Allāh, 48, 353–54

natural theology, 15–16, 32–37, 329
necessity for punishment, 145, 189
Nestorianism
    henosis ("union") of Christ's divine and human natures, 283
    sunapheia ("conjunction") of Christ's divine and human natures, 283
Nestorius, 282–83
non-Christian, use of terminology, 3n1
non-theism, 145, 173n26, 431n32
    of Buddhism, 173n26

objectification, 127, 237, 246–47
obsessions, 391–95
Origen of Alexandria, 293
original sin, classical doctrine thereof, 68, 93, 99–100, 178, 216, 320n13, 352n8, 434
    and ritualism, 326–27
    biological vs. psychodynamic interpretation thereof, 216–17
    development thereof vis-à-vis Augustine's mental health, 318–21, 323–25
    medium of transmission thereof, 320n13
    punitive consequence thereof, 434n36
    scriptural incongruence thereof, 61, 64–91, 177–81, 216–17

paganism/neo-paganism, 194, 286, 318n10
pain
    as emotional, 355
    of the Father and Spirit at the cross, 355n13
Paul of Samosata, 282
Pelagianism, 439
personhood, human
    as dependent on social interaction, 265, 273–74
    definition thereof, 273
    facets thereof, 357–58
    religious cult as necessary for, 316–17
    religious cult as unnecessary for, 316
    spiritual-transcendent as necessary for, 317–43
phenomenology, 157
Philo of Alexandria, 245
Platonism
    influence thereof on Christian theology, 40n41, 259–64, 298
    Neoplatonism, 301–2
    view of God thereof, 300–302
poverty of spirit, 74, 229n54, 278
predestination, 62, 64–91, 100, 148, 280, 363, 379, 382, 385–86, 429, 438
progressive knowledge of God as Trinity
    medical/scientific, 64
progressive revelation
    of divine sorrow and wrath, 331–32
    of eternal solace, 399–400
progressive theology, 7, 14n1, 47–48, 189n44, 268, 378
psychological availability, 227
psychological displacement, of self-worth
    in Buddhism, 167
psychological dysfunctionality
    appeasement thereof through non-retaliation, 141
    as conspiring with compulsive evil, 87–88, 109–10, 388, 434
    as constructed value system, 337–39
    as non-justification for immoral action, 416–17
    definition thereof, 319
    dysfunctional self vs. natural self, nature and evidence thereof, 337
    impact thereof on moral orientation, 179–80
    impact thereof on reciprocal loving relations, 238
    misunderstanding thereof as principle of sin, 318–26
    reason for the denial thereof, 418

vis-à-vis biblical witness to role of
  childhood, 414–15
psychological maturity, route toward,
  417
psychological projection, 318n10,
  330–31, 394
  God as, 330–31

Qur'ān, 48, 402–4

Rahner, Karl, 157, 253, 294
  "anonymous Christians", 157
  Trinitarian doctrine thereof, 253,
    293–94
  Vorgriff ("supernatural existential"),
    157
recognizing God's voice, 228n54, 316n8
rejection of God
  non-probative basis thereof, 331
regenerate, sinful desires thereof, in
  Calvinism, 225n48
regeneration, in Calvinism, why none
  may charge God for depriving
  one thereof, 67–68
relational pathology, as nurtured in
  childhood, 38–39
relationship with God, intimacy thereof,
  228n54, 316n8
religions, doctrinal differences
  affinity thereof in focus on
    forgiveness and morality,
    189–90
  as arising from revelatory
    adaptation, 173n26, 353–54
  as complementary paths to the same
    God, 256, 312n4
  compatibility thereof, 167–76, 172,
    249n84
    metaphorical, 172, 249n84
religious authority, role thereof, 248–50
religious exclusivism, etiology and
  anatomy thereof, 317–27
repentance
  vis-à-vis divine grace, 176–81
rest, for God's people, 411n14
revelation, religious claims thereof
  grounds for legitimacy thereof, 330

Sabellianism, 252
salvation
  absence of conception thereof in
    certain other religions, 256
  signification thereof, 220–23, 256,
    427–37
Schleiermacher, Friedrich Daniel Ernst,
  16n3, 95, 291n38
self-forgiveness
  as indicating pre-terrestrial human
    experience of divine atonement,
    145, 179, 189, 221–22
self-hatred, 112–13
self-love
  healthy and unwholesome, 111–12
sensibility
  as appropriateness, 110, 193, 387n13
  as emotivity, 133
  as humaneness, 4, 9, 129, 176, 246,
    382
  as logical coherence, 314, 409
  as perceptibility, 107
  as proportionality, 151, 400
Sikhism, 192
simulation, world as, 360–61
sin
  as irresponsibility, 416–17
  vis-à-vis divine being and action,
    363–64
  ways of dealing with another's
    alienation, 421–23
    crusade, 424–25
    extenuation, 424
    mercy, 424–27
    resignation/license, 424
  ways of dealing with one's own
    condemnation, 337
    criticism without
      condemnation, 337–38, 390
social messaging
  as source of psychological harm,
    201
soteriology
  dysfunctional role of ritualism in
    the context thereof, 326–27,
    427–39
speech, hurtfulness and significance
  thereof, 142n57

supernaturalist theology, 328–30
  critique thereof, 329–30

Taoism, 100n14, 191–92
temptation, minimizing thereof, 392
Tertullian, 262n6, 292
theism
  baseline conviction thereof, 35
  definition thereof, 215, 266–67, 327–28
  experiential-intellectual basis thereof, 327, 331–33, 356–61
theodicy, 13, 48–49, 52, 62, 104, 153–54, 205, 212, 214, 233
  connection building, 154
  soul-making, 154
theology of religions
  exclusivism, 155–56
  exclusivism, divine-creature, 175
  inclusivism, 156–58
  integrative and pluriform, 158–59, 175
  non-exclusivism, religious/metaphysical, 175, 318
  particularism, 175
  pluralism, 158
transactionalism, 20n10, 38–39, 338
  in the atonement, 303
transcendence, divine
  dual, 51
  formal and qualitative, 51–93
  former, 51
  non-transcendence, 51
  radical, analogical access, 51
  radical, symbolic access, 51
transcendental realism, 34n29
  compatibilist view thereof, 34n29
tree of the knowledge of good and evil
  meaning of consequence of consumption of fruit thereof, 217n32
Trinity
  as integral to the Divine Nature, 63, 107–8, 126
  difference thereof from OT monotheism, 406
  doctrine thereof, 250–56
    Islamic misconception thereof, 402–6
  emotionality as reflection thereof, 265–66
  functional equivalents thereof in other religions/humanism, 170–71
  Islamic view thereof, 402–4
  personhood within, 292–93
    hypostasis and the ill-conceived adoption thereof, 293
    prosopon/persona, 292
  progressive revelation, 406
  psychological maturity, 126, 265, 290–92, 305

unconscious, nature thereof, 419–20
unforgivable sin, biblical teaching on
  implications thereof, 163–64
unforgiveness, living with, 138
unrepentance, boundaries in light of, 142n57

Waraqa Ibn Nawfal, 48

Yahweh
  as contrasted with Greek gods, 187–88

Zoroastrianism, 192

Scripture Index

Old Testament

Genesis
15n2, 183, 197, 206

1	7, 207–8, 209n18, 243n74
1:1	243n74
1:1–2	243n74
1:1—2:3	208
1:2	243
1:26	292
1:26–27	264
1:26, 28	310
1:28–29	416
1:31	242
2	206, 243
2:2–3	208
2:5	206
2:7	211n20
2:9	207, 242
2:15–17	183
2:16–17	207
2:25	243
3	243
3:1	120
3:7	243
3:10	243
3:11	243
3:19	211n20
3:22	292
3:22–24	298
4:1–8	88, 306
4:6	308
4:6–7	203, 388
4:7	308–9
5:2	244
6:1–13	134
6:5	69, 86, 134
8:21	134, 218
9:1–4	416
9:1–7	182
9:1–17	134
11:1–9	298, 300
15:12–16	233
15:16	135n49
16	55
16:13	229
17	231
18:14	232
18:20–21	227–28
18:22–33	233n62
20:1–7	217
20:7	217
21	55
22:1–2	316n8
22:1–14	228
22:8	229
22:12	298, 300
22:14	229
25:29–34	77, 77n31
35:11–12	231
48:3–4	231
50:20	58, 386

SCRIPTURE INDEX

Exodus	15n2, 359
1:13–14	80n33
2:23–25	115, 228
3	94
3:2	345, 359
3:2–3	359
3:4	359
3:4–22	345
3:8	135n49
3:14	94
3:19–20	80
4	359
4:16	359
4:17	360
4:21–23	80
5:1–9	80
7	359
7:1	359
7:2	359
7:3–5	80
8:15	218
8:32	218
9:15	81
9:16	79–80
9:34	218
16	57
19	341
20:8–11	206
20:11	207
21:20	127
21:26–27	127
24:4	15n2
25:22	92n53
32:1–6	199
32:1–14	298
32:7–14	231
33:19	94

Leviticus	15n2
4:1—6:7	91
14:33–53	371
16:20–22	91
18	173n26
18:21	186
24	140n55
24:17–22	140n55

Numbers	15n2
8:5–19	371
13–14	412n14
14:1–24	298
14:11–20	231
19:14–20	371
20:14–21	79
23:19	347

Deuteronomy	15n2
8	369
8:3	218n34
8:17	369
13:12–18	395
17:18–20	15n2
19	140n55
19:21	140n55
20:16–18	135
28	185
28:48	243
30:11–20	185
31:9–13	15n2
31:24–26	15n2

Joshua	
2	151n66
24:15	135n49
24:26	15n2

Judges	185
4:1–10	354
11:29–40	186n38

1 Samuel	
4:1–9	186
10:25	15n2
15:29	347
16:7	376

SCRIPTURE INDEX

2 Samuel

6:6–7	92
24:15–16	227–28

1 Kings

8:27	381
17:17–24	304
17:21–22	304
19:9–18	341

2 Kings

1	318n10
3:26–27	186
4:18–37	304
4:33	304
13:20–21	304
17:7–23	186
22:8	15n2

2 Chronicles

17:9	15n2
36:17–21	139

Ezra — 186

7:6	15n2
7:10	15n2

Nehemiah — 15n2, 186

8:1–2	15n2

Esther — 15n2

Job — 73n27, 206–7, 212

34:14–15	215, 227
35:5–8	73n27
38–42	207, 212
38:4–11	206
38:12–15	206
41:11	412
42:2	232

Psalms

1	227
1:2	207
14	389
14:1–3	389
14:5	389
14:6	389
19:2	207
19:3–4	161
19:4–6	207
19:7–14	207
37:23	371
50:10–13	412
51	180
51:5	217
51:6	217
51:10	180
53	389
53:1–3	389
53:4	389
69:1–28	82
69:22–23	82
80:7	368
85:4	368
85:6	368
104:27–30	214
110:1	292
136	207
137:8–9	139
139	381
139:7–12	107
141:3	372
141:4	372

Proverbs

1:7	334n32
1:29	334n32
2:5	334n32
6:16–17	75
8:13	75, 334n32
9:10	334n32
10:27	334n32

Proverbs (continued)

14:26–27	334n32
15:16	334n32
15:33	334n32
16:6	334n32
19:23	334n32
22:4	334n32
23:17	334n32
28:13	241n70

Ecclesiastes   19n8

1:2	19n8
7:13	100
7:13–14	100
7:14	100
8:15	202n10

Isaiah   115, 345

6	73
6:1–5	346
9:6	415n18
29:10	82
29:13–14	82
44:9	211n20
45:7	100
57:3–10	401
66:1	381

Jeremiah   15n2

2:13	199
18:1–11	83n36
23:24	381
32:17	232
36:27–28	15n2

Ezekiel   345

1:26–28	346
11:19–20	370
11:21	370
14:6–11	80
16:7	243
16:22	243
16:39	243
18	59, 142, 228, 239
18:4	85
18:7	243
18:16	243
18:20	85
18:23	54
18:31	371
18:32	54
23:29	243
36	371
36:22–27	370
36:25	370–71
36:26	371

Daniel

4:29–30	74
4:31–32	74
4:35	75
4:37	75
7:13–14	171n24
9:2	15n2
9:3–23	228
10:2–14	228
12:4	15n2
12:9	15n2

Hosea   424

2:16	163
2:16–17	401
6:6	114n29, 424
11:8–9	306
13:2	401

Obadiah

1:10–14	79

Jonah

4:11	233n62

SCRIPTURE INDEX

Micah

4:4	128
6:6–7	186n38

Habakkuk

1:13	75
2:4	323

Zephaniah

3:17	306

Zechariah

3:10	128
7:12	15n2

Malachi

1:2–3	79
3:6	347

New Testament

Matthew — 48

3:1–12	425n28
3:13–17	295
3:15	146
3:16–17	230
4:1–11	218n34, 342n41
4:17	425n28
5:3	74, 229n54, 278
5:5	121
5:9	124
5:13–16	415
5:21–26	139
5:23–26	124
5:38–42	140
5:43–48	137
5:48	415
6:1–6	220
6:14–15	399
6:19–21	168
6:22–23	118
6:25–34	338
7:1	121
7:1–5	441
7:5	441
7:15–23	347
9:9–13	421
9:10–13	240
9:11	421
9:12–13	422
9:13	424
9:14–17	334
9:35–38	187, 427
10:6	187
10:26–31	92
10:38–39	21
11:27	288
11:28–30	42
11:29	146, 223
12:1–21	119
12:15–21	39–40, 121
12:22–32	163, 342
13:11	384
13:24–30	233n62
13:36–43	213n21, 233n62, 235n64
13:41–42	213n21
14:22–33	146
16:13–20	341
16:21	341
17:1–8	295
18:5–6	414, 417
18:15–17	121
18:21–35	137n52, 399
19:13–14	362n19
19:16–30	285, 388
19:21	324
19:26	232
19:27	154
19:29	154
21:33–41	231
21:33–44	315
22:1–14	235n64, 436n38
22:14	437n38
22:34–40	112n27
22:37–40	117
23	150
23:1–36	186–87

SCRIPTURE INDEX

Matthew (continued)

23:3	334
23:4	42
23:37–39	150
24	279
24:36–51	235n64
25	86n42
25:14–30	222, 235n64, 411n13, 436n38
25:31–46	86n42, 164, 235n64, 240, 277
26:14–16	387
26:36–39	296
26:41	368
26:47–54	296
26:52–56	230n55
26:53	128
26:57–68	141
27:11–14	141
27:46	228, 230
28:11–15	357
28:16–17	342

Mark

2:1–12	144n60, 357n15
2:5	433
2:14–17	421
3:22–30	163
4:11	384
5:21–24	304
5:35–43	304
6:5–6	231n56
7:19	357n15
8:34–38	336
9:38–41	164
10:18	118, 164
10:45	39, 77
14:36	232
14:53–65	141
15:1–5	141
15:39	287
16:15–18	146

Luke

	15n2
1:37	232
3:21–28	244
4:18–19	115
5:16	285
5:27–32	421
6:20	278
7:11–17	304
7:36–50	240
8:10	384
9:21–22	131
9:22	150
9:51	131, 150
9:51–56	240, 318n10
10:17–20	123
12:2–3	150
12:10	163
12:11–12	297
12:13–21	387
15	55
15:1–2	74
15:17	73
16:19–31	164, 289
17:7–10	219, 413
18:7–8	358
18:9–14	221, 241n70
18:18–30	240
19:1–10	240
19:11–27	222, 231, 411n13
22:24–27	77
22:32	368
22:66–71	141
23:1–5	141
23:28–31	279
23:34	427
23:42–43	238n66
23:46	228

John

	15n2, 303
1:1	285
1:5	118
1:12–13	57
1:18	288, 295
1:47	128
2:1–11	334
2:12–17	126n41

3:16–21	42
4:24	331
5:17–18	357n15
5:17–30	294
5:19	304
5:19–30	295
5:21	304
5:22–29	305
5:26	305
6:25–34	57
6:37	57–58, 74
6:44	57–58
6:45	57, 368
6:65	368
7:16	304
8:1–11	121, 240
8:2–11	152
8:34	389
9:39–41	41
10:10	136, 236
11:1–44	304
11:22	304
11:41–42	304
11:43–44	304
12:15–21	334
12:24–26	336
12:27–30	295, 341
13:1	150, 287
13:21–30	299
13:34	117, 416
13:34–35	127
14:6–11	294
14:6–14	295
14:12	146
14:16–17	296
14:26	297
15:12–17	150
15:18—16:4	195
15:26	297
16:7	146
16:7–15	297
16:8–11	122n36, 250
16:9	225n48
16:32–33	195
17	151n67
17:3	255
17:4	295
17:6	295
17:20–23	127
17:21	127n42
17:23	127n42
18:33–38	141
18:36	91n52, 396, 398

Acts 187

1:24–26	96
2:23	58, 385
2:36–38	177
3:13–15	385
3:18	385
4:28	385
5:1–11	86
5:32	219n35
7:49	381
9:1–9	277
10:34–35	159, 161
10:36	115
10:38	115, 146
12:1–17	228
17:22–30	177n30
17:22–31	159, 162, 187
17:24–25	412
17:26–27	160
17:27–28	160
17:28	107, 230
26:19–20	425n28

Romans 45

1	162
1:16–17	288, 322–23, 430
1:17	323, 363
1:18–23	35, 188
1:18–32	86, 187, 239
1:19–20	83, 161–62
1:20	35
1:31	361
2	83, 353, 390
2:1–11	168, 432
2:1–16	73
2:2–11	233
2:4	149, 180
2:5	177
2:6–7	168

SCRIPTURE INDEX

Romans (continued)

2:6–11	59
2:6–29	376
2:10	168
2:12–16	351, 390, 431
2:14–15	162n14
2:15	108
2:24	390
2:26	162n14
2:27	390
3	83
3:1–2	162n14
3:3	390
3:9	390
3:10–12	389
3:20	178
3:21–28	430
3:22–26	177
3:23–26	86
3:27	178
4	362
4:5	430
4:25	59
5:6	215
5:6–8	72n26, 114
5:9	432
5:12	216
5:12—6:1	387
5:17	363
5:19	431
6	382
6:1–14	437
6:1—7:6	58n12
6:3–4	362
6:6	59
6:8	59, 362
6:11	59
6:12–16	389
6:15–16	388
7	86
7:7–13	367
7:7–24	244
7:7–25	367, 407
7:7—8:1	217n32
7:11	367
7:13–25	86, 226, 430n30
7:15	87
7:16	86
7:18	86
7:19	87
7:22	86
7:23	86–87
7:24–25	244, 430n30
7:25	88
8	369
8:1	390
8:19–22	341n40
8:19–30	148
8:32	149
8:37	369
9	369
9:6–9	77
9:6–24	76
9:6–29	82n36
9:10–13	77
9:11–12	78
9:13	79
9:14	79
9:15–16	79
9:16	369
9:17	80
9:19	81
9:20	81
9:20–21	81
9:22–24	81
10:2–4	82
10:5–13	288
10:9	45, 288
11:7–10	82
11:20	81
11:20–24	82
11:25	384
11:29	79n32
11:32	81
12:2	244
12:3	151–52
12:4–5	151
12:10	152
12:12	228
12:18	39, 376
13:1–7	376
13:14	324
14:4	375

14:8	364
14:17	39
16:25–26	384

1 Corinthians

1–2	369
1:5	369
1:12	369
1:18–25	286
1:30	431
2:1	384
2:6	427
2:6–8	427
2:7	384
2:8	116
2:15	441
3	411n13, 437
3:4	369
3:10–15	223n43
4	369
4:1	384
4:6	369
4:7	343, 368, 413
4:8–13	369
5	121
5:1	121
5:1–5	239
5:7	420
6:12–20	437
7:3–5	30
10:31	352n8
12:3	35n30
13:13	315
14:33	39n39
15:20–23	58
15:20–28	305n65
15:51	384
15:56	217n32
15:56–57	367

2 Corinthians

1:3–4	228
2:5–11	121
3	369
3:3	329
3:5	369
3:6	117
3:17	123
4:4	55, 188n43, 264
4:5–6	264
4:14	58
5:17–18	180
5:21	363, 431
8:9	152
12:1–10	230

Galatians

2:20	362
3:1–6	57
5:16–24	407
5:19–21	90
5:22	39n39
6:1	119, 121
6:7–8	86, 90

Ephesians

1:9	384
1:13	349
2	218
2:1–9	223n43
2:3	142
2:4–7	61
2:8–9	215
2:8–10	218
2:10	179, 219
3:1	123n37
3:3–4	384
3:9	384
4:1–16	151n67
4:6	143n58
4:13	417
5:13–14	118
5:32	384
6:18–20	123n37
6:19	384

Philippians

1:6	366n25
1:12–14	123n37
2:2–4	336
2:12	437n38
2:12–13	224, 391
3:9	431
3:10–14	407
4:8	436

Colossians

1:15–16	153
1:16	302n62
1:17	153
1:21–23	144
1:26–27	384
2:2	384
2:12–13	362
3:1	362
3:3	362, 420
3:5	420
4:3	123n37, 384
4:18	123n37

1 Thessalonians

1:10	432
5:19	222

2 Thessalonians

1:7–9	213
1:8	213n21
2:1–12	384
2:8	213n21

1 Timothy

1:8–11	86n42, 90, 136, 184
2:1–2	68n23
2:1–4	223n43
2:3–4	228
2:4	68n23
2:8–15	223n43
3:9	384
3:16	384
4:2	88
4:16	223n43
6	346
6:10	387
6:13–16	345
6:16	384

Titus

2:14	224

Philemon

1:9–10	123n37

Hebrews

	45, 136, 264, 295, 386, 432
1:3	55, 263, 295, 357n15
3:7–19	432
3:7—4:13	412n14
3:8	432
3:13	432
4:12–13	376
4:15	136
5:7	230n55
5:7–8	299
5:7–10	128, 296
6:4–8	86, 221n40, 432
6:8	432
9:27	164
10:26	432
10:26–31	86, 432
11:3	vi, 35
12:2–17	433
12:3	433
12:5–11	433
12:14–17	433
13:2	228

SCRIPTURE INDEX

James

1:5	88
1:12–17	75
1:13	80n33, 136
1:13–15	87n44, 219
1:13–18	100
1:14	368
1:19–21	223n43
2	86n42
2:14	349
2:14–26	215, 349
2:15–16	349
2:17	349
2:18	349
2:19	349
2:20	349
2:21	349
2:22	349
2:23	349
2:24	349
2:25	349
2:26	349
3:13–16	124
3:13—4:2	136
3:17–18	124
4:2	203
4:6	75

1 Peter

2:19–23	130
3:8–22	223n43
3:13	224
4:3	224
4:12–19	223n43

2 Peter

1:3–4	219, 222
1:3–11	436
1:5–7	219
1:8–11	219
1:10	222
3:8	346
3:9	55, 68n23, 142, 186, 228, 239

1 John

1:5—2:11	221
2:19	220
2:22	221
3:1–10	437
3:4	389
3:4–10	221
3:7	314
3:8	389
3:11–21	390
3:24	314
4:1–3	221
4:1–6	314
4:2–3	35n30
4:7	304
4:7–8	314
4:7–21	303
4:7—5:5	221
4:8	71, 112, 405
4:9	304
4:9–11	314
4:12	314
4:16	71, 112, 314, 405
4:18	73, 168
4:19	416
5:1	221
5:10	221

Jude 213n21

1:14–15	213n21
1:23	85

Revelation 195, 345, 398

1:20	384
4:2–3	346
4:11	227
6:9–11	93n55, 289
8:1–5	228
8:6—9:21	213n21
10:7	384
12	234
13	195
17	384
19	213n21

Revelation (continued)

19:11–16	213
19:15	213n21
20:11–15	235n64
21	398
21:4	398
21:12	235n64
22:15	235n64

www.ingramcontent.com/pod-product-compliance
Lightning Source LLC
Chambersburg PA
CBHW052046290426
44111CB00011B/1639